Current Readings in Child Development

Third Edition

Judy S. DeLoache

Sarah C. Mangelsdorf

Eva Pomerantz

University of Illinois, Champaign

Allyn and Bacon

Boston London Toronto Sydney Tokyo Singapore

Copyright © 1998, 1994, 1992 by Allyn & Bacon
A Viacom Company
160 Gould Street
Needham Heights, Massachusetts 02194-2130

Internet: www.abacon.com
America Online: keyword: College Online

ISBN 0-205-27955-4

Printed in the United States of America

10 9 8 7   06 05 04 03

Contents

PREFACE

For the editors of this book of readings, as well as the authors whose articles are reprinted in it, there is nothing so fascinating as the mysterious and miraculous process of child development. We hope that reading these articles makes this process seem a little less mysterious, but no less miraculous.

This book is designed to introduce students to some of the most interesting and important current research in the field of developmental science. It contains 25 outstanding articles. Some are original research reports reprinted from scientific journals; others are integrative summaries of research in particular areas. *Current Readings in Child Development* is intended for use as a supplementary text in undergraduate courses in developmental science (developmental psychology, child development, psychology, human development, etc.).

Several criteria and good intentions guided our selections. Because we want this reader to represent the *current* state of developmental science, we included only articles published from 1989 to the present. The other two primary criteria were that the research reported or summarized should have *scientific merit* and that the article should be relatively *readable*. In a book of readings targeted for undergraduate students, there is little point in including papers that, however important, are too technical. We also tended to select relatively brief articles, both to make them more useful to students and to enable us to include a wider variety of papers in the book. The general *importance of the topic* led us to select articles from areas in which there is currently a high level of interest and research activity. *Influence on the field* was another important criterion; we considered the impact of the specific article, of the author's work in general, and of the overall area of study. Some articles represent one form of influence, others different ones. *Comprehensiveness* was, of course, important for the articles as a whole. We tried to achieve a final set that illustrated different areas of child development, different theories, different methodologies, and so on.

We are pleased with the selections that are reprinted here and hope you will find them interesting and useful. At the same time, we regret that, because of page limitations, many important areas and many outstanding investigators are not represented.

To The Student

Reading the articles in this book will deepen your understanding of the field of child development. Your class ans developmental textbook gives you a broad overview of the field, and this book of readings introduces you to current scientific publications by developmental researchers. You will gain a fuller appreciation of what some of the major questions and debates are all about, and you will learn how scientists go about trying to answer those questions.

Because this may be your first experience reading primary source materials, we have tried to provide you with some help. First, we have tried to choose articles that will be interesting to you and relatively easy to read and understand. Second, we have written introductions to each of the articles. In each we give some context for the article and provide you with some pointers to help you read it. Almost all of our selections include some technical and challenging material. You may find the Results sections of the journal articles difficult, especially if you have not yet taken a statistics course. You should, however, be able to get the main points of all the articles by concentrating primarily on the Introduction and Discussion sections. Finally, to help you assess your understanding of each article we have included some self-test questions. The answers to the multiple-choice questions can be found at the end of the book.

To The Instructor

This book of readings is intended to supplement your class in child development and give your students a much deeper appreciation for the field of developmental science than is possible with only a textbook and lectures. In the introductions to each of the individual articles, we provide some context for the article and make it inviting to the student. In addition to highlighting important points about the article itself, we have tried to reinforce concepts the student may encounter in the textbook for the course (for example, aspects of research design and methodology, theoretical debates). In addition, we have introduced some concepts that we suspect may not be covered by the text. Hence, this reader will not only deepen but also broaden your students' knowledge.

The readings are ordered according to a topical format, but it should be simple to rearrange them into a chronological format, if that is how you prefer to organize your course.

Acknowledgements

We thank Gwen Kenney and Terry Sturdyvin for their invaluable assistance in completing this reader. We also thank all of the authors who granted permission for their work to be reprinted in this book.

ARTICLE 1

Children of the Garden Island

Emmy E. Werner

Reprinted from: *Scientific American*, 1989, *260*, 107-111.
Copyright © 1989 by Scientific American. Reprinted with permission.

This article was carefully selected as your introduction to this book of readings. It exemplifies the practice, as well as the spirit, of developmental science.

Change and continuity are both at the heart of the study of child development. We are always asking what changes and what stays the same with age. Which factors facilitate change, and which promote stability? In this article, Emmy Werner summarizes a massive project--the Kauai Longitudinal Study--investigating the long-term consequences of early stress and rearing conditions. She and her colleagues have examined the relations between health status at birth, early home environment, and eventual outcome.

With respect to method, this study employs a longitudinal design--the same individuals are studied at different ages (times). One of the several remarkable methodological features of this study is its length. There are surprisingly few studies of the same individuals from birth through adulthood. Although such studies are important, they are very difficult and expensive to do. Another feature is the extraordinary success these investigators had in keeping subjects in their study. A common problem with longitudinal research is subject attrition: People drop out of the study for a variety of reasons (moving, lack of interest, various life problems). Notice the lengths to which Werner and her colleagues went to recruit and retain their subjects.

With respect to the spirit of developmental science, one of our ultimate goals is to improve the outcome of development. Werner's research tells us some important things about long-term prediction. Developmental outcome depends on many factors--both negative factors such as birth problems and unstable families that place young children at risk, and positive factors such as nurturance and emotional support that serve a protective function. The vulnerability or resilience of individual children is thus a result of many variables. (As you will see, the concepts of vulnerability and resilience are central to several of the articles in this book.)

The bottom-line message of this study is both heartening and sobering. Although we have learned a great deal from it about what factors improve developmental outcomes, we have yet to figure out how to make those health-promoting conditions available to all children.

Children of the Garden Island

In 1955, 698 infants on the Hawaiian island of Kauai became participants in a 30-year study that has shown how some individuals triumph over physical disadvantages and deprived childhoods

by Emmy E. Werner

Kauai, the Garden Island, lies at the northwest end of the Hawaiian chain, 100 miles and a half-hour flight from Honolulu. Its 555 square miles encompass mountains, cliffs, canyons, rain forests and sandy beaches washed by pounding surf. The first Polynesians who crossed the Pacific to settle there in the eighth century were charmed by its beauty, as were the generations of sojourners who visited there after Captain James Cook "discovered" the island in 1778.

The 45,000 inhabitants of Kauai are for the most part descendants of immigrants from Southeast Asia and Europe who came to the island to work on the sugar plantations with the hope of finding a better life for their children. Thanks to the islanders' unique spirit of cooperation, my colleagues Jessie M. Bierman and Fern E. French of the University of California at Berkeley, Ruth S. Smith, a clinical psychologist on Kauai, and I have been able to carry out a longitudinal study on Kauai that has lasted for more than three decades. The study has had two principal goals: to assess the long-term consequences of prenatal and perinatal stress and to document the effects of adverse early rearing conditions on children's physical, cognitive and psychosocial development.

The Kauai Longitudinal Study began at a time when the systematic exami-

nation of the development of children exposed to biological and psychosocial risk factors was still a bit of a rarity. Investigators attempted to reconstruct the events that led to physical or psychological problems by studying the history of individuals in whom such problems had already surfaced. This retrospective approach can create the impression that the outcome is inevitable, since it takes into account only the "casualties," not the "survivors." We hoped to avoid that impression by monitoring the development of all the children born in a given period in an entire community.

We began our study in 1954 with an assessment of the reproductive histories of all the women in the community. Altogether 2,203 pregnancies were reported by the women of Kauai in 1954, 1955 and 1956; there were 240 fetal deaths and 1,963 live births. We chose to study the cohort of 698 infants born on Kauai in 1955, and we followed the development of these individuals at one, two, 10, 18 and 31 or 32 years of age. The majority of the individuals in the birth cohort—422 in all—were born without complications, following uneventful pregnancies, and grew up in supportive environments.

But as our study progressed we began to take a special interest in certain "high risk" children who, in spite of exposure to reproductive stress, discordant and impoverished home lives and uneducated, alcoholic or mentally disturbed parents, went on to develop healthy personalities, stable careers and strong interpersonal relations. We decided to try to identify the protective factors that contributed to the resilience of these children.

Finding a community that is willing or able to cooperate in such an effort is not an easy task. We chose Kauai for a number of reasons, not the least of which was the receptivity of the island population to our endeavors. Coverage by medical, pub-

lic-health, educational and social services on the island was comparable to what one would find in communities of similar size on the U.S. mainland at that time. Furthermore, our study would take into account a variety of cultural influences on childbearing and child rearing, since the population of Kauai includes individuals of Japanese, Pilipino, Portuguese, Chinese, Korean and northern European as well as of Hawaiian descent.

We also thought the population's low mobility would make it easier to keep track of the study's participants and their families. The promise of a stable sample proved to be justified. At the time of the two-year follow-up, 96 percent of the living children were still on Kauai and available for study. We were able to find 90 percent of the children who were still alive for the 10-year follow-up, and for the 18-year follow-up we found 88 percent of the cohort.

In order to elicit the cooperation of the island's residents, we needed to get to know them and to introduce our study as well. In doing so we relied on the skills of a number of dedicated professionals from the University of California's Berkeley and Davis campuses, from the University of Hawaii and from the island of Kauai itself. At the beginning of the study five nurses and one social worker, all residents of Kauai, took a census of all households on the island, listing the occupants of each dwelling and recording demographic information, including a reproductive history of all women 12 years old or older. The interviewers asked the women if they were pregnant; if a woman was not, a card with a postage-free envelope was left with the request that she mail it to the Kauai Department of Health as soon as she thought she was pregnant.

Local physicians were asked to submit a monthly list of the women who were coming to them for prenatal care. Community organizers spoke to wom-

EMMY E. WERNER is professor of human development and research child psychologist at the University of California, Davis. She received her Ph.D. from the University of Nebraska in 1955 and then joined the Institute of Child Development at the University of Minnesota; she served as visiting scientist at the perinatal research branch of the National Institutes of Health from 1959 to 1962 and as an associate research child psychologist in the School of Public Health at the University of California, Berkeley, between 1965 and 1969. Werner has taught at Davis since 1962.

n's groups, church gatherings, the county medical society and community leaders. The visits by the census takers were backed up with letters, and milk cartons were delivered with a printed message urging mothers to cooperate. We advertised in newspapers, organized radio talks, gave slide shows and distributed posters.

Public-health nurses interviewed the pregnant women who joined our study in each trimester of pregnancy, noting any exposure to physical or emotional trauma. Physicians monitored any complications during the prenatal period, labor, delivery and the neonatal period. Nurses and social workers interviewed the mothers in the postpartum period and when the children were one and 10 years old; the interactions between parents and offspring in the home were also observed. Pediatricians and psychologists independently examined the children at two and 10 years of age, assessing their physical, intellectual and social development and noting any handicaps or behavior problems. Teachers evaluated the children's academic progress and their behavior in the classroom.

From the outset of the study we recorded information about the material, intellectual and emotional aspects of the family environment, including stressful life events that resulted in discord or disruption of the family unit. With the parents' permission we also were given access to the records of public-health, educational and social-service agencies and to the files of the local police and the family court. My collaborators and I also administered a wide range of aptitude, achievement and personality tests in the elementary grades and in high school. Last but not least, we gained the perspectives of the young people themselves by interviewing them at the age of 18 and then again when they were in their early 30's.

Of the 698 children in the 1955 cohort, 69 were exposed to moderate prenatal or perinatal stress, that is, complications during pregnancy, labor or delivery. About 3 percent of the cohort—23 individuals in all—suffered severe prenatal or perinatal stress; only 14 infants in this group lived to the age of two. Indeed, nine of the 12 children in our study who died before reaching two years of age had suffered severe perinatal complications.

Some of the surviving children became "casualties" of a kind in the next two decades of life. One out of every six children (116 children in all) had physical or intellectual handicaps of perinatal or neonatal origin that were diagnosed between birth and the age of two and that required long-term specialized medical, educational or custodial care. About one out of every five children (142 in all) developed serious learning or behavior problems in the first decade of life that required more than six months of remedial work. By the time the children were 10 years old, twice as many children needed some form of mental-health service or remedial education (usually for problems associated with reading) as were in need of medical care.

By the age of 18, 15 percent of the young people had delinquency records and 10 percent had mental-health problems requiring either in- or outpatient care. There was some overlap among these groups. By the time they were 10, all 25 of the children with long-term mental-health problems had learning problems as well. Of the 70 children who had mental-health problems at 18, 15 also had a record of repeated delinquencies.

As we followed these children from birth to the age of 18 we noted two trends: the impact of reproductive stress diminished with time, and the developmental outcome of virtually every biological risk condition was dependent on the quality of the rearing environment. We did find some correlation between moderate to severe degrees of perinatal trauma and major physical handicaps of the central nervous system and of the musculoskeletal and sensory systems; perinatal trauma was also correlated with mental retardation, serious learning disabilities and chronic mental-health problems such as schizophrenia that arose in late adolescence and young adulthood.

But overall rearing conditions were more powerful determinants of outcome than perinatal trauma. The better the quality of the home environment was, the more competence the children displayed. This could already be seen when the children were just two years old: toddlers who had experienced severe perinatal stress but lived in middle-class homes or in sta-

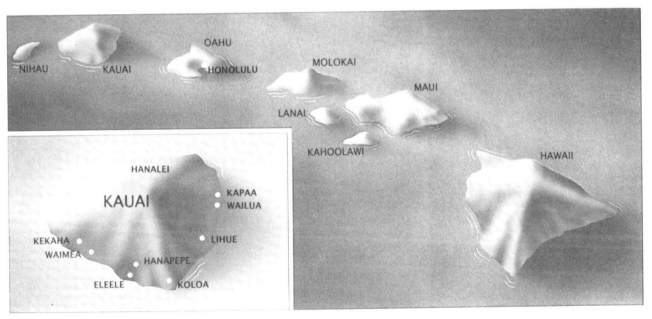

KAUAI, the Garden Island, lies at the northwest end of the Hawaiian archipelago. The towns that participated in the Kauai Longitudinal Study are shown in the inset. Lihue is the county seat; it is about 100 miles from Honolulu, the capital of Hawaii.

ble family settings did nearly as well on developmental tests of sensory-motor and verbal skills as toddlers who had experienced no such stress.

Prenatal and perinatal complications were consistently related to impairment of physical and psychological development at the ages of 10 and 18 only when they were combined with chronic poverty, family discord, parental mental illness or other persistently poor rearing conditions. Children who were raised in middle-class homes, in a stable family environment and by a mother who had finished high school showed few if any lasting effects of reproductive stress later in their lives.

How many children could count on such a favorable environment? A sizable minority could not. We designated 201 individuals—30 percent of the surviving children in this study population—as being high-risk children because they had experienced moderate to severe perinatal stress, grew up in chronic poverty, were reared by parents with no more than eight grades of formal education or lived in a family environment troubled by discord, divorce, parental alcoholism or mental illness. We termed the children "vulnerable" if they encountered four or more such risk factors before their second birthday. And indeed, two-thirds of these children (129 in all) did develop serious learning or behavior problems by the age of 10 or had delinquency records, mental-health problems or pregnancies by the time they were 18.

Yet one out of three of these high-risk children—72 individuals altogether—grew into competent young adults who loved well, worked well and played well. None developed serious learning or behavior problems in childhood or adolescence. As far as we could tell from interviews and from their record in the community, they succeeded in school, managed home and social life well and set realistic educational and vocational goals and expectations for themselves when they finished high school. By the end of their second decade of life they had developed into competent, confident and caring people who expressed a strong desire to take advantage of whatever opportunity came their way to improve themselves.

They were children such as Michael, a boy for whom the odds on paper did not seem very promising. The son of teen-age parents, Michael was born prematurely, weighing four pounds five ounces. He spent his first three weeks of life in a hospital, separated from his mother. Immediately after his birth his father was sent with the U.S. Army to Southeast Asia, where he remained for two years. By the time Michael was eight years old he had three siblings and his parents were divorced. His mother had deserted the family and had no further contact with her children. His father raised Michael and his siblings with the help of their aging grandparents.

Then there was Mary, born after 20 hours of labor to an overweight mother who had experienced several miscarriages before that pregnancy. Her father was an unskilled farm laborer with four years of formal education. Between Mary's fifth and 10th birthdays her mother was hospitalized several times for repeated bouts of mental illness, after having inflicted both physical and emotional abuse on her daughter.

Surprisingly, by the age of 18 both Michael and Mary were individuals with high self-esteem and sound values who cared about others and were liked by their peers. They were successful in school and looked forward to the future. We looked back at the lives of these two youngsters and the 70 other resilient individuals who had triumphed over their circumstances and compared their behavioral characteristics and the features of their environment with those of the other high-risk youths who developed serious and persistent problems in childhood and adolescence.

We identified a number of protective factors in the families, outside the family circle and within the resilient children themselves that enabled them to resist stress. Some sources of resilience seem to be constitutional: resilient children such as Mary and Michael tend to have characteristics of temperament that elicit positive responses from family members and strangers alike. We noted these same qualities in adulthood. They include a fairly high activity level, a low degree of excitability and distress and a high degree of sociability. Even as infants the resilient individuals were described by their parents as "active," "affectionate," "cuddly," "easygoing" and "even-tempered." They had no eating or sleeping habits that were distressing to those who took care of them.

The pediatricians and psychologists who examined the resilient children at 20 months noted their alertness and responsiveness, their vigorous play and their tendency to seek out novel experiences and to ask for help when they needed it. When they entered elementary school, their classroom teachers observed their ability to concentrate on their assignments and noted their problem-solving and reading skills. Although they were not particularly gifted, these children used whatever talents they had effectively. Usually they had a special hobby they could share with a friend. These interests were not narrowly sex-typed; we found that girls and boys alike excelled at such activities as fishing, swimming, horseback riding and hula dancing.

We could also identify environmental factors that contributed to these children's ability to withstand stress. The resilient youngsters tended to come from families having four or fewer children, with a space of two years or more between themselves and the next sibling. In spite of poverty, family discord or parental mental illness, they had the opportunity to establish a close bond with at least one caretaker from whom they received positive attention during the first years of life.

The nurturing might come from substitute parents within the family (such as grandparents, older siblings, aunts or uncles) or from the ranks of regular baby-sitters. As the resilient children grew older they seemed to be particularly adept at recruiting such surrogate parents when a biological parent was unavailable (as in the case of an absent father) or incapacitated (as in the case of a mentally ill mother who was frequently hospitalized).

Maternal employment and the need to take care of younger siblings apparently contributed to the pronounced autonomy and sense of responsibility noted among the resilient girls, particularly in households where the father had died or was permanently absent because of desertion or divorce. Resilient boys, on the other hand, were often firstborn sons who did not have to share their parents' attention with many additional children in the household. They also had some male in the family who could serve as a role model (if not the father, then a grandfather or an uncle). Structure and rules in the household and assigned chores were part of the daily routine for these boys during childhood and adolescence.

Resilient children also seemed to find a great deal of emotional support outside their immediate family. They tended to be well liked by their classmates and had at least one close friend, and usually several. They relied on an informal network of neighbors, peers and elders for counsel and support in times of crisis and transition. They seem to have made school a home away from home, a refuge from a disordered household. When we interviewed them at 18, many resilient youths mentioned a favorite teacher who had become a role model, friend and confidant and was particularly supportive at times when their own family was beset by discord or threatened with dissolution.

For others, emotional support came from a church group, a youth leader in the YMCA or YWCA or a favorite minister. Participation in extracurricular activities—such as 4-H, the school band or a cheerleading team, which allowed them to be part of a cooperative enterprise—was also an important source of emotional support for those children who succeeded against the odds.

With the help of these support networks, the resilient children developed a sense of meaning in their lives and a belief that they could control their fate. Their experience in effectively coping with and mastering stressful life events built an attitude of hopefulness that contrasted starkly with the feelings of helplessness and futility that were expressed by their troubled peers.

In 1985, 12 years after the 1955 birth cohort had finished high school, we embarked on a search for the members of our study group. We managed to find 545 individuals—80 percent of the cohort—through parents or other relatives, friends, former classmates, local telephone books, city directories and circuit-court, voter-registration and motor-vehicle registration records and marriage certificates filed with the State Department of Health in Honolulu. Most of the young men and women still lived on Kauai, but 10 percent had moved to other islands and 10 percent lived on the mainland; 2 percent had gone abroad.

We found 62 of the 72 young people we had characterized as "resilient" at the age of 18. They had finished high school at the height of the energy crisis and joined the work force during the worst U.S. recession since the Great Depression. Yet these 30-year-old men and women seemed to be handling the demands of adulthood well. Three out of four (46 individuals) had received some college education and were satisfied with their performance in school. All but four worked full time, and three out of four said they were satisfied with their jobs.

Indeed, compared with their low-risk peers from the same cohort, a significantly higher proportion of high-risk resilient individuals described themselves as being happy with their current life circumstances (44 percent versus 10 percent). The resilient men and women did, however, report a significantly higher number of health problems than their peers in low-risk comparison groups (46 percent versus 15 percent). The men's problems seemed to be brought on by stress: back problems, dizziness and fainting spells, weight gain and ulcers. Women's health problems were largely related to pregnancy and childbirth. And although 82 percent of the women were married, only 48 percent of the men were. Those who were married had strong commitments to intimacy and sharing with their partners and children. Personal competence and determination, support from a spouse or mate and a strong religious faith were the shared qualities that we found characterized resilient children as adults.

We were also pleasantly surprised to find that many high-risk children who had problems in their teens were able to rebound in their twenties and early thirties. We were able to contact 26 (90 percent) of the teen-age mothers, 56

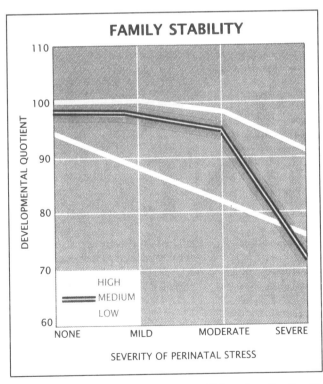

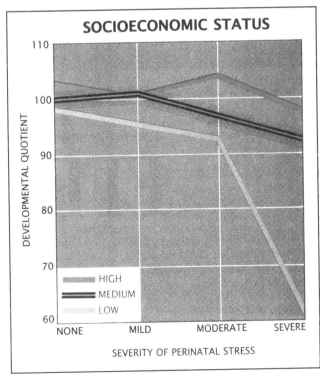

INFLUENCE OF ENVIRONMENTAL FACTORS such as family stability (*left*) or socioeconomic status (*right*) appears in infancy. The "developmental quotients" derived from tests given at 20 months show that the rearing environment can buffer or worsen the stress of perinatal complications. Children who had suffered severe perinatal stress but lived in stable, middle-class families scored as well as or better than children in poor, unstable households who had not experienced such stress.

(80 percent) of the individuals with mental-health problems and 74 (75 percent) of the former delinquents who were still alive at the age of 30.

Almost all the teen-age mothers we interviewed were better off in their early thirties than they had been at 18. About 60 percent (16 individuals) had gone on to additional schooling and about 90 percent (24 individuals) were employed. Of the delinquent youths, three-fourths (56 individuals) managed to avoid arrest on reaching adulthood. Only a minority (12 individuals) of the troubled youths were still in need of mental-health services in their early thirties. Among the critical turning points in the lives of these individuals were entry into military service, marriage, parenthood and active participation in a church group. In adulthood, as in their youth, most of these individuals relied on informal rather than formal sources of support: kith and kin rather than mental-health professionals and social-service agencies.

Our findings appear to provide a more hopeful perspective than can be had from reading the extensive literature on "problem" children that come to the attention of therapists, special educators and social-service agencies. Risk factors and stressful environments do not inevitably lead to poor adaptation. It seems clear that, at each stage in an individual's development from birth to maturity, there is a shifting balance between stressful events that heighten vulnerability and protective factors that enhance resilience.

As long as the balance between stressful life events and protective factors is favorable, successful adaptation is possible. When stressful events outweigh the protective factors, however, even the most resilient child can have problems. It may be possible to shift the balance from vulnerability to resilience through intervention, either by decreasing exposure to risk factors or stressful events or by increasing the number of protective factors and sources of support that are available.

It seems clear from our identification of risk and protective factors that some of the most critical determinants of outcome are present when a child is very young. And it is obvious that there are large individual differences among high-risk children in their responses to both negative and positive circumstances in their caregiving environment. The very fact of individual variation among children who live in adverse conditions suggests the need for greater assistance to some than to others.

If early intervention cannot be extended to every child at risk, priorities must be established for choosing who should receive help. Early-intervention programs need to focus on infants and young children who appear most vulnerable because they lack—permanently or temporarily—some of the essential social bonds that appear to buffer stress. Such children may be survivors of neonatal intensive care, hospitalized children who are separated from their families for extended periods of time, the young offspring of addicted or mentally ill parents, infants and toddlers whose mothers work full time and do not have access to stable child care, the babies of single or teen-age parents who have no other adult in the household and migrant and refugee children without permanent roots in a community.

Assessment and diagnosis, the initial steps in any early intervention, need to focus not only on the risk factors in the lives of the children but also on the protective factors. These include competencies and informal sources of support that already exist and that can be utilized to enlarge a young child's communication and problem-solving skills and to enhance his or her self-esteem. Our research on resilient children has shown that other people in a child's life—grandparents, older siblings, day-care providers or teachers—can play a supportive role if a parent is incapacitated or unavailable. In many situations it might make better sense and be less costly as well to strengthen such available informal ties to kin and community than it would to introduce additional layers of bureaucracy into delivery of services.

Finally, in order for any intervention program to be effective, a young child needs enough consistent nurturing to trust in its availability. The resilient children in our study had at least one person in their lives who accepted them unconditionally, regardless of temperamental idiosyncracies or physical or mental handicaps. All children can be helped to become more resilient if adults in their lives encourage their independence, teach them appropriate communication and self-help skills and model as well as reward acts of helpfulness and caring.

Thanks to the efforts of many people, several community-action and educational programs for high-risk children have been established on Kauai since our study began. Partly as a result of our findings, the legislature of the State of Hawaii has funded special mental-health teams to provide services for troubled children and youths. In addition the State Health Department established the Kauai Children's Services, a coordinated effort to provide services related to child development, disabilities, mental retardation and rehabilitation in a single facility.

The evaluation of such intervention programs can in turn illuminate the process by which a chain of protective factors is forged that affords vulnerable children an escape from adversity. The life stories of the resilient individuals on the Garden Island have taught us that competence, confidence and caring can flourish even under adverse circumstances if young children encounter people in their lives who provide them with a secure basis for the development of trust, autonomy and initiative.

FURTHER READING
KAUAI'S CHILDREN COME OF AGE. Emmy E. Werner and Ruth S. Smith. The University of Hawaii Press, 1977.
VULNERABLE BUT INVINCIBLE: A LONGITUDINAL STUDY OF RESILIENT CHILDREN AND YOUTH. Emmy E. Werner and Ruth S. Smith. McGraw-Hill Book Company, 1982.
LONGITUDINAL STUDIES IN CHILD PSYCHOLOGY AND PSYCHIATRY: PRACTICAL LESSONS FROM RESEARCH EXPERIENCE. Edited by A. R. Nichol. John Wiley & Sons, Inc., 1985.
HIGH RISK CHILDREN IN YOUNG ADULTHOOD: A LONGITUDINAL STUDY FROM BIRTH TO 32 YEARS. Emmy E. Werner in American Journal of Orthopsychiatry, Vol. 59, No. 1, pages 72–81; January, 1989.

Questions for Self-Study

Multiple Choice:

1. Which of the following was one of the main conclusions from this research?

    A.   The long-term effects of prenatal and perinatal stress were more serious than the immediate impact.
    B.   The developmental outcome of every biological risk condition depended on rearing conditions.
    C.   The investigators were able to predict with surprising accuracy the developmental outcome of an individual based on his or her condition at birth.
    D.   Early stress had no effect on eventual outcome.

2. Which of the following was *not* cited as a source of resilience?

    A.   temperament
    B.   the presence of several supportive siblings
    C.   nurturance from at least one adult
    D.   emotional support outside the family

3. Which of the following is *not* true?

    A.   Overall, most of the subjects in this study who had undergone difficulty in their teens were better off as adults.
    B.   A generally poor outcome was seen for children who had experienced severe perinatal stress and then grew up in low SES families.
    C.   The majority of the children who were considered to be "vulnerable" because of having multiple risk factors nevertheless experienced few serious developmental problems.

Essay:

1. A good friend calls you in great distress because she has just given birth to a premature baby and there were some perinatal complications as well. Based on Werner's article, what could you tell your friend to reassure her? What advice might you give her?

2. We think it was Pearl Bailey who said, "I've been rich and I've been poor, and I can tell you, honey--rich is better." How is being poor worse in terms of recovery from early stress?

ARTICLE 2

Cultural Variation in Infants' Sleeping Arrangements: Questions of Independence

Gilda A. Morelli, Barbara Rogoff, David Oppenheim, and Denise Goldsmith

Reprinted from: *Developmental Psychology*, 1992, *28*, 604-613.

Imagine yourself, happily married and living in a cozy two-bedroom home, just bringing home a new baby. Where will the baby sleep? Will you take your newborn into bed with you and your spouse, put the baby in a bassinet in your bedroom, or will the infant have his or her own room?

Did you answer these questions easily? Are you fully comfortable with your response? Our best guess is that the majority of our readers, like most North Americans, reject the idea of co-sleeping with an infant, do not have to think very hard to answer these questions, and are pretty certain that what they know would be best for both the baby and the rest of the family.

We are thus confident that most of our readers would be in a very small minority worldwide with respect to their beliefs about this aspect of child rearing. In most societies, today and throughout history, infants sleep with one or both of their parents, in some cases for several years. This practice is a preference, not a necessity; even when there is plenty of room for infants to sleep elsewhere, they share the parental bed.

Co-sleeping is thus a good illustration of the concept of *cultural relativity*, the fact that there is enormous variation in the beliefs and practices of different societies. What one cultural group considers to be the obvious, normal way to treat children is viewed by a different group as downright peculiar and possibly even deviant. As you will see in this article, people who think infants should not sleep alone regard the standard North American practice of isolating even little babies as unnatural and cruel--possibly even abusive.

An important point to note as you read this article is how cultural practices arise from cultural beliefs and values. U.S. families tend to place very high value on independence, which leads them to believe that sleeping apart is a good way to help infants develop self-reliance. Mayan families place higher value on close relationships and believe that sleeping together is a good way to promote emotional attachment.

Another point to notice is that both practices have virtues and drawbacks. There is no perfect way to raise a child.

Developmental Psychology
1992, Vol. 28, No. 4, 604–613

Cultural Variation in Infants' Sleeping Arrangements: Questions of Independence

Gilda A. Morelli
Boston College

Barbara Rogoff
University of Utah

David Oppenheim
Department of Psychiatry
University of Colorado Health Sciences Center

Denise Goldsmith
University of Utah

This study examines the decisions of middle-class U.S. and Highland Mayan parents regarding sleeping arrangements during their child's first 2 years and their explanations for their differing practices. All 14 Mayan children slept in their mothers' beds into toddlerhood. None of the 18 U.S. infants slept in bed with their mothers on a regular basis as newborns, although 15 slept near their mothers until age 3 to 6 months, when most were moved to a separate room. The Mayan parents explained their practices in terms of the value of closeness with infants; the U.S. parents explained their practices in terms of the value of independence for infants. The U.S. families, but not the Mayan families, used bedtime routines and objects to facilitate the transition to sleep.

It was time to give him his own room . . . his own territory. That's the American way.

Reflections of a middle-class U.S. mother

Among middle-class families and child-care experts in the United States, it is assumed that the proper sleeping arrangement for infants and parents is separate. The purpose of this article is to examine this assumption as a cultural practice. A sociocultural approach involves understanding how practices within a community relate to other aspects of the community's functioning, such as adult work roles, physical space arrangements, climate, and values and goals regarding desired characteristics of citizens. One of the most valuable aspects of comparisons across cultural communities is that they make us aware of the cultural basis for and the assumptions underlying our own practices, whoever we are (Cole, 1985; Munroe, Munroe, & Whiting, 1981; Rogoff, 1990; Rogoff & Morelli, 1989; B. B. Whiting & Edwards, 1988).

In this study, we review work demonstrating that the middle-class U.S. practice of separating infants from their mothers is unusual compared with the practice in most communities around the world, and we examine speculations regarding val-

ues and other practices that may be associated. Then we make an explicit comparison of practices and rationales described by parents of infants in two communities: a small Guatemalan Mayan town and a middle-class sample from a U.S. city.

Folk wisdom in the United States considers the early nighttime separation of infants from their parents as essential for the infants' healthy psychological development. This widespread belief is reflected in the advice parents have received since the early 1900s from child-rearing experts regarding cosleeping. Spock (1945) wrote, "I think it's a sensible rule not to take a child into the parents' bed for any reason" (p. 101). Brazelton (1978, 1979) and Ferber (1986), pediatricians and writers nationally known as specialists on parenting, also warned parents of the dangers of sleeping with their infants. The concerns of such authors included possible smothering by a restless parent (Bundesen, 1944), the increased likelihood of catching a contagious illness (Holt, 1957), the difficulty of breaking the habit when the child grows older (Spock, 1945), and sexual overstimulation for the oedipal child (Spock, 1984). Although several accounts now acknowledge the value placed on cosleeping by some families (Brazelton, 1990), or advocate the practice (Thevinin, 1976), pediatricians generally advise parents to avoid cosleeping (Lozoff, Wolf, & Davis, 1984).

Research indicates that cosleeping is not commonly practiced by middle- to upper-class U.S. families. Lozoff et al. (1984) found that only 35% of urban Caucasian 6- to 48-month-olds slept with their parents for all or part of the night on a regular basis. Crowell, Keener, Ginsburg, and Anders (1987) reported even lower figures: A mere 11% of the 18- to 36-month-olds they studied shared a bed with their parents 3 or more nights a week, and only 15% shared a room with them. Valsiner and Hall (1983) found that 18 out of 19 infants from well-educated U.S. families slept in a room separate from their parents from before 3 months of age. Over half of the infants studied by

This study was conducted while Gilda A. Morelli was a National Institute of Mental Health postdoctoral fellow at the University of Utah. Parts of the data reported were presented in Phoenix, Arizona, in November 1988, at the American Anthropological Association meeting. Completion of the work was made possible by a Boston College Faculty Research grant to Gilda A. Morelli.

We would like to thank Alison Nash and Miyukui Nakagawa for their help in the initial planning of this study and David Wilkie and Paula Ivey for their comments on an earlier version of the article.

Correspondence concerning this article should be addressed to Gilda A. Morelli, Department of Psychology, Boston College, Chestnut Hill, Massachusetts 02167.

Hong and Townes (1976) slept in their own rooms by 2 months of age, 75% by 3 months, and 98% by 6 months. Other researchers have noted that by 6 months, middle-class U.S. infants' designated sleeping place is in a room separated from their parents (Keener, Zeanah, & Anders, 1988; Richman, Miller, & Solomon, 1988; B. B. Whiting & Edwards, 1988). From these and other studies it appears that in the U.S. middle class, cosleeping is not a frequently occurring event in infancy and early childhood (Mandansky & Edelbrock, 1990; Rosenfeld, Wenegrat, Haavik, Wenegrat, & Smith, 1982).

In many non-U.S. communities it is customary for infants to sleep with their mothers for the first few years of life, at least in the same room and usually in the same bed. J. W. M. Whiting (1964) reported that infants sleep in bed with their mothers in approximately two thirds of the 136 societies he sampled around the world, and in the remainder the babies were generally in the same room with their mothers. Infants regularly slept with a parent until weaning in all but 1 (the United States) of the 12 communities studied by B. B. Whiting and Edwards (1988); in the U.S. community no cosleeping was observed. In a survey of 100 societies, American parents were the only ones to maintain separate quarters for their babies (Burton & Whiting, 1961; see also Barry & Paxson, 1971; McKenna, 1986). These findings are consistent with other work on sleeping arrangements in urban Korea (Hong & Townes, 1976) and urban and rural Italy (Gaddini & Gaddini, 1971; Gandini, 1990; New, 1984).

Communities that practice cosleeping include both highly technological and less technological communities. Japanese urban children usually sleep adjacent to their mothers in early childhood and generally continue to sleep with a parent or an extended family member until the age of 15 (Caudill & Plath, 1966; Takahashi, 1990). Parents often separate in order to provide all children with a parental sleeping partner when family size makes it difficult for parents and children to share a single room. Space considerations appear to play a minor role in cosleeping practices for Japanese families (Caudill & Plath, 1966).

Within the United States, demographic, ethnic, and economic correlates of cosleeping have been identified. There is less cosleeping by mothers with some college education than by mothers with a high school education (Wolf & Lozoff, 1989). Black U.S. children are more likely than White U.S. children to fall asleep with a caregiver present, to have their beds in their parents' room, and to spend all or part of the night cosleeping with their parents (Lozoff et al., 1984; Ward, 1971). Thirty-six percent of infants growing up in eastern Kentucky shared their parents' beds as newborns, and 48% shared their parents' room. Over 65% of infants from this community slept with or near their parents through the first 2 years of life (Abbott, 1992); again, space did not seem to be the issue.

Previous literature has identified a stress on independence training as being connected with middle-class parents' avoidance of cosleeping (Munroe et al., 1981). Kugelmass (1959) advocated separate rooms for children on grounds that it would enable them to develop a spirit of independence. The rare middle-class U.S. families who do practice cosleeping often recognize that they are violating cultural norms (Hanks & Rebelsky, 1977). In contrast, Brazelton (1990) noted that "the Japanese think the U.S. culture rather merciless in pushing small children toward such independence at night" (p. 7). Parents in communities where cosleeping is common may regard cosleeping as important for the development of interpersonal relationships (Caudill & Plath, 1966).

In the present study, we examine differences between a U.S. middle-class community and a non-Western community in the sleeping arrangements of infants, including where the babies sleep and nighttime feeding and waking practices, as well as parents' rationales for and comfort with their infants' sleeping arrangements. We are particularly interested in the values expressed by parents regarding the consequences for children of cosleeping or sleeping apart. We also investigate practices that may be associated with sleeping arrangements, such as special activities occurring around bedtime. The transition to sleep may be a difficult process for young children that is eased by the presence of their caregivers or by substitute attachment objects or special bedtime activities (Albert, 1977; Wolf & Lozoff, 1989).

Although middle-class U.S. parents and child-care specialists regard sleeping problems as among the most common disturbances of infancy, our goal is not to prescribe any changes but rather to come to a broader understanding of cultural practices in which middle-class U.S. and Mayan families, like all other families, participate.

Method

Participants

Eighteen Caucasian, middle-class mothers living in a U.S. city (with 7 girls and 11 boys aged 2 to 28 months, median age = 16 months) and 14 Mayan mothers living in a rural Guatemalan community (with 7 girls and 7 boys aged 12 to 22 months, median age = 19 months) were interviewed on topics related to the sleeping arrangements of their youngest child.

U.S. families were randomly selected from birth information supplied by the Bureau of Vital Records and were invited to take part in the study. Mayan families were selected from a small town in highland Guatemala. The families from the two communities were similar in number of children (Mdn = 2, range = 2–7 for the U.S. sample; Mdn = 3, range = 1–9 for the Mayan sample). Approximately one third of the children were firstborn in both communities. The U.S. mothers averaged 30 years of age (range = 22–39, based on 13 respondents) and the Mayan mothers averaged 26 years (range = 19–42). The U.S. mothers had completed more years of schooling, with a median of 14 grades (range = 12–18, based on 14 respondents), compared with a median of 3 grades for the Mayan mothers (range = 0–9). All of the Mayan mothers were the primary daytime caregivers for their toddlers; two thirds of the U.S. mothers were. Most families included a father; all of the 18 U.S. fathers and 11 of the 14 Mayan fathers were living with the child and mother. The religious affiliations of the families reflected those of their communities. Over half of the U.S. families were Mormon (58%, based on 12 respondents), and the remainder were Catholic, Protestant, or Jewish; over half of the Mayan families were Catholic (64%), and the remainder were Protestant.

Procedure

Parents were interviewed in their homes, with family and community members often included in the session. A North American researcher familiar with the language, community, and families interviewed the Mayan sample, with a community member assisting in translation when parents preferred speaking Mayan. A second North American researcher interviewed the U.S. sample.

Family sleeping arrangements at the time of the interview were determined by asking parents to draw a map of their home indicating relative positions of rooms as well as beds and identifying each person's present sleeping location. Parents were asked about their infant's sleeping locations from the time of birth, about other practices associated with sleeping arrangements (e.g., night feedings), and why they made the choices they did. Questions were grouped topically, but the interviewer used her judgment to decide the order in which they were asked. Information on family background was also gathered. The interview was tailored in ways appropriate to each community. It took approximately 60 min to interview an American family. Mayan interviews took longer (approximately 120 min) because the questions were embedded in a larger study.

Sleeping Arrangement Variables

Questions on infants' sleeping locations, night feedings, and bedtime routines were parallel in the two communities. Questions exploring rationale for and comfort with decisions were tailored to each community, because the practices and issues were different for each.

Infant's sleeping location is categorized as being in the mother's bed (which we term *cosleeping,* after Lozoff et al.'s, 1984, definition), in the mother's room, or in another room. We also report any changes in location since the infant's birth and information on who else besides the mother shared the infant's bed or room.

Night feedings includes information on whether the baby is breast or bottle fed, where night feedings occur (in mother's bed, mother's room, or another room), and where the baby is put to sleep following night feedings.

Bedtime routines are reported in terms of whether the infant fell asleep alone or in someone's company, whether the infant fell asleep at the same time as the mother or separately, whether the infant received special bedtime activities (e.g., bedtime story, lullaby, bathing or toothbrushing routines), and whether the infant used a security object for falling asleep.

Sleeping arrangement issues and reflections differ in format in the two communities because of their very different practices. For the Mayan families, we report on the issues that appear when toddlers are shifted away from cosleeping with the mother, usually at age 2 or 3, and on some of the Mayan parents' reflections on U.S. middle-class infants' sleeping arrangements.

For the U.S. families, we report the parents' rationales for the infant's sleeping location (and changes in location), their comfort with the infant's sleeping location, their perceptions of the relation between the baby's sleeping location and development, and their attitudes toward cosleeping. Table 1 lists coded categories and representative statements by U.S. parents.

Reliability

Reliability estimates were unnecessary for the data that did not involve judgments by the researchers (e.g., sleeping location, night feedings, bedtime routines). The reflections of the U.S. parents on sleeping arrangements were grouped into coding categories requiring judgments; 50% of them were selected for reliability assessment using percentage agreement scores. The values ranged from 75% to 100%, with a median of 88%.

Results

The practices of the Mayan and U.S. middle-class families with regard to sleeping locations, night feedings, and bedtime routines are reported first. We then follow up the differences in practices by examining parents' reflections on the different issues with questions tailored to the community's practices.

Sleeping Location

Mayan families. All 14 Mayan mothers slept in the same bed with their infants through the 1st year of life and into the 2nd year (see Table 2); 1 child had spent some time sleeping apart from her mother, on a cot in the same room, but was now sleeping with her mother again. In this case, the sleeping arrangement reflected changes in the presence of the father, from whom the mother was now separated.

Most of the Mayan toddlers (8 of them) also slept in the same bed with their fathers. Of the 6 who did not share a bed with their fathers, 3 had fathers sleeping in another bed in the same room (in 2 cases, father was sleeping with other young children), and the other 3 involved absent fathers. Four of the toddlers had a sibling (newborn to 4 years of age) in the same bed with them and their mothers, and of these, 2 also had the father in the same bed. Ten of the 14 toddlers had siblings sleeping in the same room with them, either in the same bed or another bed. Of the 4 toddlers who had no siblings sleeping in the same room, all were only children; one of these had paternal uncles sleeping in the same room.

U.S. families. In none of the 18 U.S. families did parents sleep with their newborns on a regular basis (see Table 2). Rather, most mothers and fathers (15 families) chose to share a room with their newborn infants, often placing them in a bassinet or crib near the parents' bed. This was a temporary arrangement; by 3 months of age 58% of the babies were already sleeping in separate rooms. This figure climbed to 80% by the 6th month of life. When the babies were moved to a room apart from their parents, firstborns were placed in a room of their own, but most second- and laterborns (89%) were moved into rooms with siblings. However, none of them shared a bed with a sibling.

In 3 of the 18 U.S. families, parents chose not to share a room with their babies from the time the babies were brought home from the hospital. These 3 newborn infants slept in their own rooms, despite the fact that 2 of them had siblings with whom they could have shared a room. For 1 family this meant keeping the infant in the living room.

Of the 15 families in which parents had slept near their newborn infants and then moved their babies to a separate room, 3 moved the infants back in the second half year of their baby's lives. Two babies were moved to cribs located in their parents' rooms; 1 baby was moved to her parents' bed. In addition, 1 family moved their child from a separate bed in the parents' room to the parents' bed when the child was 1 year old.

Night Feedings

Mayan families. The pattern of night feeding arrangements in the Mayan families was for the baby or toddler to sleep with the mother until shortly before the birth of another child (about age 2 or 3) and to nurse on demand. The mothers reported that they generally did not notice having to feed their babies in the

Table 1

Issues Related to Sleeping Arrangements, Coding Categories, and Associated Representative Statements: U.S. Sample

Topic	Coding category	Representative statement by parents
Reasons for sleeping near baby	Pragmatic (e.g., reference to temporary phenomenon such as illness, room renovations, or convenience)	"My husband's mother . . . decided to come to visit, so he (baby) stayed (in parent's room) until she left."
	Developmental (e.g., reference to vulnerability or infant features associated with physical or psychological attributes)	"I could look over and see, yes he is still alive. He's still there, he's still breathing."
	Affectionate/emotional (security, closeness, comfort)	"I think he was able to look over and feel comfortable. It was a good experience for him, and for me, for the closeness."
Sleeping near mother and baby's development	Develop security or closeness	"I think that being in our room was probably healthy for him . . . he could see our bed . . . and feel more comfortable."
Reasons for moving baby out of mother's room	Pragmatic (e.g., reference to temporary phenomenon such as illness, room renovations, or convenience)	"It is kind of a strain for a couple to tiptoe in (the bedroom) and be quiet."
	Developmental (e.g., reference to infant features associated with physical or psychological attributes)	"My baby was sleeping through the night, he didn't need me anymore."
	Foster independent or autonomous behavior	"It was time to give him his own space, his own territory."
	Fear of establishing a difficult-to-break habit	"She just might as well get used to it (sleeping by self)."
Sleeping apart from mother and baby's development	Develop independent or autonomous behavior	"I think it would have made any separation harder if he wasn't even separated from us at night."
Comfort with sleeping apart from mother	Comfortable	"It was not bad because we put him right across the hall. I wouldn't say a big adjustment."
	Ambivalent	"There is good and bad both ways."
	Uncomfortable	"But I don't know how they are doing. I can't check up on them. No it is not comfortable having (him) in the other room."
Reasons for not sleeping with the baby	Fear of establishing a difficult-to-break habit	"Once you start it (cosleeping) it will continue. They (friends who cosleep) are sorry now that they have started it because now he is older and they can't get him out."
	Safety issues	"We might roll over him, hurt him . . . he could get smothered."
	Uncomfortable with idea	"I . . . don't think that I ever want him right in the same bed as me. I don't really know why."
	Concerns about encouraging dependency	"I think that he would be more dependent . . . if he was constantly with us like that" (i.e., asleep near them).

night. Mothers said that they did not have to waken, just to turn and make the breast accessible. Hence night feedings were not an issue for the Mayan mothers or for their infants and toddlers.

U.S. families. All but 1 of the 18 U.S. mothers reported having to stay awake during night feedings (which, for most mothers, lasted 6 months or so). Ten mothers chose not to feed their babies in their rooms, even though 7 of them had infants sleeping there and 8 of them were breastfeeding. Two mothers (both breastfeeding) fed infants in the parental room, but not in the parental bed; and 6 mothers (all breastfeeding) elected to feed their babies in the parental bed, but 5 of them regularly returned babies to their own beds when finished. The 1 mother whose infant regularly remained in bed with her following feed-

ings was the only mother who said that nightly feedings did not bother her.

Bedtime Routines

Mayan families. The idea that sleeping arrangements were not an issue for the Mayan families is supported by the lack of bedtime routines carried out in the nightly transition to sleep. There was not a separate routine to coax the baby to sleep. Most of the babies simply fell asleep when sleepy, along with the rest of the family or before if they got tired. Seven of the babies fell asleep at the same time as their parents, and most of the rest fell asleep in someone's arms. Ten of them were nursed to sleep (as

Table 2
Sleeping Locations in the Two Communities

	U.S. (n = 18)		Mayan (n = 14)	
Location	0–3 months	After 6 months	0–3 months	After 6 months
In mother's bed, with father and/or sibling	0	2	10	10
In mother's bed, with no other bedmates	0	0	4	4
In separate bed, in mother's room	15	2	0	0
In another room, with a bedmate	0	0	0	0
In own bed in another room, with a roommate	0	6	0	0
In another room, alone	3	8	0	0

they are nursed on demand during the daytime as well). Of the 4 who were no longer nursing, 1 fell asleep alone with a bottle, 1 fell asleep with a bottle and his mother going to bed with him, and 2 who had been nursed to sleep until recently (and were being weaned) usually fell asleep on their own but were cuddled by their father or older brother on the occasions when they needed company at bedtime.

None of the babies received a bedtime story; there were no reports of bathtime or toothbrushing in preparation for bed; none of the babies sucked their thumbs; only 1 was reported to use a security object for falling asleep (a little doll—this belonged to the 1 child who had for a time had a bed by herself!). There was thus no focus on objects as comfort items for falling asleep.

None of the Mayan families sang special children's lullabies to the babies at bedtime; some laughed at the idea. However, 4 of the mothers admitted with embarrassment that they sometimes sang their babies church songs at bedtime. (One added that she does this when she feels badly about not having taken the baby out during the day.) The babies were not changed into pajamas in preparation for bed. (They do not have specialized nightclothes; nor do the parents.) However, 11 of them were changed into their oldest clothes for sleeping. The other 3 just slept in the clothes they had worn during the day. Thus it appears that no special preparations or coaxing are needed for these babies, whose sleeping occurs in the company of the same people with whom they spend the day.

U.S. families. Events surrounding bedtime for the U.S. families played a significant role in the organization of family evening activities. Besides the daily evening activity of putting on nightclothes and brushing teeth, 10 of the 18 parents engaged in additional routines such as storytelling. Routines varied in their degree of elaborateness, with some parents spending just a few minutes reading a story to their babies and other parents investing a fair amount of time getting their child ready for sleep. One mother jokingly said, "When my friends hear that it is time for my son to go to bed, they teasingly say 'See you in an hour.'"

Once infants were in bed, 11 were expected to fall asleep by themselves. It is interesting that 5 of the 8 infants who fell asleep alone took a favorite object such as a blanket to bed with them (data are missing for 3 children). By comparison, only 2 of the 6 infants who fell asleep in the company of another person (data are missing for 1 child) needed to do the same.

Reflections of Parents on Sleeping Arrangements

Mayan families. Most of the families regarded their sleeping arrangements as the only reasonable way for a baby and parents to sleep. In addition, in five interviews the subject of how U.S. families handle sleeping arrangements came up. Invariably, the idea that toddlers are put to sleep in a separate room was received with shock, disapproval, and pity. One mother responded, "But there's someone else with them there, isn't there?" When told that they are sometimes alone in the room the mother gasped and went on to express pity for the U.S. babies. Another mother responded with shock and disbelief, asked whether the babies do not mind, and added with feeling that it would be very painful for her to have to do that. The responses of the Mayan parents gave the impression that they regarded the practice of having infants and toddlers sleep in separate rooms as tantamount to child neglect. Their reactions and their accounts of their own sleeping arrangements seemed to indicate that their arrangements were a matter of commitment to a certain kind of relationship with their young children and not a result of practical limitations (such as number of rooms in the house).

In Mayan families, sleeping arrangements are not an issue until the child is displaced from the mother's side by a new baby. At the time or before the new baby is born, the toddler is weaned and may be moved to sleep beside the father in the same bed or in another bed in the same room. One mother and father told us that their little boy got very angry at his mother (when the next child arrived) and even cried when he was moved to his father's bed; he wanted to be the last born—he did not want someone else to take his place beside his mother. For most families, though, this transition is usually made without difficulty. Parents sometimes try to prevent any difficulties by getting the child accustomed to sleeping with another family member before the new baby is born.

The transition is sometimes difficult for Mayan mothers and fathers. Mothers may regret letting the child move from their care to that of another family member, and fathers may lose sleep as they often become responsible for the displaced child. One father of a toddler told us that his older son, whose wife was expecting a second child in 4 months, needed to move their 2-year-old firstborn to another bed soon, even though she did not want to move. The older man told us that the firstborn needed to become accustomed to sleeping apart from the mother or the father would have trouble later. "I know," said the older man, "because I went through this . . . If the first child doesn't sleep through the night, apart from the parents, when the new child comes, the father suffers. He has to get up in the night to give the child something."

If there are older siblings, they often take care of the displaced child if needed during the night, allowing the father to sleep. Of the 10 Mayan families with older siblings, in 5 of them the older siblings had moved to sleep with the father when our subjects were born (3 in the same bed with mother and the new baby, 2 with father in another bed in the same room), in 2 they had moved to sleep with a sibling in the same room, in 2 they had moved to a separate bed in the same room, and in 1 they slept with the mother and the new baby as father slept in a separate bed in the same room. It is noteworthy that even when the children are displaced from their mother's side, they still sleep in the same room with her, usually at someone else's side.

U.S. families.[1] U.S. parents chose to sleep near their newborn infants for pragmatic reasons (mentioned by 78%, e.g., "Because I nurse them . . . it is sort of convenient to have them here") as well as for developmental and affectionate reasons (57% and 64% mentioned these). Of the parents who slept near their babies starting at birth, an overwhelming majority (92%) felt that sleeping near infants helped foster the development of an affectionate tie between them and their babies. (Table 1 contains a description of coding categories and representative statements by parents.)

Although these parents acknowledged that sleeping near their infants was a meaningful experience for both them and their babies, all but 1 family decided to move their infants to separate quarters within the 1st year of life (most moves occurred during the first 3 to 6 months).[2] When asked about the reasons for shifting sleeping quarters, parents often talked about the infant's developmental readiness for separation (69%): "She didn't need to be watched as close"; "He was old enough to be by himself." This suggests that a perceived decrease in the vulnerability of the infant and readiness for separation played an important role in the parents' decision to move the infant out of the parents' room. Pragmatic factors (e.g., "It was time for me to go back to work") were cited as important in the decision-making process by 54% of the families. Fostering independence and preventing conflict over separation were given as reasons for moving the baby out of the parents' room by 38% and 15% of the families, respectively. Most U.S. families did not consider the transition from sleeping near parents to sleeping apart from them in these early months to be stressful for the infants. One family speculated that a baby might find the move stressful if the baby was a firstborn.

Twelve of the 14 families who moved their babies out of their rooms expressed satisfaction with their decision.[3] Many emphasized that the move allowed continued proximity to their babies. Half of the parents told us that the baby's room was close to their room, making it easy for them to monitor their infant's movements. Some families also made a regular habit of keeping doors slightly ajar so that they could better hear their babies' cries. Just 2 mothers who moved their babies out of their room were unhappy with their decision. For 1 mother, the baby's move to the living room severely hampered her daytime activities.

Three parents participating in the study never had their infants sleep in the same room with them. Two of the 3 families made this choice because of concerns related to independence training. All 3 families were comfortable with their decision to maintain separate sleeping quarters; 2 families commented that the rooms were sufficiently close to allow them to hear their infants in case of an emergency.

Most of the 17 families who slept in different rooms from their infants (from birth, or within months following the baby's birth) focused on issues related to independence training when discussing what their practices meant for their baby. Sixty-nine percent of these families believed that it was important for their infants' developing independence and self-reliance to sleep apart from them, with some reporting that separations at night made daytime separations easier and would help reduce their babies' dependence on them.

The findings suggest that encouraging independence during infancy is an important goal for many U.S. families and that parents believe that sleeping apart helps train children to be independent. But the age at which parents think it is appropriate for infants to sleep apart is somewhat variable, ranging from 0 to usually 3 to 6 months. This range of variability is narrow compared with worldwide sleeping practices.

Sixteen of the 18 U.S. mothers reported that they would not want to sleep with their baby on a regular basis. The explanations for avoiding cosleeping included the fear of establishing a habit that would be difficult to break (50%; e.g., "She would like it and not want to leave"), concern about encouraging dependency in their baby (19%), safety reasons (44%; e.g., "I was so afraid that I would crush him"), or simply being uncomfortable with the idea (44%). However, the majority of parents (77%) did report allowing occasional night visits, often as a way to comfort their infants. But some families felt that it was just not acceptable to bring a baby into the parental bed for any reason.

---

[1] Some of the findings reported in this section involve a few cases of missing data. The percentages do not include these cases.

[2] One family made cosleeping a regular family practice when their son was 1 year of age, after having had the infant in a separate bed in the parents' room. The mother already had a history of falling asleep with the infant while nursing; the decision was one of convenience, prompted by the baby's increasing resistance to sleeping alone. Nonetheless, the parents were ambivalent about their decision to cosleep. They felt that cosleeping provided their son with emotional security but, at the same time, they wanted their privacy.

[3] The 3 families who made additional changes in their babies' sleeping arrangements after their infants had been moved to separate rooms were unhappy about their decisions, although they reported that their decisions were necessary (because of medical concerns or space issues). One mother exclaimed, "I am a human being, and I deserve some time and privacy to myself."

Sleeping within listening distance (but not within touch) of babies during the first months of life is a practice preferred by most of the U.S. middle-class mothers participating in the study. As parental perceptions of the developing infant shifted, it seemed increasingly inappropriate to the U.S. mothers for their babies to be within their beds or bedrooms. Cosleeping was often seen as a bad habit that is difficult to break or as a practice that impedes the development of independence.

Discussion

Mayan and U.S. middle-class families differed in the way they managed their infants' and young children's sleeping arrangements. Cosleeping, a practice found in many communities worldwide, was common in the Mayan community (Burton & Whiting, 1961; B. B. Whiting & Edwards, 1988; J. W. M. Whiting, 1964; see also Barry & Paxson, 1971; McKenna, 1986). Mayan infants slept with their mothers, and often their fathers and siblings, from birth onward, with changes in sleep location not expected until around the time of the birth of a sibling.

None of the middle-class U.S. parents, by comparison, coslept with their newborn infants on a regular basis. Rather, many parents chose to sleep near their babies in the same room but moved them to separate rooms by 3 to 6 months of age. Some parents, however, chose not to share a room even with their newborn infants. The pattern observed in our U.S. sample is similar to what has been described for other Caucasian middle- and upper-class families living in the United States (Hong & Townes, 1976; Keener et al., 1988; Richman et al., 1988; Valiner & Hall, 1983; B. B. Whiting & Edwards, 1988). U.S. middle-class parents may differ somewhat in their sleeping arrangements for their newborn infants, but they are working toward a common goal, which is to have infants sleep in rooms of their own as early as possible. In fact, it seems as though U.S. parents are more comfortable with the idea of newborn infants sleeping in a room alone than with the idea of 1-year-olds sharing a room with their parents.

The few U.S. parents who had difficulty achieving the goal of sleeping apart from their babies and had moved them back to the parents' room after they had already been sleeping in separate quarters felt their decision was necessary but were unhappy about it. Discussion of their infants' present sleeping locations suggested that these parents knew that they were going against conventional practices and were reminded of it by family and community members alike, who expressed surprise and concern about the consequences of the parents' decision for both the infants' and the parents' well-being.

The practice of sleeping with babies may relate to concerns with infant survival. According to LeVine (1980), concerns about survival take precedence during infants' first years of life and shape infants' early caregiving environment. In our middle-class U.S. sample, many parents' decisions regarding newborns were based on their perceptions of infant vulnerability. U.S. parents were comforted by the fact that they could check up on their babies during the night to make sure that they were still breathing. (But note that U.S. parents chose not to sleep with their babies.) Once parents felt that their babies' health was not in jeopardy (around the 3rd to 6th month of life), they expected

them to sleep apart. The Mayan practice of cosleeping may help minimize threats to infant survival, which are considerably greater than in the U.S. middle class because of malnutrition and illness.

McKenna (1986) argued that cosleeping was a panhuman practice with survival value for infants during much of our evolutionary past (see also Konner & Super, 1987). His view is based on the claim that infants rely on cues from parents when sleeping to help them regulate their breathing, allowing them to survive "breathing control errors" (p. 53) that might play a role in sudden infant death syndrome. Evidence that infants in some communities wake and feed about every 4 hours at night (as they do in the daytime) for at least the first 8 months of life adds to the argument that forcing babies to be alone through the night may go beyond the limits of some infants' physiological systems (McKenna, 1986; Super & Harkness, 1982).

Decisions about infants' sleeping arrangements, like other parenting decisions, also relate to the community's values and goals regarding desired characteristics of citizens. Some Mayan parents who reflected on the possibility of sleeping apart from their infants and toddlers emphasized qualities related to *interdependence*. It seems that their arrangements reflect commitment to this type of relationship with their young children. Speculations at one interview lend support to this idea:

> Upon being asked how she teaches her 13-month-old that there are some things not to handle, the mother said she tells her, "Don't touch it, it's no good, it could hurt you," and the baby nods seriously at mother and obeys, and knows not to touch it. (This was a common statement by the Mayan mothers.)

> The interviewer commented that U.S. babies don't understand so young, and instead of understanding and obeying when they are told not to touch something, they might get more interested in it. With much feeling, another mother who was present at the interview (in which we reported on U.S. sleeping arrangements) speculated that perhaps U.S. children do that because of the custom of separating children from parents at night. "In our community the babies are always with the mother, but with North Americans, you keep the babies apart. Maybe that's why the children here understand their mothers more; they feel close. Maybe U.S. children feel the distance more." She went on to speculate that if children do not feel close, it will be harder for them to learn and understand the ways of the people around them.

In many respects, Mayan infants and toddlers were regarded as not yet accountable (they were not punished for misdeeds, being considered unable to understand) and not yet ready to be treated as individuals who could be separated from their families, especially their mothers. On the other hand, the mothers generally reported that their infants and toddlers understood social rules and prohibitions from an early age. Almost all of the Mayan mothers reported that they could trust their young children not to put objects in their mouths and not to touch prohibited objects. Contrast this with the vigilance with which U.S. parents watch over their children around small objects until age 2 or 3. The mothers in our U.S. sample reported that they did not trust their young children with small objects. This difference is consistent with the Mayan mothers' speculation that the relationships fostered in sleeping close with babies may relate to the Mayan babies' learning from those around them (see also Rogoff, Mosier, Mistry, & Göncü, in press, on Mayan babies' keenness of observation and alertness to their social surroundings).

The relation between cosleeping and interdependence was noted by Caudill and Plath (1966) in their work on Japanese families. Japanese parents believe that their infants are born as separate beings who must develop interdependent relationships with community members to survive; cosleeping is thought to facilitate this process (Caudill & Weinstein, 1969). In contrast, U.S. parents believe that infants are born dependent and need to be socialized to become independent. Abbott (1992) argues that the Eastern Kentucky practice of parents sleeping with or near their children through the first 2 years of life is a strategy used by parents to foster the development of interdependence. Our U.S. middle-class mothers indicated that having newborns sleep in the parents' room fostered their feelings of closeness and the newborn's sense of security and emotional attachment. However, for the U.S. middle-class families, the fostering of closeness in this fashion seemed to be limited to the newborn period and involved parents sleeping in sight or hearing of but not in contact with their newborns.

In criticizing cosleeping, many U.S. mothers talked about the need to train babies to be independent and self-reliant from the first few months of life, and they reported concern with establishing a habit that would be difficult to break. A number of authors share this view (Edelman, 1983; Hoover, 1978; Spock, 1945). This reveals an assumption that from birth children should become accustomed to the requirements of later life, an assumption that child-rearing practices in infancy should be continuous with those of childhood (Benedict, 1955). This is an assumption that is not shared by many communities where infants are treated differently than young children; in such communities infants are assumed not to have sense or to understand and to have needs different than those of children. Rather than making the break in closeness with mother at or shortly after birth, infants are treated as part of a mother–infant unit until about the end of the 2nd year (when the appearance of a new baby and the need for weaning often occur). This latter view of infancy is consistent with Mayan beliefs and practices surrounding sleeping arrangements and with Kawakami's (1987) statement regarding Japanese child rearing: "An American mother–infant relationship consists of two individuals. . . . On the other hand a Japanese mother–infant relationship consists of only one individual, i.e., mother and infant are not divided" (p. 5).

Loss of privacy and associated concerns about sexual intimacy were also mentioned by some of the U.S. mothers when discussing their decision not to sleep with their babies on a regular basis. One U.S. mother said, "My husband did not like that idea (cosleeping). He was afraid that it would be unnatural, too much intimacy." It appears that unlike the Mayan community, who view sleeping as a social activity, some U.S. families see sleeping as a time for conjugal intimacy.

It is possible that spending extended periods of time alone may provide training in self-comforting and self-regulation (LeVine, 1980, 1990; Munroe et al., 1981). Although many U.S. parents believe that their infants are asleep during the night, this is not always true. Anders (1979) found that 78% of 9-month-olds were not removed from their cribs from midnight to 5 a.m., satisfying conventional criteria for sleeping through

the night. Yet 57% of these infants woke up during these hour When babies wake in the absence of a caregiver, they are respon sible for dealing with their own emotional or physiological di tress (e.g., fear, hunger, cold). The fear of sleeping alone was we put by one U.S. middle-class 3-year-old who developed nigh mares and trouble sleeping. He went into his parents' room an complained, "If there was a human in the same room, I wouldn't be 'fraid." When he was moved into his baby brother room, his sleeping troubles disappeared (V. K. Magarian, pe sonal communication, July 1991).

However, Wolf and Lozoff (1989) questioned the relation be tween sleeping alone and independence training. They note that "if leaving children to fall asleep alone truly fosters inde pendence, it is perhaps surprising that during historical perioc in the U.S. in which 'independence' was most vividly demor strated, such as the colonial period or the westward movemen children were not likely to fall asleep alone" (p. 292). It might b that infants and young toddlers who sleep alone during th night find it more difficult (rather than easier, as assumed b middle-class parents) to separate from their parents during th day (E. Z. Tronick, personal communication, September 1991

The struggle seen around bedtime between many U.S. mid dle-class parents and their children may be related to the stress infants experience when required to make the transition t sleep without assistance (Albert, 1977; see also LeVine, 1990). may also reflect a conflict of goals, with parents wanting thei child to go to sleep as soon as possible, and the child wanting t delay bedtime as long as possible because of fears engendere by having to sleep on his or her own (Gandini, 1986). For th U.S. toddlers, bedtime was associated with separation from fam ily social life: All toddlers went to bed earlier than their par ents, and most were expected to fall asleep alone, in their ow rooms. Anders (1979) and LeVine (1990) reported similar find ings. In contrast, most Mayan babies went to sleep when thei parents did or fell asleep in the midst of ongoing social activity This is consistent with a general pattern, observed in communi ties around the world, in which there is little distinction be tween daytime and nighttime events for infants and toddler (LeVine, 1990).

Bedtime routines, common in many U.S. families, including those we observed, are thought to help ease the child's nightly transition from being with others to being alone (Albert, 1977; Crowell et al., 1987; Lozoff et al., 1984). Many of the U.S. children who were expected to fall asleep alone took objects to bed with them that were seen by their parents as offering solace to their children. This finding replicates that of Wolf and Lozoff (1989), who found that middle-class children who did not have an adult present as they fell asleep were more likely to use transitional objects or to suck their thumbs at night. The nightly passage to sleep appears to be difficult for young children who have to do it alone; security objects and bedtime routines may be used to help infants in the transition to sleep. This view is consistent with findings showing that infants who sleep near or with their parents tend not to use transitional objects (Gaddini & Gaddini, 1971; Hong & Townes, 1976) and with our finding that Mayan toddlers did not use security objects for falling asleep.

It is interesting from a cultural perspective that some parents would prefer that their children become attached to and dependent on an inanimate object (e.g., a blanket) rather than a person. U.S. parents feel obliged, in many cases, to avoid giving their children comfort during the night or while getting to sleep. One mother reported putting a pillow over her head to drown out the sounds of her crying baby as she fell asleep—consistent with the advice of some child-rearing specialists (such as Ferber, 1986).

The Mayan infants, who generally go to sleep with the rest of the family or in the company of a family member, appear not to experience bedtime as an issue for negotiation with parents or as a time of stress. However, Mayan families face a transition at age 2 or 3 when a new sibling is expected and toddlers are weaned from the breast and their mother's bed. Parents report attempts to prevent difficulties at this transition by moving the child from the mother's side to sleep with another person before the new baby is born. Most children are reported to make the transition without difficulty.

The Mayan children generally continue to sleep with others throughout their childhoods. In a study of 60 9-year-olds in this Mayan community, only 8% were in a bed by themselves, and none were in a separate bedroom (Rogoff, 1977). Most (63%) shared a bed with siblings, 20% shared a bed with one or both parents, and 8% shared a bed with a grandmother or aunt. The idea of sleeping alone was disagreeable to the Mayan 9-year-olds, who expressed pity for U.S. 9-year-olds when told that they sleep in rooms of their own. And Mayan adults often find a sleeping companion if for some reason their family is away. Sleeping alone is seen as a hardship.

In both the middle-class U.S. and the Mayan communities, sleeping arrangements reflect child-rearing goals and values for interpersonal relations. It is not our aim to determine causality in the patterns we observed or to make recommendations for change in either community. It is instructive simply to note the patterns and to come to a broader understanding of cultural practices in which all families participate. In the Mayan community, infants and toddlers sleep with their mothers, and when a new baby appears they make a transition to sleeping with another family member or to a separate bed in the same room. Bedtime has social continuity with the relationships in which the Mayan children participate throughout the day and is not specially marked with transition routines or aided by attachment objects. In the U.S. middle-class community, infants generally sleep in a room separate from their parents by the second half of the 1st year of life. Infants seem to adjust to the changes made in their sleeping arrangements and may develop sleep patterns and rhythms similar to those of family members as they make adjustments associated with sleeping separate from their parents. The transition to sleep and to spending long hours alone is eased by attachments to objects and by special transition routines at bedtime. The transition is often stressful for parents and children alike, with parents at times acting in an adversarial role with their children in order to force adherence to what is seen by many as a cultural imperative—children sleeping alone—that aids in developing self-reliance and independence, personal characteristics valued by the community.

References

Abbott, S. (1992). Holding on and pushing away: Comparative perspectives on an Eastern Kentucky child-rearing practice. *Ethos, 20,* 33–65.

Albert, S. (1977). *Rites of passage: Study of children's bedtime rituals.* Paper presented at the 85th Annual Convention of the American Psychological Association, San Francisco, CA.

Anders, T. (1979). Night-waking in infants during the first year of life. *Pediatrics, 63*(6), 860–864.

Barry, H., & Paxson, L. (1971). Infancy and early childhood: Cross-cultural codes 2. *Ethnology, 10,* 466–508.

Benedict, R. (1955). Continuities and discontinuities in cultural conditioning. In M. Mead & M. Wolfenstein (Eds.), *Childhood in contemporary cultures* (pp. 21–30). Chicago: University of Chicago Press.

Brazelton, T. (1978, October). Why your baby won't sleep. *Redbook,* p. 82.

Brazelton, T. (1979, June). What parents told me about handling children's sleep problems. *Redbook,* pp. 51–54.

Brazelton, T. B. (1990). Parent–infant cosleeping revisited. *Ab Initio, 2*(1), pp. 1, 7.

Bundesen, H. (1944). *The baby manual.* New York: Simon & Schuster.

Burton, R., & Whiting, J. (1961). The absent father and cross-sex identity. *Merrill-Palmer Quarterly, 7,* 85–95.

Caudill, W., & Plath, D. (1966). Who sleeps by whom? Parent–child involvement in urban Japanese families. *Psychiatry, 29,* 344–366.

Caudill, W., & Weinstein, H. (1969). Maternal care and infant behavior in Japan and America. *Psychiatry, 32,* 12–43.

Cole, M. (1985). The zone of proximal development. Where culture and cognition create each other. In J. V. Wertsch (Ed.), *Culture, communication, and cognition: Vygotskian perspectives* (pp. 146–161). Cambridge, England: Cambridge University Press.

Crowell, J., Keener, M., Ginsburg, N., & Anders, T. (1987). Sleep habits in toddlers 18 to 36 months old. *American Journal of Child and Adolescent Psychiatry, 26*(4), 510–515.

Edelman, G. N. (1983, November). When kids won't sleep. *Parents Magazine,* pp. 74–77.

Ferber, R. (1986). *Solve your child's sleep problems.* New York: Simon & Schuster.

Gaddini, R., & Gaddini, E. (1971). Transitional objects and the process of individuation. *Journal of the American Academy of Child Psychiatry, 9,* 347–365.

Gandini, L. (1986, September). *Parent–child interaction at bedtime: Strategies and rituals in families with young children.* Paper presented at the European Conference on Developmental Psychology, Rome, Italy.

Gandini, L. (1990). Children and parents at bedtime in two cultures. *Ab Initio, 2*(1), pp. 5, 7.

Hanks, C., & Rebelsky, F. (1977). Mommy and the midnight visitor: A study of occasional co-sleeping. *Psychiatry, 40,* 277–280.

Holt, E. (1957). *How children fail.* New York: Dell.

Hong, K., & Townes, B. (1976). Infants' attachment to inanimate objects: A cross-cultural study. *Journal of the American Academy of Child Psychiatry, 15,* 49–61.

Hoover, M. B. (1978, November). Does your bed belong to baby? *Parents Magazine,* p. 129.

Kawakami, K. (1987, July). *Comparison of mother–infant relationships in Japanese and American families.* Paper presented at the meeting of the International Society for the Study of Behavioral Development, Tokyo, Japan.

Keener, M. A., Zeanah, C. H., & Anders, T. F. (1988). Infant temperament, sleep organization, and parental interventions. *Pediatrics, 81*(6), 762–771.

Konner, M. J., & Super, C. M. (1987). Sudden Infant Death Syndrome: An anthropological hypothesis. In C. M. Super (Ed.), *The role of culture in developmental disorder* (pp. 95–108). San Diego, CA: Academic Press.

Kugelmass, N. (1959). *Complete child care.* New York: Holt, Rinehart, & Winston.

LeVine, R. (1980). A cross-cultural perspective on parenting. In M. D. Fantini & R. Cardenas (Eds.), *Parenting in a multicultural society* (pp. 17–26). San Diego, CA: Academic Press.

LeVine, R. (1990). Infant environments in psychoanalysis. In J. W. Stigler, R. A. Shweder, & G. Herdt (Eds.), *Cultural psychology: Essays on comparative human development* (pp. 454–474). Cambridge, England: Cambridge University Press.

Lozoff, B., Wolf, A., & Davis, N. (1984). Cosleeping in urban families with young children in the United States. *Pediatrics, 74*(2), 171–182.

Mandansky, D., & Edelbrock, C. (1990). Cosleeping in a community sample of 2- and 3-year-old children. *Pediatrics, 86,* 197–280.

McKenna, J. (1986). An anthropological perspective on the Sudden Infant Death Syndrome (SIDS): The role of parental breathing cues and speech breathing adaptations. *Medical Anthropology, 10*(1), 9–92.

Munroe, R. L., Munroe, R. H., & Whiting, J. W. M. (1981). Male sex-role resolutions. In R. H. Munroe, R. L. Munroe, & B. B. Whiting (Eds.), *Handbook of cross-cultural human development* (pp. 611–632). New York: Garland.

New, R. (1984). *Italian mothers and infants: Patterns of care and social development.* Unpublished doctoral dissertation, School of Education, Harvard University.

Richman, A. L., Miller, P. M., & Solomon, M. J. (1988). The socialization of infants in suburban Boston. In R. A. LeVine, P. M. Miller, & M. M. West (Eds.), *Parental behavior in diverse societies* (pp. 65–74). San Francisco: Jossey-Bass.

Rogoff, B. (1977). *A portrait of memory in cultural context.* Unpublished doctoral dissertation, Harvard University.

Rogoff, B. (1990). *Apprenticeship in thinking: Cognitive development in social context.* New York: Oxford University Press.

Rogoff, B., & Morelli, G. (1989). Perspectives on development from cultural psychology. *American Psychologist, 44,* 343–348.

Rogoff, B., Mosier, C., Mistry, J., & Göncü, A. (in press). Toddlers' guided participation with their caregivers in cultural activity. In E. Forman, N. Minick, & A. Stone (Eds.), *Contexts for learning: Sociocultural dynamics in children's development.* New York: Oxford University Press.

Rosenfeld, A., Wenegrat, A., Haavik, D., Wenegrat, B., & Smith, C. (1982). Sleeping patterns in upper-middle-class families when the child awakens ill or frightened. *Archives of General Psychiatry, 39,* 943–947.

Spock, B. J. (1945). *The common sense book of child and baby care.* New York: Duell, Sloan, & Pearce.

Spock, B. J. (1984, December). Mommy, can I sleep in your bed? *Parents Magazine,* p. 129.

Super, C. M., & Harkness, S. (1982). The infant's niche in rural Kenya and metropolitan America. In L. L. Adler (Ed.), *Cross-cultural research at issue* (pp. 47–55). San Diego, CA: Academic Press.

Takahashi, (1990). Are the key assumptions of the "Strange Situation" procedure universal? A view from Japanese research. *Human Development, 33,* 23–30.

Thevinin, T. (1976). *The family bed: An age old concept in childrearing.* Minneapolis, MN: Author.

Valsiner, J., & Hall, D. (1983). *Parents' strategies for the organization of child–environment relationships in home settings.* Paper presented at the Seventh Biennial Meeting of the International Society for the Study of Behavioural Development, Munchen, Bundesrepub, Germany.

Ward, M. C. (1971). *Them children.* New York: Holt, Rinehart, & Winston.

Whiting, B. B., & Edwards, C. (1988). *Children of different worlds: The formation of social behavior.* Cambridge, MA: Harvard University Press.

Whiting, J. W. M. (1964). The effects of climate on certain cultural practices. In W. H. Goodenough (Ed.), *Explorations in cultural anthropology: Essays in honor of George Peter Murdock* (pp. 511–544). New York: McGraw-Hill.

Wolf, A., & Lozoff, B. (1989). Object attachment, thumbsucking, and the passage to sleep. *Journal of the American Academy of Child and Adolescent Psychiatry, 28,* 287–292.

Received January 3, 1992
Accepted January 5, 1992 ∎

Multiple Choice:

1. Which of the following was NOT reported in this article?

   A. Mayan infants were more likely than U.S. infants to share a bed with their mothers.
   B. U.S. mothers were more often awake for night feedings than were Mayan mothers.
   C. Elaborate bedtime rituals were established by the Mayan mothers to help their babies fall asleep with them.
   D. Mayan and U.S. mothers were equally certain that their style of sleeping arrangements was best for their babies.

2. The authors stress that different child care practices, such as sleeping arrangements, ultimately reflect deep cultural values. Which of the following values did they suggest was especially important in the behavior of the U.S. families?

   A. close emotional attachment
   B. independence
   C. safety
   D. avoidance of stress

Essay:

1. According to this article, security objects, such as favorite blankets and toys, are commonly used to facilitate bedtime for U.S. infants and young children, but not for Mayans. How is this difference in children's bedtime behavior related to the standard sleeping arrangements in their culture?

2. This article introduced you to a child care practice that is very different from what most North American parents do. Did you find yourself questioning any of your assumptions about how babies should be cared for as you read this selection? Why do you think it is so difficult for parents to follow a caretaking practice that differs from what others in their culture commonly do?

ARTICLE 3

Mothers' Alcohol Consumption During Pregnancy: Effects on Spatial-Visual Reasoning in 14-Year-Old Children

Earl Hunt, Ann P. Streissguth, Beth Kerr, and Heather Carmichael Olson

Reprinted from: *Psychological Science*, 1995, 6, 339-342.
Copyright © 1995 by the American Psychological Society.
Reprinted with the permission of Cambridge University Press.

The most rapid period of human development occurs before birth as the single cell that results from the union of the mother's egg and father's sperm becomes a baby with millions of cells. All the organ systems of the body are formed, as well as every neuron the individual will ever have. The fetus begins moving in the 6th week, and by 12 weeks most of the reflexes it will have at birth are present. For the last three months of life in the womb, the fetus can hear the mother's heart beat and the gurglings of her digestive system, as well as some sounds from the external world.

With so much development occurring in so short a time, it is a wonder that it usually comes off without a hitch. Normal fetal development can be derailed, however, if the mother is exposed to any of a variety of *teratogens*--agents from the external world that can harm a fetus.

A teratogen we have known about for many years is alcohol, which can have a dramatic, negative effect on prenatal development: Infants whose mothers are alcoholic (who regularly drink to excess) are at risk for *fetal alcohol syndrome*. Although this syndrome was discovered some time ago, it was not clear that lower levels of alcohol consumption would necessarily be bad; many teratogens have an effect only if one receives a high dose.

The point of this article (and others by Dr. Streissguth and her colleagues) is that less extreme drinking habits can also have a negative impact on development. The important results are summarized in the figure accompanying the article. It shows that the performance of 14-year-old adolescents on a test of spatial-visual reasoning was directly related to how much their mothers drank while pregnant with these now teenagers. Adolescents whose mothers had consumed little or no alcohol performed the task very accurately, taking time to analyze the stimuli before responding. Adolescents whose mothers had drunk more responded more rapidly, but less accurately.

We all know the admonition, "If you drink, don't drive." You should also emblazon on your memory the mantra, "If you are pregnant, don't drink."

Research Article

MOTHERS' ALCOHOL CONSUMPTION DURING PREGNANCY:
Effects on Spatial-Visual Reasoning in 14-Year-Old Children

Earl Hunt, Ann P. Streissguth, Beth Kerr, and Heather Carmichael Olson

University of Washington

Abstract—*Fourteen-year-old adolescents' behavior on a spatial-visual reasoning task was associated with self-report of their mothers' alcohol consumption during pregnancy, 15 years earlier. The task was arranged so that it was possible to evaluate the examinees' tendency to respond rapidly and less accurately, or slowly and more accurately. The greater the mother's reported drinking, the faster and less accurately the adolescent responded. The decrement in visual-spatial reasoning related to alcohol appears to be linked to a tendency toward impulsive responding.*

The children of women who consume high levels of alcohol during pregnancy are at risk of an identifiable birth defect known as fetal alcohol syndrome. This syndrome is characterized by growth impairment, craniofacial anomalies, central nervous system dysfunction, and sometimes mental retardation. Do children also incur a risk at lower levels of prenatal alcohol exposure?

To answer this question, Streissguth and her colleagues have conducted a longitudinal study of approximately 500 children, all born in Seattle in 1974 and 1975. The details of this sample have been published elsewhere (Streissguth, Barr, Bookstein, & Sampson, 1993; Streissguth, Barr, Sampson, Bookstein, & Darby, 1989). Previous analyses of this longitudinal sample have documented associations between moderate levels of maternal alcohol ingestion and children's physiognomy, cognitive performance, and school performance in the first 11 years of life (Carmichael Olson, Sampson, Barr, Streissguth, & Bookstein, 1992; Streissguth et al., 1993). We report here an association between "social" levels of maternal alcohol consumption and one of the major dimensions of human cognition: spatial-visual reasoning (Carroll, 1993). The association, though present, is not direct. It depends on the tendency of the adolescent to react either quickly or more reflectively to complex visual-spatial problems.

METHOD

Subjects

The subjects studied were 442 members (236 males and 206 females) of the longitudinal panel referred to.[1] Children were

contacted through their parents and asked to participate in approximately 4 hr of testing. The test session included a set of tasks intended to evaluate attention and memory (Streissguth et al., 1994; Streissguth, Bookstein, Sampson, & Barr, in press), a set of tests to evaluate cognitive and motor performance (Feldman, Kerr, & Streissguth, 1995), an assessment of physical growth and dysmorphology (Sampson, Bookstein, Barr, & Streissguth, 1994), and a series of questionnaires and rating scales on behavioral and learning problems (Carmichael Olson et al., 1995). The visual-spatial task described here was the second in the battery, being preceded only by the serial-choice reaction time task described by Feldman et al. (1995).

Measures

The task used was a computer-presented version of what are known as form board tests. Such tests are widely used to evaluate spatial visualization (Pellegrino & Kail, 1982). The particular procedure we utilized (Pellegrino, Hunt, Abate, & Farr, 1987) has been used in several studies. Information on maternal alcohol use and other health-related data and demographics were derived from personal interviews conducted in the mothers' homes when they were 5 months pregnant (for details, see Streissguth et al., 1993).

Procedure

The test was administered as the second test in the 4-hr testing session. The testing procedure is illustrated in Figure 1. First, the examinee was shown from two to six triangles and squares, drawn on the computer display. An example is shown in the top panel of Figure 1. Letters were marked on some of the borders of the triangles and squares. The task was to imagine what larger figure would be produced if the triangles and squares were joined along the appropriate lettered sides. The task is rather like trying to determine what a jigsaw puzzle will look like after its pieces are combined. The examinee studied the display of pieces until he or she decided what the final figure would look like, and then depressed the space bar on the computer's keyboard. Examinees could study a display for up to 1 min, but in practice few took this long.

When the space bar was depressed, the display changed to an unfilled polygon, as shown in the bottom half of Figure 1. The examinee then pressed a key on the computer's keyboard

---

Address correspondence to Earl Hunt, Department of Psychology NI-25, University of Washington, Seattle, WA 98195.

1. There are 464 active participants in the longitudinal study. All were interviewed and tested as part of the larger study, but there were 20 subjects for whom some of the relevant data were missing. The most

frequently missing variable was father's education, which was missing for 14 subjects. In addition, we did not analyze the data from 2 subjects who have been diagnosed with fetal alcohol syndrome.

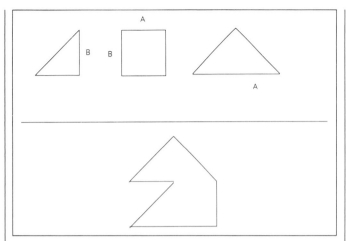

Fig. 1. A form board visual-spatial reasoning task. A participant first viewed the figures in the top row and was asked to image the figures as being joined along the matching lettered lines. After the participant indicated that he or she had done this "in the mind's eye," the top row of figures was removed from view and the bottom figure was shown. The participant indicated whether or not the bottom figure was identical to the figure that would be produced by joining the top figures as indicated. In this example, the answer is "yes."

to indicate whether or not the figure was the one that would be formed by joining elements as indicated in the previous display.[2] The task had five levels, corresponding to the number of component elements (2–6), and 8 different problems were presented for each level of the task, for a total of 40 problems. Within levels, half the items were correctly answered "same" and half "different."

The procedure produces two variables of interest, the study time used to examine the first display and the number of correct judgments of whether or not the pieces in the first display could be joined to form the figure in the second display. Both these variables have been shown to be reliable markers of spatial-visual reasoning (Hunt, Pellegrino, Frick, Farr, & Aldteron, 1988).

RESULTS

Study time increased and the number of correct answers decreased as the number of pieces in the first display increased ($p < .001$ for each). The relevant data are displayed in Table 1. Males took less time than females in the study phase ($p < .001$) and marginally answered more items correctly ($p < .07$). These findings mirror those of many other studies using form board tasks (Halpern, 1992; Pellegrino & Kail, 1982).

Performance correlated with two demographic variables, father's and mother's level of education, and with two measures of mother's self-reported drinking behavior, the average number of drinks taken per occasion of drinking in the month or so

prior to the discovery of pregnancy (ADOCC-P) and the average number of drinks taken during midpregnancy (ADOCC-D). These alcohol consumption measures were reported previously (Streissguth et al., 1993).[3] The correlations between these variables are shown in Table 2. This table also shows the residual correlations between the drinking variables and the two performance measures, after allowance has been made for parental education. (This covariate was used because of the many studies showing that cognitive performance can often be predicted from measures of parental performance.) As the table shows, allowing for parental education made little change in the correlations, because the original and residual scores are themselves correlated at $r > .9$. Because the ADOCC-P and ADOCC-D scores are highly correlated ($r = .81$), we discuss our results in terms of the relation between the ADOCC-D score (alcohol consumption by mothers during midpregnancy) and the cognitive performance scores.

Table 2 shows a positive relationship between study time for the first display and the number of correct choices made when the second display was exposed. This is evidence of a speed-accuracy trade-off. Observers who spend more time accumulating information are more accurate when they respond. Such trade-offs have long been known to characterize choice reaction time tasks such as this one (Pachella, 1974).

The speed-accuracy curve expresses the relative frequency of a correct choice, $P(c)$, as a function of the study time. Such curves are typically negatively accelerated, rising from a starting point of .5, the guessing probability in our study, to 1.0. Therefore, we estimated the speed-accuracy curve by the equation

$$P(c) = (1 - e^{-\phi x}) + .5\, e^{-\phi x}, \qquad (1)$$

where x is study time in seconds, e is the Naperian constant, and ϕ is a rate parameter to be estimated from the data. Intuitively, the first term of the right-hand expression of Equation 1 is the probability that a person will know the correct answer after having studied the component pieces for x seconds, the second term is the probability that the person does not know the right answer but will guess correctly, and the rate parameter, ϕ, indicates how rapidly the person's chance of getting an item correct increases as he or she continues to look at the display.

Equation 1 was fit separately to the data from the male and female examinees. The equation fit both sets of data. The rate parameter was .061 for males ($SE = .003, p < .001$) and .042 for females ($SE = .003, p < .001$). The difference between the two was reliable ($p < .005$). In nonmathematical terms, males exhibited a sharper trade-off of speed for accuracy than did fe-

---

2. The examinee pressed the "S" key to indicate that the correct figure was being shown, and the "K" key if it was not. These keys had been marked "S" (same) and "D" (different), respectively.

3. In previous reports on this longitudinal study, a variety of composite scores have represented drinking behavior, including composites involving nonlinear transformations of the original scores. The composite scores were related to the behavioral measures in substantially the same way as the measures reported here. Therefore, we used the ADOCC-D score because it emphasizes the amount drunk when a person drinks, rather than the average consumption over some period of time. Previous research has highlighted the importance of this type of exposure measure as a predictor of alcohol's effects.

Table 1. *Mean study time (in seconds) and mean number of correct answers as a function of number of pieces in the initial display*

	Number of pieces				
Measure	Two	Three	Four	Five	Six
Study time					
Male	3.162	5.646	9.021	12.862	15.391
Female	3.501	6.358	10.553	15.140	18.207
Number correct					
Male	6.27	6.35	5.28	5.18	4.88
Female	6.11	6.20	4.88	5.15	4.13

Note. Study times are the means of the median times for each individual within each condition.

males, as shown graphically in Figure 2. Note, though, that although the trade-off is sharper for males than for females, the males were more accurate than the females at all time intervals. This finding is consistent with several studies showing that men, on the average, outperform women on spatial-visual tasks of this nature (Halpern, 1992).

Maternal drinking behavior was negatively related to both study time and the number of correct choices, suggesting that the maternal-drinking variables may have influenced the location of the examinees on the speed accuracy curve. To investigate this question, we projected each individual's performance data (study time and percentage of correct choices) onto the speed-accuracy curve, and then computed the relationship between reported drinking during pregnancy and position on the curve, where position is equivalent to the distance along the speed-accuracy function from the intercept to an individual's predicted position on the curve. The correlations were .21 ($p <$ .002) for males and .13 ($p <$ .07) for females. The difference between the two correlations is not reliable ($t <$ 1.0). The weighted mean correlation between speed-accuracy position and reported drinking, calculated from the separate estimates, is .17 ($p <$ .001).

There were differences in where males and females positioned themselves on the speed-accuracy curves: Females tended to spend more time in the study phase than males, $F(1, 440) >$ 10, $p <$ .002. There were no reliable correlations between reported drinking and the residual for either study time or accuracy of choice, after allowing for the effects of the speed-accuracy trade-off.

Figure 2 shows these effects graphically, with separate plots for males and females. In this figure, maternal drinking habits have been grouped into four levels: abstainers ($n =$ 53 males, 48 females), light drinkers (less than two drinks per occasion; $n =$ 106 males, 89 females), moderate drinkers (from two to less than four drinks per occasion; $n =$ 66 males, 63 females), and heavy drinkers (four or more drinks per occasion; $n =$ 11 males, 6 females). The figure shows a clear association between sex, maternal drinking behavior during pregnancy, and speed-accuracy performance of the 14-year-old participants. The heavier the maternal drinking, the more the adolescents positioned themselves in the "impulsive" area of high-speed, low-accuracy responding. The mean values for seven of the eight groups shown in Figure 2 are within 1 standard deviation of the values predicted for the groups from the speed-accuracy curve. The only exception is for the small ($n =$ 6) group of females whose mothers were heavy drinkers.

Table 2. *Correlations between drinking measures, parental education, and speed-accuracy measures after adjustment for parental education level*

	ADOCC-P	ADOCC-D	FathED	MothED	Study time	Number correct	Residual study time
ADOCC-P							
ADOCC-D	.81						
FathED	−.19	−.14					
MothED	−.15	−.14	.64				
Study time	−.16	−.17	.21	.23			
Number correct	−.16	−.13	.35	.36	.52		
Residual study time	−.12	−.13	0	0	.97	.44	
Residual number correct	−.09	−.07	0	0	.46	.92	.47

Note. A correlation of .10 is reliable at the .05 level for a sample of this size. ADOCC-P = average number of drinks per occasion of drinking in the month or so prior to the discovery of pregnancy; ADOCC-D = average number of drinks per occasion of drinking during midpregnancy; FathED = father's level of education; MothED = mother's level of education.

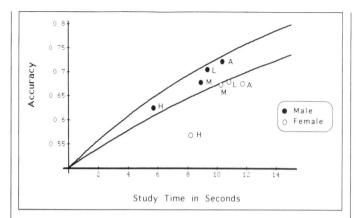

Fig. 2. Relation between maternal drinking behavior, gender, and position on the speed-accuracy curve. Speed-accuracy curves are shown separately for males and females. Points shown are the means for offspring of abstainers (A), light drinkers (L), moderate drinkers (M), and heavy drinkers (H). Because of the convexity of the speed-accuracy curve based on individual examinees' data, one would expect the means for the groups to lie slightly below the speed-accuracy curve itself.

DISCUSSION

The results indicate that there is an association between moderate amounts of maternal alcohol ingestion during pregnancy and the manner in which the offspring approach a spatial-visual task 15 years later. Basically, the more drinking the mother reported, the faster and less accurately the adolescent responded. This observation is consistent with several other findings from this cohort. When the children were age 11, prenatal alcohol exposure was related to teachers' ratings of impulsivity and disorganization (Carmichael Olson et al., 1992). A neuropsychological study of these adolescents at age 14 showed that heavy maternal drinking was associated with fluctuations of attention (Streissguth et al., 1994). The consistency of our present results with these observations is evidence that our results are unlikely to have arisen by chance, a problem that is always of concern in large multivariate studies.

Our results are also consistent with some observations by Schandler, Brannock, Cohen, and Mendez (1993), using a quite different spatial task. They found that the children of alcoholics tended to make rapid, erroneous responses, compared with the children of nonalcoholics. We extend these results by observing a similar effect on a more widely used spatial reasoning task than that developed by Schandler et al., and by finding a similar effect with much lower levels of alcohol consumption.

Whether or not alcohol ingestion is a causal factor and whether genetic or social variables associated with maternal drinking also produce impulsivity are questions for future research. These two explanations are not mutually exclusive.

Acknowledgments—This research was supported by the National Institute on Alcohol Abuse and Alcoholism, Grant AA01455-01-18 to the University of Washington, A.P. Streissguth, principal investigator. We are happy to acknowledge the assistance of Helen Barr, Derek Chung, Julie Feldman, Paul Sampson, and Michael Scott.

REFERENCES

Carmichael Olson, H., Sampson, P.D., Barr, H.M., Streissguth, A.P., & Bookstein, F.L. (1992). Prenatal exposure to alcohol and school problems in late childhood: A longitudinal prospective study. *Development and Psychopathology, 4,* 341–359.

Carmichael Olson, H., Streissguth, A.P., Sampson, P.D., Barr, H.M., Bookstein, F.L., & Theide, K. (1995, February). *Prenatal alcohol exposures and behavioral and learning problems in early adolescence.* Paper presented at the annual meeting of the International Neuropsychology Society, Seattle, WA.

Carroll, J.B. (1993). *Human cognitive abilities.* Cambridge, England: Cambridge University Press.

Feldman, J., Kerr, B., & Streissguth, A.P. (1995). Correlational analyses of procedural and declarative learning performance. *Intelligence, 20,* 87–114.

Halpern, D.F. (1992). *Sex differences in cognitive abilities* (2nd ed.). Hillsdale, NJ: Erlbaum.

Hunt, E., Pellegrino, J.W., Frick, R.W., Farr, S., & Aldteron, D. (1988). The ability to reason about movement in the visual field. *Intelligence, 12,* 77–100.

Pachella, R. (1974). The interpretation of reaction time in information processing research. In B.H. Kantowitz (Ed.), *Human information process: Tutorials in performance and cognition* (pp. 41–82). Hillsdale, NJ: Erlbaum.

Pellegrino, J.W., Hunt, E., Abate, R., & Farr, S. (1987). A computer based test battery for the assessment of static and dynamic spatial reasoning abilities. *Behavioral Research Methods, Instrumentations, and Computers, 19,* 231–236.

Pellegrino, J.W., & Kail, R., Jr. (1982). Process analysis of spatial aptitude. In R.J. Sternberg (Ed.), *The psychology of human intelligence* (Vol. 1, pp. 311–365). Hillsdale, NJ: Erlbaum.

Sampson, P.D., Bookstein, F.L., Barr, H.M., & Streissguth, A.P. (1994). Prenatal alcohol exposure, birthweight, and measures of child size from birth to age 14 years. *American Journal of Public Health, 84,* 1421–1428.

Schandler, S.L., Brannock, J.C., Cohen, M.J., & Mendez, J. (1993). Spatial learning deficits in adolescent children of alcoholics. *Journal of Experimental and Clinical Psychopharmacology, 1,* 207–214.

Streissguth, A.P., Barr, H.M., Bookstein, F.L., & Sampson, P.D. (1993). *The enduring effects of prenatal alcohol exposure on child development: Birth through 7 years.* Ann Arbor: University of Michigan Press.

Streissguth, A.P., Barr, H.M., Sampson, P.D., Bookstein, F.L., & Darby, B.L. (1989). Neurobehavioral effects of prenatal alcohol: Part I. Literature review and research strategy. *Neurotoxicological Teratology, 11,* 461–476.

Streissguth, A.P., Bookstein, F.L., Sampson, P.D., & Barr, H.M. (in press). Attention: Prenatal alcohol and continuities of vigilance and attentional problems from 4 through 14 years. *Development and Psychopathology.*

Streissguth, A.P., Sampson, P.D., Carmichael Olson, H., Bookstein, F.L., Barr, H.M., Scott, M., Feldman, J., & Mirsky, A.F. (1994). Maternal drinking during pregnancy and attention/memory performance in 14 year old children: A longitudinal prospective study. *Alcoholism: Clinical and Experimental Research, 18,* 202–218.

(RECEIVED 7/18/94; ACCEPTED 12/14/94)

Multiple Choice:

1. Which of the following describes the usual relation between speed and accuracy?

    A. In general, individuals who respond quickly on most tasks tend to be highly accurate as well.
    B. There is a trade off--as the speed of response increases, so does the number of errors.
    C. Responding impulsively with the first thing that comes to mind usually pays off.
    D. Speed and accuracy are unrelated in most psychological tests.

2. This is a *longitudinal* study because:

    A. the same individuals were tested multiple times
    B. the research has continued over many years
    C. a very large sample was studied
    D. both questionnaire and direct observation data were obtained
    E. all of the above

Essay:

1. According to Table 2, both fathers' and mothers' educational level was negatively correlated with the amount that mothers drank during mid-pregnancy; that is, the higher the education level of either parent, the less alcohol the mother consumed. What might contribute to this relation?

ARTICLE 4

The Improvising Infant: Learning about Learning to Move

Esther Thelen

This selection is very different from any other in this reader. It is a chapter from a book of mini-autobiographies by prominent developmental researchers. We chose this article because it illustrates so many aspects of the process of doing research.

First, it introduces you to a researcher, Dr. Esther Thelen, whose career was initially motivated by simple curiosity--the best of all beginnings for a scientist. Second, the value of careful observation is illustrated: How else could one notice the relation between leg movements of wasps and waifs. Third, it shows the virtue of keeping an open mind so that you can see familiar things in a new light and can move beyond your former ideas. Fourth, as you read this selection, you can follow the chain of logic by which Dr. Thelen proceeds from one study to the next. And what clever studies they are: Surely you will never forget the researcher who tested a hypothesis about fat legs by putting babies in a fish tank! Fifth, Dr. Thelen's research reveals how fruitful it can be to apply an analogy from one domain (the actions of springs and levers) to help understand something in quite a different area (infant stepping movements). Sixth, you see how a specific theoretical approach can organize one's thinking: Dr. Thelen's deep appreciation of the complexity of development found an intellectual home in the dynamical systems approach (a version of chaos theory).

Our final reason for including this biographical selection is its illustration of the fact that development can meander. Although Dr. Thelen is currently a prominent and influential developmental psychologist, she did not start out with that goal in mind. At this point, you may know exactly what you want to do with the rest of your life. Or you may not. But, as Dr. Thelen's life path shows, you don't necessarily have to know your destination at the outset to end up at a very satisfying place.

The Improvising Infant: Learning about Learning to Move

———— ❖ ————

I hope that readers will learn from this book not only how people conduct research but also something about how people conduct lives. I am sure that within the chapters of this book are stories of researchers whose lives have followed a singular vision, a burning question, or a straight path from college to graduate school to a position at a research university. I suspect that my story is equally represented—and probably even more likely among women. It is in some ways an unscripted story, because it did not follow the conventional ways of academic training and careers. But as I reflect on where my questions have led me, I also see a theme played out in my work.

I like the musical metaphor used by Mary Catherine Bateson in her book *Composing a Life*. In this book, she tells the stories of five women, of my generation and older, as they seek a coherent life in times when women's roles and expectations are rapidly changing. She likens their lives not so much to a structured musical score, where the notes and chords follow a planned and logical sequence, but to improvisation. The women in Bateson's book did not so much play out their lives according to the conventional scores of their age, gender, education, backgrounds, or even larger visions, but composed them from the opportunities and constraints of their daily situations and what they brought to those situations. As each personal victory or tragedy unfolded, the women opportunistically seized upon it and used it to build. The improvisational metaphor is especially apt; like good jazz, the notes and riffs of everyday life may seem unplanned, but from them comes a coherent structure. The secret seems to be the ability to improvise as circumstances change: to explore, select, and use what the situation affords us. (Later, I will argue that this metaphor applies just as well to infants learning motor skills; hence the title of this essay.)

In my scientific life, I see both the big themes and lots of improvisation. Every day seems a lot like improvisation, but the themes also come through, especially when writing an essay like this one, when one tries to make sense of the local encounters and chance events. Some themes of my scientific life are: (1) I like to describe behavior as it plays out through time, (2) I like to try and construct a "big picture" from data, and (3) I have enjoyed crossing disciplinary boundaries.

FROM BIOLOGY TO PSYCHOLOGY

I could not have identified these themes when I was an undergraduate biology major at the University of Wisconsin in the early 1960s; I had not yet composed them. But they—and the more compelling dynamics of family—must have fed my decision not to go to graduate school in molecular or cellular biology, exciting new areas in which I had done well as an undergraduate. Although I had enjoyed my classes and lab work, it just didn't feel right to continue. The questions were not right for me. I never thought much about psychology. I blush to admit that although I have now taught in a psychology department for over fifteen years, I never had an undergraduate psychology class! At the time, academic psychology was dominated by the behaviorists, and I knew enough about the work to be decidedly underwhelmed.

So instead of graduate training, I chose the more traditional path of supporting my husband's professional career (he is a historian), and soon after, of starting a family. What did get me back to science was a confluence of largely chance events. The first was the winter of 1970 in Madison, Wisconsin, one of the coldest and snowiest on record. My husband was a visiting professor and I was home with two preschoolers. To go out, it took an hour to bundle up the kids, and that was *if* I could start the car and shovel out the driveway. I resolved that when we returned to our home in Columbia, Missouri (which was a lot warmer!), I would "take a class" as a way of expanding my interests beyond jello cubes and *Sesame Street.* I have often reminded my children that they were entirely responsible for my career.

Well, what class was the bored housewife to take? The second chance event was the class I eventually chose, animal behavior, taught in the biology department at the University of Missouri, where my husband was on the faculty. I loved it! The class was taught by Fritz Walther, a classical ethologist trained by Konrad Lorenz himself. Professor Walther made me see the coherence of behavior and biology, and I immediately recognized that this was the level at which I had questions to ask. Ethologists carefully watched animals as they lived out their complex lives. They described behavior as their subjects sought food, avoided predators, found mates, and raised their young. Then the ethologists asked about what *caused* the animals to act in this way: What triggered behavior, how did it evolve, and how did it develop? These are the questions that motivate me to this day.

Although a theme was beginning to emerge from the notes, I cannot remember actually ever deciding to become a researcher and faculty member, and sometimes I am even sort of surprised at how I went from League of Women Voters meetings to addressing large audiences at scientific meetings. What happened was that one class led to another and I ended up in graduate school. I went to the University of Missouri because that was where we happened to be. Maybe if I had been more driven by the vision of career rather than just doing interesting things, I would have made different choices. But as it was, I tried to do the best I could with what circumstances offered.

My graduate training was an amalgam of biology and psychology. This was also unplanned. I was interested in behavior, and they taught more about behavior in the psychology department than in biology. These local decisions—to take this class or that, work on this problem or that, had both good and bad consequences. Because I was following my own interests and fashioning my own program, I fell between the mentoring cracks. I never belonged to a real "lab," or had an intense intellectual relationship with a close group of colleagues and mentors, although I had fine, supportive teachers. I did not feel especially deprived at the time. Now I can see that this situation allowed me much room for improvisation and discovery. Like sensitive parents, my professors provided help and facilitation but let me find my own way.

FROM INSECTS TO BABIES?

The theme that emerged from that first course in animal behavior until the present is an overarching interest in patterns of behavior and their change over time. It all began in an unlikely species—a tiny, parasitic wasp. My professor, Donald Farish, was interested at the time in how patterns of behavior could reveal phylogenetic relationships; that is, how behavior rather than anatomical structure could tell about the evolution of species. The behavior was grooming. It turns out that, in the family Hymenoptera, the bees and wasps, you can describe an evolutionary "family tree" just as well on grooming patterns, the ways in which these creatures rub their antennae, legs, and bodies, as on fixed anatomical features.

For my master's thesis, however, I looked in detail at the structure of grooming movements in one species of wasp that lived by laying eggs on other insect larvae. The tiny critters went through a real grooming dance;

first they rubbed the antennae, then the head, then the front legs in a certain pattern, and so on. It looked like their nervous systems played a tape, and out came not just the pattern of a single type of movement, but also an elaborate sequence. Did the sequence come entirely from the tape inside the nervous system, or was there something about cleaning the antennae that triggered cleaning the head?

To test this, I did the logical experiment. I cut off the wasps' antennae. Sure enough, the insects waved their legs and cleaned the air where their antennae were supposed to be—it must be the tape. But no, when I looked really closely at the structure and sequencing of "air grooming," it was different from that of intact wasps. There must also be feedback from the groomed structures. This is a theme that has recurred over and over in looking at patterned behavior. Yes, there is internal structure, but no movements occur without information from the outside. But as for improvisation, insects don't do very much of it.

Although it may seem implausible to jump from some of the simplest animals to the most complex, it was a natural transition for me to go from insects to infants. I was taking and much enjoying a course in developmental psychology—another fortuitous event. As I read the famous developmental psychologist Jean Piaget's description of "circular reactions"— actions that infants repeat over and over again, I was reminded of the stereotyped movement sequences I was seeing in the little wasps. Do human infants do the same kind of repeated motor sequences? I wrote a paper on the topic for the class and discovered that, yes, people for a long time had noticed rhythmic movements in normal infants, but also in infants and children in institutions, as well as in people with mental retardation and other handicaps such as autism. There were explanations based on animal behavior, speculations coming from Freudian theory, and theories grounded in medical neurology, but really, not much was known.

Well, I reasoned, what a good topic for a dissertation! It would combine my background in behavioral biology with my newly emerging interest in developmental psychology. Since none of my professors objected, I forged ahead.

AN INFANT ETHOLOGIST

In many ways, my dissertation research set the direction of my research career. I began, as I still begin now, as a good ethologist. In order to understand behavior you have to know what it looks like. You need to see what form the behavior takes, how frequently and under what circumstances it is performed, and how it changes. So I undertook a longitudinal study of observing twenty normal infants in their homes every two weeks over their first year to chart these "rhythmic stereotypies" in their natural setting. It was a big job; my assistants and I would visit two homes every day, lugging a box of toys to keep the siblings happy, a Bayley test kit to keep track of the babies' developmental progress, and a heavy reel-to-reel video recorder and camera. We became like members of the families and shared many experiences, including one time, even being attacked by fleas deposited by the family pets! As we watched everyday family life, we detailed, both by a sampled frequency count and by a detailed narrative, the episodes of repetitive movements performed by the infants.

In addition to the pleasure of watching our little subjects grow and develop, I learned a great deal from this intensive period of observation. I did not enter into the observations with a theoretical bias, perhaps a benefit from not having a single, dominant mentor. I learned how to watch behavior very patiently and carefully. I completed the study having gained some understanding of infant rhythmicities. But, as in any good research, it also raised a lot more questions. I became convinced that the previous explanations of rhythmicities were insufficient, and that maybe accounts of other aspects of infant development were incomplete as well.

SHAKE, RATTLE, AND ROLL

What I found was that these perfectly normal infants spent a lot of time moving their limbs and bodies in rhythmic, stereotyped ways. They moved nearly every body part: We saw kicking, rocking, swaying, banging, waving, bouncing, and jumping movements. Some of these movements are pictured in Figure 2-1. All the babies did them, although some more than others. But what was most intriguing was that these movements were associated with distinct developmental periods. In particular, infants performed these oscillating movements when they had some emerging control of that body part or posture, but before they became really skilled. For instance, infants swayed back and forth just after they learned to sit, but not after they were sitting in a stable and comfortable manner. They rocked back and forth just after they could get up on their hands and knees but before they actually crawled well. They banged their arms and waved their toys after they could reach and grab, but before they had fine manipulation skills.

I saw these rhythmic movements like a window opening on the process of developing skills. At these points of transition, when control was just emerging, the system said "Do something"—try to crawl, find out about this interesting toy—but the infant's brain could not yet tell the muscles precisely when and how much to contract to actually get those arms and legs going right. So the system, given a general "go" signal, does what limbs and muscles can do—oscillates like a spring that has been pulled tight and released. When the baby has learned the right muscle settings, she or he now can do more interesting things than repeat a goalless movement, and the stereotyped behaviors normally stop.

But what makes an infant do a particular rhythmic movement at a particular time? When I looked at the real-life situations that were associated

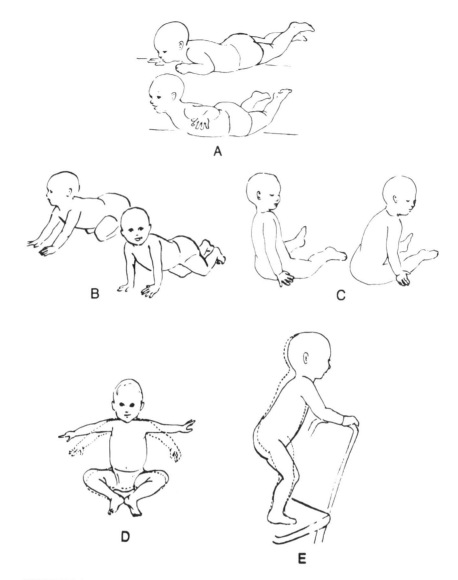

FIGURE 2-1
Infants performing rhythmic stereotypies of their legs, arms, and torsos in various postures.

with bouts of stereotyped movement, I saw that they were not randomly performed. Infants often did these movements when they were excited, or when they were drowsy. (Indeed, adults perform rhythmic movements under similar circumstances; some normal adults report rocking or head banging when drowsy, and many people jump up and down when they are really excited, or bang their fists when angry.) And although most of the movements seemed almost involuntary, frequently infants seemed to "take over" the movement for some seemingly intentional action. A little boy, for example, banged his hand against his tray and kicked his feet in between spoonfuls of food. He seemed to be communicating his impatience to his mother, who was feeding him.

Infants' abilities to take some action, adapt it to serve a new purpose, and then modify that action to better fit the new purpose is another developmental theme that came from my dissertation and has carried through my later research. Here, in fact, is the improvisation theme: Play a melody, explore how you can change it. As I will explain, this capacity to move bits and pieces of behavior around, so to speak, has important implications for understanding how the brain and the body work.

THE ORGANIZATION OF INFANT MOVEMENTS

When I finished my Ph.D. dissertation, I was not in a very good position to find a job. I was trained in a strange combination of fields, and I had no group of well-known mentors to recommend me. Luckily, and again, by chance, a few people in the psychology department and the administration of the University of Missouri liked what I had done as a student, and offered me a half-time faculty position. The only lab space available was a funny little house next to the main psychology building. Maybe the building's history explained why it was vacant: Many years ago, the psychology building housed the University of Missouri Medical School and my lab was the morgue, where the dissections were done. The tile walls, cement floors, and drains were not ideal for a baby lab, but with carpets and colorful posters, it would do. I was thrilled to be able to continue to do research. (I now have a beautiful watercolor painting of the little house hanging in my living room, a gift from a former student.)

As I said before, my dissertation raised many intriguing questions. The first thing I wanted to know was how infants actually did these movements. What did the movements look like in time and space? How were they controlled? I knew very little about motor control in general, and so in order to answer these questions I had to begin to learn about an entirely new field.

I started by looking at leg kicking because it was a very rhythmical behavior that infants did all the time, and about which I could find no previous studies. Videotape was just becoming easy to use in the lab; so, using an enormous Sony 3/4-inch video recorder, I devised a system to analyze infant leg movements. It was very primitive compared to the expensive computer-assisted devices I now have, just a plexifilm grid placed over the video monitor. As I advanced the videotape frame-by-frame, I could track the x,y coordinates of little squares of tape we put on the babies' legs. By knowing the position of the joint and the videoframe, I could reconstruct the path of the limb over time. (The fancy devices work on the very same principle.)

What my students and I discovered confirmed my earlier impression that common infant kicking was indeed very organized. Infants were not just flailing around. The movements were quite precisely timed—about one-third of a second to flex the leg toward the body, and a little longer to extend it back out, and the kicks occurred in rhythmic bouts, one kick after another. When infants kicked at a faster rate, the actual movement times did not change much, but the time *between* kicks became shorter. This is exactly what happens as people *walk* faster; the swing of their legs forward does not become much quicker at all, but the time between swings decreases. Maybe I had found the motor tape in young infants that later controlled locomotion! Perhaps there was a program inside the baby, just waiting to play out, like the tiny wasps' grooming.

THE MYSTERY DEEPENS

I did not hold onto the motor tape theory very long. My students and I looked more closely at these movements, into the actual muscle patterns controlling these kicks. We used tiny electrodes to sense the muscle contractions on infants' legs. (Electromyography, or EMG, detects muscle activity in the same way as an EKG records heart activity by detecting minute electrical changes in the body.) What we found was that although the patterns of leg movements were quite organized and even looked programmed, in comparison, the muscle patterns were very unspecific. When babies flexed their legs in a kick, all the muscles fired at the same time, including muscles that normally flex *and* those that normally extend the leg. Even more surprising, was when the infants extended their legs after the flexion, no muscles contracted at all. What could be going on? How could the movements have more organization than the patterns of muscle contraction that produced them? If there were a tape, it would not be a very precise one; nothing inside was apparently timing the movements.

This single discovery cascaded into a new way of thinking about motor development, and indeed, about thinking about development in general. Some other processes must be involved in producing leg movement patterns because they were *more* than just muscle contraction patterns. But it took another set of experiments to sharpen my theoretical focus.

THE CASE OF THE DISAPPEARING REFLEX

One of the long-held mysteries of early development is the Case of the Disappearing Reflex. If you hold newborn infants upright by supporting them under the armpits, and then lower their feet to the table, they will take "steps"—an alternating kind of march that is always quite surprising to see, because newborn infants normally are so uncoordinated. Within a month or two, however, this early reflex disappears and can no longer be elicited. Traditionally, psychologists and pediatricians have assumed that the reflex disappears because it is inhibited by other parts of the brain as the infants mature.

But as I looked at the hours of videotape of infants kicking their legs, infants ranging in age from 2 weeks to over 6 months, I was struck by an incongruity. Kicking looked a lot like stepping lying down. Or stepping looked a lot like kicking standing up. But babies never stopped kicking. It not only did not disappear, it increased in frequency.

When my graduate student, Donna Fisher, and I carefully compared the movement and EMG patterns in very young infants, we found no difference between those of kicking and of stepping. They were one and the same movement done in different postures. Yet as they got older, infants stopped the movements when we stood them up and resumed them when we lay them back down. How could the maturing brain exert this inhibitory influence in one posture and not another? It did not make sense.

*T*HINKING ABOUT SPRINGS AND LEVERS

I tried to back off from the traditional neurological explanation and think about *all* the things that were going on in this puzzling story. What was happening to infants as they got older in addition to changes in their brains? One obvious change was that during the first few months of life, when the stepping reflex disappears, babies grow very rapidly. They get much heavier. With a bit of detective work in the literature, I discovered that most of this postnatal growth is in subcutaneous fat tissue, rather than in muscle. So the legs were getting heavier, but not proportionately stronger.

For the next piece of the puzzle, I consulted with a biomechanist, someone who studies the mechanical actions of the body. Yes, he confirmed, if you think of the leg segments as levers, it would be true that lifting legs when upright takes more strength than when lying down. This is because gravity helps to flex the leg when infants are supine, but only opposes movement when they are upright.

So it began to make sense. Before infants developed fat legs, they had no problem moving them from either position. But as their legs got fat and heavy faster than their muscle strength increased, infants could no longer lift them to step when upright. However, they had no trouble kicking when supine. The stepping reflex did not really disappear, it was just masked by the changes in other systems. This led to several simple predictions, which we tested by experiments.

My favorite is the fish tank experiment. Heavy legs should not pose a problem underwater, because limbs become buoyant. If leg mass inhibits movements, infants who no longer step "on land" should step fine when their legs are submerged. So we bought the largest fish tank we could afford. It was a bit tricky explaining to parents why we wanted to hold their 2-month-old infants in torso-deep warm water in a large fish tank, but they all agreed. And, as predicted, our wet and slippery subjects all stepped like crazy.

Thinking about legs acting like levers made me aware of theories that suggested that limbs also can behave like springs. Muscles can store energy when stretched, and then spring back and even oscillate when released, just like an ordinary spring. The spring model could help explain kicking and, in particular, why I found precisely timed flexions and extensions in the movements themselves, but no alternating patterns of muscle contractions. When a spring (or a pendulum) oscillates, it does so with a particular timed cycle; indeed springs and pendulums are used as timekeepers inside clocks. But there is no clock itself inside the spring. The timing comes from the physical characteristics of the spring; its degree of springiness and its damping characteristics, and the fact that it stores energy when it is stretched. Likewise, the timing of kicking may come, not from a clock inside the infant, but from the leg acting as a spring. All the infant needs to do is stretch the spring (add energy by contracting muscles) and the pattern emerges as the spring oscillates. Perhaps springs had something to do with all the rhythmic behaviors I had observed in my dissertation research; when infants do not have very good control over a limb or posture, adding energy to the system may reveal its natural oscillations.

Springs and levers may seem far removed from developmental psychology, but they opened my eyes to how multidetermined behavior and its change must be. Some contributions to development may not be immediately obvious—like body fat! So I began to look for a way to conceptualize development that gave equal status to all the contributing factors.

TOWARD A SYSTEMS APPROACH

In nearly every textbook of child development, the authors devote an early chapter to the physical growth of infants. Motor development is often included as part of physical growth. In some ways this distinction tells readers that while physical growth and motor skill are necessary for psychological growth, they are also separate from it. A common message is that motor skill development, like growth, *just happens* as time passes: As the brain gets bigger and better, it instructs the body to do more and more complicated things. Psychological growth, the traditional view holds, is more complex and interactive.

It was my confrontation with the reality of legs as springs and levers that made me think that this traditional view was wrong. First, the body could not just be waiting around to be told what to do. In fact, it is because limbs and bodies are physical things—levers and elastic springs that are subject to gravity, that generate forces and move through space and time—that the brain *cannot* know ahead of time what to tell the body. How can the brain know in advance how much force to exert in what direction to get a limb of a particular mass and elasticity to a particular place, especially when those properties are changing rapidly? The traditional view has got it backward, I thought: The body has to instruct the brain. Infants have to learn about their own bodies in particular situations in order to acquire such skills as sitting or walking or reaching for things.

Second, in development, *everything* counts! It is not enough to ascribe change to just the nervous system, because behavior emerges from interactions. There are times when infants move their legs when lying down, or when submerged, but not when held erect. Can we say that babies "have" upright stepping because they can step under some circumstances? It is the wrong question. What we can say is, the system product of a heavy 3-month-old held upright is no movement of the legs. Under water, the very same system reorganizes to produce stepping motions. The behavior resides not in the infant, nor in the fish tank, but in the entire baby-in-context situation. Behavior does not live in disembodied form. Rather, it organizes itself in the real circumstances from whatever capabilities are available in the organism in relation to a task and a set of physical constraints. I like to use a term coined by Peter Kugler and Michael Turvey—*soft-assembly*—meaning that the actions you see are never wired into the system in a rigid fashion, but tacked together at the moment out of available components. Sometimes the assembly is very stable and looks the same from time to time. Walking is a good example of a stable assembly. But even stable behaviors are never *exactly* the same. People can and do make frequent subtle adjustments to meet different conditions as they walk, or even to express different moods.

Thinking about behavior in this way profoundly changes the way we think about development. To return to my musical metaphor, the infant's first year is not so much the playing out of a previously written score, but an improvisation. At any point in time, the infant has certain abilities and particular needs and desires; for example, to put interesting things in her mouth, or to keep Mom talking and smiling at him. What babies do is assemble the best they have at the time to attempt the task—an improvisation—and then as they repeat and repeat the attempts, they learn. Over time the match between their attempts and the world gradually improves and we say they become skilled. And as they master one task, it opens up new tasks. For instance, learning to crawl tremendously increases the number of opportunities to learn about the world as infants can then move themselves from one place to another. It is the challenge of the task that keeps development moving forward, not a little clock inside the baby.

*D*EVELOPMENTAL DYNAMICS

I came to articulate the account of development in the previous paragraphs because I could not find an existing theoretical framework that fit the data I was gathering in my lab. More formally, my thinking has been influenced greatly by theoretical advances in other fields, notably from a mathematical and physical theory of complexity called "dynamical systems" or "chaos" theory. I first heard of dynamical systems because a few researchers, notably Scott Kelso, Michael Turvey, and Peter Kugler, were applying dynamics to adult motor behavior. It was very difficult for me to understand at first, but as I learned more and more, I became increasingly excited, and convinced that it would be very useful for understanding baby movements as well.

Many readers will have read James Gleick's popular book, *Chaos*, or seen a *Nova* program on television proclaiming this "new science." Dynamical systems theories are a departure from conventional approaches because they seek to understand the overall behavior of a system, not by dissecting it into parts, but by asking how and under what circumstances the parts *cooperate* to produce a whole pattern.

There are many kinds of dynamical systems and many applications, from weather patterns to brain waves, but for human development, a few general principles are important. First is the importance of time—dynamic means changing over time, and dynamic systems are those that act over time. Second, is the notion of "self-organization," that is that patterns can emerge from complex systems without a blueprint existing beforehand. Good examples are the patterns in clouds, snowflakes, or water flowing over a stream bed. Likewise, biological systems may exhibit complex patterns over time without a little person inside telling the parts what to do. Recall infants' legs showing regular movements from their springlike behavior. The pattern is self-organized. And third is that these systems may be "nonlinear." A system is linear when the strength of a response is proportional to the strength of the stimulus: For every amount of x, there is a proportional change in y. Nonlinearity means that sometimes just a little change in the stimulus will lead to a disproportional response, or even a shift into an entirely new kind of response. When systems show these kinds of nonlinear responses, the component parts may reorganize to a new form: A simple example is freezing water. As the temperature of the air is lowered, liquid water gets colder. At 32 degrees Fahrenheit, a phase shift occurs and the water changes into ice.

The lesson from dynamical systems is that to understand how a complex system behaves, we must understand its dynamics, that is, how it behaves over time and under different conditions. When is it stable and when does it change? In development, we are especially interested in phase shifts, or when the infant acquires new skills, skills like reaching and walking or learning words, that were not there before. When we see this transition, we then want to understand why and how the system reorganized. It is obviously more complex than lowering the temperature! But this way of thinking about systems and how they are organized is very useful.

Much of my work since moving to Indiana University in 1985 has been inspired by dynamical systems thinking. It is a very powerful metaphor. Once I began to look at things "dynamically" I could not go back to the more traditional approaches. Students and colleagues have told me the same thing, that seeing behavior as fluid and time-based changes their interpretations of phenomena they are studying. Dynamic systems thinking also affects the way you conduct developmental studies, because it naturally leads to longitudinal experiments where subjects are followed intensively to track behavioral changes over time. (I realized only recently that I had been conducting dynamic systems studies all along, beginning with my dissertation. I just did not know it!)

USING DYNAMICS: BABIES ON TREADMILLS

One of the most fun series of studies coming from this dynamic inspiration has been with babies on treadmills. I can't remember exactly why I thought it might be interesting to put a baby on a treadmill. I think I was looking for a way to restore the lost stepping reflex. I had no idea whether it would work and there is no way of testing the effect of a treadmill without a treadmill. So we designed and built a baby-scaled treadmill that could sit on a table top. We recruited our first subject; I don't know what we said to convince the parents and the Human Subjects Committee that it was perfectly safe. You can imagine our excitement and delight when the baby who was about 7 months old and, who didn't move a muscle when held upright without the treadmill, responded immediately to the treadmill with beautifully coordinated and alternating steps! With my colleague Beverly Ulrich, who has collaborated on most of these studies, I have tested many dozens of infants ranging from 1 month to 1 year of age, and nearly every one steps on a treadmill. It is quite remarkable to see because the infants don't seem to be intentionally "walking," yet their movements are quite mature-looking. Like adults, infants take more steps when you speed up the treadmill and even are able to coordinate their steps when each foot is on a separate treadmill belt going at different speeds. Figure 2-2 is an illustration of a baby on a treadmill.

The treadmill studies were important theoretically because they demonstrated again the principle of soft-assembly. Obviously infants were not designed to have treadmill stepping. Possibly no infants in human history ever faced a treadmill before. Yet, given this environmental context—stretch legs back on a moving belt—infants improvise a new and very coordinated behavior. What they do have in place are neuromuscular pathways that respond to this task, but the behavior resides in the combination of the infant and the treadmill—it self-organizes in this situation. In fact, what Beverly Ulrich and I later found was that many components contribute to treadmill stepping, including having legs with the right amount of "springiness" to benefit from the action of the treadmill.

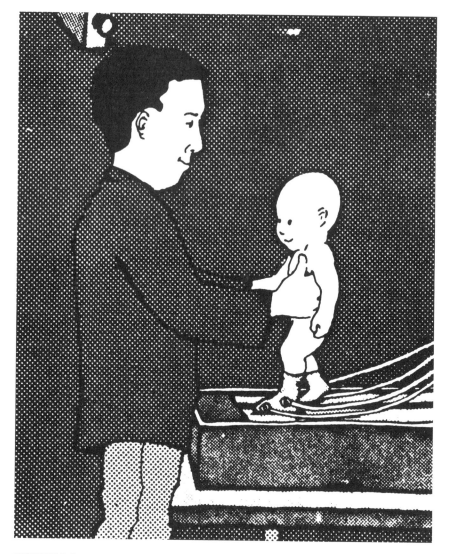

FIGURE 2-2

Infant being tested on the treadmill. The wires are connected to devices that help track the movements in time and space.

*I*MPROVISING LIVES

My current research follows the same overall pattern of first describing the developmental dynamics of an infant motor skill, and then trying to uncover what causes a new behavior to appear and become more skilled. My students and I have just completed a longitudinal study of how infants learn to reach. As we watched babies struggle hard to gain control of their arms, it was again clear how much of this is a problem-solving exercise, a problem each infant has to solve for himself or herself. This leads to more questions about how they discover a solution, and then how they remember it, and generalize it to other, similar situations.

In all this, however, I have come to appreciate more and more the value of improvisation not only for infants as they learn new skills, but for all of us as we live our lives. This is not to say we should not plan our futures and save our money, but rather that part of life should be taking advantage of opportunities that come along. One of the great joys of a research career is the freedom to follow silly ideas like putting babies in tanks of water or on treadmills on the chance they may do something interesting. Sometimes nothing will happen. However, I always teach my students to look just as carefully at the things that don't work out as at the experiments that work perfectly well because we can learn just as much. Improvisation means risk. Experiments might not work, and often infants try to walk and fall down. But improvisation also is our only means of discovery.

SUGGESTED READINGS

The August 1993 issue of *Child Development* has a special section entitled "Developmental Biodynamics: Brain, Body, Behavior Connections," edited by Esther Thelen and Jeffrey Lockman. The twelve articles and commentary are a good place to see the range of work now being conducted in early perceptual-motor development, and the implications for the field of child development in general.

Also:

GIBSON, E. J. (1988). Exploratory behavior in the development of perceiving, acting, and the acquiring of knowledge. *Annual Review of Psychology, 39,* 1–41.

OYAMA, S. (1985). *The Ontogeny of information: Development systems and evolution.* New York: Cambridge University Press.

THELEN, E. (1992). Development as a dynamic system. *Current Directions in Psychological Science, 1,* 189–193.

——— (1994). *A dynamic systems approach to the development of cognition and action.* Cambridge, MA: MIT Press/Bradford Books.

Multiple Choice:

1.   Dr. Thelen applied dynamical systems theory to the study of:

      A.   evolutionary psychology
      B.   musical ability
      C.   muscular development
      D.   motor development

2.   According to Dr. Thelen, one reason the stepping reflex disappears is that:

      A.   infants' legs become too heavy to lift
      B.   the waning of this lower level reflex is part of the human motor program
      C.   rhythmic stereotypic movements always disappear early in development
      D.   Dr. Thelen cut off wasps' antennae

Essay:

1.   Esther Thelen did a study (not mentioned in this chapter) in which she attached little weights to the ankles of babies and observed how it affected their leg kicking. Why do you think she did this? Hint--this study tested the same idea that Dr. Thelen tested by suspending 2-month-olds in water.

ARTICLE 5

Early Experience and Emotional Development: The Emergence of Wariness of Heights

Joseph J. Campos, Bennett I. Bertenthal, and Rosanne Kermoian

Reprinted from *Psychological Science*, 1992, *3*, 61-64.
Copyright © 1992 by the American Psychological Society.
Reprinted with the permission of Cambridge University Press.

In studying development (and anything else, for that matter), it is difficult to consider numerous factors all at once. Consequently, we tend to study development in one domain relatively separate from development in other domains. One of the special strengths of this article is that it breaks across topical boundaries and presents research relevant to motor, perceptual, and emotional development. This is the model researchers should attempt to emulate more often. We need to acknowledge and study the complexity of development, rather than try to oversimplify it and consequently miss its richness.

Parents are always excited when their infant achieves a new motor milestone, but this article stresses that the onset of independent locomotion--crawling--leads to other developmental advances. The authors used converging research operations to attempt to clarify the nature of the relation between self-produced locomotion and fear of heights.

By approaching the same question from four different directions, they were able to conclude that crawling experience--that is, moving one's self through the environment--leads infants to develop wariness and subsequent avoidance of heights. To reach such a conclusion, these investigators showed (1) an association between crawling and a measure of wariness of height, (2) acceleration of the onset of wariness as a function of extra experience, (3) delay as a function of deprivation of experience, and (4) a stronger relation of experience than age with the onset of fear.

This article thus illustrates the importance and difficulty of establishing causal relationships. Two variables (such as crawling and fear) can be associated with one another without either of them causing the other; for example, a third factor could be responsible for both. By their careful and clever series of experiments, the authors of this article were able to conclude that in this particular case, locomotor development induces emotional development.

Symposium on Emotion

EARLY EXPERIENCE AND EMOTIONAL DEVELOPMENT:
The Emergence of Wariness of Heights

Joseph J. Campos,[1] Bennett I. Bertenthal,[2] and Rosanne Kermoian[1]

[1]*University of California at Berkeley,* [2]*University of Virginia*

Abstract—*Because of its biological adaptive value, wariness of heights is widely believed to be innate or under maturational control. In this report, we present evidence contrary to this hypothesis, and show the importance of locomotor experience for emotional development. Four studies bearing on this conclusion have shown that (1) when age is held constant, locomotor experience accounts for wariness of heights; (2) "artificial" experience locomoting in a walker generates evidence of wariness of heights; (3) an orthopedically handicapped infant tested longitudinally did not show wariness of heights so long as he had no locomotor experience; and (4) regardless of the age when infants begin to crawl, it is the duration of locomotor experience and not age that predicts avoidance of heights. These findings suggest that when infants begin to crawl, experiences generated by locomotion make possible the development of wariness of heights.*

Between 6 and 10 months of age, major changes occur in fearfulness in the human infant. During this period, some fears are shown for the first time, and many others show a step-function increase in prevalence (Bridges, 1932; Scarr & Salapatek, 1970; Sroufe, 1979). These changes in fearfulness occur so abruptly, involve so many different elicitors, and have such biologically adaptive value that many investigators propose maturational explanations for this developmental shift (Emde, Gaensbauer,

This research was supported by grants from the National Institutes of Health (HD-16195, HD-00695, and HD-25066) and from the John D. and Catherine T. MacArthur Foundation.

Address requests for reprints to Joseph J. Campos, Institute of Human Development, 1203 Tolman Hall, University of California at Berkeley, Berkeley, CA 94720.

& Harmon, 1976; Kagan, Kearsley, & Zelazo, 1978). For such theorists, the development of neurophysiological structures (e.g., the frontal lobes) precedes and accounts for changes in affect.

In contrast to predominantly maturational explanations of developmental changes, Gottlieb (1983, 1991) proposed a model in which different types of experiences play an important role in developmental shifts. He emphasized that new developmental acquisitions, such as crawling, generate experiences that, in turn, create the conditions for further developmental changes. Gottlieb called such "bootstrapping" processes probabilistic epigenesis. In contrast to most current models of developmental transition, Gottlieb's approach stresses the possibility that, under some circumstances, psychological function may precede and account for development of neurophysiological structures.

There is evidence in the animal literature that a probabilistic epigenetic process plays a role in the development of wariness of heights. Held and Hein (1963), for instance, showed that dark-reared kittens given experience with active self-produced locomotion in an illuminated environment showed avoidance of heights, whereas dark-reared littermates given passive experience moving in the same environment manifested no such avoidance. In these studies, despite equivalent maturational states in the two groups of kittens, the experiences made possible by correlated visuomotor responses during active locomotion proved necessary to elicit wariness of heights.

So long as they are prelocomotor, human infants, despite their visual competence and absence of visual deprivation, may be functionally equivalent to Held and Hein's passively moved kittens. Crawling may generate or refine skills sufficient for the onset of wariness of heights. These skills may include improved calibration of distances, heightened sensitivity to visually specified self-motion, more consistent coordination of

visual and vestibular stimulation, and increased awareness of emotional signals from significant others (Bertenthal & Campos, 1990; Campos, Hiatt, Ramsay, Henderson, & Svejda, 1978).

There is anecdotal evidence supporting a link between locomotor experience and development of wariness of heights in human infants. Parents commonly report that there is a phase following the acquisition of locomotion when infants show no avoidance of heights, and will go over the edge of a bed or other precipice if the caretaker is not vigilant. Parents also report that this phase of apparent fearlessness is followed by one in which wariness of heights becomes quite intense (Campos et al., 1978).

In sum, both the kitten research and the anecdotal human evidence suggest that wariness of heights is not simply a maturational phenomenon, to be expected even in the absence of experience. From the perspective of probabilistic epigenesis, locomotor experience may operate as an organizer of emotional development, serving either to induce wariness of heights (i.e., to produce a potent emotional state that would never emerge without such experience) or to facilitate its emergence (i.e., to bring it about earlier than it otherwise would appear). The research reported here represents an attempt to determine whether locomotor experience is indeed an organizer of the emergence of wariness of heights.

Pinpointing the role of locomotion in the emergence of wariness of heights in human infants requires solution of a number of methodological problems. One is the selection of an ecologically valid paradigm for testing wariness of heights. Another is the determination of an outcome measure that can be used with both prelocomotor and locomotor infants. A third is a means of determining whether locomotion is playing a role as a correlate, an antecedent, an inducer, or a facilitator of the onset of wariness of heights.

The ecologically valid paradigm we selected for testing was the visual cliff (Walk, 1966; Walk & Gibson, 1961)—a large, safety-glass-covered table with a solid textured surface placed immediately underneath the glass on one side (the "shallow" side) and a similar surface placed some 43 in. underneath the glass on the floor below on the other side (the "deep" side).

To equate task demands for prelocomotor and locomotor infants, we measured the infants' wariness reactions while they were slowly lowered toward either the deep or the shallow side of the cliff. This descent procedure not only allowed us to assess differences in wariness reactions as a function of locomotor experience in both prelocomotor and locomotor infants but also permitted us to assess an index of depth perception, that is, a visual placing response (the extension of the arms and hands in anticipation of contact with the shallow, but not the deep, surface of the cliff [Walters, 1981]).

To assess fearfulness with an index appropriate to both pre- and postlocomoting infants, we measured heart rate (HR) responses during the 3-s period of descent onto the surface of the cliff. Prior work had shown consistently that heart rate decelerates in infants who are in a state of nonfearful attentiveness, but accelerates when infants are showing either a defensive response (Graham & Clifton, 1966) or a precry state (Campos, Emde, Gaensbauer, & Henderson, 1975).

To relate self-produced locomotion to fearfulness, we used a number of converging research operations. One was an *age-held-constant design,* contrasting the performance of infants who were locomoting with those of the same age who were not yet locomoting; the second was an analog of an experiential *enrichment* manipulation, in which infants who were otherwise incapable of crawling or creeping were tested after they had a number of hours of experience moving about voluntarily in walker devices; the third was an analog of an experiential *deprivation* manipulation, in which an infant who was orthopedically handicapped, but otherwise normal, was tested longitudinally past the usual age of onset of crawling and again after the delayed acquisition of crawling; and the fourth was a *cross-sequential lag design* aimed at teasing apart the effects of age of onset of locomotion and of duration of locomotor experience on the infant's avoidance of crossing the deep or the shallow side of the cliff to the mother.

EXPERIMENT 1: HR RESPONSES OF PRELOCOMOTOR AND LOCOMOTOR INFANTS

In the first study, a total of 92 infants, half locomoting for an average of 5 weeks, were tested at 7.3 months of age. Telemetered HR, facial expressions (taped from a camera under the deep side of the cliff), and the visual placing response were recorded. Each infant was lowered to each side of the cliff by a female experimenter, with the mother in another room.

As predicted from the work of Held and Hein (1963), locomotor infants showed evidence of wariness of heights, and prelocomotor infants did not. Only on deep trials did the HR of locomotor infants accelerate significantly from baselevels (by 5 beats/min), and differ significantly from the HR responses of prelocomotor infants. The HR responses of prelocomotor infants did not differ from baselevels on either the deep or shallow sides. Surprisingly, facial expressions did not differentiate testing conditions, perhaps because the descent minimized the opportunity to target these expressions to social figures.

In addition, every infant tested, regardless of locomotor status, showed visual placing responses on the shallow side, and no infant showed placing responses on the deep side of the cliff. Thus, all infants showed evidence for depth perception on the deep side, but only locomotor infants showed evidence of fear-related cardiac acceleration in response to heights.

EXPERIMENT 2: ACCELERATION OF LOCOMOTOR EXPERIENCE

Although correlated, the development of locomotion and the emergence of wariness of heights may be jointly determined by a third factor that brings about both changes. Disambiguation of this possibility required a means of providing "artificial" locomotor experience to infants who were not yet able to crawl. This manipulation was achieved by providing wheeled walkers to infants and testing them after their mothers had reported at least 32 hr of voluntary forward movement in the device.

Infants who received walkers were divided into two groups: prelocomotor walkers ($N = 9M, 9F$, Mean Age = 224 days, Walker Experience = 47 hr of voluntary forward movement) and locomotor walkers ($N = 9M, 7F$, Mean Age = 222 days, Walker Experience = 32 hr). The performance of infants in these two groups was compared with the performance of age-matched subjects, also divided into two groups: prelocomotor controls ($N = 9M, 9F$, Mean Age = 222 days) and locomotor controls ($N = 9M, 7F$, Mean Age = 222 days). The average duration of crawling experience was only 5 days in the locomotor walker and the locomotor control groups. All infants were tested using the same procedure as in the prior study. No shallow trials were administered in order to minimize subject loss due to the additional testing time required for such trials.

As revealed in Figure 1, the three groups of infants with any type of locomotor experience showed evidence of cardiac acceleration, whereas the prelocomotor control infants did not. It is noteworthy that all 16 infants in the locomotor walker group (who had a "double dosage" of locomotor experience consisting of walker training and some crawling) showed HR accelerations upon descent to the cliff. Planned comparisons revealed significant differences between (1) all walker infants and all controls, (2) all spontaneously locomoting infants and prelocomotor controls, and (3) prelocomotor walkers and prelocomotor controls. These findings show that the provision of "artificial" locomotor experience may facilitate or induce wariness of heights, even for infants who otherwise have little or no crawling experience. Locomotor experience thus appears to be an antecedent of the emergence of wariness.

EXPERIMENT 3: DEPRIVATION OF LOCOMOTOR EXPERIENCE

Although Experiment 2 showed that training in locomotion accelerates the

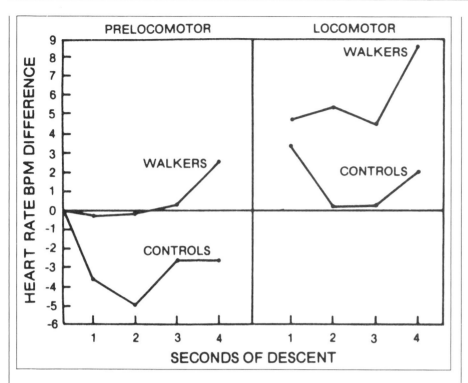

Fig. 1. Heart rate response while the infant is lowered toward the deep side of the visual cliff as a function of locomotor experience. The left panel contrasts the performance of prelocomotor infants with and without "artificial" walker experience. The right panel contrasts the performance of crawling infants with and without "artificial" walker experience. Heart rate is expressed as difference from baseline in beats/min.

onset of wariness of heights, it is possible that this response would eventually develop even in the absence of locomotor experience. To determine whether the delayed acquisition of crawling precedes the delayed emergence of wariness of heights, we longitudinally tested an infant with a peripheral handicap to locomotion. This infant was neurologically normal and had a Bayley Developmental Quotient of 126, but was born with two congenitally dislocated hips. After an early operation, he was placed in a full body cast. The infant was tested on the visual cliff monthly between 6 and 10 months of age using the procedures described above. While the infant was in the cast, he showed no evidence of crawling. At 8.5 months of age (i.e., 1.5 months after the normative age of onset of locomotion), the cast was removed, and the infant began crawling soon afterward.

This infant showed no evidence of differential cardiac responsiveness on the deep versus shallow side of the cliff until 10 months of age, at which time his HR

accelerated markedly on the deep side, and decelerated on the shallow. Although we cannot generalize from a single case study, these data provide further support for the role of self-produced locomotion as a facilitator or inducer of wariness of heights.

EXPERIMENT 4: AGE OF ONSET OF LOCOMOTION VERSUS LOCOMOTOR EXPERIENCE

In the studies described so far, HR was used as an imperfect index of wariness. However, we felt that a study using behavioral avoidance was needed to confirm the link between locomotor experience and wariness of heights. We thus used the locomotor crossing test on the visual cliff, in which the infant is placed on the center of the cliff, and the mother is instructed to encourage the infant to cross to her over either the deep or the shallow side. In this study, we also assessed separately the effects of age of onset of crawling (early, normative, or

late) and of duration of locomotor experience (11 or 41 days), as well as their interaction, using a longitudinal design.

The results of this study demonstrated a clear effect of locomotor experience independent of the age when self-produced locomotion first appeared. This effect of experience was evident with both nominal data (the proportion of infants who avoided descending onto the deep side of the cliff on the first test trial) and interval data (the latency to descend from the center board of the visual cliff onto the deep side on deep trials minus the latency to descend onto the shallow side on shallow trials). At whatever age the infant had begun to crawl, only 30% to 50% of infants avoided the deep side after 11 days of locomotor experience. However, after 41 days of locomotor experience, avoidance increased to 60% to 80% of infants. The latency data revealed a significant interaction of side of cliff with locomotor experience, but not a main effect of age, nor of the interaction of age with experience. The results of this study further suggest that locomotor experience paces the onset of wariness of heights.

PROCESSES UNDERLYING THE DEVELOPMENT OF WARINESS OF HEIGHTS

The pattern of findings obtained in these four studies, taken together with the animal studies by Held and Hein (1963), demonstrates a consistent relation between locomotor experience and wariness of heights. We propose the following interpretations for our findings.

We believe that crawling initially is a goal in itself, with affect solely linked to the success or failure of implementing the act of moving. Locomotion is initially not context dependent, and infants show no wariness of heights because the goal of moving is not coordinated with other goals, including the avoidance of threats. However, as a result of locomotor experience, infants acquire a sense of both the efficacy and the limitations of their own actions. Locomotion stops being an end in itself, and begins to be goal corrected and coordinated with the environmental surround. As a result, infants begin to show wariness of heights once locomotion becomes context dependent (cf. Bertenthal & Campos, 1990).

The context-dependency of the infants' actions may come about from falling and near-falling experiences that locomotion generates. Near-falls are particularly important because they are frequent, they elicit powerful emotional signals from the parent, and they set the stage for long-term retention of negative affect in such contexts.

There is still another means by which the infant can acquire a sense of wariness of depth with locomotion. While the infant moves about voluntarily, visual information specifying self-movement becomes more highly correlated with vestibular information specifying the same amount of self-movement (Bertenthal & Campos, 1990). Once expectancies related to the correlation of visual and vestibular information are formed, being lowered toward the deep side of the cliff creates a violation of the expected correlation. This violation results from the absence of visible texture near the infant when lowered toward the deep side of the cliff, relative to the shallow side. As a consequence, angular acceleration is not detected by the visual system, whereas it is detected by the vestibular system. This violation of expectation results in distress proportional to the magnitude of the violation. A test of this interpretation requires assessment of the establishment of visual-vestibular coordination as a function of locomotor experience and confirmation that wariness occurs in contexts that violate visual-vestibular coordination.

LOCOMOTOR EXPERIENCE AND OTHER EMOTIONAL CHANGES

The consequences of the development of self-produced locomotion for emotional development extend far beyond the domain of wariness of heights. Indeed, the onset of locomotion generates an entirely different emotional climate in the family. For instance, as psychoanalytic theories predict (e.g., Mahler, Pine, & Bergman, 1975), the on-set of locomotion brings about a burgeoning of both positive and negative affect—positive affect because of the child's new levels of self-efficacy; negative affect because of the increases in frustration resulting from thwarting of the child's goals and because of the affective resonance that comes from increased parental expressions of prohibition (Campos, Kermoian, & Zumbahlen, in press). Locomotion is also crucial for the development of attachment (Ainsworth, Blehar, Waters, & Wall, 1978; Bowlby, 1973), because it makes physical proximity to the caregiver possible. With the formation of specific attachments, locomotion increases in significance as the child becomes better able to move independently toward novel and potentially frightening environments. Infants are also more sensitive to the location of the parent, more likely to show distress upon separation, and more likely to look to the parent in ambiguous situations.

Locomotion also brings about emotional changes in the parents. These changes include the increased pride (and sometimes sorrow) that the parents experience in their child's new mobility and independence and the new levels of anger parents direct at the baby when the baby begins to encounter forbidden objects. It seems clear from the findings obtained in this line of research that new levels of functioning in one behavioral domain can generate experiences that profoundly affect other developmental domains, including affective, social, cognitive, and sensorimotor ones (Kermoian & Campos, 1988). We thus propose that theoretical orientations like probabilistic epigenesis provide a novel, heuristic, and timely perspective for the study of emotional development.

REFERENCES

Ainsworth, M.D.S., Blehar, M., Waters, E., & Wall, S. (1978). *Patterns of attachment*. Hillsdale, NJ: Erlbaum.

Bertenthal, B., & Campos, J.J. (1990). A systems approach to the organizing effects of self-produced locomotion during infancy. In C. Rovee-Collier & L.P. Lipsitt (Eds.), *Advances in infancy research* (Vol. 6, pp. 1–60). Norwood, NJ: Ablex.

Bowlby, J. (1973). *Attachment and loss: Vol. 2. Separation*. New York: Basic Books.

Bridges, K.M. (1932). Emotional development in early infancy. *Child Development, 3,* 324–341.

Campos, J.J., Emde, R.N., Gaensbauer, T.J., & Henderson, C. (1975). Cardiac and behavioral interrelationships in the reactions of infants to strangers. *Developmental Psychology, 11,* 589–601.

Campos, J.J., Hiatt, S., Ramsay, D., Henderson, C., & Svejda, M. (1978). The emergence of fear of heights. In M. Lewis & L. Rosenblum (Eds.), *The development of affect* (pp. 149–182). New York: Plenum Press.

Campos, J.J., Kermoian, R., & Zumbahlen, R.M. (in press). In N. Eisenberg (Ed.), *New directions for child development*. San Francisco: Jossey-Bass.

Emde, R.N., Gaensbauer, T.J., & Harmon, R.J. (1976). Emotional expression in infancy: A biobehavioral study. *Psychological Issues* (Vol. 10, No. 37). New York: International Universities Press.

Gottlieb, G. (1983). The psychobiological approach to developmental issues. In P. Mussen (Ed.), *Handbook of child psychology: Vol. II. Infancy and developmental psychobiology* (4th ed.) (pp. 1–26). New York: Wiley.

Gottlieb, G. (1991). Experiential canalization of behavioral development: Theory. *Developmental Psychology 27,* 4–13.

Graham, F.K., & Clifton, R.K. (1966). Heartrate change as a component of the orienting response. *Psychological Bulletin, 65,* 305–320.

Held, R., & Hein, A. (1963). Movement-produced stimulation in the development of visually-guided behavior. *Journal of Comparative and Physiological Psychology, 56,* 872–876.

Kagan, J., Kearsley, R., & Zelazo, P.R. (1978). *Infancy: Its place in human development*. Cambridge, MA: Harvard University Press.

Kermoian, R., & Campos, J.J. (1988). Locomotor experience: A facilitator of spatial cognitive development. *Child Development, 59,* 908–917.

Mahler, M., Pine, F., & Bergman, A. (1975). *The psychological birth of the human infant*. New York: Basic Books.

Scarr, S., & Salapatek, P. (1970). Patterns of fear development during infancy. *Merrill-Palmer Quarterly, 16,* 53–90.

Sroufe, L.A. (1979). Socioemotional development. In J. Osofsky (Ed.), *Handbook of infant development* (pp. 462–516). New York: Wiley.

Walk, R. (1966). The development of depth perception in animals and human infants. *Monographs of the Society for Research in Child Development, 31*(Whole No. 5).

Walk, R., & Gibson, E. (1961). A comparative and analytical study of visual depth perception. *Psychological Monographs, 75*(15, Whole No. 5).

Walters, C. (1981). Development of the visual placing response in the human infant. *Journal of Experimental Child Psychology, 32,* 313–329.

Multiple Choice

1. According to the concept of "probabilistic epigenesis":

   A. development in one area can create the opportunity for development in other areas
   B. locomotor experience can induce emotional development.
   C. wariness of heights may emerge as a function of crawling experience.
   D. all of the above.

2. Which of the following was not mentioned by the authors of this article as a behavior exhibited by infants on the visual cliff?

   A. heart-rate acceleration
   B. placing responses with hands and feet
   C. crying
   D. avoidance of crawling onto the deep side

3. Which of the following standard developmental designs was not used in any of the studies reported here?

   A. cross-sectional
   B. age-held-constant
   C. enrichment
   D. cross-sequential lag

Essay

1. For parents, the onset of upright locomotion--walking--is an even more memorable motor milestone than the beginning of crawling. What new experiences does a novice walker have? What changes in other areas of development might result from independent walking?

ARTICLE 6

Nutrition and Child Development:
More Food for Thought

Marian Sigman

Reprinted from: *Current Directions*, 1995, *4*, 52-55.
Copyright © 1995 by the American Psychological Society.
Reprinted with the permission of Cambridge University Press.

Although most of us do not live to eat, we all must eat to live. And we must eat well to think well, according to this article.

Given the fundamental importance of eating, it is somewhat surprising that until recently there was little research on nutrition-related behavior. In recent years, developmental scientists have become avidly interested in topics such as the origins of children's food preferences, how children regulate the amount they eat, and the precursors of obesity and eating disorders such as anorexia and bulimia. Although such topics are important in affluent societies, much of the rest of the world is concerned on a daily basis with just getting enough to eat.

This article summarizes research conducted all around the world on the effects of inadequate nutrition on cognitive development. Cognitive abilities can suffer as a consequence of not enough food, a poor quality diet, and insufficient vitamins and minerals. Improvement can be achieved through supplementing the diets of children and mothers.

A particularly interesting feature of this article is the discussion of the complex ways in which nutrition can affect mental development. For example, one hypothesis is that the small size and delayed motor skills of malnourished infants may lead others to treat them as if they were younger than they actually are, thus depriving them of appropriate stimulation. Another suggestion is that when parents are forced to spend a substantial amount of time and energy trying to obtain food, their children may have to take on increased family responsibilities even though they have diminished energy due to lack of food. The important point here is that mild to moderate malnutrition can affect cognitive development in a variety of both direct and indirect ways.

Throughout this reader, you will see that most developmental phenomena turn out to be highly complex with many different factors interacting to influence how change occurs.

Nutrition and Child Development: More Food for Thought

Marian Sigman

For many years, the specific effects of mild-to-moderate protein-energy malnutrition, poor-quality diet, and sporadic food shortages on children's development were unknown. Although the serious consequences of severe malnutrition early in life had been identified, the extent to which milder deprivation compromises the child's development was unclear. In an earlier issue of this journal, Ricciuti outlined some of the issues[1] but, in my view, underestimated the detrimental effects of undernutrition as well as the beneficial effects of supplementation. The aims of this review are, first, to summarize a series of studies that have identified some of the nutritional and psychological mechanisms underlying the effects of undernutrition and, second, to present the findings on supplementation in a more positive light.

Mild-to-moderate malnutrition is difficult to study for several reasons. First, unlike serious malnutrition, which can be identified by the physical condition of the individual, mild protein-energy malnutrition and inadequacy of diet cannot always be identified by anthropometry (i.e., measuring physical size or condition). In addition, there are no clinical or biochemical indicators diagnostic of mild-to-moderate malnutrition. For these reasons, anthropometry and biochemical and clinical markers need to be supple-

Marian Sigman is Professor of Psychology and Psychiatry at the University of California at Los Angeles. Address correspondence to Marian Sigman, Department of Psychology, University of California, Los Angeles, CA 90024.

mented with information about food intake. Because of problems with subjects' varying recall of food consumption and judgments about what should be recorded, self-report measures are often invalid. Therefore, accurate studies require observation and measurement of nutritional intakes. These procedures need to be conducted quite regularly so that the family becomes familiar with the observers and their methods.

The second difficulty in studying malnutrition is that it occurs in conjunction with other forms of deprivation. Within any community, the least well-fed individuals are likely to have the fewest social and economic resources. Because malnutrition accompanies (and sometimes causes) poor health, the confounding of the effects of diet and illness must be addressed. Thus, detailed information about the social experiences, education, and health of individuals studied is required.

HUMAN NUTRITION COLLABORATIVE RESEARCH SUPPORT PROGRAM (CRSP)

In the early 1980s, a three-country study was organized to investigate the functional effects of nutrition with particular emphasis on child development. In Kenya, Egypt, and Mexico, the study examined families that were likely to conceive a child within the study period or that already had either infants beginning the 2nd year of life or young school-age children. Nutritional level was assessed over the course of a year with monthly 2-day home observations of food consumed as well as monthly anthropometry of all family members. Blood levels of var-

ious nutrients were also assessed on a regular basis. The social and economic conditions of the family were measured, and a home visitor recorded illness weekly. Physical examinations of the children were carried out monthly.

In each of the three countries, we followed a group of toddlers for a year beginning at 18 months of age (and the Kenyan toddlers to age 5 years) and a group of young school age children for a year. Cognitive abilities were assessed with similar methods across the three countries although some of the items were adapted to be appropriate to a particular culture. The Bayley Mental Scale was administered at ages 24 and 30 months in Egypt and Kenya and at 30 months in Mexico. A measure of symbolic play was administered at age 30 months in Egypt and Kenya. More advanced cognitive abilities were measured among the schoolchildren (as well as the Kenyan toddlers followed to age 5 years) with a battery of subtests drawn from the Wechsler Intelligence Scale for Children-Revised, the Raven's Progressive Matrices, and a verbal comprehension scale. Social and behavioral outcomes were also assessed, but the methods used varied across the three countries. For this reason, I discuss here only the associations of nutrition with cognitive outcomes.

Although nutritional levels varied widely across the three countries, a measure of diet quantity and a measure of diet quality could be designed for each locale. *Diet quantity*, as defined by adequacy of protein-energy intake, was only weakly and variably related to cognitive outcomes.[2] In both Kenya and Egypt, toddlers with more adequate protein-energy intakes showed more symbolic play at 30 months. In addition, the Egyptian toddlers had higher scores on the 24-month Bayley Scale, although the Kenyan toddlers did not. Protein-calorie intakes were not associated with any toddler abilities in Mexico nor with the abil-ties of the school-age children in any of the countries.

In contrast, *diet quality*, as defined mostly by the availability of animal products, proved to be important for the development of cognitive abilities in the toddlers and the school-age children.[3] Toddlers with better quality diets had higher Bayley scores at 24 months in Egypt and at 30 months in Mexico. In Kenya, Bayley scores were not associated with diet quality. However, those Kenyan toddlers who had higher intakes of animal products showed more symbolic play at 30 months and had higher scores on cognitive measures at 5 years of age than toddlers with lower intakes of animal products. School-age children with better quality diets also performed better on the cognitive batteries in Kenya and Mexico. Egyptian schoolgirls with better quality diets had more advanced verbal abilities than less well-fed schoolgirls.

Preliminary studies have been carried out to determine the particular micronutrients that are associated with scores on the developmental and cognitive scales. In general, animal products were important not so much as a source of energy or protein but as a source of vitamins and minerals otherwise restricted in local diets. School-age cognitive scores were associated with intakes of calcium, animal-source iron, B12 and other B vitamins, and vitamin D in Kenya; with calcium, animal-source iron and zinc, vitamin A, and vitamin B12 in Egypt; and with animal-source iron and zinc in Mexico. Although the micronutrients important for development appear to be similar in the three countries, deficiencies in different micronutrients could have similar effects on physical and mental development. Moreover, the bioavailability of a particular micronutrient often depends on the intake of other nutrients. For these reasons, it may be more useful to conceive of diet quality in terms of a continuum ranging from diets consisting of plant staples to more diversified diets including animal-source food products rather than in terms of amounts of a specific micronutrient or set of micronutrients.

Relationships between diet quality and behavior emerged early in life.[4] In both Mexico and Egypt, infants whose mothers were better fed throughout pregnancy performed better on a newborn neurological examination than the infants of less well-fed mothers. These associations were independent of birth weight and gestational age. The quality of maternal nutrition throughout the first 6 months of the infant's life was also correlated with behavioral development.

As mentioned earlier, it is important to consider possible confounds that could account for the association between animal product intakes and cognitive outcomes. In the CRSP study, intake of animal products, socioeconomic status, family rearing style, parental abilities and education, and length of child's schooling all contribute independently to cognitive scores. This evidence for the independent contribution of micronutrients to the development of children depends on statistical control of variables, which is less convincing than experimental control. For this reason, intervention studies are needed. There are only a few supplementation studies that have examined experimentally the effects of diet quality or of specific micronutrients (usually iron) on development. As an example, in a study of iron-deficient anemic infants aged 12 to 18 months in Indonesia, the mean Bayley Mental score increased nearly 20 points with 4 months of iron supplementation while the placebo group showed no change in score.[5]

STUDIES OF THE EFFECTS OF SUPPLEMENTATION

In most supplementation studies, pregnant women, infants, or mothers and children were provided with diets enriched in calories, protein, or both. Infants given enriched diets in Jamaica, Indonesia, and Colombia developed somewhat more advanced motor and performance abilities than infants whose diets were not enriched. Enriched maternal diets during pregnancy and lactation had similar effects on infants in Taiwan.[6] In a study in New York, infants' cognitive abilities were partly measured by the rate with which the infants stopped looking at a repeated stimulus (habituation) and the extent of recovery of attention to a changed stimulus (dishabituation).[7] Infants whose mothers were given supplemental protein showed faster habituation and stronger dishabituation and longer periods of play (but not better motor abilities) than infants whose mothers had lower protein intakes. The mean developmental quotient (DQ) of supplemented 24-month-olds in Jamaica was 100 (SD = 13), whereas the mean DQ of the control group was 92 (SD = 8). Although Ricciuti argued that the small magnitude of this difference makes its functional significance questionable, this effect size is considered large in the psychological literature and compares favorably to the usual effect size for early interventions. Moreover, developmental delays in this early period are likely to interfere with later exploration and learning so that the long-term consequences may be even more marked.

The results of the one long-term supplementation study, carried out in Guatemala from 1969 to 1977, substantiate this hypothesis. In this extensive project, a high-calorie, high-protein supplement was made available on a daily basis to all the inhabitants of two villages for 8 years, while a low-calorie supplement was available to all the inhabitants of two other villages. Early publications from this project presented somewhat contradictory findings. However, a recent reanalysis of the data shows significant effects of the high-calorie supplementation on infant and preschool cognitive tests.[8] The experimental group had better motor abilities at 2 years and better perceptual organization and verbal skills at ages 4 and 5 years than the control group. Moreover, in a follow-up conducted in 1988–1989, adolescents in the experimental group had higher scores on tests of numeracy, vocabulary, and reading achievement than the control adolescents. These effects were strongest in children from families with the lowest socioeconomic status. Thus, long-term supplementation beginning in pregnancy and continuing through the early years of children's lives had consequences for adolescent cognitive abilities even though food supplementation had been discontinued about 12 years earlier.

NUTRITION AND HEALTH

Both adequate nutrition and good health appear to be important for children's development.[9] In the Kenyan study, healthy girls in both the preschool and school-age samples were more cognitively able than girls who suffered frequent illnesses. Frequency of illness and diet quality made independent contributions to the variance in cognitive scores. In Egypt, cognitive abilities in toddlers were a function of both health and the quality of child rearing.

WHY SHOULD NUTRITION AFFECT MENTAL DEVELOPMENT?

One major theory explaining the effect of malnutrition on mental development is that limited food intake compromises the child's active exploration and learning, which in turn leads to mental deficiencies. Pollitt and colleagues[8] have proposed a two-step process in which early malnutrition retards physical

and motor development so that the infant is small in size and delayed in motor abilities. Subsequently, infants who are small and motorically immature are cared for in ways appropriate for younger infants, which further limits their cognitive and verbal development. There is indirect support for this hypothesis in that the positive effects of supplementation are mostly confined to locomotor and performance skills in infants under 15 months of age. After 15 months, some supplementation studies have shown improvement in cognitive skills as well.[10] Other support for this hypothesis was found in the CRSP: Poorly fed toddlers in both Kenya and Egypt were cared for in ways that may be detrimental to development.[11]

This theory does not suggest that early physical and motor retardation accounts for all the effects of limited diet on cognitive development, however. At older ages, malnutrition undoubtedly continues to interfere with learning. For example, in Kenya, regardless of height, a marker of past nutrition, school-age children with poor diets were inactive and uninvolved in the classroom and playground and less intellectually skillful than better fed children.

The other major theory explaining the link between malnutrition and intellectual retardation is that malnutrition causes structural changes in the central nervous system. At present, there is little support for this explanation in studies of humans, partly because it is so difficult to prove.

INFLUENCES OF THE SOCIAL AND EDUCATIONAL ENVIRONMENT

Adequacy of the social and educational environment is as significant as nutrition for mental development (or possibly more significant). In both Kenya and Egypt, toddlers

were more verbally and socially adept if their caregivers talked to and responded to them frequently over the course of the year than if they were ignored.[12] Toddlers' cognitive abilities at 30 months were best predicted when the influence of the caregiving environment and nutritional factors were combined. In the Jamaican intervention study, a home-based program for encouraging maternal play with infants affected overall abilities as much as food supplementation. The effects of stimulation and supplementation were additive, so that the group with both interventions had a mean DQ 15 points higher than the control group at 24 months of age.

During the school years, education continues to be at least as critical as nutrition for cognitive development. In underdeveloped countries, school attendance is irregular because families do not have money for school supplies and fees and because children are needed for work at home. In the CRSP, length of schooling was one of the strongest correlates of children's cognitive abilities in both Mexico and Kenya. The combination of food quality and length of schooling was a better predictor of cognitive abilities than either variable alone in the Mexican boys and the Kenyan schoolchildren of both sexes. In the Guatemalan study, children who attended school for the most years had the strongest benefit from dietary supplementation.

Temporary food shortages disrupt the functioning of school-age children in ways that may interfere with their school learning. A drought in Africa during 1984 provided the unfortunate opportunity to investigate the effects of a temporary food shortage on the families involved in the Kenyan research project.[13] During the 4 months before food aid could be obtained, the food intakes of the mothers and school-age children declined, while the food available to toddlers remained stable. The play-

Published by Cambridge University Press

round activity, social involvement, and classroom attentiveness of the school-age children, particularly those whose food intake suffered the most, showed declines in this period. Cognitive skills measured concurrently did not change, although mathematics skills assessed several years later were lower for the children who had suffered the most during the drought. The change in behavior may be attributable to lack of energy due partly to lack of food and partly to the increased family responsibilities the children had to shoulder as their parents tried to find food.

CONCLUSION

The current research literature suggests that mild-to-moderate protein-energy malnutrition, quality of diet, and food shortages compromise childhood cognitive development. Intervention studies are needed to confirm experimentally the findings from correlational studies. It is not clear that protein and calories available in relatively affluent countries are adequate. Problems with quality of diet and sporadic food shortages imperil children worldwide. Nutrition is not the sole area of concern, as the studies reviewed here give strong indications that children's rearing and learning environments are critical for their cognitive development. Research is needed to spell out the factors that facilitate and hinder children's development not only in developing countries but also in deprived communities in the industrialized world.

Acknowledgments—Some of the research reported on in this article was supported by U.S. Agency for International Development Contract DAN1309-G-SS-80 and the Ford Foundation (Nairobi, Kenya).

Notes

1. H.N. Ricciuti, Nutrition and mental development, *Current Directions in Psychological Science*, 2, 43–46 (1993).

2. M. Sigman, C. Neumann, M. Baksh, N. Bwibo, and M.A. McDonald, Relations between nutrition and development of Kenyan toddlers, *Journal of Pediatrics*, 115, 357–364 (1989); T.D. Wachs, W. Moussa, Z. Bishry, F. Yunis, A. Sobhy, G.P. McCabe, N.W. Jerome, O.M. Galal, G. Harrison, and A. Kirksey, Relations between nutrition and cognitive performance in Egyptian toddlers, *Intelligence*, 17, 151–172 (1993); L.H. Allen, J.R. Backstrand, A. Chavez, and G.H. Pelto, *People Cannot Live by Tortillas Alone: The Results of the Mexico Nutrition CRSP*, final report to the U.S. Agency for International Development, Washington, DC (1992).

3. M. Sigman, M.A. McDonald, C. Neumann, and N. Bwibo, Prediction of cognitive competence in Kenyan children from toddler nutrition, family characteristics and abilities, *Journal of Child Psychology and Psychiatry*, 32, 307–320 (1991); M. Sigman, C. Neumann, A.A.J. Jansen, and N. Bwibo, Cognitive abilities of Kenyan children in relation to nutrition, family characteristics, and education, *Child Development*, 60, 1463–1474 (1989); S.Y. Oh, *Nutrition and psychological performance in Mexican school-age children*, unpublished doctoral dissertation, University of Connecticut, Storrs (1990); T.D. Wachs, Z. Bishry, W. Moussa, and F. Yunis, *Relation of specific nutrients to cognition and adaptive behavior of undernourished Egyptian school children*, paper presented at the meeting of the Society for Research in Child Development, New Orleans (March 1993).

4. Allen, Backstrand, Chavez, and Pelto, note 2; A. Kirksey, A. Rahmanifar, T.D. Wachs, G.P. McCabe, N.S. Bassily, Z. Bishry, O.M. Galal, G.G. Harrison, and N.W. Jerome, Determinants of pregnancy outcome and newborn behavior of a semirural Egyptian population, *American Journal of Clinical Nutrition*, 54, 657–667 (1991). The infant data have not yet been analyzed for the Kenyan sample.

5. P. Idjradinata and E. Pollitt, Reversal of developmental delays in iron-deficient anaemic infants treated with iron, *Lancet*, 341, 1–4 (1991).

6. See, e.g., S.M. Grantham-McGregor, C.A. Powell, S.P. Walker, and J.H. Hines, Nutritional supplementation, psychological stimulation and mental development of stunted children: The Jamaican study, *Lancet*, 338, 1–5 (1991); D.P. Waber, L. Vouri-Christiansen, N. Ortiz, J.R. Clement, N.E. Christiansen, J.O. Mora, R.B. Reed, and M.G. Herrera, Nutritional supplementation, maternal education and cognitive development of infants at risk of malnutrition, *American Journal of Clinical Nutrition*, 34, 807–813 (1981); B.K. Joos, E. Pollitt, W.H. Mueller, and D.L. Albright, The Bacon Chow Study: Maternal nutritional supplementation and infant behavioral development, *Child Development*, 54, 669–676 (1983).

7. D. Rush, Z. Stein, and M. Susser, *Diet and Pregnancy: A Randomized Control Trial of Nutritional Supplements* (Alan R. Liss, New York, 1980).

8. E. Pollitt, K. Gorman, P. Engle, R. Martorell, and J. Rivera, Early supplementary feeding and cognition: Effects over two decades, *Monographs of the Society for Research in Child Development*, 58(6, Serial No. 235, 1993).

9. C. Neumann, M.A. McDonald, M. Sigman, N. Bwibo, and M. Marquardt, Relationships between morbidity and development in mild-to-moderately malnourished Kenyan toddlers, *Pediatrics*, 88, 934–942 (1991); T.D. Wachs, W. Moussa, Z. Bishry, F. Yunis, A. Sobhy, G. McCabe, N. Jerome, O. Galal, G. Harrison, and A. Kirksey, Relation of rearing environment to adaptive behavior of Egyptian toddlers, *Child Development* (in press).

10. Motor development may genuinely be more retarded by undernutrition in the first 15 months of life than mental development is. The difficulty, however, is that measures of mental development have largely been confined to infant developmental scales, which are not very sensitive measures of cognitive abilities. Attentional measures have been shown to be sensitive measures of cognitive abilities in early infancy; see M.H. Bornstein and M.D. Sigman, Continuity in mental development from infancy, *Child Development*, 57, 251–274 (1986). When attentional measures are used, infants' information processing abilities vary with nutrition as early as 5 months; see S.A. Rose, Relation between physical growth and information processing in infants born in India, *Child Development*, 65, 889–903 (1994).

11. T.D. Wachs, M. Sigman, Z. Bishry, W. Moussa, C. Neumann, N. Bwibo, and M.A. McDonald, Caregiver-child interaction patterns in two cultures in relation to nutritional intake, *International Journal of Behavioral Development*, 15, 1–8 (1992).

12. M. Sigman, C. Neumann, E. Carter, D.J. Cattle, S. D'Souza, and N. Bwibo, Home interactions and the development of Embu toddlers in Kenya, *Child Development*, 59, 1251–1261 (1988); Wachs et al., note 9.

13. M.A. McDonald, M. Sigman, M.P. Espinosa, and C. Neumann, Impact of a temporary food shortage on children and their mothers, *Child Development*, 65, 404–415 (1994).

Multiple Choice:

1. In a study of nutrition and cognitive development in three countries:

   A. the *quantity* of food available to developing children was of utmost importance.

   B. dietary *quality* was important for cognitive development in toddlers and school-age children.

   C. the single most important factor was the amount of *protein* in the children's diet.

   D. the results were so complex and so variable across the different countries that it was difficult to draw any firm conclusions.

2. Which of the following is NOT correct with respect to the effect of dietary supplementation?

   A. Supplementing the diets of pregnant or nursing mothers has little or no effect on their infants' development, but increasing the protein calorie content of infant formula is effective.

   B. Guatemalan adolescents whose diets had been supplemented for the first eight years of life performed better on several cognitive assessments.

   C. Larger effects of supplementation occur for children in families of lower socioeconomic status.

   D. Combining food supplementation with educational programs for parents was more effective than either intervention alone.

Essay:

1. In underdeveloped countries, length of time that children spend in school is one of the strongest correlates of cognitive abilities. What are four factors mentioned in the article that contribute to this relation? Can you think of other ways that length of schooling would affect and reflect children's cognitive development? (Hint: Remember to consider the fact that this relation could occur for a variety of reasons--children who are brighter to begin with may stay in school longer; greater school experience may facilitate cognitive performance; other factors, such as nutritional status, may affect both involvement in school and general cognitive ability; and so on.)

ARTICLE 7

How Do Infants Learn About the Physical World?

Renée Baillargeon

Reprinted from: *Current Directions*, 1994, *3*, 133-140.
Copyright © 1994 by the American Psychological Society.
Reprinted with the permission of Cambridge University Press.

What happens to an object when it becomes invisible--does it still exist? Can an object float in mid-air? Can it remain stable if only a tiny bit of it rests on a surface? What will happen if a ball collides with another ball or with an object with wheels? If you see a soft cloth with a lump under it, what do you assume?

It doesn't take a rocket scientist to answer these questions. Adults have highly stable expectations about physical events. What, if any, of these expectations do infants share?

Not many years ago, the assumption--based largely on Piaget's theory of sensorimotor intelligence--was that young infants know very little about the physical world and that they only very gradually build up knowledge about it. However, research by Renée Baillargeon and a number of other investigators has established that infants actually have some of the same knowledge that adults do.

The program of research described in this article illustrates how empirical investigations and theoretical ideas are interwoven. Baillargeon's early work was designed to test an important aspect of Piaget's theory--the idea that young infants do not realize that objects that disappear from view continue to exist. According to Piaget's concept of *object permanence*, only after eight months can babies mentally represent an object that they can no longer see or touch. Baillargeon's initial studies (using the rotating screen procedure described in this article) established that infants as young as 4-1/2 months of age can mentally represent an invisible object. The results of those early studies suggested further questions that she then followed up. Gradually, the emerging pattern of results led her to formulate a new view of infants' knowledge about the physical world. She proposes that infants first form a simple core concept about a particular physical phenomenon and then they gradually identify factors that affect their initial concept. This article describes what babies first know about several phenomena and how that core knowledge is gradually elaborated.

How Do Infants Learn About the Physical World?

Renée Baillargeon

Until recently, young infants were assumed to lack even the most fundamental of adults' beliefs about objects. This conclusion was based largely on analyses of young infants' performance in object manipulation tasks. For example, young infants were said to be unaware that an object continues to exist when masked by another object because they consistently failed tasks that required them to search for an object hidden beneath or behind another object.[1]

In time, however, researchers came to realize that young infants might fail tasks such as search tasks not because of limited physical knowledge, but because of difficulties associated with the planning and execution of action sequences. This concern led investigators to seek alternative methods for exploring young infants' physical knowledge, methods that did not depend on the manipulation of objects.

Infants' well-documented tendency to look longer at novel than at familiar events[2] suggested one alternative method for investigating young infants' beliefs about objects. In a typical experiment, infants are presented with two test events: a possible and an impossible event. The possible event is consistent with the expectation or belief examined in the experiment; the impossible event, in contrast, violates this ex-

Renée Baillargeon is a Professor of Psychology at the University of Illinois at Urbana-Champaign. Address correspondence to Renée Baillargeon, Department of Psychology, University of Illinois, 603 East Daniel, Champaign, IL 61820.

pectation. The rationale is that if infants possess the belief being tested, they will perceive the impossible event as more novel or surprising than the possible event, and will therefore look reliably longer at the impossible than at the possible event.

Using this violation-of-expectation method, investigators have demonstrated that even very young infants possess many of the same fundamental beliefs about objects as adults do.[3,4] For example, infants aged 2.5 to 3.5 months are aware that objects continue to exist when masked by other objects, that objects cannot remain stable without support, that objects move along spatially continuous paths, and that objects cannot move through the space occupied by other objects.

The repeated demonstration of sophisticated physical knowledge in early infancy has led investigators in recent years to focus their efforts in a new direction. In addition to exploring what infants know about the physical world, researchers have become interested in the question of how infants attain their physical knowledge.

My colleagues and I have begun to build a model of the development of young infants' physical reasoning.[5–7] The model is based on the assumption that infants are born not with substantive beliefs about objects (e.g., intuitive notions of impenetrability, continuity, or force), as researchers such as Spelke[8] and Leslie[9] have proposed, but with highly constrained mechanisms that guide the development of infants' reasoning about objects. The model is derived from findings concerning infants' intuitions about different

physical phenomena (e.g., support, collision, and unveiling phenomena). Comparison of these findings points to two developmental patterns that recur across ages and phenomena. We assume that these patterns reflect, at least indirectly, the nature and properties of infants' learning mechanisms. In this review, I describe the patterns and summarize some of the evidence supporting them.

FIRST PATTERN: IDENTIFICATION OF INITIAL CONCEPT AND VARIABLES

The first developmental pattern is that, when learning about a new physical phenomenon, infants first form a preliminary, all-or-none concept that captures the essence of the phenomenon but few of its details. With further experience, this *initial* concept is progressively elaborated. Infants slowly identify discrete and continuous *variables* that are relevant to the initial concept, study the effects of those variables, and incorporate this accrued knowledge into their reasoning, resulting in increasingly accurate predictions over time.

To illustrate the distinction between initial concepts and variables, I summarize experiments on the development of young infants' reasoning about support phenomena (conducted with Amy Needham, Julie DeVos, and Helen Raschke), collision phenomena (conducted with Laura Kotovsky), and unveiling phenomena (conducted with Julie DeVos).[3,5–7]

Support Phenomena

Our experiments on young infants' ability to reason about support phenomena have focused on simple problems involving a box and a platform. Our results indicate that by 3 months of age, if not before, infants expect the box to fall if it loses all ontact with the platform and to remain stable otherwise. At this stage, any contact between the box and the platform is deemed sufficient to ensure the box's stability. At least two developments take place between 3 and 6.5 months of age. First, infants become aware that the locus of contact between the box and the platform must be taken into account when judging the box's stability. Infants initially assume that the box will remain stable if placed either on the top or against the side of the platform. By 4.5 to 5.5 months of age, however, infants come to distinguish between the two types of contact and recognize that only the former ensures support. The second development is that infants begin to appreciate that the amount of contact between the box and the platform affects the box's stability. Initially, infants believe that the box will be stable even if only a small portion (e.g., the left 15%) of its bottom surface rests on the platform (see Fig. 1). By 6.5 months of age, however, infants expect the box to fall unless a significant portion of its bottom surface lies on the platform.

Fig. 1. Paradigm for studying infants' understanding of support phenomena. In both events, a gloved hand pushes a box from left to right along the top of a platform. In the possible event (top), the box is pushed until its leading edge reaches the end of the platform. In the impossible event (bottom), the box is pushed until only the left 15% of its bottom surface rests on the platform.

These results suggest the following developmental sequence. When learning about the support relation between two objects, infants first form an initial concept centered on a distinction between contact and no contact. With further experience, this initial concept is progressively revised. Infants identify first a discrete (locus of contact) and later a continuous (amount of contact) variable and incorporate these variables into their initial concept, resulting in more successful predictions over time.

Collision Phenomena

Our experiments on infants' reasoning about collision events have focused on simple problems involving a moving object (a cylinder that rolls down a ramp) and a stationary object (a large, wheeled toy bug resting on a track at the bottom of the ramp). Adults typically expect the bug to roll down the track when hit by the cylinder. When asked how far the bug will be displaced, adults are generally reluctant to hazard a guess (they are aware that the length of the bug's trajectory depends on a host of factors about which they have no information). After observing that the bug rolls to the middle of the track when hit by a medium-size cylinder, however, adults readily predict that the bug will roll farther with a larger cylinder and less far with a smaller cylinder made of identical material.

Our experiments indicate that by 2.5 months of age, infants already possess clear expectations that the bug should remain stationary when not hit (e.g., when a barrier prevents the cylinder from contacting the bug) and should be displaced when hit. However, it is not until 5.5 to 6.5 months of age that infants are able to judge, after seeing that the medium cylinder causes the bug to roll to the middle of the track, that

the bug should roll farther with the larger but not the smaller cylinder (see Fig. 2). Younger infants are not surprised to see the bug roll to the end of the track when hit by either the larger or the smaller cylinder, even though all three of the cylinders are simultaneously present in the apparatus, so that their sizes can be readily compared, and even though the infants have no difficulty remembering (as shown in other experiments) that the bug rolled to the middle of the track with the medium cylinder. These results suggest that prior to 5.5 to 6.5 months of age, infants are unaware that the size of the cylinder can be used to reason about the length of the bug's trajectory.

One interpretation of these findings is that when learning about collision events between a moving and a stationary object, infants first form an initial concept centered on a distinction between impact and no impact. With further experience, infants begin to identify variables that influence this initial concept. By 5.5 to 6.5 months of age, infants realize that the size of the moving object can be used to predict how far the stationary object will be displaced. After seeing how far a stationary object travels with a moving object of a given size, infants readily use this information to calibrate their predictions about how far the stationary object will travel with moving objects of different sizes.

Unveiling Phenomena

Our experiments on unveiling phenomena have involved problems in which a cloth cover is removed to reveal an object. Our results indicate that by 9.5 months of age, infants realize that the presence (or absence) of a protuberance in the cover signals the presence (or absence) of an object beneath the cover. Infants are surprised to see a toy retrieved from under a cover that lies flat on a surface, but not from

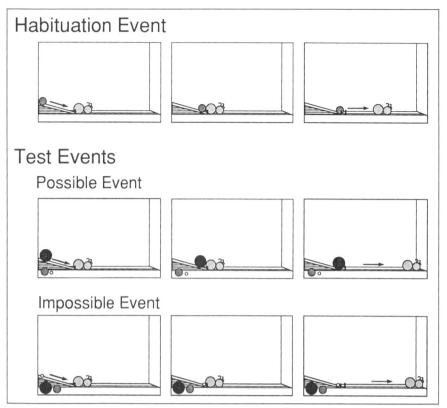

Habituation Event

Test Events

Possible Event

Impossible Event

Fig. 2. Paradigm for studying infants' understanding of collision phenomena. First, infants are habituated to (i.e., repeatedly shown) an event in which a blue, medium-size cylinder rolls down a ramp and hits a bug resting on one end of a track; the bug then rolls to the middle of the track. In the test events, two new cylinders are introduced, and the bug now rolls to the end of the track. The cylinder used in the possible event is a yellow cylinder larger than the habituation cylinder; the cylinder used in the impossible event is an orange cylinder smaller than the habituation cylinder.

under a cover that displays a marked protuberance.

At this stage, however, infants are not yet aware that the size of the pro-

tuberance in the cover can be used to infer the size of the object beneath the cover. When shown a cover with a small protuberance, they are not

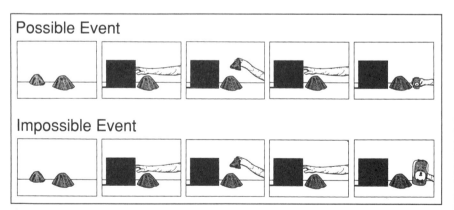

Possible Event

Impossible Event

Fig. 3. Paradigm for studying infants' understanding of unveiling phenomena. Infants first see two identical covers placed side by side; both covers display a small protuberance. Next, a screen hides the left cover, and a gloved hand reaches behind the screen twice in succession, reappearing first with the cover and then with a small (top) or a large (bottom) toy dog. Each dog is held next to the visible cover, so that their sizes can be readily compared.

surprised to see either a small or a large toy retrieved from under the cover. Furthermore, providing infants with a reminder of the protuberance's size has no effect on their performance. In one experiment, for example, infants saw two identical covers placed side by side; both covers displayed a small protuberance (see Fig. 3). After a few seconds, a screen hid the left cover; the right cover remained visible to the right of the screen. Next, a hand reached behind the screen's right edge twice in succession, reappearing first with the cover and then with a small (possible event) or a large (impossible event) toy dog. Each dog was held next to the visible cover, so that their sizes could be readily compared. At 9.5 months of age, infants judged that either dog could have been hidden under the cover behind the screen. At 12.5 months of age, however, infants showed reliable surprise at the large dog's retrieval.

Together, these results suggest the following developmental sequence. When learning about unveiling phenomena, infants first form an initial concept centered on a distinction between protuberance and no protuberance. Later on, infants identify a continuous variable that affects this concept: They begin to appreciate that the size of the protuberance in the cover can be used to infer the size of the object under the cover.

Comments

How can the developmental sequences described in this section be explained? As I mentioned earlier, we assume that these sequences reflect not the gradual unfolding of innate beliefs, but the application of highly constrained, innate learning mechanisms to available data. In this approach, the problem of explaining the age at which specific initial concepts and variables are understood is that of determining (a) what data—observations or manipulations—are necessary for learning and (b) when these data become available to infants.

For example, one might propose that 3-month-old infants have already learned that objects fall when released in midair because this expectation is consistent with countless observations (e.g., watching their caretakers drop peas in pots, toys in baskets, clothes in hampers) and manipulations (e.g., noticing that their pacifiers fall when they open their mouths) available virtually from birth. Furthermore, one might speculate that it is not until 6.5 months that infants begin to appreciate how much contact is needed between objects and their supports because it is not until this age that infants have available pertinent data from which to abstract such a variable. Researchers have reported that the ability to sit without support emerges at about 6 months of age; infants then become able to sit in front of tables (e.g., on a parent's lap or in a high chair) with their upper limbs and hands relieved from the encumbrance of postural maintenance and thus free to manipulate objects.[10] For the first time, infants may have the opportunity to deposit objects on tables and to note that objects tend to fall unless significant portions of their bottom surfaces are supported. In the natural course of events, infants would be unlikely to learn about such a variable from observation alone because caretakers rarely deposit objects on the edges of surfaces. There is no a priori reason, however, to assume that infants could not learn such a variable if given appropriate observations (e.g., seeing that a box falls when released on the edge of a platform). We are currently conducting a "teaching" experiment to investigate this possibility; our preliminary results are extremely encouraging and suggest that very few observations may be necessary to set infants on the path to learning.

SECOND PATTERN: USE OF QUALITATIVE AND QUANTITATIVE STRATEGIES

In the previous section, I proposed that when learning about a novel physical phenomenon, infants first develop an all-or-none initial concept and later identify discrete and continuous variables that affect this concept. The second developmental pattern suggested by current evidence concerns the strategies infants use when reasoning about continuous variables. Following the terminology used in computational models of everyday physical reasoning,[11] a strategy is said to be *quantitative* if it requires infants to encode and use information about absolute quantities (e.g., object A is "this" large or has traveled "this" far from object B, where "this" stands for some absolute measure of A's size or distance from B). In contrast, a strategy is said to be *qualitative* if it requires infants to encode and use information about relative quantities (e.g., object A is larger than or has traveled farther than object B). After identifying a continuous variable, infants appear to succeed in reasoning about the variable qualitatively before they succeed in doing so quantitatively.

To illustrate the distinction between infants' use of qualitative and quantitative strategies, I report experiments on the development of infants' ability to reason about collision phenomena (conducted with Laura Kotovsky), unveiling phenomena (conducted with Julie DeVos), and barrier phenomena.[3,5–7]

Collision Phenomena

As I explained earlier, 5.5- to 6.5-month-old infants are surprised, after observing that a medium-size cylinder causes a bug to roll to the middle of a track, to see the bug roll farther when hit by a smaller but not

a larger cylinder. Such a finding suggests that by 5.5 to 6.5 months of age, infants are aware that the size of the cylinder affects the length of the bug's trajectory.

In these initial experiments, the small, medium, and large cylinders were placed side by side at the start of each event, allowing infants to compare their sizes directly. In subsequent experiments, only one cylinder was present in the apparatus in each test event. Under these conditions, 6.5-month-old infants were no longer surprised when the small cylinder caused the bug to roll to the end of the track; only older, 7.5-month-old infants showed surprise at this event.

Our interpretation of these results is that at 5.5 to 6.5 months of age, infants are able to reason about the cylinder's size only qualitatively: They can predict the effect of modifications in the cylinder's size only when they are able to encode such modifications in relative terms (e.g., "this cylinder is smaller than the one used in the last trial"). When infants are forced to encode and compare the absolute sizes of the cylinders, because the cylinders are never shown side by side, they fail the task. By 7.5 months of age, however, infants have already overcome this initial limitation and succeed in the task even when they must rely on their representation of the absolute size of each cylinder to do so.[12]

Unveiling Phenomena

In the previous section, I reported that 9.5-month-old infants are not surprised to see either a small or a large toy dog retrieved from under a cover with a small protuberance, even when a second, identical cover is present. Unlike these younger infants, however, 12.5-month-old infants *are* surprised when the large dog is brought into view. This last finding suggests that by 12.5 months of age, infants are aware that the size

Published by Cambridge University Press

of the protuberance in a cloth cover can be used to infer the size of the object under the cover.

In our initial experiment, 12.5-month-old infants were tested with the second cover present to the right of the screen (see Fig. 3). Subsequent experiments were conducted without the second cover (see Fig. 4, top panel) or with the second cover placed to the left, rather than to the right, of the screen (see Fig. 4, bottom panel); in the latter condition, infants could no longer compare in a single glance the size of the dog to that of the cover. Our results indicated that 12.5-month-old infants fail both of these conditions: They no longer show surprise when the large dog is retrieved from behind the screen. By 13.5 months of age, however, infants are surprised by the large dog's retrieval even when no second cover is present.

These results suggest that at 12.5 months of age, infants are able to reason about the size of the protuberance in the cover only qualitatively: They can determine which dog could have been hidden under the cover only if they are able to compare, in a single glance, the size of the dog with that of a second, identical cover (e.g., "the dog is bigger than the cover"). When infants are forced to represent the absolute size of the protuberance in the cover, they fail the task. By 13.5 months of age, however, infants have already progressed beyond this initial limitation; they no longer have difficulty representing the absolute size of the protuberance and comparing it with that of each dog.

Barrier Phenomena

Our experiments on barrier phenomena have focused on problems involving a moving object (a rotating screen) and a stationary barrier (a large box). In the test events, infants first see the screen lying flat against the apparatus floor; the box stands clearly visible behind the screen. Next, the screen rotates about its distant edge, progressively occluding the box. At 4.5 months of age, infants expect the screen to stop when it reaches the occluded box; they are surprised if the screen rotates unhindered through a full 180° arc. However, infants are initially poor at predicting at what point the screen should encounter the box and stop. When shown a possible event in which the screen stops against the box (112° arc) and an impossible event in which the screen stops after rotating through the top 80% of the space occupied by the box (157° arc), 6.5-month-old infants give evidence of detecting this 80% violation, but 4.5-month-old infants do not: They judge both the 112° and the 157° stopping points to be consistent with the box's height and location (see Fig. 5).

In subsequent experiments, we examined whether 4.5-month-old infants would succeed in detecting the 80% violation if provided with a second, identical box. In one condition, this second box was placed to the right of and in the same frontoparallel plane as the box behind the screen (see Fig. 6, left panel). In the possible event, the screen stopped when aligned with the top of the second box; in the impossible event, the screen rotated past the top of the second box. In another condition, the second box was placed to the right of but slightly in front of the box behind the screen (see Fig. 6, right panel). In this condition, the screen

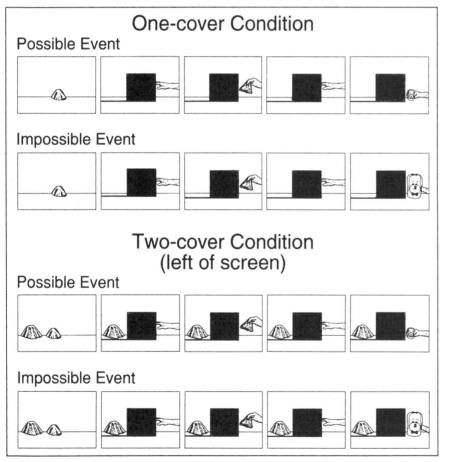

Fig. 4. Further experiments examining infants' understanding of unveiling phenomena. These test events are identical to those depicted in Figure 3 except that only one cover is used (top) or the second, identical cover is placed to the left of the screen (bottom). In the latter condition, infants can no longer compare in a single glance the height of the dog to that of the second cover.

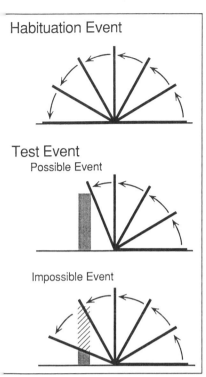

Habituation Event

Test Event
Possible Event

Impossible Event

Fig. 5. Paradigm for studying infants' understanding of barrier phenomena. Infants are first habituated to a screen that rotates through a 180° arc, in the manner of a drawbridge. Next, a large box is placed behind the screen. In the possible event, the screen stops when it encounters the box (112° arc); in the impossible event, the screen stops after rotating through the top 80% of the space occupied by the box (157° arc).

rotated past the top of the second box in each test event. The infants succeeded in detecting the 80% violation in the first but not the second condition.

These results suggest that at 4.5 months of age, infants are able to reason about the box's height and location only qualitatively: They can predict the screen's stopping point only when they are able to rely on a simple alignment strategy (e.g., "the screen is aligned with the top of the visible box"). By 6.5 months of age, however, infants have already progressed beyond this point; they can use their representations of the occluded box's height and distance from the screen to estimate, within broad limits, at what point the screen will stop.

Comments

How should the developmental sequences described in this section be explained? We think it unlikely that these sequences reflect the maturation of infants' general quantitative reasoning or information processing because the same pattern recurs at different ages for different phenomena. What phenomenon-specific changes could account for the findings reported here? At least two hypotheses can be advanced. On the one hand, it could be that when first reasoning about a continuous variable, infants either do not spontaneously encode information about this variable or do not encode this information swiftly enough or precisely enough for it to be of use in the tasks examined here (e.g., infants do not encode the size of the protuberance in the cover and hence are unable to judge which dog could have been hidden beneath it). On the other hand, infants could encode the necessary quantitative information but have difficulty accessing or processing this information in the context of deriving new and unfamiliar predictions (e.g., infants encode the protuberance's size and realize that they must compare it with that of the dog, but are thwarted in performing this comparison by the added requirement of having to retrieve part of the information from memory). Future research will no doubt help determine which, if either, of these hypotheses is correct.

CONCLUDING REMARKS

I have argued that in learning to reason about a novel physical phenomenon, infants first form an all-or-none concept and then add to this initial concept discrete and continuous variables that are discovered to affect the phenomenon. Furthermore, I have proposed that after identifying continuous variables, infants succeed in reasoning first qualitatively and only later quantitatively about the variables.

This sketchy description may suggest a rather static view of development in which accomplishments, once attained, are retained in their initial forms. Nothing could be further from the truth, however. Our data suggest that the variables infants identify evolve over time, as do the qualitative and quantitative strategies infants devise. When judging whether a box resting on a platform is stable, for example, infants initially focus exclusively on the amount of contact between the box's bottom surface and the platform, and as a consequence treat symmetrical and asymmetrical boxes alike. By the end of the 1st year, however, infants appear to have revised their definition of this variable to take into account the shape (or weight distribution) of the box.[5] Similarly, evidence obtained with the rotating-screen paradigm suggests that infants' quantitative reasoning continues to improve over time (e.g., 6.5-month-old infants can detect 80% but not 50% violations, whereas 8.5-month-old infants can detect both), as does their qualitative reasoning (e.g., 6.5-month-old infants will make use of a second box to detect a violation even if this second box differs markedly in color from the box behind the screen, whereas 4.5-month-old infants will not).[3]

The model of the development of infants' physical reasoning proposed here suggests many questions for future research. In particular, what are the innate constraints that guide this development? Are infants born with core principles (e.g., intuitive notions of impenetrability and continuity) that direct their interpretations of physical events? Or are infants, as I suggested earlier, equipped primarily with learning mechanisms that are capable, when applied to coherent sets of observations, of producing appropriate generalizations? What

Published by Cambridge University Press

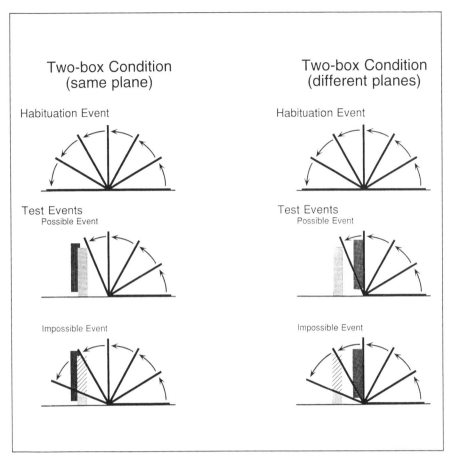

Two-box Condition (same plane)

Habituation Event

Test Events
Possible Event

Impossible Event

Two-box Condition (different planes)

Habituation Event

Test Events
Possible Event

Impossible Event

Fig. 6. Further experiments examining infants' understanding of barrier phenomena. These events are identical to those depicted in Figure 5 except that a second, identical box stands to the right of and in the same fronto-parallel plane as the box behind the screen (left) or to the right and in front of the box behind the screen (right).

evidence would help distinguish between these two views?

Some insight into this question may be gained by considering two predictions that proponents of the innate-principles view might offer. The first prediction is that when reasoning about a physical event involving a core principle, infants should succeed at about the same age at detecting all equally salient violations of the principle. Thus, researchers who deem impenetrability a likely core principle might expect infants who realize that a small object cannot pass through a gapless surface to understand also that a large object cannot pass through a small gap; provided that the two situations violate the impenetrability principle to a similar degree, they would be expected to yield identical interpretations. The second prediction is that infants should succeed at about the same age at reasoning about different physical events that implicate the same underlying core principle. Thus, it might be proposed that infants who are successful at reasoning about objects' passage through gaps should be just as adept at reasoning about objects' entry into containers, because both phenomena would trigger the application of the impenetrability principle.

The model presented here departs systematically from the two predictions just described. First, the model predicts explicitly that when reasoning about physical events, infants succeed in detecting certain types of violations before others. Thus, in contrast to the innate-principles view, the model would expect infants to recognize that a small object cannot pass through a gapless surface before they recognize that a large object cannot pass through a smaller gap. This developmental sequence would be cast in terms of the formation of an initial concept centered on a distinction between gap and no gap, followed by the identification of size as a continuous variable relevant to the phenomenon.

Second, the present model also diverges from the prediction that different physical events that implicate the same core principle should be understood at about the same age. The results summarized in the preceding sections and elsewhere[6]—such as the finding that unveiling tasks yield the same developmental patterns as rotating-screen tasks, but at much later ages—suggest that infants respond to physical events not in terms of abstract underlying principles, but in terms of concrete categories corresponding to specific ways in which objects behave or interact. Thus, according to our model, it would not be at all surprising to find that infants succeed in reasoning about gaps several weeks or months before they do containers; the order of acquisition of the two categories would be expected to depend on the content of infants' daily experiences. The model does not rule out the possibility that infants eventually come to realize that superficially distinct events—such as those involving gaps and containers, or rotating screens and cloth covers—can be deeply related; unlike the innate-principles view, however, the model considers such a realization a product, rather than a point of departure, of learning.

One advantage of the view that infants process physical events in terms of concrete categories focusing on specific types of interactions between objects is that this view makes it possible to explain incorrect interpretations that appear to stem from miscategorizations of events. Pilot data collected in our laboratory suggest that young infants expect a moving object to stop when it encounters a tall, thin box but not a short, wide box, even when the latter is considerably larger in volume than the former. We suspect that infants are led by the dominant vertical axis of the tall box to perceive it as a wall-like, immovable object, and hence categorize the event as an instance of a barrier phenomenon; in contrast, infants tend to view the wide box as a movable object, and hence categorize the event as an instance of a collision phenomenon, resulting in incorrect predictions.

The foregoing discussion highlighted several types of developmental sequences that would be anticipated in an innate-mechanisms view but not (without considerable elaboration) in an innate-principles view. To gain further insight into the nature and origins of these developmental sequences, we have adopted a dual research strategy. First, we are examining the development of infants' understanding of additional physical phenomena (e.g., gap, containment, and occlusion phenomena) to determine how easily these developments can be captured in terms of the patterns described in the model and to compare more closely the acquisition time lines of phenomena that are superficially distinct but deeply related. Second, as was alluded to earlier, we are attempting to teach infants initial concepts and variables to uncover what kinds of observations, and how many observations, are required for learning. We hope that the pursuit of these two strategies will eventually allow us to specify the nature of the learning mechanisms that infants bring to the task of learning about the physical world.

Acknowledgments—This research was supported by grants from the Guggenheim Foundation, the University of Illinois Center for Advanced Study, and the National Institute of Child Health and Human Development (HD-21104). I would like to thank Jerry DeJong, for his support and insight, and Susan Carey, Noam Chomsky, Judy DeLoache, Cindy Fischer, John Flavell, Laura Kotovsky, Brian Ross, and Bob Wyer, for many helpful comments and suggestions.

Notes

1. J. Piaget, *The Construction of Reality in the Child* (Basic Books, New York, 1954).

2. E.S. Spelke, Preferential looking methods as tools for the study of cognition in infancy, in *Measurement of Audition and Vision in the First Year of Postnatal Life*, G. Gottlieb and N. Krasnegor, Eds. (Ablex, Norwood, NJ, 1985).

3. R. Baillargeon, The object concept revisited: New directions in the investigation of infants' physical knowledge, in *Visual Perception and Cognition in Infancy*, C.E. Granrud, Ed. (Erlbaum, Hillsdale, NJ, 1993).

4. E.S. Spelke, K. Breinlinger, J. Macomber, and K. Jacobson, Origins of knowledge, *Psychological Review, 99*, 605–632 (1992).

5. R. Baillargeon, L. Kotovsky, and A. Needham, The acquisition of physical knowledge in infancy, in *Causal Understandings in Cognition and Culture*, G. Lewis, D. Premack, and D. Sperber, Eds. (Oxford University Press, Oxford, in press).

6. R. Baillargeon, A model of physical reasoning in infancy, in *Advances in Infancy Research*, Vol. 9, C. Rovee-Collier and L. Lipsitt, Eds. (Ablex, Norwood, NJ, in press).

7. R. Baillargeon, Physical reasoning in infants, in *The Cognitive Neurosciences*, M.S. Gazzaniga, Ed. (MIT Press, Cambridge, MA, in press).

8. E.S. Spelke, Physical knowledge in infancy: Reflections on Piaget's theory, in *The Epigenesis of Mind: Essays on Biology and Cognition*, S. Carey and R. Gelman, Eds. (Erlbaum, Hillsdale, NJ, 1991).

9. A.M. Leslie, ToMM, ToBy, and Agency: Core architecture and domain specificity, in *Causal Understandings in Cognition and Culture*, G. Lewis, D. Premack, and D. Sperber, Eds. (Oxford University Press, Oxford, in press).

10. P. Rochat and A. Bullinger, Posture and functional action in infancy, in *Francophone Perspectives on Structure and Process in Mental Development*, A. Vyt, H. Bloch, and M. Bornstein, Eds. (Erlbaum, Hillsdale, NJ, in press).

11. K.D. Forbus, Qualitative process theory, *Artificial Intelligence, 24*, 85–168 (1984).

12. This example focused exclusively on the size of the cylinder, but what of the distance traveled by the bug in each event? It seems likely that infants encode this information not in quantitative terms (e.g., "the bug traveled x as opposed to y distance"), but rather in qualitative terms, using as their point of reference the track itself (e.g., "the bug rolled to the middle of the track"), their own spatial position (e.g., "the bug stopped in front of me"), or the brightly decorated back wall of the apparatus (e.g., "the bug stopped in front of such-and-such section of the back wall").

Questions for Self Study

Multiple Choice:

1. Which of the following would be the best name for the method used in the research summarized in this article?

    A. habituation
    B. violation of expectancy
    C. object manipulation
    D. object permanence

2. According to Baillargeon, infants first form a core concept about a given physical phenomena. Which of the following does NOT characterize core concepts?

    A. qualitative knowledge only
    B. all-or-none
    C. highly detailed
    D. relative information

3. Which of the phenomena covered in this article requires the infant to draw an *inference* about the existence and size of an invisible object?

    A. unveiling
    B. support
    C. collision
    D. barrier

Essay:

1. What everyday events in the life of young infants might help them acquire the knowledge revealed in these experiments?

ARTICLE 8

The Credible Shrinking Room: Very Young Children's Performance With Symbolic and Nonsymbolic Relations

Judy S. Deloache, Kevin F. Miller, and Karl S. Rosengren

Reprinted from: *Psychological Science*, 1997, *8*, 308-313.
Copyright © 1997 by the American Psychological Society.
Reprinted with the permission of Cambridge University Press.

One message we hope you will take away from reading this article is that doing research can be fun!

These researchers invented a shrinking machine--or at least they convinced 2-1/2-year-old children that they had such a marvelous machine. The children accepted the idea that the machine could cause a troll doll to shrink into a tiny toy and a tent-like room to become a miniature room.

This Machiavellian maneuver was designed to test a theoretical prediction. Previous research had established that very young children have difficulty using what they know about a scale model to figure out something about the room that it stands for. This study established that 2-1/2-year-old children could successfully reason from a scale model to a room when they thought that the model *was* the room after having been shrunk; because these children thought the room and model were the same thing, they readily transferred what they knew about one to the other. Performance of the same age group was much poorer when there was a symbolic relation between the two spaces, that is, when the model "stood for" the room.

This study thus illustrates that figuring out how symbols are related to what they stand for can be quite challenging for young children. It is a challenge that must be surmounted, since mastering a variety of symbols and symbol systems is crucial for learning throughout the rest of life. Indeed, there is nothing more important for human cognition and communication than mastering the symbols used by one's culture.

This study involved a mild deception, but before any of these toddlers took part in it, their parents were fully informed about the nature of the study and gave their permission for their child's participation. All research involving human subjects must obtain the *informed consent* of the participants or, for children, of their parents. Everyone has the right to refuse to participate and, if they do participate, to withdraw their permission at any time for any reason. Infants and toddlers sometimes withdraw from studies in fairly dramatic fashion--by crying, for example, a sure sign they do not consent to further participation.

Research Article

THE CREDIBLE SHRINKING ROOM:
Very Young Children's Performance With Symbolic and Nonsymbolic Relations

Judy S. DeLoache, Kevin F. Miller, and Karl S. Rosengren
University of Illinois at Urbana-Champaign

Abstract—*Becoming a proficient symbol user is a universal developmental task in the first years of life, but detecting and mentally representing symbolic relations can be quite challenging for young children. To test the extent to which symbolic reasoning per se is problematic, we compared the performance of 2½-year-olds in symbolic and nonsymbolic versions of a search task. The children had to use their knowledge of the location of a toy hidden in a room to draw an inference about where to find a miniature toy in a scale model of the room (and vice versa). Children in the nonsymbolic condition believed a shrinking machine had caused the room to become the model. They were much more successful than children in the symbolic condition, for whom the model served as a symbol of the room. The results provide strong support for the role of dual representation in symbol understanding and use.*

Nothing so distinguishes humans from other species as the creative and flexible use of symbols. Abstract concepts, reasoning, scientific discovery, and other uniquely human endeavors are made possible by language and a panoply of symbolic tools, including numbers, alphabets, maps, models, and various notational systems. The universality and centrality of symbolic representation in human cognition make understanding its origins a key developmental issue.

How do children master the symbolic artifacts of their culture? They must start by recognizing that certain entities should be interpreted and responded to primarily in terms of what they stand for—their referents—rather than themselves. This is obviously a major challenge in the case of completely arbitrary symbol–referent relations. Nothing about the appearance of a numeral or a printed word suggests what it represents. Hence, it is not surprising that children have to be explicitly taught and only gradually learn the abstract relations between numerals and quantities and between printed and spoken words.

In contrast, it is generally taken for granted that highly iconic symbols (i.e., symbols that resemble their referents) are understood easily and early. Recent research, however, reveals that this assumption is unwarranted: A high degree of similarity between a symbol and its referent is no guarantee that young children will appreciate the symbol–referent relation. For example, several studies have established that very young children often fail to detect the relation between a realistic scale model and the room it represents (DeLoache, 1987, 1989, 1991; DeLoache, Kolstad, & Anderson, 1991; Dow & Pick, 1992; Marzolf & DeLoache, 1994; Uttal, Schreiber, & DeLoache, 1995). Most 2½-year-old children give no evidence of understanding that the model and room are related or that what they know about one space can be used to draw an inference about the other.

Address correspondence to Judy DeLoache, Psychology Department, University of Illinois, 603 East Daniel, Champaign, IL 61820; e-mail: jdeloache@s.psych.uiuc.edu.

Children just a few months older (3-year-olds) readily exploit this symbol–referent relation.

Why is a highly iconic relation that is so transparent to older children and adults so opaque to very young children? Many theorists have characterized symbols as possessing dual reality (Gibson, 1979; Gregory, 1970; Potter, 1979). According to the *dual representation* hypothesis (DeLoache, 1987, 1991, 1995a, 1995b), it is the double nature of symbols that poses particular difficulty for young children. To understand and use a symbol, one must mentally represent both the symbol itself and its relation to the referent. Thus, one must achieve dual representation, thinking about the concrete features of the symbol and the abstract relation between it and something else at the same time.

According to this hypothesis, the more salient the concrete aspects of a symbol are, the more difficult it is to appreciate its abstract, symbolic nature. Thus, young children's attention to a scale model as an interesting and attractive object makes it difficult for them to simultaneously think about its relation to something else. The philosopher Langer (1942) seemed to have something similar in mind when she noted that a peach would make a poor symbol because people care too much about the peach itself.

The research reported here constitutes an extremely stringent test of this hypothesis. We compared 2½-year-old children's performance in two tasks in which they had to detect and exploit the relation between a scale model and a room. In both tasks, children had to use their knowledge of where a toy was hidden in one space to infer where to find an analogous toy in the other space. In one task, there was a symbolic relation between the model and the room, whereas the other task involved a nonsymbolic relation between the same two entities. If achieving dual representation is a key obstacle in early symbolic reasoning, then performance should be superior in the nonsymbolic task, which does not require dual representation. We made this prediction even though the nonsymbolic task involved convincing children of an impossible scenario—that a machine could cause the room to shrink into the model.

Our reasoning was that if a child believes that the model is the large room after having been shrunk, then there is no symbolic relation between the two spaces; to the credulous child, the model simply *is* the room (albeit dramatically different in size). Thus, if the room is shrunk after a large toy has been hidden in it, finding a miniature toy in the model is, from the child's perspective, primarily a memory task. Dual representation is not necessary. Note that in both tasks, children must use the correspondence between the hiding places in the two spaces; their memory representation of the toy hidden behind a full-sized chair in the room must lead them to search behind the miniature chair in the model. In the symbolic task, the child knows there are two chairs, so he or she must represent the relation between them. In the nonsymbolic task, however, the child thinks there is only one chair. Superior performance in the nonsymbolic, shrinking-room task would thus provide strong support for the dual representation hypothesis.

METHOD

Subjects

The subjects included 15 children (29–32 months, $M = 30$ months) in the symbolic condition and 17 (29–33 months, $M = 31$ months) in the nonsymbolic condition. Names of potential subjects came from files of birth announcements in the local newspaper, and the majority of the children were middle class and white.

Materials

The same two spaces were used for both tasks. The larger space was a tentlike portable room (1.9 m × 2.5 m) constructed of plastic pipes supporting white fabric walls (1.9 m high) with a brown cardboard floor. The smaller space was a scale model (48.3 cm × 62.9 cm, with walls 38.1 cm high) of the portable room, constructed of the same materials. The room held several items of furniture (fabric-covered chair, dresser, set of shelves, basket, etc.); the model contained miniature versions of these items that were highly similar in appearance (e.g., same fabric on the chairs) to their larger counterparts. The relative size and spatial arrangement of the objects were the same in the two spaces, and the model was always in the same spatial orientation as the room. This model and room have been used in several previous studies (DeLoache et al., 1991; Marzolf & De-Loache, 1994). Figures 1a, 1b, and 1c show the arrangement of the room and model for the two tasks.

Procedure

Symbolic task

In this task (which was very similar to that used in the previously cited model studies), each child was given an orientation that began with the introduction of two troll dolls referred to as "Big Terry" (21 cm high) and "Little Terry" (5 cm). The correspondence between the room (described as "Big Terry's room") and the model ("Little Terry's room") and between all of the objects within them was fully and explicitly described and demonstrated by the experimenter.

On the first of four experimental trials, the child watched as the experimenter hid the larger doll somewhere in the room (e.g., behind the chair, in the basket). The child was told that the smaller toy would be hidden in the "same place" in the model. The child waited (10–15 s) as the miniature toy was hidden in the model in the adjoining area (Fig. 1a) and was then encouraged to retrieve it. The experimenter reminded the child of the corresponding locations of the two toys: "Can you find Little Terry? Remember, he's hiding in the same place in his little room where Big Terry's hiding in his big room." If the child failed to find the toy on his or her first search, increasingly direct prompts were given until the child retrieved the toy. On the second trial, the hiding event occurred in the model instead of the room. Thus, the child watched as the miniature toy was hidden in the model, and he or she was then asked to retrieve the larger toy from the room. The space in which the hiding event occurred again alternated for the third and fourth trials.[1]

To succeed, children in the symbolic task had to realize that the room and model were related. If they did, they could figure out where to search for the target toy, even though they had not actually seen it being hidden. If they failed to represent the model–room relation, they had no way of knowing where to search. Based on numerous previous studies with this basic task, we expected a low level of performance from our 2½-year-old subjects (DeLoache, 1987, 1989, 1991; De-Loache et al., 1991; Dow & Pick, 1992; Marzolf & DeLoache, 1994).

Nonsymbolic task

The initial arrangement for this task is shown in Figure 1b. In the orientation to the task, each child was introduced to "Terry" (the larger troll doll) and to "Terry's room" (the portable room). In the ensuing practice trial, the child watched as the experimenter hid the troll in the room and then waited for a count of 5 before searching. The children always succeeded in this simple memory-based retrieval (100% correct).

Next, the child was shown a "machine that can shrink toys" (actually an oscilloscope with flashing green lights—the solid rectangle in Fig. 1b). The troll doll was placed in front of it, a switch was turned on, and the child and experimenter retreated to an adjoining area and closed the door to the lab. During a delay of approximately 10 s, the child heard a tape of computer-generated tones, which were described as the "sounds the shrinking machine makes while it's working." When the sounds stopped, the child returned to the lab to find a miniature troll (5 cm high) in the place the larger one had previously occupied. Figures 1d and 1e depict the shrinking machine with the troll before and after the shrinking event.

The child was then told that the machine could also make the troll get larger, and the process was repeated in reverse, ending with the large troll again standing in front of the machine. For the final part of the orientation, the same shrinking and enlarging demonstrations were performed with "Terry's room." The shrinking machine was aimed at the room, and the child and experimenter waited in the adjoining area, listening to a longer (38-s) tape of the same computer sounds. When the door to the lab was opened, the scale model was revealed sitting in the middle of the area previously occupied by the room (Fig. 1c). The sight of the small model in place of the large room was very dramatic. The process was then repeated in reverse, resulting in the room replacing the model.[2]

---

1. There were two major differences between the current symbolic task and the standard model task used in previous research: First, the hiding event alternated from trial to trial between model and room. In the standard task, it always occurs in one space or the other for a given child. In studies in which half the children see the hiding event in the room and the other half in the model, there has never been any difference in performance as a function of this variable. Second, in the standard task, children always perform two retrievals: For example, after seeing the toy being hidden in the model, they first search for the larger toy in the room and then return to the model to retrieve the toy they originally observed being hidden. However, the performance of the 2½-year-olds tested in the current study did not differ from that of a group tested in the standard model task using all the same materials.

2. An elaborate scenario supported the shrinking and enlarging events. When the child first saw the artificial room, it was surrounded on three sides by black curtains, which were visible only on the sides in front of the portable room (Fig. 1b). For each shrinking event, as soon as the child had left the lab, one assistant turned on a tape recorder to begin the shrinking-machine sounds (thereby concealing any noises made in the lab). Two other assistants pulled the artificial room behind the curtains, and the first placed the model, with the miniature troll in the appropriate position, in the center of the space formerly occupied by the room. In the enlarging events, the model was replaced by the room.

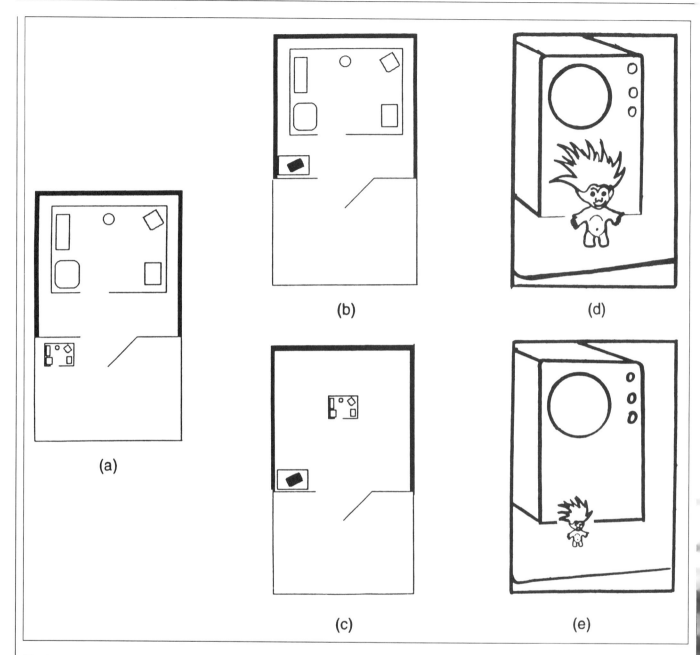

Fig. 1. Physical arrangements for the symbolic and nonsymbolic tasks. For the symbolic task (a), the portable room was located in a large lab, surrounded on three sides by opaque curtains (represented by heavy lines); the model was located in an adjoining area. The nonsymbolic task began with the arrangement shown in (b); before the first shrinking event, the portable room was located in the lab, partially surrounded by curtains, just as it was for the symbolic task. The only difference was the presence of the shrinking machine, represented by the dark rectangle, sitting on a table. In the aftermath of the shrinking event, depicted in (c), the model sat in the middle of the area previously occupied by the portable room. The sketches in (d) and (e) show Terry the Troll before and after the demonstration shrinking event.

On the first of four trials, the child watched as the larger doll was hidden in the room (the same hiding places were used as in the symbolic task), and the child was instructed to remember where it was hidden. After a 38-s delay, again spent waiting in the adjoining area listening to the sounds of the shrinking machine, the child entered the lab, where the model had replaced the portable room. The child was encouraged to find the doll: "Can you find Terry? Remember where we hid him? That's where he's hiding." The miniature troll was, of course, hidden in the model in the place that corresponded to where the child had seen the larger troll being hidden in the room. On two of the four trials, the room and large troll were shrunk, alternating with two trials in which the model and miniature troll were enlarged. A different hiding place was used on each trial.

To assess the extent to which the children accepted our shrinking-machine scenario, the experimenter and each child's accompanying parent independently rated the child on a 5-point scale, with 1 indicating that the child "firmly believed" that the machine really did shrink the objects and 5 indicating that the child "firmly did not believe" it. The average ratings were 1.1 and 1.5 for the experimenter and parents, respectively. There was only one child that the observing adults judged to be at all skeptical. The children generally reacted to the shrinking events with interest and pleasure, but not astonishment. Several children made revealing comments, such as "I want to make it big [little] again," and, while listening to the sounds of the shrinking machine, "It's working to make it big." In addition, when the children later told other family members about the session, they typically talked about the troll or the room "getting little." None ever described the situation as pretend or as a trick. We therefore feel confident that our subjects believed that the model and room were actually the same thing, which means that the shrinking-room task was, as intended, nonsymbolic (involving an identity rather than a symbolic relation).[3]

We wish to emphasize that it is unlikely that the a priori prediction of superior performance in the nonsymbolic task would be made on any basis other than the dual representation hypothesis. Indeed, various aspects of the procedures would lead to the opposite expectation. For example, getting and keeping toddlers motivated in experimental situations is always a challenge; and the shrinking-room task was more complicated, required more verbal communication, and took longer than the standard symbolic task. In addition, the delay between the hiding event and the opportunity to search for the toy was substantially longer in the shrinking-room task (ca. 50–60 s) than in the standard symbolic task (ca. 10–15 s). Delays between hiding and retrieval are known to cause the performance of even older children to deteriorate dramatically in the standard model task (Uttal et al., 1995).

RESULTS

The critical question was whether performance in the nonsymbolic (shrinking-room) condition would be superior to performance in the symbolic (model) condition. Figure 2 shows the mean number of errorless retrievals (searching first at the correct location) achieved in the two tasks.

The children in the symbolic task achieved a mean of only 0.8 errorless retrievals over four trials ($SE = 0.2$), a rate not different from chance. (We conservatively estimated chance at 25%, based on our use of four hiding places; however, it is actually lower because there are additional possible hiding places.) Individual performance in this task was similarly poor: Six of the 15 children never found the toy, and 6 retrieved it only once. No child succeeded on more than two of the four trials. These children understood that they were supposed to search for a hidden toy on each trial, and they were happy to do so, but they apparently failed to realize that their knowledge of one space could be applied to the other.

The poor performance of the children in the symbolic task (19%) is exactly what would be expected from previous model studies. In

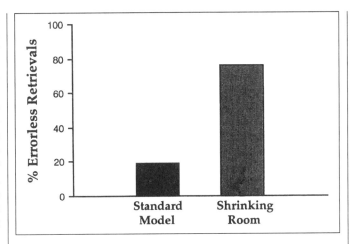

Fig. 2. Mean number of errorless retrievals (searching first in the correct location) in the symbolic and nonsymbolic tasks.

research in our own and other labs using a variety of different models and rooms, 2½-year-olds reliably average around 20% successful retrievals.

In contrast, children in the nonsymbolic task were very successful. Performance in the nonsymbolic (shrinking-room) condition was well above chance—3.1 errorless retrievals ($SE = 0.2$)—and significantly better than the performance of the children in the symbolic condition. Twelve of the 17 subjects achieved three or more errorless retrievals, and 7 of those had perfect scores. The difference between the two tasks was the only significant result in a 2 (task) × 2 (gender) analysis of variance, $F(1, 28) = 51.5, p < .0001$. Performance did not differ on trials in which the hiding event occurred in the room and the child searched in the model versus trials in which the hiding and search spaces were the reverse.

The main result of this study has been replicated, both in an additional study with 2½-year-olds and in two studies in which the same logic was applied to a different age group. Using two different, more difficult versions of the model task, we found the same pattern of results with 3-year-olds as occurred with the 2½-year-olds in the present study—significantly better performance in the nonsymbolic, shrinking-room version than in the symbolic model task (DeLoache, 1995a; Marzolf, 1994).

DISCUSSION

We conclude that a major challenge to detecting and using symbolic relations stems from their inherent dual reality and the necessity of achieving dual representation (DeLoache, 1987, 1995a, 1995b). The model task was more difficult than the shrinking-room task because the former required dual representation, whereas the latter eliminated the need for it. The research reported here provides strong support for a theoretical account of early symbol understanding and use in which young children's ability to use symbols is considered to be limited by several factors, a key one being the difficulty of achieving dual representation (DeLoache, 1995a, 1995b). Relatively limited information processing capacity makes it difficult for younger children to keep two representations active at the same time, and limited cognitive flexibility makes it especially difficult for them to mentally represent a single entity in two different ways.

---

3. The parents of all the participants in this study were fully informed of the procedures to be followed, and a parent was present throughout each experimental session. The children's assent was always obtained before the sessions began. After the completion of their sessions, the children in the nonsymbolic (shrinking-room) condition were debriefed: They were shown the two dolls and the model and room together, and the experimenter explained that the machine did not really shrink or enlarge them.

The study reported here provides especially strong support against criticism of this theoretical account of early symbol use. It has been claimed that the use of a symbol such as a scale model requires nothing more than simply detecting some kind of correspondence between the symbol and referent (Blades & Spencer, 1994; Lillard, 1993; Perner, 1991). One claim is that the child succeeds on each trial by noticing that the current hiding place of the miniature toy corresponds to the full-sized hiding place of the larger toy, without ever appreciating the higher level relation between the two spaces.

The simple correspondence view cannot explain the current results. For one thing, it offers no account of how children's performance depends on the kind of relation that must be represented. In both tasks, corresponding items in the two spaces must be mentally linked; memory for the object concealing the original toy must support a search at the corresponding object. The challenge in the nonsymbolic task is simply to recognize that object in its new form. The challenge in the symbolic task is to represent the relation between that object and the other one it stands for.

Furthermore, simply detecting the correspondence between matching items does not support successful performance in the symbolic task. In a recent study (DeLoache, 1995a), 2½-year-old children readily matched the items in the room to the corresponding items in the model, yet still failed the subsequent standard model task. Establishing object correspondences is thus necessary but not sufficient for reasoning from one space to the other. Although the simple correspondence account has the appearance of parsimony, because it posits a lower level explanation than dual representation, it cannot account for results presented here and elsewhere in support of dual representation (DeLoache, 1991; Marzolf & DeLoache, 1994).

At the most general level, the research reported here indicates that it is the nature of a child's mental representation of the relation between two entities that governs the child's ability to reason from one to the other. Very young children can reason successfully based on an identity relation, even when it results from the complex and novel scenario of a shrinking machine. They fail to appreciate a symbolic relation between the same two entities, even though it is explained and demonstrated. Despite the importance and universality of symbolization, very young children are quite conservative when it comes to interpreting novel objects as symbols.

The dual representation hypothesis, which received strong support from the study reported here, has important practical implications. For example, it calls into question the assumption commonly made by educators that children will readily comprehend the meaning of manipulables—concrete objects used to instantiate abstract mathematical concepts (Uttal, Scudder, & DeLoache, 1997). One must take care to ensure that children appreciate the relation between, for example, the size of blocks and numerical quantities before using the blocks for teaching purposes. Similar doubt is cast on the widespread practice of using anatomically explicit dolls to interview young children in child-abuse investigations. Young children's difficulty with dual representation suggests that the relevant self–doll relation may not be clear to them; if so, using dolls may not be helpful and might even be counterproductive. Recent research has supported this conjecture: Several studies have reported no advantage to using dolls to interview 3-year-old children about events they have experienced (Bruck, Ceci, Francoeur, & Renick, 1995; DeLoache, Anderson, & Smith, 1995; DeLoache & Marzolf, 1995; Goodman & Aman, 1990; Gordon et al., 1993).

One other aspect of the results reported here merits attention. The 2½-year-old children had no difficulty dealing with the size transformations supposedly effected by the shrinking machine. This finding is consistent with research showing that very young children represent and rely on geometric features of a space (Hermer & Spelke, 1994). The children's ability to mentally scale the two spaces in the present research may have been assisted by the fact that the size transformations preserved the geometric properties of the original space, including its overall shape, the relative sizes and positions of the objects, and the distances among them.

Spatial representations other than scale models also pose problems for young children. Only with difficulty can 3-year-olds use a simple map to locate a hidden object, and their ability to do so is easily disrupted (Bluestein & Acredolo, 1979). Older preschool children often fail to interpret aerial photographs consistently (Liben & Downs, 1992); they may, for example, describe one feature of an aerial photo correctly as a river but another as a piece of cheese. Thus, figuring out the nature and use of spatial symbols is a persistent challenge for young children.

The current study, along with other research on the early understanding and use of symbols, makes it clear that one can never assume that young children will detect a given symbol–referent relation, no matter how transparent that relation seems to adults or older children. Young children may perceive and form a meaningful interpretation of both the symbol and the entity it stands for without representing the relation between them.

Acknowledgments—The research reported here was supported in part by Grant HD-25271 from the National Institute of Child Health and Human Development. This article was completed while the first author was a fellow at the Center for Advanced Study in the Behavioral Sciences with financial support from the John D. and Catherine T. MacArthur Foundation, Grant No. 95-32005-0. We thank R. Baillargeon and G. Clore for helpful comments on this article and K. Anderson and N. Bryant for assistance in the research.

REFERENCES

Blades, M., & Spencer, C. (1994). The development of children's ability to use spatial representations. In H. Reese (Ed.), *Advances in child development and behavior* (Vol. 25, pp. 157–199). New York: Academic Press.

Bluestein, N., & Acredolo, L. (1979). Developmental change in map reading skills. *Child Development, 50,* 691–697.

Bruck, M., Ceci, S.J., Francoeur, E., & Renick, A. (1995). Anatomically detailed dolls do not facilitate preschoolers' reports of a pediatric examination involving genital touching. *Journal of Experimental Psychology: Applied, 1,* 95–109.

DeLoache, J.S. (1987). Rapid change in the symbolic functioning of very young children. *Science, 238,* 1556–1557.

DeLoache, J.S. (1989). Young children's understanding of the correspondence between a scale model and a larger space. *Cognitive Development, 4,* 121–139.

DeLoache, J.S. (1991). Symbolic functioning in very young children: Understanding of pictures and models. *Child Development, 62,* 736–752.

DeLoache, J.S. (1995a). Early symbolic understanding and use. In D. Medin (Ed.), *The psychology of learning and motivation* (Vol. 33, pp. 65–114). New York: Academic Press.

DeLoache, J.S. (1995b). Early understanding and use of symbols. *Current Directions in Psychological Science, 4,* 109–113.

DeLoache, J.S., Anderson, K., & Smith, C.M. (1995, April). *Interviewing children about real-life events.* Paper presented at the annual meeting of the Society for Research in Child Development, Indianapolis, IN.

DeLoache, J.S., Kolstad, D.V., & Anderson, K.N. (1991). Physical similarity and young children's understanding of scale models. *Child Development, 62,* 111–126.

DeLoache, J.S., & Marzolf, D.P. (1995). The use of dolls to interview young children. *Journal of Experimental Child Psychology, 60,* 155–173.

Dow, G.A., & Pick, H.L. (1992). Young children's use of models and photographs as spatial representations. *Cognitive Development, 7,* 351–363.

Gibson, J.J. (1979). *The ecological approach to visual perception.* Boston: Houghton Mifflin.

Goodman, G.S., & Aman, C. (1990). Children's use of anatomically detailed dolls to recount an event. *Child Development, 61,* 1859–1871.

Gordon, B.N., Ornstein, P.A., Nida, R.E., Follmer, A., Crenshaw, M.C., & Albert, G. (1993). Does the use of dolls facilitate children's memory of visits to the doctor? *Applied Cognitive Psychology, 7,* 459–474.

Gregory, R.L. (1970). *The intelligent eye.* New York: McGraw-Hill.

Hermer, L., & Spelke, E. (1994). A geometric process for spatial reorientation in young children. *Nature, 370,* 57–69.

Langer, S.K. (1942). *Philosophy in a new key.* Cambridge, MA: Harvard University Press.

Liben, L.L., & Downs, R.M. (1992). Developing an understanding of graphic representations in children and adults: The case of GEO-Graphics. *Cognitive Development, 7,* 331–349.

Lillard, A.S. (1993). Pretend play skills and the child's theory of mind. *Child Development, 64,* 348–371.

Marzolf, D.P. (1994, April). *Representing and mapping relations in a symbolic task.* Paper presented at the International Conference on Infant Studies, Paris.

Marzolf, D.P., & DeLoache, J.S. (1994). Transfer in young children's understanding of spatial representations. *Child Development, 64,* 1–15.

Perner, J. (1991). *Understanding the representational mind.* Cambridge, MA: Bradford Books/MIT Press.

Potter, M.C. (1979). Mundane symbolism: The relations among objects, names, and ideas. In N.R. Smith & M.B. Franklin (Eds.), *Symbolic functioning in childhood* (pp. 41–65). Hillsdale, NJ: Erlbaum.

Uttal, D.H., Schreiber, J.C., & DeLoache, J.S. (1995). Waiting to use a symbol: The effects of delay on children's use of models. *Child Development, 66,* 1875–1891.

Uttal, D.H., Scudder, K.V., & DeLoache, J.S. (1997). Manipulatives as symbols: A new perspective on the use of concrete objects to teach mathematics. *Journal of Applied Developmental Psychology, 18,* 37–54.

(RECEIVED 8/25/96; ACCEPTED 12/20/96)

Multiple Choice:

1.   Why did these investigators think that telling the toddlers in this study that a machine could shrink a room would make it easier for them to reason between the two spaces?

      A.   The children would not have to represent the symbolic relation between room and model.
      B.   The children would interpret the task as a pretend game and hence enjoy it more.
      C.   It would help the children remember the hiding event.

2. This study was a test of:

      A.   sensorimotor thought
      B.   map reading
      C.   symbolic play
      D.   dual representation

Essay:

1.   Magicians hate to perform for very young children. Does the 2-1/2-year-olds' acceptance of the shrinking machine scenario give you a clue as to why this is true?

2.   How can you reconcile this article, in which toddlers gullibly accepted the idea of a shrinking machine, with the one by Baillargeon, in which infants seem to know a surprising amount about the nature of the physical world?

ARTICLE 9

The Development of Children's Knowledge about Inner Speech

John H. Flavell, Frances L. Green, Eleanor R. Flavell, and James B. Grossman

Reprinted from: *Child Development*, 1997, *68*, 39-47.
Copyright © 1997 by the Society for Research in Child Development.
Reprinted with permission.

Among the many things that people need to know--and hence that children must come to know--one of the most important is how the mind works. To go about our everyday lives we do not, of course, have to have scientific knowledge about the mind, but we do need what is called a *folk psychology*, a set of beliefs that we can use to understand, interpret, and predict our own and other people's thoughts and actions. What would it be like not to understand how beliefs relate to behavior, how desire relates to choice, or how conscious thought differ from dreams? Children only slowly come to understand these and many other aspects of the mind and mental activity.

This article is part of what has recently been an extremely active area of research on the development of children's *theory of mind*. Previous research has established that young children have limited understanding of how the mind represents reality. For example, it is not until around the age of four that children understand the relation between appearance and reality. They then come to realize that appearances can deceive, that is, an object can look like something other than what it really is, so one's perception of what it is can be wrong. At about the same age, children also appreciate the possibility of *false belief*--the fact that one can believe and act on the basis of something that is not true.

Even after these advances, older preschool children seem to have remarkably little insight into other aspects of the mental world. For example, John Flavell and his colleagues have found that 4- and 5-year-olds do not realize that there is always something going on in the head of anyone who is not asleep (although we sometimes doubt this ourselves when we survey students in an early morning class). By seven years of age, children can generally give reasonable accounts of these and other activities.

In this *cross-sectional* study, Flavell and his colleagues examine what children know about inner speech. Hearing a voice in your head can be a sign of schizophrenia, or it can be perfectly normal--depending on whose voice you hear. *Inner speech* refers to the reflections, self-instructions, musings, and so forth that occur during most of our waking time. Although adults can easily become aware of and reflect upon their own inner speech, the preschool children in this research could not. An older group of 6- to 7-year-olds had knowledge of inner speech similar to that of adults.

Child Development, February 1997, Volume 68, Number 1, Pages 39–47

The Development of Children's Knowledge about Inner Speech

John H. Flavell, Frances L. Green, Eleanor R. Flavell, and James B. Grossman

Two studies demonstrated that preschool children have little knowledge and awareness of inner speech. Study 1 showed that, in contrast to 6- to 7-year-olds and adults, 4-year-olds usually did not infer that a person silently engaged in such intrinsically verbal mental activities as reading, counting, or recalling items from a shopping list was saying things to herself. They also tended to deny that covert speech is a possible human activity. Study 2 demonstrated that 4- and 5-year-olds are much poorer than adults at detecting their own inner speech. Children seem to acquire this sort of knowledge and awareness during the early school years, perhaps through experiencing their own inner speech while reading, writing, adding, and subtracting.

INTRODUCTION

Research on the development of children's naive theory of mind or folk psychology has shown that they are in possession of some impressive basic knowledge about the mental world by the age of 4 or 5 years (Astington, 1993; Bartsch & Wellman, 1995; Lewis & Mitchell, 1994; Perner, 1991; Wellman & Gelman, 1992). Most important, they show by their performance on false-belief, appearance-reality, Level 2 perspective-taking, and other tasks that they have acquired something akin to a mental-representational conception of the mind. Thus, they understand that people act on the basis of their beliefs, even when those beliefs are false, and that how things seem or appear may vary with the perceiver's perspective and may also differ from how things really are.

However, studies have also revealed a number of major limitations on preschoolers' theory-of-mind competencies. For example, Flavell, Green, and Flavell (1993, 1995, 1996) have shown that older preschoolers lack important knowledge and abilities concerning their own and other people's ongoing mental activities. They are largely unaware of the fact that people experience a flow of ideation (William James's *stream of consciousness*) even when not engaged in cognitive tasks. Even more surprising, preschoolers may fail to assume that anything is going on in the minds of people who are engaged in such obviously (to us) cognitive activities as looking, listening, reading, and talking. Children of this age are also very poor introspectors of their own mental activity, frequently failing to report experimentally induced mental content that children of 7 or 8 years of age find very easy to report. Finally, unpublished research by Flavell, Green, and Flavell indicates that older preschoolers lack a clear understanding of the differences in mental activity and mental experience between being conscious (awake) and being unconscious (in a deep, dreamless sleep).

The main purpose of the present studies was to assess preschoolers' knowledge of inner speech or verbal thought, a very important and frequently occurring form of mental activity. There are several reasons why preschoolers might be largely unaware even of the existence of internal verbal events.

1. Several lines of evidence suggest that preschoolers may engage in less inner speech or verbal thought than older children and adults, at least in task situations. First, there is now considerable research support for Vygotsky's (1962) well-known claim that children's private, self-directed speech tends to become more covert—more "inner"—during the elementary school years (Diaz & Berk, 1992). Second, research on the development of memory strategies has shown a similar increase during this same age period in children's tendency to covertly rehearse stimulus names (Flavell, Miller, & Miller, 1993, chap. 6). Finally, children are generally thought to become more reflective as they grow older, and much of that increased reflection would undoubtedly be verbal in nature. This is not to suggest that preschoolers do not engage in inner speech at all but only to suggest that they may engage in it less or differently than their elders. On the contrary, they must be doing some kind of covert verbal encoding whenever they produce or comprehend speech (Hitch, Halliday, Schaafstal, & Heffernan, 1991). There is also experimental evidence that preschoolers subvocalize. In memory studies using electromyography or other methods, researchers have shown that preschoolers may subvocalize the names of the to-be-remembered items when the items are first presented even though, unlike older children, they may not continue to rehearse them subsequently (Garrity, 1975; Hitch, Halliday, Dodd, & Littler, 1989; Hitch et al., 1991; Hulme, Sil-

vester, Smith, & Muir, 1986; Locke & Fehr, 1970). They will definitely subvocalize words when the memory items are words rather than depicted objects (Hitch et al., 1989, 1991). Other studies have demonstrated that 5-year-olds can be successfully trained to engage in covert as well as overt verbal rehearsal in recall tasks (Johnston & Conning, 1990; Johnston, Johnson, & Gray, 1987).

2. Preschoolers' limited introspection skills should reduce the likelihood of their being consciously aware of whatever inner speech or verbal thought they do engage in.

3. Their extensive experience with overt talking coupled with their inexperience with silent reading might lead them to assume that speech could not be speech if it were not overt. If so, the very notion of inner, soundless speech might be almost unthinkable for them.

4. Just as preschoolers may believe that an activity could not be simultaneously linguistic and covert, as just proposed, so also might they believe that an activity could not be simultaneously linguistic and intellectual. That is, although they know that there are certain acts called thinking and certain acts called talking, they may not realize that the two can coexist in the same act in the form of verbal thinking.

STUDY 1

Two hypotheses were tested in this study. The main one (inner-speech hypothesis) was that 4-year-olds would have relatively little knowledge about inner speech and would show this lack of knowledge in two ways. First, they would be less likely than older children and adults to believe that it is possible for people to talk to themselves silently, "up in their heads." Second, they were also predicted to be less likely than older participants to infer the presence of inner speech in an experimenter who was engaged in a mental activity that would clearly require it, for example, silently trying to recall items on a shopping list. Similar tests were made of a secondary hypothesis derived from speculation 4 above, namely, that 4-year-olds would be less likely than older persons to believe that an individual who is talking aloud could also be thinking at the same time (simultaneous-talk-and-think hypothesis).

Method

Participants

The participants consisted of 20 4-year-olds, 20 6- to 7-year-olds, and 20 adults. The younger children were drawn from a university laboratory preschool and were mostly from middle-class families. Half were males and half females, and their mean age was 4 years 8 months (range = 4 years 2 months to 4 years 11 months). The older children were drawn from two private elementary schools and were of similar SES. Eleven were female and nine male, and their mean age was 7 years 1 month (range = 6 years 3 months to 7 years 10 months). The adult group consisted of 13 female and 7 male college students. Two female experimenters, hereafter referred to as E1 and E2, tested all of the participants.

Procedure

Training and pretest. To insure that the younger children were willing to answer questions with both "yes" and "no" answers, participants were asked four training questions about the possibility of both mental and physical activities. Feedback was given for these four questions. Three additional questions about thinking and talking (questions 3, 6, and 7) provided tests of our hypotheses. No feedback was given for these three questions. E1 began the testing session by saying, "You know, [participant's name], people *can* do lots of different things, can't they? They *can* drive cars, they *can* smile, they *can* sing songs. There are also things people can*not* do. They can*not* fly like a bird, they can*not* walk through walls, and they can*not* talk as loud as thunder. Now I'm going to ask you some questions about what people *can* and can*not* do."

> 1. Can a person eat ice cream? That's right/ Actually a person *can* do that.
> 2. Can a person stand on one foot all day long? That's right/ Actually a person can*not* do that.
> 3. Can a person say the words to a story up in his head, without moving his lips? OK.
> 4. At the very same tiny minute, can a person feel happy, sad, and mad, all at once? That's right/ Actually a person can*not* do that.
> 5. Can a person have dreams? That's right/ Actually a person *can* do that.
> 6. Can a person tell himself things or talk to himself up in his head? OK.
> 7. When a person is talking out loud, can he be thinking at the same time? OK.

Questions 6 and 7 were asked in counterbalanced order, and the other five questions were asked in the order shown.

Main tasks. Four tasks followed the pretest: two, blocked together, in which E2 sat silently while thinking (Silent) and two, also blocked together, in which she muttered continuously while thinking (Talk). The order of the tasks within the blocks was counterbalanced. Half the participants in each age group received the Silent tasks first, and half received the Talk tasks first.

In one of the Silent tasks (Store), E2 said, "You know, E1, this morning my friend asked me to buy some things for her at the grocery store. I didn't write down what she asked for." E1 responded, "Uh oh. Well, E2, try to remember all the things she asked you to buy." E2 said, "Hmm. This is going to take some time. Give me a few minutes." She then turned her back to the participant and E1 and said, "It's hard to remember exactly what she said." E1 paused a few seconds and then asked, "Right now, is E2 thinking, up in her head, or not? That's right/ Actually she *is* thinking. Is she just thinking, up in her head, or is she also saying things to herself, up in her head?" If participants answered, "Also saying things," E1 asked, "What is she talking about, up in her head?" If they answered, "Just thinking," E2 asked, "What is she thinking about, up in her head?" In this and all the other tasks, the choices within the test questions were counterbalanced across participants. In the other Silent task (Bicycle), E2 silently planned how she would tell her husband about some damage she had accidentally caused to his bicycle.

In one of the Talk tasks (Books), E1 said, "E2, I know you read lots of good books last year. Try to remember your three favorite books." E2 said, "Hmm, this is going to take some time. Give me a few minutes." She turned her back to E1 and the participant, while continuing to talk: "It's hard to remember exactly what I read. What was the name of that book I read about farming? It was the name of a place. Hmm." With E2 continuing to mutter audibly in this fashion, E1 asked, "Right now, is E2 talking or not? That's right, she *is* talking. Is she just talking or is she also thinking, up in her head?" As in the Silent tasks, participants were then asked for the content of E2's talking if they responded "Just talking," or the content of her thinking if they responded "Also thinking." In the other Talk task (Doctor), E2 continued to mutter aloud as she wrestled with the problem of what she would say to her sick son to persuade him to go see the doctor.

Additional tasks. The testing session ended with the administration, in random order, of two additional Silent tasks and one additional Talk task that we thought might be easier for young children than the four main ones. The Silent tasks concerned E2's covert verbal activity ("also saying things to herself, up in her head?") while silently counting an array of ob-

Table 1   Percentage of Correct Responses to Tests of the Inner Speech Hypothesis in Study 1

Test	Age		
	4 Years	6–7 Years	Adult
Question 3	20*	65	90*
Question 6	45	95*	100*
Store	35	55	85*
Bicycle	25*	65	75*
Count	30	80*	100*
Read	30	90*	95*

Note: Percentages significantly ($p < .05$) larger or smaller than chance expectations of 50% according to the binomial table are marked with an asterisk.

jects (Count) or while silently reading a story book (Read). At the end of the Read task a more direct question was asked: "She's still reading. Is she saying any story words to herself right now, or not?" Preschoolers have had some experience with the intrinsically verbal activities of counting and reading, and even if they haven't done them silently themselves, they have certainly observed others doing them silently. They might, therefore, have had the experience of hearing numbers and other words in their heads in these situations and therefore be more willing to admit that E2 was talking to herself. In the additional Talk task (Shoe), E2 reported that she felt something inside her shoe and then repeatedly said, "I wonder what it can be. I can't imagine what it is." We thought the repeated use of "wonder" and "imagine" might help the 4-year-olds realize that E2 must be thinking as well as talking.

Results and Discussion

Table 1 shows how each age group responded to the six tests of the inner-speech hypothesis: the two initial questions about whether it would be possible for a person to engage in inner speech; following these, the two main Silent tasks concerning E2's inner speech; and last, the two additional, supposedly easier Silent tasks. The data from all six tests strongly support the hypothesis that 4-year-olds have little knowledge or awareness of inner speech. On none of these tests did the 4-year-old participants show above-chance (50%) correct responding and on two (Question 3, Bicycle) they performed significantly worse than chance. Thus, only a minority of these preschoolers said that a person could say the words to a story up in his head without moving his lips (Question 3) or could tell himself things or talk to himself up in his head (Question 6). Similarly, fewer

Table 2 Percentage of Correct Responses to Tests of the Simultaneous-Talk-and-Think Hypothesis in Study 1

	Age		
Test	4 Years	6–7 Years	Adult
Question 7	15*	60	100*
Books	60	90*	100*
Doctor	65	95*	100*
Shoe	55	80*	100*

Note: Percentages significantly ($p < .05$) larger or smaller than chance expectations of 50% according to the binomial table are marked with an asterisk.

than one-third of them said that E2 was saying things to herself while trying to silently recall her shopping list (Store), silently plan a persuasive message (Bicycle), silently count an array of objects (Count), or silently read a book (Read). To our surprise, they proved to be no more likely to infer inner speech when E2 was silently counting and reading than in the other two Silent tasks, despite the obviously verbal nature of these two activities. Recall that at the end of the Read task participants were asked an even more direct and specific question about inner speech: "She's still reading. Is she saying any story words to herself right now, or not?" Only six of the 20 4-year-olds said that she was, whereas 19 6- to 7-year-olds and 19 adults did so ($p < .001$, Fisher exact test).

There was also clear improvement with age on each of these tests. Chi-square or Fisher tests were carried out on the six rows of Table 1, and all of these age trends were statistically significant. If one accepts correct responding to at least five of these six tests as a criterion of awareness of inner speech, then 1 4-year-old, 11 6- to 7-year-olds, and 16 adults showed this awareness: $\chi^2(2) = 23.44$, $p < .001$. If the criterion is relaxed to at least four of six responses correct, the numbers per group become 4, 14, and 20: $\chi^2(2) = 28.13$, $p < .001$. It appears, then, that whereas few of the 4-year-olds gave evidence of this awareness, more than half of the 6- to 7-year-olds did. Some adult participants responded "could be" rather than "yes" to some of the Main tasks. We decided to be conservative and score these responses as incorrect. Had we scored them as correct, however, the adults' Store and Bicycle percentages correct would have risen to 100% and 85%, respectively, making the age differences even more marked.

As Table 2 shows, the secondary, simultaneous-talk-and-think hypothesis was also supported by the data. On none of the four tests of this hypothesis did the 4-year-olds respond significantly better than would be expected by chance, and on one (Question

7) they performed significantly worse. Only three of the 20 4-year-olds (15%) appeared to believe that a person could be thinking at the same time he or she was talking out loud (Question 3). Likewise, only 55%–65% said that E2 was also thinking while verbally puzzling aloud over various problems (Books, Doctor, Shoe tasks). As with the Silent tasks, the Talk task that we thought would be the easiest of the three because of E2's repeated use of "wonder" and "imagine" (Shoe) did not prove to be any easier than the other two. These results together with those of the Read task are reminiscent of Flavell et al.'s (1995, Study 7) finding that preschoolers often fail to ascribe concurrent mental activity to a person who is talking or reading.

There was also a clear improvement with age on these four measures. Chi-square or Fisher tests of the four rows in Table 2 showed significant age trends in each case. The numbers of participants per age group responding correctly to all four tests were 1, 11, and 20 from youngest to oldest group, $\chi^2(2) = 36.30$, $p < .001$. Lowering the criterion to three or more tests correct, the corresponding figures were 8, 16, and 20, $\chi^2(2) = 19.09$, $p < .001$. In addition, on those tasks in which 4-year-olds did correctly say that E2 was thinking as well as talking, they responded incorrectly 25% of the time when subsequently asked what she was thinking about, whereas the older participants never did. This suggests that some of the younger children's correct responses may not have been based on the knowledge under study. Thus, similar to what was found with the inner-speech measures, only a few of the 4-year-olds but more than half of the 6- to 7-year-olds gave clear evidence of knowing that people may think while talking.

Finally, a 3 (age) × 2 (task: Silent versus Talk) × 2 (order: Silent tasks first versus Talk tasks first) mixed ANOVA performed on responses to the four main tasks yielded significant main effects for age, $F(2, 54) = 8.51$, $p < .001$, for task, $F(1, 54) = 22.01$, $p < .001$, and for order, $F(1, 54) = 9.90$, $p < .01$, plus a significant age × order interaction, $F(2, 54) = 5.63$, $p < .01$. The two main Talk tasks (Books, Doctor) proved to be significantly easier than the two main Silent tasks (Store, Bicycle). One possible reason for this might have been that there were more available clues that E2 was thinking while talking aloud (e.g., she was obviously wrestling with a problem) than that she was talking silently while thinking. Another reasonable possibility is that children of this age are more aware that people think than that they talk covertly. As to the significant age × order interaction, this was because the 10 4-year-olds who received the Talk tasks before the Silent tasks performed better on both types of tasks than the 10 who received the Silent tasks first. However, the former subgroup also performed better on the three pretest questions (3, 6, and 7) that preceded the Talk and Silent tasks, suggesting that the order effect may have been just a sampling error.

STUDY 2

As suggested in the introduction (point 2), young children may be unaware of the existence of inner speech in part because their limited introspective skills tend to prevent them from noticing its presence on those occasions when they engage in it themselves. Study 2 was designed to test the hypothesis that they have considerable difficulty in noticing their own inner speech. Preschool children and adults were given four silent (no-talking-aloud) thinking tasks, two designed to engender inner speech and two designed to engender visual imagery. Immediately following each task participants were asked if they had solved it by subvocalizing or by visualizing. The prediction was that, in contrast to the adults, the preschoolers would be poor at recognizing which type of processing they had just done on each task.

Method

Participants

The participants consisted of 18 4-year-olds, 18 young 5-year-olds, and 18 adults, drawn from the same sources as the participants in Study 1. The 4-year-old group consisted of 10 girls and 8 boys; their mean age was 4 years 7 months (*range* = 4 years 5 months to 4 years 11 months). The 5-year-old group comprised 8 girls and 10 boys, mean age of 5 years 2 months (*range* = 5 years 0 months to 5 years 5 months). The adults were 11 female and 7 male college students. Two additional 4-year-olds and four 5-year-olds failed the introductory practice task and thus were not included in the study. One experimenter (male) tested all the participants.

Procedure

The participants were first given a practice task to acquaint them with the procedure. On the pretext of keeping their thinking secret from a puppet, they were encouraged to think about their teacher's name silently, up in their heads. Then the puppet was put in a box so he could not hear and the participants were asked what name they had just been thinking

Table 3 Percentage of Correct Responses to Verbal and Visual Tasks in Study 2

Test	Age		
	4 Years	5 Years	Adult
Verbal, name	40	55	78*
Verbal, age	55	55	72
Visual, house	50	78*	100*
Visual, face	61	83*	100*

Note: Percentages significantly ($p < .05$) larger or smaller than chance expectations of 50% according to the binomial table are marked with an asterisk.

of, and then whether they had thought of it by forming a picture of it in their head or by saying it to themselves in their head. No corrective feedback was provided in the case of incorrect answers to these questions. If a child was unable to think about the teacher's name without saying it out loud, the task was repeated using a friend's name instead. If a child responded incorrectly a second time, he or she was dropped from the study.

Four tasks of the same general sort followed, two Verbal and two Visual. In one of the Verbal tasks (Name), participants were asked to think silently about how their name sounds. They were then asked how they had thought about it: "Did you say your name to yourself in your head, or did you have a picture of your name in your head?" In the other Verbal task (Age) they thought silently about how old they were and then were asked a similar two-choice question. In one Visual task (House) they thought silently about how their house looked and then were asked whether, while doing so, they had had a picture of their house in their head or had said "house" to themselves in their head. In the other Visual task (Face) they thought silently about their mother's face and were asked a similar question. If a child said an answer aloud prematurely or indicated that he or she was unable to perform the requested task, then a back-up task was administered. Three 4-year-olds and one 5-year-old needed to be given a total of two back-up tasks each, all of which they were able to perform. The order of the four tasks and the order of options within each question ("say" versus "picture") were determined randomly for each participant, with each age group sharing the same set of random orders.

Results and Discussion

Table 3 shows how the participants in each age group performed on the two Verbal and the two Viual tasks. A 3 (age) × 2 (task: Verbal versus Visual) mixed ANOVA performed on responses to these tasks yielded as significant effects only a main effect for age, $F(2, 51) = 10.20$, $p < .001$, and for task, $F(1, 51) = 8.77$, $p < .01$. Tukey tests showed that the adults performed significantly ($p < .05$) better than the 4-year-olds on both Verbal and Visual tasks; no other pairwise age comparisons were significant. One 4-year-old, 5 5-year-olds, and 11 adults chose "correctly," as we defined correctness, on all four tasks: $\chi^2(2) = 13.05$, $p < .01$. Related t tests showed that the adults and the 5-year-olds, but not the 4-year-olds, performed significantly better on the Visual tasks than on the Verbal ones: for the adults, $t(17) = 3.00$, $p < .01$; for the 5-year-olds, $t(17) = 2.30$, $p < .05$.

It is apparent from Table 3 and the foregoing analyses that, consistent with our hypothesis, the 4-year-olds gave no evidence of knowing when they had just verbalized rather than visualized and when they had just done the opposite. In contrast, Table 3 shows that the adults usually reported having verbalized rather than visualized on the Verbal tasks (the 72% in Table 3 is near-significantly ($p < .10$) better than chance) and always reported having visualized rather than verbalized on the Visual ones. The performance of the 5-year-olds was intermediate. Like the 4-year-olds, they did not report verbalization significantly more often than visualization on the Verbal tasks. Like the adults, however, they did usually report having visualized on the Visual tasks. Finally, recall that all participants were given a Verbal practice task at the beginning of the testing session. The age trend for that task was quite similar to that for the two subsequent Verbal tasks: 60%, 50%, and 83% from youngest to oldest age group.

We were surprised that even a minority of the adults reported having thought of their name and their age via imagery rather than via inner speech on the Verbal tasks, whereas they never did the opposite on the Visual tasks. Perhaps we should not have been wholly surprised. Being skilled readers, the adults could have visualized the letters forming their name and the digits representing their age rather than, or in addition to, saying them to themselves. Indeed, three adults claimed to have both verbalized and visualized on one of their two Verbal tasks. This strategy would obviously have been much less available to preliterate preschoolers; even if a precocious few could have visualized the written version of their *own* name and age, surely none would have been able to visualize the written version of their *teacher's* name. In contrast, subvocalizing "house" and "face" on the Visual tasks would seem useless and therefore much

less likely to occur. Another possibility is that some participants may have experienced the sound of their name and their age as something heard internally rather than something said internally, that is, as acoustic imagery rather than inner speech. If so, this could also have depressed the number of verbalization choices on the Verbal tasks.

The age trend for the Visual tasks shown in Table 3 is consistent with a recent finding by Estes and Buchanan (1993). These investigators gave 4-, 5-, 6-, and 20-year-old participants extensive experience with a computer game in which Shepard-type mental rotation could be a useful solution procedure. They found an increase with age in the percentage of participants whose reaction time patterns indicated that they were, in fact, using this visualization strategy. More to the present point, they also found a marked increase with age in the percentage of these "rotators" who, when questioned, showed some awareness that they had been mentally rotating the stimulus. Similar to what was found in the present study, awareness was rare in the 4-year-old group, fairly common among the 5-year-olds, and very common among the 6-year-olds and adults. Likewise, Estes, Wellman, and Woolley (1989) found that preschoolers were usually able to "make a picture in your head" of familiar objects and also visualize movements or transformations of these objects, for example, visualizing the opening and closing of a pair of imaged scissors. These results support Harris's (1995, p. 100) recent conjecture that children may be able to introspect mental imagery somewhat earlier and more easily than they can introspect other kinds of mental processes.

As Table 3 shows, on the Verbal tasks the child participants did not report having said their name and age to themselves more often than would be expected by chance. Could that be because they did not, in fact, subvocalize these words and therefore had nothing to report? We think that this is extremely unlikely. The children generally seemed to understand the tasks and seemed to be trying to think about what they had been asked to think about. Indeed, even if they had not tried to, it seems likely that the task instruction alone (e.g., "I want you to think about how your name sounds") would have automatically triggered some mental attention to whatever they were asked to think about. If this is true, it is hard then to imagine how they could have silently thought about how their name sounds and how old they are without verbalizing these words to some extent. For preliterate thinkers, especially, there appears to be no other feasible way to represent them. We believe, rather, that their chance level of performance was due to their failure to notice or remember their covert verbalizations.

GENERAL DISCUSSION

The results of these two studies indicate that preschool children's knowledge of inner speech is extremely limited. Study 1 showed that preschool participants tend not to infer the presence of inner speech in another person who is silently trying to solve a verbal problem, even though the person's solution efforts would necessarily require verbalization. Indeed, the majority of Study 1 preschoolers apparently did not believe that people can talk to themselves or say words covertly; that is, they seemed unaware that such an activity as inner speech is even possible. Likewise, they showed little understanding that people can also be thinking while talking aloud, even when the people are obviously talking their way through a problem. The latter finding also suggests that they would have little awareness of the possibility of covert verbal thought. Study 2 showed that preschoolers also tend to be very poor at detecting the presence of inner speech in themselves when they are engaged in a task that elicits such speech. This result is consistent with other recent findings (Flavell et al., 1995) of poor introspective abilities in children of this age. Gopnik (1993) and Wimmer and Hartl (1991) have presented arguments and evidence against the traditional Cartesian assumption that the human mind is transparent to itself. The Study 2 results, together with those of Flavell et al. (1995), offer additional evidence that this assumption is wrong, at least in the case of young children.

It might be argued that the complexity of the questions they were asked rather than their lack of knowledge about inner speech was primarily responsible for the preschoolers' poor performance on our tasks. However, there are several facts that make this seem an unlikely explanation of our results. First, recall that only 6 of the 20 4-year-olds (30%) in Study 1 correctly answered the direct question asked at the end of the Read task ("Is she saying any story words to herself right now, or not?"), even though it is structurally simpler than the other questions. Second, all 20 of the Study 1 4-year-olds correctly said yes in response to control questions 1 and 5 and no in response to control questions 2 and 4. These questions are not, on average, structurally simpler than test questions 3, 6, and 7 (compare the complexity of 4 with that of 3 and 6, for instance), and yet the 4-year-

olds found them much easier than the test question (Table 1). In addition, their perfect performance on the four control questions shows that they were quite willing to answer questions either affirmatively or negatively, depending upon the content of the question. Third, in one of Flavell et al.'s studies (1995, p. 46), 20 4-year-olds were asked two control questions very similar in structure to those employed in the Main and Additional tasks of Study 1. For example, one was: "——— [E2's name] is holding a crayon, isn't she? Is she just holding the crayon or is she holding the pencil too?" For one of these questions, E was seen holding just the first-named of the two objects; for the other, she was seen holding both. Despite the structural complexity of these questions, all 20 4-year-olds answered both correctly. This suggests that it was the content rather than the structure of our questions that made them difficult for our preschool participants. One could also object that the preschoolers might not understand the "up in her head" phrase in the Study 1 inner-speech questions, but they had just agreed that E2 was "thinking, up in her head." Because of this priming, together with the finding that children of this age usually do understand that thinking is a silent activity carried on inside one's head (Flavell et al., 1995), the general meaning of "activity X, up in her head" should have been clear to them. If it was in fact clear to them, then it is hard to see why they would deny that E2 was "also saying things to herself, up in her head" unless they simply did not believe that she was. Finally, if the 4-year-olds in Study 1 really possessed significant knowledge about inner speech one would think that at least one of our six questions would have liberated it. As Table 1 shows, however, none of these questions were correctly answered by more than a minority of the 4-year-olds. These arguments and evidence, together with those cited previously, support the conclusion that children of this age really do lack knowledge and awareness of inner speech.

When do children begin to acquire such knowledge and awareness? There is evidence that they make considerable progress during the early elementary school years. In Study 1, 6- to 7-year-olds proved to be more aware than 4-year-olds of the existence of inner speech and also more able to infer its presence in another person. Flavell et al. (1995, Studies 12 and 13) found that 7- to 8-year-olds were considerably better than 5-year-olds at reporting their recent thoughts, at least some of which were verbal in nature. Siegler and his co-workers (Siegler, 1996) have found that early elementary school children are able to report quite accurately the strategies they use when adding, subtracting, telling time, and memorizing number sequences. These strategies include such inner-speech processes as covert counting and verbal rehearsal. It is reasonable to think that experience in elementary school would foster awareness of inner speech. Reading, writing, and arithmetic—the basic staples of primary grade education—all require considerable private speech on the part of the learner. Furthermore, the speech becomes progressively covert with increasing practice and expertise. This is as true for the speech involved in these activities as it is for the self-regulatory speech studied by the Vygotskyans. One can easily imagine children initially noticing that they talk aloud or half-aloud to themselves as they add and subtract numbers and read and write words, and later noticing that they still talk to themselves, but now often covertly, as they become more skilled at these activities. Recall in this connection that the 6- to 7-year-olds in Study 1 performed significantly above chance only on the Count and Read Silent tasks, the ones that entailed these school activities. As they become increasingly aware of the existence of inner speech as a cognitive activity and increasingly able to notice its occurrence when they engage in it, they should come to realize that it occurs frequently and can take many forms: rehearsing the past or planning the future, verbal problem solving, daydreaming and fantasizing, worrying and obsessing, and so forth. And with this realization, they will have learned a lot about what people's inner lives are like.

ACKNOWLEDGMENTS

This research was supported by National Institute of Mental Health Grant MH 40687. We are grateful to the children, teachers, and parents of Bing School of Stanford, Keys School of Palo Alto, California, and The Phillips Brooks School of Menlo Park, California, whose cooperation made this study possible.

ADDRESSES AND AFFILIATIONS

Corresponding author: John H. Flavell, Department of Psychology, Building 420, Stanford University, Stanford, California 94305-2130; e-mail: francie@ psych. stanford.edu. Frances L. Green, Eleanor R. Flavell, and James B. Grossman are also at Stanford University.

REFERENCES

Astington, J. W. (1993). *The child's discovery of the mind.* Cambridge, MA: Harvard University Press.

Bartsch, K., & Wellman, H. M. (1995). *Children talk about the mind.* New York: Oxford University Press.

Diaz, R. M., & Berk, L. E. (1992). *Private speech: From social interaction to self-regulation.* Hillsdale, NJ: Erlbaum.

Estes, D., & Buchanan, L. (1993, March). *Mental rotation and metacognition in early childhood.* Paper presented at the meeting of the Society for Research in Child Development, New Orleans.

Estes, D., Wellman, H. M., & Woolley, J. P. (1989). Children's understanding of mental phenomena. In H. Reese (Ed.), *Advances in child development and behavior* (Vol. 22). New York: Academic.

Flavell, J. H., Green, F. L., & Flavell, E. R. (1993). Children's understanding of the stream of consciousness. *Child Development, 64,* 387–398.

Flavell, J. H., Green, F. L., & Flavell, E. R. (1995). Young children's knowledge about thinking. *Monographs of the Society for Research in Child Development, 60*(1, Serial No. 243).

Flavell, J. H., Green, F. L., & Flavell, E. R. (1996). The development of children's knowledge about attentional focus. *Developmental Psychology, 31,* 706–712.

Flavell, J. H., Miller, P. H., & Miller, S. A. (1993). *Cognitive development* (3d ed.). Englewood Cliffs, NJ: Prentice-Hall.

Garrity, L. I. (1975). An electromyographical study of subvocal speech and recall in preschool children. *Developmental Psychology, 11,* 274–281.

Gopnik, A. (1993). How we know our minds: The illusion of first-person knowledge of intentionality. *Behavioral and Brain Sciences, 16,* 1–14.

Harris, P. L. (1995). Commentary. *Monographs of the Society for Research in Child Development, 60*(1, Serial No. 243).

Hitch, G. J., Halliday, M. S., Dodd, A., & Littler, J. E. (1989). Development of rehearsal in short-term memory: Differences between pictorial and spoken stimuli. *British Journal of Developmental Psychology, 7,* 347–362.

Hitch, G. J., Halliday, M. S., Schaafstal, A. M., & Heffernan, T. M. (1991). Speech, "inner speech," and the development of short-term memory: Effects of picture-labeling on recall. *Journal of Experimental Child Psychology, 51,* 220–234.

Hulme, C., Silvester, J., Smith, S., & Muir, C. (1986). The effects of word length on memory for pictures: Evidence for speech coding in young children. *Journal of Experimental Child Psychology, 41,* 61–75.

Johnston, R. S., & Conning, A. (1990). The effects of overt and covert rehearsal on the emergence of the phonological similarity effect in 5-year-old children. *British Journal of Developmental Psychology, 8,* 411–418.

Johnston, R. S., Johnson, C., & Gray, C. (1987). The emergence of the word length effect in young children: The effects of overt and covert rehearsal. *British Journal of Developmental Psychology, 5,* 243–248.

Lewis, C., & Mitchell, P. (Eds.). (1994). *Children's early understanding of mind: Origins and development.* Hillsdale, NJ: Erlbaum.

Locke, J. L., & Fehr, F. S. (1970). Young children's use of

the speech code in a recall task. *Journal of Experimental Child Psychology, 10,* 367–373.

Perner, J. (1991). *Understanding the representational mind.* Cambridge, MA: MIT Press.

Siegler, R. S. (1996). *Emerging minds: The process of change in children's thinking.* New York: Oxford University Press.

Vygotsky, L. S. (1962). *Thought and language.* Cambridge, MA: MIT Press.

Wellman, H. M., & Gelman, S. A. (1992). Cognitive development: Foundational theories of core domains. In M. R. Rosenzweig & L. W. Porter (Eds.), *Annual review of psychology.* Palo Alto, CA: Annual Reviews.

Wimmer, H., & Hartl, M. (1991). Against the Cartesian view on mind: Young children's difficulty with own false beliefs. *British Journal of Developmental Psychology, 9,* 125–138.

Multiple Choice:

1. Which developmental theorist was concerned with inner speech?

   A.   Piaget
   B.   Freud
   C.   Erickson
   D.   Vygotsky

2. Which of the following do 4-year-olds think is engaging in inner speech?

   A.   a person who is reading
   B.   a person who is talking
   C.   themselves when they are asked to think about how old they are.
   D.   all of the above
   E.   none of the above

Essay:

1. Studying what children know about what goes on "up in their heads" is quite challenging. Go back through this article and notice all the things that these researchers did to try to make sure their results would tell them what children believe about inner speech, that is, that the children's responses would not be due to something other than what the authors wanted to study.

ARTICLE 10

The Psychological and Social Origin
of Autobiographical Memory

Katherine Nelson

Reprinted from: *Psychological Science*, 1993, *4*, 7-14.
Copyright © 1993 by the American Psychological Society.
Reprinted with the permission of Cambridge University Press.

What is your earliest memory? I am quite confident that if we could survey every reader of this page, almost no one would report a memory from before the age of two, a small number would describe an experience they had between two and three, and most would report earliest memories originating from when they were four, five, or six.

This phenomenon, which has eternally fascinated people, was called "infantile amnesia" by Freud. Psychologists have offered many different explanations for the fact that we have no conscious memories of our earliest experiences. Most of these accounts propose that early in life memories are encoded differently from how they are encoded later. For example, Piaget, as well as others, emphasized the role of language, arguing that experiences in the first two years or so are primarily encoded non-verbally and are inaccessible to conscious, verbal recall later in life.

Nelson offers quite a different account of the infantile amnesia phenomenon, although her account still assigns a central role to language. She proposes that the development of autobiographical memory is a function of social interaction. Young children learn to talk about the past with their parents. As a result, language gradually becomes available as a means of gaining access to the child's representational system.

THE PSYCHOLOGICAL AND SOCIAL ORIGINS OF AUTOBIOGRAPHICAL MEMORY

By Katherine Nelson

Recent research on young children's memory for personal episodes provides new insights into the phenomenon of infantile amnesia, first identified by Freud. New research indicates that children learn to share memories with others, that they acquire the narrative forms of memory recounting, and that such recounts are effective in reinstating experienced memories only after the children can utilize another person's representation of an experience in language as a reinstatement of their own experience. This competence requires a level of mastery of the representational function of language that appears at the earliest in the mid to late preschool years.

Remembering past events is a universally familiar experience. It is also a uniquely human one. As far as we know, members of no other species possess quite the same ability to experience again now, in a different situation and perhaps in a different form, happenings from the past, and know that the experience refers to an event that occurred in another time and in another place. Other members of the animal kingdom . . . cannot travel back into the past in their own minds. (Tulving, 1983, p. 1)

This passage introducing Tulving's book on episodic memory makes a strong claim, similar to the more familiar claim of the uniqueness of human language. If remembering past events is uniquely human, as Tulving claims, the point calls out for further investigation. What is the significance of this ability for human social and psychological functioning? How and why does it arise phylogenetically and ontogenetically? Is it related to other uniquely human functions such as language, symbolic cognitive processing, and the establishment of complex cultures?

Tulving's claim is controversial, and has been argued extensively (see commentators on Tulving, 1984). For the purposes of this article, I take it as an assumption to be examined, but I confine the assumption only to the late-developing type of episodic memory that humans possess, namely, autobiographical memory. And I examine the assumption in the course of addressing the question of why a specific kind of episodic memory—autobiographical memory—may develop in human childhood.

For the developmental account outlined here, it is important to distinguish not only between semantic and episodic memory, as Tulving has, but also between generic event memory, episodic memory, and autobiographical memory, taking autobiographical memory as a subtype of episodic. *Generic event memory* (not specifically considered by Tulving) provides a schema derived from experience that sketches the general outline of a familiar event without providing details of the specific time or place when such an event happened, whether once or many times. A basic type of this kind of general schema is the *script* (Schank & Abelson, 1977) that specifies the sequence of actions and empty slots for roles and props that may be filled in with default values, in the absence of specifications. Generic event memory may also be considered for some purposes a type of semantic memory in that it crosscuts the distinctions that Tulving set forth.

Both of Tulving's memory types (and those considered in this article) fall under the *declarative* memory system distinguished by Squire (1992) or the *explicit* memory system described by Schacter (1992), which involve conscious recollection of previous experiences. The present distinctions among memory types are adopted primarily for the purpose of interpreting the developmental research and providing an explanation for the establishment of a "life history" memory.

In contrast to generic event memory, an *episodic* memory has the phenomenal characteristic of referring to something that happened once at a specific time and place. But the specific identification of time and place does not seem to be necessarily part of episodic recall, although adults can often reconstruct an episodic memory from different types of cues, and find a way of identifying a specific time and place at which a specific event was experienced, even if the location is not available in declarative form. All that seems to truly distinguish episodic recall from generic event memory is the sense that "something happened *one* time" in contrast to the generic "things happen this way." Yet it is not at all clear that this somewhat vague impression (of "one time") will

Address correspondence to Katherine Nelson, City University of New York Graduate Center, 33 West 42nd St., New York, NY 10036.

85

bear the weight of Tulving's claim of human uniqueness. We simply do not know whether other animals, or even human infants, experience a phenomenal difference between remembering and knowing, differentiating between one-time happenings and usual happenings. They very well might.

Equally important, not all episodic memory is *autobiographical memory*. This point is critical to the theoretical and empirical explication of the development of autobiographical memory. To take a simple example, what I ate for lunch yesterday is today part of my episodic memory, but being unremarkable in any way, it will not, I am quite sure, become part of my autobiographical memory. It has no significance to my life story beyond the general schema of lunch. In contrast, the first time I presented a paper at a conference is part of my autobiographical memory: I remember the time, place, and details of the program and participants, and I have a sense of how that experience fits into the rest of my personal life story. It is important to make this distinction at the outset, because, as recent research has established, very young children do have episodic memories, but do not yet have autobiographical memory of this kind.

Autobiographical memory as used here is specific, personal, long-lasting, and (usually) of significance to the self-system. Phenomenally, it forms one's personal life history. Prior to the development of this system, memories do not become part of a personally known life history, although of course they may be important in other ways to one's life, and one may derive a strong sense of one's early history from hearing about it from other people.

Autobiographical memory has its onset during the early childhood years. Surprisingly, it is only recently that this onset has been thought of in developmental terms. In the past, it has usually been conceived of in terms of childhood (or infantile) amnesia, the phenomenon, first identified by Freud (1963) and familiar to all who reflect on it, that memories for events from the early years of our lives—before about 3 to 4 years—are not available to adult consciousness, although many memories from later childhood usually are easily called up.

The onset of autobiographical memory is simply the inverse of infantile amnesia. In the present framework, the critical questions are when and why an autobiographical system—in which some memories are retained for a lifetime—becomes differentiated from a general episodic system.

Most of the research on childhood amnesia—the period of life before the onset of autobiographical memory—has come from studies of adults' recall of childhood memories, beginning with a questionnaire study by Henri and Henri in 1897 (see review by Dudycha & Dudycha, 1941). As in many studies that followed, they asked adults ($N = 120$) to recall their earliest memories from childhood and reported the data in terms of the number of childhood memories from a given age range. No memories were reported from before 2 years, but 71% of the subjects had some memories from the period between 2 and 4 years of age. Summarizing over a large number of such studies, Pillemer and White (1989) found that the earliest memory is reported on average at about 3½ years. They noted that there are actually two phases of childhood amnesia, the first a total blocking of memories, usually prior to about 3 years, and the second, between 3 and 6 years, a significant drop-off of accessible memories relative to later memories. Such a pattern has been verified by the analysis of the forgetting curve for adult recall of childhood memories (Wetzler & Sweeney, 1986). However, it is important to note also that there is considerable variability both in age of earliest memory—from 2 years to 8 years or even later—and in number of memories reported from early childhood. In the early empirical literature on the topic, the age of earliest memory has been negatively correlated with IQ, language ability, and social class, and females tend to have earlier memories than males.

It is commonly objected that the data on early childhood memories are unreliable and unverifiable, but for the following reasons these objections do not invalidate the conclusions drawn. First, those who can reliably date their memories—because they experienced moves or other disruptions during early childhood—or whose parents can verify events (Usher & Neisser, 1991) exhibit the same general age relations as those suggested by the overall research. For example, it is rare to find anyone who claims to remember a specific incident from before the age of 2 years. Moreover, a study of memory for the birth of a sibling, which could be definitively dated, showed the same age relation as the questionnaire data: Children could remember the event if it occurred when they were 3 years or older, but not before that age (Sheingold & Tenney, 1982).

The validity of any given memory is not relevant within the present theoretical framework. Although the validity of a memory may be of concern if one is interested in such issues as whether children are reliable witnesses, it is of less concern if one is interested in when they begin to retain memories in the autobiographical memory system. Memories do not need to be true or correct to be part of that system.

The term childhood amnesia implies that something was there and is lost. This in turn implies that we need to find an explanation either in terms of loss or in terms of some force that interferes with retrieval of memories that still exist, as Freud proposed. The alternative possibility explored here is that something develops that leads to a new organization of memory or the establishment of a new memory system or function. These possibilities can be evaluated only in terms of the study of memory during the period prior to and subsequent to the emergence of autobiographical memory. The adult research, on the basis of which so much of the discussion has been based, can tell us only that the phenomenon is real; it cannot reveal anything about its development.

EVIDENCE FROM DEVELOPMENTAL RESEARCH

Research on memory in very early childhood is very recent, coming mostly from the past 15 years. My colleagues and I began investigations of children's event memory in the mid-1970s, and our early studies revealed that 3-year-olds are quite good at telling what happens in general in a familiar event such as having lunch at the preschool or going to McDonald's, but they are relatively poor at telling what happened on one particular occasion (Nelson, 1978; Nelson & Gruendel, 1981). These early findings suggested to us an explanation for infantile amnesia, namely, that children do not preserve episodic memories, although they may remember bits of information from specific events in their schematic event memory. In early childhood, we believed, all information retained from experience is absorbed by the generic memory system. Recently, Gopnik and Graf (1988) and Perner (1991) have suggested similar "overwrite" mechanisms.

However, this hypothesis—that young children have generic memory only—has not stood up to empirical test. Subsequent research indicated that very young children do remember novel events, within limits, and sometimes quite readily report episodes that they find interesting (Hudson, 1986; Ratner, 1980). When asked about routine events, they simply give routine answers, but when asked about novel events, they are sometimes able to respond with details even when as young as 2½ years. More recent research has verified that children do have specific episodic memories and can remember them for extensive periods—sometimes as long as 2 years—prior to the age of the earliest autobiographical memories reported by adults (see Fivush & Hudson, 1990, for reviews). Why do these memories not persist into later childhood and adulthood?

Not only does this research invalidate the proposal that memory is at first completely generic, but it calls into question some other theoretical proposals as well. For example, there is nothing in this recent evidence to support the idea that young children's memories are especially threatening, either positively or negatively affect laden, as Freud's theory would suggest.

Schachtel (1947) and Neisser (1962) suggested that autobiographical memories are the outcome of a reconstructive process based on schemas or frames of reference, along the lines suggested by Bartlett (1932). Remembering, then, involves *reconstructing* past events using presently existing schemas, and the claim is that adult schemas are not "suitable receptacles" for early childhood experience; "adults cannot think like children" and thus cannot make use of whatever fragments of memories they may retain. In this view, socialization and the impact of language force a drastic change in the child's schemas at age 6.

The recent developmental data cast doubt on this proposal as well. Although very young children often need extensive probing to elicit their memories, suggesting that they may retain only random and unschematized fragments, there is also evidence of specific episodic memories that have the same form as we might find in older children. A fragment from a 2½-year-old girl talking to herself when alone in her room is illustrative:

We *bought* a baby, cause, the well because, when she, well, we *thought* it was for Christmas, but *when* we went to the s-s-store we didn't have our jacket on, but I saw some dolly, and I *yelled* at my mother and said I want one of those dolly. So after we were finished with the store, we went over to the dolly and she *bought* me one. So I have one.

In this example, Emily was recounting to herself what apparently was a significant episode in her life (she had not rehearsed this recent episode with her parents or others; see Nelson, 1989, for further details). This recount is well organized, with clear and concise temporal and causal sequencing. It—and others like it—does not suggest that the preschool child's schemas are dramatically different from those of the older child and adult.

Indeed, recent reports of young children's free recall of salient episodic memories (Engel, 1986; Hudson, 1990; Tessler, 1991) support the conclusion that the basic ways of structuring, representing, and interpreting reality are consistent from early childhood into adulthood. These studies indicate that young children, in both their script recounts and their specific memory recounts, typically tell their stories in a sequence that accurately reflects the sequence of the experience itself and that has the same boundaries that seem natural to adult listeners (Nelson, 1986).

Of course, there may be other differences between adult and child memories, including what is noticed and remembered of an event. The extensive cuing and probing often required to elicit details from a young child suggest that adult and child may have different memories of the same event. An analysis of the content of crib talk (talk to self alone before sleep) by the child Emily, recorded from 21 to 36 months, supports the suggestion that adult and child may focus on different events and different aspects of events. Emily's memories were concerned mostly with the quotidian, unremarkable, routines of her life. They were not concerned with the truly novel events of her life (from the adult's point of view), such as the birth of her baby brother or her airplane trips to visit relatives (Nelson, 1989). Thus, interest in–and therefore memory for—aspects of experience that seem unremarkable to adults, and indifference to what adults find interesting, as well as lack of facility with language and differences in the knowledge base, may account for why children sometimes seem to have organized their knowledge in a different form or have remembered only fragments from an episode that adults consider memorable.

In summary, recent research on episodic memory in early childhood indicates that children have at least some well-organized specific and general event memories, similar to those of adults; thus, the suggestion that a schematic reorganization may account for infantile amnesia is not supported. However, recent research that has shown that children learn to talk about their past experiences in specific ways does provide some clues as to what may be developing and how.

NARRATIVE CONSTRUCTION OF MEMORY

Over the past decade, a number of researchers have studied the ways in which parents engage in talking about the past with their very young children. These studies, some focused on the specific language forms used, others on the content of talk, and still others on narrative forms and differences in communicative styles, have revealed the active role that parents play in framing and guiding their children's formulation of "what happened."

Hudson (1990) concluded from a study of her own daughter's memory talk between 21 and 27 months that eventually Rachel began to "interpret the conversations not as a series of questions to be answered but as an *activity of remembering*" (p. 183). Hudson endorses a *social interaction model* of the development of autobiographical memory, a model that Pillemer and White (1989) and Fivush and Reese (1991) have also invoked. In this view, children gradually learn the forms of how to talk about memories with others, and thereby also how to formulate their own memories as narratives. The social interaction model differs from the schematic change model in that it claims that children learn *how* to formulate their memories and thus retain them in recoverable form.

Several studies at the City University of New York (and elsewhere) have found that parents not only engage in memory talk but also differ among themselves in the number of memory-relevant questions they ask, the kind of memory they attempt to elicit, and the ways in which they frame the talk. Engel (1986) studied mother–child conversations about past episodes with children from 18 months to 2 years and identified two styles of mother talk, one described as *elaborative,* the other more *pragmatic.* The elaborative mothers tended to talk about episodes in narrative terms of what happened when, where, and with whom. Pragmatic mothers referred to memory primarily in instrumental terms, such as "where did you put your mittens?" For pragmatic mothers, memory is useful for retrieving information relevant to ongoing activities. For elaborative mothers, memory provides the basis for storytelling, constructing narratives about what mother and child did together in the there and then. Engel found that children of elaborative mothers contributed more information to the memory talk at 2 years than children of pragmatic mothers.

Tessler (1986, 1991) studied the effect of adult talk during an experience on children's subsequent memory for the experience in two naturalistically designed experiments. She observed differences in mother's style of interaction similar to those identified by Engel, and found that children of narrative (or elaborative) mothers remembered more from a trip to a natural history museum a week later, when probed with a standard set of questions, than did children of pragmatic-type mothers. Most strikingly, none of the children remembered any of the objects that they viewed in the museum if they had not talked about them together with their mothers. In a second study, Tessler found that there was no difference between children experiencing different types of interaction with mothers during an event in recognizing elements of the experience, but there were differences in the amount of information recalled from the experience, with the children of narrative mothers recalling significantly more. Again, things that were not talked about were not recalled. These findings indicate not only that talk about the past is effective in aiding the child to establish a narrative memory about the past, but that talk during a present activity serves a similar purpose. In both cases, adults who present the activity in a narrative format, in contrast to a focus on identification and categorization, appear to be more effective in establishing and eliciting memories with their young children. Could this be important in establishing an autobiographical memory system? The social interaction hypothesis would certainly suggest so.

EFFECTS OF LANGUAGE ON MEMORY

What is it that talking about events—past and present—contributes to memory? The social interaction hypothesis emphasizes learning to structure memories in narrative form. Another suggestion might be the effects of rehearsal. However, there are two indications that rehearsal is not the major contributor. First, children are frequently unresponsive to maternal probing (Fivush & Fromhoff, 1988), suggesting that often the event being talked about was not what the child remembered but what the adult remembered. Second, available evidence suggests that events that do seem rehearsed are not subsequently remembered. For example, Emily sometimes recounted an event many times during an evening's session of crib talk but did not apparently remember the event months later (Nelson, 1989) or when probed years later (Nelson, unpublished data). Emily seemed to be attempting to understand the events she took part in, and to use them in her representation of her world, but not for holding on to memories of specific episodes. Long-term follow-up studies of memories rehearsed in early childhood are obviously important but are very rare. In one instance, similar to the findings from Emily, J.A. Hudson (personal communication, April 1992) has indicated that her daughter at 8 years remembers nothing of the events they rehearsed together when she was 2.

In a unique follow-up study, Hudson and Fivush (1991) reported on the long-term memories of sixth graders for a class trip they took as kindergartners. Some memories of the trip could be retrieved when the children were probed and viewed pictures taken at the time, but none of the children spontaneously recalled the event. These children would have been on the edge of the amnesia barrier at age 5 or 6 when they experienced the event; however, the trip may not have seemed personally significant, or may have been absorbed into the generic memory of class trips as years went by.

A possible function of memory talk distinct from rehearsal is that of reinstatement. Reinstatement is a concept that has been invoked in infant memory studies by Rovee-Collier and Hayne (1987). The idea is that a learned response (e.g., kicking to make a mobile move) that would otherwise be lost over time may be reinstated and thus preserved if a part of the context is re-presented within a given time period. A study by Fivush and Hamond (1989) with 2-year-old children found a similar effect; specific memories that tended to be lost over a period of weeks could be retained if they were reinstated by providing an experience similar to the original event at least once within a specific period of time—in this case, 2 weeks. In a memory test 3 months later, children whose memory had been reinstated remembered significantly more than children who had not had this experience. Equally important, the reinstated group remembered as much at 3 months as they had at 2 weeks; that is, there was no subsequent loss.

FUNCTIONS OF EARLY MEMORY

At this point, it may be possible to construct an integrated picture of the development of memory in early childhood and the establishment of an autobiographical memory system. The proposal rests on the assumption that the basic episodic memory system is part of a general mammalian learning-memory adaptive function for guiding present action and predicting future outcomes. The most useful memory for this function is generic memory for routines that fit recurrent situations, that is, a general event schema (or script) memory system. Memory for a specific episode presumably becomes part of that system when a new situation is encountered, and thus it becomes apparent that a new schema must be established. A new experience alerts the organism (person, animal) to set up a new schema, which at first may be equivalent to an episodic memory, but with further experience with events of the same kind comes to be more and more scriptlike. Indeed, research on novel and repeated events with preschool children found that this was precisely what happened (Hudson & Nelson, 1986). The more frequently an event (such as going to the beach or the zoo) had been experienced, the more scriptlike the child's account became. Events experienced five or more times tended to be formulated in general present-tense terms and to confuse slot-fillers (e.g., animals seen) for different episodes of the event.

This general scheme leaves us with a problem, however: How is the basic memory system to know whether a novel event is the first of a recurrent series of events that should therefore be remembered (i.e., schematized for future reference) or is an aberration that is of no functional significance? (Of course, if the aberration is life-threatening, it is likely to be entered into the general memory and knowledge system as important information for that reason alone.) The point is, the system cannot know on the basis of one encounter what significance the event might have with respect to future encounters.

The solution for a limited memory system is either to integrate the new information as part of the generic system or to keep the novel memory in a separate, temporary, episodic memory for a given amount of time to determine if it is the first of a series of recurrent events and thus should become part of the generic system. Then, if the event reoccurs, the memory may be transferred to the more permanent generic memory system. If a similar event does not recur during that test period, the episode is dropped from memory as of no adaptive significance.

Reinstatement would play an important part in this proposal. Reinstatement signals that the episode is not a one-time occurrence and thus the memory should be retained for future reference. Reinstatement would extend the amount of time that a memory is held in the episodic system, as found by Rovee-Collier and Hayne (1987) and by Fivush and Hamond (1989). In the basic functionally based system being described here, all memory is either generic knowledge—scriptlike—or temporarily episodic. The basic episodic system is claimed to be a *holding pattern,* not a permanent memory system. I suggest that this basic system characterizes human infants and young children and probably our close primate relatives as well, and perhaps other mammals.

Thus far then, the proposed system can account for the good generic event memory found in early childhood, as well as the availability of episodic memories that may persist for 6 months, or longer if there are conditions of reinstatement. But this proposal does not account for the establishment of an autobiographical memory system in which some specific memories may persist for a lifetime. This raises the question as to what function the autobiographical system serves beyond that of the long-lasting generic plus temporary episodic system just described.

The claim here is that the initial functional significance of autobiographical memory is that of sharing memory with other people, a function that language makes possible. Memories become valued in their own right—not because they predict the future and guide present action, but because they are shareable with others and thus serve a social solidarity function. I suggest that this is a universal human function, although one with variable, culturally specific rules. In this respect, it is analogous to human language itself, uniquely and universally human but culturally—and individually—variable. I suggest further that this social function of memory underlies all of our storytelling, history-making narrative activities, and ultimately all of our accumulated knowledge systems.

The research briefly reviewed here supports these speculations. Children learn to engage in talk about the past, guided at first by parents who construct a narrative around the bits and pieces contributed by the child (Eisenberg, 1985; Engel, 1986; Hudson, 1990). The timing of this learning (beginning at about 2½ years and continuing through the preschool years) is consistent with the age at which autobiographical memory begins to emerge. The fact that the adult data suggest a two-phase process, as noted earlier, including the absence of memories in the first 2 to 3 years, followed by a sparse but increasing number of memories in the later preschool years, supports the supposition that the establishment of these memories is related to the experience of talking to other people about them. Also, the variability in age of onset of autobiographical memory (from 2 to 8 years or later) and its relation to language facility is consistent with the idea that children's experiences in sharing memories of the right kind and in the right form contribute to the establishment of autobiographical memory.

The social interaction hypothesis outlined earlier clearly fits these data well. This proposal is not simply one of cultural transmission or socialization, but rather a dialectical or Vygotskian model in which the child takes over the forms of adult thought through transactions with adults in activity contexts where those forms are employed—in this case, in the activities where memories are formed and shared. The problem that the child faces in taking on new forms and functions is to coordinate earlier memory functions with those that the adult displays, incorporating adult values about what is important to remember, and the narrative formats for remembering, into his or her own existing functional system.

This, then, is the functional part of the proposal, suggesting that sharing memories with other people performs a significant social-cultural function, the acquisition of which means that the child can enter into the social and cultural history of the family and community. However, identifying this function, and some of the social-linguistic experiences that support it, does not in itself explain why personal autobiographical memories continue to persist. For that explanation we must call on an additional function of language.

Recall that reinstatement through action was shown to be effective in establishing the persistence of a memory of an event. I hypothesize that an important development takes place when the process of sharing memories with others through language becomes available as a means of reinstating memory. (See also Hudson, 1990.) Further, I suggest that language as a medium of reinstatement is not immediately available when mothers and their young children first begin to exchange talk about a remembered experience.

Rather, reinstatement through language requires a certain level of facility with language, and especially the ability to use the verbal representation of another person to set up a representation in one's own mental representation system, thus recognizing the verbal account as a reinstatement of one's prior experience. Using another person's verbal representation of an event as a partial reinstatement of one's own representation (memory) depends on the achievement of language as a representational system in its own right, and not only as either an organizing tool or a communication tool. This achievement is, I believe, a development of the late preschool years (Nelson, 1990).

In summary, the theoretical claim here is that language opens up possibilities for sharing and retaining memories in a culturally shared format for both personal and social functions. Sharing memory narratives is important to establish the new social function of autobiographical memory, as well as to make reinstatement through language possible. Following Vygotsky's (1978) model of internalization, after overt recounting becomes established, covert recounting or reexperiencing to oneself may take place, and take on the function of reinstatement.

If memory is not talked about, to oneself or to others, should it persist? Once an autobiographical memory system is established, it takes on a personal as well as a social value in defining the self, as other scholars (e.g., Fivush, 1988) have recently argued. Thus, replaying a memory, even without talking about it specifically, overtly or covertly, might well reinstate it and cause it to persist, once the autobiographical system is set in motion.

A number of lines of research are suggested by this proposal. For example, a shift in linguistic communities should disrupt autobiographical memory, because of its dependence on linguistic representations, and there is some evidence from D. Pillemer's (personal communication, March 1990) work that such is the case. Also, the number of recounting opportunities should be important, and this might be variable across families and communities. Deaf children of hearing parents might be expected to be delayed in establishing early memories because of their lack of opportunities to engage in talk about past experiences. Cultural differences in discourse practices might be expected to lead to differences in autobiographical memory. Most of our present evidence is from middle-class Western children. In other cultures, for example, cultures that discourage children's participation in adult talk, such as the Mayan (Rogoff & Mistry, 1990), autobiographical memory might be a very late development, or take on different cultural forms such as shared myths.

To conclude, autobiographical memory may be thought of as a function that comes into play at a certain point in human childhood when the social conditions foster it and the child's representational system is accessible to the linguistic formulations presented by other people.

Finally, to return to Tulving's claim, memory, that is, autobiographical memory, "is a universally familiar experience. It is also a uniquely human one." It is uniquely human because of its dependence on linguistic representations of events, and because human language itself is uniquely human. As Miller (1990) has recently stressed, human language is unique in serving the dual function of mental representation and communication. These dual functions make possible its use in establishing the autobiographical memory system. And because such memory is at once both personal and social, it enables us not only to cherish our private memories, but also to share them with others, and to construct shared histories as well as imagined stories, in analogy with reconstructed true episodes. Once the child has begun to share memories with others, he or she is well on the way to sharing all of the accumulated cultural knowledge offered at home, in school, or in the larger world.

Acknowledgments—This article is based on a paper presented at the International Conference on Memory at the University of Lancaster, July 1991. I thank Marcia Johnson, Robyn Fivush, and Judith Hudson for their helpful comments and ideas, and Minda Tessler for permitting me to report her unpublished research and for goading me over the years to reconsider the central importance of socially shared memory.

REFERENCES

Bartlett, F.C. (1932). *Remembering: A study in experimental and social psychology*. Cambridge, England: Cambridge University Press.

Dudycha, G.J., & Dudycha, M.M. (1941). Childhood memories: A review of the literature. *Psychological Bulletin, 38,* 668–682.

Eisenberg, A.R. (1985). Learning to describe past experiences in conversation. *Discourse Processes, 8,* 177–204.

Engel, S. (1986). *Learning to reminisce: A developmental study of how young children talk about the past.* Unpublished doctoral dissertation, City University of New York Graduate Center, New York.

Fivush, R. (1988). The functions of event memory: Some comments on Nelson and Barsalou. In U. Neisser & E. Winograd (Eds.), *Remembering reconsidered: Ecological and traditional approaches to the study of memory* (pp. 277–282). New York: Cambridge University Press.

Fivush, R., & Fromhoff, F.A. (1988). Style and structure in mother-child conversations about the past. *Discourse Processes, 11,* 337–355.

Fivush, R., & Hamond, N.R. (1989). Time and again: Effects of repetition and retention interval on two year olds' event recall. *Journal of Experimental Child Psychology, 47,* 259–273.

Fivush, R., & Hudson, J.A. (Eds.). (1990). *Knowing and remembering in young children.* New York: Cambridge University Press.

Fivush, R., & Reese, E. (1991, July). *Parental styles for talking about the past.* Paper presented at the International Conference on Memory, Lancaster, England.

Freud, S. (1963). Three essays on the theory of sexuality. In J. Strachey (Ed.), *The standard edition of the complete works of Freud* (Vol. 7). London: Hogarth Press.

Gopnik, A., & Graf, P. (1988). Knowing how you know: Young children's ability to identify and remember the sources of their beliefs. *Child Development, 59,* 1366–1371.

Hudson, J.A. (1986). Memories are made of this: General event knowledge and the development of autobiographic memory. In K. Nelson, *Event knowledge: Structure and function in development* (pp. 97–118). Hillsdale, NJ: Erlbaum.

Hudson, J.A. (1990). The emergence of autobiographic memory in mother-child conversation. In R. Fivush & J.A. Hudson (Eds.), *Knowing and remembering in young children* (pp. 166–196). New York: Cambridge University Press.

Hudson, J.A., & Fivush, R. (1991). As time goes by: Sixth graders remember a kindergarten experience. *Applied Cognitive Psychology, 5,* 347–360.

Hudson, J.A., & Nelson, K. (1986). Repeated encounters of a similar kind: Effects of familiarity on children's autobiographical memory. *Cognitive Development, 1,* 253–271.

Miller, G.A. (1990). The place of language in a scientific psychology. *Psychological Science, 1,* 7–14.

Neisser, U. (1962). Cultural and cognitive discontinuity. In T.E. Gladwin & W. Sturtevant (Eds.), *Anthropology and human behavior* (pp. 54–71). Washington, DC: Anthropological Society of Washington.

Nelson, K. (1978). How young children represent knowledge of their world in and out of language. In R.S. Siegler (Ed.), *Children's thinking: What develops?* (pp. 225–273). Hillsdale, NJ: Erlbaum.

Nelson, K. (1986). *Event knowledge: Structure and function in development.* Hillsdale, NJ: Erlbaum.

Nelson, K. (Ed.). (1989). *Narratives from the crib.* Cambridge, MA: Harvard University Press.

Nelson, K. (1990). Event knowledge and the development of language functions. In J. Miller (Ed.), *Research on child language disorders* (pp. 125–141). New York: Little, Brown & Co.

Nelson, K., & Gruendel, J. (1981). Generalized event representations: Basic building blocks of cognitive development. In M. Lamb & A. Brown (Eds.), *Advances in developmental psychology* (Vol. 1, pp. 131–158). Hillsdale, NJ: Erlbaum.

Perner, J. (1991). *Understanding the representational mind.* Cambridge, MA: MIT Press.

Pillemer, D.B., & White, S.H. (1989). Childhood events recalled by children and adults. In H.W. Reese (Ed.), *Advances in child development and behavior* (Vol. 21, pp. 297–340). New York: Academic Press.

Ratner, H.H. (1980). The role of social context in memory development. In M. Perlmutter (Ed.), *Children's memory: New directions for child development* (Vol. 10, pp. 49–68). San Francisco: Jossey-Bass.

Rogoff, B., & Mistry, J. (1990). The social and functional context of children's remembering. In R. Fivush & J.A. Hudson (Eds.), *Knowing and remembering in young children* (pp. 197–223). New York: Cambridge University Press.

Rovee-Collier, C., & Hayne, H. (1987). Reactivation of infant memory: Implications for cognitive development. In H.W. Reese (Ed.), *Advances in child development and behavior* (Vol. 20, pp. 185–283). New York: Academic Press.

Schachtel, E. (1947). On memory and childhood amnesia. *Psychiatry, 10,* 1–26.

Schacter, D.L. (1992). Understanding implicit memory. *American Psychologist, 47,* 559–569.

Schank, R.C., & Abelson, R.P. (1977). *Scripts, plans, goals, and understanding.* Hillsdale, NJ: Erlbaum.

Sheingold, K., & Tenney, Y.J. (1982). Memory for a salient childhood event. In U. Neisser (Ed.), *Memory observed* (pp. 201–212). San Francisco: W.H. Freeman.

Squire, L.R. (1992). Memory and the hippocampus: A synthesis from findings with rats, monkeys, and humans. *Psychological Review, 99,* 195–231.

Tessler, M. (1986). *Mother-child talk in a museum: The socialization of a memory.* Unpublished manuscript, City University of New York Graduate Center, New York.

Tessler, M. (1991). *Making memories together: The influence of mother-child joint encoding on the development of autobiographical memory style.* Unpublished doctoral dissertation, City University of New York Graduate Center, New York.

Tulving, E. (1983). *Elements of episodic memory.* New York: Oxford University Press.

Tulving, E. (1984). Precis of *Elements of episodic memory* with open peer commentary. *Behavioral and Brain Sciences, 7,* 223–268.

Usher, J.A., & Neisser, U. (1991). *Childhood amnesia in the recall of four target events* (Emory Cognition Project Report No. 20). Atlanta: Emory University, Department of Psychology.

Vygotsky, L.S. (1978). *Mind in society: The development of higher psychological processes.* Cambridge, MA: Harvard University Press.

Wetzler, S.E., & Sweeney, J.A. (1986). Childhood amnesia: An empirical demonstration. In D.C. Rubin (Ed.), *Autobiographical memory* (pp. 191–201). New York: Cambridge University Press.

Questions for Self-Study

Multiple Choice:

1. According to Nelson, autobiographical memory is a form of:

    A.   generic event memory.
    B.   semantic memory.
    C.   implicit memory.
    D.   episodic memory.

2. Which of the following is NOT an important element in Nelson's account of the origins of autobiographical memory?

    A.   narrative structure
    B.   reinstatement
    C.   memory span
    D.   scripts

3. Nelson believes _____ is crucial to the development of autobiographical memory:

    A.   social interaction
    B.   talk about the past
    C.   parental guidance
    D.   all of the above

Essay:

1. Imagine a toddler telling her mother about her day at the child care center. What sort of events might the child report that she would remember into adulthood? What aspects of the interaction with her mother could assist the child to remember events?

ARTICLE 11

"I Hardly Cried When I Got My Shot!" Influencing Children's Reports about a Visit to Their Pediatrician

Maggie Bruck, Stephen J. Ceci, Emmett Francoeur, and Ronald Barr

Reprinted from: *Child Development*, 1995, *66*, 193-208.

Can children "tell the truth, the whole truth, and nothing but the truth?" Never before has this question seemed so important as we have come to realize that sexual abuse is much more common than had previously been believed. Society has the double responsibility of identifying anyone guilty of sexually abusing a child, while avoiding false accusations of innocent people. Children's testimony is often important in the investigation of possible abuse and in court proceedings, so it is imperative that we know as much as possible about children as witnesses. Developmental psychologists have become very active in studying children's eyewitness testimony.

This article examines young children's *suggestibility*--the tendency for one's memory for an event to be influenced by misleading suggestions (whether given intentionally or not). Although suggestibility can be a factor in memory reports by people of any age, young children are thought to be especially susceptible. In this study some children were told that a painful shot they had received during a pediatric visit had not hurt them at all. The children's subsequent memory was affected by this and other misleading information they were repeatedly given some time after the event.

These findings are important because leading and misleading questions are common in investigations of suspected abuse. Furthermore, children are often asked the same questions over and over by many different people, and the questioning may take place weeks, months, and even years after the event. The improvement of interview procedures for use with children is a high priority for many developmental memory researchers, as well as professionals (clinical psychologists, social workers, police) who deal with allegations of child abuse.

"I Hardly Cried When I Got My Shot!" Influencing Children's Reports about a Visit to Their Pediatrician

Maggie Bruck

McGill University

Stephen J. Ceci

Cornell University

Emmett Francoeur

Montreal Children's Hospital

Ronald Barr

Montreal Children's Hospital

BRUCK, MAGGIE; CECI, STEPHEN J.; FRANCOEUR, EMMETT; and BARR, RONALD. *"I Hardly Cried When I Got My Shot!" Influencing Children's Reports about a Visit to Their Pediatrician.* CHILD DEVELOPMENT, 1995, **66**, 193–208. We examined, in 2 phases, the influence of postevent suggestions on children's reports of their visits to a pediatrician. Phase 1 examined the effect of giving one of 3 types of feedback to 5-year-old children immediately following their Diphtheria Pertussis Tetanus (DPT) inoculation. Children were given pain-affirming feedback (the shot hurt), pain-denying feedback (the shot did not hurt), or neutral feedback (the shot is over). 1 week later, they did not differ in their reports concerning how much the shot hurt or how much they cried. In Phase 2, the same children were visited approximately 1 year after their inoculation. During 3 separate visits, they were either given additional pain-denying or neutral feedback. They were also given misleading or nonmisleading information about the actions of the pediatrician and the assistant. Children given pain-denying feedback reported that they cried less and that the shot hurt less than did children given neutral feedback. Those who were given misleading information about the actions of the assistant and the pediatrician made more false allegations about their actions than did children who were not given this information. These results challenge the view that suggestibility effects are confined to peripheral, nonaction events; in this study children's reports about salient actions involving their own bodies in stressful conditions were influenced.

Studies of children's suggestibility have been conducted since the turn of the twentieth century. For the first 80 years, researchers examined the influences of a single misleading suggestion on children's reports of neutral, nonscripted, and often uninteresting events that occurred in a laboratory setting (e.g., Binet, 1900). The results of these studies consistently indicated that children were suggestible and, moreover, that they were more suggestible than adults (see Ceci & Bruck, 1993, for review). These results are of importance to theoretical issues concerning whether suggestions alter children's reports because of children's desire to comply with adult authority figures who supplied the erroneous suggestions (i.e., a social explanation) or because of the effects of one or more cognitive factors, such as trace alteration, source misattributions, or reasoning-

This research was supported by a National Health and Welfare Scholar Award to M. Bruck and by grant 0GP000A1181 from the Natural Sciences and Engineering Research Council to M. Bruck, and by NICHHD RO1 HD 25775 to Stephen J. Ceci. Laurie Hellstrom, Sandy Gabriel, Vicky Murphy, and Merav Jacobs were the excellent research assistants who are described throughout the paper. We thank Steve Lindsay, Peter Ornstein, and other reviewers for their helpful comments on this manuscript. Send correspondence to Maggie Bruck, Psychology Department, McGill University, 1205 Docteur Penfield Avenue, Montreal, Quebec, H3A 1B1, Canada. E-mail address: bruckhebb.psych.mcgill.ca based inferences (see Ceci & Bruck, 1993).

Despite their theoretical importance, however, these studies have been criticized for their limited practical and legal relevance regarding the reliability of the child witness. Specifically, it is argued that the procedures used in laboratory studies are so qualitatively different from those that pertain to the child witness that the results do not permit inferences about children's suggestibility in more authentic circumstances.

Some researchers claim that these studies are not forensically relevant because they do not examine how children respond to questions about salient events involving their own body that occurred in personally experienced, stressful situations. Because salient information is given privileged encoding (Strangor & McMillan, 1992), it is thought that suggestibility effects might be greatly diminished under such situations. In order to address these issues, more recent studies have focused on asking children misleading questions about being touched. In some of these studies, children are questioned about an embarrassing or stressful medical procedure such as an inoculation or a genital examination (Goodman, Hirschman, Hepps, & Rudy, 1991; Saywitz, Goodman, Nicholas, & Moan, 1991). It has been found that children rarely make false claims about touching and particularly about sexual touching in response to a single misleading question in a single interview. According to these researchers, the results of earlier studies overestimated children's suggestibility (e.g., Melton, 1992).

This line of study, however, does not examine the effects of a planted suggestion on children's recall; it merely examines how children answer misleading questions about a medical procedure. Phase 1 of the present study addresses this issue. It examines the influence of a postevent suggestion on children's recall of their reactions to a somewhat stressful medical procedure, an inoculation.

A different set of concerns about the validity of earlier studies of children's suggestibility focuses on the argument that the interviewing procedures of such studies were so much less intense than those that bring children to court as to result in a potential *underestimation* of children's suggestibility (Raskin & Esplin, 1991; Steller, 1991). The interview procedures of traditional laboratory studies are qualitatively different from forensic interviews in several ways. First,

children who come to court are often questioned weeks, months, or even years after the occurrence of an event (as opposed to several minutes or days later). Suggestibility effects may be more salient after long delays because the original memory trace has faded sufficiently to allow a more complete penetration of the suggestion than might occur after shorter delays (Loftus, Miller, & Burns, 1978). Second, child witnesses are rarely interviewed only one time, by one interviewer, under nonstressful neutral conditions. They are interviewed many times about the same events by child protection workers, law enforcement officers, therapists, lawyers, and parents (e.g., Goodman et al., 1992; Gray, 1993). The incessant use of leading questions and suggestions in these interviews may result in a qualitatively different type of report distortion than that which arises from a single misleading question in a single postevent interview. Third, an examination of the interviews of some child witnesses reveals that the term "suggestive interview" describes more than the use of misleading questions. Rather, implicit and explicit suggestions can be woven into the fabric of the interview through the use of bribes, threats, repetitions of certain questions, and the inductions of stereotypes and expectancies (Ceci & Bruck, 1993).

Although it is very difficult to create experimental conditions that reflect the confluence of these variables, the results of recent studies indicate that children who are repeatedly given suggestions in multiple interviews prior to and following the occurrence of an event will eventually make many false allegations about the perpetrators of the event and will report inaccurate details that are nevertheless consistent with the event (Ceci, Leichtman, & White, in press). Also, when questioned by interviewers who have a particular bias or incorrect information about an event, children's reports eventually come to resemble the interviewer's interpretation of the event (e.g., Ceci et al., in press; Goodman & Clarke-Stewart, 1991; Pettit, Fegan, & Howie, 1990). One important caveat, however, is that conclusions about the influences of repeated suggestions within and across interviews are based on interviews about unpredictable (i.e., nonscripted) and low-stress events. Although some researchers claim that suggestibility is diminished or nonexistent for central and personally experienced actions, especially those involving their bodies (Melton, 1992; Saywitz et al., 1991) or for highly predictable scripted events, such as a visit to their pediatrician (see Hudson, Fivush, & Kuebli, 1992), the effects of repeated suggestions on children's recalls of such events are simply not known. These issues are addressed in Phase 2 of the present study. Approximately 1 year after their inoculation, children were given repeated suggestive interviews. The effects of these interviews on their subsequent reports of personally experienced, predictable, and salient events were examined.

Phase 1

METHOD

Design

Five-year-old children were given one of three types of feedback immediately after receiving a Diphtheria Pertussis Tetanus (DPT) inoculation at their pediatrician's office. Children were told that the shot hurt, that the shot did not hurt, or that the shot was over. One week later, these children were asked how much the shot hurt and how much they cried.

Subjects

Subjects were between 54 and 70 months at the time of their medical visit. All were patients of the same pediatrician (E. Francoeur). The social class backgrounds of the children were normally distributed. Most of the children were Caucasian. None of the children had undergone major medical procedures or exhibited unusual developmental histories.

Although 83 children were given feedback immediately following the inoculation, only 75 were included in the data analysis. Subjects were omitted either because they refused to interact with the research assistant at the 1-week follow-up visit, their parents interfered with the experimental procedures, or the parents could not reschedule the 1-week follow-up appointment. These omitted subjects were equally distributed across the three feedback conditions.

Procedures

Parental assistance.—A research assistant (RA) described the aims and procedures of the study to the parents when they arrived at the pediatrician's office for their child's medical examination. While their child was occupied in the playroom in another part of the waiting room, parents were told that they could comfort their child nonverbally during the inoculation procedure, but they were asked not to say anything to their child other than, "It's OK. It's over now." Parents were told about the three types of feedback, but they were not told which one their child would receive.

Six parents refused to participate. Those who agreed to participate were given a diary and asked to record for 1 week, the day, date, time, and summary of any conversations, complaints, or reactions related to the inoculation.

Medical examination and inoculation.—The pediatrician carried out a routine medical examination. The RA was not present for this part of the visit. After the examination, the parent and child entered the "inoculation room" where they were met by the RA, who talked to the child about a poster on the wall. Approximately 5 min later, the pediatrician entered the room. After reminding the parent how to comfort the child, he gave the child an oral polio vaccine and then the DPT inoculation. The RA coded the child's level of distress at the time of inoculation. She also timed the number of seconds between the inoculation and the child's leaving the inoculation room, which occurred only after the child stopped crying and said he or she was ready to participate in the next part of the study. The entire procedure was audio-recorded for subsequent coding and reliability checking.

Postinoculation feedback.—After the child had calmed down, the RA took the child and parent to a third room where she randomly assigned the child to one of three feedback conditions. Children in the pain-denying (i.e.,"no-hurt") feedback condition were told:

Your shot didn't seem to hurt you at all. You acted like a big kid, and a very brave kid! It doesn't hurt big kids when they get a shot. Here's a lollipop and a sticker for being such a big kid and for not letting it hurt.[1]

Children in the pain-affirming (i.e.,"hurt") feedback condition were told:

Your shot seemed to hurt you a lot. But you know,

---

[1] Children who received feedback that was totally inconsistent with how they acted during their shot never resisted our erroneous feedback. Preschoolers' willingness not to challenge obviously discrepant feedback has been found in numerous other studies (e.g., Ceci, Ross, & Toglia, 1987) and may be a source of their vulnerability.

it hurts kids when they get a shot. So it's OK that it hurt a lot. Here's a lollipop and a sticker because it hurt so much.

Children in the neutral feedback condition were told:

Your shot—it's over now. You know, lots of kids today get shots. Its all over now and here's a lollipop and a sticker."

The RA then read the child a story about a child who goes out to play and falls out of a tree. In the story, the mother gives the child feedback consistent with the feedback the RA had just given the subject. The RA pointed out that the story character acted just like the actual child when the inoculation was given. The pediatrician was not in the room for the feedback or the story.

One-week follow-up interview.—One week later, a different research assistant (blind to the feedback condition) visited the child at home. The child was taught to use a rating scale and then to indicate how much the shot had hurt and how much he or she cried at the time of the shot. The Peabody Picture Vocabulary Test (PPVT-R), a test of receptive vocabulary that correlates highly with verbal intelligence (Dunn & Dunn, 1981), was also administered at this time. The diaries were collected from the parents. Seventy-eight percent had been filled out: 69% in the "no hurt" condition, 79% in the "hurt" condition, and 88% in the neutral condition.

Measures

Distress ratings.—The Torrance Global Mood Scale (Torrance, 1968) was adapted for this study to describe the distress levels of children during the inoculation. This seven-point scale rates the child's distress on the basis of facial features, verbalizations, and degree of crying. The lowest rating of "1" is given to children who are attentive, happy, and interested. A rating of "4" characterizes unhappy, worried, or anxious children who do not cry. Finally, children who scream and who are held down receive a rating of "7."

Research assistants were trained to use the rating scale by viewing videotapes of children being prepared for anesthesia and then rating these children's levels of distress. Training was complete when their ratings were identical to those of the principal investigator for 18 children. During the actual experiment, the pediatrician provided distress ratings for 32 of the subjects. In all cases, these ratings were identical to those of the research assistant.

How Much Did It Hurt Scale.—This scale was adapted from "Hester's Poker Chip Tool" (Hester, 1979). The child was shown five piles of poker chips, each representing a different level of hurt. The first pile contained one white poker chip. The next piles contained one red chip, two red chips, three red chips, and four red chips, respectively. The experimenter explained to the child that the white chip shows no hurt at all, that the pile with one red chip shows a little bit of hurt, that two red chips shows a little bit more hurt, that three red chips shows even a little more, and that the pile with four red chips shows all the hurt you can have.

The child was then asked to use the chips to show how much it hurts when the experimenter gently taps the child's arm, and when the child falls off a bike onto the sidewalk. The procedure was repeated if the child did not use more chips for the second than for the first question. Children were then asked to use the chips to show how much it hurt when they got their shot.

Hester (1979) found that children's ratings of hurt, obtained after an inoculation, were highly correlated with measures of children's distress during the inoculation.

How Much Did You Cry Scale.—Children were shown six cartoon faces of a child. The faces ranged in intensity from a very happy, smiling face (face 1) to a very unhappy face shedding many tears (face 6). These faces were arranged on one piece of paper in descending order from happy to sad. The experimenter gave verbal description for each face (e.g., "This face is smiling a lot"; "This face is crying a little"; "This face is crying the most"). The child was asked to point to the face that shows "what you look like when you are having a lot of fun," and "when a sharp knife cuts your finger." This procedure was repeated if the child did not point to one of the happy and then one of the sad faces. The child was then asked to point to the face that showed "what you looked like when you got your shot."

Peabody Picture Vocabulary Test (PPVT-R).—This standardized test of receptive vocabulary (Dunn & Dunn, 1981) was used to assess overall verbal ability. The child is asked to identify from among four pictorial alternatives the one that corresponds to an orally presented word.

TABLE 1

Summary of Results for Phase 1

	FEEDBACK		
	No Hurt (n = 24)	Hurt (n = 25)	Neutral (n = 26)
Age (months)	61 (.6)	62 (.7)	60 (.5)
% females	54	48	46
Distress rating	4.3 (.3)	4.6 (.3)	4.4 (.3)
Seconds to calm after shot	92 (7.4)	90 (7.1)	90 (8.4)
PPVT (raw scores)	61 (2.8)	61 (3.1)	62 (2.8)
How much hurt	3.5 (.3)	3.5 (.3)	3.6 (.3)
How much cry	2.9 (.4)	3.6 (.4)	3.2 (.4)
Days of postinoculation pain	2.5 (.3)	2.8 (.3)	2.8 (.3)

NOTE.—Standard errors are presented in parentheses. Days of postinoculation pain was based on parent diary reports.

RESULTS

The three feedback groups did not differ significantly in terms of age, gender, distress ratings, and PPVT-R scores (see Table 1). The distress ratings indicate that on average the children were unhappy and worried. However, there was much variation within each group, with some children appearing unaffected during the procedure whereas others screamed and raged.

Two separate one-way analyses of variance were carried out to examine the effect of feedback condition on children's ratings of how much the shot hurt and how much they cried. The mean responses for each scale are shown in Table 1. The results can be summarized simply: There was no significant effect of feedback condition for either the Hurt scale ($p > .96$) or the Cry scale ($p > .25$).

Examination of the parent diaries indicated that, on average, children experienced 2–3 days of discomfort following the shot (see Table 1). The number of days of discomfort was not associated with the children's hurt or cry ratings nor with their group membership (all $ps > .66$).

The children's postinoculation conversations about the shots, as recorded in the parent diaries, reveal that they often received feedback inconsistent with that of the experimental condition. One-third of the children who had been told by the experimenter that the shot hurt were later told by parents, friends, or other adults that they had been very brave or that shots don't hurt. Similarly, 33% of the children who had been told by the experimenter that the shot didn't

hurt were later told by parents or adults that shots really do hurt. Finally, 20% of the children given neutral feedback by the experimenter were later given feedback consistent with the "hurt" or "no-hurt" condition. Because the parent who filled out the diary was not privy to all conversations that the child had about the shot or may not have recorded all conversations, the above figures probably underestimate the number of children who received feedback inconsistent with that of the experimental condition.

DISCUSSION

Providing suggestive feedback to children concerning how much a shot hurt did not influence their reports of how much the shot hurt or of the more objective measure, how much they cried. These nonsignificant results do not reflect children's difficulties in using the scales to rate their memories, because their ratings of how much they cried and hurt were positively correlated with their distress ratings at the time of the inoculation: $r = .65$ and $.27$, respectively ($ps < .05$). Thus, these ratings reflect the children's behavior during the inoculation procedure and their ability to use the scales accurately.

These results indicate that the children in this study could not be easily influenced to make inaccurate reports concerning significant and stressful procedures involving their own bodies. Several factors may have contributed to these results. First, a review of the parent diaries revealed that the experimental suggestion may have been ineffective because it was only one of different types of feedback that the child received after the shot. Second, although the inoculation itself was not very painful, most children experienced several days of discomfort following the shot, according to the parent diaries. It is possible that the discomfort after the inoculation may have overridden the potential influence of the suggestion.

Finally, providing children with approximately 1–2 min of feedback immediately following a somewhat stressful experience may not be sufficient to influence their reports. As indicated above, children may not give sway to a single suggestion in a single interview when the event involves their own bodies.

Phase 2

In Phase 2, we examined the influence of multiple suggestive interviews, which occurred many months after the inoculation, on children's recall of the inoculation. In addition to examining the effects of repeated feedback on children's subsequent reports of how they acted during the inoculation, we also examined the effects of repeated misinformation on children's reports of salient and personally experienced events during the inoculation visit.

Few studies have examined the wide-reaching effects of misinformation on subsequent reports; most have merely examined whether misinformation is directly incorporated into children's false reports. In Phase 2, we examined whether misleading information about specific events promoted children's false reports about the suggested events as well as about other logically related events. This objective was motivated by previous findings that preschool children possess strong "implicational structures" that guide their probabilistic reconstruction of the past and that at times this deployment of normal inferential processes can lead to unwarranted conclusions (Ceci, Caves, & Howe, 1981).

In Phase 2, we also attempted to isolate some of the characteristics that differentiate children who fall sway to misinformation from those children who resist misinformation. First, we examined the relation between suggestibility and memory of the target events. Even though theorists differ in their accounts of suggestibility effects, most predict a negative correlation between memory of the original event and suggestibility. For example, according to Loftus's memory impairment view (1992), weak

traces of the original event permit the erroneous suggestion easier access and incorporation into memory, thus "overwriting" or erasing the original trace. According to the demand characteristic view of McCloskey and Zaragoza (1985; Zaragoza, 1991), children who have no memory of an event may be more likely to accept the suggestions of a trustworthy interviewer in order to provide a response and please the interviewer. Despite these predictions, there has been little developmental evidence to show that suggestibility is highest when memories are weakest (see Ceci & Bruck, 1993).

Next, we examined the relation between suggestibility and children's stress levels at the time of the inoculation. There is considerable debate concerning the association between stress and children's suggestibility. Some researchers claim that high stress levels increase children's suggestibility (e.g., Peters, 1991), some claim that high stress levels are associated with lower suggestibility (e.g., Goodman et al., 1991), and some researchers find no consistent association between the two (see Ceci & Bruck, 1993).

Finally, we examined the relation between suggestibility and IQ. Many earlier studies report robust negative correlations between IQ and children's suggestibility (see Ceci & Bruck, 1993): Children with lower IQ scores were more suggestible. However, these studies often entailed paper and pencil tests of both suggestibility and IQ, thus raising the possibility that literacy skills accounted for the common variance between IQ and suggestibility measures. The correlation may also reflect the common variance due to memory in both the suggestibility and intelligence tests since many of these earlier studies focused on children's memories of peripheral events.

METHOD

Design and Hypotheses

Four to 18 months after their inoculation (average delay = 11 months), children who participated in Phase 1 of this study were given one of two types of feedback concerning how they felt and acted when they received their inoculation. Some children were given "positive" feedback; they were told that they acted brave and that they did not cry at all. Other children were given "neutral" feedback; that is, they were given no feedback about how they acted at the time of the shot. Children were given the same feedback in three different visits spread out over a 2-week period. On the fourth visit, children were asked to rate how much the shot had hurt and how much they had cried 1 year previously. If children cannot be influenced to make inaccurate statements about bodily events, then positive feedback should have no effect on their subsequent reports of how much the shot hurt and how much they cried.

During the three interviews, children were also provided with different types of information about who carried out different actions during the inoculation visit. There were two between-subject factors (information about the RA, information about the pediatrician), each with two levels (misleading, no information). These two factors were completely crossed; thus children were assigned to one of four groups. Children in group 1 were falsely reminded that the RA had given them their inoculation and oral vaccine, and that the pediatrician had shown them a poster, given them treats, and read them a story during the inoculation visit. Children in group 2 were falsely reminded that the RA had given them their inoculation and their oral vaccine, and that *someone* had shown them a poster, given them treats, and read them a story. The reverse held for children in group 3, who were told that someone had given them an inoculation and an oral vaccine but falsely reminded that the pediatrician had shown them a poster, given them treats, and read them a story. Children in group 4 were given no misinformation and were simply reminded that someone had given them an inoculation and an oral vaccine, and that someone had shown them a poster, given them treats, and read them a story. In the fourth and final visit, children recalled the details of their inoculation visit.

An implication from past research is that misleading information should not influence the accuracy of children's reports if it is incongruent with children's scripted expectations or if it involves central actions and personally experienced events (Goodman, Rudy, Bottoms, & Aman, 1990; Saywitz et al., 1991). We predicted that these statements do not generalize to conditions when children are repeatedly interviewed after a long delay. Furthermore, we predicted that misinformation not only affects children's reports about the suggested events but also about other logically related events. Thus, children who were told that the RA had given them their shot and oral vaccine were predicted to report later that the RA had given them a shot, an oral vaccine, *and* a checkup.

Subjects

Parents whose children had participated in Phase 1 were sent a letter describing the goals and general procedures of Phase 2. In order to avoid possible contamination, parents were not given examples of the actual feedback or misinformation that might be given to their child. Sixty-six of the 83 Phase 1 children were retested. Two families had moved, and two families refused to have their children retested. The remaining 13 families could not be conveniently scheduled.

Children were assigned to a positive feedback condition ("you were brave, it didn't hurt, you didn't cry") or to a neutral feedback condition.[2] The assignment procedure was constrained to equate the two groups in terms of (a) interval between Phase 1 and Phase 2, (b) gender, (c) distress rating at the time of inoculation, and (d) feedback condition of Phase 1 (i.e., the three feedback conditions of Phase 1 were fully crossed with the two feedback conditions of Phase 2).

The two feedback conditions in Phase 2 were fully crossed with four other conditions which differed in the amount of misinformation given about the RA and the pediatrician. Thus, subjects were assigned to one of these four conditions to equate for Phase 2 feedback conditions as well as for gender and for the interval between Phase 1 and Phase 2. In order to conform to the matching criteria and to include all 66 subjects, not all cells had equal numbers of subjects. Eighteen children were given misleading information about the RA (+RA) and about the pediatrician (+P). This group is referred to as +RA+P. Sixteen children were given misleading information about the RA (+RA), but no information about the pediatrician (−P). This group is referred to as +RA−P. Fifteen children were given no information about the RA but misleading information

---

[2] A third condition, "hurt" feedback was not used in this study. We felt that it was unethical to attempt to convince children 1 year later that their prior doctor's visit had been very painful, particularly for those who had not reacted with great distress.

about the pediatrician ($-RA+P$). Seventeen children were given no information about the RA or about the pediatrician ($-RA-P$).

Procedures: Session 1

Session 1 consisted of four components: eliciting children's recall of their inoculation visit, giving children positive or neutral feedback about how they acted during the inoculation, providing children misleading or no information about the RA, and giving children misleading or no information about the pediatrician.

Recall of inoculation.—The interviewer (who did not participate in Phase 1) visited the children either at their preschool or home. She told the children that she worked with their pediatrician and asked them to tell everything they could remember about the time they got their shot (Free Recall). If the child did not mention the RA, she or he was asked if she or he remembered anyone else at the office during that visit. The experimenter then told the child that the RA works at the pediatrician's office and that the RA was at the pediatrician's office when the child got the shot.

Children were shown a photograph of the pediatrician along with three other foils; they were asked to point to and name anyone they knew in the lineup. All children correctly selected and named the pediatrician. Similarly, they were shown a photograph of the RA along with three foils. If the child did not select the correct photograph, this information was provided. (Only 35% of the children selected the correct picture of the RA.) The target photographs were kept in front of the child for the rest of the interview.

Feedback about reactions to shot.

Next, children were given positive or neutral feedback about their reactions to their shot. The following is part of the positive feedback given in Session 1:

Laurie (RA) and Dr. F . . . said that when you got your shot, you were really a brave kid. They said you didn't cry at all when you got your shot. It was like it didn't even hurt you at all.

The following is part of the neutral feedback given in Session 1:

Laurie (RA) and Dr. F . . . said they remembered the day you went to get your shot. They said that first you came into the office and Maureen, the secretary, talked to your Mom (or Dad).

Information about the research assistant.—Next, children were given misleading or no information about who gave them their shot. The following is a segment of the misleading-information script given to children in conditions $+RA+P$ and $+RA-P$:

Laurie (RA) . . . gives kids their shots. She gave you your shot. Laurie said that she remembered when she gave you your shot, but she couldn't remember whether she gave you something to drink. When Laurie gave you your shot, did she give you something to drink?

The following is part of the script given to children who received no information about who gave them the shot—children in conditions $-RA+P$ and $-RA-P$:

Laurie (RA) and Dr. F . . . said that when kids get shots they sometimes get something to drink. They couldn't remember whether you got something to drink when you got your shot. Did you drink something?

Information about the pediatrician.—Next, children were given misleading or no information about who showed them the poster. The following is part of the misleading sequence in conditions $+RA+P$ and $-RA+P$.

Dr. F . . . said he showed you a big picture on the wall in the room where you got your shot. And Dr. F. talked to you about the picture on the wall. What was in the picture that Dr. F showed you?

The following is part of the sequence in conditions which provided no information about who showed the poster (conditions $+RA-P$ and $-RA-P$).

Laurie and Dr. F said there was a big picture on the wall in the room where you got your shot. They said that someone talked to you about the picture on the wall. What was in that picture?

In between these exchanges the experimenter talked to the child about common events and played Legos with the child. The entire session lasted approximately 45 min. In this and all subsequent interviews, no adults or other children were present. This and all other sessions were audiotaped and later transcribed.

Procedures: Sessions 2 and 3

The same procedures were followed for Sessions 2 and 3 as for Session 1, except that children were not asked to recall the inoculation visit. At the beginning of each session, the experimenter showed the photographs of the RA and the pediatrician, leaving them out for the whole session and pointing to them when appropriate. She played with the child while conducting the interview. Each session lasted approximately 45 min. Sessions were separated by approximately 5 days.

Feedback about reactions to shot.—The feedback (positive or neutral) was repeated in each of these sessions with a different script but with the same concepts as those used in the first session.

Information about RA.—In Session 2, children who were misled about the RA were told that she gave them their shot, and this time they were also told that she also gave them their oral vaccine. As part of this script, they were also asked:

When Laurie (RA) gave you the shot, was your mom or dad with you?

Children who were given no information about who gave them the shot were told that someone gave them a shot and an oral vaccine. They were asked:

When you got your shot, was your mom or dad with you?

In Session 3, children who were given misleading information about the RA were reminded that the RA gave them a shot. As part of the script, the children were asked:

Did anybody listen to your heart or look in your ears, when Laurie (RA) gave you your shot?

Children who were given no information about the RA were asked if anybody listened to their heart or looked in their ears.

Information about the pediatrician.—In Session 2, children who were given misleading information about the pediatrician were reminded that he had shown them a poster and were told that he usually gives kids treats. As part of the script, the children were asked:

Did Dr. F give you any treats?

Children who were given no information about the pediatrician were reminded that someone had shown them a poster and were told that children usually get treats after their shots. These children were asked if they got treats.

In Session 3, children who were given misleading information about the pediatrician were falsely reminded that the pediatrician had given them a treat and also read them a story. They were asked to recall the details of the story that Dr. F had read. Children given no information about the pediatrician were reminded that someone had given them a treat and read them a story. They were asked to recall the details of the story.

Procedures: Session 4

The fourth and final visit occurred 5 days after Session 3. The same experimenter who questioned the children in the first three sessions served as the interviewer.

Recall of Phase 1.—Children were first asked to try to tell everything they could remember when they had their shot. Next, the children were shown photographs of the pediatrician and of the RA and asked to tell everything that the RA did and everything that the pediatrician did. If a child did not name the agent of the shot, oral vaccine, checkup, poster, treat, or story event in either the free recall or open-ended photo-prompt questions, then the experimenter explicitly asked him or her to name the agent (e.g., "Who gave you your shot?").

Ratings of hurt and crying.—Using the same procedures described in Phase 1, children used the Hurt scale and the Cry scale to show how much the shot had hurt and how much they had cried when they got their shot. After the study was completed, parents were sent a letter summarizing the results.

Measures

The number of target details that the child reported in the free recall at the beginning of Session 1 and of Session 4 were counted. There were six target details: the oral vaccine, the shot, the checkup, the poster, the treats, and the story. The agent of these actions did not have to be reported in order for the detail to be coded as present. Two raters scored the recall data. The proportion of agreements across raters was .98; discrepancies were resolved through discussion.

The number of false reports of the agents of these six target actions that were elicited through free recall, photo-prompt, or explicit questions in Session 4 was counted.

The number of visits to the pediatrician between Phase 1 and Phase 2, as indicated

103

TABLE 2

SUMMARY OF NEUTRAL AND POSITIVE FEEDBACK RESULTS FOR PHASE 2

	FEEDBACK	
	Positive (n = 33)	Neutral (n = 30)
Age (months)	72 (.7)	73 (.7)
Months since shot	11.1 (.6)	11.7 (.6)
% females	50	48
Distress rating at time of shot	4.5 (.2)	4.4 (.3)
Seconds to calm after shot	85 (5.3)	89 (8.0)
PPVT (raw scores)	61 (2.8)	61 (2.3)
Doctor visits between Phase 1 and Phase 2	2.6 (.6)	2.5 (.5)
Hurt—1 week	3.7 (.3)	3.3 (.3)
Hurt—1 year	1.9 (.2)	2.5 (.2)
Cry—1 week	3.6 (.4)	3.0 (.3)
Cry—1 year	2.7 (.3)	3.6 (.2)

NOTE.—Standard errors are presented in parentheses.

by the pediatrician's records, was also counted.

Results

Effects of feedback on children's hurt and cry ratings.—Two separate two-way analyses of variance with repeated measures were carried out to examine the degree to which children's reports of how they acted during the inoculation changed as a function of feedback condition. The dependent variable in the first analysis was children's ratings of how much the shot hurt, and the dependent variable in the second analysis was children's ratings of how much they cried. The independent variables were the feedback conditions for Phase 2 (positive vs. neutral) and the repeated measure, time of rating (1 week after the shot vs. approximately 1 year after the shot).[3] Three children who had not been tested 1 week after the shot because of scheduling difficulties were excluded from these analyses. Thus, there were 30 children in the neutral feedback group and 33 children in the positive feedback group. Results of these analyses along with background characteristics of these children are presented in Table 2. Before

the feedback was given for Phase 2, children in these two groups did not differ on any of the background variables.

For the "hurt" analysis, there was a significant main effect of time, $F(1, 61) = 35.32$, $p < .001$, and a significant interaction between feedback condition and time, $F(1, 61) = 6.04$, $p < .02$. Post hoc Neuman-Keuls tests carried out on the interaction revealed that the children in the positive and neutral feedback conditions produced similar hurt ratings 1 week following the shot; however, children who were given three sessions of positive feedback approximately 1 year after the shot reported less hurt than children not given this feedback. Although both groups of children showed significant reductions in their ratings of hurt in the year following their shot, planned comparison tests indicated that the reductions were significantly greater in the positive feedback condition than in the neutral feedback condition.

Similarly, for the "cry" scale analysis, there was a significant feedback × time interaction, $F(1, 60) = 9.04$, $p < .004$. Post hoc Neuman-Keuls tests indicated that 1 week after the shot, the ratings of the two feedback

[3] Analyses of how much the shot hurt and how much the child cried were rerun including a third independent variable—feedback condition of Phase 1 (no-hurt, hurt, and neutral) and a fourth independent variable—the four different combinations of misleading and no information concerning the actions of the RA and the pediatrician. These two factors were never significant nor did they ever interact with the repeated measure of time of testing or with the feedback condition of Phase 2 (all $ps > .47$). For clarity the results of these analyses are not reported in the text.

TABLE 3

CHARACTERISTICS OF CHILDREN RECEIVING MISINFORMATION OR NO INFORMATION
ABOUT THE RESEARCH ASSISTANT AND THE PEDIATRICIAN

	CONDITION			
	+RA+P (n = 18)	+RA−P (n = 16)	−RA+P (n = 15)	−RA−P (n = 17)
Age (months)	73 (1.2)	72 (.8)	72 (1.2)	71 (1.0)
Months since shot	10.5 (.8)	12.0 (.7)	12.0 (.7)	10.7 (1.0)
% females	50	50	47	53
Distress rating at time of shot	3.7 (.3)	4.4 (.4)	4.7 (.3)	4.9 (.3)
Seconds to calm after shot	75 (7.7)	85 (10.6)	98 (10.3)	94 (8.8)
PPVT (raw scores)	56 (3.6)	63 (4.5)	59 (3.7)	64 (2.6)
Doctor visits between Phase 1 and Phase 2	2.6 (1.0)	2.7 (.6)	1.7 (.3)	2.8 (.8)

NOTE.—Standard errors are presented in parentheses.

groups were equivalent; however, after 1 year and repeated suggestions, children in the positive feedback group reported significantly less crying than children in the neutral group. Also, there was no change in the absolute magnitude of the ratings for the neutral group from 1 week to 1 year, thus indicating highly stable reports. Children in the positive group, however, reported significantly less crying after 1 year than after 1 week. Thus, repeated positive feedback 1 year after the shot produced substantial reductions in children's reports of their distress during the inoculation procedure.

Effects of misinformation on reports of central actions and persons.—Background characteristics of the children in each of the four different misleading/no information conditions are presented in Table 3. The children were equated by design in terms of months since the shot and gender. They also had similar PPVT scores at Phase 1, and the same number of visits to their pediatrician between Phase 1 and Phase 2. However, children in condition +RA+P had significantly lower distress ratings at the time of the shot than did children in conditions −RA−P and −RA+P, $F(3, 65) = 2.70$, $p < .05$. There were no between-group differences in terms of number of seconds to calm after the shot.

Three separate chi-square analyses were carried out to compare the percentage of children in each of the four conditions who falsely reported at the fourth and final interview that the RA (a) gave them a shot, (b) gave them the oral vaccine, and (c) looked in their ears and nose (or any other action involved in a general medical checkup; Fig. 1).

Children in conditions +RA+P and +RA−P who were given misleading information about the RA were more likely than children not given this misinformation to falsely report in Session 4 that the RA had given them a shot, $\chi^2(3) = 13.41$, $p < .003$. Only one child inaccurately reported that the RA had given the shot when no information was provided, compared to 11 (32%) children in the two +RA misinformation conditions. The results of the analysis of the oral vaccine data just missed traditional levels of significance, $\chi^2(3) = 6.97$, $p < .07$. However, the analysis is significant when the two +RA conditions are collapsed and compared to the two collapsed −RA conditions. Five children (16%) in the −RA conditions inaccurately reported that the RA administered the oral vaccine, compared with 42% of the children in the +RA conditions, $\chi^2(1) = 4.92$, $p < .03$. Finally, none of the children in the two −RA conditions said that the RA gave them a checkup, compared to 38% of the children in the two +RA conditions who had been told that the RA gave them a shot and the oral vaccine. Further

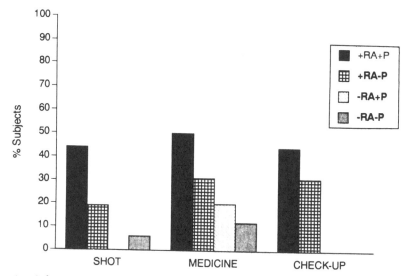

FIG. 1.—Subjects (%) in each condition who incorrectly reported the research assistant

analyses revealed no differences in the false reports of children in the +RA+P and +RA−P conditions.

Three separate chi-square analyses were carried out to compare the percentage of children in each of the four conditions who falsely reported at the fourth and final interview that the pediatrician had (a) shown the poster, (b) given treats, and (c) read a story.

As shown in Figure 2, children who were given no information about the RA and the pediatrician (condition −RA−P) were significantly less likely than children in the other three conditions to report falsely that the pediatrician had shown the poster, $\chi^2(3) = 10.51$, $p < .01$, given treats, $\chi^2(3) = 12.02$, $p < .01$, or told a story, $\chi^2(3) = 8.68$, $p < .03$. There were no significant differences in the response rates of the other three groups.

Characteristics of suggestible children.—For each of the six target events, children who were given misleading information about the agent of that event were classified, based on their Session 4 reports, as giving a false report (nonresistors) or re-

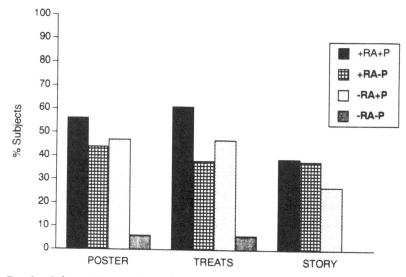

FIG. 2.—Subjects (%) in each condition who incorrectly reported the pediatrician

sisting misleading information about the agent (resistors). For each target event, a series of analyses of variance were carried out to rule out the possibility that the differences between resistors and nonresistors occurred as a function of a number of potentially confounding variables, namely, visits to the pediatrician between Phase 1 and Phase 2, age at Phase 1, age at Phase 2, and interval between Phase 1 and Phase 2. None of these differences were significant, thus ruling out potential confounds.

In the next set of analyses, the effects of memory, stress, and IQ on susceptibility to misleading information were investigated. For each of the target events, analyses of variance were carried out to compare resistors' and nonresistors' distress ratings during inoculation, seconds to calm after inoculation, PPVT score at Phase 1, number of target events recalled in Session 1, and correct identification of the photo of the RA in Session 1. The first two variables assess stress at the time of inoculation, the third variable assesses verbal IQ, and the last two variables assess children's memories of the target events. Only two of the 30 analyses yielded significant results. In both cases, susceptibility to suggestion was associated with higher stress at the time of the inoculation. Specifically, children who fell sway to the suggestion about the RA giving them a shot (nonresistors) took longer to calm after the inoculation, $F(1, 33) = 7.61$, $p < .01$, than children who resisted. Similarly, children who falsely reported that the RA gave them a checkup (nonresistors) took longer to calm after the inoculation than did resistors, $F(1, 33) = 3.99$, $p < .05$.

Characteristics of suggestible versus inaccurate children.—We attempted to delineate those variables that differentiated misled children who gave inaccurate reports from children who gave inaccurate reports in the absence of a misleading suggestion (i.e., those in the no-information conditions). The only significant variable was the spontaneity of the children's false allegations. In the fourth and final visit, children were asked to remember everything they could about their visit to the pediatrician (free recall, Session 4). They were then shown pictures of the RA and the pediatrician and asked to tell everything that each did during the visit. If the children did not name the agent of a target action (shot, oral vaccine, checkup, poster, treat, story), they were asked to provide a name (e.g., "Who gave you the shot?"). Summing over the six target actions, children gave 28 inaccurate reports when they had been given *no* information about the actors. In 27 of these cases, the incorrect target name was supplied in response to the specific question, "Who . . . ?" Thus only one false allegation was spontaneous. In contrast, misled children made 85 false allegations; 41 (48%) of these were spontaneous, occurring in reports to open-ended questions. In nine cases these occurred in response to "Tell me everything that happened," whereas 32 false reports were in response to the second open-ended question, "Tell me everything he or she did." When children made false allegations in response to the latter question, the information about the actor was not provided in response to the first question. Thus, in the present study, children who were given misleading information were much more likely to make spontaneous false allegations than children who were not given this information.

General Discussion

The results of this study place boundaries on children's suggestibility. First, the results of Phase 1 indicate that giving 5-year-old children a single suggestion in the course of a single interview about how they acted during a distressing event, immediately following that event, has little if any influence on their report of how they acted a week later. These results are not consistent with other studies that *have* found suggestibility effects for children of this age (e.g., Ceci et al., 1987). However, in most of these other studies children's suggestibility was assessed by a response to misleading information about either neutral or peripheral events (e.g., Ceci et al., 1987, misled children about the contents of a story character's breakfast). In contrast to studies that have found suggestibility effects for peripheral details, Phase 1 of the present study found no effects of suggestion on children's recall of a salient event that involved their own bodies, their own feelings, and their own actions. Moreover, these other studies presented misleading information to nondistressed children who may have been better able to process the suggestions than did children in the present study, who were still upset by the shot when the misleading information was first given. Taken together, these data indicate that 5-year-old children are not sponges soaking up misinformation from the environment and incorporating it into their reports. Both their affective states and the nature of the event being recalled seem to have buffered them from succumbing to the suggestions about their expressed pain.

While the data from Phase 1 portray 5-year-olds as resistant to a salient postevent suggestion about their bodies, the data from Phase 2 show that there is somewhat greater latitude in the scope of children's suggestibility than indicated either in Phase 1 or, more generally, in the developmental literature. First, we found that under certain circumstances 6-year-old children's reports concerning their own bodies can be influenced. That is, children who were provided with repeated positive feedback about how they had acted during their inoculation reported significantly less crying and hurt than children not provided with this feedback. Second, we also found that children's reports of salient events can be influenced by repeated suggestions. For example, approximately one-third of all children who were provided misleading information about the gender of the person who administered the shot incorrectly reported being inoculated by a female research assistant rather than by a male pediatrician.[4] Significantly, we found that children will even incorporate such central misinformation into their responses to open-ended questions and not just in response to yes/no questions. This is something that has not heretofore been found, since the popular wisdom is that, although children do not provide much information in response to open-ended questions, what they do provide is highly accurate (e.g., Goodman et al., 1990).

Although we did not directly manipulate the variables, we suggest that the difference in the pattern of results obtained in Phase 1 and Phase 2 reflects the confluence of three factors. The first factor concerns the time between the original event and the suggestions. We interviewed subjects in Phase 2 from 4 to 18 months after the shot. Perhaps this was enough time for the original memories to be weakened so that erroneous feedback could interfere with them or, if there was no longer any original memory, fill the void.

A second factor concerns the distress levels of the children at the time of the first suggestion, which immediately followed the administration of the shot in Phase 1. Many of the children were moderately to severely distressed as a result of their shot, and consequently may not have accurately processed the pain-affirming or pain-denying feedback of Phase 1. In Phase 2, the suggestions were given many months after the shot, when the children were no longer distressed. Thus, suggestions may have been more effective in Phase 2.

Third, our success in influencing children's reports in Phase 2 was achieved largely because of the nature of the repeated suggestions. These suggestions did not take the form of one sentence or of one misleading question but, rather, were woven into the experimenter's conversations with the children within and across interviews. In doing this, we deliberately tried to mimic interviews that child witnesses may undergo with their parents, law enforcement officials, or therapists.

In Phase 2, we also examined the associations between children's suggestibility, IQ, and two measures of stress (seconds to calm and ratings of stress) with six different dependent measures, thus yielding 18 analyses. Only two of the 18 analyses were significant, and both of these involved the link between stress and suggestibility. Children who fell sway to Phase 2 suggestions took longer to calm after their inoculation than children who resisted these suggestions. This finding is consistent with the assumption that high stress levels lower the efficiency with which information is processed (Peters, 1991), making children more susceptible to suggestibility, even when questioned a long time after the event.

We now turn to a more direct consideration of the mechanisms that may account for children's suggestibility in Phase 2. Throughout this paper we have consistently used the phrase "influence children's reports" as opposed to "influence children's memories." The former phrase implies that children's ratings and reports *may* have reflected genuine memory or cognitive change as a result of initial attempts to comply with the suggestions of the experimenter, but they also may only have reflected children's

---

[4] One might argue that our subjects were easily misled because since receiving their DPT shot, they had visited a female health professional who had given them a shot. However, an inspection of the children's records did not indicate any subsequent shots. Therefore, the DPT vaccination was a unique event for these children.

attempt to comply with the suggestions of the experimenter. The experimenter who obtained the final reports was the same person who gave the original erroneous suggestions in Phase 2, so it is possible that children may have been more likely to comply than if two different experimenters had been used. The present experimental procedure limits our ability to shed light on this distinction because the interviewing procedures were purposely designed to be similar to those that occur in some legal contexts where children's reports emerge after repeated interviews with the same individuals.

Nevertheless, two pieces of evidence indicate that, in addition to social processes, memory or cognitive changes in the form of reasoning-based inferential processes may account for some of the results of Phase 2. First, a substantial percentage of children given the misleading information that the RA had given them both the shot and the oral vaccine later reported that she had also given them a checkup, although this particular misinformation had never been provided to any of the children. These results may reflect cognitive mechanisms involving children's attempts to make the RA's actions congruent with those of someone who administers shots and oral vaccines (i.e., a pediatrician). It appears that children were using their expectations, based on the previous two weeks of suggestions, to construct a congruent script (e.g., Ceci et al., 1981). They filled in gaps that were consistent with, but not necessarily implied by, the suggestion. If social forces alone were operating to produce children's erroneous reports (e.g., a desire to please the interviewer), it is unclear why they would falsely report in Session 4 that the RA checked their ears and throat, since these actions had never been suggested to them by an adult.

Second, children who were given misleading information about the RA but no misleading information about the pediatrician (condition + RA – P) gave as many inaccurate reports about the pediatrician as did children who were given misleading information about the pediatrician (conditions + RA + P and – RA + P). Children's use of expectations to fill in gaps when a script is incomplete could explain these results. Many children know that when they visit the pediatrician, he always does something (see Ornstein, Larus, & Clubb, 1991). Thus, when told that the RA performed some of the actions that a pediatrician usually performs, the children may have attempted to find something else for their pediatrician to do, even if it involved showing them a poster, giving them treats, and telling a story. Conversely, children who were given no information about the RA and misleading information about the pediatrician (condition – RA + P) did not claim that the RA gave them a shot, perhaps because the children had no expectancy about the role and associated actions of the RA. Taken together, this pattern of performance would appear to implicate some cognitive mechanisms in children's false reports, whereby they restructure their reports in order to make them consistent with the suggestions as well as with their more general expectations about visiting a pediatrician. It is not easy to envision how an exclusively social mechanism could account for these asymmetrical results.

In summary, the results of this experiment indicate that 6-year-old children can be misled about salient events involving their own bodies when repeatedly provided with misinformation about the event after a lengthy delay. Furthermore, repeated misinformation also increases children's false reports about other salient events for which no misinformation is provided. These results challenge the view that suggestibility effects are confined to peripheral, neutral, and nonmeaningful events.

References

Binet, A. (1900). *La suggestibilité*. Paris: Schleicher Freres.

Ceci, S. J., & Bruck, M. (1993). The suggestibility of the child witness: A historical review and synthesis. *Psychological Bulletin, 113,* 403–440.

Ceci, S. J., Caves, R., & Howe, M. J. (1981). Children's memory for information incongruent with their long term knowledge. *British Journal of Psychology, 72,* 443–450.

Ceci, S. J., Leichtman, M., & White, T. (in press). Interviewing preschoolers: Remembrance of things planted. In D. P. Peters (Ed.), *The child witness in context: Cognitive, social, and legal perspectives.* Holland: Kluwer.

Ceci, S. J., Ross, D., & Toglia, M. (1987). Age differences in suggestibility: Psycholegal implications. *Journal of Experimental Psychology: General, 117,* 38–49.

Dunn, L. M., & Dunn, L. M. (1981). *Peabody Picture Vocabulary Test—Revised.* Circle Pines, MN: American Guidance Service.

Child Development

Goodman, G. S., & Clarke-Stewart, A. (1991). Suggestibility in children's testimony: Implications for child sexual abuse investigations. In J. L. Doris (Ed.), *The suggestibility of children's recollections* (pp. 92–105). Washington, DC: American Psychological Association.

Goodman, G. S., Hirschman, J. E., Hepps, D., & Rudy, L. (1991). Children's memory for stressful events. *Merrill Palmer Quarterly, 37*, 109–158.

Goodman, G. S., Rudy, L., Bottoms, B., & Aman, C. (1990). Children's concerns and memory: Issues of ecological validity in children's testimony. In R. Fivush & J. Hudson (Eds.), *Knowing and remembering in young children* (pp. 249–284). New York: Cambridge University Press.

Goodman, G. S., Taub, E. P., Jones, D. P., England, P., Port, L., Rudy, L., & Prado, L. (1992). Testifying in Criminal Court. *Monographs of the Society for Research in Child Development, 57*(5, Serial No. 229).

Gray, E. (1993). *Unequal justice: The prosecution of child sexual abuse.* New York: Macmillan.

Hester, N. K. (1979). The preoperational child's reaction to immunization. *Nursing Research, 28*, 250–254.

Hudson, J., Fivush, R., & Kuebli, J. (1992). Scripts and episodes: The development of event memory. *Applied Cognitive Psychology, 6*, 483–505.

Loftus, E. F. (1992). When a lie becomes memory's truth: Memory distortion after exposure to misinformation. *Current Directions in Psychological Science, 4*, 121–123.

Loftus, E. F., Miller, D. G., & Burns, H. J. (1978). Semantic integration of verbal information into a visual memory. *Journal of Experimental Psychology: Human Memory and Learning, 4*, 19–31.

McCloskey, M., & Zaragoza, M. (1985). Misleading postevent information and memory for events: Arguments and evidence against the memory impairment hypothesis. *Journal of Experimental Psychology: General, 114*, 1–16.

Melton, G. (1992). Children as partners for justice: Next steps for developmentalists (pp. 153–159). *Monographs of the Society for Research in Child Development, 57*(5, Serial No. 229).

Ornstein, P., Larus, D., & Clubb, P. (1991). Understanding children's testimony: Implications of research on the development of memory. In R. Vasta (Ed.), *Annals of child development* (Vol. 8, pp. 145–176). London: Jessica Kingsley.

Peters, D. P. (1991). The influence of stress and arousal on the child witness. In J. L. Doris (Ed.), *The suggestibility of children's recollections* (pp. 60–76). Washington, DC: American Psychological Association.

Pettit, F., Fegan, M., & Howie, P. (1990). *Interviewer effects on children's testimony.* Paper presented at International Congress on Child Abuse and Neglect, Hamburg.

Raskin, D., & Esplin, P. (1991). Assessment of children's statements of sexual abuse. In J. L. Doris (Ed.), *The suggestibility of children's recollections* (pp. 153–164). Washington, DC: American Psychological Association.

Saywitz, K., Goodman, G., Nicholas, G., & Moan, S. (1991). Children's memory of a physical examination involving genital touch: Implications for reports of child sexual abuse. *Journal of Consulting and Clinical Psychology, 5*, 682–691.

Steller, M. (1991). Commentary. In J. L. Doris (Eds.), *The suggestibility of children's recollections* (pp. 106–109). Washington, DC: American Psychological Association.

Strangor, C., & McMillan, D. (1992). Memory for expectancy-congruent and expectancy-incongruent information: A review of the social and social developmental literatures. *Psychological Bulletin, 111*, 42–61.

Torrance, J. T. (1968). *Children's reaction to intramuscular injection: A comparative study of needle and jet injections.* Unpublished masters thesis, School of Nursing, Case Western Reserve University, Cleveland.

Zaragoza, M. (1991). Preschool children's susceptibility to memory impairment. In J. L. Doris (Ed.), *The suggestibility of children's recollections* (pp. 27–39). Washington, DC: American Psychological Association.

Questions for Self-Study

Multiple Choice:

1. Suggestibility effects are limited to:

   A. young children.
   B. events that do not involve bodily touching.
   C. questioning that occurs immediately after an event.
   D. children of low IQ.
   E. none of the above.

2. Which of the following was NOT found when the children were tested a year following the original check-up?

   A. Children who were told a shot had not hurt reported less crying than children who were given neutral feedback.
   B. Children who had experienced higher levels of stress at the time of the original shot were more susceptible to suggestion.
   C. Other than the painfulness of the shot, the children were generally highly resistant to the misinformation they received.

Essay:

1. Why did these researchers get different results from the immediate and the delayed interviews?

2. What would you say is the good news and what is the bad news that this article has for interviewing children about potential abuse?

ARTICLE 12

Becoming a Native Listener

Janet F. Werker

Reprinted from: *American Scientist*, 1989, 77, 54-59.
Copyright © 1989 by the Sigma Xi Society.
Reprinted with permission of *American Scientist*,
Journal of Sigma Xi, The Scientific Research Society.

Language is our crowning glory. It is species specific and species universal. Many animals have very complex systems of communication, but none even begins to rival human language. And all humans, except those who are severely retarded or suffer from some other defect, acquire language.

Research has established that human infants are exquisitely sensitive to the sounds of human language. Newborns can discriminate, for example, between "ba" and "da." Infants make such distinctions in the same way that adults do--they both show *categorical perception* of speech sounds.

More remarkable still is the finding described by Janet Werker in this article. Babies are actually better at making these distinctions than adults are. While adults can make many fine distinctions between speech sounds that are meaningful in their own language, they fail to discriminate between many other sounds that do not carry meaning for them. Because "ra" and "la" do not occur in their language, for example, Japanese adults and children cannot readily discriminate one from the other. Japanese babies can.

Werker describes how infants' universal phonetic sensitivity gradually declines until they perceive only the distinctions made in the language being spoken around and to them. We are so used to thinking of development as getting better, it is fascinating to encounter an example where development means getting worse.

Note the theoretical model shown in Figure 4 summarizing the various ways that experience can affect perceptual development. This model makes it clear that the relation between experience and development is quite complex.

If you read this article carefully enough, you may figure out how to pronounce "Nthlakapmx." If you do, please let us know.

Becoming a Native Listener

Janet F. Werker

The syllables, words, and sentences used in all human languages are formed from a set of speech sounds called phones. Only a subset of the phones is used in any particular language. Adults can easily perceive the differences among the phones used to contrast meaning in their own language, but young infants go much farther: they are able to discriminate nearly every phonetic contrast on which they have been tested, including those they have never before heard. Our research has shown that this broad-based sensitivity declines by the time a baby is one year old. This phenomenon provides a way to describe basic abilities in the young infant and explore the effects of experience on human speech perception.

To put infants' abilities in perspective, adult speech perception must be understood. The phones that distinguish meaning in a particular language are called phonemes. There is considerable acoustic variability in the way each individual phoneme is realized in speech. For example, the phoneme /b/ is very different before the vowel /ee/ in "beet" from the way it is before the vowel /oo/ in "boot." How do adults handle this variability? As first demonstrated in a classic study by Liberman and his colleagues (1967), they treat these acoustically distinct instances of a single phoneme as equivalent. This equivalency is demonstrated in the laboratory by presenting listeners with a series of pairs of computer-synthesized speech stimuli that differ by only one acoustic step along a physical continuum and asking them first to label and then to try to discriminate between the stimuli. Adult listeners are able to discriminate reliably only stimuli that they have labeled as different—that is, they cannot easily discriminate between two acoustically different stimuli that they labeled /pa/, but they can discriminate between two similar stimuli if one is from their /ba/ category and one from their /pa/ category.

The phenomenon by which labeling limits discrimination is referred to as categorical perception. This has obvious advantages for language processing. It allows a listener to segment the words he hears immediately according to the phonemic categories of his language and to ignore unessential variations within a category.

Given that adults perceive speech categorically, when do such perceptual capabilities appear? To find out, Eimas and his colleagues (1971) adapted the so-called high-amplitude sucking procedure for use in a speech discrimination task. This procedure involves teaching infants to suck on a pacifier attached to a pressure transducer in order to receive a visual or auditory stimulus. After repeated presentations of the same sight or sound, the sucking rate declines, indicating that the infants are becoming bored. The infants are then presented with a new stimulus. Presumably, if they can discriminate the new sight or sound from the old, they will increase their sucking rate.

In Eimas's experiment, infants one and four months old heard speech sounds that varied in equal steps from /ba/ to /pa/. Like adults, they discriminated between differences in the vicinity of the /ba/-/pa/ boundary but were unable to discriminate equal acoustic changes from within the /ba/ category. Rather than having to learn about phonemic categories, then, infants seem capable of grouping speech stimuli soon after birth.

Experiments in the 17 years since Eimas's original study have shown that infants can discriminate nearly every phonetic contrast on which they are tested but are generally unable to discriminate differences within a single phonemic category (for a review, see Kuhl 1987). That is, like adults, infants perceive acoustically distinct instances of a single phoneme as equivalent but easily discriminate speech sounds from two different categories that are not more acoustically distinct.

Of special interest are demonstrations that young infants are even able to discriminate phonetic contrasts not used in their native language. In an early study, Streeter (1976) used the high-amplitude sucking procedure to test Kikuyu infants on their ability to discriminate the English /ba/-/pa/ distinction, which is not used in Kikuyu. She found that the infants could discriminate these two syllable types. Similar results have been obtained from a variety of laboratories using other nonnative phonetic contrasts (Lasky et al. 1975; Trehub 1976; Aslin et al. 1981; Eilers et al. 1982). This pattern of results indicates that the ability to discriminate phones from the universal phonetic inventory may be present at birth.

Developmental changes

Given these broad-based infant abilities, one might expect that adults would also be able to discriminate nearly all phonetic contrasts. However, research suggests that adults often have difficulty discriminating phones that do not contrast meaning in their own language. An

> *How does experience listening to a particular language modify an infant's perceptual abilities?*

English-speaking adult, for example, has difficulty perceiving the difference between the two /p/ phones that are used in Thai (Lisker and Abramson 1970). So too, a Japanese-speaking adult initially cannot distinguish between the English /ra/ and /la/, because Japanese uses a single phoneme intermediate between the two English phonemes (Miyawaki et al. 1975; MacKain et al. 1981). This pattern of extensive infant capabilities and more limited capabilities in the adult led to the suggestion that infants may have a biological predisposition to perceive all possible phonetic contrasts and that there is a decline in this universal phonetic sensitivity by adulthood as a function of acquiring a particular language (Eimas 1975; Trehub 1976).

My work has been designed to explore this intriguing possibility. In particular, I wanted to trace how speech perception changes during development. Are infants actually able to discriminate some pairs of speech sounds better than adults, or have they simply been tested with more sensitive procedures? If infants do have greater discriminative capacities than adults, when does the decline occur and why?

The first problem that my colleagues and I faced was to find a testing procedure which could be used with infants, children of all ages, and adults. We could then begin a program of studies comparing their relative abilities to perceive the differences between phonetic contrasts of both native and nonnative languages.

The testing routine we chose is a variation of the so-called infant head turn procedure (for a complete description, see Kuhl 1987). Subjects are presented with several slightly different versions of the same phoneme (e.g., /ba/) repeated continuously at 2-sec intervals. On a random basis every four to twenty repetitions, a new phoneme is introduced. For example, a subject will hear "ba," "ba," "ba," "ba," "ba," "da," "da." Babies are conditioned to turn their heads toward the source of the sound when they detect the change from one phoneme to another (e.g., from "ba" to "da"). Correct head turns are reinforced with the activation of a little toy animal and with clapping and praise from the experimental assistant. Figure 1 shows a baby being tested. Adults and children are tested the same way, except that they press a button instead of turning their heads when they detect a change in the phoneme, and the reinforcement is age-appropriate.

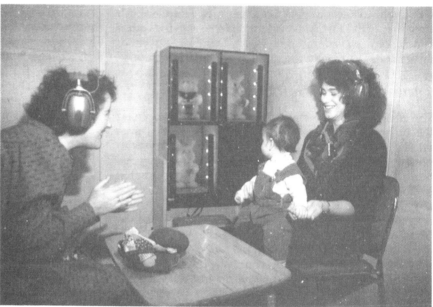

Figure 1. Human beings are born with the ability to recognize the speech sounds used in all the world's languages, even though only a portion of the sounds are used in any one language. As a baby listens to its own "native" tongue, it gradually loses the ability to discriminate sounds that are not used in that language. The author and her colleagues have elucidated this developmental change by testing infants, children, and adults with contrasting sounds in various languages. The infant shown here has learned to turn his head toward the source of the sounds when he hears a change in them. A correct head turn is reinforced by the activation of the toy animals as well as by the clapping and praise of the experimental assistant. (Photographs by Peter McLeod.)

In the first series of experiments, we compared English-speaking adults, infants from English-speaking families, and Hindi-speaking adults on their ability to discriminate the /ba/-/da/ distinction, which is used in both Hindi and English, as well as two pairs of syllables that are used in Hindi but not in English (Werker et al. 1981). The two pairs of Hindi syllables were chosen on the basis of their relative difficulty. The first pair contrasts two "t" sounds that are not used in English. In English, we articulate "t" sounds by placing the tongue a bit behind the teeth at the alveolar ridge. In Hindi, there are wo different "t" phonemes. One is produced by placing he tongue on the teeth (a dental t—written /t/). The other is produced by curling the tip of the tongue back and placing it against the roof of the mouth (a retroflex t—written /T/). This contrast is not used in English, and is in fact very rare among the world's languages.

The second pair of Hindi syllables involves different categories of voicing—the timing of the release of a consonant and the amount of air released with the consonant. Although these phonemes, called /t^h/ and /d^h/, are not used in English, we had reason to believe that they might be easier for English-speaking adults to discriminate than the /t/-/T/ distinction. The timing difference between /t^h/ and /d^h/ spans the English /t/-/d/ boundary. Moreover, this contrast is more common among the world's languages.

The results of this study, which are presented in Figure 2, were consistent with the hypothesis of universal phonetic sensitivity in the young infant and a decline by adulthood. As expected, all subjects could discriminate /ba/ from /da/. Of more interest, the infants aged six to eight months performed like the Hindi adults and were able to discriminate both pairs of Hindi speech contrasts. The English-speaking adults, on the other hand, were considerably less able to make the Hindi distinctions, especially the difficult dental-retroflex one.

Timing of developmental changes

The next series of experiments was aimed at determining when the decline in nonnative sensitivity occurs. It was originally believed that this decline would coincide with puberty, when, as Lenneberg (1967) claims, language flexibility decreases. However, our work showed that twelve-year-old English-speaking children were no more able to discriminate non-English syllables than were English-speaking adults (Werker and Tees 1983). We then tested eight- and four-year-old English-speaking children, and, to our surprise, even the four-year-olds could not discriminate the Hindi contrasts. Hindi-speaking four-year-olds, of course, showed no trouble with this discrimination.

Before testing children even younger than age four, we felt it was necessary to determine that the phenomenon of developmental loss extended to other languages. To this end, we chose a phonemic contrast from a North American Indian language of the Interior Salish family, called Nthlakapmx by native speakers in British Columbia but also referred to as Thompson.

North American Indian languages include many consonants produced in the back of the vocal tract, behind our English /k/ and /g/. The pair of sounds we chose contrasts a "k" sound produced at the velum with another "k" sound (written /q/) produced by raising the back of the tongue against the uvula. Both are glottalized—that is, there is an ejective portion (similar to a click) at the beginning of the release of the consonants.

Again, we compared English-speaking adults, infants from English-speaking families, and Nthlakapmx-speaking adults in their abilities to discriminate this pair of sounds (Werker and Tees 1984a). As was the case with the Hindi syllables, both the Nthlakapmx-speaking adults and the infants could discriminate the non-English phonemes, but the English-speaking adults could not.

If infants do have greater discriminative capacities than adults, when does the decline occur and why?

We were now satisfied that there is at least some generality to the notion that young infants can discriminate across the whole phonetic inventory but that there is a developmental decline in this universal sensitivity. Our next series of experiments involved testing children between eight months and four years of age to try to determine just when the decline in sensitivity might start. It quickly became apparent that something important was happening within the first year of life. We accordingly compared three groups of infants aged six to eight, eight to ten, and ten to twelve months. Half of each group were tested with the Hindi (/ta/-/Ta/) and half with the Nthlakapmx (/ki/-/qi/) contrast.

As shown in Figure 3, the majority of the six-to-eight-month-old infants from English-speaking families could discriminate the two non-English contrasts, whereas only about one-half of the eight-to-ten-month-olds could do so. Only two out of ten ten-to-twelve-month-olds could discriminate the Hindi contrast, and only one out of ten the Nthlakapmx. This provided strong evidence that the decline in universal phonetic sensitivity was occurring between six and twelve months of age. As a further test to see if this developmental change would be apparent within the same individuals, six infants from English-speaking families were tested at two-month intervals beginning when they were about six to eight months old. All six infants could discriminate both the Hindi and Nthlakapmx contrasts at the first testing, but by the third testing session, when they were ten to twelve months old, they were not able to discriminate either contrast.

To verify that the decline in nonnative sensitivity around ten to twelve months was a function of language experience, we tested a few infants from Hindi- and Nthlakapmx-speaking families when they reached eleven to twelve months old. As predicted, these infants were still able to discriminate their native contrasts, showing quite clearly that the decline observed in the infants from English-speaking families was a function of specific language experience. Since doing these studies, we have charted the decline between six and twelve months old using a computer-generated set of synthetic syllables which model another pair of Hindi sounds not used in English (Werker and Lalonde 1988).

Janet F. Werker is an assistant professor of developmental psychology at the University of British Columbia. She received a B.A. from Harvard University and a Ph.D. in psychology from the University of British Columbia in 1982. She was an assistant professor of psychology at Dalhousie University from 1982 to 1986, and joined the faculty at the University of British Columbia in 1986. The research reported here was supported by the Natural Sciences and Engineering Research Council of Canada and the Social Science and Humanities Research Council. In addition, portions of this work were made possible by an NICHD grant to Haskins Laboratories. Address: Department of Psychology, University of British Columbia, Vancouver, British Columbia, V6T 1Y7, Canada.

115

How does experience affect development?

A theoretical model for considering the possible effects of experience on perceptual development was suggested by Gottlieb in 1976. As expanded by both Gottlieb (1981) and Aslin (1981), the model includes several roles experience might—or might not—play, as shown in Figure 4.

Induction refers to cases in which the emergence and form of a perceptual capability depend entirely on environmental input. In this case, an infant would not show categorical perception of speech sounds without prior experience. Attunement refers to a situation in which experience influences the full development of a capability, enhancing the level of performance; for example, categorical boundaries between phonetic contrasts might be sharper with experience than without. In facilitation, experience affects the rate of development of a capability, but it does not affect the end point. If this role were valid, speech perception would improve even without listening experience, but hearing specific sounds would accelerate the rate of improvement. Maintenance/loss refers to the case in which a perceptual ability is fully developed prior to the onset of specific experience, which is required to maintain that capability. Without adequate exposure an initial capability is lost. Finally, maturation refers to the unfolding of a perceptual capability independent of environmental exposure. According to this hypothetical possibility, the ability to discriminate speech sounds would mature regardless of amount or timing of exposure.

Our work is often interpreted as an illustration of maintenance/loss, since it suggests that young infants can discriminate phonetic contrasts before they have gained experience listening but that experience hearing the phones used in their own language is necessary to maintain the ability to discriminate at least some pairs of phones.

Support for this view was provided by another study in which we tested English-speaking adults who had been exposed to Hindi during the first couple of years of life and had learned their first words in Hindi but had little or no subsequent exposure. These subjects could discriminate the Hindi syllables much more easily than other English-speaking adults, and performed virtually as well as native Hindi speakers on the discrimination task (Tees and Werker 1984). This is consistent with the view that early experience functions to maintain perceptual abilities, suggesting that no further experience is necessary to maintain them into adulthood.

Recovery of sensitivity

Our early work led us to believe that the loss of nonnative sensitivity is difficult to reverse in adults. In one study, we tested English-speaking adults who had studied Hindi for various lengths of time. Adults who had studied Hindi for five years or more were able to discriminate the non-English Hindi syllables, but those who had studied Hindi for one year at the university level could not do so. In fact, even several hundred trials were insufficient to teach English-speaking adults to discriminate the more difficult Hindi contrasts (Tees and Werker 1984). This implies that while the ability is recoverable,

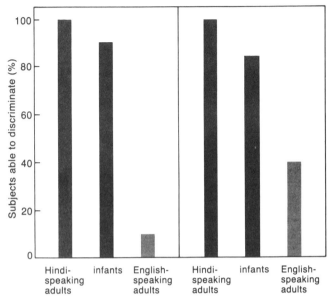

Figure 2. When tested on their ability to discriminate two Hindi syllables that are not used in English, six-to-eight-month-old infants from English-speaking families do nearly as well as Hindi-speaking adults. English-speaking adults, however, have great difficulty with this discrimination task, depending on the degree of difference from English sounds. The graph on the left shows a contrast involving two "t" sounds, one dental (i.e., made with the tip of the tongue touching the upper front teeth) and the other retroflex (made with the tongue curled back under the palate). This contrast is rare in the world's languages. The contrast in the graph on the right involves two kinds of voicing, a phenomenon that is less unusual and thus somewhat more recognizable to English-speaking adults. (After Werker et al. 1981.)

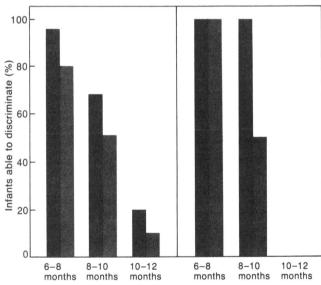

Figure 3. Infants show a decline in the universal phonetic sensitivity demonstrated in Figure 2 during the second half of their first year, as shown here in the results of experiments performed with babies from English-speaking families and involving non-English syllables from Hindi (*dark gray bars*) and Nthlakapmx, a language spoken by some native Indians in British Columbia (*light gray bars*). The graph on the left gives results from experiments with three groups of infants aged six to eight months, eight to ten months, and ten to twelve months. The graph on the right gives results from testing one group of infants three times at the appropriate ages. None of the latter group were able to discriminate either of the non-English contrasts when they were ten to twelve months old. (After Werker and Tees 1984a.)

116

onsiderable experience is required. Similar conclusions an be drawn from a study by MacKain and her colleagues (l981), who tested Japanese speakers learning nglish. Only after one year of intensive English training n the United States could they discriminate /ra/ from /la/.

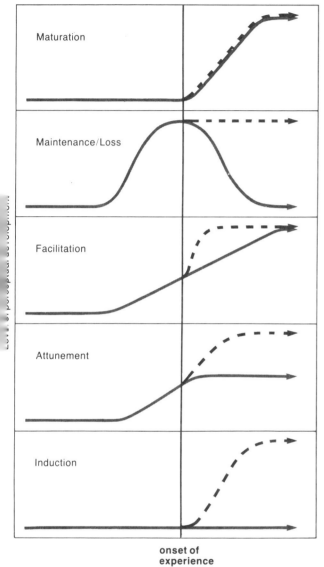

onset of
experience

Figure 4. Researchers have suggested several roles that experience might—or might not—play in the development of particular perceptual capabilities. These possibilities are shown graphically here: red curves represent development after the onset of experience, and gray curves represent development in the absence of experience. Induction refers to cases in which a capability depends entirely on experience. Attunement refers to a situation in which experience makes possible the full development of a capability. In facilitation, experience affects only the rate of development of a capability. Maintenance/loss refers to the case in which a capability is fully developed before the onset of experience, but experience is necessary to maintain the capability. Maturation refers to the development of a capability independent of experience. The phenomenon of universal phonetic sensitivity followed by a narrowing of sensitivity to native language sounds appears to illustrate maintenance/loss, since it suggests that young infants can discriminate phonetic contrasts before they have gained experience listening but that experience with language is necessary to maintain the full ability. (After Aslin l98l; Gottlieb 1981.)

The question still remained whether recovery of nonnative sensitivity results from new learning in adulthood or from a latent sensitivity. To explore this question, we asked English-speaking adults to discriminate both the full syllables of the difficult Hindi and Nthlakapmx phonemes and shortened portions of the syllables which do not sound like speech at all but contain the critical acoustic information specifying the difference between the phonemes (Werker and Tees 1984b). Subjects were first tested on the shortened stimuli and then on the full syllables. To our surprise, they were able to discriminate the shortened stimuli easily but were still not able to discriminate the full syllables, even immediately after hearing the relevant acoustic information in shortened form. This finding reveals that the auditory capacity for discriminating the acoustic components of these stimuli has not been lost but that it is difficult to apply when processing language-like sounds.

In a further set of experiments, we attempted to make English-speaking adults discriminate the full-syllable nonnative stimuli (Werker and Logan 1985). One task involved presenting adults with pairs of stimuli and asking them to decide simply if the stimuli were the same or different, a test that proved to be much more sensitive than the head turn procedure. In this "same/different" task, listeners have to compare only two stimuli at a time. Moreover, if the interval between the two stimuli is short enough, listeners can hold the first stimulus in auditory memory while comparing it to the second. In the head turn task, on the other hand, listeners have to compare each stimulus to a whole set of variable stimuli and judge whether it is a member of the same category.

We found that English-speaking adults could discriminate the Hindi syllables when tested in the same/different procedure, particularly after practice. Thus there was evidence that adults can discriminate nonnative contrasts if tested in a more sensitive procedure. Similar results have been reported by other researchers (Pisoni et al. l982). This suggests that the developmental changes between infancy and adulthood should be considered a language-based reorganization of the categories of communicative sounds rather than an absolute loss of auditory sensitivity. The increasing reliance on language-specific categories accounts for the age-related decline, implying that maintenance has its effect at the level of linguistic categories rather than simple peripheral auditory sensitivity (see Best et al. 1988).

Parallels in speech production

It is interesting to compare our findings of developmental changes in speech perception to recent work on speech production. Although it is impossible to survey this substantial literature here, there appear to be systematic regularities in the repertoire of sounds produced at different stages of babbling. These regularities may reflect vocal tract and neuromuscular maturation, with phones appearing as a child develops the ability to articulate them (Locke 1983). In contrast to early work suggesting that the sounds produced during babbling gradually narrow to those that are used in the language-learning environment, recent research shows very little influence from the native language on vocal development during the babbling stage. This conclusion is particularly strong for consonants. However, it is clear that after the acquisition of the first word children's vocal productions start becoming differentiated on the basis of language experience. That is, once a child begins to talk, the sounds produced conform more and more closely to the subset of phones used in his native language. The stage at which these changes occur is consistent with our work showing universal sensitivity in early infancy followed by only language-specific sensitivity beginning around ten to twelve months.

This leads us to believe that just as a reorganization of language production is related to the emergence of the first spoken word, so too the reorganization of perceptual abilities may be related to the emergence of the ability to understand words. By the time he is one year old, a child understands a fair amount of spoken language, even though he may produce only a few words. We are currently conducting experiments to see if the reorganization of speech perception is related to the emerging ability to understand words. This work will add another piece to the solution of the puzzle of how early sensitivity to all language sounds becomes limited to the functional categories that are necessary for communicating in one's own language.

References

Aslin, R. N. 1981. Experiential influences and sensitive periods in perceptual development: A unified model. In *Development of Perception*, ed. R. N. Aslin, J. R. Alberts, and M. R. Petersen, vol. 2, pp. 45–94. Academic Press.

Aslin, R. N., D. B. Pisoni, B. L. Hennessy, and A. J. Perey. 1981. Discrimination of voice onset time by human infants: New findings and implications for the effect of early experience. *Child Devel.* 52: 1135–45.

Best, C. T., G. W. McRoberts, and N. N. Sithole. 1988. The phonological basis of perceptual loss for non-native contrasts: Maintenance of discrimination among Zulu clicks by English-speaking adults and infants. *J. Exper. Psychol.: Human Percept. Perform.* 14:345–60.

Eilers, R. E., W. J. Gavin, and D. K. Oller. 1982. Cross-linguistic perception in infancy: Early effects of linguistic experience. *J. Child Lang.* 9:289–302.

Eimas, P. D. 1975. Developmental studies in speech perception. In *Infant Perception: From Sensation to Cognition*, ed. L. B. Cohen and P. Salapatek, vol. 2, pp. 193–231. Academic Press.

Eimas, P. D., E. R. Siqueland, P. W. Jusczyk, and J. Vigorito. 1971. Speech perception in infants. *Science* 171:303–06.

Gottlieb, G. 1976. The roles of experience in the development of behavior and the nervous system. In *Studies on the Development of Behavior and the Nervous System*, ed. G. Gottlieb, vol. 3, pp. 1–35. Academic Press.

———. 1981. Roles of early experience in species-specific perceptual development. In *Development of Perception*, ed. R. N. Aslin, J. R. Alberts, and M. R. Petersen, vol. 1, pp. 5–44. Academic Press.

Kuhl, P. K. 1987. Perception of speech and sound in early infancy. In *Handbook of Infant Perception*, ed. P. Salapatek and L. Cohen, vol. 2, pp. 275–382. Academic Press.

Lasky, R. E., A. Syrdal-Lasky, and R. E. Klein. 1975. VOT discrimination by four to six and a half month old infants from Spanish environments. *J. Exper. Child Psychol.* 20:215–25.

Lenneberg, E. H. 1967. *Biological Foundations of Language.* Wiley.

Liberman, A. M., F. S. Cooper, D. P. Shankweiler, and M. Studdert-Kennedy. 1967. Perception of the speech code. *Psychol. Rev.* 74:431–61.

Lisker, L., and A. S. Abramson. 1970. The voicing dimension: Some experiments in comparative phonetics. In *Proceedings of the 6th International Congress of Phonetic Sciences*, pp. 563–67. Prague: Academia.

Locke, J. L. 1983. *Phonological Acquisition and Change.* Academic Press.

MacKain, K. S., C. T. Best, and W. Strange. 1981. Categorical perception of English /r/ and /l/ by Japanese bilinguals. *Appl. Psycholing.* 2:269–90.

Miyawaki, K., et al. 1975. An effect of linguistic experience: The discrimination of [r] and [l] by native speakers of Japanese and English. *Percept. Psychophys.* 18:331–40.

Pisoni, D. B., R. N. Aslin, A. J. Perey, and B. L. Hennessy. 1982. Some effects of laboratory training on identification and discrimination of voicing contrasts in stop consonants. *J. Exper. Psychol.: Human Percept. Perform.* 8:297–314.

Streeter, L. A. 1976. Language perception of two-month old infants shows effects of both innate mechanisms and experience. *Nature* 259:39–41.

Tees, R. C., and J. F. Werker. 1984. Perceptual flexibility: Maintenance or recovery of the ability to discriminate non-native speech sounds. *Can. J. Psychol.* 34:579–90.

Trehub, S. 1976. The discrimination of foreign speech contrasts by infants and adults. *Child Devel.* 47:466–72.

Werker, J. F., J. H. V. Gilbert, K. Humphrey, and R. C. Tees. 1981. Developmental aspects of cross-language speech perception. *Child Devel.* 52:349–53.

Werker, J. F., and C. E. Lalonde. 1988. The development of speech perception: Initial capabilities and the emergence of phonemic categories. *Devel. Psychol.* 24:672–83.

Werker, J. F., and J. S. Logan. 1985. Cross-language evidence for three factors in speech perception. *Percept. Psychophys.* 37:35–44.

Werker, J. F., and R. C. Tees. 1983. Developmental changes across childhood in the perception of non-active speech sounds. *Can. J. Psychol.* 37:278–86.

———. 1984a. Cross-language speech perception: Evidence for perceptual reorganization during the first year of life. *Infant Behav. Devel.* 7:49–63.

———. 1984b. Phonemic and phonetic factors in adult cross-language speech perception. *J. Acoustical Soc. Am.* 75:1866–78.

Questions for Self-Study

Multiple Choice

1. Adults can easily discriminate between some speech stimuli that are one acoustic step apart but are unable to distinguish between other stimuli that are also only one step different. This phenomenon is:

   A. acoustic equivalence.
   B. phonemic sensitivity.
   C. phonetic equilibration.
   D. categorical perception.

2. What procedure was used in Werker's research on speech perception in infants?

   A. conditioning.
   B. habituation.
   C. perception.
   D. same/different matching.

3. Which of the following is true?

   A. Young infants can distinguish more phonetic contrasts than adults can.
   B. The universal phonetic sensitivity of infants begins to decline at approximately two years of age.
   C. Young infants from English speaking families can discriminate non-English syllables better than adults can, and they are especially good at discriminating English syllables.
   D. All of the above.

Essay

1. What are the implications of universal phonetic sensitivity in infancy for language learning and instruction?

2. Study the model of the different possible effects of experience on perceptual development (Figure 4). Can you apply this model to a different phenomenon such as color perception? For each curve, describe what the relation would be between color perception and visual experience if that curve were true.

Multiple Choice:

1. Adults can easily discriminate between some speech stimuli that are one acoustic step apart but are unable to distinguish between other stimuli that are also only one step different. This phenomenon is:

    A. acoustic equivalence.
    B. phonemic sensitivity.
    C. phonetic equilibration.
    D. categorical perception.

2. What procedure was used in Werker's research on speech perception in infants?

    A. conditioning
    B. habituation
    C. perception
    D. same/different matching

3. Which of the following is true?

    A. Young infants can distinguish more phonetic contrasts than adults can.
    B. The universal phonetic sensitivity of infants begins to decline at approximately two years of age.
    C. Young infants from English speaking families can discriminate non-English syllables better than adults can, and they are especially good at discriminating English syllables.
    D. All of the above.

Essay:

1. What are the implications of universal phonetic sensitivity in infancy for language learning and instruction?

2. Study the model of the different possible effects of experience on perceptual development (Figure 4). Can you apply this model to a different phenomenon such as color perception? For each curve, describe what the relation would be between color perception and visual experience if that curve were true.

ARTICLE 13

Babbling in the Manual Mode:
Evidence for the Ontogeny of Language

Laura Ann Petitto and Paula F. Marentette

Reprinted from: *Science*, 1991, *251*, 1493-1496.
Copyright © 1991 by the American Association for the Advancement of Science.
Reprinted with permission.

"Ma-ma-da-da-da-buh-buh . . ."

Utterances like this one are produced by all human infants who have been exposed to a spoken language and who have no problems with their speech apparatus. It has generally been assumed that babbling is specifically a speech phenomenon, that is, its onset reflects the maturation of the articulatory mechanisms involved in producing human speech.

Petitto and Marentette wondered if babbling might be specific to language, but not to speech. They asked a simple but theoretically important question: Would infants learning a non-vocal language (such as ASL-American Sign Language) babble?

They painstakingly studied the manual behavior of a small number of deaf and hearing infants. Their remarkable discovery is that deaf infants who are exposed to ASL appear to babble with their hands. The majority of the manual gestures they make resemble units of signs, just as vocal babbling produces recognizable syllables. These manual gestures also display many additional characteristics of babbling.

This result is fascinating in its own right, but it also has profound implications for our understanding of language and language development. As the authors point out, these results suggest that our innate language capacity is less clearly tied to speech than we have assumed. It may be that human infants are predisposed not to learn to speak a language, but to learn to produce whatever meaningful linguistic system they experience.

Babbling in the Manual Mode: Evidence for the Ontogeny of Language

LAURA ANN PETITTO* AND PAULA F. MARENTETTE

Infant vocal babbling has been assumed to be a speech-based phenomenon that reflects the maturation of the articulatory apparatus responsible for spoken language production. Manual babbling has now been reported to occur in deaf children exposed to signed languages from birth. The similarities between manual and vocal babbling suggest that babbling is a product of an amodal, brain-based language capacity under maturational control, in which phonetic and syllabic units are produced by the infant as a first step toward building a mature linguistic system. Contrary to prevailing accounts of the neurological basis of babbling in language ontogeny, the speech modality is not critical in babbling. Rather, babbling is tied to the abstract linguistic structure of language and to an expressive capacity capable of processing different types of signals (signed or spoken).

A KEY FEATURE OF HUMAN DEVELOP-
ment is the regular onset of vocal
babbling well before infants are able
to utter recognizable words (1). Vocal babbling is widely recognized as being continuous with later language acquisition (2).
The prevailing view is that the structure of
vocal babbling is determined by development of the anatomy of the vocal tract and
the neural mechanisms subserving the motor control of speech production (3, 4). In
brain-based theories of language representation, it is argued that the human language
capacity has a unique link to innate mechanisms for producing speech (5); it has also
been argued that human language has been
shaped by properties of speech (6).

Although there is general agreement that
humans possess some innately specified
knowledge about language (7), the maturation of the human language capacity may
not be uniquely tied to the maturation of
speech-specific production mechanisms.
Naturally evolved human signed languages
exist that are organized identically to spoken
languages (for example, phonology, mor-
phology, syntax, and semantics) (8). If babbling is due to the maturation of a language
capacity and the articulatory mechanisms
responsible for speech production, then it
should be specific to speech. However, if
babbling is due to the maturation of a
brain-based language capacity and an expressive capacity capable of processing different types of signals, then it should occur
in spoken and signed language modalities.

Hearing infants between 7 and 10 months

of age begin to produce a type of vocaliza-
tion described as reduplicated or syllabic
babbling, for example, "dadadada" or "ba
bababa" (9). Syllabic vocal babbling is characterized by (i) use of a reduced subset of
possible sounds (phonetic units) found in
spoken languages (10), (ii) syllabic organization (well-formed consonant-vowel clus-
ters) (11), and (iii) use without apparent
meaning or reference (12). Other properties
include reduplication, well-defined age of
onset, characteristic stages (12), and continuity of phonetic form and syllabic type
within an individual child's babbling and
first words (2).

In this study, experimental and naturalistic data were collected from five infants, each
videotaped at three ages (approximately 10,
12, and 14 months). Two subjects were
profoundly deaf infants of deaf parents (D1
and D2), acquiring American Sign Language (ASL) as a first language. Three control subjects were hearing infants of hearing
parents (H1, H2, H3), acquiring spoken
language with no exposure to a signed language (13, 14).

In studies of vocal babbling, investigators
typically transcribe all acoustic forms or
sounds produced over a period of time (15)
and analyze all acoustic forms that are not
words to see if they have any systematic
organization. If systematic organization is
found, the investigator determines whether
the organization has phonetic and syllabic
features common to spoken languages (2).

We analyzed the deaf and hearing infants'
manual activities in an identical manner.
First, all of the infants' manual activities
were transcribed and entered into a comput-

Department of Psychology, McGill University, Mon-
tréal, Québec, Canada H3A 1B1.

*To whom correspondence should be addressed.

22 MARCH 1991

er database (16) with a transcription system that we had devised and tested (17). In this system, the precise physical form of the child's every manual activity is coded with diacritics that represent internal features of the hand or hands, such as its handshape and location in space. The precise manner of use is also coded for each manual activity, including whether the form was used with or without objects in hand, used referentially, used communicatively, had conventional meaning, or was a standard sign in ASL (a sign has identical linguistic properties to a word in spoken languages) (18). Second, we further analyzed all manual activities that were not ASL signs and were not pointing to objects to determine whether they had any systematic organization. If so, we analyzed these activities to determine whether they had unique organizational properties or whether they shared phonetic and syllabic organization common to signed languages (19, 20). Attribution of manual babbling was applied only to forms that fulfilled the same criteria as vocal babbling. This transcription system permitted direct comparisons of the manual activities of the deaf and hearing infants. The reliability of rating for two independent coders ranged from 82 to 95% (21).

The results yielded two types of manual activity: syllabic manual babbling and gestures (for example, raising arms to be picked up and holding a cup to lips as if to drink). Both types were observed in deaf and hearing infants. The manual activities identified as syllabic manual babbling (i) were produced with a reduced subset of combinatorial units that were members of the phonetic inventory of signed languages (20), (ii)

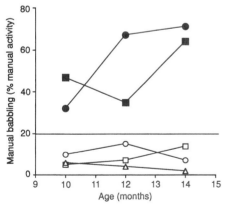

Fig. 1. Manual babbling as a percent of manual activity [manual babbling/(manual babbling + gesture)]. Open symbols represent the hearing children and closed symbols represent the deaf children (□, H1; △, H2; ○, H3; ●, D1; and ■, D2). The required syllabic ratio is 20% (line) syllabic to total vocal utterances for children to be classed in the syllabic vocal babbling stage of language acquisition (7). The deaf children met and surpassed this ratio in their manual babbling, but the hearing children did not.

Table 1. Tokens of gestures and manual babbling produced by each child over the three taping sessions.

Child	Gesture	Manual babbling
Hearing		
H1	98	10
H2	195	8
H3	121	14
Deaf		
D1	101	80
D2	122	111

demonstrated syllabic organization seen only in signed languages, and (iii) were produced without meaning or reference. By contrast, gestures were not constructed from a restricted set of combinatorial units, had no principled internal organization, and were used referentially (22).

Hearing and deaf infants produced similar types and quantities of gestures during the three sessions. However, they differed in their production of manual babbling (Table 1). Manual babbling accounted for 32 to 71% of manual activity in deaf infants and a mere 4 to 15% of the manual activity of hearing infants (Fig. 1).

In manual babbling, the deaf infants used a reduced subset of the phonetic units found in ASL (23): 32% (13/40) of the handshapes (20) that make up the phonetic inventory of adult ASL (Fig. 2). Of these 13 handshapes, 6 were used 75% of the time: 5, 52, A, A2, O, and G (24). The deaf infants produced 54% (13/24) of ASL's movements (20); the three most frequently used were the closing of a handshape, movement toward the body, and an up-and-down movement. Most of the deaf children's manual babbling (98%, 188/191) was produced within a restricted space in front of the body. In addition, each infant had an individual preference regarding the location (20): most of D1's manual babbling was produced in the space in front of the midtorso (neutral space), whereas the majority of D2's manual babbling involved contact with the head, ears, and face region. Similarly, hearing infants demonstrate clear individual preferences in the phonetic content of their vocal babbling (25).

The manual babbling of the deaf infants contained four syllable types (20), a subset of which were used more frequently (Fig. 3). D1 predominantly produced syllables involving secondary movement in the form of handshape change (69%). D2 predominantly produced syllables involving path movement (69%).

The deaf infants' manual babbling demonstrated four other properties observed in hearing children's vocal babbling. First,

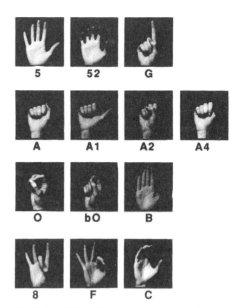

Fig. 2. The 13 handshape primes produced by the deaf children in their manual babbling. The handshape A4 does not occur in adult ASL; it is a possible but nonexistent phoneme.

reduplication occurred in 47% of the tokens of sign babbling produced by the deaf infants (26). Second, by age 10 months, the deaf infants were well into the syllabic manual babbling stage, which occurred at the same time as in hearing infants (ages 7 to 10 months). Third, the deaf infants progressed through stages of manual babbling similar to the stages of vocal babbling observed in hearing infants, and on a similar time course. Hearing children produce vocal jargon babbling (meaningless babbling sequences that sound like sentences; onset 12 to 14 months) (12); similarly, the deaf infants produced manual jargon babbling (onset 12 to 14 months). They produced phonologically possible, but nonexisting, forms in the ASL lexicon; the forms maintained the rhythm and duration of rudimentary ASL sentences and were similar to hearing infants' use of stress and intonation in vocal jargon babbling (12). Fourth, there was a continuity between the phonetic and syllabic forms used in the deaf infants' manual babbling and their first signs. For each infant, the most frequent phonetic units in his or her manual babbling were also the most frequent in his or her first signs: the 5 handshape was most frequent for both D1 [manual babbling (m.b.) = 27%, signs (s.) = 43%] and D2 (m.b. = 29%, s. = 54%); the most frequent movement type produced by D1 was the closing of a handshape (m.b. = 55%, s. = 36%), and D2's most frequent movement type was movement toward the signer (m.b. = 29%, s. = 40%); D1 continued to produce signs in neutral space (m.b. = 82%, s. = 59%), and D2 maintained a preference for locations in the head and face area (m.b. = 51%, s. = 53%). As for syllables, D1 continued to prefer handshape-change syllables (m.b. = 69%, s. = 44%), and D2 continued to prefer location-change syllables (m.b. = 69%, s. = 58%). Thus, like hearing infants (2), deaf infants produce their first signs from the pool of phonetic and syllabic types rehearsed in their babbling. Further, the deaf infants' first signs and the hearing infants' first words occurred at similar ages: D1 (10 months, 10 days), D2 (11 months, 28 days), H1 (11 months, 6 days), H2 (12 months, 11 days), H3 (12 months, 14 days).

The hearing infants in this study produced few instances of manual babbling (Table 1). They used an even smaller subset of phonetic units than did deaf infants, displaying only three handshapes (F, O, bO; 80%, 28/35) (27), one movement (thumb to digit contact plus repeated rub; 84%, 27/32) and one location (neutral space; 100%, 32/32). Further, they used primarily one syllable type (handshape change; 88%, 28/32). This is similar to deaf infants' limited production of syllabic vocal babbling, which also shows little variation in form and a very reduced set of consonants and vowels (11, 28).

Our data do not support the notion that babbling is determined by motor developments of the articulatory mechanisms subserving speech production (4). Instead, babbling is an expression of an amodal, brain-based language capacity that is linked to an expressive capacity capable of processing speech and sign. Despite radical differences

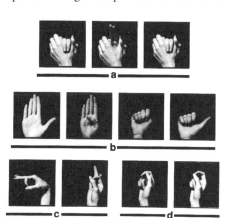

Fig. 3. Examples of syllable types in manual babbling. In real time these are continuous forms; in order to demonstrate the handshapes that occur, the forms have been presented as sequences of static pictures. All forms were reduplicated; only the basic unit is presented here. (**a**) A two-handed handshape-change syllable. (**b**) A unimanual, bisyllabic, handshape-change production involving four distinct handshapes. (**c**) An orientation-change syllable produced by a flexing of the wrist. (**d**) A handshape-change syllable typically produced by the hearing children, which is much less complex than that shown in example (**b**).

between the motoric mechanisms that subserve signed and spoken languages, deaf and hearing infants produce identical babbling units. Both manual and vocal babbling contain units and combinations of units that are organized in accordance with the phonetic and syllabic properties of human language. Thus, the form and organization of babbling is tied to the abstract linguistic structure of language.

Infants appear to be innately predisposed to discover the particular patterned input of phonetic and syllabic units (29, 30), that is, particular patterns in the input signal that correspond to the temporal and hierarchical grouping and rhythmical characteristics in natural language phonology. We suggest that this predisposition is a property of an amodal language capacity. Patterned input in either the signed or spoken modalities with phonetic and syllabic organization can serve as the vehicle for language production and reception, thereby triggering a babbling stage (31). Babbling is thus the mechanism by which infants discover the map between the structure of language and the means for producing this structure. The production of babbling units helps infants to identify the finite inventory of basic units, and the permissible combination of these units, from which language will be constructed (29). By attending to particular patterned input, infants can begin to acquire the basic forms of language well before they have mastered adult knowledge of language structure and meaning.

Similarities in the time course, structure, and use of manual and vocal babbling suggest that there is a unitary language capacity that underlies human signed and spoken language acquisition. Like other systems identified in evolutionary biology (32), the language capacity appears to be both constrained and flexible. It is internally constrained with regard to the structures that it can realize (phonetic and syllabic units), yet, in the face of environmental variation, it appears to be flexible with regard to the expressive modality it can adopt to realize this capacity (signed or spoken).

REFERENCES AND NOTES

1. E. H. Lenneberg, *Biological Foundations of Language* (Wiley, New York, 1967).
2. M. M. Vihman et al., *Language* **61**, 397 (1985).
3. J. L. Locke, *Phonological Acquisition and Change* (Academic Press, New York, 1983).
4. J. M. Van der Stelt and F. J. Koopmans-van Bienum, in *Precursors of Early Speech*, B. Lindblom and R. Zetterstrom, Eds. (Stockton, New York, 1986), pp. 163–173.
5. A. M. Liberman and I. G. Mattingly, *Cognition* **21**, 1 (1985); *Science* **243**, 489 (1989).
6. P. Lieberman, *The Biology and Evolution of Language* (Harvard Univ. Press, Cambridge, MA, 1984).
7. N. Chomsky, *Behav. Brain Sci.* **3**, 1 (1980); L. Gleitman, *Cognition* **10**, 103 (1981).
8. E. S. Klima and U. Bellugi, *The Signs of Language* (Harvard Univ. Press, Cambridge, MA, 1979).
9. D. K. Oller, in *Production*, vol. 1 of *Child Phonology*, G. Yeni-Komshian, J. F. Kavanagh, C. A. Ferguson, Eds. (Academic Press, New York, 1980), pp. 93–112.
10. Cross-linguistic evidence suggests that infants use a universal subset of possible consonants during babbling (3).
11. D. K. Oller and R. E. Eilers, *Child Dev.* **59**, 441 (1988).
12. L. Elbers, *Cognition* **12**, 45 (1982).
13. Subjects' gender, native language, and age at each taping were as follows: D1 (female, ASL, 10 months, 10 days; 12 months, 0 days; 14 months, 17 days); D2 (male, ASL, 9 months, 26 days; 11 months, 29 days; 13 months, 23 days); H1 (female, French, 9 months, 27 days; 11 months, 27 days; 14 months, 14 days); H2 (female, French, 10 months, 10 days; 12 months, 14 days; 15 months, 7 days); H3 (male, English, 11 months, 9 days; 12 months, 8 days; 13 months, 29 days).
14. Videotaped sessions commenced with a period in which the infant and parent played freely. Then there was an elicitation task, in which common baby toys were held in the infant's sight but out of reach for 10 s and then were given to the infant. Finally, each infant was observed in solitary play. Sessions were conducted in the infant's native language (signed or spoken).
15. Vegetative sounds, such as crying or belching, are not transcribed because they are unrelated to an infant's prelinguistic development.
16. Manual activities such as scratching or eye-rubbing were not transcribed (15).
17. L. A. Petitto, in *The Development of Language and Language Researchers: Essays in Honor of Roger Brown*, F. S. Kessel, Ed. (Erlbaum, Hillsdale, NJ, 1988), pp. 187–221.
18. "Used referentially" refers to manual activity that was used in relation to a referent in the world. "Used communicatively" refers to manual activity that was produced with clear communicative intent (fixed eye gaze at adult). The term "has conventional meaning" refers to manual activity with established cultural meaning that was not the standard sign in ASL. For example, the manual activity used to convey the concept "quiet" (index to pursed lips while producing a "shhh" sound) is used by children and adults (deaf and hearing) to indicate "quiet," but the sign QUIET in ASL is produced with an entirely different handshape and movement.
19. We further transcribed the data utilizing a notational system analogous to the International Phonetic Alphabet for spoken languages [W. C. Stokoe, D. C. Casterline, C. G. Croneberg, *A Dictionary of American Sign Language on Linguistic Principles* (Linstok Press, Silver Spring, MD, 1976)].
20. As in spoken languages, signed languages are constructed from a finite set of meaningless units (phonetic units); the subset of units used for production of a particular language is its phonetic inventory. ASL's phonetic inventory is drawn from the four parameters of a sign—handshape, movement, location, and palm orientation—each of which contains a restricted set of phonetic units (for example, a set of handshapes, a set of movements). Phonetic units are further organized into structured units called syllables [S. K. Liddell, *Language* **60**, 372 (1984)]. A well-formed syllable has a handshape, a location, and a path movement (change in location) or secondary movement (change in handshape or orientation). This yields at least four syllable types: (i) path movement, (ii) secondary movement (handshape change), (iii) secondary movement (orientation change), and (iv) path and secondary movement combined.
21. One of each infant's three videotapes (selected across all three ages) was transcribed by two coders. Reliability was calculated based on coders' percent agreement on whether a manual activity had occurred and on the precise content of a manual activity; thus, the full range of infant manual activity is represented in the figures provided.
22. Unlike words or signs, gestures (i) had unrestricted forms; (ii) violated natural-kind boundaries (events, objects, possessions, and locations) typically ob-

served in hearing [J. Huttenlocher and P. Smiley, *Cognit. Psychol.* **19**, 63 (1987)] and deaf infants; (iii) were used in communicatively restricted contexts (typically requests); and (iv) showed no semantic or structural developmental progression (17).

23. Just as hearing infants do not babble in specific languages (10), deaf infants do not babble in ASL or any other sign language. Deaf infants acquiring two distinct sign languages (ASL and Langue des Signes Québécoise) also use a common subset of possible phonetic units [L. A. Petitto and P. F. Marentette, in preparation; L. A. Petitto, *Cognition* **27**, 1 (1987)].

24. These symbols represent the meaningless alphanumeric labels used for notation of the restricted set of handshapes in signed languages (20).

25. M. M. Vihman, C. A. Ferguson, M. Elbert, *Appl. Psycholinguist.* **7**, 3 (1986).

26. Percent reduplicated vocal babbling has not been reported to our knowledge.

27. This ratio is divided by 35 instead of 32 because some instances of manual babbling involved more than one handshape.

28. That infants produce occasional babbling forms in the modality that does not carry linguistic input appears to be the vestige of their potential to have produced language in either modality. This babbling is unproductive because of the lack of systematic input.

29. P. W. Jusczyk, in *Invariance and Variability in Speech Processes*, J. Perkell and D. H. Klatt, Eds. (Erlbaum, Hillsdale, NJ, 1986), pp. 1–19.

30. J. Mehler, G. Lambertz, P. Jusczyk, C. Amiel-Tison, *C. R. Acad. Sci. Ser. III Sci. Vie* **303** , (no. 15), 637 (1986).

31. Hearing children of deaf parents, acquiring both signed and spoken languages, produce babbling and other linguistic milestones in both modalities on an identical time course (P. F. Marentette and L. A. Petitto, in preparation).

32. M. Shatz, *Merrill-Palmer Q.* **31**, 211 (1985).

33. We thank K. Dunbar, M. Bruck, S. Waxman, R. Wise, and anonymous reviewers for comments on versions of this paper. Supported by the Natural Sciences Engineering Research Council of Canada, McGill IBM Cooperative Project, and McDonnell-Pew Centre Grant in Cognitive Neuroscience.

21 August 1990; accepted 19 February 1991

Multiple Choice:

1. Which of the following is not a characteristic of both vocal and manual babbling?

    A. different set of units than used in the language
    B. well-formed syllables
    C. reduplication
    D. use without meaning

2. The claim that our brain-based language capacity is *amodal* means that:

    A. infants are predisposed to learn any spoken language they experience.
    B. deaf infants can learn to speak if given adequate training.
    C. infants are capable of processing both speech and sign.
    D. deaf and hearing infants babble equally well in both vocal and manual modalities.
    E. both C and D.

Essay:

1. Often in developmental science, we learn a great deal about normal development by studying atypical development. Discuss how studying the development of sign language in deaf children can give us a better understanding of spoken language development in hearing children.

ARTICLE 14

Temperament and the Reactions to Unfamiliarity

Jerome Kagan

Reprinted from: *Child Development*, 1997, *68*, 139-143.
Copyright © 1997 by the Society for Research in Child Development.
Reprinted with Permission.

When you started college, did you love going to big parties to meet new people, or was that your idea of a nightmare? There are clear differences in how humans react to meeting new people, going to new places, and doing new things. For some of us, the novelty is exciting and fun, for others it is aversive. Jerome Kagan has spent the last 20 years studying shyness and why some children are more shy than others. He and his colleagues are now convinced that there is a biological basis for shyness, that is, some children are born more reactive to unfamiliar people and things, whereas other children are less reactive from birth. He believes differences in brain anatomy may be responsible.

Kagan and his colleagues have conducted *longitudinal* research in which they follow the same children over time, so they are able to ask: "Do highly reactive or fearful babies turn into fearful, shy children?" The answer to this question, like the answer to many complex psychological questions, is yes and no. Yes, in that children who had been classified as highly reactive to novelty as infants talked less when they interacted with an unfamiliar female experimenter at 4-1/2 years of age than children did who were rated as less reactive as infants. No, in that only around 20% of the highly fearful infants were described as highly fearful over the period of 4 months to 4-1/2 years. But it is noteworthy that only one fearful infant became an uninhibited or bold 4-year-old. Thus, an extremely fearful infant is unlikely to become the most talkative outgoing child in his or her preschool class, nor will the fearless infant become extremely shy and withdrawn.

Kagan also suggests that these early differences in shyness may predispose children to develop different sorts of emotional problems. He is in no way suggesting that shyness or lack of it *is* an emotional problem; rather, he thinks that in interaction with various environmental factors, some children will develop emotional problems, and that these early differences may play a part in the type of problems they develop. Thus, a shy, fearful child is more likely to develop problems with anxiety, whereas an uninhibited, bold child may be more prone to engage in dangerous, risky activities. Because uninhibited, bold children are not prone to experience anxiety, they may develop conduct disorders if they grow up in environments in which it is easy to engage in dangerous activities. The bottom line is that to understand children's personality development, we must consider both temperament and social environment.

Child Development, February 1997, Volume 68, Number 1, Pages 139–143

Temperament and the Reactions to Unfamiliarity

Jerome Kagan

The behavioral reactions to unfamiliar events are basic phenomena in all vertebrates. Four-month-old infants who show a low threshold to become distressed and motorically aroused to unfamiliar stimuli are more likely than others to become fearful and subdued during early childhood, whereas infants who show a high arousal threshold are more likely to become bold and sociable. After presenting some developmental correlates and trajectories of these 2 temperamental biases, I consider their implications for psychopathology and the relation between propositions containing psychological and biological concepts.

INTRODUCTION

A readiness to react to events that differ from those encountered in the recent or distant past is one of the distinguishing characteristics of all mammalian species. Thus, the events with the greatest power to produce both an initial orienting and sustained attention in infants older than 3 to 4 months are variations on what is familiar, often called discrepant events (Fagan, 1981; Kagan, Kearsley, & Zelazo, 1980). By 8 months of age, discrepant events can produce a vigilant posture of quiet staring and, occasionally, a wary face and a cry of distress if the event cannot be assimilated easily (Bronson, 1970). That is why Hebb (1946) made discrepancy a major basis for fear reactions in animals, why a fear reaction to strangers occurs in the middle of the first year in children growing up in a variety of cultural settings, and, perhaps, why variation in the initial behavioral reaction to novelty exists in almost every vertebrate species studied (Wilson, Coleman, Clark, & Biederman, 1993).

Recent discoveries by neuroscientists enrich these psychological facts. The hippocampus plays an important role in the detection of discrepant events (Squire & Knowlton, 1995). Projections from the hippocampus provoke activity in the amygdala and lead to changes in autonomic function and posture and, in older children, to reflection and anticipation (Shimamura, 1995). Because these neural structures and their projections are influenced by a large number of neurotransmitters and neuromodulators, it is reasonable to expect inherited differences in the neurochemistry of these structures and circuits and, therefore, in their excitability. Variation in the levels of, or receptors for, corticotropin releasing hormone, norepinephrine, cortisol, dopamine, glutamate, GABA, opioids, acetylcholine, and other molecules might be accompanied by differences in the intensity and form of responsivity to unfamiliarity (Cooper, Bloom, & Roth, 1991). This speculation is supported by research with infants and children (Kagan, 1994). This article summarizes what has been learned about two temperamental types of children who react in different ways to unfamiliarity, considers the implications of these two temperamental categories for psychopathology, and comments briefly on the relation between psychological and biological constructs.

INFANT REACTIVITY AND FEARFUL BEHAVIOR

About 20% of a large sample of 462 healthy, Caucasian, middle-class, 16-week-old infants became both motorically active and distressed to presentations of brightly colored toys moved back and forth in front of their faces, tape recordings of voices speaking brief sentences, and cotton swabs dipped in dilute butyl alcohol applied to the nose. These infants are called high reactive. By contrast, about 40% of infants with the same family and ethnic background remained motorically relaxed and did not fret or cry to the same set of unfamiliar events. These infants are called low reactive. The differences between high and low reactives can be interpreted as reflecting variation in the excitability of the amygdala and its projections to the ventral striatum, hypothalamus, cingulate, central gray, and medulla (Amaral, Price, Pitkanen, & Carmichael, 1992; Davis, 1992).

When these high and low reactive infants were observed in a variety of unfamiliar laboratory situations at 14 and 21 months, about one-third of the 73 high reactives were highly fearful (4 or more fears), and only 3% showed minimal fear (0 or 1 fear) at both ages. By contrast, one-third of the 147 low reactives were minimally fearful at both ages (0 or 1 fear), and only 4% displayed high levels of fear (Kagan, 1994).

The profiles of high and low fear to unfamiliar

events, called inhibited and uninhibited, are heritable, to a modest degree, in 1- to 2-year-old middle-class children (DiLalla, Kagan, & Reznick, 1994; Robinson, Kagan, Reznick, & Corley, 1992). Further, high reactives show greater sympathetic reactivity in the cardiovascular system than low reactives during the first 2 years (Kagan, 1994; Snidman, Kagan, Riordan, & Shannon, 1995).

As children approach the fourth and fifth years, they gain control of crying to and reflex retreat from unfamiliar events and will only show these responses to very dangerous events or to situations that are not easily or ethically created in the laboratory. Hence, it is important to ask how high and low reactive infants might respond to unfamiliar laboratory situations when they are 4–5 years old. Each species has a biologically preferred reaction to novelty. Rabbits freeze, monkeys display a distinct facial grimace, and cats arch their backs. In humans, restraint on speech seems to be an analogue of the immobility that animals display in novel situations (Panksepp, Sacks, Crepeau, & Abbott, 1991), for children often become quiet as an initial reaction to unfamiliar situations (Asendorpf, 1990; Kagan, Reznick, & Gibbons, 1989; Kagan, Reznick, & Snidman, 1988; Murray, 1971). It is also reasonable to expect that the activity in limbic sites provoked by an unfamiliar social situation might interfere with the brain states that mediate the relaxed emotional state that is indexed by smiling and laughter (Adamec, 1991; Amaral et al., 1992).

When the children who had been classified as high and low reactive were interviewed at $4\frac{1}{2}$ years of age by an unfamiliar female examiner who was blind to their prior behavior, the 62 high reactives talked and smiled significantly less often (means of 41 comments and 17 smiles) than did the 94 low reactives (means of 57 comments and 28 smiles) during a 1 hour test battery: $F(1, 152) = 4.51$, $p < .05$ for spontaneous comments; $F(1, 152) = 15.01$, $p < .01$ for spontaneous smiles. Although spontaneous comments and smiles were positively correlated ($r = 0.4$), the low reactives displayed significantly more smiles than would have been predicted from a regression of number of smiles on number of spontaneous comments. The high reactives displayed significantly fewer smiles than expected. Every one of the nine children who smiled more than 50 times had been a low reactive infant.

However, only a modest proportion of children maintained an extreme form of their theoretically expected profile over the period from 4 months to $4\frac{1}{2}$ years, presumably because of the influence of intervening family experiences (Arcus, 1991). Only 19% of the high reactives displayed a high level of fear at both 14 and 21 months (>4 fears), together with low

values (below the mean) for both spontaneous comments and smiles at $4\frac{1}{2}$ years. But not one low reactive infant actualized such a consistently fearful and emotionally subdued profile. By contrast, 18% of low reactive infants showed the opposite profile of low fear (0 or 1 fear) at both 14 and 21 months together with high values for both spontaneous smiles and spontaneous comments at $4\frac{1}{2}$ years. Only one high reactive infant actualized that prototypic, uninhibited profile. Thus, it is uncommon for either temperamental type to develop and to maintain the seminal features of the other type, but quite common for each type to develop a profile that is characteristic of the less extreme child who is neither very timid nor very bold.

The $4\frac{1}{2}$-year-old boys who had been high reactive infants had significantly higher resting heart rates than did low reactives, but the differences between high and low reactive girls at this older age took a different form. The high reactive girls did not show the expected high negative correlation (-0.6 to -0.8) between heart rate and heart rate variability. It is possible that the greater sympathetic reactivity of high reactive girls interfered with the usual, vagally induced inverse relation between heart rate and heart rate variability (Porges, Arnold, & Forbes, 1973; Richards, 1985).

Honest disagreement surrounds the conceptualization of infant reactivity as a continuum of arousal or as two distinct categories. The raw motor activity score at 4 months formed a continuum, but the distribution of distress cries did not. Some infants never fretted or cried; others cried a great deal. A more important defense of the decision to treat high and low reactivity as two distinct categories is the fact that within each of the two categories variation in motor activity and crying was unrelated to later fearfulness or sympathetic reactivity. If reactivity were a continuous trait, then a low reactive infant with extremely low motor and distress scores should be less fearful than one who showed slightly more arousal. But that prediction was not affirmed. Second, infants who showed high motor arousal but no crying or minimal motor arousal with frequent crying showed developmental profiles that were different from those who were categorized as low or high reactive. Finally, high and low reactives differed in physical and physiological features that imply qualitatively different genetic constitutions. For example, high reactives have narrower faces than low reactives in the second year of life (Arcus & Kagan, 1995). Unpublished data from our laboratory reveal that the prevalence of atopic allergies among both children and their parents is significantly greater among high than low reactive infants. Studies of monozygotic and dizygotic same-sex twin pairs reveal significant heritability for inhibited and uninhibited behavior in the second year of life (Robinson et al., 1992). These facts imply that the two temperamental groups represent qualitatively different types and do not lie on a continuum of arousal or reactivity to stimulation.

The decision to regard individuals with very different values on a construct as members of the discrete categories or as falling on a continuum will depend on the scientists' purpose. Scientists who are interested in the relation, across families and genera, between brain size and body mass treat the two measurements as continuous. However, biologists interested in the maternal behavior of mice and chimpanzees regard these two mammals as members of qualitatively different groups. Similarly, if psychologists are interested in the physiological foundations of high and low reactives, it will be more useful to regard the two groups as categories. But those who are giving advice to mothers who complain about the ease of arousal and irritability of their infants may treat the arousal as a continuum.

IMPLICATIONS

The differences between high reactive–inhibited and low reactive–uninhibited children provoke speculation on many issues; I deal briefly with implications for psychopathology and the relation between psychological and biological propositions.

Anxiety Disorder

The high reactive infants who became very inhibited 4-year-olds—about 20% of all high reactives—have a low threshold for developing a state of fear to unfamiliar events, situations, and people. It is reasonable to expect that these children will be at a higher risk than most for developing one of the anxiety disorders when they become adolescents or adults. The childhood data do not provide a clue as to which particular anxiety profile will be most prevalent. However, an extensive clinical interview with early adolescents (13–14 years old), who had been classified 11 years earlier (at 21 or 31 months) as inhibited or uninhibited (Kagan et al., 1988), revealed that social phobia was more frequent among inhibited than among uninhibited adolescents, whereas specific phobias, separation anxiety, or compulsive symptoms did not differentiate the two groups (Schwartz, personal communication). This intriguing result, which requires replication, has interesting theoretical ramifications.

Research with animals, usually rats, suggests that acquisition of a fear reaction (e.g., freezing or potentiated startle) to a conditioned stimulus (light or tone) that had been paired with electric shock is mediated by a circuitry that is different from the one that mediates the conditioned response to the context in which the conditioning had occurred (LeDoux, 1995).

Davis (personal communication) has found that a potentiated startle reaction in the rat to the context in which light had been paired with shock involves a circuit from the amygdala to the bed nucleus of the stria terminalis and the septum. The potentiated startle reaction to the conditioned stimulus does not require that circuit. A phobia of spiders or bridges resembles an animal's reaction of freezing to a conditioned stimulus, but a quiet, avoidant posture at a party resembles a fearful reaction to a context. That is, the person who is extremely shy at a party of strangers is not afraid of any particular person or of the setting. Rather, the source of the uncertainty is a situation in which the shy person had experienced anxiety with other strangers. Thus, social phobia may rest on a neurophysiology that is different from that of specific phobia.

Conduct Disorder

The correlation between social class and the prevalence of conduct disorder or delinquency is so high it is likely that the vast majority of children with these profiles acquired their risk status as a result of life conditions, without the mediation of a particular temperamental vulnerability. However, a small proportion—probably no more than 10%—who began their delinquent careers before age 10, and who often committed violent crimes as adolescents, might inherit a physiology that raises their threshold for the conscious experience of anticipatory anxiety and/or guilt over violating community standards for civil behavior (Tremblay, Pihl, Vitaro, & Dubkin, 1994). Damasio (1994) and Mountcastle (1995) have suggested that the surface of the ventromedial prefrontal cortex receives sensory information (from the amygdala) that originates in the peripheral targets, like heart, skin, gut, and muscles. Most children and adults who think about committing a crime experience a subtle feeling that accompanies anticipation of the consequences of an antisocial act. That feeling, which might be called anticipatory anxiety, shame, or guilt, provides an effective restraint on the action. However, if a small proportion of children possessed a less excitable amygdala, or a ventromedial surface that was less responsive, they would be deprived of the typical intensity of this feeling and, as a result, might be less restrained than the majority (Kochanska, Murray, Jacques, Koenig, & Vandegeest, 1996; Zahn-Waxler, Cole, Welsh, & Fox, 1995). If these children are reared in homes and play in neighborhoods in which antisocial behavior is socialized, they are unlikely to become delinquents; perhaps they will become group leaders. However, if these children live in families that do not socialize aggression consistently and play in neighborhoods that provide temptations for antisocial behavior, they might be candidates for a delinquent career.

Biology and Psychology

The renewed interest in temperament has brought some psychologists in closer intellectual contact with neuroscientists. Although this interaction will be beneficial to both disciplines, there is a tension between traditional social scientists who describe and explain behavioral and emotional events using only psychological terms and a smaller group who believe that an acknowledgment of biological events is theoretically helpful. The recent, dramatic advances in the neurosciences have led some scholars to go further and to imply that, in the future, robust generalizations about psychological processes might not be possible without study of the underlying biology (LeDoux, 1995).

Although some neuroscientists recognize that the psychological phenomena of thought, planning, and emotion are emergent—as a blizzard is emergent from the physics of air masses—the media suggest, on occasion, that the biological descriptions are sufficient to explain the psychological events. This publicity creates a misperception that the biological and psychological are competing explanations when, of course, they are not. Vernon Mountcastle notes that although "every mental process is a brain process, . . . not every mentalistic sentence is identical to some neurophysiological sentence. Mind and brain are not identical, no more than lung and respiration are identical" (Mountcastle, 1995, p. 294).

Some neuroscientists, sensing correctly the community resistance to a strong form of biological determinism, are emphasizing the malleability of the neuron's genome to environmental events. A few neurobiologists have come close to declaring that the human genome, like Locke's image of the child's mind, is a tabula rasa that is subject to continual change. This position tempts citizens unfamiliar with neuroscience to conclude that there may be a linear cascade that links external events (e.g., loss of a loved one) directly to changes in genes, physiology, and, finally, behavior, with the psychological layer (e.g., a mood of sadness) between brain physiology and

apathetic behavior being relatively unimportant. This error is as serious as the one made by the behaviorists 60 years ago when they assumed a direct connection between a stimulus and an overt response and ignored what was happening in the brain. Both corpora of evidence are necessary if we are to understand the emergence of psychological qualities and their inevitable variation. "The phenomena of human existence and experience are always simultaneously biological and social, and an adequate explanation must involve both" (Rose, 1995, p. 380).

ACKNOWLEDGMENTS

This paper represents portions of the G. Stanley Hall Lecture delivered at the annual meeting of the American Psychological Association, New York City, August 1995. Preparation of this paper was supported, in part, by grants from the John D. and Catherine T. MacArthur Foundation, William T. Grant Foundation, and NIMH grant 47077. The author thanks Nancy Snidman and Doreen Arcus for their collaboration in the research summarized.

ADDRESS AND AFFILIATION

Corresponding author: Jerome Kagan, Harvard University, Department of Psychology, Cambridge, MA 02138; e-mail: JK@WJH.HARVARD.EDU.

REFERENCES

Adamec, R. E. (1991). Anxious personality and the cat. In B. J. Carroll & J. E. Barrett (Eds.), *Psychopathology in the brain* (pp. 153–168). New York: Raven.

Amaral, D. J., Price, L., Pitkanen, A., & Carmichael, S. T. (1992). Anatomical organization of the primate amygdaloid complex. In J. P. Aggleton (Ed.), *The amygdala* (pp. 1–66). New York: Wiley.

Arcus, D. M. (1991). *Experiential modification of temperamental bias in inhibited and uninhibited children*. Unpublished doctoral dissertation, Harvard University.

Arcus, D. M., & Kagan, J. (1995). Temperament and craniofacial variation in the first two years. *Child Development, 66,* 1529–1540.

Asendorpf, J. B. (1990). Development of inhibition during childhood. *Developmental Psychology, 26,* 721–730.

Bronson, G. W. (1970). Fear of visual novelty. *Developmental Psychology, 2,* 33–40.

Cooper, J. R., Bloom, F. E., & Roth, R. H. (1991). *Biochemical basis of neuropharmacology*. New York: Oxford University Press.

Damasio, A. (1994). *Descartes' error*. New York: Putnam.

Davis, M. (1992). The role of the amygdala in conditioned

fear. In J. P. Aggleton (Ed.), *The amygdala* (pp. 256–305). New York: Wiley.

DiLalla, L. F., Kagan, J., & Reznick, J. S. (1994). Genetic etiology of behavioral inhibition among two year olds. *Infant Behavior and Development, 17,* 401–408.

Fagan, J. F. (1981). Infant intelligence. *Intelligence, 5,* 239–243.

Hebb, D. O. (1946). The nature of fear. *Psychological Review, 53,* 259–276.

Kagan, J. (1994). *Galen's prophecy.* New York: Basic.

Kagan, J., Kearsley, R. B., & Zelazo, P. R. (1980). *Infancy.* Cambridge, MA: Harvard University Press.

Kagan, J., Reznick, J. S., & Gibbons, J. (1989). Inhibited and uninhibited types of children. *Child Development, 60,* 838–845.

Kagan, J., Reznick, J. S., & Snidman, N. (1988). Biological bases of childhood shyness. *Science, 240,* 167–171.

Kochanska, G., Murray, K., Jacques, T. Y., Koenig, A. L., & Vandegeest, K. A. (1996). Inhibitory control in young children and its role in emerging internalization. *Child Development, 67,* 490–507.

LeDoux, J. E. (1995). In search of an emotional system in the brain. In M. S. Gazzinaga (Ed.), *The cognitive neurosciences* (pp. 1049–1062). Cambridge, MA: MIT Press.

Mountcastle, V. (1995). The evolution of ideas concerning the function of the neocortex. *Cerebral Cortex, 5,* 289–295.

Murray, D. C. (1971). Talk, silence, and anxiety. *Psychological Bulletin, 75,* 244–260.

Panksepp, J., Sacks, D. S., Crepeau, L. J., & Abbott, B. B. (1991). The psycho and neurobiology of fear systems in the brain. In M. R. Denny (Ed.), *Fear, avoidance, and phobias* (pp. 17–59). Hillsdale, NJ: Erlbaum.

Porges, S. W., Arnold, W. R., & Forbes, E. J. (1973). Heart rate variability: An index of attention responsivity in human newborns. *Developmental Psychology, 8,* 85–92.

Richards, J. E. (1985). Respiratory sinus arrhythmia predicts heart rate and visual responses during visual attention in 14 to 20 week old infants. *Psychophysiology, 22,* 101–109.

Robinson, J. L., Kagan, J., Reznick, J. S., & Corley, R. (1992) The heritability of inhibited and uninhibited behavior A twin study. *Developmental Psychology, 28,* 1030–1037.

Rose, R. J. 1995. Genes and human behavior. In J. T. Spence J. M. Darley, & D. P. Foss (Eds.), *Annual review of psychology* (pp. 625–654). Palo Alto, CA: Annual Reviews.

Shimamura, A. P. (1995). Memory and frontal lobe function. In M. S. Gazzinaga (Ed.), *The cognitive neurosciences* (pp. 803–814). Cambridge, MA: MIT Press.

Snidman, N., Kagan, J., Riordan, L., & Shannon, D., 1995. Cardiac function and behavioral reactivity in infancy. *Psychophysiology, 31,* 199–207.

Squire, L. R., & Knowlton, B. J. (1995). Memory, hippocampus, and brain systems. In M. S. Gazzinaga (Ed.), *The cognitive neurosciences* (pp. 825–838). Cambridge, MA: MIT Press.

Tremblay, R. E., Pihl, R. O., Vitaro, F., & Dubkin, P. L. (1994). Predicting early onset of male antisocial behavior from preschool behavior. *Archives of General Psychiatry, 51,* 732–739.

Wilson, D. S., Coleman, K., Clark, A. B., & Biederman, L. (1993). Shy-bold continuum in pumpkinseed sunfish (*Lepomis gibbosus*): An ecological study of a psychological trait. *Journal of Comparative Psychology, 107,* 250–260.

Zahn-Waxler, C., Cole, P., Welsh, J. D., & Fox, N. A. (1995). Psychophysiological correlates of empathy and prosocial behavior in preschool children with behavioral problems. *Development and Psychopathology, 7,* 27–48.

Multiple Choice:

1. In Kagan's longitudinal study of reaction to novelty he found that:

   A. children who were highly reactive or fearful in infancy were highly reactive or fearful at 4-1/2 years of age.
   B. children who were highly reactive or fearful in infancy talked and smiled less with an adult stranger at 4-1/2 years of age.
   C. there was little stability in shyness in early childhood; shy children often became very outgoing, and fearless kids often became very fearful.
   D. shyness was stable for girls in the preschool years, but not for boys.

2. Kagan suggests that shy, fearful children who develop emotional problems are most likely to develop:

   A. depression.
   B. anxiety.
   C. conduct disorders.
   D. obsessive compulsive disorder.

Essay:

1. Kagan ends his article with a quote, "The phenomena of human existence and experience are always simultaneously biological and social, and an adequate explanation must involve both." What does he mean by this? How do the findings from his longitudinal research on shyness support this?

2. Discuss some of the differences between the high reactive-inhibited (fearful) and the low reactive-uninhibited (fearless or bold) children from infancy through age 4-1/2 years.

ARTICLE 15

Maternal Representations of Attachment During Pregnancy Predict the Organization of Infant-Mother Attachment at One Year of Age

Peter Fonagy, Howard Steele, and Miriam Steele

Reprinted from: *Child Development*, 1991, *62*, 891-905.
Copyright © 1991 by the Society for Research in Child Development.
Reprinted with permission.

Do you think that the relationship you have with your mother is a lot like the relationship she had with her parents, or is it very different? These researchers examine how mothers' recollections or memories about their relationships with their parents during childhood are related to their own relationships with their children (specifically, to the kind of relationship their own babies will have with them).

The researchers interviewed mothers shortly before the birth of their first child. Using a standard set of questions called the Adult Attachment Interview, they asked the mothers questions about their childhoods and early relationships. When the children were one year old, the researchers observed the mothers and children in the Strange Situation, a laboratory procedure involving short separations from and reunions with the parent. The way the child responds to these separations and reunions is used to assess the quality of the relationship. The mothers' memories about their own parents or their "working models of attachment" assessed during pregnancy accurately predicted about 75% of the time whether their infants would establish secure or insecure attachments to them.

What is particularly interesting, however, is that it was not just a "happy childhood" that predicted that infants and their mothers would form "secure" attachment relationships; it was whether the mothers had a *coherent* view of their childhood, in other words, whether their stories or memories "made sense." Although the majority of the women in the study described their childhoods in ways that were coherent, some women did not. For example, there were some mothers who said they had had a "perfect childhood," but then went on to tell stories about their parents that revealed that their parents were often cold and rejecting. These mothers were more likely to have children who were insecurely attached.

Thus, there is some continuity in relationships across generations. We are not, however, doomed to repeat bad relationships. Even adults who have experienced abuse and neglect as children may go on to be loving parents, as long as they face their past and acknowledge how it affected them.

Maternal Representations of Attachment during Pregnancy Predict the Organization of Infant-Mother Attachment at One Year of Age

Peter Fonagy

The Anna Freud Center

Howard Steele

University College London

Miriam Steele

The Anna Freud Center

FONAGY, PETER; STEELE, HOWARD; and STEELE, MIRIAM. *Maternal Representations of Attachment during Pregnancy Predict the Organization of Infant-Mother Attachment at One Year of Age.* CHILD DEVELOPMENT, 1991, **62**, 891–905. While strong retrospective and concurrent associations between maternal and infant patterns of attachment have been noted, this is one of the first reports of a prospective investigation of such associations. The Adult Attachment Interview was administered to 100 mothers expecting their first child, and, at 1-year follow-up, 96 of these were seen with their infants at 12 months in the Strange Situation. Maternal representations of attachment (autonomous vs. dismissing or preoccupied) predicted subsequent infant-mother attachment patterns (secure vs. insecure) 75% of the time. These observed concordances, as well as the discordances, are discussed in terms of the uniquely powerful contribution the Adult Attachment Interview makes to the study of representational and intergenerational influences on the development of the infant-mother attachment.

There is increasing evidence of an association between the way in which a mother recalls her own childhood experience and the quality of the relationship existing between her and her child (Grossmann, Fremmer-Bombik, Rudolph, & Grossmann, 1988; Main & Goldwyn, 1984, in press–a; Main, Kaplan, & Cassidy, 1985; Morris, 1981; Ricks, 1985). The notion of intergenerational concordance in relationship patterns has a distinguished history in the psychoanalytic literature (Bowlby, 1973, 1988; Emde, 1988; Fraiberg, Adelson, & Shapiro, 1975; Freud, 1940/1964) as well as in epidemiological research (Frommer & O'Shea, 1973; Rutter & Madge, 1976; Rutter, Quinton, & Liddle, 1983). More recently, developmental psychologists, in searching for the roots of individual differences in infant patterns of attachment, have begun to explore the influence of the mother's childhood experience and personality structure on the child-mother relationship (Belsky & Isabella, 1988; Grossmann et al., 1988; Haft & Slade, 1989; Main et al., 1985; Ricks, 1985; Spieker & Booth, 1988; Sroufe, 1985).

John Bowlby's attachment theory provides a plausible explanation for the social transmission of relationship patterns across generations. Child-caregiver interaction patterns are internalized early in life and guide

The research was supported by a Commonwealth Scholarship to H. Steele and a Social Sciences and Humanities Research Council of Canada Doctoral Fellowship to M. Steele and grants from the Nuffield Foundation, the Central Research Fund of the University of London, and the Collaborative Research Fund of the Anna Freud Centre. The interest of families participating in the research is gratefully acknowledged. Recruitment of subjects was facilitated by H. Brant and A. McMeeking in the Department of Obstetrics and Gynecology, University College Hospital. Mary J. Ward provided training in the coding of the Strange Situation. Karen Pinder, Arabella Kurtz, and Gemma Rocco assisted with data collection and compilation. For comments on earlier drafts and for their support and sustained interest in the work, the authors thank Mary Main, John Bowlby, and George Moran. The authors thank Anna Higgitt for her continued interest and involvement in the research. Address correspondence to P. Fonagy or M. Steele, 12 Maresfield Gardens, the Anna Freud Center, Hampstead, London, NW3, UK.

the infant's expectations, and evaluations, of relationship experiences. While these internal representations can be modified by current experience, they are considered resistant to change. They continue to influence relationships throughout childhood, across the lifespan, and even into the next generation (Bowlby, 1973, 1988). This article addresses the issue of how expectant mothers' mental representations of attachment may be seen to influence the subsequent quality of the infant-mother relationship.

Attachment research was substantially advanced by the development of a structured interview for classifying an adult's mental representations concerning relationships. The Adult Attachment Interview (George, Kaplan, & Main, 1985) consists of a series of questions and probes designed to elicit as full a story as possible about the individual's childhood attachment experiences and evaluations of the effects of those experiences on present functioning. The manner in which these experiences are conveyed, rather than the nature of the experiences themselves, yields an overall classification of the adult's current state of mind with respect to attachment. It has been suggested that these classifications— Dismissing (D), Preoccupied (E), or Autonomous (F)—bear a systematic association to the Strange Situation classifications of infant patterns of attachment—Avoidant (A), Resistant (C), or Secure (B), respectively (Ainsworth & Eichberg, in press; Main & Goldwyn, in press–a; Main et al., 1985).

Mothers whose interviews are classified Autonomous show objectivity and balance in discussing their childhood experiences, whether favorable or unfavorable, and present a narrative picture that is both coherent and believable. Mothers whose interviews are rated as Dismissing seem cut off from the emotional nature of childhood attachment experiences. Their current state of mind with respect to attachment is variously characterized by idealization, derogation, insistence on the inability to recall, and cognitive formulations divorced from affect. Mothers whose interviews are classified Preoccupied are over involved with their sometimes traumatic childhood experiences at the time of the interview. These experiences appear often to have involved role reversal in which they have assumed the role of parenting the parent(s). Their mind appears overwhelmed and confused by the topic of attachment, evidenced in the interview context by incoherence and preoccupying anger or passivity.

We may understand the relation between mothers' state of mind with respect to attachment and the possible influence of this on maternal behavior and infant security in the following way. Interviews classified Autonomous point to mothers whose minds are not taken up with unresolved concerns regarding their childhood experience and are therefore free to respond to their child's attachment cues. Interviews classified Dismissing indicate a reluctance to acknowledge attachment needs that may make such mothers—who often seem to share a history of rejection by their own mothers— insensitive and unresponsive to their infants' signals. Interviews classified Preoccupied suggest that mothers are likely to provide an inconsistent, confused picture for their infants, giving rise to an anxiously resistant pattern where infants' attempts to deal with their attachment needs are easily frustrated.

Main and Goldwyn (in press–a) report a concordance coefficient of .61 (kappa) between mother and child attachment classification. The figure is particularly impressive since these interviews were conducted with parents of 6-year olds and then correlated with their child's security of attachment as measured 5 years previously (Main et al., 1985). These results have been confirmed by an independent group of investigators (Grossmann et al., 1988). However, the retrospective nature of both these studies permits no control for the possibility that mothers' recollections may have been moderated by their evolving relationship with their children. As Sroufe (1985) suggested, a prospective study is the ideal method for assessing the significance of mothers' relationship histories. The attachment theory model of intergenerational concordance predicts that there should be an association between a prenatal assessment of maternal representations of relationships and the subsequent quality of the infant-mother attachment. This article presents findings of a prospective study that examined the association between primiparous mothers' Adult Attachment Interviews, assessed during pregnancy, and Strange Situation assessments of the infant-mother attachment relationship assessed at 1 year.

Method

Subjects.—One hundred pregnant women were recruited for the London Parent-Child Project. Recruitment for "a study aimed at better understanding how one's own experience of childhood influ-

ences the parenting of the next generation"
took place during prenatal classes at the obstetrics and gynecology department of University College Hospital. Selection criteria
included primiparous status, current cohabi-
tation with the father of the child, fluency
in the English language, and age above 20.
About 50% of those to whom the study was
described agreed to participate. Of the group
who declined participation, some did not
meet the selection criteria, while others
could not obtain agreement from their hus-
bands/partners, despite their interest in participating. A sizable minority were simply
not responsive to the idea of participation in
the research.

The expectant mothers' ($N = 100$) median age was 31 (range, 22–42). Eighty-two
of the women were married to the expectant
father at the time of recruitment or married
subsequently. At prenatal assessment, median length of residence together was 5
years (range, 1–19). The sample turned out
to be a well-educated, white, middle-class
group with 70 of the women holding university degrees; all 100 were high school graduates. Twenty-one of the women represented
social class I (professional and managerial),
65 social class II (intermediate occupations),
nine social class III (skilled occupations),
and five social class IV (partly skilled occupations), according to the criteria of the Office of Population Censuses and Surveys
(1980). The Registrar General's classification
includes a separate 12-point coding of subjects' occupation, allowing for further coding
into lower, middle, and upper income
groups. Sixty-five of the women were in the
middle income group, 21 were in the upper
income group, and 14 were in the lower income group. Seventy-five of the expectant
mothers were from England, 10 from Scot-
land or Ireland, and 15 were born outside
the United Kingdom. This latter group was
primarily Anglo-Saxon or European with
only a few from genuinely different cultures.

Between prenatal and 1-year assessments, attrition was low. One mother was
excluded from the study because she had
twins. Data from one subject were eliminated because she was recently bereaved.
Strange Situation data were unavailable for
a further two cases because of technical difficulties. Of the 96 children seen in the laboratory, 46 were girls and 50 were boys. No
child had significant auditory or visual handicap. One child (classified secure with
mother in the Strange Situation) was born
with a cystic hygroma and received consid-

erable medical attention with multiple hos-
pitalizations.

Design.—During the last trimester of a
first pregnancy, the Adult Attachment Interview (George et al., 1985) was administered
to 100 women; 98 were interviewed in their
homes, and two were interviewed in the laboratory. While the laboratory setting is normally to be preferred in AAI research, in the
present study interviews in the home were
favored for the added degree of personal
contact involved. To maintain continuity
with the sample, all subjects were contacted
by telephone and by post at 3 months postpartum. At 12 months postpartum, all the
families were invited to the laboratory for
the first time, where 96 children were assessed with mother in the Strange Situation.

*Adult Attachment Interview proce-
dure.*—The interview administered to all
subjects closely followed the schedule outlined by George et al. (1985). The Adult Attachment Interview is a structured interview
consisting of 18 questions. All interviews
were conducted by the same female interviewer and lasted from 30 min to 2 hours,
with most lasting approximately 45 min. The
interviewer, while trying to put the inter-
viewee at ease, asked only the questions and
the relevant probes without looking at the
interview text. The interviews were audio-
recorded and later transcribed verbatim.

The Adult Attachment Interview is
structured entirely around the topic of attachment, principally, the individual's relationship to mother and to father (and/or to
alternative caregivers) during childhood.
Subjects are asked both to describe their relationship with their parents during childhood and to provide specific biographical
episodes to support global evaluations. Ultimate classification depends on the goodness
of fit between semantic evaluations and episodic memories.

The interviewer asks directly about
childhood experiences of rejection; being
upset, ill, and hurt; as well as loss, abuse,
and separations. In addition, the subject is
asked to offer explanations for the parents'
behavior and to describe the current relationship with their parents and the influence
they consider their childhood experiences to
have on current behavior and, in the present
study, future parenting style.

All 100 interviews were independently
rated by four judges (Miriam Steele, Howard
Steele, and Peter Fonagy, who had received

training from Mary Main, and Anna Higgitt, who received training from MS, HS, and PF). The rating procedure followed the established guidelines (see Main & Goldwyn, in press–b), and all raters independently studied and rated all interviews. Reliability coefficients were calculated by computing agreements between each possible pair of raters (six estimates) and choosing the median as indicator of reliability. Levels of agreement among the four raters' readings of the interviews were consistently high: On the three-way classifications, median kappa = .90 (range, .72–.92) as well as on the scales for Probable Past Experience, median r = .84 (range, .69–.97) and Present State of Mind, median r = .81 (range, .68–.94).

Each interview was rated on a series of 9-point scales according to criteria specified by Main and Goldwyn (in press–b) where every second point had specific operational definitions. Three of these scales concerned the adult's probable childhood experience of having been parented in a (1) loving, (2) rejecting, or (3) role-reversing manner. The adult's probable experience with each parent was rated separately. A further five scales pertained to subjects' current state of mind with respect to attachment: (4) idealization, (5) preoccupying anger, (6) derogation, (7) insistence on the inability to recall, and (8) the overall coherence of the interview. Notably, preoccupying anger is to be distinguished from derogation. The anger scale is thought to be most relevant to the Preoccupied classification in its actively resentful (E2) rather than passive form (E1). Derogation, by contrast, is regarded as indicative of the Dismissing classification, derogation or devaluing of attachment being an attempt to distance oneself from attachment-related feelings including anger. Furthermore, maternal anger is expected to correlate with infant resistance in its active, angry form (C1), while maternal derogation is expected to correlate with infant avoidance.

After assigning Probable Experience and State of Mind scale ratings to an interview transcript, the judge then assigned each interview to one of three categories reflecting the individual's overall organization of thought concerning attachment: (1) Dismissing of attachment "D," (2) Preoccupied with or entangled by past attachments "E," or (3) Freely valuing, secure, or autonomous with respect to attachment "F." It is to be noted that in addition to assigning a D/E/F

classification, the judge also decided on the appropriateness of an alternative classification of Unresolved (U) with respect to past trauma or loss. This is consistent with the observed associations between the U interview status and the recently discovered "disorganized" pattern of infant attachment (Main & Hesse, in press). In this article we report only the major D/E/F classifications and not the alternative U classification as this latter issue is peripheral to the major question under investigation, that is, can previously reported retrospective patterns be observed prospectively?

The AAI ratings by the four raters were averaged. The associations between the AAI scales were examined by computing product-moment correlations across the 100 interviews. Table 1 displays these correlations. In light of the relatively high correlations between scales, a multivariate approach was adopted in all further analyses involving the AAI scale scores.

A discriminant function analysis was performed to identify which of the AAI scales made the most important contributions to the categorization of the interviews. Two significant canonical variables were extracted (canonical correlations = .809 and .617, $p \le .001$, respectively). The first variable appeared to distinguish the Autonomous (F) group from the other two groups (D, E), while the second differentiated between the Preoccupied (E) and Dismissing (D) groups. Correlations between AAI scale scores and canonical variables indicated that coherence of discourse, a loving past relationship with mother and father, and the absence of role reversal contributed highly to the first canonical variable. Present anger, good recall, and the absence of derogation made the most important contribution to the second canonical variable. The complete discriminant function accurately classified 89 of the 100 cases.

Strange Situation procedure.—It is already well established that the Strange Situation is a reliable and valid instrument with which to assess the quality of child-mother attachments (Ainsworth, Blehar, Waters, & Wall, 1978). This 20-min laboratory-based assessment involves two brief separations and two 3-min reunions with the parent. Focus is on the infant's behavior, especially during the reunions, where individual differences are measured in terms of the strategies employed to cope with this stressful situation (i.e., introduction to an unfamiliar

TABLE 1

PRODUCT-MOMENT CORRELATION MATRIX OF THE RATING-SCALE SCORES
OF 100 ADULT ATTACHMENT INTERVIEWS

	LOVING		REJECTING		ROLE REVERSING	
	Mother	Father	Mother	Father	Mother	Father
Loving^F	.67**					
Rejecting^M	−.84**	−.57**				
Rejecting^F	−.43**	−.81**	.48**			
Reversal^M	−.27*	−.46**	.24	.39**		
Reversal^F	−.25	−.13	.23	.11	.42**	
Coherence	.55**	.49**	−.44**	−.31*	−.32*	−.29*
Poor recall	−.38**	−.48**	.21	.35**	.15	.12
Idealization^M	−.03	−.25	−.02	.23	.07	.15
Idealization^F	−.21	.07	.22	−.13	−.20	.18
Anger^M	−.54**	−.31*	.62**	.13	.13	.25
Anger^F	−.28*	−.45**	.34**	.45**	.35**	.34**
Derogation^M	−.67**	−.40**	.68**	.28*	.12	.17
Derogation^F	−.27*	−.58**	.23	.60**	.23	.17

	Coherence	Inability to Recall	IDEALIZATION		CURRENT ANGER		Derogation
			Mother	Father	Mother	Father	
Poor Recall	−.45**						
Idealization^M	−.38**	.31*					
Idealization^F	−.25	.14	.37**				
Anger^M	−.48**	.08	−.11	.19			
Anger^F	−.26	.12	.00	−.13	.58**		
Derogation^M	−.39**	.22	−.16	.20	.48**	.31*	
Derogation^F	−.28*	.27*	.19	−.13	.21	.63**	.48**

NOTE.—^M = mother-probable experience with or state of mind concerning; ^F = father-probable experience with or state of mind concerning.
* $p \leq .01$, two-tailed.
** $p \leq .001$, two-tailed.

place and person, and two brief separations from mother). Of the three major patterns of response, two are thought to reflect an anxious attachment to the parent (either avoidant or resistant) and one is understood to indicate a secure attachment to the parent. Infants whose attachment is coded avoidant tend to appear undistressed during separation and to avoid proximity to the parent upon reunion. Infants whose attachment is coded resistant tend to be distressed by separation and to seek contact during reunion, but rather than being settled by the parent's return, they resist the contact they also seek and are unable to be comforted. Infants whose attachment is coded secure may or may not be distressed by separation, but upon reunion are pleased to see the parent and, if distressed, are easily comforted. Strange Situation assessments, videotaped and audiotaped when the infants were between 12 and 13 months, were subsequently coded by raters blind to the mothers' interview data. Proximity seeking, contact main-

tenance, resistance, and avoidance during each of the two reunions were coded on the seven-point scales developed by Ainsworth et al. (1978). In addition, all infants were assigned to one of three classifications: secure, avoidant, or resistant. Mary J. Ward coded 35 of the tapes in the context of training three independent coders to high levels of major category agreement, median $r = .88$ (range, .84–.92). On the remaining 61 tapes, median interrater reliability was .91 (range, .88–.94), and on interactive behavior ratings, median interrater reliability .88 (range, .85–.91). All Strange Situation tapes were coded by at least two independent coders, both blind to mothers' interview classification, and assigned to one of the three major categories. Disagreements between the two primary raters were conferenced in discussions with a third trained rater, also blind to mothers' interview classification.

Following the Strange Situation procedure, both parents were independently interviewed using a semistructured interview with two major components. The first concerned the presence of major life events or difficulties, including deaths, separations, or changes in employment or financial circumstances. The second aspect of the interview concerned a more detailed inquiry into the individual's experience of the transition to parenthood. Interviews were transcribed; the analysis of the experience of parenthood, however, is not yet complete.

Results

The results are presented in three sections. The first examines the concordance between mothers' Adult Attachment Interview classifications, assessed prenatally, and infants' security of attachment to mother, assessed in the Strange Situation at 12 months. The second examines the particular characteristics of mothers whose interviews were classified secure but whose children were classified insecurely attached in the Strange Situation. The third section considers the distinguishing features of mothers whose prenatal interviews were classified insecure but whose children were classified securely attached in the Strange Situation. For all results reported, analyses were repeated excluding those mothers ($N = 15$) born outside the United Kingdom or Ireland in order to control for the possible influence of cultural factors. Mention is made only where the analyses on the homogeneously U.K./Irish group ($N = 81$) differ from those attained for the larger London sample ($N = 96$).

1. *The intergenerational concordance.*—Of those adult attachment interviews for which Strange Situation data were available ($N = 96$), 59 were classified Autonomous, 22 Dismissing, and 15 Preoccupied with respect to attachment. The prediction that a mother's organization of thought concerning relationships, assessed prior to the birth of her child, is associated to her child's security of attachment at 1 year was impressively confirmed. Seventy-five percent of secure mothers had securely attached children; 73% of mothers Dismissing or Preoccupied with respect to attachment had insecurely attached children. The overall two-way (secure-insecure) match between mothers' prenatal interviews and children's security of attachment was 75% (kappa = .48, $p \le .001$, 52% expected by chance alone). The three-way match was 66% (kappa = .38, $p \le .001$, 44% expected). Table 2 shows the observed and expected frequencies for the three-way comparisons be-

tween mothers' classification on the Adult Attachment Interview and the infants' Strange Situation classification.

Examination of the observed and expected frequencies in Table 2 clarifies which AAI classifications were found to have particular value for predicting Strange Situation results from prenatal assessments. Autonomous adult classification increases the likelihood of secure infant classification while reducing that of anxious avoidant. Dismissing classification substantially increases the likelihood of anxious avoidant classification while reducing the probability of observing a secure infant pattern of attachment. The Preoccupied classification was of some help in predicting insecure infant status but failed to distinguish anxious-avoidant and anxious-resistant groups. Infants classified insecure resistant could not be predicted on the basis of the classifications of the prenatal AAIs shown in Table 2.

Because of colinearity among the scales, the following transformations were performed. Scores on the loving and the reflexed rejection scales were combined separately with respect to the subject's experience with her mother and father. Reversal, idealization, derogation, and anger scores were combined for the two parents. The means and standard deviations of the AAI scale scores grouped according to the child's Strange Situation classification are shown in Table 3. The eight variables were submitted to one-way multivariate analyses of variance which yielded a significant Wilks's lambda (lambda = .746, approximate $F = 1.72$, $df = 16,172$, $p \le .05$). Univariate F tests were performed to examine which of the variables contributed to these group differences. Anxious-resistant and secure children had mothers who recalled their relationship with their mothers as significantly more loving and less rejecting. Idealization was highest among mothers of avoidant and resistant children. Inability to recall was particularly marked among mothers of avoidant children. Coherence was highest among mothers of securely attached infants, significantly distinguishing them from mothers of avoidantly attached infants.

Table 4 portrays the association between prenatal Adult Attachment Interview classification and mean interactive behavior ratings for first and second reunions in the Strange Situation at 1 year. A multivariate analysis of variance was performed which yielded a significant Wilks's lambda (lambda

TABLE 2

Associations between 96 Mothers' Prenatal Adult Attachment Interview
Classifications and the Strange Situation Classifications of Their Infants
at 12 Months

Infants' Strange Situation Classifications	Mothers' Adult Attachment Interview Classifications		
	Dismissing ($N = 22$)	Autonomous ($N = 59$)	Preoccupied ($N = 15$)
Avoidant ($N = 30$) ...	15 (6.9)	8 (18.4)	7 (4.7)
Secure ($N = 55$)	5 (12.6)	45 (33.8)	5 (8.6)
Resistant ($N = 11$) ...	2 (2.5)	6 (6.8)	3 (1.7)

	D/E/F → A/C/B Three-Way	F/non-F → B/non-B Two-Way
Observed match ...	66%	75%
Expected match....	44%	52%
Kappa	.38	.48
Chi²	27.6 ($df = 4$), $p \leq .001$	22.54 ($df = 1$), $p \leq .001$

Note.—Expected frequencies appear in parentheses. Predicted cells are underscored.

$= .701$, approximate $F = 2.12$, $df = 16,172$, $p \leq .01$), indicating that the child's reunion behavior, particularly during the second reunion, was well predicted by the mother's Adult Attachment Interview classification. Univariate ANOVAs performed to explore this association provided strong evidence for the hypothesis that contact maintenance in both Strange Situation reunions would be most marked in infants of mothers whose prenatal interviews were judged Autonomous, while avoidance, as predicted, was most apparent in children of mothers whose interviews were classified Dismissing. Notably, children of mothers whose interviews were classified Preoccupied showed a significantly elevated level of resistance to contact in the second reunion, but not in the first. Similarly, avoidance ratings significantly distinguished Dismissing from Autonomous interviews, but only in the second reunion. This underscores the importance of using two reunions in the assessment of the child's security of attachment.

2. *Maternal attachment security and insecurely attached children.*—Fourteen (24%) of the mothers whose interviews were classified Autonomous had insecurely attached infants, eight avoidant and six resistant. Exploration of this difference initially focused on the incidence of major life events over the year intervening between pregnancy and 1-year assessments. One of the 45 and two of the 14, both mothers of avoidantly attached infants, reported having experienced stressful life events (e.g., loss of a

loved one, marital strife) during the first year of the child's life. Subsequent analyses of the maternal security/infant insecurity issue were performed with these individuals excluded, as it was felt that the incidence of life events could obscure the picture of the predictive value of the AAI. We also considered the possibility that some of these Autonomous mothers of anxiously attached children may not have been mainstream F's (i.e., F3) in the AAI system of subclassification. Exploration of this possibility led to a counterintuitive finding. Seventy-five percent of Autonomous mothers with anxiously attached children had prototypical Autonomous interviews (F3a or F3b), whereas only 36% of Autonomous mothers with securely attached children had interviews so classified, $\chi^2(1) = 4.24$, $p \leq .05$. Multivariate analysis of variance was then performed to test the hypotheses that the two Autonomous groups could be differentiated on the basis of their AAI scale scores. The analysis yielded a marginally significant Wilks's lambda (lambda $= .80$, approximate $F = 2.53$, $df = 8,47$). Table 5 shows the results of the comparisons between the AAI scale scores assigned to the interviews of each of these interview groups. Individual F tests revealed that the group with insecurely attached infants were consistently rated as somewhat more positive, both in terms of the Probable Experience and the State of Mind scales. They were rated lower in terms of role-reversing experiences with their parents ($p \leq .05$). In terms of their present state of mind, this group was also distinguished

TABLE 3

MEAN SCALE-SCORE RATINGS OF MOTHERS' ATTACHMENT INTERVIEWS GROUPED BY INFANTS' CHILD-MOTHER STRANGE SITUATION CLASSIFICATIONS (N = 96)

AAI Scales	Avoidant (A) (N = 30)	Resistant (C) (N = 11)	Secure (B) (N = 55)	ANOVA F (df = 2,93)	Pair-Wise Comparisons		
					A vs. C	A vs. B	C vs. B
Probable experience:							
Loving/nonrejecting[M] ...	5.82 (1.64)	7.21 (1.11)	6.54 (1.83)	3.20*	3.26**	2.12*	N.S.
Loving/nonrejecting[F] ...	5.52 (1.87)	6.60 (1.88)	6.34 (1.61)	2.71	N.S.	N.S.	N.S.
Role reversing[B]	2.06 (1.12)	2.01 (1.01)	1.87 (1.14)	< 1	N.S.	N.S.	N.S.
State of mind:							
Idealization of[B]	3.31 (1.23)	3.57 (1.18)	2.79 (.91)	4.01*	N.S.	2.11*	N.S.
Derogation of[B]	2.21 (1.22)	1.52 (.88)	1.83 (.79)	2.73	N.S.	N.S.	N.S.
Current anger at[B]	2.32 (1.42)	1.84 (1.27)	2.28 (1.30)	< 1	N.S.	N.S.	N.S.
Poor recall[C]	3.90 (1.44)	3.36 (1.26)	3.21 (1.19)	3.10*	N.S.	2.23*	N.S.
Coherence[G]	4.83 (1.34)	5.57 (1.36)	5.96 (1.22)	7.76***	N.S.	3.05***	N.S.

NOTE.—Standard deviations appear in parentheses. Results of pair-wise comparisons by separate variance analysis are expressed as t values with Bonferronized significance levels. [M] = mother, [F] = father, [B] = both parents, [G] = global state of mind.

* $p \leq .05$.
** $p \leq .01$.
*** $p \leq .001$.

TABLE 4

MEAN SCORES FOR REUNION BEHAVIOR DURING THE STRANGE SITUATION AT 12 MONTHS BY MOTHERS' PRENATAL ADULT ATTACHMENT INTERVIEW CLASSIFICATION

	DISMISSING (D) (N = 22)	PREOCCUPIED (E) (N = 15)	AUTONOMOUS (F) (N = 59)	OVERALL F (df = 2,93)	PAIR-WISE COMPARISONS		
					D vs. E	D vs. F	E vs. F
First reunion:							
Proximity and contact seeking ...	1.95 (1.05)	2.74 (2.12)	2.84 (1.62)	2.50	N.S.	N.S.	N.S.
Contact maintenance	1.23 (.53)	2.00 (1.56)	2.49 (1.98)	4.40**	1.73	4.38***	N.S.
Resistance to contact	1.14 (.35)	1.54 (1.12)	1.62 (1.19)	N.S.	N.S.	N.S.	N.S.
Avoidance of proximity	4.32 (1.43)	3.80 (1.70)	3.22 (1.79)	2.51	N.S.	N.S.	N.S.
Second reunion:							
Proximity and contact seeking ...	2.82 (1.33)	3.17 (1.90)	3.93 (1.69)	2.51	N.S.	N.S.	N.S.
Contact maintenance	2.32 (1.91)	3.40 (2.33)	3.91 (2.35)	4.05*	N.S.	3.13**	N.S.
Resistance to contact............	1.96 (1.70)	3.27 (1.94)	1.97 (1.28)	4.83**	1.94	N.S.	2.19*
Avoidance of proximity	4.00 (1.48)	3.13 (1.73)	2.63 (1.72)	5.44**	N.S.	3.50***	N.S.

NOTE.—Standard deviations appear in parentheses. Pair-wise comparisons are expressed as t values for separate variance with Bonferronized significance levels.
* p ≤ .05.
** p ≤ .01.
*** p ≤ .001.

143

TABLE 5

MEAN AAI SCALE SCORES FOR AUTONOMOUS MOTHERS WITH SECURELY AND
INSECURELY ATTACHED CHILDREN

	Autonomous Mothers with Securely Attached Infants (N = 44)	Autonomous Mothers with Insecurely Attached Infants (N = 12)	ANOVA F (df = 1,54)
Probable experience scales:			
Loving/Nonrejecting[M] ..	6.94 (1.68)	7.16 (1.00)	1.77
Loving/Nonrejecting[F] ...	6.70 (1.42)	6.96 (.94)	2.91
Role reversing[B]	1.68 (.76)	1.31 (.52)	4.51*
State-of-mind scales:			
Idealization[B]	2.50 (.84)	3.13 (.92)	3.46*
Derogation[B]	1.72 (.82)	1.37 (.34)	2.14
Anger[B]	2.45 (.99)	1.48 (.75)	4.32*
Coherence.....................	6.36 (.94)	6.42 (.57)	< 1
Poor recall....................	2.95 (.99)	3.04 (.95)	< 1

NOTE.—Standard deviations appear in parentheses. [M] = mother, [F] = father, [B] = both parents.
* $p \leq .05$.

by their significantly lower rating on the scale for current anger ($p \leq .05$).

Of the 11 infants classified anxious resistant in the sample, four were assigned to the passive-resistant (C2) subclass, and all four of these infants belonged to mothers whose prenatal interviews had been classified Autonomous. This is noteworthy because it puts in perspective the significantly lower ratings for preoccupying anger among these mothers. Indeed, *low* maternal anger is an expected correlate of the C2 infant subclassification (Main & Goldwyn, in press–b).

A further comparison was made in order to consider whether these mothers whose interviews were rated so positively and classified Autonomous, but whose infants were observed to be anxiously attached, were more prone to have avoidant or resistant infants. Here it was revealed that the presence of the resistant infant pattern was beyond that which would be expected by chance: six, or 55%, of the 11 children classified resistant belonged to this group of Autonomous mothers, while of the 30 children classified avoidant only six, or 20%, belonged to this group (Fisher exact $p \leq .05$).

3. *Maternal attachment insecurity and securely attached children.*—Of those mothers whose prenatal interviews were classified as Dismissing of attachment (N = 22), five (23%) had securely attached infants. Of the 15 mothers classified as Preoccupied, five (33%) had securely attached infants. Thus, 27% of mothers whose interviews were classified as Dismissing or Preoccu-

pied had securely attached children. In post-hoc exploration of this anomaly, it was noted that maternal interview classifications appeared to be associated with the country and culture of upbringing of the mother. While only 27 (33%) of the 81 U.K./Irish-born mothers were classified insecure, 11 (73%) of the 15 subjects born outside the United Kingdom and Ireland were so classified (Fisher exact $p \leq .01$). However, this possible overextension of the insecure classification in the case of non-U.K./Irish subjects could not account for the insecure-mother/secure-child form of discordance. Of the 27 U.K./Irish mothers who were classified Dismissing or Preoccupied, 82% had infants coded insecurely attached; of the 11 non-U.K./Irish mothers in the same group, 55% of the infants were coded insecure (Fisher exact N.S.).

Consideration was also given to the possibility that the maternal insecurity/infant insecurity type of discordance may have been due to the insecure attachment classification being overextended to those subjects belonging to the lower social classes and/or income groups. There was, however, no association between a mother's demographic characteristics and either her or her infant's attachment classification.

Discussion

Based on prenatal administration of the Adult Attachment Interview to 96 primiparous mothers, we were able, in 75% of the cases, to successfully predict whether an infant would be coded securely or insecurely attached (B/non-B) to mother at 1 year in the Strange Situation. These figures are consistent with those obtained in retrospective (Main & Goldwyn, in press–a, 75% [A/B/C]; Grossmann et al., 1988, 77% [B/non-B]) and concurrent (Ainsworth & Eichberg, in press, 80% [A/B/C/D]) administrations of these instruments. Other ongoing research involving prenatal administration of the AAI also suggests that it is possible to predict infant-mother patterns of attachment from pregnancy assessments (e.g., Ward, Botyanski, Plunket, & Carlson, 1991). Unlike past retrospective and concurrent investigations, we did not find the Preoccupied classification to be singularly predictive of the resistant infant classification. The Autonomous and Dismissing interview classifications were powerfully predictive of the secure and avoidant infant classifications, respectively.

The reported accuracy of prediction is impressive when compared with past attempts at identifying determinants of infants' security of attachment in prospective investigations. Previous reports have failed to provide strong evidence of a predictive association between expectant mothers' developmental history and infants' security of attachment (e.g., Belsky & Isabella, 1988). The significance of mothers' developmental history is unlikely to be fully captured unless we are clear about what in an individual's developmental history is of importance for facilitating infants' security of attachment. Predictive power resides, it seems, not in the quality of past experience but in the overall organization of mental structures underlying relationships and attachment-related issues.

The present investigation has additional importance in that it originates in London, where Adult Attachment Interview research has not previously been reported. The frequency distribution of AAI categories as well as Strange Situations, however, matched closely the reports of middle-class samples from North American cities. This reflects the ubiquity of the Bowlby-Ainsworth attachment paradigm and the generalizability of Main's approach to its assessment in adulthood.

Our results indicate that the mother of the securely attached child is able to fluently convey a global representation (whether favorable or unfavorable) of what her relationship to each parent was like during her childhood. At the same time, she is able to provide specific memories that support and elaborate on the global representation of her parents. In presenting to the interviewer her account of her development within her family of origin, she demonstrates an understanding of her own personal development that includes an awareness of the multiple motives (conscious and perhaps unconscious) that guided her parents' behavior toward her. Upon reading the transcript, one is not inclined to derive conclusions different from those being presented by the subject. In other words, there is little idealization of the past, no insistence on an inability to recall, and, overall, there are no significantly distorting mental processes at work. The subject clearly has access to, and is able to express, her feelings without being overwhelmed by them; she is autonomous and freely valuing of attachment—and therefore the prediction, which the present study confirms, that such a woman was substantially more likely to bring to the Strange Situation assessment at 1 year a child who would be classified securely attached to mother. The likely pathways for this effect involve sensitive and responsive patterns of mother-child behavior observed more frequently in women classified as Secure-Autonomous on the Adult Attachment Interview (Crowell & Feldman, 1988; Haft & Slade, 1989). Conversely, mothers classified Dismissing on the Adult Attachment Interview have been shown to manifest a lack of attunement in mother-infant interactions (Haft & Slade, 1989) and restricted patterns of communication between child and parent (Grossmann, 1989).

While mothers of infants who would develop a secure or anxious-avoidant attachment were distinguishable before the child was born, the present study could not easily identify mothers of children who would develop an anxious-resistant attachment. Exploration of the results did, however, reveal two significant associations between infant resistance and maternal interview status. Ratings of infant resistance during the second reunion in the Strange Situation were predictable on the basis of the Preoccupied interview classification. The second observed association between infant resistance and maternal interview status involved the apparent discordance between Autonomous interviews and anxious Strange Situation patterns. The anxious-resistant pattern was significantly associated with a particular type of maternal interview response. This was a response likely to be rated as suggestive of a supportive attachment history, a state of mind typified by low preoccupying anger, some idealization, and an overall impression of security. This was a picture derived from the pregnancy assessment. On the basis of what we subsequently observed in the Strange Situation, we would suggest that there was something fragile about the prenatal interview not detected in our initial ratings of these interviews, which foreshadowed difficulties in adjustment to the caregiving role. This suggestion is consistent with previous findings from prospective longitudinal investigations. Spieker and Booth (1988) found that mothers of resistant infants (unlike mothers of avoidant infants) differed little prenatally from mothers whose infants were classified secure. But a certain fragility, unseen before the child was born, appeared postnatally: they expressed satisfaction with their life and with their infants' temperament despite having higher scores on the Beck Depression Inventory and less confidence in themselves as mothers. This same paradoxical pattern emerged in the present sample where those mothers whose interviews were classified as Autonomous during pregnancy but had insecurely attached children were revealed as presenting a particularly positive picture of their childhood during their prenatal interview. We informally observed in the interview conducted at the time of the Strange Situation, consistent with Spieker and Booth's findings, that these were mothers for whom the maternal experience involved considerable disillusionment, but this requires further systematic investigation. Perhaps the antecedents of the resistant coding are best understood as part of an evolving pattern of a less than successful adaptation to motherhood. This is in accord with the view that mothers of anxiously resistant children have a sensitive set of attachment-related beliefs, but are unable to act consistently on these beliefs (Ainsworth et al., 1978). In other words, it may be worth exploring the hypothesis that there seems to be a certain attachment-related state of mind, perhaps particular to pregnancy, characterized by a somewhat exaggerated secure pattern, which is subsequently associated with infant insecurity. This infant insecurity is perhaps especially prone to take the form of passive resistance and may be mediated by maternal difficulties in adjustment to the caregiving role.

The quality of prediction in any prospective investigation will be moderated by possibilities of change in the mother. The likelihood of change may be substantially increased over the year in which a woman becomes a mother (Benedek, 1959). We cannot be certain at this point in time to what extent the mismatch between apparently heightened security in pregnancy and infants' insecurity at 1 year is due to long-lasting alterations in mental structure (perhaps induced by the transition to motherhood) and to what extent it is due more to transitory shifts (e.g., postpartum depression or lack of support from spouse). A readministration of the Adult Attachment Interview to this group and a matched control group of mothers would yield information as to the extent and nature of possible changes in mental representations of attachment relationships and attachment-related concerns.

Just as the transition to parenthood may occasion disappointment and an inability to consistently employ an appropriate mothering repertoire, so too may entry into the parental role lead to positive alterations in mental structure. This was perhaps operative in those mothers whose prenatal interviews were classified insecure but whose children were later classified as securely attached. We are not proposing that internal working models necessarily change as a function of the initial parenting experience. Yet the accessibility or level of activation of aspects of these mental models may be heightened or attenuated as a function of expectations or events. Particular representations active at any one time exerting control over attachment-related cognitions and behaviors may perhaps be best conceived of as "attachment states." These attachment states are to be distinguished from the underlying organization and structure of the internal working model, which may be thought of as predisposing the individual to particular types of behaviors, analogous to the function of personality traits. Comprehensive models of attachment will need to increasingly focus on the processes by which changes may occur in the representational processes influencing attachment-related feelings, cognitions and behaviors. There are a number of clinical service approaches that have begun to incorporate the systematic consideration of these representational processes on the quality of parent-child relationships (Aber & Baker, 1990; Greenspan & Lieberman, 1988; Nezworski, Tolan, & Belsky, 1988; Stern-Bruschweiler & Stern, 1989). The further development and refinement of these clinical/service approaches may be facilitated by careful use of the Adult Attachment Interview along with the delineation of pertinent situational, person-based, and interactional influences (Sameroff & Chandler, 1975).

In assessing the origins of observed discordances between maternal working models of relationships and infants' security of attachment, we need to distinguish possible errors of measurement from the likelihood of alterations in mental structure. A general, possibly limiting factor that awaits confirmation is the test-retest reliability of the instrument. Another measurement issue, which emerges from the current findings, concerns mothers' place of birth. When this does not coincide with the mainstream culture, it may lead to an underestimation of the extent of mothers' security/autonomy. Also, certain methodological limitations arise from pregnancy administrations of the Adult Attachment Interview. In the present study, the mothers were not probed specifically for fear of loss of the child, an expected correlate of avoidance in infancy (Main & Goldwyn, in press–b), which when present in significant measure automatically leads the AAI judge to assign the Insecure-Dismissing classification. One disadvantage, then, of using this measure prospectively is that attachment states that are activated by the presence of an infant cannot be assessed and may lead to inaccurate classification.

It is worth noting that the present report does not include consideration of forthcoming pieces of data that may help to elucidate the current portrait of family relationship patterns. It may be that some of the reported discordances will become more comprehensible when data pertaining to the expected match between maternal lack of resolution of mourning and infant disorganization are taken into consideration (Main & Hesse, 1990). It is also likely that consideration of the Adult Attachment classification of the father may provide information pertinent to the origins of discordance. Past studies have shown that a good marriage with attendant social support is capable of mitigating the influence of institutional background on child rearing (Quinton & Rutter, 1988) and to also permit a break from the cycle of abuse (Egeland, Jacobvitz, & Sroufe, 1988). It may therefore be necessary to take into account both parents' mental representations not only of their respective attachment histories but also their representations of one another and of the child (Aber, Slade, Berger, & Kaplan, 1985; Bretherton, Biringen, Ridgeway, Maslin, & Sherman, 1989) if a com-

prehensive account of the influence of past relationships on present and future relationships is to be provided (Stevenson-Hinde, 1988, 1990).

In summary, the present study provides evidence for lawful continuities in the nature and quality of parent-child relationships across generations. The Adult Attachment interview was shown to be capable of identifying prenatally infants whose attachment to mother is more likely to assume an anxious as opposed to secure form. Many previous studies have shown how these infant patterns of attachment make certain, less than adaptive, developmental pathways more likely (Sroufe, 1988). The availability of an instrument capable of identifying mothers at high risk of evolving such patterns of relationships with their children calls for replication and extension. In addition, it creates new possibilities for preventive work addressed at both attachment-related behaviors and mental representations.

References

Aber, J. L., & Baker, A. J. L. (1990). Security of attachment in toddlerhood: Modifying assessment procedures for joint clinical and research purposes. In M. Greenberg, D. Cicchetti, & E. M. Cummings (Eds.), *Attachment in the preschool years: Theory, research, and intervention* (pp. 427–460). Chicago: University of Chicago Press.

Aber, J. L., Slade, A., Berger, B., Bresgi, I., & Kaplan, M. (1985). *The parent development interview: Manual and administration procedures.* New York: Barnard College, Department of Psychology.

Ainsworth, M. D. S., Blehar, M. C., Waters, E., & Wall, S. (1978). *Patterns of attachment: A psychological study of the Strange Situation.* Hillsdale, NJ: Erlbaum.

Ainsworth, M. D. S., & Eichberg, C. G. (in press). Effects on infant-mother attachment of mother's unresolved loss of an attachment figure or other traumatic experience. In P. Marris, J. Stevenson-Hinde, & C. Parkes (Eds.), *Attachment across the life cycle.* New York: Routledge.

Belsky, J., & Isabella, R. (1988). Maternal, infant, and social-contextual determinants of attachment security. In J. Belsky & T. Nezworski (Eds.), *Clinical implications of attachment* (pp. 41–94). Hillsdale, NJ: Erlbaum.

Benedek, T. (1959). Parenthood as a developmental phase. *Journal of the American Psychoanalytic Association, 7,* 389–417.

Bowlby, J. (1973). *Attachment and loss: Vol. 2.*

Separation, anxiety and anger. New York: Basic.

Bowlby, J. (1988). *A secure base: Clinical applications of attachment theory.* London: Routledge.

Bretherton, I., Biringen, Z., Ridgeway, D., Maslin, C., & Sherman, M. (1989). Attachment: The parental perspective. *Infant Mental Health Journal,* 10(3), 203–221.

Crowell, J. A., & Feldman, S. S. (1988). Mothers' internal models of relationships and children's behavioral and developmental status: A study of mother-child interaction. *Child Development,* 59, 1273–1285.

Egeland, B., Jacobvitz, D., & Sroufe, L. A. (1988). Breaking the cycle of abuse. *Child Development,* 59, 1080–1088.

Emde, R. N. (1988). Development terminable and interminable: I. Innate and motivational factors from infancy. *International Journal of Psychoanalysis,* 69, 23–42.

Fraiberg, S. H., Adelson, E., & Shapiro, V. (1975). Ghosts in the nursery: A psychoanalytic approach to the problem of impaired infant-mother relationships. *Journal of the American Academy of Child Psychiatry,* 14, 387–422.

Freud, S. (1964). An outline of psychoanalysis. In J. Strachey (Ed. and Trans.), *The standard edition of the complete psychological works of Sigmund Freud* (Vol. 23, pp. 137–207). London: Hogarth. (Original work published 1940).

Frommer, E. A., & O'Shea, G. (1973). Antenatal identification of women likely to have problems in managing their infants. *British Journal of Psychiatry,* 123, 149–156.

George, C., Kaplan, N., & Main, M. (1985). *The Adult Attachment Interview.* Unpublished manuscript, University of California at Berkeley, Department of Psychology.

Greenspan, S., & Lieberman, A. (1988). A clinical approach to attachment. In J. Belsky & T. Nezworski (Eds.), *Clinical implications of attachment* (pp. 387–424). Hillsdale, NJ: Erlbaum.

Grossmann, K. (1989, September). *Avoidance as a communicative strategy in attachment relationships.* Paper presented at the Fourth World Congress for Infant Psychiatry and Allied Disciplines, Lugano, Switzerland.

Grossmann, K., Fremmer-Bombik, E., Rudolph, J., & Grossmann, K. E. (1988). Maternal attachment representations as related to patterns of infant-mother attachment and maternal care during the first year. In R. A. Hinde & J. Stevenson-Hinde (Eds.), *Relationships within families: Mutual influences* (pp. 241–260). Oxford: Clarendon.

Haft, W., & Slade, A. (1989). Affect attunement and maternal attachment: A pilot study. *Infant Mental Health Journal,* 10(3), 157–172.

Main, M., & Goldwyn, R. (1984). Predicting rejection of her infant from mother's representation of her own experience: Implications for the abused-abusing intergenerational cycle. *Child Abuse and Neglect,* 8, 203–217.

Main, M., & Goldwyn, R. (in press-a). Interview-based adult attachment classifications: Related to infant-mother and infant-father attachment. *Developmental Psychology.*

Main, M., & Goldwyn, R. (in press-b). Adult attachment rating and classification systems. In M. Main (Ed.), *A typology of human attachment organization assessed in discourse, drawings and interviews* (working title). New York: Cambridge University Press.

Main, M., & Hesse, E. (1990). Parents' unresolved traumatic experiences are related to infant disorganized attachment status: Is frightened and/or frightening parental behavior the linking mechanism? In M. Greenberg, D. Cicchetti, & E. M. Cummings (Eds.), *Attachment in the preschool years: Theory, research, and intervention* (pp. 161–182). Chicago: University of Chicago Press.

Main, M., Kaplan, N., & Cassidy, J. (1985). Security in infancy, childhood and adulthood: A move to the level of representation. In I. Bretherton & E. Waters (Eds.), Growing points of attachment theory and research (pp. 66–104). *Monographs of the Society for Research in Child Development,* 50(1–2, Serial No. 209).

Morris, D. (1981). Attachment and intimacy. In G. Stricker & M. Fisher (Eds.), *Intimacy* (pp. 305–323). New York: Plenum.

Nezworski, T., Tolan, W., & Belsky, J. (1988). Intervention in insecure infant attachment. In J. Belsky & T. Nezworski (Eds.), *Clinical implications of attachment* (pp. 352–386). Hillsdale, NJ: Erlbaum.

Office of Population Censuses and Surveys (1980). *Classification of occupations and coding index.* London: Her Majesty's Stationery Office.

Quinton, D., & Rutter, M. (1988). *Parenting breakdown: The making and breaking of intergenerational links.* Brookfield, VT: Gower.

Ricks, M. (1985). The social transmission of parental behavior: Attachment across generations. In I. Bretherton & E. Waters (Eds.), Growing points of attachment theory and research (pp. 211–227). *Monographs of the Society for Research in Child Development,* 50(1–2, Serial No. 209).

Rutter, M., & Madge, N. (1976). *Cycles of disadvantage: A review of research.* London: Heinemann.

Rutter, M., Quinton, D., & Liddle, C. (1983). Parenting in two generations: Looking backwards and looking forwards. In N. Madge (Ed.), *Families at risk* (pp. 60–98). London: Heinemann.

Sameroff, A. J., & Chandler, M. J. (1975). Reproductive risk and the continuum of caretaking causality. In F. D. Horowitz (Ed.), *Review of child development research* (Vol. 4, pp. 187–244). Chicago: University of Chicago Press.

Spieker, S., & Booth, C. (1988). Maternal antecedents of attachment quality. In J. Belsky & T. Nezworski (Eds.), *Clinical implications of attachment* (pp. 95–135). Hillsdale, NJ: Erlbaum.

Sroufe, L. A. (1985). Attachment classifications from the perspective of infant-caregiver relationships and infant temperament. *Child Development, 56,* 1–14.

Sroufe, L. A. (1988). The role of infant-caregiver attachment in development. In J. Belsky & T. Nezworski (Eds.), *Clinical implications of attachment* (pp. 18–38). Hillsdale, NJ: Erlbaum.

Stern-Bruschweiler, N., & Stern, D. (1989). A model for conceptualizing the role of the mother's representational world in various mother-infant therapies. *Infant Mental Health Journal,* 10(3), 142–156.

Stevenson-Hinde, J. (1988). Individuals in relationships. In R. A. Hinde & J. Stevenson-Hinde (Eds.), *Relationships within families: Mutual influences* (pp. 68–80). Oxford: Clarendon.

Stevenson-Hinde, J. (1990). Attachment within family systems: An overview. *Infant Mental Health Journal,* 11(3), 218–227.

Ward, M., Botyanski, N., Plunket, S., & Carlson, E. (1991). *The predictive and concurrent validity of the Adult Attachment Interview for adolescent mothers.* Paper presented at the meeting of the Society for Research in Child Development, Seattle.

Multiple Choice:

1. In Fonagy et al.'s study of mothers' representations of attachment, they found that:

    A. if mothers had negative childhood memories, their children were insecurely attached.
    B. mothers' representations of their childhood accurately predicted infant-caregiver attachment in all cases.
    C. if mothers' descriptions of their childhoods are coherent and believable, their children are most likely to be securely attached.
    D. if mothers were abused as children, their children were likely to be rated as "avoidant" in the Strange Situation.

2. Which of the following statements best describes the major conclusion from this study?

    A. Childhood experiences affect what kind of parent you will become--if you had a bad childhood your child will likely be insecurely attached.
    B. Childhood experiences have little association with the kind of relationship you will have with your child.
    C. What best predicts the kind of relationship you will have with your child is what sort of sense you have made of your childhood, be it bad or good.
    D. If you are still angry at your parents when you are an adult, your child will probably have a resistant/ambivalent attachment relationship with you.

Essay:

1. Fonagy and his colleagues state "Predictive power resides, it seems, not in the quality of past experience but in the overall organization of mental structures underlying relationships and attachment related issues." What do they mean by this?

2. Why do you think these investigators interviewed all of their subjects before they had their first child, as opposed to once they were already parents? What difference might this make?

ARTICLE 16

Developmental Change in Children's Assessment of Intellectual Competence

Deborah Stipek and Douglas Mac Iver

Reprinted from: *Child Development*, 1989, *60*, 521-538.

...re has important implications for how we deal with challenges. ...who view themselves as incompetent are far more vulnerable ...as competent. Unfortunately, as children get older, they ...re incompetent.

...dren's self-perceptions? Deborah Stipek and Douglas Mac ...ir *view* of their social environment and their *actual* social

... of their social environment, Stipek and Mac Iver point out that ...y change as they make their way through elementary school and into junior high school. For example, younger children view ability as something that may be increased through hard work. For them, failure can be easily remedied by simply trying harder. This understanding of ability protects them against perceiving themselves as incompetent because when they learn that they are not doing well, they simply conclude that they need to try harder. Older children, however, tend to view ability as something that cannot be influenced by effort. These children often conclude that hard work is necessary only for children who are not smart; thus, when they learn that they are not doing well, they assume that it means that they are not smart.

Stipek and Mac Iver argue that children's *actual* social environment also changes. For example, teachers give younger children lots of positive feedback, but very little negative feedback and most of this feedback is for how hard they try, rather than for their performance. Thus, teachers may lead younger children to evaluate their abilities positively, even when they are not performing very well. In contrast, teachers supply older children with a mixture of positive and negative feedback, mainly about their performance. This more realistic feedback may lead children to become less positive about themselves.

Developmental Change in Children's Assessment of Intellectual Competence

Deborah Stipek and Douglas Mac Iver

University of California, Los Angeles

STIPEK, DEBORAH, and MAC IVER, DOUGLAS. *Developmental Change in Children's Assessment of Intellectual Competence*. CHILD DEVELOPMENT, 1989, **60**, 521–538. This review analyzes what is known about how children's judgments of their intellectual competence and their definition and criteria for evaluating competence change with age and experience in achievement contexts. Research documenting an age-related decline in children's average ratings of their intellectual ability is interpreted in terms of developmental changes in children's concept of ability and the criteria they use to evaluate ability. The studies reviewed suggest that children's concept of ability becomes more differentiated with age and that children do not develop a concept of ability as a stable trait until late in elementary school. Research also indicates that the criteria children use to assess intellectual competence shift over the elementary school years—from effort, social reinforcement, and mastery to objective and normative information. Changes in ability assessments are considered in the context of age-related changes in children's cognitive abilities and in the nature of their educational environments.

How do children define and assess their intellectual competence, and how does the assessment process change with age? What implications do changes in the assessment process have for the conclusions children draw about their competence?

These questions have both theoretical and practical significance. Self-perceptions of ability figure prominently in virtually every cognitive theory of achievement motivation, including self-efficacy theory (Bandura, 1982), self-worth theory (Covington & Beery, 1976), and attribution theory (Dweck & Reppucci, 1973; Weiner, 1986). In all of these theories, ability perceptions are assumed to affect behavior and learning, and thus to have practical, educational importance.

This review summarizes what is known about how children's judgments of their academic competence and their definition and criteria for assessing competence change with age and experience in achievement contexts. We interpret these changes in ability assessments in terms of age-related changes in children's cognitive abilities and in the nature of their educational environments.

Children's Ratings of Competence

In many studies of children's self-perceptions of competence, including one with a large sample of 650 second through fifth graders (Marsh, Barnes, Cairns, & Tidman, 1984), ratings are close to the maximum in the early elementary grades and decline, on average, thereafter (Benenson & Dweck, 1986; Eshel & Klein, 1981; Nicholls, 1978, 1979; Pintrich & Blumenfeld, 1985; Stipek, 1981; Stipek & Tannatt, 1984). This decline in perceived competence is also evident in the proportion of self-congratulatory and self-critical statements students spontaneously make in the classroom (Frey & Ruble, 1987).

There is some evidence for a particularly steep decline in early adolescence. Harter, Whitesell, and Kowalski (1987) and Simmons and her colleagues (Simmons, Blyth, Van Cleave, & Bush, 1979; Simmons, Rosenberg, & Rosenberg, 1973) have found precipitous declines in academic self-esteem at the seventh grade, particulary for girls. Studies of children's perceptions of their math ability have also found relatively dramatic declines from the sixth to the seventh grade (Eccles et

The authors are grateful to Denise Daniels, Deborah Phillips, and John Weisz for helpful comments on previous drafts of this paper. Address correspondence to Deborah Stipek, Graduate School of Education, UCLA, Los Angeles, CA 90024.

[*Child Development*, 1989, **60**, 521–538. © 1989 by the Society for Research in Child Development, Inc.

al., 1983). Although perceived academic competence typically declines with age, a bias toward a positive evaluation does not disappear. In one study of early adolescents, for example, less than 17% of the seventh graders ranked themselves below the middle of the class in math ability (Eccles, 1986).

Researchers have found declines over the elementary school years in students' ratings on several general dimensions of competence, including physical (Marsh et al., 1984) and social competence (Ausubel, Schiff, & Glasser, 1952). The declines in perceived competence found among older children may be more task specific. For example, Eccles et al. (1983) found a decline from fifth through twelfth grade in perceived competence in math but not in English.

The generality of the decline in perceived competence during elementary school suggests that it may be caused by general changes in cognitive processing abilities and widespread changes in the educational environment that occur as children advance through the elementary grades. The greater specificity of later declines in perceived competence suggests that they may be explained primarily by experiences tied to certain academic subjects.

The evidence also suggests that young children's uniformly high self-ratings apply only when the question is posed at a very general level (e.g., how smart/good in sports/pretty are you?). Children may be slightly more realistic when they are asked to rate specific, observable outcomes or familiar skills (e.g., whether they get stars on their papers, know the names of colors, know the alphabet, can catch a ball). For example, no decline was found between preschool and second grade (Harter & Pike, 1984) or from third to ninth grade (Harter, 1982b) in the average scores of several large samples of children who completed Harter's Perceived Competence Scales, which ask questions about specific skills. Perhaps young children are aware of which skills they have and which skills they lack, but these specific assessments do not affect their judgment of their overall competence. Studies examining evaluations of specific skills and general competencies for the same children would provide more direct evidence on this interpretation.

It would also be useful to examine the effect of children's judgments about specific versus global competencies on task behavior. Since global competency ratings are uniformly high among preschool children, they

could not explain much of the variance in young children's task behavior. However, both younger and older children's behavior might be affected by perceptions of specific competencies. This is assumed by intrinsic motivation theorists, who claim that under optimal conditions (e.g., when external evaluation is not emphasized) children choose tasks that challenge their current skill level (see Stipek, 1988). To make appropriate choices, they would have to judge the difficulty of a task in relation to their own skills. Studies involving observations of children's performance on tasks and their subsequent task selections would provide evidence on their ability to make valid judgments.

Although most young children rate their *own* competence high, their ratings of *classmates'* competence are not higher than older children's ratings (Stipek & Tannatt, 1984). Moreover, their self-ratings are not invariably high. Stipek and Daniels (1988) found that the ability ratings of children in highly academic kindergartens, in which normatively based evaluative feedback (both positive and negative) was very salient, rated themselves at the same level as the fourth graders.

These results suggest that young children's typically high ratings of their competence cannot be explained by a response bias (i.e., always selecting the high end of the scale) or by an inability to process evidence to the contrary. How might we, then, explain the positive bias in young children's perceptions of their general academic competence and the steady and pervasive decline in these perceptions? One explanation concerns the way children define academic competence.

Conceptions of Academic Competence

Young children's conception demic ability are different from th children and adults in at lea According to research review definitions of academic comp inclusive than adults'. Also, a ferentiated from effort for you they do not have a concept of abil ble trait that limits the effectiveness

Definitions of Academic Competence
   Differentiation of academic and social dimensions.—Studies have shown that academic and social competence are not well differentiated in young children. In an interview study conducted by Stipek and Tannatt (1984), 40% of the preschool-age children and 15% of the kindergarten and first-grade chil-

dren referred to social behavior when they were asked to explain the "smartness" ratings they gave their classmates. Thus, according to some children, a smart classmate shared his or her toys and a classmate who was not smart bit other children (see also Stipek, 1981).

Children's concept of academic competence becomes better differentiated from social competence over the course of the elementary school years. In a study by Yussen and Kane (1985), 76% of the first graders, 44% of the third graders, and 35% of the sixth graders claimed that sharing was a quality that distinguished between average and smart people. Research using Marsh's Self-Description Questionnaire found that self-ratings of competence in math and reading, physical ability, and relations with peers were more differentiated in fourth and fifth grade than in second grade (Marsh et al., 1984).

The young child's poorly differentiated concept of ability is consistent with Werner's (1957) claim that, "Whenever development occurs, it proceeds from a state of relative globality and lack of differentiation, articulation and hierarchic integration" (p. 126). However, it may also be partly an artifact of the verbal assessment methods that have been used to examine ability conceptions. Children may make distinctions that are not incorporated into their vocabulary. For example, they may differentiate between social competence and academic performance in school, but use the word "smart" to refer to both. Studies that rely less on children's understanding of particular words could clarify previous findings. One could assess, for example, whether children's choice of playmates versus work partners (on academic tasks) is influenced by classmates' social behavior versus academic performance. It would also be useful to observe from which classmates children seek help on school tasks. Children who seek help from academically successful rather than popular classmates or best friends presumably differentiate, at some level, between intellectual and social competence.

Children may differentiate the cognitive from the social domain in ratings of their own competence sooner than in ratings of their peers' competence. Preschool- and kindergarten-age children's self-ratings on Harter's Pictorial Scale of Perceived Competence and Social Acceptance resulted in separate cognitive and social factors (Harter & Pike, 1984). Also, when children were asked to explain their *own* smartness ratings in Stipek's interview studies, only a few children at all ages referred to their social competence as an explanation (Stipek, 1981; Stipek & Tannatt, 1984).

The more pronounced confounding of social and cognitive competencies when judging peers than when judging the self may be related to young children's egocentrism and the importance of peers' social behavior toward them. Young children may be more concerned about whether their classmates bite or share their toys than they are about whether their classmates know their numbers or the alphabet. Consequently, when asked to evaluate their peers on any dimension, they may focus on social behavior.

Differentiation of intellectual competence from work habits.—Even after children have begun to differentiate social and cognitive competence, they do not have a concept of intellectual competence that is as narrow as that of most adults. In Stipek's interview studies, many of the second and third graders discussed work habits (e.g., neatness, effort) to explain their assessments of their own and their peers' ability in school (Stipek, 1981; Stipek & Tannatt, 1984).

Young children of elementary school age may also confuse intellectual competence with general conduct, such as following school rules. Blumenfeld, Pintrich, Meece, and Wessels (1982) found that second graders' but not sixth graders' ability perceptions were negatively related to the proportion of conduct-related criticism they received.

Development of a Concept of Ability as a Stable Trait

In addition to having a more global concept of ability, young children do not differentiate between effort and ability in the same way that older children and adults do. Dweck (1986; Dweck & Bempechat, 1983) refers to young children's undifferentiated concept of ability as an "instrumental-incremental" concept; ability is similar to a skill, and it is increased through one's own instrumental behavior, like practice and effort. According to the differentiated concept of ability, which Dweck refers to as an "entity" concept, ability is a stable trait, unaffected by effort. The more ability an individual has, the more performance is facilitated by effort. If two people exert the same amount of effort, the person with the most ability will perform the best; if two people perform the same, the person who exerted the least amount of effort is highest in ability. Assessing ability using an entity concept requires interpersonal comparisons.

Nicholls (1978; see also Nicholls & Miller, 1984a, 1984b) has studied children's concept of ability and their understanding of ability as a stable trait by showing them films of children doing math problems with varying levels of effort and success. The youngest children in Nicholls's studies (aged 5 and 6) do not distinguish among effort, ability, and outcome; they reason that if a person succeeded, he must be smart and he must have tried hard. If two children in the film received the same score but differed in effort, young subjects often invent effort-related explanations (e.g., she must have started earlier or he must have been thinking while fiddling). Children from about the age of 7 to 10 distinguish effort and outcome as a cause and effect, but ability "in the sense of capacity which can increase or limit the effectiveness of effort" is not understood (p. 812) (see also Karabenick & Heller, 1976; Kun, 1977; Kun, Parsons, & Ruble, 1974).

In addition to understanding that ability facilitates or limits the effectiveness of effort, an entity or differentiated concept of ability requires an understanding that the strength of the relation between a task outcome and a person's ability level depends to some degree on the difficulty level of the task. Adults recognize that good performance on an easy task does not indicate high ability, and poor performance on a very difficult task does not indicate low ability. Young children's judgments regarding the difficulty level of a task depend on their perception of their own ability to complete the task (Nicholls & Miller, 1984a, 1984b). Most first- and second-grade children use objective criteria (e.g., number of puzzle pieces) to assess the difficulty level of a task (Nicholls & Miller, 1984a, 1984b). Not until after about the second grade do children use normative information to infer the difficulty level of a task. From then on, a hard task is one that most children their age cannot do (Nicholls, 1978, 1980). This understanding is a prerequisite to an entity concept of ability.

Dweck's and Nicholl's work on the development of an entity concept of ability is related to research on children's use of stable traits to explain behavior on other dimensions (e.g., niceness). Some researchers claim that children as young as kindergarten age interpret behavior in terms of stable traits (e.g., Heller & Berndt, 1981), although most find significant increases in the use of dispositional attributions, especially after about the age of 7 (e.g., Livesley & Bromley, 1973; Rholes & Ruble, 1984).

A concept of ability as a stable trait may emerge later than other personality traits because it requires a higher level of cognitive development. To recognize niceness as a stable trait children need to recognize consistency in behavior over time and across situations, and to attribute the consistency to the person. A concept of *ability* as a stable trait requires, in addition, an understanding of the reciprocal relation between effort and ability—that ability limits the effectiveness of effort, and that effort is more facilitative of performance in high-ability than in low-ability individuals. Nicholls (1978) suggests that this mature understanding of ability requires the formal operational capacity to coordinate proportional relations (Inhelder & Piaget, 1958). He points out that an understanding of the relation between effort and ability is analogous to achieving equilibrium in Inhelder and Piaget's balance problem. The outcome in the balance task can only be predicted accurately by combining, proportionally, weight and distance of weight from the fulcrum, just as outcomes on achievement tasks can only be predicted by combining, proportionally, effort and ability.

Research in which children are asked to predict academic performance from previous performance (e.g., Heller & Berndt, 1981) does not necessarily test their understanding of a mature concept of ability. Children may predict future performance that is consistent with past performance but base their prediction on an entirely different attribute, such as typical effort (i.e., Jill did well on academic tasks in the past; she must be a hard worker, and therefore will continue to do well). It would be useful in future research to assess children's reasons for their predictions. Also, research on children's concept of ability as a trait has concentrated on intellectual ability. Consequently, we do not know to what degree the concept of ability as a stable trait varies across domains. It would be useful to study this concept in other domains, such as athletics, music, or art.

The development of a concept of ability as a stable trait is especially important to understand because it has implications for children's behavior in academic contexts. Two studies have demonstrated that young children's persistence on academic tasks does not decline as a consequence of failure until the fifth or sixth grade (Miller, 1985; Rholes, Blackwell, Jordan, & Walters, 1980). And Miller (1985) provides direct evidence indicating that the debilitating effect of failure is associated with the development of a concept of ability as a stable trait.

TABLE 1

CONCEPTIONS OF ABILITY

Preschool–Second Grade	Third–Sixth Grade	Junior High
Behaviors Included		
Social behavior, work habits, and conduct	Academic perfor-mance; to a lesser degree, social be-havior and work habits	Academic perfor-mance
Differentiation among Academic Subjects		
Undifferentiated	Partially differenti-ated	Fully differentiated
Definition of Ability		
"Incremental"—in-creases through practice and effort	Primarily Incremen-tal; developing concept of ability as a stable trait	"Entity"—a stable trait unaffected by effort

Summary

The research reviewed in this section suggests important developmental changes in the way in which children conceptualize intellectual ability. Children in preschool (and to some degree in the first year or two of elementary school) have a very global concept of ability that includes social behavior, work habits, and conduct, and they concep-tualize ability as a skill that is increased by practice and effort. Over the elementary school years, children's definition of aca-demic ability becomes narrower. However, not until early adolescence do children fully differentiate ability, in the sense of capacity, from effort. These changes are summarized in Table 1.

That young children define intellectual competence in terms of social behavior, effort, and work habits does not, alone, explain why most have positive perceptions of their com-petence. Certainly not all kindergarten chil-dren behave appropriately and work hard all of the time. Next, we consider differences in the criteria younger and older children use to evaluate intellectual competence that may help explain the age-related decline in ability ratings.

Criteria for Assessing Intellectual Competence

Information relevant to one's intellectual competence can come in many forms. Some tasks (e.g., puzzles) provide immediate feed-back regarding mastery or nonmastery. In school, children often receive objective feed-back from teachers, such as the number of

spelling words they spelled incorrectly on a spelling test. And they receive direct social reinforcement and criticism. Competency in-formation is contained in symbolic feedback, for example, stars, stickers, happy faces, and grades. The amount of effort expended on tasks can also provide information on intel-lectual competence. There are many other sources of information in school, such as abil-ity-group placement and work displayed on bulletin boards. Some forms of ability-related information are more subtle—for example, whom the teacher calls on to answer difficult questions, how long the teacher waits for a response, or to whom the teacher offers help (Weinstein & Middlestadt, 1979).

With all of these types of information, students can base their ability judgments on intra- or on interindividual comparisons. They can observe changes over time or differ-ences across subject areas in these sources of information about their own competence, or they can compare these indices of their own ability with similar information about class-mates.

There are systematic age differences in how children process different types of infor-mation about intellectual competence and in children's propensity to make intra- versus in-terindividual comparisons. We review in this section what is known about these develop-mental changes.

Sources of Information

Mastery information.—Mastery involves meeting some goal or performance standard. Examples could be completing a puzzle or spelling 80% of the words on a spelling test correctly. Before about the age of 7 or 8, children rely considerably on mastery standards to assess their ability. In interview studies, young children frequently refer to particular tasks that they can do to justify the high competence ratings they give themselves (Blumenfeld, Pintrich, & Hamilton, 1986; Stipek, 1981).

Young children cite mastery as evidence of their competence, but preschool-age children do not seem to accept nonmastery as evidence of incompetence, at least not in any long-term sense. Studies have shown that failure experiences do not dampen preschool-age children's ability judgments and future expectations (see Stipek, 1984a, 1984b, for reviews). We suspect that when young children rate their competency high on a task they have just failed several times, they mean that they will be competent with a little practice and effort.

Social versus objective feedback.—Positive social feedback (i.e., praise) also seems to affect young children's ability judgments more than it affects older children's. Lewis, Wall, and Aronfreed (1963), for example, gave first and fifth graders a binary probability choice task. Whereas social and correctness feedback had about the same effect on fifth graders' choices, social feedback had a much stronger effect than the correctness feedback on the first graders' choices. In a study of preschool children, Graziano (1986) reports that subjects adjusted the relative amount of reward (stars) they gave themselves and another child as a function of whether an adult verbally reinforced their own or the other child's performance on a previous task, even when the subject's performance was objectively equal to the other child's. Spear and Armstrong (1978) also report that kindergartners and first graders were more responsive to social reinforcement than fourth, fifth, and sixth graders.

Adult evaluation may be more salient for younger than older children because, until children reach concrete operations, they attribute virtually full evaluative and moral authority to adults. Furthermore, guided by what Kohlberg (1969) refers to as the "good boy" or "good girl" principle of moral behavior, they are especially concerned about pleasing adults.

Preoperational thinking may contribute to young children's exclusive attention to praise. First, preoperational thinking is dominated by perceptually salient information

(Piaget, 1950). Since preoperational children have difficulty coordinating two or more dimensions simultaneously, they base their judgments on the most salient feedback and disregard other information. In contrast, the concrete-operational child should be able to process social and objective feedback simultaneously and draw inferences about ability from both. Our argument is analogous to Piaget's observations regarding children's moral reasoning. He claims that preoperational children focus on a perceptually salient outcome (e.g., a large inkblot) and cannot coordinate that information with another, more subtle variation (e.g., intention) in their moral judgments (Piaget, 1932).

Less is known about children's use of criticism in their ability judgments. The finding reported by Blumenfeld et al. (1982) —that second graders' ability ratings were associated with the amount of conduct-related criticism they received—suggests that by second grade children do consider negative social feedback in their self-assessments. Pintrich and Blumenfeld (1985), however, found no relation between second and sixth graders' ability ratings and the amount of work and behavioral criticism they received.

There is apparently a decline with age in the relative weight given to social reinforcement relative to objective feedback. In addition to the studies discussed above, which found that young children attend primarily to social feedback, Stipek (1987) found that kindergarten children's ability ratings were little affected by objective feedback. But, as is found in most studies, the upper-elementary-school-age children's judgments were affected by objective information on performance.

In addition to a decline in the relative weight given to social feedback, there is evidence for a change in the way social feedback is interpreted by children. Meyer et al. (1979, Experiment 2) found in an experimental study that adults and students in the eighth grade or above interpreted praise for success on an easy task to indicate low ability. Younger children accepted praise at face value; they assumed that praise indicated high ability regardless of the task.

Barker and Graham (1987) replicated these developmental differences in the effect of praise on children's ability judgments, and also demonstrated that blame following failure was interpreted differently by younger and older children. Eleven- and 12-year-olds interpreted an angry teacher response following a child's failure to indicate high ability, whereas younger children interpreted the angry response to suggest low ability.

These findings on children's interpretation of teacher feedback are no doubt related to developmental changes (discussed above) in children's understanding that success on easy tasks requires less ability than success on difficult tasks and that, given equal outcomes, effort and ability are inversely related. Both young and older children understand that teachers praise success and express anger for failure when they perceive a child to have exerted high or low effort, respectively (Harari & Covington, 1981). But apparently only older children understand that when success on an easy task requires high effort (and is thus praiseworthy) or when failure on an easy task is not attributed to low effort (and therefore is not responded to with anger), the person is low in ability.

Practically, the research reviewed here suggests that during the first few years in school, children's ability judgments are significantly and positively affected by teacher praise, even if the praise is contradicted by other evidence, such as objective-task outcomes. The ability judgments of children in the middle and upper elementary grades are positively affected by praise, but praise is considered in conjunction with other information. In junior high, praise has a positive or negative effect on ability judgments, depending on the context, for example, whether the task was perceived to be easy or difficult.

Symbols.—Grades are no doubt the most commonly used symbol of academic performance in school. However, stickers, stars, happy faces, and other symbols are also used, especially in the early elementary grades. There is some evidence to suggest that children as young as kindergarten age incorporate some symbolic feedback, such as stars, into their ability judgments (Stipek, 1987) but do not attend to and may not even understand letter grades (Stipek & Daniels, 1988).

Entwistle and Hayduk (1978) found that children's expected grades did not correlate significantly with their previous grades until the end of the second grade. Nicholls (1978, 1979) has found that children's self-ratings of ability were not significantly related to grades given by the teacher until the third or fourth grade.

In contrast to younger children, there is evidence that upper elementary students rely heavily on grades to evaluate their ability. Blumenfeld et al. (1986) report that the per-

centage of children referring to grades when asked "How do you know when someone is smart?" more than doubled (from 15.2% to 38.6%) from second to fifth grade. Furthermore, Mac Iver (1988) found greater variability (a larger variance) in sixth graders' math-ability perceptions in classrooms with higher variance in report card grades. Mac Iver (1987) also demonstrated that when grades were given frequently, relatively untalented sixth graders were less likely to believe that they were mastering their assignments or outperforming others than when grades were given infrequently. Finally, upper-elementary-school-age children's self-ratings of ability correlate highly with their grades (Nicholls, 1978, 1979).

There are several explanations for younger children's greater attention to symbolic rewards, such as stars and happy faces, than to letter grades. First, stars and happy faces may be intrinsically appealing to young children, whereas the value of the letter "A" has to be learned. Second, stars and happy faces are either present or not. An understanding of letter grades requires an understanding of an ordinal scale. Children may need concrete operations, especially seriation (e.g., "B" is simultaneously better than "C" and worse than "A"), to fully grasp the meaning of letter grades. Third, grades are typically based on a normative standard. Thus, an "A" is valuable because it is given only to the best performers. Children's increasing attention to grades is no doubt related to a shift (discussed later) from mastery to normative criteria for assessing performance.

Effort.—For young children, effort is one of the primary indicators of intellectual competence. People who work hard are smart, regardless of other evidence to the contrary. Thus, a young child who believes that she is a hard worker (based on self-observations and social feedback) may consider herself smarter than a "goof-off," even if the "goof-off" obtains higher levels of objective success (Nicholls & Miller, 1984b).

Similarly, if young children assume that effort almost inevitably leads to skill improvement, they may conclude that they are competent at frequently practiced tasks, even if their actual skill gains in some of these tasks have been barely noticeable. Some support for this conjecture comes from Harter and Pike's (1984) study. Thirty-four percent of the preschool through second-grade children they interviewed explained high self-perceptions of cognitive competence by citing habitual engagement in activities that foster skill development (e.g., "I practice a lot," "I read a lot at home"). The fact of practicing alone seemed to indicate competence to these children.

Finally, because young children do not perceive high effort to be indicative of low ability, they may judge their competence to be just as high on tasks that require them to exert sustained effort as on tasks that they can complete without much effort. In contrast, once children understand the inverse relationship between effort and ability (above the age of 10), they may conclude that they are less competent on tasks that require them to work hard than on those that are easy for them (see Kun, 1977; Nicholls & Miller, 1984b; Surber, 1980).

Other sources.—There are many other indicators of competence available in classrooms. Research by Weinstein and her colleagues (Weinstein, Marshall, Sharp, & Botkin, 1987; Weinstein & Middlestadt, 1979) has shown that throughout the elementary school years, students are aware that teachers treat high-ability students differently from low-ability students. For example, high-ability students are perceived to be granted special privileges, to be given more autonomy, to be helped less, and to be given more time to answer questions in class. However, Weinstein et al. (1987) reported that the first and third graders in their sample were less likely than the fifth graders to perceive negative teacher treatment of *themselves.* Thus, although children are aware of teacher differential treatment toward low and high achievers as early as first grade, they may not incorporate "negative" treatment in their perceptions of their own ability until a few years later.

As mentioned above, children can use all of these sources of information about their ability to make both intra- and interindividual comparisons. We discuss next developmental research on children's tendency to compare their own performance across time and across subject areas (intraindividual comparisons) with their tendency to compare their performance with that of their classmates (interindividual comparisons).

Intraindividual Comparisons
Over time.—Young children seem to perceive improvement as evidence of competence, but they do not necessarily see a lack of improvement as evidence of low competence. Many studies find that young children's expectations for success on specific tasks are not dampened by failure to improve (see Stipek, 1984b, for a review). Thus, for example, if pre-

school-age, and to some degree kindergarten and first-grade children, fail a task on as many as four trials, they continue to expect to do well on the next trial (Stipek & Hoffman, 1980). This research has to be viewed cautiously, however, because it is based on children's verbal statements. Even if failure does not affect verbally stated expectations or perceptions of competence, it might affect persistence, enthusiasm, or achievement-related emotions, such as shame.

An asymmetry in the incorporation of improvement but not nonimprovement in children's competency judgments could be explained by their "incremental" concept of ability. Thus, improvement in skill level or objective successes indicates competence; failure to improve does not indicate incompetence; it indicates that greater effort or more practice is needed to succeed.

Improvement continues to be used as evidence of ability throughout elementary school (France-Kaatrude & Smith, 1985; Mac Iver, 1984, 1987; Reuman, 1986). However, unlike children in the first few grades of elementary school, who may not lower their ability estimates as a consequence of "nonimprovement," older elementary-school children see nonimprovement as being especially diagnostic of a lack of ability (Mac Iver, 1984).

Mastery and improvement continue to play a role in older children's ability assessments, but research reviewed later indicates that their importance diminishes relative to social comparison information as children progress through school.

Across domains.—It is not likely that young children make across-domain comparisons in their ability judgments, even implicitly. First, as discussed above, their definition of ability is not well differentiated across performance domains. There is also some evidence that young children have difficulty acknowledging "contradictory" assessments (e.g., being good at math but bad at reading), presumably because preoperational thought precludes them from coordinating different perceptual attributes simultaneously. For example, Harter (1982a) reports that preoperational children find it difficult to acknowledge that they can feel smart and dumb at the same time. Thus, a bright dyslexic 6-year-old claims that he is "all dumb," even though he is able to perform competently in certain subjects. If children do not differentiate competence across different domains, they should not be able to use across-domain comparisons to assess competence.

The evidence suggests that children do not begin to base their ability judgments on across-domain comparisons in performance until the late elementary grades. In Marsh's research, verbal and math self-assessments were substantially correlated in the early elementary grades (Marsh, 1986; Marsh, Smith, & Barnes, 1985). But by the fifth and sixth grades, perceptions of verbal and mathematic abilities were uncorrelated, despite a correlation in actual relative standing (Marsh, 1986). If students relied solely on social comparison or objective feedback in forming estimates of their math and verbal abilities, these estimates would be highly correlated. Marsh proposes that older students engage in internal, across-domain comparisons. Thus, they compare their skills and achievement in math with their skills and achievement in reading, and they use this internal, relativistic comparison as one basis for their competence judgments in both domains.

In addition to helping students identify areas of strength and weakness, across-domain comparisons may help generally low-performing students maintain moderately high self-ability ratings in those domains in which they are relatively more competent. Mac Iver (1987) found evidence for this in his study of upper-elementary-school students. Many of the relatively low-performing students who believed that they were competent in math indicated that they based their math ability judgment on across-domain comparisons.

In summary, during the first few grades in school, children use across-time comparisons in their ability assessments. Across-domain comparisons donot appear to influence ability judgments until upper elementary school. Both types of intraindividual comparisons figure in the ability assessments of older children and adolescents, although they are considered in conjunction with interindividual criteria.

Interindividual Comparisons
One of the most important developmental changes in the ability-assessment process concerns the use of social comparative information. Research suggests that children as young as preschool age engage in and make inferences from social comparisons. For example, an observation study demonstrated that preschool-age children make social comparisons, and they make competitive, "besting" verbal statements (Mosatche & Bragonier, 1981). Heckhausen (1984) reports, furthermore, that by the age of 3 children reveal, in their emotional responses, that they differentiate between tasks that they complete before or after an adult finishes an identical task.

Both of these studies, however, involved direct comparisons with one other person, and neither involved an ability judgment. There is considerable evidence suggesting that children generally do not use group normative information or social comparative feedback to assess their intellectual ability until after the first year or two of elementary school (Aboud, 1985; Boggiano & Ruble, 1979; Nicholls, 1978; Ruble, Boggiano, Feldman, & Loebl, 1980; Ruble, Parsons, & Ross, 1976).

A study by Ruble et al. (1980) is illustrative. First- and second-grade children were given tasks in groups of four. The outcome of the task was ambiguous so that the experimenter could give children predetermined but believable information about their own and the other three children's performance. Subjects were either told that they had succeeded or that they had failed; in each of the success and failure conditions, children were either given no information about the other children's performance, were told that all of the other children had succeeded, or were told that all of the other children had failed. The first graders' subsequent ratings of their ability on the task were affected by whether they succeeded or failed, but not by the information about other children's performance. Second graders' ratings were influenced both by their own outcome and the normative information.

Research is inconsistent with regard to the exact age at which children use social comparison information to judge their ability. Ruble's research (e.g., Ruble et al., 1980) suggests that this does not occur until about the second grade. However, a few studies have found that kindergartners' (Stipek, 1987) and first graders' (Levine, Snyder, & Mendez-Caratini, 1982) self-evaluations are affected by information about how their performance compares to other children's. And by kindergarten, children are able to correctly order themselves and other children in terms of their performance or ability on a concrete observable dimension (e.g., running; Morris & Nemcek, 1982).

Research is needed to make sense of the inconsistencies in the results of studies of social comparison. Existing studies have, for the most part, asked *whether* young children use social comparative information in their judgments of their abilities. In future research, it would be fruitful to examine systematically the conditions under which children do or do not use such information. We suspect that such variables as the nature of the information (e.g., whether it is concrete or abstract, presented visually or verbally) and children's motivation for comparing (e.g., whether they are choosing a partner for future tasks as in the Levine et al. study; whether they are evaluating real classmates or hypothetical peers) affect their use of social comparative information. But these and other variables have not been systematically varied in extant studies.

While the evidence on whether children use social comparison to evaluate their competencies in the first few grades of school is inconsistent, there is clear evidence of a sharp increase in children's use of social comparison information in about the second or third grade (Aboud, 1985; France-Kaatrude & Smith, 1985; Ruble et al., 1980; Stipek & Tannatt, 1984). Above about the second grade, children's ability judgments are consistently affected by normative information, and they begin to explain their self-perceptions of smartness in social comparative terms.

Furthermore, there is evidence that older children are more skilled than younger children at obtaining (Ruble, Feldman, & Boggiano, 1976) and interpreting (Aboud, 1985; Ruble, 1983) social comparative information. First, upper-elementary-school children are more likely than younger children to compensate for nonability-related performance factors when inferring ability from social comparison information. For example, in one study, fifth but not second graders compensated for a disadvantage in the amount of time they were given to work on a test in judging their performance relative to a peer (Aboud, 1985).

Second, as children develop, their social comparison choices become more differentiated. Whereas children in the primary grades have been characterized as making indiscriminate comparisons (e.g., Suls & Sanders, 1982), by fifth and sixth grade, children show more interest in comparing with a peer than with an inferior younger or a superior older child (France-Kaatrude & Smith, 1984). Presumably older children are more discriminatory because they have developed a concept of ability as a stable and valued trait, and they are more likely to use social comparison for the purpose of judging their own ability (Ruble, 1983). Their normative, "entity" definition of ability requires them to hold constant nonability-related factors affecting performance, such as age or experience. They compare performance with peers that are similar to themselves in nonability-related factors because they understand that this comparison provides the clearest information on their own ability.

Although upper-elementary-school students are more likely to incorporate social comparative information in their judgments of competence, and more likely to make appropriate comparisons and inferences, they do not necessarily display more overt social comparison behavior than children in the earlier grades. Ruble and Frey (1987) describe a developmental shift from "overt to covert comparison, and from boorish braggadocio to questions requiring little self-disclosure" (Ruble & Frey, 1987, p. 94).

Students' attention to social comparison information increases even more upon entry to junior high school (Feldlaufer, Midgley, & Eccles, 1988). For example, students say that they compare their report card grades with others more after the transition to junior high school than before. Similarly, according to teacher reports, seventh graders ask, "How am I doing in math compared to other students?" more frequently than do sixth graders. As with elementary-school-age children, the increased concern regarding social norms is not accompanied by increases in overt competition (Feldlaufer et al., 1988).

During the junior and senior high school years, there may be an increasing tendency for students to use evaluative criteria that place their achievement into a broader context than their classroom. For example, students' perceptions of competence may be increasingly influenced by their official standing within their school according to grade point average, and their success in gaining and maintaining membership in school-wide honor societies. By the final years of high school, students' competence perceptions may be affected by standardized achievement test scores, the outcomes of scholarship competitions, college admissions, and other indicators of their achievement in relation to national norms. For most, a shift toward use of such criteria in evaluating competence would provoke further decreases in their perceptions of their ability.

Summary
The developmental shifts found in the criteria children use to assess their academic ability and in their bases for comparison (see Tables 2, 3), in conjunction with changes in their definition of academic ability, help explain the average developmental decline in ability ratings. Children from preschool until

TABLE 2

CRITERIA FOR ASSESSING ABILITY

Preschool–Second Grade	Third–Sixth Grade	Junior High
	Social Reinforcement	
At face value	At face value	Interpreted as a function of other factors, such as the difficulty of the task
	Mastery	
But *not* nonmastery	And nonmastery	And nonmastery
	Symbols	
Stars and happy faces, but not grades	Grades	Grades
	Objective Feedback	
Positive only	Positive and negative	Positive and negative
	Effort	
More effort indicates higher ability	More effort indicates higher ability	More effort for the same outcome indicates lower ability

about the second grade apparently base their ability judgments primarily on social reinforcement and on mastery. As we shall see in the next section, social reinforcement is probably plentiful in early childhood, and since young children accept praise at face value, its importance is not diminished by the fact that the task was easy or that all children were praised. All young children's skills improve. Given their definition of ability as something that is improved by practice and effort, "non-mastery" indicates, for the younger child, only that ability has not yet been demonstrated. All that is needed is a little more prac-

tice. Consequently, if young children focus on such intraindividual comparisons, they should conclude that they are competent.

As Nicholls and Miller (1984b) point out, development brings its discontents. Children develop a definition of ability as a stable trait, unaffected by effort, and their criteria for evaluation shift from intraindividual to social comparisons. Consequently, some children must conclude that they are low in ability. The relatively low-performing older children's only hope of maintaining perceptions of themselves as competent is to take across-

TABLE 3

BASIS OF COMPARISON

Preschool–Second Grade	Third–Sixth Grade	Junior High
	Intraindividual	
Over time (improvement, but *not* failure to improve)	Over time (improvement *and* failure to improve)	Over time (improvement *and* failure to improve)
...	Across domain	Across domain
	Interindividual	
With one other person	With multiple others	With multiple others
Very narrow frame of reference	Narrow frame of reference (primarily classroom)	Broad frame of reference (school and beyond)

domain comparisons into consideration, and, according to Mac Iver's (1984, 1987) research, this is exactly what some students do.

The role of cognitive development has been emphasized in the literature on age-related changes in children's ability judgments (e.g., Nicholls & Miller, 1984b; Surber, 1984). However, researchers have also speculated that changes in children's definitions of competence and self-ratings of ability are to some degree a consequence of systematic shifts in the activities, organization, evaluation practices, and ability-grouping patterns that children are exposed to in school (e.g., Eccles, Midgley, & Adler, 1984; Higgins & Parsons, 1983; Rosenholtz & Simpson, 1984b; Stipek, 1984a; Stipek & Daniels, 1988). The next section describes what is known about age-related changes in children's educational environments that might contribute to the developmental shifts described above in children's assessments of their intellectual competence.

Age-related Change in the Availability and Salience of Ability-relevant Information

Preschool and Early Elementary School Years

In the family setting, most children have the opportunity to compare their performance with both older and younger people and to discover that there are striking improvements in performance and ability level as one gets older (Eccles et al., 1984). Upon entry into an age-stratified environment, children are able to make the additional discovery that there are differences in performance, even among individuals of the same age. However, in typical preschools, and to some degree in early elementary classrooms, individual differences in performance are not emphasized and most evaluative feedback is positive.

Preschool teachers usually accept a child's product as satisfactory as long as the child has devoted a reasonable amount of time to working on it (Apple & King, 1978; Potter, 1982; see also Blumenfeld et al., 1982). Although young children receive some "midtask corrections," most children end up receiving positive feedback on most tasks because they eventually complete the tasks, and nearly all products are considered acceptable. Furthermore, observation studies suggest that preschool teachers rarely comment negatively on a child's ability. Given the uniformly high levels of positive performance feedback most preschool students receive and teachers' emphasis on individual accomplishments, it is not surprising that (1) they have high perceptions of their intellectual competence, and (2) their self-assessments do not emphasize social comparisons.

The nature of tasks given to children shifts gradually across the early elementary school years (Eccles et al., 1984; Higgins & Parsons, 1983; Rosenholtz & Simpson, 1984b). Tasks involving intellectual skills become more frequent. Children are increasingly given tasks where there is a single "right answer" and where success and failure on the task are not obvious without outside evaluation. They encounter ability grouping (Hallinan & Sorensen, 1983) and other public evidence (e.g., star charts) of their own and classmates' skills (Higgins & Parsons, 1983). Finally, children are increasingly asked to do the same tasks at the same time (using the same methods) as their classmates. This shift toward regimented intellectual tasks reinforces young children's heavy reliance on adults' evaluations and makes it easier for children to make meaningful comparisons with classmates.

In spite of the shift toward standardized intellectual tasks and the increasing availability of relative performance information in the first few years of elementary school, the emphasis throughout this period is primarily on children's acquisition of the "student" role, and not on academic performance. Teachers in early elementary school focus their socializing on good work habits, respect toward teachers, and consideration and cooperativeness toward classmates (Blumenfeld, Hamilton, Bossert, Wessels, & Meece, 1983; Brophy & Evertson, 1978; Higgins & Parsons, 1983). Consistent with this emphasis, teachers reinforce effort and hold students accountable for finishing their work more frequently in the earlier than in the later grades (Blumenfeld et al., 1983). Similarly, the report card grades that early elementary school teachers assign are mediated by the child's conduct to a much larger degree than in later grades (e.g., Entwistle & Hayduk, 1978). And although normative information is more available in the early elementary grades than in preschool, it is not usually made salient. The academic environment, therefore, supports young children's inclusion of social behavior, work habits, and effort in their definitions of competence, and it usually does not encourage social comparison.

Upper Elementary School

During the upper elementary school years, the amount of positive reinforcement declines (Pintrich & Blumenfeld, 1985).

Evaluation also becomes more frequent and increasingly emphasizes students' relative performance (Blumenfeld et al., 1983; Gullickson, 1985; Hill & Wigfield, 1984). During early elementary school, any hardworking and respectful student is likely to receive good grades, but in upper elementary school, as grades come to emphasize one's relative performance on tests and assignments, the grades of average- and below-average-ability students start to fall. The impact of declining grades on these students' self-perceptions may be exacerbated by concurrent increases in the use of competitive activities in the classroom (e.g., spelling bees, math "baseball," science fair contests, etc.). Ability grouping is also more likely to be extended to subjects other than reading in the upper elementary grades. All of these practices conspire to foster interindividual comparisons.

As formal performance evaluations become more frequent and ability grouping is extended to more subjects, it also becomes easier for students to make "across-domain" comparisons in their performance. Research has shown that the more frequently teachers assign grades on classwork, the more their students rely on across-domain comparisons to infer ability (Mac Iver, 1987). Grades facilitate across-domain comparisons because they provide a standardized summary of performance in each subject. Similarly, multiple-subject ability grouping allows students to compare the level of their group placement across subjects.

Children are also exposed to a broader range of activities, tasks, and subjects in upper elementary school than in the primary grades (Higgins & Parsons, 1983). These age-related increases in the breadth of children's activities may contribute to the increase in self-concept differentiation that occurs during this period (Marsh et al., 1984), as well as an increase in across-domain comparisons.

In the upper elementary grades, teacher-student relationships become "much less personalized and more focused on teaching and learning" (Brophy & Evertson, 1978, p. 312). Private social interactions with the teacher tend to be replaced by briefer, less personal public exchanges. The changes in teacher-student interaction patterns coincide with a decrease in individualization and an increase in the use of whole-group instruction (Brophy & Evertson, 1978). This shift in the nature of teacher-student interactions may prompt students to decrease their reliance on informal social feedback as a criterion for self-evalua-

tion and lead them to focus increasingly on grades.

In many instances, the upper elementary students within a given age/grade cohort will have spent several years together (Higgins & Parsons, 1983, p. 25). They will, therefore, have had repeated opportunities over a period of several years to compare their performances (and their ability-group placements) with a fairly constant set of "similar others." The high stability of students' relative performance and ability-group assignments within and across school years (Hallinan & Sorensen, 1983) may foster the development of a concept of ability as a stable trait that is differentiated from effort. After observing high "interteacher reliability" in the performance evaluations and ability-group placements that teachers have given them over the years, low-ability students will find it increasingly difficult to maintain high levels of optimism regarding their future competence.

Middle and Junior High School

Changes in task organization at the middle or junior high level are a continuation of changes that began in elementary school (Feldlaufer et al., 1988; Rounds & Osaki, 1982). In junior high school, small-group instruction is no longer common and individualized instruction is hardly ever observed. All students within a given classroom typically work on the "same assignment at the same time, using the same textbooks, and receiving the same homework assignment" (Eccles & Midgley, in press). Furthermore, there is little variety in the nature of these common tasks. The tasks used to teach a given subject tend to tap a narrow range of students' skills and usually define only a limited range of performance dimensions as being important for judging success or failure.

It has been suggested that the visibility and usefulness of social comparison is higher under these conditions than when students are allowed to choose from several alternative assignments that vary somewhat on the sorts of skills necessary for success. Social comparison is more salient when task structures are undifferentiated because undifferentiated task structures reduce intraindividual variation in performance across time, while making inequalities in performance across students more interpretable (outcomes are more comparable, more salient, and more public; e.g., Blumenfeld et al., 1982; Marshall & Weinstein, 1984; Pepitone, 1972; Rosenholtz & Simpson, 1984a, 1984b; Rosenholtz & Wilson, 1980).

TABLE 4

EDUCATIONAL CONTEXT

Preschool–Second Grade	Third–Sixth Grade	Junior High
	Evaluation	
Corrective	Mastery and normative feedback	Normative feedback
Based on effort and completeness	Based on effort and performance (tests and assignments)	Based on performance (primarily tests)
Mostly positive	Positive and negative	Positive and negative (stringent)
	Tasks	
Individualized	Individualized and uniform	Uniform
	Class Structure	
Individualized and small groups	Small groups and whole class	Whole class
Within-class ability grouping in reading	Within-class ability grouping in reading and math	Between-class ability grouping
	Range of Activities	
Narrow	Broader	Broad
	Relationship with Teacher	
Individual, social interactions	Individual and group interactions; more focused on academic issues	Group interactions; formal; academic-related

Some evidence suggests that junior high school teachers use more stringent criteria in assessing student competency (Eccles & Midgley, in press). For example, students, on average, receive poorer grades and competency ratings in junior high school than in elementary school, even though their performance on cognitive and achievement tests generally improves (Finger & Silverman, 1966; Kavrell & Petersen, 1984; Nottlemann, 1987; Reuman, Mac Iver, Eccles, & Wigfield, 1987). Grades are also based more narrowly on test performance in junior high, compared to the multiple criteria (assignments, class discussion, papers) used in elementary school (Gullickson, 1985). Thus, students in junior high school have fewer opportunities to compensate for low test performance.

Summary

The task structures, evaluation practices, and teacher-student relationships in classrooms change as children progress through school in such a way as to increasingly emphasize individual differences in performance (see Table 4). The shift toward whole-group instruction and uniformity in assignments increases the salience of and opportunities for social comparison. In conjunction with the shift toward more rigorous grading, this change in task structure makes it increasingly difficult for average- and below-average students to maintain high perceptions of competence.

Conclusion

It is clear from this review that developmental change in the way children evaluate ability is best understood in terms of a child-by-environment interaction. Consider, as an example, the development of a concept of ability as a normatively distributed, stable trait. An entity concept of ability requires certain cognitive competencies that are not fully developed until formal operations. Cognitive development, however, does not explain the whole story. Dweck and her colleagues (Dweck & Leggett, 1988) have found systematic differences among upper elementary school-age children in the degree to which they have an entity versus an incremental theory of ability. These individual differences are most likely related to variables in the achievement environments children have experienced—such as the degree of variability in tasks, the stability of ability groups, and the salience of social comparative information. Indeed, Rosenholtz and Simpson (1984b) argue that an entity concept of ability is, itself, a social construction perpetuated by a particular kind of educational context. Thus, cognitive development *allows* children to evaluate ability in terms of a stable, normatively distributed trait; the degree to which children actually develop an entity concept of ability probably depends on the achievement environment. We recommend future research that examines child-by-environment interactions directly, such as by assessing simultaneously the effects of age and the achievement context on children's evaluations of intellectual competence.

The research reviewed here also has practical implications. If children evaluate intellectual competence differently at different ages, then instructional practices that maximize self-confidence and positive motivation for children in one age group may not be appropriate for children in another age group. More developmental research that examines the effects of classroom practices on children's perceived competence and achievement behavior would help teachers tailor instructional approaches to optimize motivation in children of different ages.

References

Aboud, F. (1985). The development of a social comparison process in children. *Child Development, 56,* 682–688.

Apple, M., & King, N. (1978). What do schools teach? In G. Willis (Ed.), *Qualitative evaluation: Concepts and cases in curriculum criticism* (pp. 444–465). Berkeley, CA: McCutchan.

Ausubel, D., Schiff, H., & Glasser, E. (1952). A preliminary study of the developmental trends in socioempathy: Accuracy of perception of own and others' sociometric status. *Child Development, 23,* 111–128.

Bandura, A. (1982). Self-efficacy mechanism in human agency. *American Psychologist, 37,* 122–147.

Barker, G., & Graham, S. (1987). Developmental study of praise and blame as attributional cues. *Journal of Educational Psychology, 79,* 62–66.

Benenson, J., & Dweck, C. (1986). The development of trait explanations and self-evaluations in the academic and social domains. *Child Development, 57,* 1179–1187.

Blumenfeld, P., Hamilton, V., Bossert, S., Wessels, K., & Meece, J. (1983). Teacher talk and student thought: Socialization into the student role. In J. M. Levine & M. C. Wang (Eds.), *Teacher and student perceptions: Implications for learning* (pp. 143–192). Hillsdale, NJ: Erlbaum.

Blumenfeld, P., Pintrich, P., & Hamilton, V. (1986). Children's concepts of ability, effort, and conduct. *American Educational Research Journal, 23,* 95–104.

Blumenfeld, P., Pintrich, P., Meece, J., & Wessels, K. (1982). The formation and role of self-perceptions of ability in elementary classrooms. *Elementary School Journal, 82,* 401–420.

Boggiano, A., & Ruble, D. (1979). Competence and the overjustification effect: A developmental study. *Journal of Personality and Social Psychology, 37,* 1462–1468.

Brophy, J., & Evertson, C. (1978). Context variables in teaching. *Educational Psychologist, 12,* 310–316.

Covington, M., & Berry, R. (1976). *Self-worth and school learning.* New York: Holt, Rinehart & Winston.

Dweck, C. (1986). Motivational processes affecting learning. *American Psychologist, 41,* 1040–1048.

Dweck, C., & Bempechat, J. (1983). Children's theories of intelligence: Consequences for learning. In S. Paris, G. Olson, & H. Stevenson (Eds.). *Learning and motivation in the classroom* (pp. 239–255). Hillsdale, NJ: Erlbaum.

Dweck, C., & Reppucci, N. (1973). Learned helplessness and reinforcement responsibility in children. *Journal of Personality and Social Psychology, 25,* 109–116.

Dweck, C., & Leggett, E. (1988). A social-cognitive approach to motivation and personality. *Psychological Review, 95,* 256–273.

Eccles, J. (1986). *Wave 3 codebook for student and individual assessment questionnaires: Transitions in early adolescence project* (V5157: SA4Rank Self in Math). (Available from Jacquelynne Eccles, 5201 Institute for Social Research, University of Michigan, Ann Arbor, MI 48106-1248.)

Eccles, J., Adler, T., Futterman, R., Goff, S., Kaczala, M., Meece, J., & Midgley, C. (1983). Expectancies, values, and academic behaviors. In J. Spence (Ed.), *Achievement and achievement motivation* (pp. 75–146). San Francisco: W. H. Freeman.

Eccles, J., & Midgley, C. (in press). Stage environment fit: Developmentally appropriate classrooms for early adolescents. In R. P. Ames & C. Ames (Eds.), *Research on motivation in education: Vol. 3.* New York: Academic Press.

Eccles, J., Midgley, C., & Adler, T. (1984). Grade-related changes in the school environment: Effects on achievement motivation. In J. G. Nicholls (Ed.), *Advances in motivation and achievement: Vol. 3. The development of achievement motivation* (pp. 283–331). Greenwich, CT: JAI.

Entwistle, D., & Hayduk, L. (1978). *Too great expectations: Young children's academic outlook*. Baltimore, MD: Johns Hopkins University Press.

Eshel, Y., & Klein, Z. (1981). Development of academic self-concept of lower-class and middle-class primary school children. *Journal of Educational Psychology*, **73**, 287–293.

Feldlaufer, H., Midgley, C., & Eccles, J. (1988). Student, teacher, and observer perceptions of the classroom environment before and after the transition to junior high school. *Journal of Early Adolescence*, **8**, 133–156.

Finger, J., & Silverman, M. (1966). Changes in academic performance in junior high school. *Personnel and Guidance Journal*, **45**, 157–164.

France-Kaatrude, A., & Smith, W. (1984, May). *Social comparison and task persistence in children*. Paper presented at Midwestern Psychological Association, Chicago.

France-Kaatrude, A., & Smith, W. (1985). Social comparison, task motivation, and the development of self-evaluative standards in children. *Developmental Psychology*, **21**, 1080–1089.

Frey, K., & Ruble, D. (1987). What children say about classroom performance: Sex and grade differences in perceived competence. *Child Development*, **58**, 1066–1078.

Graziano, W. (1986, May). *Children's peer relations: A natural boundary area for social and developmental psychology*. Invited address presented at the annual meeting of the Western Psychological Association, Seattle.

Gullickson, A. (1985). Student evaluation techniques and their relationship to grade and curriculum. *Journal of Educational Research*, **79**, 96–100.

Hallinan, M., & Sorensen, A. (1983). The formation and stability of instructional groups. *American Sociological Review*, **48**, 838–851.

Harari, O., & Covington, M. (1981). Reactions to achievement from a teacher and a student perspective: A developmental analysis. *American Educational Research Journal*, **18**, 15–28.

Harter, S. (1982a). A cognitive-developmental approach to children's use of affect and trait labels. In F. Serafica (Ed.), *Social cognition and social relations in context* (pp. 27–61). New York: Guilford.

Harter, S. (1982b). The perceived competence scale for children. *Child Development*, **53**, 87–89.

Harter, S., & Pike, R. (1984). The pictorial scale of perceived competence and social acceptance for young children. *Child Development*, **55**, 1969–1982.

Harter, S., Whitesell, N., & Kowalski, P. (1987). *The effects of educational transitions on children's perceptions of competence and motivational orientation*. Manuscript submitted for publication.

Heckhausen, H. (1984). Emergent achievement behavior: Some early developments. In J. Nicholls (Ed.), *Advances in motivation and achievement: Vol. 3. The development of achievement motivation* (pp. 1–32). Greenwich, CT: JAI.

Heller, K., & Berndt, T. (1981). Developmental changes in the formation and organization of personality attributions. *Child Development*, **52**, 552–558.

Higgins, E., & Parsons, J. (1983). Social cognition and the social life of the child: Stages as subcultures. In E. T. Higgins, D. N. Ruble, & W. W. Hartup (Eds.), *Social cognition and social development: A sociocultural perspective* (pp. 15–62). New York: Cambridge University Press.

Hill, K., & Wigfield, A. (1984). Test anxiety: A major educational problem and what can be done about it. *Elementary School Journal*, **85**, 105–126.

Inhelder, B., & Piaget, J. (1958). *The growth of logical thinking from childhood to adolescence*. New York: Basic.

Karabenick, J., & Heller, K. (1976). A developmental study of effort and ability attributions. *Developmental Psychology*, **12**, 559–560.

Kavrell, S., & Petersen, A. (1984). Patterns of achievement in early adolescence. In M. L. Maher (Ed.), *Advances in motivation and achievement* (pp. 1–35). Greenwich, CT: JAI.

Kohlberg, L. (1969). Stage and sequence: The cognitive-developmental approach to socialization. In D. Goslin (Ed.), *Handbook of socialization theory and research* (pp. 347–480). Chicago: Rand-McNally.

Kun, A. (1977). Development of magnitude-covariation and compensation schemata in ability and effort attributions of performance. *Child Development*, **48**, 862–873.

Kun, A., Parsons, J., & Ruble, D. (1974). Development of integration processes using ability and effort information to predict outcome. *Developmental Psychology*, **10**, 721–732.

Levine, J., Snyder, H., & Mendez-Caratini, G. (1982). Task performance and interpersonal attraction in children. *Child Development*, **53**, 359–371.

Lewis, M., Wall, M., & Aronfreed, J. (1963). Developmental change in the relative values of social and nonsocial reinforcement. *Journal of Experimental Psychology*, **66**, 133–137.

Livesley, W., & Bromley, D. (1973). *Person perception in childhood and adolescence*. New York: Wiley.

Mac Iver, D. (1984, April). *Information use in self-assessments of ability*. Paper presented at the annual meeting of the American Educational Research Association, New Orleans.

Mac Iver, D. (1987). Classroom factors and student characteristics predicting students' use of achievement standards during ability self-assessment. *Child Development, 58,* 1258–1271.

Mac Iver, D. (1988). Classroom environments and the stratification of students' ability perceptions. *Journal of Educational Psychology, 80,* 495–505.

Marsh, H. (1986). Verbal and math self-concepts: An internal/external frame of reference model. *American Educational Research Journal, 23,* 129–149.

Marsh, H., Barnes, J., Cairns, L., & Tidman, M. (1984). Self-description questionnaire: Age and sex effects in the structure and level of self-concept for preadolescent children. *Journal of Educational Psychology, 76,* 940–956.

Marsh, H., Smith, I., & Barnes, J. (1985). Multidimensional self-concepts: Relationships with sex and academic achievement. *Journal of Educational Psychology, 77,* 581–596.

Marshall, H., & Weinstein, R. (1984). Classroom factors affecting students' self-evaluations: An interactional model. *Review of Educational Research, 54,* 301–325.

Meyer, W., Bachmann, M., Biermann, V., Hempelmann, P., Ploger, F., & Spiller, H. (1979). The informational value of evaluative behavior: Influence of praise and blame on perceptions of ability. *Journal of Educational Psychology, 71,* 259–268.

Miller, A. (1985). A developmental study of the cognitive basis of performance impairment after failure. *Journal of Personality and Social Psychology, 49,* 529–538.

Morris, W., & Nemcek, D. (1982). The development of social comparison motivation among preschoolers: Evidence of a stepwise progression. *Merrill-Palmer Quarterly, 28,* 413–425.

Mosatche, H., & Bragonier, P. (1981). An observational study of social comparison in preschoolers. *Child Development, 52,* 376–378.

Nicholls, J. (1978). The development of the concepts of effort and ability, perceptions of academic attainment and the understanding that difficult tasks require more ability. *Child Development, 49,* 800–814.

Nicholls, J. (1979). Development of perception of own attainment and causal attributions for success and failure in reading. *Journal of Educational Psychology, 71,* 94–99.

Nicholls, J. (1980). The development of the concept of difficulty. *Merrill-Palmer Quarterly, 26,* 271–281.

Nicholls, J., & Miller, A. (1984a). Conceptions of ability and achievement motivation. In R. Ames & C. Ames (Eds.), *Research on motivation in education: Vol. 1. Student motivation* (pp. 39–73). New York: Academic Press.

Nicholls, J., & Miller, A. (1984b). Development and its discontents: The differentiation of the concept of ability. In J. Nicholls (Ed.), *Advances in motivation and achievement: Vol. 3. The development of achievement motivation* (pp. 219–250). Greenwich, CT: JAI.

Nottlemann, E. (1987). Competence and self-esteem during transition from childhood to adolescence. *Developmental Psychology, 23,* 441–450.

Pepitone, E. (1972). Comparison behavior in elementary school children. *American Educational Research Journal, 9,* 45–63.

Piaget, J. (1932). *The moral judgment of the child.* London: Kegan Paul.

Piaget, J. (1950). *The psychology of intelligence.* New York: Harcourt, Brace.

Pintrich, P., & Blumenfeld, P. (1985). Classroom experience and children's self-perceptions of ability, effort, and conduct. *Journal of Educational Psychology, 77,* 646–657.

Potter, E. (1982, March). *Demands upon children regarding quality of achievement: Standard setting in preschool classrooms.* Paper presented at the annual meeting of the American Educational Research Association, New York.

Reuman, D. (1986). Motivational implications of ability grouping in sixth-grade mathematics: A strong inference approach to theories of achievement motivation. *Dissertation Abstracts International, 47,* 1315B. (University Microfilms No. 86-12, 609)

Reuman, D., Mac Iver, D., Eccles, J., & Wigfield, A. (1987, April). Change in students' mathematics motivation and behavior at the transition to junior high school. In C. Midgley (Chair), *Early adolescence: School, psychological, and social transitions.* Symposium conducted at the annual meeting of the American Educational Research Association, Washington, DC.

Rholes, W., Blackwell, J., Jordan, C., & Walters, C. (1980). A developmental study of learned helplessness. *Developmental Psychology, 16,* 616–624.

Rholes, W., & Ruble, D. (1984). Children's understanding of dispositional characteristics of others. *Child Development, 55,* 550–560.

Rosenholtz, S., & Simpson, C. (1984a). Classroom organization and student stratification. *Elementary School Journal, 85,* 21–37.

Rosenholtz, S., & Simpson, C. (1984b). The formation of ability conceptions: Developmental trend or social construction? *Review of Educational Research, 54,* 31–63.

Rosenholtz, S., & Wilson, B. (1980). The effect of classroom structure on shared perceptions of ability. *American Educational Research Journal, 17,* 75–82.

Rounds, T., & Osaki, S. (1982). *The social organization of classroom: An analysis of sixth- and seventh-grade activity structures* (Report EPSSP-82-5). San Francisco: Far West Laboratory.

Ruble, D. (1983). The development of social comparison processes and their role in achievement-related self-socialization. In E. T. Higgins, D. N. Ruble, W. W. Hartup (Eds.), *Social cognition and social development: A sociocultural perspective* (pp. 134–157). New York: Cambridge University Press.

Ruble, D., Boggiano, A., Feldman, N., & Loebl, J. (1980). A developmental analysis of the role of social comparison in self-evaluation. *Developmental Psychology, 16,* 105–115.

Ruble, D., Feldman, N., & Boggiano, A. (1976). Social comparison between young children in achievement situations. *Developmental Psychology, 16,* 105–115.

Ruble, D., & Frey, K. (1987). Social comparison and self-evaluation in the classroom: Developmental changes in knowledge and function. In J. C. Masters & W. P. Smith (Eds.), *Social comparison, social justice, and relative deprivation: Theoretical, empirical, and policy perspectives* (pp. 81–104). Hillsdale, NJ: Erlbaum.

Ruble, D., Parsons, J., & Ross, J. (1976). Self-evaluative responses of children in an achievement setting. *Child Development, 47,* 990–997.

Simmons, R., Blyth, D., Van Cleave, E., & Bush, D. (1979). Entry into early adolescence: The impact of school structure, puberty, and early dating on self-esteem. *American Sociological Review, 44*(6), 948–967.

Simmons, R., Rosenberg, M., & Rosenberg, F. (1973). Disturbance in the self-image at adolescence. *American Sociological Review, 39*(5), 553–568.

Spear, P., & Armstrong, S. (1978). Effects of performance expectancies created by peer comparison as related to social reinforcement, task difficulty, and age of child. *Journal of Experimental and Child Psychology, 25,* 254–266.

Stipek, D. (1981). Children's perceptions of their own and their classmates' ability. *Journal of Educational Psychology, 73,* 404–410.

Stipek, D. (1984a). The development of achievement motivation. In R. Ames & C. Ames (Eds.), *Research on motivation in education: Vol. 1. Student motivation* (pp. 145–174). New York: Academic Press.

Stipek, D. (1984b). Young children's performance expectations: Logical analysis or wishful thinking? In J. Nicholls (Ed.), *The development of achievement motivation* (pp. 33–56). Greenwich, CT: JAI.

Stipek, D. (1987). Emotional responses to objective and normative performance feedback. *Journal of Applied Developmental Psychology, 8,* 183–195.

Stipek, D. (1988). *Motivation to learn: From theory to practice.* Englewood Cliffs, NJ: Prentice-Hall.

Stipek, D., & Daniels, D. (1988). Declining perceptions of competence: A consequence of changes in the child or the educational environment? *Journal of Educational Psychology, 80,* 352–356.

Stipek, D., & Hoffman, J. (1980). Development of children's performance-related judgments. *Child Development, 51,* 912–914.

Stipek, D., & Tannatt, L. (1984). Children's judgments of their own and their peers' academic competence. *Journal of Educational Psychology, 76,* 75–84.

Suls, J., & Sanders, G. (1982). Self-evaluation through social comparison: A developmental analysis. In L. Wheeler (Ed.), *Review of personality and social psychology* (Vol. 3, pp. 171–197). Beverly Hills, CA: Sage.

Surber, C. (1980). The development of reversible operations in judgments of ability, effort, and performance. *Child Development, 51,* 1018–1029.

Surber, C. (1984). The development of achievement-related judgment processes. In J. Nicholls (Ed.), *Advances in motivation and achievement: Vol. 3. The development of achievement motivation* (pp. 137–184). Greenwich, CT: JAI.

Weiner, B. (1986). *An attributional theory of motivation and emotion.* New York: Springer-Verlag.

Weinstein, R., Marshall, H., Sharp, L., & Botkin, M. (1987). Pygmalion and the student: Age and classroom differences in children's awareness of teacher expectations. *Child Development, 58,* 1079–1093.

Weinstein, R., & Middlestadt, S. (1979). Student perceptions of teacher interactions with male high and low achievers. *Journal of Educational Psychology, 71,* 421–431.

Werner, H. (1957). The concept of development from a comparative and organismic point of view. In D. Harris (Ed.), *The concept of development* (pp. 125–148). Minneapolis: University of Minnesota Press.

Yussen, S., & Kane, P. (1985). Children's conception of intelligence. In S. R. Yussen (Ed.), *The growth of reflection in children* (pp. 207–241). Orlando, FL: Academic Press.

Multiple Choice:

1. Stipek and Mac Iver suggest that the trend for children to view their abilities negatively as they progress through elementary school and into junior high school is due to:

    A. biological changes at this time.
    B. changes in the classroom at this time.
    C. children's gender.
    D. all of the above.

2. Research indicates that as children get older, they:

    A. become more likely to compare their performance to that of others.
    B. view schoolwork as more important.
    C. pay less attention to the feedback that their teachers give them.
    D. get stars and happy faces instead of grades.

Essays:

1. Imagine that you are a fifth grade teacher. What practices might you implement to help your students maintain the positive self-perceptions they had when they were younger?

2. What might some of the benefits be of older children's negative perceptions of their abilities? That is, how might older children's views of themselves be more beneficial than younger children's views?

ARTICLE 17

Children's Reasoning about Interpersonal and Moral Conflicts

Judith G. Smetana, Melanie Killen, and Elliot Turiel

Reprinted from: *Child Development*, 1991, *62*, 629-644.
Copyright © 1991 by the Society for Research in Child Development.
Reprinted with permission.

Heading the list of universal goals of parents is the survival and health of their children. Almost as prominent a goal is that their children should share their moral and ethical values. The thought that our children might not adopt the moral principles we hold dear is much more disturbing than the idea that they might differ from us in almost any other way.

Not surprisingly, many developmental psychologists have been concerned with issues of moral development. The best-known theorist in this domain is Lawrence Kohlberg, who proposed qualitatively distinct stages in the development of moral judgment. The stages progress from judgments about moral dilemmas based on the consequences of actions to judgments based on conformity to social rules to judgments based on abstract ethical principles.

Carol Gilligan has taken issue with Kohlberg's stage theory of moral judgment, arguing that it is gender-biased. She claims that for females, morality is defined less in terms of justice and rights and more in terms of interpersonal commitment and concern for others.

The authors of this article studied school children's judgments about a variety of situations involving conflicts between justice and interpersonal relations. They report that both boys and girls of all the ages they studied used both justice and interpersonal considerations in their reasoning. Which particular concern was uppermost depended on the specific situation.

Children's Reasoning about Interpersonal and Moral Conflicts

Judith G. Smetana

University of Rochester

Melanie Killen

Wesleyan University

Elliot Turiel

University of California, Berkeley

SMETANA, JUDITH G.; KILLEN, MELANIE; and TURIEL, ELLIOT. *Children's Reasoning about Interpersonal and Moral Conflicts.* CHILD DEVELOPMENT, 1991, **62**, 629–644. 2 studies were conducted to determine if children make judgments about both justice and interpersonal relations in conflictful situations. In Study 1, 48 subjects (24 males and 24 females) in the third, sixth, and ninth grades (mean ages = 8.40, 11.38, 14.38 years) were administered 2 stories entailing conflicts between justice and interpersonal concerns. Children judged and justified acts in 4 conditions systematically varying interpersonal and justice concerns. Children generally gave priority to justice and rights over friendship, based primarily on considerations of welfare or rights. In Study 2, 76 subjects (39 males and 37 females) in the third, sixth, and ninth grades (mean ages = 9.08, 12.10, 14.92 years) were presented with 3 stories entailing conflicts between justice and interpersonal relations. Subjects gave greater priority to interpersonal considerations in Study 2 than in Study 1, and their evaluations varied according to the salience of the different concerns. In both studies, few gender differences were obtained. The results demonstrate that across development, concerns with justice and interpersonal relationships coexist in judgments of male and female children, and that the ways they are applied depend on the situation.

A complex and vexing problem for moral theory and research on social development is the connection between interpersonal relationships and particularistic or generalized moral obligations. Interpersonal and moral considerations are important aspects of social interactions that can be in conflict. On the one hand, it is recognized that persons in close relationships (e.g., friends, family) have special obligations to each other. On the other hand, concerns with issues like justice, rights, and welfare are thought to entail obligations that often transcend particular interpersonal ties. For example, from the moral point of view, there are problems with favoritism in the distribution of goods, or with granting certain rights to and ensuring the welfare of only some people (such as friends, family, or members of one's racial and ethnic group) and not others. At the same time, subordinating the interests of close relations in favor of abstract moral claims of strangers is problematic, certainly from a subjective perspective, and perhaps from an ethical one (Scheffler, 1988; Williams, 1981).

The link between interpersonal relationships and considerations of justice, rights, or welfare has been considered in several approaches to social and moral development (e.g., Damon, 1977; Selman, 1980). In particular, there is an ongoing debate regarding how to best characterize the development of justice and interpersonal concerns. Gilligan (1982) has argued that Kohlberg's (1969, 1971) formulation of stages of moral development fails to adequately distinguish a morality of justice from a morality of care in interpersonal concerns and that, in Kohlberg's sequence, the latter is relegated to lower stages. Gilligan and her colleagues (e.g., Gilligan & Attanucci, 1988) propose that interpersonal concerns and jus-

We thank Patricia Barasch, Jennifer Lewis, Kathleen McBrien, Toni Saunders, Loree Vaillancour, and Jenny Yau for their assistance with the research. Reprint requests should be sent to Judith G. Smetana, Graduate School of Education and Human Development, University of Rochester, Rochester, NY 14627.

tice constitute two distinct types of moral orientation linked to gender, and that each type can take a different developmental trajectory in different individuals. For the most part, morality in males is dominated by concerns with justice and rights; for females it is dominated by concerns with care in interpersonal relationships.[1]

In the present research, we explored the proposition that concerns with interpersonal relationships and justice coexist within individuals (males and females) across development, and that the ways they are applied or coordinated may partially depend on parameters of the situation in which judgments are made. This perspective is adopted from research demonstrating that children form domains of social knowledge, including morality (justice, rights, welfare), social convention, and psychological issues (Nucci, 1981; Smetana, 1985; Turiel, 1983; Turiel, Smetana, & Killen, 1991). The research indicates that individuals hold heterogeneous social orientations and coordinate and weigh different situational features when evaluating situations that entail social conflicts.

For most people, maintaining and fostering interpersonal relationships is a central social consideration. However, judgments about justice or welfare can apply to persons in close relationships and to those with lesser or no interpersonal ties. Therefore, concerns with interpersonal relations can be in conflict with justice, rights, or welfare considerations in at least two ways. Justice or welfare considerations can conflict with an interpersonal concern that is morally neutral or even negative (e.g., giving priority to a friend in distributing resources when a stranger has a more just claim). There also

can be a conflict in the application of justice or welfare considerations in interpersonal and impersonal relationships (e.g., choosing between helping a sibling or a stranger when both are in need). If interpersonal and justice considerations do coexist in males and females, then we would expect that the ways these considerations are applied by them will, at least in part, depend on the situation (e.g., the nature of the relationship, the salience of an injustice). For instance, in situations in which the justice considerations are not in strong conflict with interpersonal considerations, females and males might give priority to justice and rights over interpersonal concerns, whereas in other situations, they might give priority to maintaining interpersonal relationships over justice. Our proposition, therefore, differs from the proposition that features of the situations (for instance, the type of dilemma) interact with subjects' gender in influencing responses of justice or care (Miller & Luthar, 1989; Pratt et al., 1988; Rothbart et al., 1986; Walker et al., 1987), as well as the proposition that the moral status of each type of orientation is culturally determined (Miller, Bersoff, & Harwood, 1990).

Two studies were undertaken in the present research. One aim was to ascertain if females and males differentiate justice concerns from concerns with maintaining and fostering interpersonal relationships, and if their judgments are influenced by situational features. In this regard, we distinguished among maintenance of relationships, concerns with welfare (avoiding harm to others), and justice or rights. It should be noted, therefore, that this research was not designed as a direct test of Gilligan's

[1] Gilligan's (1977, 1982) propositions have led to a number of investigations and reanalyses of existing data. Lyons (1983) reports data supporting Gilligan's propositions, although her scoring system has been criticized by Walker, de Vries, and Trevethan (1987); other studies using Lyons's scoring system on small samples (Gilligan & Attanucci, 1988) suggest that most adults use both orientations, but that females are more likely to focus on care, and males are more likely to focus on justice. Based on an extensive review and meta-analysis of studies using Kohlberg's assessments, Walker (1984) concludes that the overall pattern of studies provides no evidence for the sex differences suggested by Gilligan. (Walker's conclusions have been questioned by Baumrind [1986]; also see Walker's [1986a] rebuttal.) Several studies (Pratt, Golding, & Hunter, 1984; Walker, 1986b, 1989; Walker et al., 1987) examining the justice versus care orientation as scored within Kohlberg's system failed to find support for the predicted pattern of sex differences. Gibbs, Arnold, and Burkhart (1984) found no overall stage differences between males and females, but they interpret significant differences in the types of reasons males and females at Stage 3 endorse as consistent with Gilligan's thesis. Finally, several studies have found that type of dilemma (e.g., hypothetical vs. real-life), rather than gender, influences justice and care responses (Pratt, Golding, Hunter, & Sampson, 1988; Rothbart, Hanley, & Albert, 1986), although other studies found more equivocal support for such differences (Ford & Lowery, 1986; Walker, 1989; Walker et al., 1987). These two sets of studies, however, found no sex differences within orientations.

hypotheses since our definition of interpersonal concerns differs somewhat from hers. Gilligan's care orientation focuses primarily on positive responsiveness to others (though her definition does include a concern with maintaining relationships). Study 1 examined interpersonal concerns in the context of avoiding harm or unfairness to others. This was done in order to assess whether children differentiate justice and concerns with maintaining relationships.

In Study 1, the situations initially presented to children posed justice or rights considerations in conflict with interpersonal expectations (from a close friend) serving motives of self-interest. Therefore, in these situations justice and rights considerations were in conflict with interpersonal expectations which did not have compelling welfare, justice, or rights components. In addition, the salience of each type of consideration was systematically varied either by changing the interpersonal relationship (from close friend to sibling to acquaintance) or by changing the magnitude of the violation of justice or rights. It was expected that females and males would give priority to the justice or rights considerations in the initially presented situations, and that their judgments would change in accord with shifts in the salience of the situational components.

Study 2 included stronger conflicts between justice and claims of an interpersonal nature by presenting situations in which the interpersonal expectations were positive in their intent and goals (not motivated by self-interest). Study 2 more directly pertains to Gilligan's care orientation than Study 1, since concerns with welfare, justice, and rights could be applied to interpersonal relations and impersonally. Our expectation was that situational features would be more important than gender in children's justice or interpersonal considerations.

Study 1

One aim of Study 1 was to ascertain whether, in certain situations, both males and females make judgments based primarily on justice and rights, even in interpersonal contexts. Toward this end, children were presented with hypothetical situations which posed the possibility of committing a transgression to maintain a friendship by furthering the self-interest of the friend. For each of two types of transgression, unequal distribution (fairness) and stealing (property

rights), children were presented with a conflict (referred to as the Initial Situation), and their evaluations and reasoning were assessed. A further aim of Study 1 was to determine whether judgments are influenced by changes in the salience of the interpersonal or fairness/rights components. The salience of the components in each situation were systematically varied by presenting children with different information.

The interpersonal components of the situations were varied by altering only the type of relationship depicted. In one variation, the interpersonal relationship was described as between acquaintances (thus decreasing the salience), and in the other, the relationship was described as involving siblings (thus increasing the salience). The salience of the fairness or rights components was varied by changing the magnitude of the transgression. In the situation pertaining to unequal distribution, the salience of the fairness component was increased by depicting the transgression as more severe than in the Initial Situation, whereas in the stealing situation, the transgression was depicted as less severe. As previous research has shown that stealing is evaluated as more wrong than unequal distribution (Smetana, 1981; Smetana, Kelly, & Twentyman, 1984), this was done to counterbalance differences between the two situations in the magnitude of the transgression depicted. Second, the type of transgression was varied to assess additional fairness or rights transgressions. Thus, in one variation, physical harm was pitted against maintaining a friendship, whereas in the other variation a trust violation was pitted against maintaining a friendship.

Subjects evaluated what the story protagonist should do and provided justifications for their choices. In addition, the ways that children weighed the different alternatives were also examined by coding whether children discussed both fairness/rights and the interpersonal choices in making their judgments or whether they considered only one alternative. This was done as a further test of the hypothesis that children separate and distinguish between fairness/rights and interpersonal issues.

It was expected that in the Initial Situations, children would generally judge that fairness or rights considerations should have priority over friendship expectations. However, in situations in which the interpersonal considerations were more salient (e.g., the sibling condition) and/or the fairness/rights components were less salient, it was expected that children would give priority to maintaining the interpersonal relationship. Finally, it was expected that children would give priority to justice/rights when these considerations were made more salient.

METHOD

Subjects

Subjects in this study were 48 children evenly divided into eight males and eight females at the third, sixth, and ninth grades (mean ages = 8.40, 11.38, 14.38 years, respectively). Subjects, who were middle class and from different ethnic groups, came from one elementary school and one junior high school in the San Francisco Bay area.

Procedure

Each subject was individually administered questions pertaining to two hypothetical situations by a female interviewer who was blind to the hypotheses of the study. The interviews took approximately 35 min and were tape-recorded and transcribed. Each situation began with an initial description of a conflict between a fairness or rights precept and an expectation from a friend (the Initial Situation). The story descriptions, questions, and salience variations are summarized in Table 1. Story 1 depicts a child who is requested by a friend to distribute candy unequally. Story 2 depicts a child who is asked by a friend to steal for her. For the Initial Situations, subjects were asked to make judgments as to what the protagonist should do and why. Then, subjects were asked about two interpersonal variations of the Initial Situation: whether the transgression should be done (a) for an acquaintance and (b) for a sibling (referred to as the Acquaintance and Sibling conditions, respectively). Finally, subjects were presented with two variations in fairness and rights that increased the magnitude of the transgressions. First, the amount of need was varied. In the distributive justice story, a situation of greater need of distribution (increased salience of fairness) was described, and the stealing story, a situation of less need for the goods (increased salience of property rights) was described (Greater Need and Less Need conditions, respectively). In another variation, the type of act was changed to depict physical harm (instead of distributive justice) and violating a trust (instead of stealing). These changes in the type of act were made to include more than one stimulus item for each story (Physical Harm and Trust Violation Conditions, respectively). For each story, five sets of judgments and justifications were obtained (Table 1).

Coding and Reliability

Responses were coded using three systems developed for this study but based on previous work (Davidson, Turiel, & Black, 1983; Killen, 1990). Twelve protocols, four from subjects at each grade level, were randomly selected to refine the coding systems.

TABLE 1

STORY THEMES AND CONDITIONS FOR STUDY 1

Sharing Story

Initial Situation: Bob brings candy to share with everyone. His close friend George does not want Bob to give candy to Tim. George and Tim do not get along and Tim has been picking on George.
Interpersonal condition—Acquaintance: Bob is asked by an acquaintance (who does not get along with Tim) to not share with Tim.
Interpersonal condition—Sibling: Bob is asked by his brother (who does not get along with Tim) to not share with Tim.
Greater Need condition: Bob, who is in charge of distributing lunches, does not give one to Tim because he had picked on George.
Physical Harm condition: Bob inflicts physical harm on Tim to please George.

Stealing Story

Initial Situation: Pat asks her close friend Diane to steal a set of pens accessible to Diane and needed by Pat.
Interpersonal condition—Acquaintance: Diane is asked by an acquaintance to take pens.
Interpersonal condition—Sibling: Diane is asked by her sister to take pens.
Less Need condition: Diane is asked to take a pack of gum for her friend.
Trust condition: Diane is asked to break a promise in order to engage in an activity with her friend.

The coders, all of whom were females, were unaware of the study's hypotheses and subjects' gender. First, *judgments* as to what the protagonist should do were coded dichotomously as (1) affirming the choice of fairness (sharing) or rights (not stealing), or (2) affirming the interpersonal choice. The second coding, referred to as *coordination of components*, assessed the extent to which children integrated different choices when evaluating the conflicts. Responses were coded into two categories: a focus on both considerations and a focus on only one element. Third, *justifications* for choices were coded into five categories: (a) *fairness-welfare*: fairness ("it's not fair"), physical welfare ("she'll get hurt"), and psychological welfare ("he'll feel bad"); (b) *interpersonal*: maintain friendship/familial relationships or establish friendship ("it's the best thing to do so that they can stay friends"); (c) *psychological*: dispositional or personality characteristics of an actor as basis for evaluating an act ("if he doesn't give the candy to George he would become a greedy person and grow up to be mean"); (d) *conventional*: violation of a social norm ("he would be breaking the school rule"); and (e) *personal*: act within individual jurisdiction ("he can do whatever he wants; it's up to him to decide"). In coding justifications, we followed the procedure used in previous research (Davidson et al., 1983) of combining fairness and welfare responses (welfare is defined as acts that negatively affect another's physical or psychological well-being). There were no differences on the major study variables (age, sex, or condition) between fairness and welfare responses. In Story 1, fairness and welfare responses occurred in equal frequencies. Story 2 resulted in greater use of fairness (79%) than welfare (21%) responses.

Interrater reliability between two coders using 12 protocols in coding judgments, coordination of components, and justifications (using Cohen's kappa) was .80, .83, and .82, respectively.

RESULTS

Judgments

Table 2 displays the percentage of children at each age who give priority to sharing equally (Story 1) and not stealing (Story 2) for each condition. Responses for each story were analyzed by a 3 (grade) × 2 (sex) × 5 (salience condition) repeated-measures analysis of variance (ANOVA) with condition as the repeated measure. Responses

were arcsine-transformed to correct for nonnormality, which may sometimes occur with the use of percentages (Winer, 1971). In these and other analyses, Duncan multiple-range tests and Bonferroni *t* tests were performed to test for significant between-subjects and within-subjects effects, respectively.

Story 1: Sharing.—As can be seen in Table 2, for the most part the majority of subjects gave priority to the act of sharing (83% in the Initial Situation; 87% overall). However, responses did vary by salience condition, $F(4,164) = 13.98$, $p < .0001$. As expected, Bonferroni *t* tests showed that greater priority was given to avoiding the transgression in the Physical Harm condition (98%) than in the Initial Situation (83%) or in the Sibling condition (74%; p's < .005). In addition, greater priority was given to sharing in the Greater Need condition (94%) than in the Sibling condition ($p < .005$). There were no significant main effects for sex (females = 93%; males = 84%) or grade (91%, 88%, and 87% for third, sixth, and ninth grades, respectively), and sex did not interact significantly with condition or grade.

Story 2: Stealing.—As with sharing, there was a main effect for salience condition, $F(4,164) = 15.16$, $p < .0001$. As expected, Bonferroni *t* tests indicated that children more frequently gave priority to the prescription against stealing in the Acquaintance condition (89%) or in the Less Need condition (81%) than when asked to steal by a friend as described in the Initial Situation (51%; p's < .005). In addition, children more frequently judged it wrong to steal in the Acquaintance condition than in the Sibling condition (60%), or to break a promise in the Trust Violation condition (43%; p's < .005). Children also judged it more wrong to steal in the Less Need condition than to break a promise in the Trust Violation condition ($p < .005$). There was no significant main effect for sex (males = 58%, females = 70% giving priority to not stealing). However, responses varied by grade, $F(2,41) = 17.80$; $p < .0001$. Third graders gave greater priority to not stealing than did sixth and ninth graders (90%, 59%, 44%, respectively).

There was a significant grade × condition interaction, $F(8,164) = 2.21$, $p < .05$. In the Initial Situation, third graders gave greater priority to not stealing than did sixth or ninth graders, $F(2,41) = 6.68$, $p < .01$. In the Trust Violation condition, third graders

Child Development

TABLE 2

RESPONSES (in %) AFFIRMING SHARING AND NOT STEALING

STORY AND CONDITION	GRADE 3		GRADE 6		GRADE 9		
	Males	Females	Males	Females	Males	Females	TOTAL
Sharing story:							
Initial Situation	100	88	63	88	86	75	83
Interpersonal—Acquaintance	75	100	88	100	100	100	94
Interpersonal—Sibling	88	75	63	100	43	75	74
Greater Need	100	88	88	100	86	100	94
Physical Harm[a]	100	100	88	100	100	100	98
Stealing Story:							
Initial Situation	88	75	13	75	14	38	51
Interpersonal—Acquaintance	100	100	75	100	71	88	89
Interpersonal—Sibling	88	75	13	88	43	50	60
Less Need	100	100	63	88	71	63	81
Trust Violation[b]	88	88	50	25	0	0	43

[a] The Physical Harm condition was in place of Sharing.
[b] The Trust Violation condition was in place of Not Stealing.

more frequently judged it wrong to break a promise than did sixth or ninth graders, and sixth graders more frequently judged it wrong to break a promise than did ninth graders, $F(2,41) = 23.39$, $p < .0001$. Furthermore, in the Less Need condition, third graders gave greater priority to not stealing than did ninth graders, $F(2,41) = 3.19$, $p < .05$. A similar finding was obtained for the Sibling condition, which approached significance, $F(2,41) = 3.00$, $p < .06$.

Coordination of Components

In order to assess whether subjects considered the two components in arriving at their choices, analyses were performed on the percentage of responses entailing a consideration of both fairness/rights and interpersonal components. A 3 (grade) × 2 (sex) × 5 (salience condition) repeated-measures ANOVA with condition as the repeated measure was performed separately upon arcsine-transformed responses for each story.

Story 1: Sharing.—The majority of responses (72% overall) indicated a consideration of the two components in making judgments, although this varied by salience condition, as indicated by a significant main effect, $F(4,164) = 8.15$, $p < .0001$. Subjects more frequently considered both fairness and interpersonal components in the Initial Situation (92%) and the Sibling condition (81%) than in the Greater Need condition (50%).

Sex was not significant in this analysis. However, age differences were obtained. Sixth and ninth graders considered both components to a greater extent than did third

graders, $F(2,41) = 10.30$, $p < .001$ (79%, 84%, 52%, respectively). A grade × condition interaction, $F(8,164) = 3.24$, $p < .05$, indicated that differences occurred in the Acquaintance condition, $F(2,41) = 8.89$, $p < .001$, the Greater Need condition, $F(2,41) = 6.87$, $p < .01$, and the Physical Harm condition, $F(2,41) = 5.54$, $p < .01$. In the Acquaintance and Physical Harm conditions, sixth and ninth graders considered both elements to a greater extent than did third graders (82%, 94%, 37% in the Acquaintance condition; 88%, 72%, 37% in the Physical Harm condition); in the Greater Need condition, ninth graders considered both elements to a greater extent than did third graders (80%, 19%).

Story 2: Stealing.—In this story, too, the majority of responses (63%) indicated a consideration of both components. A main effect for salience condition, $F(4,164) = 7.77$, $p < .0001$, revealed that subjects considered both components to a greater extent in the Initial Situation (91%) than in the Acquaintance, Sibling, Less Need, and Trust Violation conditions (55%, 66%, 51%, 51%, respectively; p's < .0001). A main effect for grade, $F(2,41) = 6.23$, $p < .01$, indicated that, as with the previous story, sixth and ninth graders considered both components to a greater extent than did third graders (72%, 72%, 45%, respectively).

Justifications

The justifications were separated by subjects' choices in the stories. Table 3 presents the percentage of justification categories used by subjects at each grade and for

TABLE 3

JUSTIFICATIONS (in %) AFFIRMING SHARING AND NOT STEALING

	SHARING STORY			STEALING STORY		
Grade:	3	6	9	3	6	9
Initial Situation:						
Fairness-Welfare	60	33	40	69	44	23
Interpersonal	18	12	13	12	0	3
Psychological	18	33	30	0	0	3
Other	0	0	0	0	0	3
Interpersonal—Acquaintance:						
Fairness-Welfare	57	72	43	75	66	53
Interpersonal	14	9	50	9	6	23
Psychological	11	9	0	16	16	6
Other	0	3	7	0	0	0
Interpersonal-Sibling:						
Fairness-Welfare	47	41	26	59	25	37
Interpersonal	25	16	10	0	6	3
Psychological	9	22	23	22	19	3
Other	0	9	0	0	0	0
Need:[a]						
Fairness-Welfare	92	69	73	91	69	80
Interpersonal	2	3	3	0	0	0
Psychological	3	19	7	3	6	0
Other	0	0	10	6	0	0
Physical Harm/Trust Violation:[b]						
Fairness-Welfare	71	49	76	75	31	0
Interpersonal	15	9	10	6	0	0
Psychological	15	34	12	3	6	0
Other	0	0	0	3	0	0

[a] This condition depicted greater need for the Sharing story and Lesser Need for the Not Stealing story.

[b] The Physical Harm condition was in place of Sharing and the Trust Violation condition was in place of Not stealing.

each condition for the choice to share and not steal. (Because there were so few sex differences, responses for boys and girls are combined.) Since conventional and personal justifications were used infrequently, they were combined into an Other category and dropped from further analysis. Each justification could have been used with either choice in the story (e.g., the interpersonal justification for a sharing choice or a fairness-welfare justification for an interpersonal choice). The table shows that three categories (fairness-welfare, interpersonal, and psychological) were primarily used for the sharing and not stealing choices. For each story, separate 3 (grade) × 2 (sex) × 5 (salience condition) repeated-measures multivariate analyses of variance (MANOVAs) were performed on the arcsine-transformed proportions of responses in the fairness-welfare, interpersonal, and psychological categories.[2]

Three categories (fairness-welfare, interpersonal, and personal choice) were used in explaining the interpersonal choices of not sharing and not stealing. Given their low frequency, however, these data were not statistically analyzed.

Story 1: Sharing.—The MANOVA revealed differences in justifications for the choice of sharing, $F(2,38) = 43.96$, $p < .0001$; overall, fairness-welfare justifications (54%) were used more frequently than interpersonal (12%) or psychological (20%) justifications (p's $< .0001$). There was a significant main effect for salience condition in justifications on the MANOVA, $F(8,32) = 10.03$, $p < .0001$. Bonferroni t tests revealed that children more frequently used welfare-fairness justifications in the conditions with increased salience of the fairness component: they were used more in the Greater Need and Physical Harm conditions than in

[2] Analyses of covariance indicated that all significant effects remained statistically significant with story choice controlled.

the Initial Situation (p's $< .0001$) and in the Greater Need condition than in the Sibling condition ($p < .0001$). Children more frequently used interpersonal justifications in the Initial Situation and the Acquaintance condition than in the Greater Need condition (p's $< .005$). Psychological justifications were used more frequently in the Initial Situation than in the Acquaintance or Greater Need conditions (p's $< .005$). Finally, the MANOVA also revealed a significant salience condition × grade interaction in justifications, $F(16,64) = 3.04$, $p < .001$. There were grade × condition interactions for fairness-welfare justifications, $F(8,168) = 2.93$, $p < .01$, and interpersonal justifications, $F(8,168) = 2.97$, $p < .01$. In the Initial Situation, third graders gave more fairness-welfare justifications than did sixth or ninth graders, $F(2,44) = 6.62$, $p < .01$, whereas in the Physical Harm condition, third and ninth graders gave more fairness-welfare justifications than did sixth graders, $F(2,44) = 4.08$, $p < .05$. In the Acquaintance condition, ninth graders gave more interpersonal justifications than did third or sixth graders, $F(2,42) = 5.33$, $p < .01$. No sex differences in justifications were obtained.

Story 2: Stealing.—The justifications for the choice of not stealing paralleled the sharing choice in that the fairness-welfare justification was used more often than the others, as indicated by significant differences among justifications, $F(2,40) = 124.73$, $p < .0001$ (fairness-welfare = 50%; interpersonal = 3%; psychological = 5%). The MANOVA also revealed a main effect for grade, $F(4,80) = 6.26$, $p < .001$. Third graders more frequently justified the wrongness of stealing on the basis of fairness-welfare concerns than did sixth or ninth graders, $F(2,44) = 8.51$, $p < .0001$. Finally, the MANOVA revealed a significant main effect for salience condition, $F(8,34) = 5.63$, $p < .0001$. Children more frequently used welfare-fairness justifications in the Less Need condition than in the Initial Situation or the Acquaintance condition, p's $< .005$. Children more frequently used interpersonal justifications in the Acquaintance condition than in the Greater Need condition, p's $< .005$.

DISCUSSION

Study 1 demonstrates that children of both genders make judgments about justice and rights both in situations in which justice or rights considerations were in minimal conflict with interpersonal considerations

(e.g., the Initial Situations) and in situations in which the salience of the fairness-rights and interpersonal considerations were varied (to shift the balance between the two components). For most conditions, the majority of children gave priority to the fairness and rights choices over meeting the expectations of a friend, and their fairness and welfare justifications were consonant with their evaluations. There were no gender differences in the use of either fairness or welfare justifications.

The study also demonstrated that females and males take into consideration interpersonal concerns, and that they are attuned to situational features. With regard to stealing, children gave greater priority to interpersonal relationships and judged it more acceptable to violate rights for a friend or a sibling than for an acquaintance. In turn, the salience of the fairness and rights components influenced children's judgments and reasoning. For instance, when the need to share was increased (Greater Need condition in Story 1) or when the transgressions would result in physical harm, most children subordinated the interpersonal consideration. Similarly, when a child was asked by a friend to steal something of lesser need (Story 2), most subjects did not give priority to the interpersonal consideration. Reasoning in these situations was consistent with evaluations since children used fairness-welfare justifications to an even greater extent in the conditions with increased salience of the justice or rights components.

Based on previous research (Davidson et al., 1983; Smetana, 1985; Turiel, 1983), justifications pertaining to welfare and rights were combined in these analyses and compared to interpersonal justifications, which pertained primarily to maintaining friendships. This differs from previous research more directly testing Gilligan's hypotheses, where reasoning regarding care and interpersonal relations has been combined (e.g., Gilligan & Attanucci, 1988; Lyons, 1983; Miller & Luthar, 1989; Rothbart et al., 1986; Walker et al., 1987). It is possible that this procedure underestimated the prevalence of "care" responses in our sample. However, our conclusions are based on the findings for judgments as well as justifications, and it is important to note the congruence between them.

Analyses of the coordination of components represent a more fine-grained assessment of whether children are cognizant of each component than assessments of judgments. In some conditions, children of all the ages and both genders considered both components in their judgments. However, the finding that with age children become more consistent in considering both components when the two are placed in greater conflict must be interpreted cautiously. These findings may reflect an increased cognitive capacity to coordinate components in situations with greater conflicts, or they may simply reflect an increased ability to express judgments about the two components. In any event, the findings are consistent with Walker et al. (1987), who found that individuals at higher levels of moral development evidenced substantial amounts of both response and rights orientations in their reasoning. If our results were to reflect changes in cognitive capacities, it would indicate that, with age, children take more aspects of the situation into account in making judgments. More generally, the extent to which children evaluated both components varied according to the different salience conditions. Considered in conjunction with the results from the analysis of judgments, Study 1 suggests that children focused solely on justice and rights only in situations where those claims were most compelling (e.g., in situations of greater need) and in situations where the interpersonal claims were less convincing (e.g., the Acquaintance condition).

Study 1 primarily ascertained that female and male children reason on the basis of justice, rights, and welfare when those considerations are in conflict with self-interested interpersonal expectations from friends or siblings. The study did not address how children make judgments and reason about conflicts in which the interpersonal expectations have legitimacy and in which acts are performed to be helpful, kind, or considerate to another (rather than to avoid losing a friendship). Furthermore, since the order of conditions was not varied in Study 1, it is possible that the effects found for salience conditions were due to repeatedly asking children the same questions. Finally, the results may be unreliable due to the small sample size. Study 2 was designed to address these issues.

Study 2

Study 1 established that the availability of either interpersonal or justice concepts does not differ by gender and provided a context for additional research on judgments about compelling conflicts between the two types of considerations. It is possible that females are more oriented than males to interpersonal considerations with positive intent and goals, as others (Rothbart et al., 1986) have claimed. There is no indication of this, however, from Study 1. Our hypothesis, instead, as noted earlier, is that the application of both justice and interpersonal concerns depends on elements of the situation.

The stimulus situations in Study 2 posed conflicts between justice or rights and interpersonal relationships calling for helpful or kind acts. Subjects were posed with situations in which an interpersonal act that benefits a friend or sibling entails unfairness or violation of rights toward an acquaintance or stranger. It is important to note that these stimulus situations (unlike Study 1) involve conflicts between welfare in interpersonal contexts, on the one hand, and impartial justice and rights considerations on the other. This comparison should be kept in mind when interpreting our terminology (for simplicity's sake we continue to refer to the components as interpersonal and justice/rights).

Three stories were used in Study 2. One depicted a brother's attempt to care for his vulnerable younger sister; by helping his sister the boy's action would result in unfair treatment of another female. In the second story, a girl chooses between (a) meeting a sick friend's request to help her complete a task to win a science fair contest, and (b) a boy's claim that doing so would violate the fairness of the competition. The third story was a conflict between welfare and property rights modeled after situations used by Kohlberg (1969) and Gilligan (1982), but adjusted to be more comprehensible to children. The conflict revolved around the choice to steal in order to protect the physical welfare of a sibling. We hypothesized that judgments and justifications would vary by the situation and that there would be no gender differences.

The methods of this study were similar to those of Study 1. Subjects were asked to judge and provide justifications about an Initial Situation. Then they were presented with conditions varying the salience of justice/rights and interpersonal components. Because Study 2 had three stories instead of two, the moral and interpersonal components were each varied in one condition (rather than two) to reduce the demands on the subjects. Since Study 1 indicated that nearly all children gave priority to justice/rights in the Acquaintance condition, this condition was dropped in Study 2. The interpersonal conditions thus either depicted a friend or a sibling, depending on the relationship described in the Initial Situation. This, in turn, was varied to control for order effects in each story. The justice/rights conditions in the three stories varied in depicting situations of greater need, a different act (lying), and a rule violation.

METHOD

Subjects

A different sample of subjects from those in Study 1, consisting of 76 children (39 males and 37 females), was used in Study 2. There were 13 males and 11 females at the third grade, 14 males and 12 females at the sixth grade, and 12 males and 14 females at the ninth grade (mean ages = 9.08, 12.10, 14.92 years, respectively). As in Study 1, they were of mixed ethnicity and middle class. They were recruited from two elementary schools and two junior high schools in the San Francisco Bay area.

Procedure

Subjects were individually administered questions about three hypothetical situations, presented in counterbalanced order, by two females who were blind to the hypotheses of the study. The interview took about 40 min and was tape-recorded and transcribed. The story descriptions, question, and variations in the components are summarized in Table 4. The first two stories (referred to as the music club and science club stories) depict conflicts between fairness and welfare in interpersonal relationships, and the third (the hurt brother story) depicts a conflict between protecting the physical welfare of a sibling and theft (the violation of property rights served interpersonal and welfare ends).

The situations were presented in the same way as in the previous study. To prevent fatigue because of an additional story, only one interpersonal and one justice/rights condition were presented for each story (see Table 4). Since the Initial Situations in two stories depicted sibling relationships, the relationship was varied to depict a friendship. The Initial Situation of the other story described a friendship relationship, and therefore in the interpersonal condition, a sibling relationship was described. Each story also had a different variation in the magnitude of the fairness or rights component. In the music club story, the salience of the fairness component was increased by describing a situation of greater need on the part of the girl than the sister. In the science project story, the fairness condition included the existence of an explicit rule prohibiting help for the contestants. In the hurt brother story,

TABLE 4

STORY THEMES AND CONDITIONS FOR STUDY 2

Music Club Story
Initial Situation: Sam, the leader of an afterschool club, lets his younger sister join the club to stop other children from teasing her. There is only space for one new member, and another girl is more deserving.
Interpersonal condition: Sam lets a friend into the club instead of another more deserving person.
Greater Need condition: The other girl would lose all her friends and be very unhappy if she were not in the club.

Science Project Story
Initial Situation: Amy is too sick to work on her science fair project and asks her best friend Sally to help her finish it. John, who is also competing in the science fair, thinks it would be unfair to have someone else help Amy on her project.
Interpersonal condition—Friend: Sally is asked by her younger sister to finish the work.
Rule Violation condition: The contest has an explicit rule prohibiting obtaining help.

Hurt Brother Story
Initial Situation: Walking home with his brother Jimmy, Marvin trips and cuts his leg. Very worried about his brother and not having enough money to call their mother, Jimmy goes to a store, but the storeowner won't let him use his phone. Jimmy takes $10 lying on the register to make a phone call to their mother.
Interpersonal condition—Friend: It is Jimmy's friend who is hurt rather than his brother.
Lying condition: Jimmy lies to the storeowner, telling him the $10 belongs to him.

181

TABLE 5

RESPONSES (in %) ENDORSING THE NONINTERPERSONAL CHOICE (Not Admitting Sister/
Not Taking Money/Not Helping Friend)

STORY AND CONDITION	GRADE 3		GRADE 6		GRADE 9		TOTAL
	Males	Females	Males	Females	Males	Females	
Music Club Story:							
Initial Situation	23	55	57	25	75	71	51
Interpersonal—Friend	85	100	93	92	100	100	95
Greater Need	23	55	64	33	75	71	54
Hurt Brother Story:							
Initial Situation	62	73	50	33	58	64	57
Interpersonal—Friend	77	73	29	42	50	64	55
Lying	85	100	86	83	92	100	91
Science Project Story:							
Initial Situation	15	18	36	8	17	36	22
Interpersonal Sibling	15	9	21	8	17	29	17
Rule Violation	92	91	79	75	92	86	84

the type of act was varied to depict a lie in conjunction with theft. As in Study 1, for each condition the child was asked to judge what the protagonist should do and why. Thus, for each of three stories, three sets of judgments and justifications were obtained.

Coding and Reliability

The three coding schemes from Study 1 were used. The first was a dichotomous assessment of *judgments* as to what the protagonist should do. The second was an assessment of the extent to which children integrated different choices when evaluating the conflicts (the *coordination of components* coding), with responses coded into two categories (focus on both components and focus on only one component). *Justifications* were coded using the same categories as in Study 1, with the addition of a *pragmatic* category (retribution or fear of punishment) that had not been given by subjects in Study 1. There were no age, sex, or condition effects in the comparisons of fairness and welfare justifications. Fairness and welfare justifications were used in each of the stories; they were mainly divided in accordance with choices in the stories. Interrater reliability, calculated as kappa coefficients between two coders scoring 20 protocols, was .86, .80, and .85 for judgments, coordination of components, and justifications, respectively.

RESULTS

Judgments

Table 5 displays the percentage of children at each age who gave priority to the fairness or rights choices (i.e., not admitting

the sister in the music club story, not helping the friend in the science project story, and not taking the money in the hurt brother story). The analyses were conducted on the percentage of children at each age who gave priority to the fairness or rights choices (i.e., not admitting the sister in the music club story, not helping the friend in the science project story, and not taking the money in the hurt brother story). Arcsine-transformed responses for each story were analyzed by 3 (grade) × 2 (sex) × 3 (salience condition) repeated-measures ANOVAs with condition as the repeated measure. Again, Duncan multiple-range tests and Bonferroni t tests were used to test significant effects.

Story 1: The music club story.—As seen in Table 5, subjects were evenly split in their choices for the Initial Situation (51% and 49%) and the Greater Need condition (54% and 46%). However, responses did vary by salience condition, $F(2,140) = 42.26$, $p < .0001$. The Interpersonal condition (friend rather than sibling) resulted in more frequent affirmation of the fairness choice (95%). There was also an age shift in the affirmation of the fairness choice. A main effect for grade, $F(2,70) = 4.92$, $p < .01$, indicated that ninth graders were more likely to give priority to fairness than third or sixth graders (82%, 57%, 61%, respectively). The main effect for sex was not significant, but there was a significant grade × sex interaction, $F(2,70) = 3.66$, $p < .05$. Third-grade males gave less priority to the fairness choice than did sixth- or ninth-grade males, $F(2,36) = 5.43$, $p < .01$ (44%, 71%, 83%, respectively), whereas the sixth-grade females gave less priority to the fairness choice than did ninth-grade females, $F(2,34) = 3.27$, $p < .05$.

Story 2: The science project story.— Table 5 shows that for the science project story only a minority of subjects gave priority to the fairness choice in the Initial Situation (22%) and the Interpersonal condition (17%), but this varied by condition, $F(2,140) = 105.59$, $p < .0001$. When helping the friend involved violating a rule, subjects more frequently judged it wrong to help (84%) than in the other conditions (p's $< .005$). These findings held for males and females across ages; there were no other significant main effects or interactions.

Story 3: Hurt brother story.—In this situation, too, there was a main effect for salience condition, $F(2,140) = 3.09$, $p < .05$. A greater proportion of children judged it wrong to steal in the Lying condition (91%) than in the Initial Situation (57%) or the Interpersonal condition (55%). There was a main effect for grade, $F(2,70) = 3.29$, $p < .05$. Duncan multiple-range tests indicated that third graders more frequently gave priority to not stealing than did sixth graders. No significant differences for gender were obtained.

Coordination of Components

Three (grade) $\times$ 2 (sex) $\times$ 3 (salience condition) repeated-measures ANOVAS with condition as the repeated measure were performed separately on the arcsine-transformed responses for each story. There were differences in consideration of components among the stories and between conditions within stories. In the music club story the majority of children at all ages (91%) considered both components. There were no main effects or interactions for sex, grade, or salience condition.

The science project story produced an increased use of two components with grade, as it interacted with condition. A main effect for salience condition, $F(2,140) = 11.28$, $p < .0001$, indicated that subjects considered both components more in the Initial Situation (65%), which depicted a friendship relationship, than in the Interpersonal (Sibling) condition (43%) or in the Rule Violation condition (31%). There was a significant grade $\times$ salience condition interaction, $F(2,70) = 4.06$, $p < .01$. Sixth and ninth graders more frequently considered both components of the Initial Situation than did third graders, $F(2,70) = 4.83$, $p < .01$ (77%, 77%, 42%, respectively).

In the hurt brother story, no grade or sex differences were obtained. A main effect for salience condition, $F(2,140) = 30.95$, $p < .0001$, indicated that subjects were less likely to consider two components in the Lying condition (13%) than in the Initial Situation (58%) or the Interpersonal (Friend) condition (58%).

Justifications

The percentages of use of justification categories are presented in Tables 6 and 7 as separated by subjects' choices in the stories. Since the conventional, personal, psychological, and pragmatic justification categories were used infrequently for the fairness choice, they were combined into an Other category (as discussed below, in a few conditions these were a substantial amount). In addition, the interpersonal category for the fairness or rights choices was used infrequently (see Table 6). Therefore, only the fairness-welfare justifications for the fairness choice were analyzed, using a 3 (grade) $\times$ 2 (sex) $\times$ 3 (salience condition) repeated-measure ANOVA. Since the frequency of interpersonal justifications was substantial in some conditions in Study 2, separate 3 (grade) $\times$ 2 (sex) $\times$ 3 (salience condition) repeated-measures MANOVAs were performed on the arcsine-transformed proportions of fairness-welfare and interpersonal justifications given for the interpersonal choice in each story. Few pragmatic justifications were given for the interpersonal choice, and thus they were not included in these analyses.

As we did in reporting justification category analyses in Study 1, we only highlight the major findings. For the music club story there were no sex differences in the use fairness-welfare justifications for the fairness choice. There were main effects for grade, $F(2,64) = 7.61$, $p < .001$, and salience condition, $F(2,128) = 40.00$, $p < .001$, as well as a grade $\times$ salience condition interaction, $F(4,128) = 2.64$, $p < .05$. Bonferroni t tests indicated that children used the fairness-welfare category more in the condition where the interpersonal component was less salient (Interpersonal condition with a friend; 91%) than in the Initial Situation (53%) and the Greater Need condition (44%). Second, across conditions, ninth graders used the fairness-welfare category more than did the younger subjects. The interaction reflects that in the Initial Situation ninth graders used the fairness-welfare category more than did sixth graders, $F(2,67) = 3.34$, $p < .05$, whereas in the Greater Need condi-

TABLE 6

JUSTIFICATIONS (in %) AFFIRMING THE NONINTERPERSONAL CHOICE

	MUSIC CLUB STORY			HURT BROTHER			SCIENCE PROJECT		
Grade:	3	6	9	3	6	9	3	6	9
Initial Situation:									
Fairness-Welfare	45	42	73	45	33	53	14	27	16
Interpersonal	2	0	0	0	0	0	0	0	0
Other	1	1	0	24	29	9	4	4	5
Interpersonal:[a]									
Fairness-Welfare	93	83	96	28	11	40	9	16	23
Interpersonal	2	12	0	0	9	4	0	0	0
Other	0	0	0	42	19	19	0	2	9
Moral:[b]									
Fairness-Welfare	24	34	73	26	37	42	31	46	46
Interpersonal	4	20	2	0	0	2	0	0	0
Other	12	0	8	68	49	45	56	38	44

[a] The Interpersonal condition pertained to friends in the Music Club Story and Hurt Brother Story, and to siblings in the Science Project Story.

[b] The Moral condition pertained to Greater Need in the Music Club Story, to Lying in the Hurt Brother Story, and to Rule Violation in the Science Project Story.

tion ninth graders used it more than did all the younger subjects, $F(2,69) = 9.79$, $p < .001$.

The MANOVA performed on justifications given for the interpersonal choice revealed a significant effect for type of justification, $F(1,64) = 9.42$, $p < .01$. Children used fairness-welfare justifications (20%) more than interpersonal justifications (4%) for the interpersonal choice. The MANOVA also revealed a salience condition × sex interaction in justifications, $F(2,64) = 5.36$, $p < .01$. The fairness-welfare category was used more by females than males for the in-

terpersonal choice in the Greater Need condition, $F(1,68) = 4.19$, $p < .05$.

For the science project story, there were no sex or grade effects in use of the fairness-welfare category for the fairness choice, as shown in Table 6. The only differences obtained were a main effect for salience condition on the MANOVA, $F(2,116) = 11.44$, $p < .0001$. The fairness-welfare category was used more in the Rule Violation condition (41%) than in the Initial Situation (19%) or the Interpersonal (Sibling) condition (16%), p's $< .001$. Children justified the interpersonal choices (as shown in Table 7) on the

TABLE 7

JUSTIFICATIONS (in %) AFFIRMING THE INTERPERSONAL CHOICES

	MUSIC CLUB STORY			HURT BROTHER			SCIENCE PROJECT		
Grade:	3	6	9	3	6	9	3	6	9
Initial Situation:									
Fairness-Welfare	29	35	19	26	37	38	74	46	72
Interpersonal	21	22	8	4	2	0	8	17	7
Interpersonal:[a]									
Fairness-Welfare	4	4	4	14	43	37	34	27	39
Interpersonal	0	0	0	11	14	0	34	50	20
Pragmatic	0	0	0	6	5	0	5	5	5
Moral:[b]									
Fairness-Welfare	36	32	13	0	13	2	10	13	8
Interpersonal	23	13	4	0	0	0	2	2	2

[a] The Interpersonal condition pertained to friends in the Music Club Story and Hurt Brother Story, and to siblings in the Science Project Story.

[b] The Moral condition pertained to Greater Need in the Music Club Story, to Lying in the Hurt Brother story, and to Rule Violation in the Science Project Story.

basis of fairness-welfare (36%) more than interpersonal concerns (16%), as indicated by a main effect for type of justification on the MANOVA, $F(1,58) = 17.74$, $p < .0001$. There were no sex or age effects.

In the hurt brother story, there was a somewhat different pattern of justifications than in the other stories. As shown in Table 6, there was substantial use of the pragmatic, conventional, and psychological categories (grouped as Other) in justifying the fairness choice. Furthermore, there were no main effects or interactions in the use of fairness-welfare justifications for the fairness choice. As shown in Table 7, however, there were differences between justifications for the interpersonal choice, $F(1,51) = 26.45$, $p < .0001$. Fairness-welfare (25%) was used more than interpersonal (3%) justifications ($p < .001$). There was also a main effect for salience condition in justifications, $F(2,50) = 14.20$, $p < .0001$. There was more use of the fairness-welfare category in the Initial Situation (34%) and in the Interpersonal condition (32%) than in the Lying condition (7%; p's $< .001$).

DISCUSSION

It appears that when children are faced with conflicts between fairness and positive interpersonal expectations, they make interpersonal choices to a greater extent than when the expectations are motivated by self-interest. Overall, children gave greater priority to interpersonal choices in Study 2 than in Study 1. Moreover, no gender differences were found in Study 2.

As in Study 1, a main finding of this study is that both females and males made judgments that accounted for situational features of the stories. There were differences between stories, as well as differences in accord with shifts in the salience of the interpersonal or fairness/rights considerations. In the science project story, children clearly gave priority to the interpersonal considerations. In the other two stories, children were nearly equally divided in their choices of whether to care for a sibling or meet other fairness or rights considerations.

It also appears that each of the stories tapped somewhat different judgments. In the music club story, both males and females (and especially the younger ones) were responsive to the need to care for a vulnerable younger sister. However, children gave greater priority to helping a sister than helping a friend in similar circumstances. Chil-

dren of both genders were especially responsive to the interpersonal expectations in the competitive context of the science project story since most of them, unlike in the music club story, judged it acceptable to help either a sibling or a friend. Perhaps lower priority was placed on impersonal fairness in this situation because the context of competition was not seen as including equal rights. Another difference between these two stories was that shifts in salience of the fairness or rights components resulted in children giving it greater priority only in the science project story (the Rule Violation condition).

The purpose of the hurt brother story was to assess judgments and justifications in the type of conflict used in previous discussions of gender differences. Again, no gender differences were found. Children were evenly divided in their choices regarding a sibling and a friend. There was the expected difference in salience condition; children were less likely to give priority to the interpersonal expectation when the protagonist lied as a means to help the sibling. The types of justifications used in this story indicate that it was perceived as more complex than the other stories. This story implicated additional considerations, such as the violation of laws and the possibility of punishment, and produced substantial use of pragmatic, conventional, and psychological justifications (grouped as Other). Children's perceptions of complexity in this story may account for the disparate and conflicting results obtained by other researchers using stories of this type (e.g., Baumrind, 1986; Gilligan, 1982; Walker, 1984, 1986a). That is, our results indicate that in these stories children perceive components from different domains (e.g., legal issues, sanctions), in addition to, for example, justice and care components. In the absence of systematic delineation of such components, it is possible that their salience varied from one study to another and, if so, might account for conflicting results.

The absence of gender differences in the story choices was paralleled by an absence of gender differences in justifications. Children primarily used fairness-welfare justifications to support their choices, especially in conditions with an increased salience of fairness or rights (as was also found in Study 1). It was also found that children reasoned about their interpersonal choices with fairness-welfare justifications more than interpersonal justifications. This indicates that, for both genders, interpersonal expectations are perceived to include fairness and welfare components. It should be stressed that, as in Study 1, males and females used fairness justifications to an equal extent as welfare justifications (the two were grouped in the analyses into one general category).

Finally, the main age-related findings in this study were consistent with those of Study 1. Although children of all ages were able to consider both components in some of their judgments, older children did so with greater consistency than the younger ones in the Science Project story. However, there were no significant age differences in the coordination of components in the other stories.

General Discussion

The findings of the two studies are complementary. Together, they demonstrate that children of both genders consider interpersonal relationships and justice, welfare, and rights. Moreover, in both studies children's judgments and reasoning shifted in accordance with situational variations. In Study 1, females and males generally favored the obligations of justice and rights over self-interested interpersonal expectations. It appears, therefore, that at least by middle childhood children have formed concepts of justice and rights that they apply to a range of social situations. At the same time, the concepts of justice and rights are not rigidly applied. Study 1 demonstrated that children also take interpersonal components into account, and that changes in the salience of one or the other component lead to changes in the ways they are applied.

The findings of Study 2 showed that children are responsive to more positive interpersonal expectations than those depicted in Study 1. In the context of interpersonal concerns with positive intent and goals, males and females make similar judgments and use similar reasoning categories. It must be stressed that we are not claiming that these studies demonstrate that no gender differences exist in moral orientations. More studies would be needed to even consider the possibility. Rather, we have obtained evidence that both males and females make judgments of justice, rights, and welfare, judge the necessity of maintaining interpersonal relationships, and apply concepts of justice, rights, and welfare to interpersonal relations and recognize potential conflicts

between the two. The features of a situation have a bearing on how it is approached and resolved.

It also should be noted that our studies had a different focus from most recent studies of gender differences (Baumrind, 1986; Gilligan, 1982; Walker, 1984, 1986a). We examined whether and how children use interpersonal and justice considerations in a series of situational contexts. The other studies have focused on general age-related shifts in "moral" reasoning through analyses of judgments about situations in which the interpersonal and justice components are not clearly specified or manipulated (e.g., through story comparisons or salience variations).

Therefore, the exact implications of our results for formulations (Damon, 1977; Kohlberg, 1969; Selman, 1980) of stages or levels of moral judgment about particular conflicts or dilemmas are uncertain. The findings of our studies, however, do suggest that there are not clear-cut individual or group differences regarding concerns with justice, welfare, and rights, on the one hand, and concerns with interpersonal relations, on the other hand. Each type of concern coexists in individuals' social judgments and reasoning.

References

Baumrind, D. (1986). Sex differences in moral reasoning: Response to Walker's (1984) conclusions that there are none. *Child Development*, **57**, 511–521.

Damon, W. (1977). *The social world of the child.* San Francisco: Jossey-Bass.

Davidson, P., Turiel, E., & Black, A. (1983). The effects of stimulus familiarity on the use of criteria and justifications in children's social reasoning. *British Journal of Developmental Psychology*, **1**, 49–65.

Ford, M. R., & Lowery, C. R. (1986). Gender differences in moral reasoning: A comparison of the use of justice and care orientations. *Journal of Personality and Social Psychology*, **50**, 777–783.

Gibbs, J. C., Arnold, K. D., & Burkhart, J. E. (1984). Sex differences in the expression of moral judgment. *Child Development*, **55**, 1040–1043.

Gilligan, C. (1977). In a different voice: Women's conceptions of self and of morality. *Harvard Educational Review*, **47**, 481–517.

Gilligan, C. (1982). *In a different voice: Psychological theory and women's development.* Cambridge, MA: Harvard University Press.

Gilligan, C., & Attanucci, J. (1988). Two moral orientations: Gender differences and similarities. *Merrill-Palmer Quarterly*, 34, 223–237.

Killen, M. (1990). Children's evaluations of morality in the context of peer, teacher-child, and familial relations. *Journal of Genetic Psychology*, **151**, 395–410.

Kohlberg, L. (1969). Stage and sequence: The cognitive-developmental approach to socialization. In D. A. Goslin (Ed.), *Handbook of socialization theory and research* (pp. 347–480). Chicago: Rand McNally.

Kohlberg, L. (1971). From is to ought: How to commit the naturalistic fallacy and get away with it in the study of moral development. In T. Mischel (Ed.), *Cognitive development and epistemology* (pp. 151–235). New York: Academic Press.

Lyons, N. (1983). Two perspectives: On self, relationships, and morality. *Harvard Educational Review*, 53, 125–145.

Miller, J. G., Bersoff, D. M., & Harwood, R. L. (1990). Perceptions of social responsibilities in India and in the United States: Moral imperatives or personal decisions? *Journal of Personality and Social Psychology*, **58**, 33–47.

Miller, J. G., & Luthar, S. (1989). Issues of interpersonal responsibility and accountability: A comparison of Indians' and Americans' moral judgments. *Social Cognition*, 7, 237–261.

Nucci, L. P. (1981). The development of personal concepts: A domain distinct from moral or societal concepts. *Child Development*, **52**, 114–121.

Pratt, M. W., Golding, G., & Hunter, W. J. (1984). Does morality have a gender? Sex, sex role, and moral judgment relationships across the adult lifespan. *Merrill-Palmer Quarterly*, 30, 321–340.

Pratt, M. W., Golding, G., Hunter, W., & Sampson, R. (1988). Sex differences in adult moral orientations. *Journal of Personality*, 56, 373–391.

Rothbart, M. K., Hanley, J., & Albert, M. (1986). Gender differences in moral reasoning. *Sex Roles*, 15, 645–653.

Scheffler, S. (1988). Agent-centered restrictions, rationality, and the virtues. In S. Scheffler (Ed.), *Consequentialism and its critics* (pp. 243–260). New York: Oxford University Press.

Selman, R. L. (1980). *The growth of interpersonal understanding: Developmental and clinical analyses.* New York: Academic Press.

Smetana, J. G. (1981). Preschool children's conceptions of moral and social rules. *Child Development*, 52, 1333–1336.

Smetana, J. G. (1985). Preschool children's conceptions of transgressions: The effects of varying moral and conventional domain-related attributes. *Developmental Psychology*, 21, 18–29.

Smetana, J. G., Kelly, M., & Twentyman, C. T. (1984). Abused, neglected, and nonmaltreated children's conceptions of moral and social-conventional rules. *Child Development*, 55, 277–287.

Turiel, E. (1983). *The development of social knowledge: Morality and convention.* Cambridge: Cambridge University Press.

Turiel, E., Smetana, J. G., & Killen, M. (1991). Social contexts in social cognitive development. In W. M. Kurtines & J. L. Gewirtz (Eds.), *Handbook of moral behavior and development* (Vol. **2**, pp. 307–332). Hillsdale, NJ: Erlbaum.

Walker, L. J. (1984). Sex differences in the development of moral reasoning. *Child Development*, 55, 677–691.

Walker, L. J. (1986a). Sex differences in the development of moral reasoning: A rejoinder to Baumrind. *Child Development*, 57, 522–526.

Walker, L. J. (1986b). Experiential and cognitive sources of moral development in adulthood. *Human Development*, 29, 113–124.

Walker, L. J. (1989). A longitudinal study of moral reasoning. *Child Development*, 60, 157–166.

Walker, L. J., de Vries, B., & Trevethan, S. D. (1987). Moral stages and moral orientation in real-life and hypothetical dilemmas. *Child Development*, 58, 842–858.

Williams, B. (1981). *Moral luck.* Cambridge: Cambridge University Press.

Winer, B. J. (1971). *Statistical principles in experimental design.* New York: McGraw-Hill.

Multiple Choice:

1.   The studies reported in this article focus on how children:

A.   reason about moral conflicts.
B.   behave in different situations.
C.   perceive that adults would behave in moral conflicts.
D.   all of the above.

2.   Which of the following was reported in this article?

A.   Both males and females generally relied on justice and rights in their reasoning.
B.   Interpersonal factors were sometimes given priority.
C.   Situational variables affected children's judgments.
D.   All of the above.

Essay:

1.   Is it wrong to cheat on an exam? Would you let a friend copy off your exam? Would you let your friend copy your test if the friend had been sick and missed class? What if your friend would be thrown out of school for failing the exam? How does your own thinking about these questions relate to what was reported in this article?

ARTICLE 18

Gender and Relationships: A Developmental Account

Eleanor E. Maccoby

Reprinted from: *American Psychologist*, 1990, *45*, 513-520.

Who are you? List the five most important things about yourself.

We would bet that your gender appears on your list of things most important for describing who you are. Gender is one of the most salient and fundamental aspects of identity. But how does our sex make us different from people of the opposite sex and like those of our own sex?

In this article, Eleanor Maccoby takes an unusual and interesting position with respect to sex differences. She argues that it may be a mistake to look for differences among individuals simply as a function of sex. She suggests that different social situations may heighten or suppress sex differences in behavior.

Maccoby summarizes a large array of studies to argue that differences between the sexes become more apparent when people are in both-sex groups than when they are in same-sex groups. To take one example she cites, in a preschool playgroup with both boys and girls, girls tend to stay near and interact with the teacher a lot of the time. This fact has been interpreted as evidence that girls are more dependent on adult approval than boys are, that they like to have adults organize their activities but boys don't, and so on. However, it turns out that in a girls-only group, the girls do not hover around the teacher. They roam around the room even more freely than boys do. Thus, it seems to be the presence of boys that leads little girls to seek out and stay near their teachers. A very different notion of sex differences thus arises when behavior is compared in single- and both-sex groups.

We think you will find this article thought-provoking. It offers a novel conceptualization in the age-old attempt to characterize the real differences between the sexes, one that brings a new level of clarity and coherence to the topic.

Gender and Relationships

A Developmental Account

Eleanor E. Maccoby　　*Stanford University*

ABSTRACT: This article argues that behavioral differentiation of the sexes is minimal when children are observed or tested individually. Sex differences emerge primarily in social situations, and their nature varies with the gender composition of dyads and groups. Children find same-sex play partners more compatible, and they segregate themselves into same-sex groups, in which distinctive interaction styles emerge. These styles are described. As children move into adolescence, the patterns they developed in their childhood same-sex groups are carried over into cross-sex encounters in which girls' styles put them at a disadvantage. Patterns of mutual influence can become more symmetrical in intimate male–female dyads, but the distinctive styles of the two sexes can still be seen in such dyads and are subsequently manifested in the roles and relationships of parenthood. The implications of these continuities are considered.

Historically, the way we psychologists think about the psychology of gender has grown out of our thinking about individual differences. We are accustomed to assessing a wide variety of attributes and skills and giving scores to individuals based on their standing relative to other individuals in a sample population. On most psychological attributes, we see wide variation among individuals, and a major focus of research has been the effort to identify correlates or sources of this variation. Commonly, what we have done is to classify individuals by some antecedent variable, such as age or some aspect of their environment, to determine how much of the variance among individuals in their performance on a given task can be accounted for by this so-called *antecedent* or *independent* variable. Despite the fact that hermaphrodites exist, almost every individual is either clearly male or clearly female. What could be more natural for psychologists than to ask how much variance among individuals is accounted for by this beautifully binary factor?

Fifteen years ago, Carol Jacklin and I put out a book summarizing the work on sex differences that had come out of the individual differences perspective (Maccoby & Jacklin, 1974). We felt at that time that the yield was thin. That is, there were very few attributes on which the average values for the two sexes differed consistently. Furthermore, even when consistent differences were found, the amount of variance accounted for by sex was small, relative to the amount of variation within each sex. Our conclusions fitted in quite well with the feminist zeitgeist

of the times, when most feminists were taking a minimalist position, urging that the two sexes were basically alike and that any differences were either illusions in the eye of the beholder or reversible outcomes of social shaping. Our conclusions were challenged as having both overstated the case for sex differences (Tieger, 1980) and for having understated it (Block, 1976).

In the last 15 years, work on sex differences has become more methodologically sophisticated, with greater use of meta analyses to reveal not only the direction of sex differences but quantitative estimates of their magnitude. In my judgment, the conclusions are still quite similar to those Jacklin and I arrived at in 1974: There are still some replicable sex differences, of moderate magnitude, in performance on tests of mathematical and spatial abilities, although sex differences in verbal abilities have faded. Other aspects of intellectual performance continue to show gender equality. When it comes to attributes in the personality–social domain, results are particularly sparse and inconsistent. Studies continue to find that men are more often agents of aggression than are women (Eagly, 1987; Huston, 1985; Maccoby & Jacklin, 1980). Eagly (1983, 1987) reported in addition that women are more easily influenced than men and that men are more altruistic in the sense that they are more likely to offer help to others. In general, however, personality traits measured as characteristics of individuals do not appear to differ systematically by sex (Huston, 1985). This no doubt reflects in part the fact that male and female persons really are much alike, and their lives are governed mainly by the attributes that all persons in a given culture have in common. Nevertheless, I believe that the null findings coming out of comparisons of male and female individuals on personality measures are partly illusory. That is, they are an artifact of our historical reliance on an individual differences perspective. Social behavior, as many have pointed out, is never a function of the individual alone. It is a function of the interaction between two or more persons. Individuals behave differently with different partners. There are certain important ways in which gender is implicated in social behavior—ways that may be obscured or missed altogether when behavior is summed across all categories of social partners.

An illustration is found in a study of social interaction between previously unacquainted pairs of young children (mean age, 33 months; Jacklin & Maccoby, 1978). In some pairs, the children had same-sex play partners; in others, the pair was made up of a boy and a

Copyright 1990 by the American Psychological Association, Inc. 0003-066X/90/$00.75
Vol. 45, No. 4, 513–520

girl. Observers recorded the social behavior of each child on a time-sampling basis. Each child received a score for total social behavior directed toward the partner. This score included both positive and negative behaviors (e.g., offering a toy and grabbing a toy; hugging and pushing; vocally greeting, inviting, protesting, or prohibiting). There was no overall sex difference in the amount of social behavior when this was evaluated without regard to sex of partner. But there was a powerful interaction between sex of the subject and that of the partner: Children of each sex had much higher levels of social behavior when playing with a same-sex partner than when playing with a child of the other sex. This result is consistent with the findings of Wasserman and Stern (1978) that when asked to approach another child, children as young as age three stopped farther away when the other child was of the opposite sex, indicating awareness of gender similarity or difference, and wariness toward the other sex.

The number of time intervals during which a child was simply standing passively watching the partner play with the toys was also scored. There was no overall sex difference in the frequency of this behavior, but the behavior of girls was greatly affected by the sex of the partner. With other girls, passive behavior seldom occurred; indeed, in girl–girl pairs it occurred less often than it did in boy–boy pairs. However when paired with boys, girls frequently stood on the sidelines and let the boys monopolize the toys. Clearly, the little girls in this study were not more passive than the little boys in any overall, trait-like sense. Passivity in these girls could be understood only in relation to the characteristics of their interactive partners. It was a characteristic of girls in cross-sex dyads. This conclusion may not seem especially novel because for many years we have known that social behavior is situationally specific. However, the point here is that interactive behavior is not just situationally specific, but that it depends on the gender category membership of the participants. We can account for a good deal more of the behavior if we know the gender mix of dyads, and this probably holds true for larger groups as well.

An implication of our results was that if children at this early age found same-sex play partners more compatible, they ought to prefer same-sex partners when they entered group settings that included children of both sexes. There were already many indications in the literature that children do have same-sex playmate preferences, but there clearly was a need for more systematic attention to the degree of sex segregation that prevails in

naturally occurring children's groups at different ages. As part of a longitudinal study of children from birth to age six, Jacklin and I did time-sampled behavioral observation of approximately 100 children on their preschool playgrounds, and again two years later when the children were playing during school recess periods (Maccoby & Jacklin, 1987). Same-sex playmate preference was clearly apparent in preschool when the children were approximately 4½. At this age, the children were spending nearly 3 times as much time with same-sex play partners as with children of the other sex. By age 6½, the preference had grown much stronger. At this time, the children were spending 11 times as much time with same-sex as with opposite-sex partners.

Elsewhere we have reviewed the literature on playmate choices (Maccoby, 1988; Maccoby & Jacklin, 1987), and here I will simply summarize what I believe the existing body of research shows:

1. Gender segregation is a widespread phenomenon. It is found in all the cultural settings in which children are in social groups large enough to permit choice.

2. The sex difference in the gender of preferred playmates is large in absolute magnitude, compared to sex differences found when children are observed or tested in nonsocial situations.

3. In a few instances, attempts have been made to break down children's preferences for interacting with other same-sex children. It has been found that the preferences are difficult to change.

4. Children choose same-sex playmates spontaneously in situations in which they are not under pressure from adults to do so. In modern co-educational schools, segregation is more marked in situations that have not been structured by adults than in those that have (e.g., Eisenhart & Holland, 1983). Segregation is situationally specific, and the two sexes can interact comfortably under certain conditions, for example, in an absorbing joint task, when structures and roles are set up by adults, or in nonpublic settings (Thorne, 1986).

5. Gender segregation is not closely linked to involvement in sex-typed activities. Preschool children spend a great deal of their time engaged in activities that are gender neutral, and segregation prevails in these activities as well as when they are playing with dolls or trucks.

6. Tendencies to prefer same-sex playmates can be seen among three-year-olds and at even earlier ages under some conditions. But the preferences increase in strength between preschool and school and are maintained at a high level between the ages of 6 and at least age 11.

7. The research base is thin, but so far it appears that a child's tendency to prefer same-sex playmates has little to do with that child's standing on measures of individual differences. In particular, it appears to be unrelated to measures of masculinity or femininity and also to measures of gender schematicity (Powlishta, 1989).

Why do we see such pronounced attraction to same-sex peers and avoidance of other-sex peers in childhood? Elsewhere I have summarized evidence pointing to two

Editor's note. This article was originally presented as a Distinguished Scientific Contributions award address at the meeting of the American Psychological Association in New Orleans in August 1989.

Award-based manuscripts appearing in the American Psychologist are scholarly articles based in part on earlier award addresses presented at the APA convention. In keeping with the policy of recognizing these distinguished contributors to the field, these submissions are given special consideration in the editorial selection process.

Author's note. Correspondence concerning this article should be addressed to Eleanor E. Maccoby, Department of Psychology, Stanford University, Jordan Hall, Bldg. 420, Stanford, CA 94305-2130.

factors that seem to be important in the preschool years (Maccoby, 1988). The first is the rough-and-tumble play style characteristic of boys and their orientation toward issues of competition and dominance. These aspects of male–male interaction appear to be somewhat aversive to most girls. At least, girls are made wary by male play styles. The second factor of importance is that girls find it difficult to influence boys. Some important work by Serbin and colleagues (Serbin, Sprafkin, Elman, & Doyle, 1984) indicates that between the ages of 3½ and 5½, children greatly increase the frequency of their attempts to influence their play partners. This indicates that children are learning to integrate their activities with those of others so as to be able to carry out coordinated activities. Serbin and colleagues found that the increase in influence attempts by girls was almost entirely an increase in making polite suggestions to others, whereas among boys the increase took the form of more use of direct demands. Furthermore, during this formative two-year period just before school entry, boys were becoming less and less responsive to polite suggestions, so that the style being progressively adopted by girls was progressively less effective with boys. Girls' influence style was effective with each other and was well adapted to interaction with teachers and other adults.

These asymmetries in influence patterns were presaged in our study with 33-month-old children: We found then that boys were unresponsive to the vocal prohibitions of female partners (in that they did not withdraw), although they would respond when a vocal prohibition was issued by a male partner. Girls were responsive to one another and to a male partner's prohibitions. Fagot (1985) also reported that boys are "reinforced" by the reactions of male peers—in the sense that they modify their behavior following a male peer's reaction—but that their behavior appears not to be affected by a female's response.

My hypothesis is that girls find it aversive to try to interact with someone who is unresponsive and that they begin to avoid such partners. Students of power and bargaining have long been aware of the importance of reciprocity in human relations. Pruitt (1976) said, "Influence and power are omnipresent in human affairs. Indeed, groups cannot possibly function unless their members can influence one another" (p. 343). From this standpoint, it becomes clear why boys and girls have difficulty forming groups that include children of both sexes.

Why do little boys not accept influence from little girls? Psychologists almost automatically look to the nuclear family for the origins of behavior patterns seen in young children. It is plausible that boys may have been more reinforced for power assertive behavior by their parents, and girls more for politeness, although the evidence for such differential socialization pressure has proved difficult to come by. However, it is less easy to imagine how or why parents should reinforce boys for being unresponsive to *girls*. Perhaps it is a matter of observational learning: Children may have observed that between their two parents, their fathers are more influential than their mothers. I am skeptical about such an explanation. In the first place, mothers exercise a good deal of managerial authority within the households in which children live, and it is common for fathers to defer to their judgment in matters concerning the children. Or, parents form a coalition, and in the eyes of the children they become a joint authority, so that it makes little difference to them whether it is a mother or a father who is wielding authority at any given time. Furthermore, the asymmetry in children's cross-sex influence with their peers appears to have its origins at quite an early age—earlier, I would suggest, than children have a very clear idea about the connection between their own sex and that of the same-sex parent. In other words, it seems quite unlikely that little boys ignore girls' influence attempts because little girls remind them of their mothers. I think we simply do not know why girls' influence styles are ineffective with boys, but the fact that they are has important implications for a variety of social behaviors, not just for segregation.

Here are some examples from recent studies. Powlishta (1987) observed preschool-aged boy–girl pairs competing for a scarce resource. The children were brought to a playroom in the nursery school and were given an opportunity to watch cartoons through a movie-viewer that could only be accessed by one child at a time. Powlishta found that when the two children were alone together in the playroom, the boys got more than their share of access to the movie-viewer. When there was an adult present, however, this was no longer the case. The adult's presence appeared to inhibit the boys' more power-assertive techniques and resulted in girls having at least equal access.

This study points to a reason why girls may not only avoid playing with boys but may also stay nearer to a teacher or other adult. Following up on this possibility, Greeno (1989) brought four-child groups of kindergarten and first-grade children into a large playroom equipped with attractive toys. Some of the quartets were all-boy groups, some all-girl groups, and some were made up of two boys and two girls. A female adult sat at one end of the room, and halfway through the play session, moved to a seat at the other end of the room. The question posed for this study was: Would girls move closer to the teacher when boys were present than when they were not? Would the sex composition of a play group make any difference to the locations taken up by the boys? The results were that in all-girl groups, girls actually took up locations *farther* from the adult than did boys in all-boy groups. When two boys were present, however, the two girls were significantly closer to the adult than were the boys, who tended to remain at intermediate distances. When the adult changed position halfway through the session, boys' locations did not change, and this was true whether there were girls present or not. Girls in all-girl groups tended to move in the opposite direction when the adult moved, maintaining distance between themselves and the adult; when boys were present, however, the girls tended to move *with* the adult, staying relatively close. It is worth noting, incidentally, that in all the mixed-sex groups except one, segregation was extreme; both boys and girls behaved as though there was only one playmate available to them, rather than three.

There are some fairly far-reaching implications of this study. Previous observational studies in preschools had indicated that girls are often found in locations closer to the teacher than are boys. These studies have been done in mixed-sex nursery school groups. Girls' proximity seeking toward adults has often been interpreted as a reflection of some general affiliative trait in girls and perhaps as a reflection of some aspect of early socialization that has bound them more closely to caregivers. We see in the Greeno study that proximity seeking toward adults was *not* a general trait in girls. It was a function of the gender composition of the group of other children present as potential interaction partners. The behavior of girls implied that they found the presence of boys to be less aversive when an adult was nearby. It was as though they realized that the rough, power-assertive behavior of boys was likely to be moderated in the presence of adults, and indeed, there is evidence that they were right.

We have been exploring some aspects of girls' avoidance of interaction with boys. Less is known about why boys avoid interaction with girls, but the fact is that they do. In fact, their cross-sex avoidance appears to be even stronger. Thus, during middle childhood both boys and girls spend considerable portions of their social play time in groups of their own sex. This might not matter much for future relationships were it not for the fact that fairly distinctive styles of interaction develop in all-boy and all-girl groups. Thus, the segregated play groups constitute powerful socialization environments in which children acquire distinctive interaction skills that are adapted to same-sex partners. Sex-typed modes of interaction become consolidated, and I wish to argue that the distinctive patterns developed by the two sexes at this time have implications for the same-sex and cross-sex relationships that individuals form as they enter adolescence and adulthood.

It behooves us, then, to examine in somewhat more detail the nature of the interactive milieus that prevail in all-boy and all-girl groups. Elsewhere I have reviewed some of the findings of studies in which these two kinds of groups have been observed (Maccoby, 1988). Here I will briefly summarize what we know.

The two sexes engage in fairly different kinds of activities and games (Huston, 1985). Boys play in somewhat larger groups, on the average, and their play is rougher (Humphreys & Smith, 1987) and takes up more space. Boys more often play in the streets and other public places; girls more often congregate in private homes or yards. Girls tend to form close, intimate friendships with one or two other girls, and these friendships are marked by the sharing of confidences (Kraft & Vraa, 1975). Boys' friendships, on the other hand, are more oriented around mutual interests in activities (Erwin, 1985). The breakup of girls' friendships is usually attended by more intense emotional reactions than is the case for boys.

For our present purposes, the most interesting thing about all-boy and all-girl groups is the divergence in the interactive styles that develop in them. In male groups, there is more concern with issues of dominance. Several psycholinguists have recorded the verbal exchanges that occur in these groups, and Maltz and Borker (1983) summarized the findings of several studies as follows: Boys in their groups are more likely than girls in all-girl groups to interrupt one another; use commands, threats, or boasts of authority; refuse to comply with another child's demand; give information; heckle a speaker; tell jokes or suspenseful stories; top someone else's story; or call another child names. Girls in all-groups, on the other hand, are more likely than boys to express agreement with what another speaker has just said, pause to give another girl a chance to speak, or when starting a speaking turn, acknowledge a point previously made by another speaker. This account indicates that among boys, speech serves largely egoistic functions and is used to establish and protect an individual's turf. Among girls, conversation is a more socially binding process.

In the past five years, analysts of discourse have done additional work on the kinds of interactive processes that are seen among girls, as compared with those among boys. The summary offered by Maltz and Borker has been both supported and extended. Sachs (1987) reported that girls soften their directives to partners, apparently attempting to keep them involved in a process of planning a play sequence, while boys are more likely simply to tell their partners what to do. Leaper (1989) observed children aged five and seven and found that verbal exchanges among girls more often take the form of what he called "collaborative speech acts" that involve positive reciprocity, whereas among boys, speech acts are more controlling and include more negative reciprocity. Miller and colleagues (Miller, Danaher, & Forbes, 1986) found that there was more conflict in boys' groups, and given that conflict had occurred, girls were more likely to use "conflict mitigating strategies," whereas boys more often used threats and physical force. Sheldon (1989) reported that when girls talk, they seem to have a double agenda: to be "nice" and sustain social relationships, while at the same time working to achieve their own individual ends. For boys, the agenda is more often the single one of self-assertion. Sheldon (1989) has noted that in interactions among themselves, girls are *not* unassertive. Rather, girls do successfully pursue their own ends, but they do so while toning down coercion and dominance, trying to bring about agreement, and restoring or maintaining group functioning. It should be noted that boys' confrontational style does not necessarily impede effective group functioning, as evidenced by boys' ability to cooperate with teammates for sports. A second point is that although researchers' own gender has been found to influence to some degree the kinds of questions posed and the answers obtained, the summary provided here includes the work of both male and female researchers, and their findings are consistent with one another.

As children move into adolescence and adulthood, what happens to the interactive styles that they developed in their largely segregated childhood groups? A first point to note is that despite the powerful attraction to members of the opposite sex in adolescence, gender segregation by no means disappears. Young people continue to spend a good portion of their social time with same-sex partners. In adulthood, there is extensive gender segregation in workplaces (Reskin, 1984), and in some societies and some social-class or ethnic groups, leisure time also is largely spent with same-sex others even after marriage. The literature on the nature of the interactions that occur among same-sex partners in adolescence and adulthood is quite extensive and cannot be reviewed here. Suffice it to say in summary that there is now considerable evidence that the interactive patterns found in sex-homogeneous dyads or groups in adolescence and adulthood are very similar to those that prevailed in the gender-segregated groups of childhood (e.g., Aries, 1976; Carli, 1989; Cowan, Drinkard, & MacGavin, 1984; Savin-Williams, 1979).

How can we summarize what it is that boys and girls, or men and women, are doing in their respective groups that distinguishes these groups from one another? There have been a number of efforts to find the major dimensions that best describe variations in interactive styles. Falbo and Peplau (1980) have factor analyzed a battery of measures and have identified two dimensions: one called direct versus indirect, the other unilateral versus bilateral. Hauser et al. (1987) have distinguished what they called *enabling* interactive styles from *constricting* or *restrictive* ones, and I believe this distinction fits the styles of the two sexes especially well. A restrictive style is one that tends to derail the interaction—to inhibit the partner or cause the partner to withdraw, thus shortening the interaction or bringing it to an end. Examples are threatening a partner, directly contradicting or interrupting, topping the partner's story, boasting, or engaging in other forms of self-display. Enabling or facilitative styles are those, such as acknowledging another's comment or expressing agreement, that support whatever the partner is doing and tend to keep the interaction going. I want to suggest that it is because women and girls use more enabling styles that they are able to form more intimate and more integrated relationships. Also I think it likely that it is the male concern for turf and dominance—that is, with not showing weakness to other men and boys—that underlies their restrictive interaction style and their lack of self-disclosure.

Carli (1989) has recently found that in discussions between pairs of adults, individuals are more easily influenced by a partner if that partner has just expressed agreement with them. In this work, women were quite successful in influencing one another in same-sex dyads, whereas pairs of men were less so. The sex difference was fully accounted for by the fact that men's male partners did not express agreement as often. Eagly (1987) has summarized data from a large number of studies on women's and men's susceptibility to influence and has found women to be somewhat more susceptible. Carli's work suggest that this tendency may not be a general female personality trait of "suggestibility" but may reflect the fact that women more often interact with other women

who tend to express reciprical agreement. Carli's finding resonates with some work with young children interacting with their mothers. Mary Parpal and I (Parpal & Maccoby, 1985) found that children were more compliant to a mother's demands if the two had previously engaged in a game in which the child was allowed to give directions that the mother followed. In other words, maternal compliance set up a system of reciprocity in which the child also complied. I submit that the same principle applies in adult interactions and that among women, influence is achieved in part by being open to influence from the partner.

Boys and men, on the other hand, although less successful in influencing one another in dyads, develop group structures—well-defined roles in games, dominance hierarchies, and team spirit—that appear to enable them to function effectively in groups. One may suppose that the male directive interactive style is less likely to derail interaction if and when group structural forces are in place. In other words, men and boys may *need* group structure more than women and girls do. However, this hypothesis has yet to be tested in research. In any case, boys and men in their groups have more opportunity to learn how to function within hierarchical structures than do women and girls in theirs.

We have seen that throughout much of childhood and into adolescence and adulthood as well, people spend a good deal of their social time interacting with others of their own gender, and they continue to use distinctive interaction styles in these settings. What happens, then, when individuals from these two distinctive "cultures" attempt to interact with one another? People of both sexes are faced with a relatively unfamiliar situation to which they must adapt. Young women are less likely to receive the reciprocal agreement, opportunities to talk, and so on that they have learned to expect when interacting with female partners. Men have been accustomed to counter-dominance and competitive reactions to their own power assertions, and they now find themselves with partners who agree with them and otherwise offer enabling responses. It seems evident that this new partnership should be easier to adapt to for men than for women. There is evidence that men fall in love faster and report feeling more in love than do women early in intimate relationships (Huston & Ashmore, 1986). Furthermore, the higher rates of depression in females have their onset in adolescence, when rates of cross-sex interaction rise (Nolen-Hoeksema, in press). Although these phenomena are no doubt multidetermined, the asymmetries in interaction styles may contribute to them.

To some degree, men appear to bring to bear much the same kind of techniques in mixed-sex groups that they are accustomed to using in same-sex groups. If the group is attempting some sort of joint problem solving or is carrying out a joint task, men do more initiating, directing, and interrupting than do women. Men's voices are louder and are more listened to than women's voices by both sexes (West & Zimmerman, 1985); men are more likely than women to lose interest in a taped message if it is spoken in a woman's rather than a man's voice (Robinson & MacArthur, 1982). Men are less influenced by the opinions of other group members than are women. Perhaps as a consequence of their greater assertiveness, men have more influence on the group process (Lockheed, 1985; Pugh & Wahrman, 1983), just as they did in childhood. Eagly and colleagues (Eagly, Wood, & Fishbaugh, 1981) have drawn our attention to an important point about cross-sex interaction in groups: The greater resistance of men to being influenced by other group members is found only when the men are under surveillance, that is, if others know whether they have yielded to their partners' influence attempts. I suggest that it is especially the monitoring by other *men* that inhibits men from entering into reciprocal influence with partners. When other men are present, men appear to feel that they must guard their dominance status and not comply too readily lest it be interpreted as weakness.

Women's behavior in mixed groups is more complex. There is some work indicating that they adapt by becoming more like men—that they raise their voices, interrupt, and otherwise become more assertive than they would be when interacting with women (Carli, 1989; Hall & Braunwald, 1981). On the other hand, there is also evidence that they carry over some of their well-practiced female-style behaviors, sometimes in exaggerated form. Women may wait for a turn to speak that does not come, and thus they may end up talking less than they would in a women's group. They smile more than the men do, agree more often with what others have said, and give nonverbal signals of attentiveness to what others—perhaps especially the men—are saying (Duncan & Fiske, 1977). In some writings this female behavior has been referred to as "silent applause."

Eagly (1987) reported a meta-analysis of behavior of the two sexes in groups (mainly mixed-sex groups) that were performing joint tasks. She found a consistent tendency for men to engage in more task behavior—giving and receiving information, suggestions, and opinions (see also Aries, 1982)—whereas women are more likely to engage in socioemotional behaviors that support positive affective relations within the group. Which style contributes more to effective group process? It depends. Wood, Polek, and Aiken (1985) have compared the performance of all-female and all-male groups on different kinds of tasks, finding that groups of women have more success on tasks that require discussion and negotiation, whereas male groups do better on tasks where success depends on the volume of ideas being generated. Overall, it appears that *both* styles are productive, though in different ways.

There is evidence that women feel at a disadvantage in mixed-sex interaction. For example, Hogg and Turner (1987) set up a debate between two young men taking one position and two young women taking another. The outcomes in this situation were contrasted with a situation in which young men and women were debating against same-sex partners. After the cross-sex debate, the self-esteem of the young men rose, but that of the young women declined. Furthermore, the men liked their women opponents better after debating with them, whereas the women liked the men less. In other words, the encounter in most cases was a pleasurable experience for the men, but not for the women. Another example comes from the work of Davis (1978), who set up get-acquainted sessions between pairs of young men and women. He found that the men took control of the interaction, dictating the pace at which intimacy increased, whereas the women adapted themselves to the pace set by the men. The women reported later, however, that they had been uncomfortable about not being able to control the sequence of events, and they did not enjoy the encounter as much as the men did.

In adolescence and early adulthood, the powerful forces of sexual attraction come into play. When couples are beginning to fall in love, or even when they are merely entertaining the possibility of developing an intimate relationship, each is motivated to please the other, and each sends signals implying "Your wish is my command." There is evidence that whichever member of a couple is more attractive, or less in love, is at an advantage and is more able to influence the partner than vice versa (Peplau, 1979). The influence patterns based on the power of interpersonal attraction are not distinct in terms of gender; that is, it may be either the man or the woman in a courting relationship who has the influence advantage. When first meeting, or in the early stages of the acquaintance process, women still may feel at some disadvantage, as shown in the Davis study, but this situation need not last. Work done in the 1960s indicated that in many couples, as relationships become deeper and more enduring, any overall asymmetry in influence diminishes greatly (Heiss, 1962; Leik, 1963; Shaw & Sadler, 1965). Most couples develop a relationship that is based on communality rather than exchange bargaining. That is, they have many shared goals and work jointly to achieve them. They do not need to argue over turf because they have the same turf. In well-functioning married couples, both members of the pair strive to avoid conflict, and indeed there is evidence that the men on average are even more conflict-avoidant than the women (Gottman & Levenson, 1988; Kelley et al., 1978). Nevertheless, there are still carry-overs of the different interactive styles males and females have acquired at earlier points in the life cycle. Women seem to expend greater effort toward maintaining harmonious moods (Huston & Ashmore, 1986, p. 177). With intimate cross-sex partners, men use more direct styles of influence, and women use more indirect ones. Furthermore, women are more likely to withdraw (become silent, cold, and distant) and/or take unilateral action in order to get their way in a dispute (Falbo & Peplau, 1980), strategies that we suspect may reflect their greater difficulty in influencing a male partner through direct negotiation.

Space limitations do not allow considering in any depth the next set of important relationships that human beings form: that between parents and children. Let me simply say that I think there is evidence for the following: The interaction styles that women have developed in interaction with girls and other women serve them well when they become mothers. Especially when children are young, women enter into deeper levels of reciprocity with their children than do men (e.g., Gleason, 1987; Maccoby & Jacklin, 1983) and communicate with them better. On the other hand, especially after the first two years, children need firm direction as well as warmth and reciprocity, and fathers' styles may contribute especially well to this aspect of parenting. The relationship women develop with young children seems to depend very little on whether they are dealing with a son or a daughter; it builds on maternal response to the characteristics and needs of early childhood that are found in both boys and girls to similar degrees. Fathers, having a less intimate relationship with individual children, treat young boys and girls in a somewhat more gendered way (Siegal, 1987). As children approach middle childhood and interact with same-sex other children, they develop the interactive styles characteristic of their sex, and their parents more and more interact with them as they have always done with same-sex or opposite-sex others. That is, mothers and daughters develop greater intimacy and reciprocity; fathers and sons exhibit more friendly rivalry and joking, more joint interest in masculine activities, and more rough play. Nevertheless, there are many aspects of the relationships between parents and children that do not depend on the gender of either the parent or the child.

Obviously, as the scene unfolds across generations, it is very difficult to identify the point in the developmental cycle at which the interactional styles of the two sexes begin to diverge, and more important, to identify the forces that cause them to diverge. In my view, processes within the nuclear family have been given too much credit—or too much blame—for this aspect of sex-typing. I doubt that the development of distinctive interactive styles has much to do with the fact that children are parented primarily by women, as some have claimed (Chodorow, 1978; Gilligan, 1982), and it seems likely to me that children's "identification" with the same-sex parent is more a consequence than a cause of children's acquisition of sex-typed interaction styles. I would place most of the emphasis on the peer group as the setting in which children first discover the compatibility of same-sex others, in which boys first discover the requirements of maintaining one's status in the male hierarchy, and in which the gender of one's partners becomes supremely important. We do not have a clear answer to the ultimate question of why the segregated peer groups function as they do. We need now to think about how it can be answered. The answer is important if we are to adapt ourselves successfully to the rapid changes in the roles and relationships of the two sexes that are occurring in modern societies.

REFERENCES

Aries, E. (1976). Interaction patterns and themes of male, female, and mixed groups. *Small Group Behavior, 7,* 7–18.

Aries, E. J. (1982). Verbal and nonverbal behavior in single-sex and mixed-sex groups: Are traditional sex roles changing? *Psychological Reports, 51,* 127–134.

Block, J. H. (1976). Debatable conclusions about sex differences. *Contemporary Psychology, 21,* 517–522.

Carli, L. L. (1989). Gender differences in interaction style and influence. *Journal of Personality and Social Psychology, 56,* 565–576.

Chodorow, N. (1978). *The reproduction of mothering.* Berkeley, CA: University of California Press.

Cowan, C., Drinkard, J., & MacGavin, L. (1984). The effects of target, age and gender on use of power strategies. *Journal of Personality and Social Psychology, 47,* 1391–1398.

Davis, J. D. (1978). When boy meets girl: Sex roles and the negotiation of intimacy in an acquaintance exercise. *Journal of Personality and Social Psychology, 36,* 684–692.

Duncan, S., Jr., & Fiske, D. W. (1977). *Face-to-face interaction: Research, methods and theory.* Hillsdale, NJ: Erlbaum.

Eagly, A. H. (1983). Gender and social influence. *American Psychologist, 38,* 971–981.

Eagly, A. H. (1987). *Sex differences in social behavior: A social role interpretation.* Hillsdale, NJ: Erlbaum.

Eagly, A. H., Wood, W., & Fishbaugh, L. (1981). Sex differences in conformity: Surveillance by the group as a determinant of male nonconformity. *Journal of Personality and Social Psychology, 40,* 384–394.

Eisenhart, M. A., & Holland, D. C. (1983). Learning gender from peers: The role of peer group in the cultural transmission of gender. *Human Organization, 42,* 321–332.

Erwin, P. (1985). Similarity of attitudes and constructs in children's friendships. *Journal of Experimental Child Psychology, 40,* 470–485.

Fagot, B. I. (1985). Beyond the reinforcement principle: Another step toward understanding sex roles. *Developmental Psychology, 21,* 1097–1104.

Falbo, T., & Peplau, L. A. (1980). Power strategies in intimate relationships. *Journal of Personality and Social Psychology, 38,* 618–628.

Gilligan, C. (1982). *In a different voice: Psychological theory and women's development.* Cambridge, MA: Howard University Press.

Gleason, J. B. (1987). Sex differences in parent-child interaction. In S. U. Phillips, S. Steele, & C. Tanz (Eds.), *Language, gender and sex in comparative perspective* (pp. 189–199). Cambridge, England: Cambridge University Press.

Gottman, J. M., & Levenson, R. W. (1988). The social psycho-physiology of marriage. In P. Roller & M. A. Fitzpatrick (Eds.), *Perspectives on marital interaction* (pp. 182–200). New York: Taylor & Francis.

Greeno, C. G. (1989). *Gender differences in children's proximity to adults.* Unpublished doctoral dissertation, Stanford University, Stanford, CA.

Hall, J. A., & Braunwald, K. G. (1981). Gender cues in conversation. *Journal of Personality and Social Psychology, 40,* 99–110.

Hauser, S. T., Powers, S. I., Weiss-Perry, B., Follansbee, D. J., Rajapark, D., & Greene, W. M. (1987). *The constraining and enabling coding system manual.* Unpublished manuscript.

Heiss, J. S. (1962). Degree of intimacy and male–female interaction. *Sociometry, 25,* 197–208.

Hogg, M. A., & Turner, J. C. (1987). Intergroup behavior, self stereotyping and the salience of social categories. *British Journal of Social Psychology, 26,* 325–340.

Humphreys, A. P., & Smith, P. K. (1987). Rough and tumble friendship and dominance in school children: Evidence for continuity and change with age in middle childhood. *Child Development, 58,* 201–212.

Huston, A. C. (1985). The development of sex-typing: Themes from recent research. *Developmental Review, 5,* 1–17.

Huston, T. L., & Ashmore, R. D. (1986). Women and men in personal relationship. In R. D. Ashmore & R. K. Del Boca (Eds.), *The social psychology of female–male relations* New York: Academic Press.

Jacklin, C. N., & Maccoby, E. E. (1978). Social behavior at 33 months in same-sex and mixed-sex dyads. *Child Development, 49,* 557–569.

Kelley, H. H., Cunningham, J. D., Grisham, J. A., Lefebvre, L. M., Sink, C. R., & Yablon, G. (1978). Sex differences in comments made during conflict in close relationships. *Sex Roles, 4,* 473–491.

Kraft, L. W., & Vraa, C. W. (1975). Sex composition of groups and pattern of self-disclosure by high school females. *Psychological Reports, 37,* 733–734.

Leaper, C. (1989). *The sequencing of power and involvement in boys' and girls' talk.* Unpublished manuscript (under review), University of California, Santa Cruz.

Leik, R. K. (1963). Instrumentality and emotionality in family interaction. *Sociometry, 26,* 131–145.

Lockheed, M. E. (1985). Sex and social influence: A meta-analysis guided by theory. In J. Berger & M. Zelditch (Eds.), *Status, attributions, and rewards* (pp. 406–429). San Francisco, CA: Jossey-Bass.

Maccoby, E. E. (1988). Gender as a social category. *Developmental Psychology, 26,* 755–765.

Maccoby, E. E., & Jacklin, C. N. (1974). *The psychology of sex differences.* Stanford, CA: Stanford University Press.

Maccoby, E. E., & Jacklin, C. N. (1980). Sex differences in aggression: A rejoinder and reprise. *Child Development, 51,* 964–980.

Maccoby, E. E., & Jacklin, C. N. (1983). The "person" characteristics of children and the family as environment. In D. Magnusson & V. L. Allen (Eds.), *Human development: An interactional perspective* (pp. 76–92). New York: Academic Press.

Maccoby, E. E., & Jacklin, C. N. (1987). Gender segregation in childhood. In H. W. Reese (Ed.), *Advances in child development and behavior* (Vol. 20, pp. 239–288). New York: Academic Press.

Maltz, D. N., & Borker, R. A. (1983). A cultural approach to male-female miscommunication. In John A. Gumperz (Ed.), *Language and social identity* (pp. 195–216). New York: Cambridge University Press.

Miller, P., Danaher, D., & Forbes, D. (1986). Sex-related strategies for coping with interpersonal conflict in children aged five and seven. *Developmental Psychology, 22,* 543–548.

Nolen-Hoeksema, S. (in press). *Sex differences in depression.* Stanford, CA: Stanford University Press.

Parpal, M., & Maccoby, E. E. (1985). Maternal responsiveness and subsequent child compliance. *Child Development, 56,* 1326–1334.

Peplau, A. (1979). Power in dating relationships. In J. Freeman (Ed.), *Women: A feminist perspective* (pp. 121–137). Palo Alto, CA: Mayfield.

Powlishta, K. K. (1987, April). *The social context of cross-sex interactions.* Paper presented at biennial meeting of the Society for Research in Child Development, Baltimore, MD.

Powlishta, K. K. (1989). *Salience of group membership: The case of gender.* Unpublished doctoral dissertation, Stanford University, Stanford, CA.

Pruitt, D. G. (1976). Power and bargaining. In B. Seidenberg & A. Snadowsky (Eds.), *Social psychology: An introduction* (pp. 343–375). New York: Free Press.

Pugh, M. D., & Wahrman, R. (1983). Neutralizing sexism in mixed-sex groups: Do women have to be better than men? *American Journal of Sociology, 88,* 746–761.

Reskin, B. F. (Ed.). (1984). *Sex segregation in the workplace: Trends, explanations and remedies.* Washington, DC: National Academy Press.

Robinson, J., & McArthur, L. Z. (1982). Impact of salient vocal qualities on causal attribution for a speaker's behavior. *Journal of Personality and Social Psychology, 43,* 236–247.

Sachs, J. (1987). Preschool boys' and girls' language use in pretend play. In S. U. Phillips, S. Steele, & C. Tanz (Eds.), *Language, gender and sex in comparative perspective* (pp. 178–188). Cambridge, England: Cambridge University Press.

in-Williams, R. C. (1979). Dominance hierarchies in groups of early adolescents. *Child Development, 50,* 923–935.

Serbin, L. A., Sprafkin, C., Elman, M., & Doyle, A. (1984). The early development of sex differentiated patterns of social influence. *Canadian Journal of Social Science, 14,* 350–363.

Shaw, M. E., & Sadler, O. W. (1965). Interaction patterns in heterosexual dyads varying in degree of intimacy. *Journal of Social Psychology, 66,* 345–351.

Sheldon, A. (1989, April). *Conflict talk: Sociolinguistic challenges to self-assertion and how young girls meet them.* Paper presented at the biennial meeting of the Society for Research in Child Development, Kansas City.

Siegal, M. (1987). Are sons and daughters treated more differently by fathers than mothers? *Developmental Review, 7,* 183–209.

Thorne, B. (1986). Girls and boys together, but mostly apart. In W. W. Hartup & L. Rubin (Eds.), *Relationships and development* (pp. 167–184). Hillsdale, NJ: Erlbaum.

Tieger, T. (1980). On the biological basis of sex differences in aggression. *Child Development, 51,* 943–963.

Wasserman, G. A., & Stern, D. N. (1978). An early manifestation of differential behavior toward children of the same and opposite sex. *Journal of Genetic Psychology, 133,* 129–137.

West, C., & Zimmerman, D. H. (1985). Gender, language and discourse. In T. A. van Dijk (Ed.), *Handbook of discourse analysis: Vol. 4. Discourse analysis in society* (pp. 103–124). London: Academic Press.

Wood, W., Polek, D., & Aiken, C. (1985). Sex differences in group task performance. *Journal of Personality and Social Psychology, 48,* 63–71.

Multiple Choice:

1. Which term does not go with the others?

    A. enabling style
    B. dominance hierarchies
    C. rough and tumble play
    D. task orientation

2. Which of the following is reported in this article?

    A. Both boys and girls prefer to play with other children of the same sex.
    B. Gender segregation most often occurs in sex-typed activities.
    C. Preference for same-sex playmates decreases with age.
    D. Gender segregation is prominent in highly structured classrooms, but is less strong on the playground.
    E. All of the above.

Essay:

1. Many people have the goal of achieving greater equality between the sexes. Does Maccoby's article make you more pessimistic or more optimistic in this regard? Why?

2. Maccoby describes many characteristics of same-sex and mixed-sex interactions. To what extent do these fit with your own experience? Give examples. How many of the sex differences Maccoby describes were you unaware of before reading this article?

ARTICLE 19

Gender Stereotypes During Adolescence: Developmental Changes and the Transition to Junior High School

Thomas Alfieri, Diane N. Ruble, and E. Tory Higgins

Reprinted from: *Developmental Psychology*, 1996, *32*, 1129-1137.

Do you remember moving from elementary school to junior high school? You no doubt experienced a number of changes in many aspects of your everyday life, as well as in the way you felt and thought about the world. One such change may have been the way you thought about gender. If so, it is likely that you became more flexible in your thinking.

This article is concerned with children's *gender stereotype flexibility*. Children who view feminine qualities (e.g., gentle and polite) and masculine qualities (e.g., careless and active) as characteristic of both females and males are flexible in their ideas about gender. In contrast, children are inflexible if they think only females possess feminine qualities and males possess masculine qualities. The research reported in this article finds that children become more flexible in their thinking about gender after they make the transition from elementary school to junior high school.

There are several important aspects of the design used in this research that make these findings especially compelling. First, the study included groups of children who made the transition from elementary school to junior high school at different ages. This eliminates the possibility that the observed increase in gender stereotype flexibility might have been due to age instead of the transition itself. Second, the research was *longitudinal*--the same children were assessed both before and after they made a transition. This allows for conclusions about change. Finally, the findings were replicated in three different samples of children. Replication is one of the most powerful tools in science. If a finding is correct, it should be replicable--the same result should occur whenever the same procedures are followed. If it is incorrect, it is unlikely that it will be observed again merely by chance.

Developmental Psychology
1996. Vol. 32. No. 6, 1129–1137

Gender Stereotypes During Adolescence: Developmental Changes and the Transition to Junior High School

Thomas Alfieri and Diane N. Ruble
New York University

E. Tory Higgins
Columbia University

Although much evidence suggests that gender stereotyping becomes less flexible during adolescence, results of the present study indicate that gender stereotypes may actually become more flexible at some point during certain adolescent school transitions. The authors measured the flexibility of gender stereotypes in adolescents in Grades 4 through 11, using a combined cross-sectional and longitudinal design. Results indicated that flexibility increased for stereotypes concerning the psychological attributes of men and women after the transition into junior high school, regardless of whether this transition occurred during the 7th or 8th grade. Over the remaining years of junior high and high school, stereotype flexibility decreased. These results help resolve previous inconsistencies found in the literature by suggesting when and why changes in gender stereotype flexibility versus rigidity occur during adolescence.

Adolescence, as the period of life between childhood and adulthood, is characterized by many important changes. As an individual traverses this period, beliefs held as a child may start to change. For example, young adolescents' attitudes toward social conventions are markedly different from those of children and older adolescents (Smetana, 1988). Among the most important sets of social-conventional beliefs likely to change at this time are those concerning gender. Indeed, considerable theoretical analysis suggests that adolescence is a special time for gender, a time when gender-related beliefs may become intensified (e.g., Hill & Lynch, 1983) or be transcended (e.g., Rebecca, Hefner, & Oleshansky, 1976). On the one hand, a newly emerging identity as a sexual being may lead to heightened concerns about gender role expectations and increased polarization of attitudes (Katz, 1979). On the other hand, continuing cognitive maturation should facilitate a more flexible and relativistic view of gender norms (Eccles, 1987).

The literature has shown support for both predictions. Several studies have reported increased flexibility in adolescence relative to childhood (Carter & Patterson, 1982; Katz & Ksansnak, 1994). For example, Nelson and Keith (1990) found that 8th graders held more flexible beliefs about the characteristics associated with gender (e.g., "How important is it for a man to be gentle?") than did 5th graders. In contrast, other researchers have suggested that gender-related flexibility decreases as a child enters adolescence (Galambos, Almeida, & Petersen, 1990; Guttentag & Longfellow, 1977; Hill & Lynch, 1983). For example, in a study of children in kindergarten, 3rd, 5th, and 8th grades, Stoddart and Turiel (1985) found that only kindergartners and 8th graders ranked gender role violations as more wrong than personal and conventional violations.

In this latter set of findings, the authors would appear to question conclusions from previous reviews of the gender stereotyping literature that flexibility of gender beliefs increases with age and with concomitant flexibility in cognitive operations (Eisenberg, Martin, & Fabes, 1996; Huston, 1983; Ruble & Ruble, 1982). Although several explanations could be offered for the inconsistent findings across studies, two seem particularly noteworthy. First, there is considerable variation in the exact age range that defines the stage of adolescence. Some studies are limited to late elementary school or junior high school ages (7th–8th grades), and others examine high school ages (9th–12th grades). Interestingly, on theoretical as well as empirical grounds, researchers have reason to suspect that these two periods might differ (Eccles, 1987; Katz, 1979). In particular, Katz has suggested that young adolescents may exhibit greater openness toward flexible gender roles than children but become increasingly rigid or polarized later in adolescence.

One problem in evaluating this hypothesis is that flexibility has been operationalized in many different ways; this may explain the variations observed in the above studies. It is thus noteworthy that in studies directly comparing younger and older adolescents, researchers have reported findings consistent with this hypothesis. In three studies examining beliefs about gender differentiation, 7th and 8th graders were more flexible, whereas older, high-school-aged adolescents were more rigid (Sigelman, Carr, & Begley, 1986; Ullian, 1976; Urberg, 1979). In addition, findings based on other measures of flexibility gen-

Thomas Alfieri and Diane N. Ruble, Department of Psychology, New York University; E. Tory Higgins, Department of Psychology, Columbia University.

This research was supported by two grants from the National Institute of Mental Health, Research Grant MH 37215 and Research Scientist Development Award MH 00484.

We would like to thank Faith Greulich and Judy Shim for their assistance, and Jacqueline Goodnow, Stacey Lutz, and Joel Szkrybalo for their helpful comments on earlier versions of this article. This research was inspired by the work of Roberta Simmons.

Correspondence concerning this article should be addressed to Diane N. Ruble, Department of Psychology, New York University, 6 Washington Place, 7th Floor, New York, New York 10003.

erally support this trend. Simmons and Blyth (1987) found a decrease between Grades 6 and 10 in adolescents' ratings of how often they acted like the opposite sex, although a floor effect for boys made this change significant for girls only. Emmerich and Shepard (1982) found that positive evaluations of targets whose behavior was sex appropriate (i.e., traditional) tended to increase between early and later adolescence among White participants. (Interestingly, Black participants were more likely to show a decrease.) Finally, in Biernat (1991), flexibility was operationalized as the extent to which gender-related social judgments are based on individuating information (e.g., behaviors) as opposed to biological sex. Although statistical comparisons of younger and older adolescents were not presented, an examination of the figures reveals that older adolescents were somewhat less flexible in their judgments than were younger adolescents.

A second possible reason for differing conclusions across studies is the failure to include in the design an examination of other changes during adolescence that are likely to affect a shift toward increasing flexibility or rigidity. One recent exception is a study by Galambos et al. (1990), which included an examination of pubertal status. However, the increased salience of gender and the pressure on individuals to be attractive as sexual relationships begin are the main reasons for expected increases in rigid distinctions between the sexes (Eccles, 1987; Hill & Lynch, 1983); changes in social structure, as opposed to pubertal status, are probably more closely related to the specific hypothesis of changing flexibility of gender-related beliefs. Such changes in social structure are likely to be much more evident for young adolescents who go to junior high school and are thus exposed to older children who have begun to date than for those who remain in elementary school. Thus, one possible reason for differences across studies examining 8th and 9th graders is that some may have been in elementary school and others in junior high school.

In addition to changes in exposure to older children associated with entry to junior high school, the process of the transition itself may influence the flexibility of gender beliefs. Recent theoretical analyses have suggested that the passage from one social life phase to another is marked not only by changes in actual social experiences and social regulation but also by changes in individual orientations toward information (Higgins, Loeb, & Ruble, 1995). According to a phase model of transitions described by Ruble (1994), when an individual enters a new life phase or subculture, his or her previously existing beliefs and expectations may be challenged by the social demands of the new life phase. The individual will then be stimulated to engage in active information seeking in order to form new beliefs and expectations. During this period of construction or reconstruction, preexisting beliefs and expectations are held only tentatively; yet, once the fundamental knowledge has been acquired, the individual begins to draw some conclusions to consolidate the new information. Consequently, at this second phase, the individual may be particularly motivated to support the recently formed conclusions and may show a kind of rigid adherence to or personal investment in information and activities that are consistent with them.

The transition to junior high school is likely to be an espe-cially important life phase for changes in gender beliefs (Higgins & Parsons, 1983; Meece, 1987). Junior high school differs from elementary school in that children attend school with a larger number and wider variety of peers, have more male teachers, and begin new forms of gender-related behavior such as dating. If these and other differences between the two types of schools sufficiently challenge gender beliefs, Ruble's (1994) model would predict that adolescents will engage in active information seeking to reconstruct their gender beliefs and that during this period of construction, they will be less sure about the nature of male and female characteristics than they were in elementary school.

The present study was designed to test directly these three hypotheses: (a) Differentiation in gender beliefs would decrease with age into early adolescence but then increase again during late adolescence; (b) the timing of these changes would be affected by entry into junior high school; and (c) adolescents may show a temporary increase in gender flexibility when they first enter junior high school despite moving into an environment expected to increase polarization of gender. In order to examine these hypotheses in the present study, we used a combination of cross-sectional and longitudinal designs. During the 1st year of the study, participants were students in Grades 4 through 9. A subset of the 7th, 8th, and 9th graders were followed for 2 additional years, providing information about stereotype flexibility up to Grade 11. With very few exceptions (Galambos et al., 1990; Lerner, Vincent, & Benson, 1976), researchers have not used longitudinal designs in studies of gender beliefs in children, making it difficult to draw clear conclusions about developmental change. In the present study, we could examine developmental changes by looking at both differences across students in different grades and changes in the same children as they progressed across these same grades. In addition, participants came from one of two neighboring school districts. In the first district, the transition to junior high school was between 6th and 7th grade, whereas in the second school district, the transition to junior high school was between 7th and 8th grade. By using this design, we were in a position to distinguish changing flexibilities associated with grade from those associated with the transition to junior high school. It was predicted that stereotypic flexibility would be highest in the 7th graders in the first district and in the 8th graders in the second district. In addition, we expected flexibility to decline after the 1st year of junior high school in both districts.

The measure used in the study examined flexibility of gender beliefs about stereotypic characteristics (e.g., traits, competencies, emotions). In order to test the hypotheses adequately, we needed a measure that had certain properties. First, we were interested in the social construction of gender and thus we needed a measure that explicitly assessed beliefs about characteristics that distinguish males and females. One problem with using measures of participants' interests in gender-related activities and their self-perceptions of gender-related characteristics is that the actual link between such choices and gender is unclear. As Spence (1993) has persuasively argued, a woman's self-description as emotional and her choice of nursing as a career may or may not be related to her constructions and attitudes about gender. Because a critical component of the gender-intensification hypothesis involves expectations about the nature of gender differences (Hill & Lynch, 1983), it seemed essential to measure these expectations directly rather than indirectly.

Second, we needed a measure that would allow a clear distinction between knowledge about gender stereotypic norms and flexibility in personal beliefs about those stereotypes. If students in the 1st year of junior high school are likely to say that math ability is equally characteristic of females and males, we cannot be certain that this represents a belief in gender flexibility as opposed to a lack of knowledge that math ability is stereotypically associated with males.[1] Fortunately, a procedure that can easily make this distinction has been identified and is now widely used in the literature (Serbin, Powlishta, & Gulko, 1993; Signorella, Bigler, & Liben, 1993). Specifically, participants are asked whether a particular characteristic is associated with males, females, or both. The number of "both" responses constitutes the measure of flexibility. Subsequently, participants are asked to reclassify the items as to whether they are more associated with males or females as an index of their gender knowledge.

Third, we needed a measure of flexibility that was relevant to the expected changes in adolescence and would show sufficient variability. Although the Sex Role Learning Index (Edelbrock & Sugawara, 1978) is a frequently used measure for children, it involves the categorization of objects (e.g., helmet, iron) that seemed less relevant to the changes in gender flexibility for adolescent participants. Other measures of flexibility used with elementary school children have involved stereotypes about occupations and roles. Unfortunately, several studies suggest that flexibility with such items approaches ceiling by 6th grade (e.g., Carter & Patterson, 1982; Lerner et al., 1976). Thus, we used a measure of flexibility with stereotypic characteristics (e.g., gentle, strong). Such items seem particularly relevant to the changes students may observe as they move from one social life phase to another (Higgins & Parsons, 1983) and to their changed expectations about gender related to sexuality. The items have also shown considerable variability in gender stereotyping among children in late elementary school (Serbin et al., 1993). Finally, one additional advantage of using this type of measure is that it matches most closely the measures used to study gender stereotyping among adults. In the literature on adults, researchers have amassed impressive evidence that such stereotypic expectations are a major determinant of what information is attended to and remembered about others, and of important decisions made about people in everyday interactions (Stangor & Lange, 1994).

Method

Participants

Participants were attending school in one of two adjacent school districts located in a suburb of New York City. After the superintendents and boards of education of these school districts granted permission to run the study, consent forms were mailed to the parents of all children in the appropriate grades. Approximately 25% of the eligible students received parental consent to participate in this study. This response rate is typical of public schools in the greater New York City area. The population from which these samples were drawn is quite homogeneous.

Table 1
Number of Participants by School, Grade, and Year

Grade	School District 1			School District 2	
	Year 1	Year 2	Year 3	Year 1	Year 2
			Main sample		
4	30[a]			54[a]	
5	33[a]			42[a]	
7	58[a]	54[b]	44[c]	19[a]	16[b]
8	46[a]	30	23[c]	9[a]	
9	28[a]	19	15[c]	8[a]	

Additional participants	
K–Grade 8 school	K–Grade 6 and Grades 7–9 school
6 28 28[d]	22 22[d]

Note. Each cell contains an approximately equal number of boys and girls. K = kindergarten.
[a] Participants in Analysis 1.   [b] Participants in Analysis 2.   [c] Participants in Analysis 3.   [d] Participants in Analysis 4.

Over 95% of the students in each of the school districts were White. Median annual incomes of all families in the first and second school districts were $52,200 and $56,600, respectively. Mean ages of students were as follows: 4th graders, 9.4 years; 5th graders, 10.4 years; 7th graders, 12.3 years; 8th graders, 13.3 years; 9th graders, 14.2 years.[2]

School District 1: Junior high school begins in 7th grade. In the first school district, kindergarten through 6th grades were in elementary schools, 7th and 8th grades were in a single junior high school, and 9th through 12th grades were in a single high school. One hundred ninety-five students (91 girls, 104 boys) in Grades 4, 5, 7, 8, and 9 participated in the 1st year of the study. Of the 7th, 8th, and 9th graders, 82 students (62% of the original sample) were tested again for 2 additional years. See Table 1 for a more complete breakdown of the sample.

School District 2: Junior high school begins in 8th grade. To better examine the effects of school environment on gender stereotype flexibility, a small sample of students were tested in another school district. In this second school district, kindergarten through 6th grades were in elementary schools, 7th grade was alone in a middle school, 8th and 9th grades were in a separate junior high school, and 10th through 12th grades were in a high school. One hundred thirty-two children in Grades 4, 5, 7, 8, and 9 were tested during the 1st year of the study (see Table 1 for a breakdown). Almost all of the 7th-grade children were tested again 1 year later. Only a small number of 7th-, 8th-, and 9th-grade students were available to be tested in this school district. Despite the small *n*s, all of the important data points in this study are drawn

---

[1] Indeed, in our pilot testing to select items that showed clear gender stereotypic knowledge, we were surprised at the lack of agreement shown by adolescents to items, such as "good at math," "logical," and "gives up easily," that are clearly stereotyped among adults.

[2] Sixth-grade students were not included in the study because the study was part of a larger investigation of social-cognitive changes across school transitions in which we had a sample entering school (preschool, kindergarten, and first grade) and an adolescent sample making junior high school transitions (the present sample), who were followed for 3 years. During the 1st year of the study, we collected data from 4th and 5th graders simply to provide an intermediate point of comparison.

from two cohorts, one cross-sectional and one longitudinal. (See other comments on this small sample size in the *Discussion* section and immediately below.)

Additional Participants

An additional sample of participants was tested in order to replicate the findings from the main sample and to directly test the hypotheses in sixth-grade students. The additional participants were 28 sixth graders (14 boys, 14 girls) from a private school that housed Grades kindergarten (K) through 8 and 22 sixth graders (10 boys, 12 girls) from a private school district that separated Grades K through 6 from Grades 7 through 9. Approximately 45% of all sixth graders in each school received parental permission to participate in our study. This response rate is not unusual for private schools in the New York City area but is higher than typical response rates for public schools.

The additional students were tested in early June (at the end of their 6th-grade year) and again in November of the following school year when all students were in 7th grade. Thus, the students in the school district that separated Grades K–6 from Grades 7–9 made a transition from elementary to junior high school during the course of this study, whereas the students in the school district that included Grades K–8 did not make a school transition.

Data from the additional participants differ from those in the main sample in three important ways. First, the additional participants were all from private school. Second, these students were tested approximately 3 years after the completion of the main study. Third, the time lag between testing dates was 5 months for the additional participants and 1 year for the main sample. Given these differences, the additional data are not directly comparable with the data in the original study. Thus, instead of just adding the additional participants to the main sample, the data from the additional participants are analyzed separately (see *Analysis 4*).

Measure

The measure of gender stereotyping consisted of 12 trait-related terms, half of which were masculine (e.g., explores strange places, careless, active) and half of which were feminine (e.g., gentle, polite, sad). In addition, half were positive and half were negative. Following well-established procedures (Serbin et al., 1993), participants were asked to indicate whether the items described males, females, or both. For items classified as both, participants were subsequently asked to recategorize the items with the both option removed. Selection of the both option represented gender stereotype flexibility. Classification as male or female after the both option was removed represented gender stereotype knowledge (Signorella et al., 1993).

The 12 items used in the measure were selected from previous research on gender stereotyping, and each item was shown to be highly associated with only one sex (e.g., Koblinsky, Cruse, & Sugawara, 1978; Williams, Bennett, & Best, 1975; Williams & Best, 1990).[3] Similar to the items used in the Williams et al. (1975) study, some of the traits in the current scale were expressed in terms of behaviors (e.g., runs away from scary places) whereas other traits were expressed in terms of competencies or emotions (e.g., angry). Item selection was contingent on participants' ability to consistently classify them as being stereotypically masculine or feminine. Indeed, preliminary analyses of the present set of items indicated that gender knowledge was extremely high. Across all grades, the percentages of classifications that were congruent with current gender stereotypes ranged from 81% to 97% (overall mean = 91%), which was considerably higher than the 75% cutoff used in previous research (Broverman, Vogel, Broverman, Clarkson, & Rosenkrantz, 1972). Stereotype knowledge in this sample of children and young adolescents did not vary as a function of age or sex.

Gender stereotype flexibility scores were calculated for each participant. Items were scored as 1 if the both option was initially selected and 0 if it was not. The high knowledge scores ensure that when participants are not responding with a both option, they are providing the stereotyped gender response in a vast majority of the cases. Two flexibility scores were computed for each participant. A flexibility score for the masculine stereotype was calculated by averaging the item flexibility scores for the six masculine stereotyped items, and a flexibility score for the feminine stereotype was calculated by averaging the item flexibility scores for the six feminine stereotyped items. These scores represent each participant's proportion of both responses to either the masculine or the feminine items. Higher scores represent greater stereotype flexibility. Masculine and feminine stereotype flexibility scores were correlated, $r(326) = .52, p < .001$.

Cronbach's alpha for the 12-item flexibility scores was .70 in the 1st year and .72 and .80 in the 2nd and 3rd years of the study, respectively. As an additional check on the issues of scale validity and reliability, additional data were collected on an independent sample of 140 children in Grades 6–8. Participants completed a gender stereotype scale similar to the one used in the original study; however, this modified scale contained the original 12 items as well as 12 additional items. The correlation between the flexibility score obtained from the original 12 items and the flexibility score obtained from the additional 12 items was, .77 ($p < .001$), suggesting that the present 12-item measure was adequate to assess a broad, gender-linked trait flexibility. Similar to the original sample, the flexibility scores of the new sample were reliable. The alpha coefficient of flexibility scores in the new sample (based on only the original items) was .71.

Because flexibility is intended to tap attitudes toward gender stereotypes and not knowledge of these stereotypes, convergent validity may be assessed by comparing flexibility with an established measure of gender-related attitudes. Thus, participants in the independent data set also filled out the Attitudes Toward Women Scale for Adolescents (Galambos, Petersen, Richards, & Gitelson, 1985). Although overall flexibility does not necessarily imply positive attitudes toward women, certain types of flexibility do. Specifically, classifying stereotypically positive masculine traits as describing females as well as males (i.e., both) implies a positive attitude toward women, and classifying stereotypically negative feminine traits as describing both males and females weakens the association between femininity and negativity and thereby also implies a more positive attitude toward women. As expected, positive attitudes toward women were significantly correlated with flexibility scores based on the positive masculine items ($r = .32, p < .001$) and with flexibility scores based on the negative feminine items ($r = .35, p < .001$). This pattern was the same for both boys and girls.

Procedure

The 4th- and 5th-grade students were interviewed individually. Participants were presented with three response cards reading either "men or boys," "women or girls," or "both" and the following instructions: "Now I'm going to ask you to match a phrase or word to whom you think it best describes—men or boys, women or girls, or both." Participants were further instructed to indicate their responses by pointing to the appropriate card and were then presented with the 12 items in the scale. Each item was printed on a separate index card and randomly presented to participants. After they classified all the items, the both

---

[3] Because this measure was included as part of a battery of measures assessing changes in children's perceptions of themselves and others, it was necessary to keep the measure as short as possible. Analyses on an independent sample described in the text, however, document that the measure is a good representation of gender stereotypes.

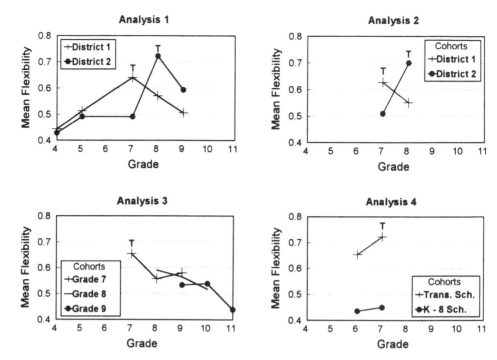

Figure 1. Mean gender stereotype flexibility by grade. Mean scores are percentages of "both" responses. Data points labeled *T* are from children who have just made the transition to junior high school. Trans. Sch. = transition school, K–8 Sch. = kindergarten through 8th-grade school.

option was removed, and participants were asked to recategorize the items originally classified as both into one of the two remaining categories: men or boys, or women or girls. Older participants were tested in group settings. Their task was the same, except that they responded in a questionnaire format. Testing for all participants (in the main study) for all years occurred during the month of October.

Results

Analysis 1: Cross-Sectional Data

The first analysis used all the data from the 1st year of testing. This analysis represented a cross-sectional test of the hypothesis that stereotype flexibility would increase on entering junior high school regardless of whether this transition occurs during the 7th or the 8th grade. An analysis of variance (ANOVA) was performed on flexibility scores from the 1st year of testing using grade (4, 5, 7, 8, or 9), and school district (transition in 7th grade or 8th grade) as between-subject variables and stereotype gender (masculine or feminine) as a within-subject variable. As predicted, this analysis produced a significant Grade × School District interaction, $F(4, 313) = 2.74$, $MSE = 0.05$, $p < .05$. Mean flexibilities, collapsed over the masculine and feminine stereotypes, for each grade in the two school districts are presented in Figure 1.

As predicted, the 1st year of junior high school was associated with an increase in gender stereotype flexibility. A planned comparison indicated that the mean flexibility score of the 7th graders in School District 1 ($M = .63$), in which junior high school began in 7th grade, was significantly higher than the mean flex-

ibility score of all the other students in this district ($M = .51$), $t(313) = 3.48$, $p < .001$. In School District 2, where 8th grade was the 1st year of junior high school, the mean flexibility score of the 8th graders ($M = .72$) was significantly higher than the mean flexibility score of all the other students in this district ($M = .50$), $t(313) = 2.79$, $p < .01$.

A series of planned comparisons between same-grade students in the two districts was also conducted. The mean flexibility score of 7th graders in School District 1 ($M = .63$) was significantly higher than the mean flexibility score of 7th graders in School District 2 ($M = .49$), $t(313) = 2.36$, $p < .05$. The mean flexibility score of the 8th graders in School District 2 ($M = .72$) was greater than and marginally significantly different from the mean flexibility score of the 8th graders in School District 1 ($M = .56$), $t(313) = 1.95$ $p < .07$. Flexibility scores of 4th, 5th, and 9th graders in the two districts were not significantly different. Grade produced a significant main effect, $F(4, 313) = 5.99$, $p < .01$. The interpretation of this main effect, however, was modified by the significant Grade × School District interaction and was discussed above. No overall differences between the two school districts or any other significant effects involving grade or school district were found. Stereotype gender also produced a significant main effect, $F(1, 313) = 5.73$, $p < .05$, with the masculine stereotype ($M = .51$) less flexible than the feminine stereotype ($M = .54$).[4]

[4] Given the small n in a few of the cells, sex of subject was not included as an independent variable in the ANOVA presented in the text. This is not a conceptual problem as sex differences in flexibility over the tran-

Analysis 2: Longitudinal Subsample

The second analysis compared data from the longitudinal subsample in School District 2 (i.e., 7th graders who were also tested in 8th grade) with the comparable sample from School District 1. This analysis represented a longitudinal test of the hypothesis that entrance into junior high school is associated with an increase in stereotype flexibility. The data from this longitudinal sample followed almost exactly the general pattern of change established in the cross-sectional sample. Mean flexibilities from the longitudinal data are presented in Figure 1. An ANOVA was conducted on the longitudinal subsample data using sex of subject and school district as between-subject variables, and year of study (in Year 1, all students were in 7th grade; in Year 2, all students were in 8th grade) and stereotype gender (masculine or feminine) as within-subject variables. This ANOVA revealed a significant interaction between school district and year of study, $F(1, 66) = 11.63$, $MSE = 0.08$, $p < .01$. The 7th graders in School District 2 increased in flexibility as they entered the 8th grade and junior high school: 7th-grade flexibility, $M = .51$; 8th-grade flexibility, $M = .71$; $t(66) = 2.88$, $p < .01$. The 7th graders in School District 1 who had already begun junior high school marginally decreased in flexibility as they entered 8th grade: 7th-grade flexibility, $M = .63$; 8th-grade flexibility, $M = .55$; $t(66) = 1.97$, $p = .053$. These results parallel those found in the cross-sectional sample. There were no other significant effects in this longitudinal subsample ANOVA.[5]

Analysis 3: Full Longitudinal Sample

The next analysis used all available data from the longitudinal sample in School District 1. Unlike students in School District 2, some of the 7th, 8th, and 9th graders in School District 1 were tested for 2 additional years. The data from this longitudinal component of the study revealed a decrease in gender stereotype flexibility in each of the three cohorts. Participants in the 7th grade were the most flexible (1st year of junior high school), and overall flexibility (collapsed over masculine and feminine flexibility) decreased with age. These data are presented in Figure 1.

An ANOVA was conducted on the longitudinal data, using sex of subject and cohort (7th, 8th, or 9th grade in 1st year of study) as between-subject variables and stereotype gender (masculine or feminine) and year of study (1st, 2nd, or 3rd) as

within-subject variables. Year of study produced a significant main effect, $F(2, 152) = 3.44$, $MSE = 0.06$, $p < .05$; Year 1, $M = .62$; Year 2, $M = .56$; and Year 3, $M = .55$. A least significant difference (LSD) test, performed at the 5% level, indicated that the Year 1 mean flexibility was significantly higher than both the Year 2 mean and the Year 3 mean. The mean-flexibility scores from Year 2 and Year 3 were not significantly different. Interactions among the variables were not significant, thus indicating similar rates of decreasing flexibility in the three cohorts.

Finally, the Sex of Subject × Stereotype Gender × Year of Study interaction was significant, $F(2, 152) = 4.07$, $p < .05$. An LSD test was performed, indicating that during the 1st year of the study, boys were less flexible with the masculine stereotype ($M = .54$) than were girls ($M = .68$). Flexibility scores of boys and girls did not differ for the feminine stereotype during the 1st year of the study, nor were there any significant differences between boys' and girls' masculine or feminine flexibility scores during the remaining years of the study.

Analysis 4: Additional Participants

The final analysis used the additional data collected from 6th-grade students at two different private schools. The results of this analysis replicate the findings presented in Analyses 1 and 2 (see Figure 1). Students who made a school transition between the Time 1 and Time 2 testing dates showed an increase in gender stereotype flexibility (Time 1, $M = .65$; Time 2, $M = .72$), whereas same-age students who attended the K–8 school did not show a statistically significant increase in flexibility over the course of the study (Time 1, $M = .44$; Time 2, $M = .45$). A repeated measures ANOVA was performed on the flexibility scores using sex of subject and type of school (transition vs. no transition) as between-subject variables and time (Time 1 or Time 2) as a within-subject variable.

This ANOVA indicated that the students who made the transition to junior high school had a significantly larger increase in stereotype flexibility than did students who did not make a school transition; the Type of School × Time interaction was significant, $F(1, 46) = 3.92$, $MSE = 0.03$, $p < .05$. Sex of student did not interact with changes in gender stereotype flexibility. Type of school did produce a significant main effect, $F(1, 46) = 15.85$, $p < .01$, with children from the transition school having higher flexibility than children from the nontransition school. The effect may be due to differences in socioeconomic status. The transition schools were located in an upper-middle-class neighborhood, and the nontransition school was located in a middle-class neighborhood. Nonetheless, the changes in flexibility over time support the hypotheses. These changes cannot be attributed to a regression toward the mean, as the group that started off high in flexibility was the one that increased in flexibility after the transition.

---

sition were not predicted. Furthermore, when sex was included in the ANOVA, the predicted Grade × School District interaction remained intact. Girls and boys did not differ in overall stereotype flexibility; mean flexibility scores for girls and boys were .53 and .51, respectively, $F(1, 303) = 0.66$, $MSE = 0.02$. There was, however, a significant Sex of Subject × Stereotype Gender interaction, $F(1, 303) = 5.69$, $MSE = 0.01$, $p < .05$. Post hoc comparisons (based on Scheffé criteria) indicated that boys were less flexible than girls on the masculine stereotype (boys, $M = .47$; girls, $M = .54$; $t[303] = 3.63$, $p < .01$), whereas boys and girls did not differ in their flexibilities on the feminine stereotype ($Ms = .55$ and .53, respectively). This interaction qualifies the stereotype gender main effect reported in the text.

---

[5] In addition to gender stereotypes, item valence was also examined. Both boys and girls were consistently most flexible with positive feminine stereotypes and least flexible with negative feminine stereotypes.

Discussion

Although some researchers have suggested that adolescence is a time of increasing stereotype flexibility, other researchers have proposed that adolescence is associated with decreasing stereotype flexibility. The present research suggests a resolution to these conflicting views. Gender stereotype flexibility may, in fact, increase or decrease during adolescence, depending on the social environment of the individual. Consistent with predictions derived from Ruble's (1994) phase model of transitions, an increase in stereotype flexibility was observed following a change in an individual's social environment, that is, the transition to junior high school. After this increase, stereotype flexibility decreased during middle and late adolescence.

The consistency of the pattern across districts varying in the timing of the junior high school transition was remarkable. In School District 1, flexibility peaked during the 7th grade, which was the beginning of junior high school. Adolescents from School District 2 showed a peak flexibility during 8th grade, which was the beginning of their junior high school. Even though only a few students from School District 2 were available for this study, the effect of school transition on stereotype flexibility was nearly perfectly replicated in both the cross-sectional and the longitudinal data. The data point represented by the small sample of 8th graders in School District 2 was replicated by the 2nd-year data for the larger sample of 7th graders. The additional data also support this pattern of change. Sixth-grade students who made a transition to junior high school in 7th grade increased in flexibility, and 6th grade students who remained in the same school in 7th grade showed no change in stereotype flexibility.

The pattern of results in this study is consistent with the finding of a recent meta-analysis in that flexibility appears to increase throughout the elementary school years (Signorella et al., 1993). Only after the 2nd year of junior high school does flexibility start to decrease. Taken together, then, the present findings support our three main predictions: (a) Flexibility in gender stereotypic beliefs increases during early adolescence but then declines, (b) the timing of these changes is linked to entry to junior high school, and (c) gender beliefs are most flexible immediately after the transition to junior high school. It is important to note that these findings are specific to one kind of gender flexibility—that concerned with beliefs about differences in the characteristics of males and females. Whether or not these same trends would be observed with other kinds of flexibility, such as personal preferences and actual behaviors, is not clear. As reviewed earlier, some studies have found a similar decline between early and later adolescence with other measures of flexibility, but the influence of the junior high context and the process of a social transition may be limited to variables related to the social construction of gender.

A brief discussion of the social environments of the 7th- and 8th-grade students may help to shed some light on the conditions that may have prompted the reevaluation of gender stereotypes. In School District 1, 7th and 8th graders were together in junior high school. In School District 2, 7th graders were alone in a middle school, and 8th and 9th graders were together in a separate junior high school. Seventh-grade students from both districts experienced a transition from an elementary school, in which they spent the majority of their days in one classroom with one teacher, to a school structure divided into periods, in which they spent each period in a different classroom studying a different subject with a different teacher. These structural changes alone, however, cannot account for the observed increase in flexibility. Students in School District 2 did not increase in stereotype flexibility when they entered the 7th grade, even though they had just experienced a transition that largely changed their daily routines. For students in both school districts, the increase in flexibility was associated with the 1st year of junior high school with older students.

Higgins and Parsons (1983) have pointed out that, in addition to understanding their newcomer status, 1st year junior high school students encounter and must accommodate to a wider range of peers, presumably with a wider range of personality types, than they did in elementary school. The present study suggests that the increase in flexibility has more to do with adapting to a newcomer status, going from being the oldest student to the youngest student, and interacting with a wide range of older peers, and presumably new norms and pressures, than it does simply with changes in daily routine.

The observed increase in flexibility appears to be temporary. As the adolescent advances through junior high and high school, stereotype flexibility decreases. According to Ruble (1994), this decrease in flexibility may reflect the consolidation of newly formed gender beliefs, expectations, and stereotyped attitudes. The pressures placed on adolescents as they are being socialized into their adult roles (Hill & Lynch, 1983) may further decrease flexibility. This socialization pressure may strengthen newly formed or reaffirmed conclusions about gender stereotypes. It may seem paradoxical that stereotype flexibility increases as children enter an environment where their older peers hold less flexible stereotypes. Ruble's model, however, does not imply that children pattern their thoughts after older peers, and the data also suggest that this is not the case. The increase in flexibility results from a motivation to learn about gender (as it exists in a junior high school subculture) after current gender beliefs (i.e., elementary school gender beliefs) are challenged by the entrance into this new life phase. Preexisting beliefs are suspended as information is gathered in order to form new conclusions about gender, leaving an individual without strong guides for gender stereotypes and producing the (temporary) increase in flexibility.

The longitudinal data did not indicate an increase in flexibility as students entered high school to parallel the increase found as students entered junior high school. Ruble's (1994) transition model may have predicted an increase in flexibility as these students entered high school, but only if the transition resulted in a new situation that sufficiently challenged the individual's current beliefs. The differences between junior high and high school may not be as great as the differences between junior high and elementary school and, therefore, may be insufficient to challenge the adolescent's current attitudes toward gender stereotypes. Moreover, a number of other important transitions are occurring at about the same time as the transition into junior high, such as the onset of puberty and dating. These additional transitions, which are no longer new to the student entering high school, may work in conjunction with the transition to junior high to prompt a reevaluation of gender stereotypes. Future research is necessary to specify more precisely the transitions related to changes in stereotype flexibility.

Although no overall sex differences in level of flexibility were found, boys tended to have lower flexibility of the masculine stereotypes compared with girls. This finding is consistent with previous literature showing stronger gender-typing among boys than girls (e.g., Frey & Ruble, 1992) and perhaps is limited to the masculine stereotype because of greater value and prestige associated with the male role (Kohlberg, 1966; Ruble & Ruble, 1982).

In conclusion, adolescence appears to be a time of decreasing flexibility of gender stereotypes. However, increases in flexibility were observed after certain types of social life transitions. The possibility exists that adolescents might conclude that stereotypes are less predictive than they thought earlier if, after the transition, they receive information that is consistent with this conclusion. Researchers and practitioners interested in implementing social programs aimed at reducing sexism and gender stereotyping may find the transition to junior high school, associated with relatively high gender stereotype flexibility, the ideal time to foster egalitarian beliefs between the sexes. The literature on gender stereotype beliefs, including the findings of this study, suggest that the information adolescents appear to receive is that gender roles are strongly proscribed, and, consequently, their stereotype flexibility decreases. Nonetheless, the present data clearly suggest that beliefs even as well established as stereotypes about the characteristics of males and females may be susceptible to change during social life transitions.

References

Biernat, M. (1991). Gender stereotypes and the relationship between masculinity and femininity: A developmental analysis. *Journal of Personality and Social Psychology, 61,* 351–365.

Broverman, I. K., Vogel, S. R., Broverman, D. M., Clarkson, F. E., & Rosenkrantz, P. S. (1972). Sex-role stereotypes: A current appraisal. *Journal of Social Issues, 28,* 59–78.

Carter, D. B., & Patterson, C. J. (1982). Sex roles as social conventions: The development of children's conceptions of sex-role stereotypes. *Developmental Psychology, 18,* 812–824.

Eccles, J. S. (1987). Adolescence: Gateway to gender role transcendence. In D. B. Carter (Ed.), *Current conceptions of sex roles and sex typing* (pp. 225–241). New York: Praeger.

Edelbrock, C., & Sugawara, A. I. (1978). Acquisition of sex-typed preferences in preschool-aged children. *Developmental Psychology, 14,* 614–623.

Eisenberg, N., Martin, C. L., & Fabes, R. A. (1996). Gender development and gender effects. In D. C. Berliner & R. C. Calfee (Eds.), *The handbook of educational psychology* (pp. 358–396). New York: Macmillan.

Emmerich, W., & Shepard, K. (1982). Development of sex-differentiated preferences during late childhood and adolescence. *Developmental Psychology, 18,* 406–417.

Frey, K. S., & Ruble, D. N. (1992). Gender constancy and the "cost" of sex-typed behavior: A test of the conflict hypothesis. *Developmental Psychology, 28,* 714–721.

Galambos, N. L., Almeida, D. M., & Petersen, A. C. (1990). Masculinity, femininity, and sex role attitudes in early adolescence: Exploring gender intensification. *Child Development, 61,* 1905–1914.

Galambos, N. L., Petersen, A. C., Richards, M., & Gitelson, I. B. (1985). The Attitudes Toward Women Scale for Adolescents (AWSA): A study of reliability and validity. *Sex Roles, 13,* 343–356.

Guttentag, M., & Longfellow, C. (1977). Children's social attributions: Development and change. In C. B. Keasey (Ed.), *Nebraska Symposium on Motivation: Social cognitive development* (Vol. 25, pp. 305–341). Lincoln: University of Nebraska.

Higgins, E. T., Loeb, I., & Ruble, D. N. (1995). The four A's of transitions. *Social Cognition, 13,* 215–242.

Higgins, E. T., & Parsons, J. E. (1983). Social cognition and the social life of the child: Stages as subcultures. In E. T. Higgins, D. N. Ruble, & W. W. Hartup (Eds.), *Social cognition and social development* (pp. 15–62). New York: Cambridge University Press.

Hill, J. P., & Lynch, M. E. (1983). The intensification of gender-related expectancies during early adolescence. In J. Brooks-Gunn & A. C. Peterson (Eds.), *Girls at puberty* (pp. 201–228). New York: Plenum.

Huston, A. C. (1983). Sex typing. In E. M. Hetherington (Ed.), *Handbook of child psychology: Socialization, personality, and social development* (Vol. 4, pp. 388–467). New York: Wiley.

Katz, P. A. (1979). The development of female identity. *Sex Roles, 5,* 155–178.

Katz, P. A., & Ksansnak, K. R. (1994). Developmental aspects of gender role flexibility and traditionality in middle childhood and adolescence. *Developmental Psychology, 30,* 272–282.

Koblinsky, S. G., Cruse, D. F., & Sugawara, A. I. (1978). Sex role stereotypes and children's memory for story content. *Child Development, 49,* 452–458.

Kohlberg, L. (1966). A cognitive-developmental analysis of children's sex-role concepts and attitudes. In E. E. Maccoby (Ed.), *The development of sex differences* (pp. 82–172). Stanford, CA: Stanford University Press.

Lerner, R. M., Vincent, S., & Benson, P. (1976). One year stability of societal and personal vocational role perceptions of females. *Journal of Genetic Psychology, 129,* 173–174.

Meece, J. L. (1987). The influence of school experiences on the development of gender schemata. In L. S. Liben & M. L. Signorella (Eds.), *New directions for child development: Vol. 38. Children's gender schemata* (pp. 57–74). San Francisco: Jossey-Bass.

Nelson, C., & Keith, J. (1990). Comparisons of female and male early adolescent sex role attitude and behavior development. *Adolescence, 25,* 183–204.

Rebecca, M., Hefner, R., & Oleshansky, B. (1976). A model of sex-role transcendence. *Journal of Social Issues, 32,* 197–206.

Ruble, D. N. (1994). A phase model of transitions: Cognitive and motivational consequences. In M. Zanna (Ed.), *Advances in experimental social psychology* (pp. 163–214). New York: Academic Press.

Ruble, D. N., & Ruble, T. L. (1982). Sex stereotypes. In A. G. Miller (Ed.), *In the eye of the beholder* (pp. 188–252). New York: Praeger.

Serbin, L. A., Powlishta, K. K., & Gulko, J. (1993). The development of sex typing in middle childhood. *Monographs of the Society for Research in Child Development, 58* (2, Serial No. 232).

Sigelman, C. K., Carr, M. B., & Begley, N. L. (1986). Developmental changes in the influence of sex-role stereotypes on person perception. *Child Study Journal, 16,* 191–205.

Signorella, M. L., Bigler, R. S., & Liben, L. S. (1993). Developmental differences in children's gender schemata about others: A meta-analytic review. *Developmental Review, 13,* 147–183.

Simmons, R. G., & Blyth, D. A. (1987). *Moving into adolescence.* New York: Aldine de Gruyter.

Smetana, J. C. (1988). Concepts of self and social conventions: Adolescents' and parents' reasoning about hypothetical and actual family conflicts. In M. R. Gunnar & W. A. Collins (Eds.), *Minnesota Sym-*

posia on Child Psychology: Vol. 21. Development during the transition to adolescence (pp. 78–122). Hillsdale, NJ: Erlbaum.

Spence, J. T. (1993). Gender-related traits and gender ideology: Evidence for a multifactorial theory. *Journal of Personality and Social Psychology, 64,* 624–635.

Stangor, C., & Lange, J. E. (1994). Mental representations of social groups: Advances in understanding stereotypes and stereotyping. In M. Zanna (Ed.), *Advances in experimental social psychology* (pp. 357–416). New York: Academic Press.

Stoddart, T., & Turiel, E. (1985). Children's concepts of cross-gender activities. *Child Development, 56,* 1241–1252.

Ullian, D. Z. (1976). The development of conceptions of masculinity and femininity. In B. Lloyd & J. Archer (Eds.), *Exploring sex differences* (pp. 25–47). New York: Academic Press.

Urberg, K. A. (1979). Sex role conceptualization in adolescents and adults. *Developmental Psychology, 15,* 90–92.

Williams, J. E., Bennett, S. M., & Best, D. L. (1975). Awareness and expression of sex stereotypes in young children. *Developmental Psychology, 11,* 635–642.

Williams, J. E., & Best, D. L. (1990). *Measuring sex stereotypes: A multination study.* Newbury Park, CA: Sage.

Received November 29, 1994
Revision Received January 2, 1996
Accepted January 2, 1996 ∎

Multiple Choice:

1. Gender stereotype flexibility refers to the view that:

   A. stereotypes can change with new experiences.
   B. both females and males may have both feminine and masculine qualities.
   C. one's gender changes when one's appearance changes.
   D. *both* young children and adults have gender-stereotypical qualities.

2. This study found that:

   A. children became more flexible in their gender stereotypes as they got older.
   B. with age, children relied more on what their friends thought about gender-related issues.
   C. children became more flexible in their gender stereotypes immediately following the transition from elementary school to junior high school.
   D. once children entered junior high school, they reverted back to the beliefs about gender they had as preschoolers.

Essay:

1. The transition from elementary school to junior high school appears to influence children' gender stereotype flexibility. What other changes throughout life might influence a person's gender stereotype flexibility?

2. What might be some of the consequences of having flexible ideas about gender? How about inflexible ideas? How might these consequences differ for females and males?

Externalizing in Preschoolers and Early Adolescents: A Cross-Study Replication of a Family Model

Nancy B. Miller, Philip A. Cowan, Carolyn Pape Cowan, E. Mavis Hetherington, and W. Glenn Clingempeel

Reprinted from: *Developmental Psychology*, 1993, *29*, 3-18
Copyright © 1993 by the American Psychological Association. Reprinted with permission.

Clinicians, teachers and parents have long been interested in trying to understand why some children "act out" (behave aggressively and destructively), whereas others do not. Psychologists refer to this type of behavior as *externalizing*. Most work in this area, including research done by Gerald Patterson and his colleagues (see Article 24), tends to point to the family as the origin of much of children's externalizing behavior. But *what* about the family is relevant?

Psychologists have proposed a variety of aspects of family functioning that may be associated with children's externalizing behavior, including inconsistent discipline, lack of parental warmth, and marital conflict. Maternal psychopathology, particularly depression, may also be associated with child behavior problems. What is particularly noteworthy about the research in this article is that these investigators look at all of these factors together--parenting style, marital quality, and parental depression--in order to better understand externalizing behavior in children.

Another important feature of this paper is that they use two samples to see whether the pattern of results is the same for preschool children and adolescents. Strikingly, the pattern is the same, although the effects are less strong for the adolescents. In both age groups, when mothers are more depressed, there tends to be less positive affect (smiling, laughter, affection) and more conflict in their marital relationships. The less positive affect there is between the spouses, the less warmth mothers show in their relationships with their children, and the more externalizing behavior children exhibit. In addition, children's externalizing behavior is directly related to conflict in the marital relationship, probably because observing marital conflict is very distressing for them. The findings are a little different for fathers. Paternal depression is associated with conflict in the couple's relationship and less control of the children, rather than less warmth as it is with mothers, but fathers' lack of control increases childrens externalizing behavior just as lack of maternal warmth does.

Can you think why parenting quality and marital quality might be less influential on teenagers' behavior than they are on preschoolers' behavior? One explanation may be that the family has less impact on children as they become increasingly independent from their parents during adolescence.

Developmental Psychology
1993, Vol. 29, No. 1, 3–18

Externalizing in Preschoolers and Early Adolescents: A Cross-Study Replication of a Family Model

Nancy B. Miller, Philip A. Cowan, Carolyn Pape Cowan, E. Mavis Hetherington, and W. Glenn Clingempeel

With families of 3½-year-olds, the direct and indirect links among parents' depression, marital quality, parenting style, and their children's externalizing behavior were examined using partial least squares analysis. No direct paths were found between parents' depression and their child's behavior. Instead, parents' depression was mediated by the quality of their relationship as a couple or by their parenting style, or by both. A replication with families of 9- to 13-year-olds supported these findings in the form of the interconnections among family variables and children's outcomes, although the magnitude of the family–child linkage was much lower than it was in the younger sample.

Children's cognitive and social competence has been found to correlate with their parents' psychological adjustment, parenting style, and, more recently, the quality of their marriage (C. P. Cowan, Cowan, Heming, & Miller, 1991; Hetherington & Clingempeel, 1992). Although the direction of influence, from child to parent or parent to child, has not been clearly established, findings have been consistent in relating children's adaptive or maladaptive behavior to parent functioning in intrapersonal, parent–child, and marital domains.

The task of describing pathways from adult functioning to children's adaptation raises both conceptual and statistical issues. Conceptually, the fact that there is a correlation between, for example, mothers' depression and children's aggression, does not tell us whether there is a direct link between maternal and child behavior or an indirect link resulting from the influence of mothers' depression on the quality of their relationships with their children. Statistically, the problem is how to analyze direct and indirect effects in nonexperimental, observation-based family studies.

The question of whether family models of children's development have the same form when children are at different developmental levels has not been given the attention it deserves. Part of the problem of comparisons across samples is that researchers studying families with children at different ages usually focus on different variables, conceptual models, and analytic approaches. In the present article, we use a similar conceptual model and identical "soft" path modeling techniques (Lohmoeller, 1989) to reduce the data and to examine links among parents' adjustment, marital quality, parenting style, and their children's externalizing behavior in two different studies—one of parents and 3½-year-olds (C. P. Cowan et al., 1991), and the other of parents and early adolescents (Hetherington & Clingempeel, 1992).

Family Correlates of Children's Development and Adaptation

Parents' Personality and Psychopathology

Research on normal families has identified few consistent connections between specific personality characteristics of parents and specific outcomes in their children (Clarke-Stewart, 1977; Parke, 1979). By contrast, it is clear from clinical samples that when one or both parents has or have been diagnosed with a serious disturbance (e.g., psychosis or depression), the children are at risk for cognitive, social, emotional, and school-related difficulties (Baldwin, Cole, & Baldwin, 1982; Cutrona & Troutman, 1986; Field, Healy, Goldstein, & Guthertz, 1990; Sameroff, Seifer, & Zax, 1982).

Studies examining the contributions of parental depression to negative child behavior have consistently shown that depressed mothers perceive the behavior of their children more negatively than those who are not depressed (Brody & Forehand, 1986; Christensen, Phillips, Glasgow, & Johnson, 1983; Forehand, Wells, McMahon, Griest, & Rogers, 1982; Schaughency & Lahey, 1985). A more serious consequence of parental depression is the growing evidence that young children of depressed parents show insecure attachment (Radke-Yarrow, Cummings, Kuczynski, & Chapman, 1985), deficits in social relations (Patterson, 1987; Zahn-Waxler, Chapman, & Cummings, 1984), and general maladaptive functioning (Keller et al., 1986). Other findings suggest that these childhood prob-

Nancy B. Miller, Department of Sociology, University of Akron; Philip A. Cowan and Carolyn Pape Cowan, Department of Psychology, University of California, Berkeley; E. Mavis Hetherington, Department of Psychology, University of Virginia; W. Glenn Clingempeel, Department of Psychology, Francis Marion College.

An earlier draft of this article was presented at the American Sociological Association Meeting, August 1991, in Cincinnati, Ohio.

Analysis of the data and preparation of this article was supported by National Institute of Mental Health (NIMH) Grant MH31109 and Spencer Foundation Grant M-1038 to Philip A. Cowan and Carolyn Pape Cowan, NIMH Training Grant MH182623 supporting the postdoctoral work of Nancy B. Miller, and a MacArthur Foundation grant to E. Mavis Hetherington and W. Glenn Clingempeel. We thank R. Frank Falk for invaluable statistical advise on our data analysis procedures.

Correspondence concerning this article should be addressed to Nancy B. Miller, Department of Sociology, University of Akron, Akron, Ohio 44325-1905.

lems are often precursors of significant psychopathology in adolescence (Cytryn, McKnew, Zahn-Waxler, & Gershon, 1985).

Parenting Styles

Recent studies suggest that the influence of parents' personality or pathology on their children occurs through disturbances in parenting behavior that affect the quality of the parent–child relationship (Belsky, Rovine, & Fish, 1989; Brunquell, Crichton, & Egeland, 1981; Susman, Trickett, Iannotti, Hollenbeck, & Zahn-Waxler, 1985). Links between positive parenting characteristics and optimal child behavior have been found for both mothers and fathers (C. P. Cowan et al., 1991; Goldberg & Easterbrooks, 1984; Heinicke, Diskin, Ramsey-Klee, & Oates, 1986).

Warmth (or acceptance) and control (or restrictiveness) are two primary variables that have been shown to reflect parents' child-rearing behaviors, attitudes, and values (Maccoby & Martin, 1983). Baumrind's (1979) research has found that authoritative parents—those whose parenting style includes both warmth and control—have children who are more competent, self-reliant, and nonaggressive than children whose parents are either authoritarian or permissive. Authoritative parents are nurturing and responsive to their children while at the same time maintaining consistent discipline and high maturity demands: They tend to provide appropriate scaffolding of their children's learning—moving in to support the child when tasks are difficult, backing away when the child is succeeding (Pratt, Kerig, Cowan, & Cowan, 1988). Baumrind's (1991) most recent findings with early adolescents continue to show that parents' responsiveness and demands are related to their children's competence and lack of problem behaviors.

Although there have been no specific pathways established between parents' behavior and a given pathological outcome, troubled parent–child relationships have been implicated in almost every major childhood psychological disorder (Rutter & Garmezy, 1984). When parents are depressed (Beardslee, Bemporad, Keller, & Klerman, 1983) or otherwise personally distressed, they tend to be less warm and nurturant (Longfellow, Zelkowitz, & Saunders, 1982; Weissman, 1983) and more inconsistent and punitive (Stoneman, Brody, & Burke, 1989; Susman et al., 1985) with their children.

Role of the Marriage

Family therapists' assumption that the parents' marriage provides the context for children's adaptation (Carter & McGoldrick, 1980; Walsh, 1982) has influenced the thinking of developmental psychologists studying nonclinic families. Some have proposed that the marital relationship provides the primary cognitive, emotional, and physical support for parents, and thus, the state of their relationship as a couple affects their parenting behaviors and, in turn, the child's adjustment (Belsky, 1984; Belsky, Youngblade, Rovine, & Volling, 1991; C. P. Cowan & Cowan, 1988; Crnic, Greenberg, Ragozin, Robinson, & Basham, 1983; Dickie, 1987). Impressive correlations between prebirth marital quality and parenting behavior with infants have been documented in several samples (Cox, Owen, Lewis, & Henderson, 1989; Grossman, Eichler, & Winikoff,

1980; Heinicke et al., 1986; Lewis, Tresch-Owen, & Cox, 1988). More harmonious marriages have been linked with developmental progress in infants and toddlers (Dickie, 1987; Easterbrooks & Emde, 1988; Goldberg & Easterbrooks, 1984) and young school-age children (Brody, Pillegrini, & Sigel, 1986; P. A. Cowan, Cowan, Schulz, & Heming, in press).

Just as some studies show that harmonious marriages promote children's competence and maturity, others demonstrate that marital conflict tends to be associated with the children's cognitive delay, school difficulties, and antisocial or withdrawn behavior in the early school years. Discord between the parents, whether married or divorced, has been implicated in poor parent–child relationships and deviant child outcomes, especially in antisocial, aggressive problem behaviors (Bond & McMahon, 1984; Emery, 1982; Gottman & Katz, 1989; Hetherington, Cox, & Cox, 1979; Keller et al., 1986; Rutter, 1978; Wallerstein & Kelly, 1980; Weissman, 1983). Parents in a distressed marriage may serve as models for negative interaction, and the emotional turmoil may limit their ability to provide adequate parenting (Krantz, 1989).

There is some evidence that a parent's psychological distress adds to marital disruption and that this may increase the risk of difficulty in the parent–child relationship. Biglan et al., (1985) found that marriages in which one spouse showed signs of depression were characterized by less self-disclosure, less problem-solving behavior, and higher rates of aggressive behavior between the parents.

A Family Model of Preschool Children's Externalizing Behavior

We know that (a) parents' adaptation as individuals and the quality of their marriage and parenting behavior are each connected to their children's developmental progress, and (b) dysfunction in each of these domains is most clearly related to their children's externalizing behavior (disobedience, aggression, temper tantrums, overactivity, and delinquency [Achenbach & Edelbrock, 1978]). What we do not know is whether the pathways from parents' distress to children's level of adaptation are direct or indirect. For example, is there a direct effect of marital conflict on children's behavior, or does parental disagreement and fighting take its toll through its impact on the parent–child relationship?

In the past decade, several researchers have proposed theoretical models that examine connections among individual characteristics of parents, dyadic relationships in the family, and the development of the child. For example, Belsky (1984) hypothesized a process model of the determinants of parenting that brings together parents' individual and marital characteristics, the child's temperament, and parental social networks. Olweus (1980) and Patterson (1987) have proposed models of boys' aggressive and antisocial behavior, respectively, that link parent and child characteristics with parenting practices. We are not aware of any previous attempts to examine the links among parents' adaptation as individuals, parenting style, and marital quality and their children's externalizing behavior within the same study or of previous attempts to compare these patterns in families with younger and older children.

Study 1 focuses on parents and their preschoolers' development. In the path analytic model to be examined here, we posit that a substantial proportion of the variance in $3\frac{1}{2}$-year-old children's aggressive, "acting-out," externalizing behavior can be accounted for by parents' distress and the quality of their relationships with their $3\frac{1}{2}$-year-olds. Specifically, we predicted that for both mothers and fathers, the parent's maladjustment as an individual, indexed by depressive symptoms, would be associated with more conflict and dissatisfaction (less positive affect) in the marriage. We expected that parents with more symptoms of depression and those with more problematic marriages would show fewer positive qualities in their parenting behavior (e.g., warmth or structuring). In turn, parents' depression, distressed marital relationships, and less effective parenting would predict higher levels of aggression in their children.

The ordering of variables in our models is based in part on our previous findings concerning the consistency of parents' adaptation over time and in part on our hypotheses about the concurrent connections among the theoretical constructs in our family model. Although we recognize that the child is an active agent in his or her own development (Lerner, 1982), our conceptual model is consistent with socialization research, predicting from parent characteristics to children's outcomes. Although we report only on concurrent data when the child is $3\frac{1}{2}$ years old, we have evidence from several studies that the characteristics of the parents examined here (depression and marital quality) are highly predictable from data obtained before the birth of the children (Belsky, Gilstrap, & Rovine, 1984; P. A. Cowan, Cowan, Schulz, & Heming, in press; Heinicke, Diskin, Ramsey-Klee, & Given, 1983; Heming, 1987; Schaefer, Edgerton, & Hunter, 1983).

The consistency of adults' adaptation and marital quality over the early years of family life supports the socialization model reflecting a theoretical time ordering for personal adjustment, marital quality, parenting style, and child outcomes. In this view, characteristics of the individual exist before his or her marriage and tend to be fairly stable. Likewise, qualities of the marriage are established before he or she enters the parenting role. Because the parent is seen as the socializing agent (Sigel, Stinson, & Kim, in press), individual parent characteristics, qualities of the marriage, and parenting practices are assumed to precede the child's behavior.

Our analysis explored both the direct and indirect pathways from parent to child within a structural equation model by using a *soft modeling* strategy. This technique is particularly suitable for studies with multiple measures where it is not known whether the factor structures are invariant (Falk & Miller, 1991; Ketterlinus, Bookstein, Sampson, & Lamb, 1989; Lohmoeller, 1989; Wold, 1980). With this method we examined the pattern of connections among multiple sources of variation in children's externalizing behavior and the differences in form and magnitude of these connections for mothers and fathers.

A Cross-Validation of the Family Model With Parents and Early Adolescents

In Study 2 we present a construct replication of the path models with data from a group of families with children approximately 8 years older than those in Study 1. The basic relation-

ships among the constructs in Study 1 were tested with data from families in another geographical area, with older children, and with different measures assessing the variables of interest. Using the same path modeling technique, we created component scores with meanings as close as possible to those used in Study 1.

A construct replication (Lykken, 1968) is a test of the cross-validation of findings. Such validation increases our confidence that the relationships found between the constructs can be used to formulate more general theories of family adaptation. Given differences in both the children's ages and the specific measures, we did not expect to find identical results; but we did expect to find support for our general hypothesis that parents' depression, marital interaction, and quality of parenting combine to account for substantial amounts of variation in the child's aggressive behavior.

Study 1: Method

Subjects

The data used in developing the model for parents and their preschoolers were selected from the Becoming a Family Project, a longitudinal research and intervention study that followed families from the mothers' late pregnancy until their children entered elementary school (C. P. Cowan, Cowan, Heming, Garrett, et al., 1985).[1] The transition to parenthood findings are reported elsewhere (C. P. Cowan, 1988; C. P. Cowan & Cowan, 1987a, 1987b; C. P. Cowan & Cowan, 1988; C. P. Cowan & Cowan, 1992; C. P. Cowan et al., 1991; P. A. Cowan & Cowan, 1990).

Data for the present study came from a follow-up assessment of these families when their first child was $3\frac{1}{2}$ years old. Of the original 72 expectant couples entering the study, 70% were reassessed at the 42-month follow-up. Attrition resulted primarily from separation and divorce (11%) and geographical relocation. Only 5% of the sample refused to participate again. Except for a tendency toward lower marital satisfaction scores at earlier assessments for the dropouts, there appears to be little difference between those who dropped out and those who continued to be involved in the study. The analyses to be presented in this article include 41 families on which complete, or nearly complete (90% or more), data were obtained during the preschool period. Missing data in these cases were replaced with the appropriate group mean for mother, father, or child.

Thirty-six of the families in our analysis were White, and 5 were either Asian, Hispanic, or Black. The average age of the children was 3 years and 8 months (range = 3.2 to 4.6 years). Their mothers averaged 32.9 years and their fathers, 34.6 years. Originally recruited through health professionals and community newsletters, parents' education level on the average included some college. At the time they entered the project, families' average income fell in the $30,000–$35,000 range.

Procedure

Parents were interviewed in their homes and were asked to complete assessment instruments individually, reporting on their own personal adjustment, the quality of the couple relationship, their parenting beliefs, and their child's behavior. In addition, mother–child and father–child dyads and mother–father–child triads were videotaped in separate sessions in an observation room in the Institute of Human Devel-

---

[1] Intervention effects were not detectable either in parents or their children at the $3\frac{1}{2}$-year follow-up (C. P. Cowan, 1988).

opment at the University of California at Berkeley. In each 30- to 40-min session, family members were asked to perform three kinds of tasks, varying in the structure of their demands.

Story task. For a more detailed description of this task, see Pratt et al. (1988). The child left the room and was told a brief story by the experimenter; the child then returned to join his or her parent. The parent's task was to get the child to tell the story—a task that proved quite frustrating for about half of the parents of 3¹/₂-year-olds.

Teaching tasks. The child was given four tasks that are difficult for a 3¹/₂-year-old to complete alone (from Block & Block, 1980), and the parents were invited to help as little or as much as they wanted to; the focus, they were told, was on how parents and children work together, not on how well the children perform. The tasks for the mother–child and father–child sessions included matching an already-constructed model using pieces of different shapes, traversing an etch-a-sketch maze, and completing a matrix on a handmade game board. In the couple–child sessions, the child was asked to match a complicated model of a train using Lego and tinker toy materials.

Sand world. In a more unstructured task, parents and children were invited to "make a world together in the sand" using a sand table and a cabinet of miniatures (people, animals, cages, trees, houses, etc.). They were given 10 min to construct their world.

The tasks, then, involved both convergent and divergent thinking, as well as work and play. In each session, behavioral ratings were made by a team composed of one male and one female rater who were unaware of any other family data.

Measures

In the analyses, there are six composited variables (theoretical constructs), created from 21 manifest variables (operational definitions) and one covariate, gender of child. All composited variables consist of multiple measures. Marital, parenting, and child behavior constructs include both self-reports and laboratory observations. Multiple method procedures reduce the bias toward inflated correlation in studies using only one measurement method.

Manifest variables were selected from measures that were related conceptually to the theoretical constructs and were shown to meet acceptable levels of reliability; that is, instruments previously had established test–retest reliability of .8, interrater reliability correlation of .7, kappa interrater agreement of .6, or internal consistency of .6 or greater. All scores demonstrated reliability, although different measures of consistency were used.

We attempted to identify three or more manifest variables for each theoretical construct that met these criteria for reliability. We were able to do so for four of the six composited variables. In the case of depression and the parenting dimension control, only two measures were identified. (See the Appendix for a description of the manifest variables.)

Parent's adjustment. Symptoms of depression were used as an index of individual parent adjustment. Mothers' and fathers' scores were obtained on two separate instruments as indicators of this construct: the Center for Epidemiological Studies in Depression Scale (Radloff, 1977) and the depression subscale from the Hopkins Symptoms Checklist (Derogatis, Lipman, & Covi, 1973).

Couple relationship. Positive affect and conflict are contrasting dimensions of couple relationship quality. Although the correlation between them is substantial in this data set ($r = -.75$ for mothers and $-.65$ for fathers), we viewed them as two separate constructs to ascertain whether they contributed differentially to variance in parenting styles and children's externalizing behavior. There were four indexes of positive affect and three indexes of couple conflict.

Parenting style. Warmth and control were the theoretical constructs chosen to represent dimensions of parenting style. They have

been identified by Baumrind (1967, 1991) as characteristics of parents of more socially and instrumentally competent children. Three measures of parent warmth and two of parent control were used.

Child's behavior. The dependent component, *externalizing behavior,* is described as angry, defiant, acting-out child behavior. It is defined by mothers' and fathers' separate reports of the child's behavior and by observers' ratings of the child's negative emotion displayed toward each parent in the parent–child laboratory sessions.

Structural Modeling

Latent variable path analysis with partial least squares (LVPLS) estimation procedure (Falk & Miller, 1992; Lohmoeller, 1984, 1989; Wold, 1975, 1982) was used to examine the relationships among parents' individual and marital adjustment, parenting style, and the child's problem behavior. In this procedure, several manifest variables (i.e., observed or measured variables) are composited to create latent variable scores. In most cases, several measurements are better than one in defining a complex theoretical construct (Rushton, Brainerd, & Pressley, 1983). Multiple measures increase variance; having three or more indicants increases stability as well. Only when measurement is simple and direct, as in age or gender, does a single variable suffice (Lavee, 1988).

One of the advantages of composited latent variable analysis is that the prediction of variables is based on the shared variance of the manifest variables. Individual variable residuals and the unreliability associated with measurement error are minimized (Harris, 1985).

In the estimation procedure, scores are computed for the composite variables on the basis of weights derived from a principal-components analysis of the measured variables. This method of data reduction creates a smaller set of theoretical variables whose relationships can be investigated without sacrificing the information available from a larger group of manifest variables. Although this procedure allows for analysis with relatively small samples, it requires that the number of subjects be adequate for the number of composited variables in the model.

We calculated the relationship between composited variables from predictor to predicted variables by using a multiple regression technique. Just as weights are adjusted to maximize a canonical correlation, the weights on composited variables are adjusted to provide the optimal linear coefficients between predictor and predicted components in the model. Composite weights provide a smoothing function that creates the plane of best fit between the constructs using the least squares criteria. The iterative process results in maximizing the prediction of the dependent composited variables from both (a) the manifest data and (b) the relationships specified in the model.

Our analyses began by specifying a fully recursive model, specifying all possible paths from left to right in the model. The covariate, gender of child, was allowed to affect each latent construct. Paths that were not of substantial size were eliminated, and the model was rerun. The test of significance on the R^2s reported used the degrees of freedom for the full model, thereby reducing the capitalization on chance for the null hypothesis that R^2 equals zero. In general, paths representing less than 10% of the variance of an endogenous variable were dropped. Only the modified models are presented. This procedure of model trimming is appropriate when hypothesized relationships are not deduced from a well-developed theory and an inductive approach must be pursued (Heise, 1975).

Study 1: Results

Latent to manifest variable loadings are shown in Table 1 for the mothers' and fathers' models. Examination of the measurement model reveals no bias in favor of either the self-report or observational method, because loadings are not consistently

Table 1

Latent Variable Path Analysis With Partial Least Squares
Component Loadings on Manifest Variables
for Sample 1 by Model

Variable	Fathers	Mothers
Parent's depression		
Fathers		
Depression scale (CES-D)	.93	
Depressive symptoms (SCL)	.90	
Mothers		
Depression scale (CES-D)		.95
Depressive symptoms (SCL)		.89
Couple's positive affect		
Fathers		
Marital adjustment (MAT)	.39	
Communication	.07	
Mothers		
Marital adjustment (MAT)		.88
Communication		.72
Observers		
Couple warmth	.90	.64
Couple cooperation	.89	.36
Couple's conflict		
Fathers		
Conflict (MAT)	.80	
Disagree about sex (MAT)	.51	
Mothers		
Conflict (MAT)		.79
Disagree about sex (MAT)		.82
Observers		
Couple conflict	.49	.49
Parenting warmth		
Fathers		
Supportive	.08	
Mothers		
Supportive		−.34
Observers		
Father's warm–responsiveness	.92	
Father's positive emotion	.93	
Mother's warm–responsiveness		.92
Mother's positive emotion		.94
Parenting control		
Fathers		
Authoritarian	−.33	
Mothers		
Authoritarian		.84
Observers		
Father's limits and demands	.96	
Mother's limits and demands		.50
Child's externalizing behavior		
Father's report		
Externalizing	.60	.40
Hyperactivity	.48	.65
Negative engagement	.44	.62
Mother's report		
Externalizing	.60	.32
Hyperactivity	.48	.58
Observer's report		
Negative emotion to father	.76	.64
Negative emotion to mother	.51	.61

Note. CES-D = Center for Epidemiological Studies Depression Scale. SCL = Hopkins Symptoms Checklist. MAT = Locke-Wallace Marital Adjustment Test.

higher for one method than the other across all constructs. Also, manifest variables seem to be reasonable indicators of their latent constructs. There are only two manifest variables in the models with loadings below .2. With loadings this low, they have very little in common with the other measures of the construct and contribute almost nothing to their respective composite score. For a more parsimonious model they could be eliminated, but for consistency across models they are maintained. Only one variable, mother's report of the child's negative engagement, was dropped because its loading was below .2 in both models.

Loadings on the parenting construct warmth reveal that mothers' and fathers' ideas about the supportive parent and their warmth and positive emotion displayed toward the child in interactions do not contribute to the definition of the construct in the same way. In the context of the other variables in the model, the behavioral ratings are the primary definer of the construct. This is also true for the control construct for fathers.

In Figure 1, relationships among symptoms of depression, couple affection and conflict, parenting warmth and structure, and the child's externalizing behavior are shown for mothers. Analysis indicates that when mothers have more depressive symptoms, there tends to be less positive affect and more conflict in the couple relationship. The less positive affect between the spouses, the less warmth she shows in the parent–child relationship and the more externalizing behavior the child exhibits. Conflict in the couple relationship does not have a path to parenting behavior; instead it leads directly to the child's externalizing behavior. Mothers of boys exercise greater control during the parent–child interaction. Forty-eight percent of the child's externalizing behavior is explained by the relationships among the variables in the mothers' model.

The path model for fathers is shown in Figure 2. Fathers' symptoms of depression are associated with conflict in the couple relationship and less control of the child. Less control on the part of the fathers, in turn, leads to more externalizing behavior in the children. Just as in the model for mothers, positive affect in the spousal relationship is related to warmth in fathers' parenting role; men's warmth in parenting is associated with less externalizing child behavior. Fathers of sons show a warmer relationship with their child than fathers of daughters. Fifty-one percent of the variance in children's externalizing behavior is explained by the fathers' model.

An overall measure of the model's fit with the data is the root-mean-square covariance (E, U). This is the average correlation between the residuals on the composited and manifest variables and represents correlation between the variables unaccounted for by the relationships specified in the model. For the two trimmed models presented, the index is .10 in each case and is interpreted as indicating an adequate or good fitting model (Falk & Miller, 1992).

Direct and Indirect Effects

Three pathways can be followed from parents' self-reported symptoms of depression to the child's behavior. One path shows that the fewer the mothers' symptoms of depression, the more they display positive affect toward their spouses. In turn, more positive affect in the couple relationship is related to warmth in

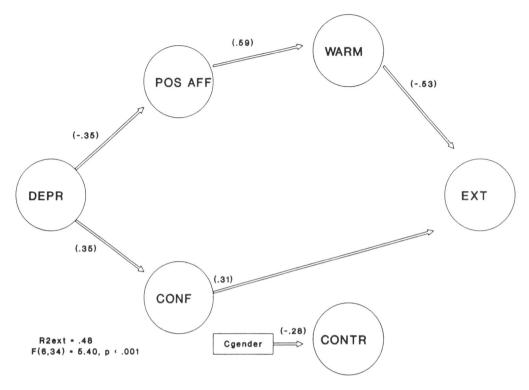

Figure 1. Path model for mothers, Sample 1. (DEPR = parent's depression; POS AFF = couple's positive affection; WARM = parenting warmth; EXT = child's externalizing behavior; CONTR = parenting control; CONF = couple's conflict; Cgender = child's gender.)

parenting, and parental warmth is associated with less acting-out behavior by the child. A second path reveals connections among mothers' depression, conflict between the parents, and the child's externalizing behavior. A third path shows connections among fathers' depression, less parental control, and more antisocial child behavior.

In these family models, the more depressive symptoms are reported by parents, the more conflictful and less positive the couple relationship. However, no direct connections are found between parents' individual adjustment and the child's behavior. The findings are consistent with two assumptions. First, it appears that parents' symptoms may have an indirect effect on children's externalizing, through their links with the quality of both marital interaction and the parent–child relationships. Second, marital relationship quality may have both direct effects on children's behavior and indirect effects through parenting style.

The correlations reported here between family variables and children's externalizing are all concurrent. It is possible to argue that aggressive children "drive" the model: They are difficult to manage; they create marital conflict; and they leave parents feeling dispirited. However, we have reported elsewhere that individual and marital data obtained from the parents in late pregnancy predicts both their depression and marital satisfaction at 18 months postpartum (Heming, 1985, 1987), as well as their observed marital warmth, conflict, and authoritarian parenting when the child is 3½ years old (P. A. Cowan, Cowan, & Kerig, 1992). Thus we find that from 17% to 30% of the varia-

tion in individual, marital, and parenting adaptation in the preschool period is not shaped by the child's characteristics.

Study 2: Replication

Although the importance of multiple corroboration of results is espoused by most researchers, examples of cross-study replications are rare. Lykken (1968) distinguished three methods of cross-validation: literal, operational, and construct replication. A construct replication differs from the former two by moving farther away from the specific methods used in the original study. Instead, the investigator takes a conceptual approach and, using a different set of methods, attempts to test the same hypotheses. In this study we attempted a construct replication of the models presented with data from a different population, with different measures of the constructs, and with children 8 years older than those in the first study.

Although the manifest variables are different in the two studies, the components that represent the constructs of interest are the same. Paths of substantial magnitude between composited variables in the fathers' and mothers' models for Sample 1 (Figures 1 and 2) were specified in the corresponding models for Sample 2. As in the original models, paths from the covariate, gender of child, were allowed to affect all composited variables.

Subjects

Families in an urban East Coast area participated in the Adaptation to Remarriage Study, a longitudinal study of early adolescent adapta-

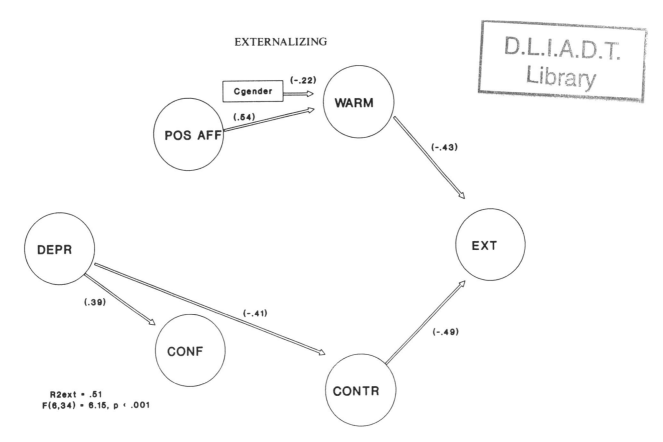

Figure 2. Path model for fathers, Sample 1. (DEPR = parent's depression; POS AFF = couple's positive affection; WARM = parenting warmth; EXT = child's externalizing behavior; CONTR = parenting control; CONF = couple's conflict; Cgender = child's gender.)

tion to divorce and remarriage (Hetherington & Clingempeel, 1992). The study focused on the effect of differential family processes on the cognitive and social development of children in three distinct family types: stepfather families; divorced, nonremarried mother-custody families; and nondivorced families. Sixty-two families from the nondivorced group on which complete data were available for all measures used in this analysis were included.

All families in Sample 2 were White, and parents had at least a high school education. Although there may have been as many as four children living in the home, only one child between the ages of 9 and 13 was assessed in each family. The average age of the children in nondivorced families was 11 years and 5 months. The age of the mothers averaged 38.2 years and the fathers, 39.9 years. Mothers' education averaged 14.9 years and fathers', 15.8 years. Average family income fell in the $25,000–$35,000 range.

Procedure

Extensive interviews, self, couple, and child assessments, and observational measures were obtained from family members at home and in the university laboratory. Videotapes of families' interaction during dinner and in problem-solving sessions involving mother–father, mother–child, father–child, and sibling–child dyads, as well as the mother–father–child triad, were rated by well-trained students using a family interaction coding system (Hetherington & Clingempeel, 1987). Twenty global dimensions of family functioning were scored after raters had watched all five taped family interaction sessions. The data presented in this article are from the first of three assessment periods in the longitudinal study.

Measures

Instruments and ratings available as measures for the theoretical constructs in the replication were, in most cases, different from those used in developing the Sample 1 models. This is not considered a disadvantage in construct replication but an indication that constructs, though measured in different ways by different researchers, still relate to other constructs in similar ways. Study 2, then, tests the robustness of the structural relationships found in Study 1.

All latent constructs consist of multiple measures and include both parents' self-report and observational indicators. For the dependent latent variable externalizing behavior, the adolescent's own record of delinquent acts was included as a measure of the construct. (See the Appendix for a description of the measures.)

Parents' adjustment. Whereas in Study 1 in which two self-reported measures of depressive symptoms were used, in Sample 2, self-report measures of parents' depression, locus of control, self-confidence, and observations of negative mood were included.

Couple relationship. A self-reported marital adjustment questionnaire was completed by parents in both Sample 1 and Sample 2 and was used as an indicant of positive affect in the couple relationship. In Sample 1, observational ratings of warmth and cooperation were used for this construct; in Sample 2, observed warmth and communication were used. Communication between the parents was an additional self-report measure in the first sample.

The conflict dimension of the couple relationship was assessed in both samples by parents' reports of their disagreements. In Sample 2 these disagreements focused primarily on parenting issues. Observers rated couple conflict in Sample 1 and hostility and coercion toward spouse in Sample 2.

Parenting style. To assess parenting dimensions in the Adaptation to Remarriage Study, we created subscales from parent reports of their emotional involvement, expression of affection, parenting practices, and child monitoring. Details of scale construction are presented in Hollier (1985). Subscale scores for parenting warmth and control are used here.

To compare parenting measures in the two samples, recall that self-report measures of parenting in Sample 1 were mothers' and fathers' ideas about parenting issues and not reports of actual child-rearing practices as they are with Sample 2's parents. Observer ratings of parental warmth were conducted in both studies. However, observed control involved limit setting and maturity demands for Sample 1's parents of preschoolers and parental influence and monitoring in Sample 2's parents of preadolescents.

Child's behavior. Externalizing child behavior was measured by parent report on a behavior checklist in both studies. In Sample 1 three factor scores—externalizing, hyperactivity, and negative engagement—were used in defining the theoretical construct; in Sample 2 a total score for externalizing behavior was used. Both samples had observer ratings of the child's negative interaction with his or her parents. Because older children are able to report on their own behavior, in Sample 2 the young adolescent's report of delinquent behavior provides an additional indicant of the construct.

Study 2: Results

Loadings of manifest variables on their respective latent variables for mothers' and fathers' models are shown in Table 2.

Although there is no method bias across all constructs, for mothers, loadings on depressive symptoms are defined more by her observed mood than by her self-report of depression and locus of control. The self-described personality factor self-confidence, however, is negatively related to her positive mood, as expected. Note that positive loadings on the control construct are observer ratings of parents trying to regulate their child's life (influence) and seeking information about his or her behavior and activities (monitoring) and not their reported attempts to control the child (attempted control of character development and attempted control of deviance).

When the models developed with families in Sample 1 were applied to Sample 2 data, the structural relationships between the theoretical variables were remarkably similar. The correlation between the five pairs of path coefficients in the mothers' models (Figures 1 and 3) is .99, and the correlation for the paths in the fathers' models (Figures 2 and 4) is .97. The relative fit index root-mean-square covariance (E, U) for the models with Sample 2 data are .09 and .08, respectively, indicating a fit of model to data that is comparable, or slightly better, than that of the original models.

In Sample 2, 34% of the variance in the children's externalizing behavior is explained in the mothers' model and 19% in the fathers' model. Three paths are consistently large (.35 or greater)

Table 2
Latent Variable Path Analysis With Partial Least Squares Component Loadings on Manifest Variables for Sample 2 by Model

Variable	Fathers	Mothers	Variable	Fathers	Mothers
Parent's depression			Parenting warmth		
Fathers			Fathers		
Depression scale (BDI)	.40		Expressive affection	.80	
Locus of control	.53		Instrumental affection	.52	
Self-confidence	.02		Rapport	.71	
Mood with mother	.80		Mothers		
Mood with child	.63		Expressive affection		.73
Mothers			Instrumental affection		.70
Depression scale (BDI)		.07	Rapport		.62
Locus of control		.07	Observers		
Self-confidence		.29	Father's warmth–involvement	.70	
Mood with father		.84	Mother's warmth–involvement		.75
Mood with child		.84	Parenting control		
Couple's positive affect			Fathers		
Fathers			Control of character	−.71	
Marital adjustment (DAS)	.49		Control of deviance	−.27	
Mothers			Mothers		
Marital adjustment (DAS)		.47	Control of character		−.40
Observers			Control of deviance		−.52
Father's warmth–involvement	.77	.83	Observers		
Father's communication	.82	.67	Father's influence	.35	
Mother's warmth–involvement	.68	.80	Father's monitoring	.64	
Mother's communication	.84	.76	Mother's influence		.75
Couple's conflict			Mother's monitoring		.78
Fathers			Child's externalizing behavior		
Disagree about adolescent issues	.62		Father's report		
Disagree about daily routines	.69		Externalizing	.75	.80
Mothers			Mother's report		
Disagree about adolescent issues		.54	Externalizing	.79	.74
Disagree about daily routines		.63	Observer's report		
Observers			Antisocial to father	.72	.77
Father's hostility	.83	.86	Antisocial to mother	.69	.76
Father's coercive behavior	.61	.63	Child's report		
Mother's hostility	.70	.62	Delinquent behavior	.48	.39
Mother's coercive behavior	.63	.62			

Note. BDI = Beck Depression Inventory. DAS = Dyadic Adjustment Scale.

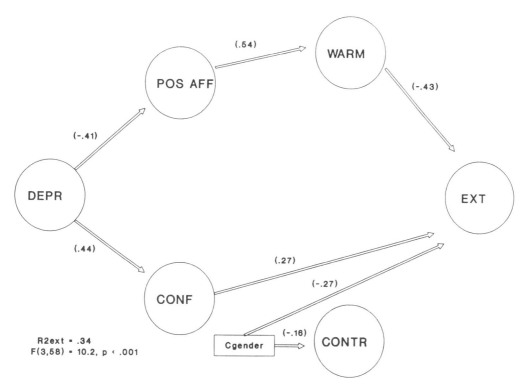

Figure 3. Path model for mothers, Sample 2. (DEPR = parent's depression; POS AFF = couple's positive affection; WARM = parenting warmth; EXT = child's externalizing behavior; CONTR = parenting control; CONF = couple's conflict; Cgender = child's gender.)

and are replicated in both models: (a) parental depression is associated with marital conflict, (b) positive affect in the couple relationship is associated with parental warmth, and (c) parental warmth contributes to lower externalizing behavior in the child.

There are meaningful differences between Sample 1 and Sample 2 with regard to the construct of control in the fathers' model. In the fathers' model with preschoolers, the path weights between depression and control and between control and externalizing behavior are substantially higher than those in the fathers' model for early adolescents. In the original model in Sample 1's families with preschoolers, the path between fathers' depressive symptoms and the tendency toward a controlling parental style has a weight of −.41. In Sample 2's families of early adolescents, the beta has a weight of only −.12. The path between fathers' control and externalizing behavior has a weight of −.49 in the model for preschoolers, suggesting that the more fathers use controlling behaviors with their preschool children, the less externalizing behavior their children display. This path is −.21 in the replication, suggesting that fathers' attempts to control may have less influence on adolescent behavior.

Even though no significant gender differences were found in preschoolers' acting-out behavior, mothers of boys were more controlling than mothers of girls, and fathers of boys were warmer than fathers of girls when they worked and played with their children. In the sample with older children but not in the preschool sample, boys displayed more externalizing behavior than girls in both mothers' and fathers' models. And, whereas

mothers were more controlling with preschoolers, mothers and fathers of adolescent boys were more controlling than parents of adolescent girls.

In families with older children, considerably more variance in the child's externalizing behavior is explained by variables in the mothers' model than by those in the fathers' model. But overall, less variance is explained in either parent's model of early adolescent problem behavior than in the models of younger children. Thus the form of the structural models replicates across samples, but the magnitude of the family–child linkages decreases as children get older.

Discussion

The across-studies replication confirms the strongest and most consistent paths in the original models. One of these is between parents' individual maladjustment and marital conflict. When mothers and fathers experience individual distress in their lives, there is more conflict in their relationship as couples. There is no direct link between parents' individual distress and the externalizing behavior of their children. Instead, the connection is mediated by the quality of the parents' relationship as a couple or with the child, or by both.

Although families in these two samples came from a non-clinic population, which may have different family process patterns than families in a clinic group, at least one study of parents with clinically diagnosed depressive disorders reported similar links between the parents' distress and the children's behavior. In that study, parents' depression had indirect effects,

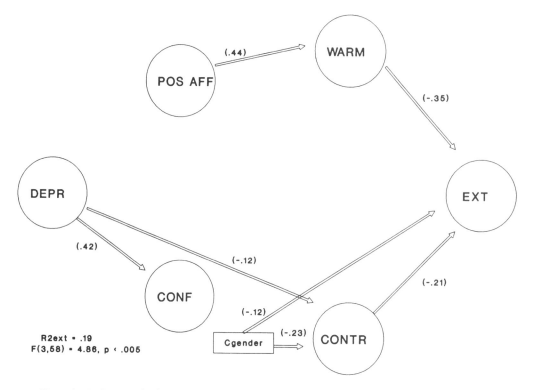

Figure 4. Path model for fathers, Sample 2. (DEPR = parent's depression; POS AFF = couple's positive affection; WARM = parenting warmth; EXT = child's externalizing behavior; CONTR = parenting control; CONF = couple's conflict; Cgender = child's gender.)

through marital discord, on children's problem behavior at school (Emery, Weintraub, & Neale, 1982). This evidence suggests that links among parents' depressive symptomatology, negative couple relationships, and children's disruptive behavior may be similar in clinic and nonclinic families. Further studies will be needed to determine whether some symptoms or conditions have this indirect linkage through the marriage while others have a direct impact on the child.

A second consistent finding is an indirect link between the quality of the couple relationship and the child's behavior. When the parents had a relationship characterized by positive, affectionate feelings for each other, their relationships with their children were warmer; and when parent–child relationships were warmer, both preschool and early adolescent children acted out less. Again, there is no direct link between parents' positive affect toward each other and the child's acting-out behavior.

Model Comparisons

Path models describing patterns in families with preschoolers accounted for more of the variance in the child's externalizing behavior than did the same models of families with early adolescents. One explanation for this finding may be that influences outside the family have a greater impact on the externalizing behavior of children as they increase in independence and in their interaction with peers, teachers, and others in their community. As children's environment grows wider, so too do the factors that affect their actions (Asher & Coie, 1990).

Because we expect differences in family process as children get older, we are not surprised to find that the relationships among fathers' depression, parental control, and the child's behavior are not as strong as in models of preschoolers. Fathers' attempts to control their adolescents' behavior may be affected less by their own psychopathology, and control itself may have other meanings to the child at this age. For example, parental control seems especially important in limiting acting-out behavior when the child is younger, but as the child approaches adolescence, strict control may evoke different and more varied responses.

Others have found that parental control is a concept with many facets. For example, Baumrind (1991) describes three distinct types of control that relate differently to adolescent behavior: restrictive, assertive, and rational. In Fauber, Forehand, Thomas, and Wierson's (1990) models of adolescent adjustment, three measures of parental discipline practices are included as mediators of the effect of couple conflict on the adolescents' adjustment. Rejection–withdrawal contributes considerably to predicting adolescents' externalizing behavior, whereas psychological control and lax control do not. Explicating and measuring multiple dimensions of control may be necessary to understand the complex relationships among parents' psychopathology, control, and their adolescent's behavior.

A comparison of the models for mothers and fathers reveals that their individual adjustment relates to marital adjustment and parenting behaviors in different ways. For mothers, the relationship between personal adjustment and parenting appears to be mediated by the qualities of the marriage; parenting behavior with the child is not linked directly with mothers' affective state. However, for fathers, personal adjustment is linked directly with the quality of their relationships with both their wives and their children, with almost equal magnitude for fathers of preschool children. Specifically, fathers' depression is associated with increased conflict in the couple relationship and with decreased parental control. This finding suggests that fathers' depression may spill over into both their marital and parental roles (P. A. Cowan, Cowan, & Kerig, 1992). Other researchers have found similar links between levels of marital interaction and parental involvement for fathers, but not for mothers (Amato, 1986; Belsky et al., 1984; Dickstein & Parke, 1988).

Studies that shed light on the process by which marriage buffers personal distress for mothers are needed to understand the role of the marital relationship in the lives of women. Likewise, we need to know more about why men who feel personally distressed seem to react similarly with their wives and children. Our findings suggest that familial relationships represent a single sphere for men when they are depressed and that improvement in their individual adjustment might have positive effects on both their marriage and their parenting behavior.

Limitations

This study is exploratory, as opposed to confirmatory, in two important ways. First, the models do not include all the relevant variables that contribute to a child's externalizing behavior. The influence of significant others, such as siblings, grandparents, and peers; the influence of socioeconomic factors; and the temperament of the child are obvious examples. Second, the study is cross-sectional. An across-occasions design would provide greater insights into the processes and mechanisms linking parents' and children's adaptation. An examination of our models with two children from the same family could highlight the impact of children's characteristics on their parents' behavior.

Although the language of pathways—predictability, direct, and indirect effects—implies causality, such interpretations are not warranted in this study. The interpretation of causality requires specific hypothesis testing from formalized theory. Such hypothesis testing might take the form of clinical interventions, either therapeutic or preventive, in which the family and child developmental consequences of improvement in individual or marital adaptation are assessed.

Likewise, the use of structural equation modeling when experimental procedures are not appropriate always limits the conclusions. Similarly, the ordering of variables and direction of relationships are difficult to establish in concomitant data sets, because the analysis of reciprocal influences requires designs that extend over several time periods. Nevertheless, path analysis is a powerful tool for structuring our suppositions and investigating direct and indirect effects.

Although this study takes a socialization perspective and emphasizes the effect of parental characteristics on the child's behavior, others (Bell, 1977; Lytton, 1990) have found evidence for a transactional model in which the children's characteristics play a major role in understanding their problem behavior. Cross-sectional studies such as ours allow researchers to analyze only one side of this transactional process; longitudinal studies will be necessary to examine the effects of both of these major influences.

Our limited sample size in the analysis of families with younger children is a frequent consequence of studies using multiple measures of mothers, fathers, and children. Although small samples have the tendency to inflate path coefficients and raise questions about the stability of prediction, replication studies—because they underscore common results—provide the best supporting evidence available for inductive findings.

Finally, because families in these samples were recruited from a middle-class, mostly White population and included only two-parent families, further study is necessary to determine the limits of generalizability to other social classes, groups, or family types.

Conclusion

Assessments of families whose first child is 3½ years old indicate that parents' individual and marital adjustment has a strong connection with the quality of their parenting styles. In turn, the quality of both the couple relationship and their parenting style is related to the emergence of the child's problem behaviors before entering elementary school. These findings suggest that parents who feel more depressed and who have less supportive couple relationships are not as warm and responsive when they interact with their children. Furthermore, when parents are not as warm and involved, their children are more likely to display problems of aggression and other negative interpersonal behavior. The replication study indicates that these important links among parents' adjustment as individuals and as couples, their parenting styles, and their child's adjustment hold true for families with 9- to 13-year-olds as well.

These findings strongly suggest that our attempts to understand children's adjustment and to develop interventions for families with aggressive, antisocial children must look beyond mothers' and fathers' parenting style to their individual and marital adjustment. Interventions that help new parents improve their personal adjustment or the quality of their marriage (e.g., C. P. Cowan, 1988) may ultimately benefit both parent–child relationships and the child's development.

References

Achenbach, T. M., & Edelbrock, C. S. (1978). The classification of child psychopathology: A review and analysis of empirical efforts. *Psychological Bulletin, 85,* 1275–1301.

Achenbach, T. M., & Edelbrock, C. S. (1979). The child behavior profile: II. Boys aged 12–16 and girls aged 6–11 and 12–16. *Journal of Consulting and Clinical Psychology, 47,* 223–233.

Amato, P. R. (1986). Marital conflict, the parent–child relationship and child self-esteem. *Family Relations, 35,* 403–410.

Asher, S. R., & Coie, J. D. (1990). *Peer rejection in childhood.* New York: Cambridge University Press.

Baldwin, A. L., Cole, R. E., & Baldwin, C. P. (1982). Parental pathology, family interaction, and the competence of the child in school. *Mono-*

graphs of the Society for Research in Child Development, 47(5, Serial No. 197).

Baumrind, D. (1967). Child care practices anteceding three patterns of preschool behavior. Genetic Psychology Monographs, 75, 43–88.

Baumrind, D. (1971). Current patterns of parental authority. Developmental Psychology Monographs, 4, 1–103.

Baumrind, D. (1978). Manual for the rating scales for parents of adolescent children. University of California, Berkeley: Family Socialization and Developmental Competence Project.

Baumrind, D. (1979). The development of instrumental competence through socialization. In A. D. Pick (Ed.), Minnesota symposia on child psychology (Vol. 7). Minneapolis: University of Minnesota Press.

Baumrind, D. (1991). Effective parenting during the early adolescent transition. In P. A. Cowan & E. M. Hetherington (Eds.), Family transitions (pp. 111–163). Hillsdale, NJ: Erlbaum.

Beardslee, W. R., Bemporad, J., Keller, M. B., & Klerman, G. L. (1983). Children of parents with major affective disorders: A review. American Journal of Psychiatry, 140, 825–832.

Beck, A. T., & Beck, R. W. (1972). Screening depressed patients in family practice: A rapid technic. Postgraduate Medicine, 52, 81–85.

Beck, A. T., Rial, W. Y., & Rickels, K. (1974). Short form of depression inventory: Cross validation. Psychological Reports, 34, 1184–1186.

Bell, R. Q. (1977). Socialization findings re-examined. In R. Q. Bell & R. V. Harper (Eds.), Child effects on adults (pp. 53–84). Hillsdale, NJ: Erlbaum.

Belsky, J. (1984). The determinants of parenting: A process model. Child Development, 55, 83–96.

Belsky, J., Gilstrap, B., & Rovine, M. (1984). The Pennsylvania infant and family development project: I. Stability and change in mother–infant and father–infant interaction in a family setting at one, three, and nine months. Child Development, 55, 692–705.

Belsky, J., Rovine, M., & Fish, M. (1989). The developing family system. In M. Gunnar (Ed.), Systems and development: Minnesota Symposium on Child Psychology (Vol. 22, pp. 119–166). Hillsdale, NJ: Erlbaum.

Belsky, J., Youngblade, L., Rovine, M., & Volling, B. (1991). Patterns of marital change and parent–child interaction. Journal of Marriage and the Family, 53, 487–498.

Biglan, A., Hops, H., Sherman, L., Friedman, L. S., Arthur, J., & Osteen, V. (1985). Problem-solving interactions of depressed women and their husbands. Behavior Therapy, 16, 431–451.

Block, J. (1965). The child-rearing practices report. Berkeley, CA: Institute of Human Development.

Block, J. H., & Block, J. (1980). The role of ego-control and ego-resiliency in the organization of behavior. In W. A. Collins (Ed.), Minnesota Symposia on Child Psychology (Vol. 13, pp. 39–101). Hillsdale, NJ: Erlbaum.

Bond, C. R., & McMahon, R. J. (1984). Relationships between marital distress and child behavior problems, maternal personal adjustment, maternal personality, and maternal parenting behavior. Journal of Abnormal Psychology, 93, 348–351.

Brody, G. H., & Forehand, R. (1986). Maternal perceptions of child maladjustment as a function of the combined influence of child behavior and maternal depression. Journal of Consulting and Clinical Psychology, 54, 237–240.

Brody, G. H., Pillegrini, A. D., & Sigel, I. E. (1986). Marital quality and mother–child and father–child interactions with school-age children. Developmental Psychology, 22, 291–296.

Brunquell, D., Crichton, L., & Egeland, B. (1981). Maternal personality and attitude in disturbances of childrearing. American Journal of Orthopsychiatry, 51, 680–691.

Carter, B., & McGoldrick, M. (Eds.). (1980). The family life cycle. New York: Gardner.

Christensen, A., Phillips, S., Glasgow, R. E., & Johnson, S. M. (1983). Parental characteristics and interactional dysfunction in families with child behavior problems: A preliminary investigation. Journal of Abnormal Child Psychology, 11, 153–166.

Clarke-Stewart, A. (1977). Child care in the family. San Diego, CA: Academic Press.

Cohler, B. J., Weiss, J. L., & Grunebaum, H. V. (1970). Child care attitudes and emotional disturbance in mothers of young children. Genetic Psychology Monographs, 82, 3–42.

Cowan, C. P. (1988). Working with men becoming fathers: The impact of a couples group intervention. In P. Bronstein & C. P. Cowan (Eds.), Fatherhood today: Men's changing role in the family (pp. 276–298). New York: Wiley.

Cowan, C. P., & Cowan, P. A. (1984). Couple communication questionnaire. University of California, Berkeley: Becoming a Family Research Project.

Cowan, C. P., & Cowan, P. A. (1987a). A preventive intervention for couples becoming parents. In C. F. Z. Boukydis (Ed.), Research on support for parents and infants in the postnatal period (pp. 225–251). Norwood, NJ: Ablex.

Cowan, C. P., & Cowan, P. A. (1987b). Men's involvement in parenthood: Identifying the antecedents and understanding the barriers. In P. Berman & F. Pedersen (Eds.), Men's transition to parenthood (pp. 145–174). Hillsdale, NJ: Erlbaum.

Cowan, C. P., & Cowan, P. A. (1988). Who does what when partners become parents: Implications for men, women, and marriage. Marriage & Family Review, 13, 1–2.

Cowan, C. P., & Cowan, P. A. (1992). When partners become parents: The big life change for couples. New York: Basic Books.

Cowan, C. P., Cowan, P. A., Heming, G., Garrett, E., Coysh, W. S., Curtis-Boles, H., & Boles, A. J. (1985). Transitions to parenthood: His, hers, and theirs. Journal of Family Issues, 6, 451–481.

Cowan, C. P., Cowan, P. A., Heming, G., & Miller, N. B. (1991). The transition from couple to family: Adaptation and distress in parents and children. In P. A. Cowan & E. M. Hetherington (Eds.), Family transitions (pp. 79–109). Hillsdale, NJ: Erlbaum.

Cowan, P. A., & Cowan, C. P. (1990). Becoming a family: Research and intervention. In I. Sigel & E. Brody (Eds.), Methods of family research (Vol. 1, pp. 1–51). Hillsdale, NJ: Erlbaum.

Cowan, P. A., Cowan, C. P., & Kerig, P. (1992). Mothers, fathers, sons, and daughters: Gender differences in family formation and parenting style. In P. A. Cowan, D. Field, D. Hansen, A. Skolnick, & G. E. Swanson (Eds.), Family, self, and society: Toward a new agenda for family research (pp. 165–195). Hillsdale, NJ: Erlbaum.

Cowan, P. A., Cowan, C. P., Schulz, M., & Heming, G. (in press). Prebirth to preschool family factors predicting children's adaptation to kindergarten. In R. Parke & S. Kellam (Eds.), Advances in family research (Vol. 4). Hillsdale, NJ: Erlbaum.

Cox, M. J., Owen, M. T., Lewis, J. M., & Henderson, V. K. (1989). Marriage, adult adjustment, and early parenting. Child Development, 60, 1015–1024.

Crnic, K. A., Greenberg, M. T., Ragozin, A. S., Robinson, N. M., & Basham, R. B. (1983). Effects of stress and social support on mothers and premature and full-term infants. Child Development, 54, 209–217.

Cutrona, C. W., & Troutman, B. R. (1986). Social support, infant temperament, and parenting self-efficacy: A medical model of postpartum depression. Child Development, 57, 1507–1518.

Cytryn, L., McKnew, D. H., Zahn-Waxler, C., & Gershon, E. S. (1985). Developmental issues in risk research: The offspring of affectively ill parents. In M. Rutter, C. E. Izard, & P. B. Read (Eds.), Depression in young people (pp. 163–188). New York: Guilford Press.

Derogatis, L. R., Lipman, R. S., & Covi, L. (1973). SCL-90: An outpatient psychiatric rating scale. *Psychopharmacology Bulletin, 9,* 13–28.

Derogatis, L. R., Lipman, R. S., Rickles, K., Uhlenhuth, E. H., & Covi, L. (1974). The Hopkins Symptom Checklist (HSCL): A measure of primary symptom dimensions. In P. Pichot (Ed.), *Psychological measurements in psychopharmacology* (pp. 79–110). Basel, Switzerland: Karger.

Dickie, J. R. (1987). Interrelationships within the mother–father–infant triad. In P. Berman & F. Pederson (Eds.), *Men's transition to parenthood* (pp. 113–143). Hillsdale, NJ: Erlbaum.

Dickstein, S., & Parke, R. D. (1988). Social referencing in infancy: A glance at fathers and marriage. *Child Development, 59,* 506–511.

Easterbrooks, M. A., & Emde, R. N. (1988). Marital and parent–child relationships: The role of affect in the family system. In R. A. Hinde & J. Stevenson-Hinde (Eds.), *Relationships in families: Mutual influences* (pp. 83–103). Oxford, England: Oxford University Press.

Emery, R. E. (1982). Interparental conflict and the children of discord and divorce. *Psychological Bulletin, 92,* 310–330.

Emery, R., Weintraub, S., & Neale, J. M. (1982). Effects of marital discord on the school behavior of children of schizophrenic, affectively disordered, and normal parents. *Journal of Abnormal Child Psychology, 10,* 215–228.

Falk, R. F., & Miller, N. B. (1991). A soft models approach to family transitions. In P. A. Cowan & E. M. Hetherington (Eds.), *Family transitions* (pp. 273–301). Hillsdale, NJ: Erlbaum.

Falk, R. F., & Miller, N. B. (1992). *A primer for soft modeling.* Akron, OH: University of Akron Press.

Fauber, R., Forehand, R., Thomas, A. M., & Wierson, M. (1990). A mediational model of the impact of marital conflict on adolescent adjustment in intact and divorced families: The role of disrupted parenting. *Child Development, 61,* 1112–1123.

Field, T., Healy, B., Goldstein, S., & Guthertz, M. (1990). Behavior-state matching and synchrony in mother–infant interactions of non-depressed versus depressed dyads. *Developmental Psychology, 26,* 7–14.

Forehand, R., Wells, K. C., McMahon, R. J., Griest, D., & Rogers, T. (1982). Maternal perceptions of maladjustment in clinic-referred children: An extension of earlier research. *Journal of Behavioral Assessment, 4,* 145–151.

Goldberg, W. A., & Easterbrooks, M. A. (1984). Role of marital quality in toddler development. *Developmental Psychology, 20,* 504–514.

Gottman, J. M. (1979). *Marital interaction: Experimental investigations.* San Diego, CA: Academic Press.

Gottman, J. M., & Katz, L. F. (1989). The effects of marital discord on young children's peer interaction and health. *Developmental Psychology, 25,* 373–381.

Grossman, F. K., Eichler, L. S., & Winikoff, S. A. (1980). *Pregnancy, birth and parenthood.* San Francisco: Jossey-Bass.

Harris, R. J. (1985). *A primer of multivariate statistics.* San Diego, CA: Academic Press.

Heinicke, C. M., Diskin, S. D., Ramsey-Klee, D. M., & Given, K. (1983). Pre-birth individual parent characteristics and family development in the first year of life. *Child Development, 54,* 194–208.

Heinicke, C. M., Diskin, S. D., Ramsey-Klee, D. M., & Oates, D. S. (1986). Pre- and postbirth antecedents of 2-year-old attention, capacity for relationships, and verbal expressiveness. *Developmental Psychology, 6,* 777–787.

Heise, D. R. (1975). *Causal analysis.* New York: Wiley.

Heming, G. (1985). *Predicting adaptation in the transition to parenthood.* Unpublished doctoral dissertation, University of California, Berkeley.

Heming, G. (1987, April). *Predicting adaptation to parenthood.* Paper presented at the meeting of the Society for Research in Child Development, Baltimore, MD.

Heming, G., Cowan, P. A., & Cowan, C. P. (1990). Ideas about parenting. In J. Touliatos, B. F. Perlmutter, & M. A. Straus (Eds.), *Handbook of family measurement techniques* (pp. 362–363). Newbury Park, CA: Sage.

Hetherington, E. M., Cox, M., & Cox, R. (1979). Family interaction and the social emotional and cognitive development of children following divorce. In V. Vaughn & T. Brazelton (Eds.), *The family: Setting priorities* (pp. 89–128). New York: Science and Medicine.

Hetherington, E. M., & Clingempeel, W. G. (1987). *Longitudinal study of adjustment to remarriage: Family interaction global coding manual.* University of Virginia, Charlottesville: Adjustment to Remarriage Project.

Hetherington, E. M., & Clingempeel, W. G. (1992). Coping with marital transitions: A family system perspective. *Monographs of the Society for Research in Child Development, 57*(2–3, Serial No. 227).

Hollier, A. E. (1985). *Parent–child relationships in the first year of remarriage.* Unpublished master's thesis, University of Virginia.

Ireton, H. R., & Thwing, E. J. (1972). *Minnesota Child Development Inventory Manual.* Minneapolis: Interpretive Scoring Systems.

Keller, M. B., Beardslee, W. R., Dorer, D. J., Lavori, P. W., Samuelson, H., & Klerman, G. R. (1986). Impact of severity and chronicity of parental affective illness on adaptive functioning and psychopathology in children. *Archives of General Psychiatry, 43,* 930–937.

Ketterlinus, R. D., Bookstein, F. L., Sampson, P. D., & Lamb, M. E. (1989). Partial least squares analysis in developmental psychopathology. *Development and Psychopathology, 1,* 351–371.

Krantz, S. E. (1989). The impact of divorce on children. In A. S. Skolnick & J. H. Skolnick (Eds.), *Family in transition* (pp. 341–363). Glenview, IL: Scott, Foresman.

Lavee, Y. (1988). Linear structural relationships (LISREL) in family research. *Journal of Marriage and the Family, 50,* 937–948.

Lerner, R. M. (1982). Children and adolescents as producers of their own development. *Developmental Review, 2,* 342–370.

Lewis, J. M., Tresch-Owen, M., & Cox, M. J. (1988). The transition to parenthood: III. Incorporation of the child into the family. *Family Process, 27,* 411–421.

Locke, H. J., & Wallace, K. M. (1959). Short marital adjustment and prediction tests: Their reliability and validity. *Marriage and Family Living, 21,* 251–255.

Lohmoeller, J. B. (1984). *LVPLS 1.6 program manual: Latent variables path analysis with partial least-squares estimation.* Cologne, Germany: Universitaet zu Koehn, Zentralarchiv fuer Empirische Sozialforschung.

Lohmoeller, J. B. (1989). *Latent variable path modeling with partial least squares.* New York: Springer-Verlag.

Longfellow, C., Zelkowitz, P., & Saunders, E. (1982). The quality of mother–child relationships. In D. Belle (Ed.), *Lives in stress: Women and depression* (pp. 163–176). Beverly Hills, CA: Sage.

Lykken, D. T. (1968). Statistical significance in psychological research. *Psychological Bulletin, 70,* 151–159.

Lytton, H. (1990). Child and parent effects in boys' conduct disorder: A reinterpretation. *Developmental Psychology, 26,* 683–697.

Maccoby, E. E., & Martin, J. A. (1983). Socialization in the context of the family: Parent–child interaction. In P. H. Mussen (Series Ed.) & E. M. Hetherington (Vol. Ed.), *Handbook of child psychology* (Vol. 4, pp. 1–101). New York: Wiley.

O'Donnell, J. P., & Van Tuinan, M. (1979). Behavior problems of preschool children: Dimensions and congenital correlates. *Journal of Abnormal Child Psychology, 7,* 61–75.

Olweus, D. (1980). Familial and temperamental determinants of aggressive behavior in adolescent boys: A causal analysis. *Developmental Psychology, 16,* 644–660.

Parke, R. D. (1979). Perspectives on father–infant interaction. In J.

Osofsky (Ed.), *Handbook of infant development* (pp. 549–590). New York: Wiley.

Patterson, G. R. (1982). *Coercive family process.* Eugene, OR: Castalia Press.

Patterson, G. R. (1987, June). *Models for the effect of divorce on mother and child.* Paper presented at the meeting of the Family Research Consortium Second Annual Summer Institute, Santa Fe, NM.

Pratt, M. W., Kerig, P., Cowan, P. A., & Cowan, C. P. (1988). Mothers and fathers teaching 3-year-olds: Authoritative parenting and adult scaffolding of young children's learning. *Developmental Psychology, 24,* 832–839.

Radke-Yarrow, M., Cummings, E. M., Kuczynski, L., & Chapman, M. (1985). Patterns of attachment in two- and three-year-olds in normal families and families with parental depression. *Child Development, 56,* 884–893.

Radloff, L. S. (1977). The CES-D scale: A self-report depression scale for research in the general population. *Applied Psychological Measurement, 1,* 385–401.

Reid, D. W., & Ware, E. E. (1974). Multidimensionality of internal versus external control: Addition of a third dimension and non-distinction of self versus others. *Canadian Journal of Behavioral Science, 6,* 131–142.

Rushton, J. P., Brainerd, C. J., & Pressley, M. (1983). Behavioral development and construct validity: The principle of aggregation. *Psychological Bulletin, 94,* 18–38.

Rutter, M. (1978). Early sources of security and competence. In J. S. Bruner & A. Garten, (Eds.), *Human growth and development* (pp. 33–61). London: Oxford University Press.

Rutter, M., & Garmezy, N. (1984). Developmental psychopathology. In P. Mussen (Ed.), *Handbook of child psychology* (Vol. 4, pp. 775–911). New York: Wiley.

Sameroff, A. J., Seifer, R., & Zax, M. (1982). Early development of children at risk for emotional disorder. *Monographs of the Society for Research in Child Development, 47*(7, Serial No. 199).

Schaefer, E. S., Edgerton, M., & Hunter, W. (1983, August). *Childrearing and child development correlates of maternal locus of control.* Paper presented at the American Psychological Association Meetings, Anaheim, CA.

Schaughency, E. A., & Lahey, B. B. (1985). Mothers' and fathers' perceptions of child deviance: Roles of child behavior, parental depression, and marital satisfaction. *Journal of Consulting and Clinical Psychology, 53,* 718–723.

Sigel, I. E., Stinson, E. T., & Kim, M. (in press). Socialization of cognition: The distancing model. In K. W. Fischer & R. Wozniak (Eds.), *Specific environments: Thinking in contexts.* Hillsdale, NJ: Erlbaum.

Spanier, G. B. (1976). Measuring dyadic adjustment: New scales for assessing the quality of marriage and similar dyads. *Journal of Marriage and the Family, 38,* 15–28.

Stoneman, Z., Brody, G. H., & Burke, M. (1989). Marital quality, depression, and inconsistent parenting: Relationship with observed mother–child conflict. *American Journal of Orthopsychiatry, 59,* 105–117.

Susman, E. J., Trickett, P. K., Iannotti, R. J., Hollenbeck, B. E., & Zahn-Waxler, C. (1985). Child-rearing patterns in depressed, abusive, and normal mothers. *American Journal of Orthopsychiatry, 55,* 237–251.

Wallerstein, J. S., & Kelly, J. B. (1980). *Surviving the break-up: How children and parents cope with divorce.* New York: Basic Books.

Walsh, F. (Ed.). (1982). *Normal family processes.* New York: Guilford Press.

Weissman, M. M. (1983). The depressed mother and her rebellious adolescents. In H. Morrison (Ed.), *Children of depressed parents: Risk, identification, and intervention* (pp. 99–113). New York: Grune & Stratton.

Wold, H. (1975). Path models with latent variables: The NIPALS approach. In H. Blalock (Ed.), *Quantitative sociology: International perspectives on mathematical and statistical model building* (pp. 307–357). San Diego, CA: Academic Press.

Wold, H. (1980). Soft modelling: Intermediate between traditional model building and data analysis. *Mathematical Statistics, 6,* 333–346.

Wold, H. (1982). Systems under indirect observation using pls. In C. Fornell (Ed.), *A second generation of multivariate analysis* (pp. 325–347). New York: Praeger.

Zahn-Waxler, C., Chapman, M., & Cummings, E. M. (1984). Cognitive and social development in infants and toddlers with a bipolar parent. *Child Psychiatry and Human Development, 15,* 75–85.

Appendix

Description of Manifest Variables

Parent's Adjustment: Study 1

Center for Epidemiological Studies Depression Scale (CES-D). The CES-D (Radloff, 1977) is a 20-item questionnaire developed to measure symptoms of depression in the general population, with reported reliability of .85. While not directly measuring clinical depression, the CES-D significantly discriminates clinically depressed and nondepressed samples. In the present study, 30% of the men and 20% of the women were classified in the distressed range when their children were $3^1/_2$ years old.

Depression subscale. The 13-item subscale for depressive symptoms from the Hopkins Symptoms Checklist (Derogatis, Lipman, & Covi, 1973) has reported test–retest reliability of .81 (Derogatis, Lipman, Rickles, Uhlenhuth, & Covi, 1974). Cronbach's alpha computed for our full sample is .91.

Couple Relationship: Study 1

The Short Marital Adjustment Test (MAT). The MAT (Locke & Wallace, 1959) is a 32-item, self-report measure of the quality of marital satisfaction used in numerous studies. It differentiates clinically distressed and nondistressed couples and is related to observed differences in marital interaction between couples above and below the cutoff (Gottman, 1979). At this assessment period, 27% of the men and 24% of the women scored in the maritally distressed range.

Observed couple warmth, cooperation, and conflict. The parental dyad was rated by observers during the mother–father–child visits on the quality of their interaction when they were with the child. Ratings were made on 5-point scales for 12 items; for each item, ratings were made of both the highest level and the typical level of the behavior under consideration. A factor analysis of the items yielded four factors: warmth (positive emotion), cooperation, conflict, and clarity of communication. Couple warmth and cooperation are used as indicants of positive affect, and conflict is used as an indicant of negative interaction in the couple relationship. Kappa reliabilities for interrater agreement are .71, .73, and .68, respectively, for these three factors.

Couple communication. This 20-item questionnaire was developed to tap the quality of, and satisfaction with, communication between the parents in four areas: (a) caring, closeness, and distance; (b) problem solving; (c) conflict and disagreement; and (d) feelings (C. P. Cowan & Cowan, 1984). The total score for each parent is used in these analyses. Alpha reliability of the scale in this study is .67.

Self-reported conflict. The conflict subscale of the Locke-Wallace marital satisfaction questionnaire assesses disagreement between spouses in 10 areas. Two items that did not contribute to internal consistency were eliminated from the subscale score, but one of these items, "disagreement between partners on sexual relations," was used as an independent index of couple conflict.

Parenting Style: Study 1

Supportive parent. The *Ideas About Parenting* questionnaire (Heming, Cowan, & Cowan, 1990) is an 80-item questionnaire developed from items on scales by Baumrind (1971), Block (1965), and Cohler, Weiss, and Grunebaum (1970) to assess parents' beliefs about raising children. This factor score includes items that describe the mother or father who believes a parent should express affection and be supportive of the child's autonomy. It consists of 9 items, including "Children should be held when they are upset so that they will be secure in their parents' love for them" and "One of the joys of parenthood is encourag-

ing a child's natural curiosity." The internal consistency of this factor is .72.

Authoritarian parent. This is a second factor score from the *Ideas About Parenting* questionnaire (Heming et al., 1990) that describes the mother or father who believes that a parent should exercise firm control. This 10-item factor consists of statements such as, "When a child is called, he or she should come immediately" and "Parents should keep a firm hold on their child's expression of angry feelings." Cronbach's alpha for this factor is .76.

Observations of parent warm–responsiveness and positive emotion. Parents' behavior toward the child across all tasks was rated on 17 items that were factor analyzed. Warm–responsiveness and positive emotion are two factor scores used as indicators of the parent warmth construct. Parent warm–responsiveness contains ratings of warmth, responsiveness, pleasure, and respect. Parent positive emotion contains ratings of anger, coldness, and displeasure; it has been reverse scored. Kappa reliabilities for interrater agreement average .61 on mothers' scales and .59 on fathers' scales for warm–responsive and .56 on mothers' and .59 on fathers' scales for positive emotion.

Observed parent limits and demands. A third factor score derived from analysis of observer ratings of parents' behavior toward the child in the parent–child laboratory sessions describes the degree to which the parent sets limits and holds high expectations for the child's behavior. Kappa reliabilities for interrater agreement on this factor average .55 for mothers' and .58 for fathers' scales.

Child's Behavior: Study 1

Externalizing, hyperactivity, and negative engagement. Three scales were created by adding items that were positively correlated and conceptually related on the Minnesota Preschool Inventory (Ireton & Thwing, 1972), with additional items from the Quay-Peterson Behavior Problem Checklist, adapted for preschool children by O'Donnell and Van Tuinan (1979). Cronbach's alphas for these scales are .75, .66, and .62, respectively.

The Externalizing scale has seven items and includes statements such as "quarrelsome, defiant; a 'troublemaker' " and "fights; hits or kicks other children." The four-item Hyperactivity scale contains items such as, "overactive; 'always on the go': 'into everything' "; and the five-item Negative Engagement scale includes "tattles" and "attention-seeking; demands adult attention verbally or physically."

Negative emotion. The two observers' ratings of the child in the laboratory sessions were summed on individual items and submitted to a principal-components analysis. Negative emotion is a factor score composed of 10 ratings on 5-point scales of items such as "highest level of anger," "highest level of anxiety," and "highest level of frustration." Two scores were used: the child's negative emotion expressed toward mother and toward father. Kappa reliabilities for ratings of child toward father are .61 and toward mother are .58.

Parents' Adjustment: Study 2

Beck Depression Inventory (BDI). The short form of the BDI consists of 13 items. In a variety of samples, it was found to correlate between .89 and .97 with the total of the 21-item BDI and between .55 and .67 with clinicians' ratings of depression (Beck & Beck, 1972; Beck, Rial, & Rickels, 1974).

Locus of control. A 32-item multidimensional version of Rotter's scale of internal versus external locus of control (Reid & Ware, 1974) includes items that assess the individual's attribution of control to fate, the social system, or the self.

Self-confidence. Personality attributes of parents were measured on a 56-item, self-sorted Q sort, adapted from Baumrind's (1978) Adult Personality Attributes. Self-confidence is one of seven factors derived from the data with loadings all above .4. It contains the following items: "likes his or her self," "feels in control of life," "self-confident, believes in abilities to achieve set goals," and "happy and contented."

Observed mood. One of the family interaction global ratings, scores on observed mood range from very negative to very positive. This variable was reverse scored so that high scores indicate a parent who appears depressed, pessimistic, and low in energy. Mood was rated separately for mothers and fathers while they engaged with each other and with the child. Reliabilities computed with Spearman's correlation are .67 and .77 for mothers and .70 and .77 for fathers.

Couple Relationship: Study 2

Dyadic Adjustment Scale (DAS). This 32-item scale assesses four basic components of marital adjustment: satisfaction, cohesion, consensus, and affectional expression. High scale reliability (.96) and content, criterion, and construct validity have been shown for the DAS (Spanier, 1976).

Warmth–involvement and positive communication. These two measures are global ratings of the parents in interaction with each other. The warmth–involvement scale measures the degree to which the parent is warm, responsive, supportive, and caring toward the other parent (Spearman's r = .87 for mothers and .86 for fathers). The positive communication scale measures the ability of the parent to communicate effectively his or her wants, needs, and point of view to the other parent and to solicit the other's views (Spearman's r = .77 for mothers and .81 for fathers).

Adolescent issues and daily routines. On the *Child-Rearing Issues* questionnaire developed for this project, parents were asked how often in the last week they had disagreements with their spouse about issues regarding the child. Twenty-two items are rated on a 7-point scale, from "more than once a week" to "not at all." The items were factored and two scales—adolescent issues and daily routines—were created by adding items. Cronbach's alphas for mothers' and fathers' reports were, respectively, .72 and .80 for adolescent issues and .58 and .85 for daily routines.

Hostility and coercive behaviors. These two observer global ratings measure the degree to which the parent displays hostile, angry, and rejecting behaviors (Spearman's r = .96 for mothers and .86 for fathers) and the degree to which attempts are made by one parent to control or change the behavior of the other by manipulation (Spearman's r = .71 for mothers and .80 for fathers).

Parenting Style: Study 2

Expressive affection, instrumental affection, and rapport. Three subscales of the parenting warmth construct assess the feelings of close-

ness each parent expressed to the child, the time parent and child spent together in mutual activities, and their communication style, respectively. For the expressive affection scale, alpha is .81 for mothers and .75 for fathers, for instrumental affection, .68 and .75, and for rapport, .76 and .82.

Attempted control of character development and attempted control of deviance. Attempts to control character development included items that assess parents' efforts to influence the child's intellectual interests, school performance, and health habits. Attempted control of deviance consisted of items indicating parents' endeavors to influence their child's choice of friends and activities at home as well as outside of the home, including involvement with tobacco, alcohol, and drugs. Cronbach's alpha is .75 and .59 for mothers and .78 and .75 for fathers for these two scales.

Warmth–involvement, parental influence, and monitoring. Reliabilities using Spearman's correlation for these three observer global rating scales are .91, .84, and .81 for mothers and .85, .83, and .73 for fathers. The warmth–involvement scale measured the degree to which a parent was caring, supportive, praising, and encouraging during interaction. The parental influence scale identified parents who were highly involved in attempts to regulate and/or control the child's life. There are two components of the monitoring scale: awareness of the child's behavior and pursuit of information regarding the child's activities. A parent who frequently showed both characteristics was rated high on monitoring.

Child's Behavior: Study 2

Externalizing behavior. The externalizing score of the Child Behavior Checklist (Achenbach & Edelbrock, 1979) was used to record the parents' perceptions of their child's adjustment. This second-order factor contains the following age-appropriate problem scales: delinquent, aggressive, and hyperactive. Test–retest reliability and interparent agreement for these problem scales have been reported as .82 and .79 for boys and .90 and .54 for girls, respectively (Achenbach & Edelbrock, 1979).

Antisocial behavior. The observer global rating scale for child's antisocial behavior measures the degree to which the child displays unpleasant, irritable, hostile, or aggressive behavior toward parents during interaction. Based on Spearman's correlation, reliability for this scale is .73 for the child's behavior toward mother and .75 for behavior toward father.

Delinquent behavior. The child's record of delinquent behavior on a 24-hr behavior checklist was included. Nine of the 31 items on the Behavior Events Inventory (described in Patterson, 1982, and modified for this study) comprised the delinquent behavior scale (α = .66). Items included "stole," "lied or cheated," "used drugs or alcohol," and "got into trouble at school."

Received October 10, 1990
Revision received December 2, 1991
Accepted May 1, 1992 ∎

Multiple Choice:

1. In this study of externalizing behavior in children, the researchers found externalizing or "acting out" to be associated with:

   A. children having difficult temperaments.
   B. parents using inconsistent discipline.
   C. parental depression, marital conflict, and poorer quality parent-child interaction.
   D. parental divorce.

2. This article had the unusual feature of studying both preschoolers and adolescents. The researchers reported that:

   A. the pattern of results was very different for the two age groups.
   B. preschoolers were more likely to demonstrate externalizing behavior than older children.
   C. the pattern of results was similar for the two age groups, but the family exerted a stronger influence on the younger children.
   D. the pattern of results was similar for the two age groups, but the family exerted a stronger influence on the older children.

Essay:

1. Why do you think the pattern of results differed in strength for the two age groups in this study? What is different about the environments of preschoolers and adolescents that might account for the differences?

2. This article suggests that there are both direct and indirect effects of family factors on children's externalizing. What is an example of a direct effect noted in this research? What is an example of an indirect effect? How are they different?

ARTICLE 21

Socialization and Development in a Changing Economy: The Effects of Paternal Job and Income Loss on Children

Vonnie C. McLoyd

Reprinted from: *American Psychologist*, 1989, *44*, 293-302.
Copyright © 1989 by the American Psychological Association. Reprinted with permission.

Throughout this book, one article after another has discussed the family as an influence--for better or for worse--on children's development. In this article, Vonnie McLoyd focuses explicitly on family effects as she examines what happens to children when their father loses his job.

As you can see from Figure 1, McLoyd offers a model of the effects of paternal job loss that includes multiple, interacting variables. One possible reaction to such a model is that it gives you a headache--it's just too complex. How can we ever hope to understand development if we have to take into account so many different variables, most of which interact with each other?

The answer is that we just simply have to. For too long, developmental scientists have looked for simple relationships--the impact of x on y, don't worry about z, or a, b, or c. But life is complex, and only by coming to grips with that complexity can we make real progress in understanding it. Thus, models like McLoyd's are a necessity, and investigators who are able to capture more of life's complexity in their work often make the greatest contributions.

McLoyd notes that a general economic decline has more impact on some groups than others. Minorities are especially hard hit, and she cites several studies of African American families.

When reading this article and thinking about the effects of income on development, keep in mind that one quarter of America's children are now living in poverty.

Socialization and Development in a Changing Economy

The Effects of Paternal Job and Income Loss on Children

Vonnie C. McLoyd   *University of Michigan*

ABSTRACT: Research on the impact of paternal job and income loss on the child is reviewed. Although some direct effects have been found, most effects are indirect and mediated through the changes that economic loss produces in the father's behavior and disposition. Fathers who respond to economic loss with increased irritability and pessimism are less nurturant and more punitive and arbitrary in their interactions with the child. These fathering behaviors increase the child's risk of socioemotional problems, deviant behavior, and reduced aspirations and expectations. The child also may model the somatic complaints of the father. The child's temperament, physical attractiveness, relationship with the mother, and degree of contact with the father are discussed as factors that condition the father's treatment of the child following economic loss. Economic hardship also may influence the child's development indirectly through the events that it potentiates (e.g., divorce) and discourages (e.g., marriage). High maternal support and experiences that encourage maturity and autonomy appear to be critical sources of psychological resilience in children who have experienced economic hardship.

This review focuses on the effects on socialization and child development of economic decline that stems from paternal job and income loss. Declines in the relative income status and economic well-being of individuals in the United States are not uncommon. In the Panel Study of Income Dynamics, 31% of individuals lived in families whose relative income position moved down at least one quintile between 1971 and 1978, and 11% moved down at least two quintiles. During the same period, about one fifth of individuals lived in families whose income relative to need declined dramatically. These fluctuations are primarily due to changes in family composition, movement into and out of the labor force, and changes in employment status, although changes in work hours and hourly wages among the continuously employed also are contributing factors (Duncan, 1984).

High rates of unemployment and job loss for fathers are a social change that characterizes the 1980s and distinguishes the decade from the previous 40 years. Back-to-back recessions in 1980 and 1981–1982, combined with management decisions to retrench and alter production methods in major manufacturing industries in response to foreign competition, resulted in an unemployment rate of 10.6% in late 1982, the highest since the Depression of the 1930s (Flaim & Sehgal, 1985). Between 1981 and 1986, 10.8 million American workers 20 years of age and over lost jobs because of plant closings, business failures, and layoffs. Those with 3 or more years of tenure on the jobs they lost (displaced workers) were without work for a median period of 18 weeks. In many cases, because wages were not restored to their previous level, reemployment only lessened rather than reversed economic decline. Of the displaced workers who found employment after losing jobs between 1981 and 1986, 30% had earnings that were 20% or more below their predisplacement earnings (Horvath, 1987).

Because most recent retrenchments have been in the manufacturing sector, where male workers predominate, rather than in the service sector, where women are more likely to be employed, most of the job loss in recent years has been among men. Afro-American men and their families experience a vastly disproportionate share of job and income loss, though we know least about how they cope with these events. This increased vulnerability to economic decline is the result of several factors including less education, less skill training, less job seniority, fewer transportable job skills, and institutional barriers deriving directly from past or present discrimination (e.g., housing patterns and information about job opportunities) (Buss & Redburn, 1983). Moreover, recent structural changes in the economy have hit Afro-American men especially hard: (a) Rates of displacement are higher and reemployment rates are lower in precisely those blue-collar occupations in which Afro-Americans are overrepresented (Simms, 1987); (b) the shift of manufacturing employment from central cities to outlying areas has been more injurious to Afro-Americans because they reside in central cities in disproportionate numbers (in 1980, 58% compared with 25% for the rest of the population); and (c) the transformation of central cities from centers of production to centers of administration has generated rapid increases in white-collar employment, but Afro-Americans rely disproportionately on blue-collar employment (Fusfeld & Bates, 1984).

Manufacturing employment is projected to decline by more than 800,000 jobs during the 1986–2000 period. As the shift from a goods-producing economy to a service economy continues, a substantial number of fathers are

Copyright 1989 by the American Psychological Association, Inc. 0003-066X/89/$00.75
Vol. 44, No. 2, 293–302

Figure 1
Conceptual Model of How Paternal Economic Loss Affects the Child

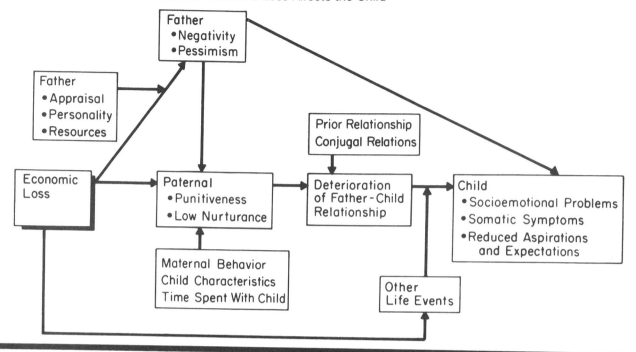

expected to be displaced, and the geographic concentration of many of the declining industries portends mass unemployment and economic decline in some localities (Kutscher, 1987). Research on the impact of paternal job and income loss on children is limited but growing, and it is largely from two periods—the 1930s and the 1980s.

Conceptual Model

The organization of this review is guided by a conceptual model, shown in Figure 1, that assumes that economic loss is a stressor, or crisis-provoking event, if it poses a situation for which the family has had little or no prior preparation. Whether job or income loss is transformed from a stressor event into a crisis that seriously undermines the functioning of the father and his family is assumed to depend on his appraisal of the event and his crisis-meeting resources (Hill, 1958; Voydanoff, 1983).

Although the workplace where job and income loss occur typically is external to the child's environment, economic loss can influence the child's development primarily through the changes it produces in the father's behavior and disposition (father mediation). This conclusion is drawn from the pioneering studies conducted

by Elder and his colleagues of families that experienced economic decline during the Depression. These studies indicated that fathers who sustained heavy financial loss became more irritable, tense, and explosive, which in turn increased their tendency to be punitive and arbitrary in the discipline of their children. These fathering behaviors were predictive of temper tantrums, irritability, and negativism in young children, especially boys, and of moodiness and hypersensitivity, feelings of inadequacy, and lowered aspirations in adolescent girls (Elder, 1979; Elder, Liker, & Cross, 1984; Elder, Nguyen, & Caspi, 1985). The parenting behavior of mothers generally was not influenced by economic hardship.

Several economic and social changes since the Depression (e.g., unemployment compensation, severance pay, and employment of spouse) are thought to mitigate the negative impact of job and income loss in today's context (Jahoda, 1979; LeGrande, 1983). Nonetheless, Elder et al.'s causal pathway linking economic loss to the child through the father's behavior has been replicated in recent studies of contemporary children (Galambos & Silbereisen, 1987a; Kelly, Sheldon, & Fox, 1985; Lempers, Clark-Lempers, & Simon, in press). Wives of unemployed men appear to be affected through a similar mediational process (Dew, Bromet, & Schulberg, 1987). The robustness of this causal pathway suggests the importance of understanding those factors that buffer psychological impairment in economically deprived fathers and contravene harsh discipline. The impact of economic loss on father-child interaction and relations is seen as variable rather than constant and is assumed to be influenced by child

Preparation of this article was supported in part by a Faculty Scholar Award in Child Mental Health from the William T. Grant Foundation.

The author is grateful to Lois Wladis Hoffman and anonymous reviewers for valuable comments on the original version of this article.

Correspondence concerning this article should be addressed to Vonnie C. McLoyd, Department of Psychology, 3433 Mason Hall, University of Michigan, Ann Arbor, MI 48109.

characteristics and the nature of the family system. The model also assumes that economic decline may influence the child's development as a result of the kinds of events it potentiates (e.g., divorce) and discourages (e.g., marriage).

In keeping with the model, the first section of this review considers the impact of job and income loss on fathers. In the second section, father–child interaction and relations in economically strapped families as well as moderating factors are discussed. The third section briefly examines selected life events potentiated by economic decline that increase children's psychological risk. Finally, the effects of economic setbacks on children's socioemotional functioning, aspirations and expectations, and physical health are reviewed.

Effects on the Father

Although most studies of psychological effects of unemployment disregard parental status, their findings concur with effects reported specifically for unemployed fathers. Besides providing material support, work structures time and provides social contacts, a sense of identity and purpose, and evidence that one is needed by others (Jahoda, 1982). It is not surprising, then, that unemployed men are more depressed, anxious, and hostile and have elevated feelings of victimization and dissatisfaction with themselves and their lives, compared with employed men. They consume more alcohol, have more somatic complaints and eating and sleeping problems, and are at higher risk of neurosis, psychoticism, and suicide (Buss & Redburn, 1983; Gary, 1985; Kasl & Cobb, 1979; Liem, 1981; Theorell, Lind, & Floderus, 1975). Decreased psychosocial adjustment is evident among Afro-American men who expect to fail in the role of primary breadwinner, father, or husband (Bowman, in press). There also is evidence that fathers are more pessimistic about life as income loss increases (Galambos & Silbereisen, 1987a). Some negative effects of unemployment are more pronounced in heads of households with dependent children, compared with those without dependents (Schlozman & Verba, 1978), probably because financial strain and feelings of failure are more acute. The findings of studies of individuals are consistent with those of aggregate studies. For example, fluctuations in unemployment rates have been linked to aggregate indices of psychological distress (e.g., admissions to psychiatric hospitals, Dooley & Catalano, 1980; Horwitz, 1984).

Recent research has demonstrated cogently that these are true effects and not simply selective factors that lead to job loss (Dew et al., 1987; Kessler, House, & Turner, 1987). Not only has unemployment been shown to be directly responsible for increasing stress symptoms, but reemployment has been demonstrated to have health-promoting, restorative effects on fathers (Liem, 1983). Collectively, these studies present strong evidence that economic decline can adversely affect mental and physical well-being. Effects appear to occur through two mechanisms. First, unemployment results in increased financial strain, which in turn undermines physical and mental

health. Second, it leaves the individual more vulnerable to the impact of unrelated life events. When financial strain is controlled, unemployed workers who have not experienced some other stressful event in the previous year have been reported to be in no worse health than the stably employed (Kessler, Turner, & House, in press-a).

Appraisal and Personality Factors

The psychological and physical health outcomes of job and income loss are not uniform, but vary depending on several cognitive, personality, and social factors. Economic loss poses a greater risk to the mental and physical health of the father and consequently the child, if the father defines job or income loss as a negative, crisis-producing event (Horwitz, 1984; Perrucci & Targ, in press), blames himself for these events (Buss & Redburn, 1983; Cohn, 1978; Ginsburg, 1942; Kasl & Cobb, 1979; Komarovsky, 1940), is prone to self-denigration (Kessler, Turner, & House, in press-b), and has rigid, traditional conjugal and family role ideologies that make role changes difficult to implement and accept (Komarovsky, 1940; Powell & Driscoll, 1973; Voydanoff, 1983). If loss of employment or income is seen as a positive event or as an event caused by external forces, it may actually strengthen family ties and boost the father's morale (Caplovitz, 1979; Little, 1976; Moen, Kain, & Elder, 1983).

Social and Financial Support

Social support has been found to insulate fathers against the negative psychological impact of unemployment (Gore, 1978; Kasl & Cobb, 1979; Kessler et al., in press-a, in press-b). Because they lessen the economic hardship caused by unemployment, greater financial assets and shorter periods of unemployment also ameliorate stress symptoms (Bakke, 1940; Gore, 1978; Kasl & Cobb, 1979; Kessler et al., in press-a, in press-b; Little, 1976). The latter two factors, combined with a reduced tendency to define job loss as a crisis of either identity or economic survival (Cohn, 1978), probably account for reduced levels of symptomatology among middle-class men (compared with working-class men) and nonminority men (compared with Afro-American men) (Buss & Redburn, 1983) who have lost jobs. As married women have entered the labor force, the proportion of unemployed husbands with a working wife (55% in 1981) has increased significantly (Klein, 1983). The wife's employment mitigates economic hardship following paternal job and income loss (Moen, 1983), though there is some tentative evidence that employment of the wife that is instigated by the husband's job loss can intensify the husband's feelings of failure (Tauss, 1976). Furthermore, if the ratio of wife's to husband's labor income increases, the restorative effects of the husband's reemployment may be attenuated (Cohn, 1978).

During the Depression, the employment of the adolescent son often eased the economic crisis for the family and appeared to facilitate the adolescent's long-term ego development (Elder, 1974). However, because children tended to give their wages to the mother rather than the father, further eroding the father's status, the child's employment often increased family tension (Cavan, 1959). Today, children's employment is less likely to reduce the family's financial strain because of a major change in the meaning of children's work. The acquisition of discretionary items for themselves, not necessities or the family's subsistence needs, is the primary reason that today's adolescent works (Greenberger, 1987). Conflict is likely to erupt if parents attempt to alter the allocation of the child's wages in favor of the family's subsistence needs.

Effects on Father–Child Interaction

Because their disposition is more likely to be gloomy and hostile, parents who have experienced job or income loss have a tendency to be less nurturant and more punitive and arbitrary in their interactions with their children (Elder et al., 1984, 1985; Goldsmith & Radin, 1987; Lempers et al., in press). However, economic setbacks do not uniformly result in this kind of paternal treatment of the child. Several factors have been found to influence the quality of father–child interaction following job and income loss.

Temperament of the Child

Elder et al. (1985, 1986) found that father mediation of economic hardship through harsh discipline was conditioned by the child's temperament. Children who were temperamentally difficult (irritable, negative, and inclined toward tantrums) at 18 months were more likely to be disciplined in an extreme (severe punishment or indifference) and arbitrary manner by financially pressed fathers 3 years later. This was true even when the father's initial level of irritability (i.e., when the child was 18 months old) was controlled, a finding that is in accord with Rutter's (1979) research with multiproblem families. It is also interesting to note that fathers who were hostile toward the child before the economy crashed were arbitrary and punitive irrespective of how the child behaved, but initially affectionate fathers behaved arbitrarily and harshly primarily in response to problematic child behavior.

Physical Attractiveness of the Child

Elder et al.'s research also showed that economically deprived fathers became more punitive and less supportive of the daughter only if she was physically unattractive. If the daughter was attractive, in some cases economic hardship actually increased supportiveness and lessened paternal harshness. It has been suggested that perhaps physical unattractiveness is a risk factor because adults assign more blame to physically unattractive children and because unattractive girls are less self-confident and assertive because they think less highly of themselves (Elder et al., 1985, 1986). In Elder et al.'s work, boys' attractiveness made no difference in the parenting outcomes of economic hardship, perhaps because physical attractiveness is less critical to boys' sense of self and less salient in others' evaluations of them.

Increase in Father–Child Contact

Unemployed fathers often cite the opportunity for increased contact with their children as a positive aspect of an otherwise negative experience. They report significant increases in the amount of time devoted to child care when asked about changes in their behavior following job loss (Warr & Payne, 1983). Jobless fathers of preschoolers report spending more time as primary caregiver and greater involvement in child rearing overall than employed fathers, and data from their wives corroborate these reports (Radin & Goldsmith, in press). However, fathers differ in the amount of time they spend with their children, and this factor may influence the impact of economic setbacks on father–child interaction and consequently the child. Because it increases the opportunity for conflict and harsh treatment of the child, greater father–child contact makes it more likely that the child will be affected by economic hardship through the changes it produces in the father.

During the Depression, adolescent girls in economically deprived families suffered considerable socioemotional distress in response to the father's harshness. In contrast, adolescent boys' functioning, which reflected greater resiliency and ego strength, was not influenced by the behavior of the father. Elder and his colleagues posit two plausible explanations for this sex difference in father mediation. First, economically strapped fathers may have directed more punitive behavior toward daughters than sons, perhaps because of the daughter's lesser size and strength and/or a greater acceptance of such abusive behavior compared with adolescent sons. Second, and more germane to this discussion, adolescent girls may have spent more time with the father and, thus, may have been exposed to more abusive parenting and family discord than adolescent boys. Adolescent girls spent substantially more time in the home doing chores to compensate for the absence of mothers who took jobs to supplement family income, whereas adolescent boys often found employment outside the home (Elder, 1974; Elder et al., 1985, 1986).

Increased father–child contact following job loss may give rise to a heightened awareness of the child's negative attributes and a less favorable perception of the child. This may contribute to withdrawal of nurturance and an increase in punitiveness by the father. In a study of involuntarily unemployed fathers previously employed in predominantly blue-collar and lower level professional occupations, Johnson and Abramovitch (1985) found that those who were primary caretakers of their children were less positive in the description of their children, attached less importance to parenting skills, and saw their unemployment as less beneficial to the child, the longer they had been unemployed. The corresponding correlations were not significant for unemployed fathers whose children were cared for primarily by someone other than the father. Because selective factors were not ruled out and the sample was small ($n = 30$), these provocative findings must be interpreted cautiously. In a follow-up study of these men six months later, Johnson and Abramovitch (1986) found a nonsignificant tendency for still-unemployed fathers to be more negative than reemployed men in the descriptions of their children, but they did not report differences between fathers who were primary caregivers and those who were nonprimary caregivers.

Unemployed fathers who assume the role of primary caregiver of preschoolers may feel behaviorally incompetent or psychologically unfit for the role (e.g., insufficient patience) or resentful about being forced into it. Even if the role of primary caregiver is viewed more positively at the outset, the new role may wear thin. As the demands of child care become more apparent and if child care responsibilities interfere with job search activities, what was initially an opportunity for greater involvement with the child may come to be seen as a burden. In addition, as the duration of unemployment increases, the father's negative feelings about his joblessness may spill over into his parenting role and rob him of the ability to enjoy the time with his child (Johnson & Abramovitch, 1985; Kanter, 1977). Increased participation in child care has been found to be associated with more positive mental health in highly educated unemployed fathers in dual-wage families—a finding that may reflect a waning of the tendency to regard caring for children as a sign of demasculinization (Shamir, 1986). However, the causal direction of this relationship is unclear, and the finding is probably not generalizable to working-class men such as those in Johnson and Abramovitch's (1985) study, who tend to have more traditional sex-role ideologies.

Extrapolating from Johnson and Abramovitch's (1985) findings, increased negative affect toward the child stemming from increased contact may be one of the mechanisms that mediate the well-documented link between unemployment and child abuse (Parke & Collmer, 1975). There are several other pathways by which the father's unemployment can lead to child abuse: (a) an increase in the father's role as disciplinarian, (b) a heightened need in fathers to exercise power because of a real or perceived status loss, (c) increased frustration brought on by financial strain, and (d) an increase in marital disputes and displacement of anger onto the child, especially if the child forms a coalition with the mother (Herrenkohl, Herrenkohl, & Egolf, 1983; Parke & Collmer, 1975). During the Depression, children whose fathers lost the greatest amount of income were most likely to perceive the mother as someone to rely on and most likely to align themselves with the mother when the parents quarreled (Elder, 1974). Taken together, this work and evidence that unemployed heads of household feel less positively about their children (Sheldon & Fox, 1983) appear to suggest that under certain conditions paternal unemployment lowers the worth of children to fathers (Siegal, 1984).

Role of the Mother

During the Depression, mothers played a pivotal role in determining how economically deprived fathers treated their children. If the mother's relationship with the child prior to the Depression was warm and affectionate, harsh treatment of the child by the father was reduced. In the face of economic loss, a family system distinguished by an aloof mother was most likely to lead to the father's maltreatment of the child. The quality of the mother–child relationship also made a difference in how income loss affected the child's behavior. Severe temper tantrums occurred only if the young child lacked a warm affective bond with the mother (Elder et al., 1986). Mothers were less supportive and protective of their young sons than their daughters, and this difference seems to explain why economic hardship during early childhood markedly increased the risk of psychological impairment in boys but was linked to personal strength and resourcefulness in girls (Elder, 1979).

Effects on the Father–Child Relationship

Given the increased tendency of unemployed fathers to behave toward their children in a rejecting, arbitrary manner, it is hardly surprising that economic losses have been found to strain the father's relationship with the child, to reduce his attractiveness to the child as a role model, companion, and confidant, and to increase the tendency of children to affiliate with peers and nonfamilial adults. The father's emotional volatility, combined with role changes and other adaptations to economic hardship, may enhance the affective status of the mother relative to the father (Elder, 1974). However, whether economic setbacks during the Depression threatened the father–child relationship depended on two factors—the quality of the father's relationship with the child before economic setbacks occurred and the affective disposition of the wife toward her husband.

Prior Father–Child Relationship

In Komarovsky's (1940) study, a positive father–child relationship prior to unemployment characterized all cases in which the fathers of young children gained status following job loss and all cases in which the fathers of children 15 years old or older maintained their parental authority (none of the latter fathers gained status). Among those fathers whose authority deteriorated subsequent to job loss, two dominant types of preunemployment father–child relationships were evident: coercive, disinterested fathers who were feared by their children and rigid, interfering fathers who commanded no respect but sought to impose on their children antiquated standards of decorum.

The Wife's Attitude

The attitude of the wife toward her husband exerted a powerful influence on the unemployed father's relationship with his child during the Depression. The mother's prominence in the child's life made it possible for her, first, to shape the child's understanding of the economic crisis and the father's ensuing behavior and, second, to modify the actions of the child toward the father. If she lost respect for her husband and blamed him for the disruption in their lives, she was unlikely either to present a sympathetic interpretation of the father's predicament or to encourage child behaviors that acknowledged the authority of the father. Within this kind of marital context, the child's relationship with the father was likely to suffer (Elder, 1974; Ginsburg, 1942). There is no compelling reason to believe that this conditioner of effects on the father–child relationship would be any less potent in the context of today's economic setbacks (for a discussion of the impact of unemployment on marital relations, see Ray & McLoyd, 1986).

Recent research findings reflect a peculiar inconsistency. Today's middle-class and working-class parents rarely report deterioration of their relationship with the child following job loss when directly asked. In fact, they are as likely or more likely to report improvement in relations with the child following job loss (Perrucci & Targ, in press; Perrucci, Targ, Perrucci, & Targ, 1987; Rayman & Bluestone, cited in Cunningham, 1983; Thomas, McCabe, & Berry, 1980), though this outcome would appear unlikely if relations were markedly distant or contentious prior to job loss (Komarovsky, 1940). In some of these studies, unemployed workers received relatively generous economic assistance following job loss (e.g., severance pay or continuation of health benefits) (Perrucci & Targ, in press), were middle class and had substantial financial assets (Thomas et al., 1980), or typically had spouses who were employed (Little, 1976). All of these factors may have mitigated family tension and discord. Also, it should be pointed out that most of these studies did not have a comparison group of employed workers.

In contrast to these benign reports from unemployed parents, when unemployed and reemployed groups are compared and the estimates of parent–child conflict are based on reports from the child, rather than the parent, differences have been found. In a recent study by Flanagan (1988b), adolescents whose parents were currently unemployed because of job loss reported more conflict with their parents than those whose parents lost jobs and had found new employment. Other researchers have found no relation between the father's employment status and children's reports of family problems (Buss & Redburn, 1983), but these reports may not reflect the quality of parent–child relationships per se. In general, the impact of economic setbacks in recent years on the father–child relationship is poorly understood because few relevant studies have been conducted and because existing studies, with notable exceptions, use severely truncated measures, ignore the child as a potential informant, lack comparison groups of employed families, and ignore conditioning factors.

Life Events Potentiated by Paternal Job and Income Loss

Unemployment may affect the child's development and his or her relationship with the father through its deterrence of marriage and ferment of marital instability. Furstenberg (1981) found that when out-of-wedlock conception occurred, marriage was much more likely to occur during the prenatal period if the father had a full-time job than if he was unemployed. Compared with those who deferred marriage, women who married prior to delivery were more likely to marry the father of the child. If she married the biological father, rather than another man, the child's cognitive and social skills were more advanced in later years, perhaps because of the continuity of the father–child relationship.

Several studies document the fact that marital dissolution is more likely if the husband is unemployed (Bishop, 1977), though the risk is probably much greater if the marriage was weak before the husband lost employment (Ray & McLoyd, 1986). When marriages end, whether through divorce, separation, or desertion, the child usually spends some time living in a single-parent household, most often (90%) headed by his or her mother (Blechman, 1982). Families headed by previously married mothers typically experience downward economic mobility. These events and circumstances have effects on both the child's development and relationship with the father (Hetherington, 1979; Weiss, 1979).

Effects on the Child

Socioemotional Functioning

Economic setbacks often require denial of money and accoutrements for social activities. These material losses, combined with embarrassment caused by the family's situation, may undermine the child's mental health and lead him or her to withdraw from peers. Children whose families have experienced job or income loss have more mental health problems (Werner & Smith, 1982) and are more depressed, lonely (Lempers et al., in press), and emotionally sensitive (Elder et al., 1985). They are less sociable and more distrustful (Buss & Redburn, 1983) and are more likely (adolescent girls) to feel excluded by peers (Elder, 1974). Parental unemployment also has been linked to low self-esteem in children, especially boys (Coopersmith, 1967; Isralowitz & Singer, 1986) and reduced competence in coping with stress (Flanagan, 1988a). Recent evidence indicates that many of these effects are mediated through the rejection and punitiveness of economically deprived parents (Elder et al., 1985; Lempers et al., in press). High maternal support and experiences that encourage maturity and autonomy appear to be critical sources of psychological resilience in economically deprived children (Elder, 1979).

If economic hardship can decrease peer affiliation, it also can increase it, especially in boys (Elder et al., 1985). The child's dependency on peers may make him or her highly susceptible to negative peer pressure. Children in families experiencing economic loss, compared with children in economically stable families, report performing more socially disapproved acts and violating more school rules (Flanagan, 1988b). Werner and Smith's (1982) longitudinal study of the children of Kauai, Hawaii, indicated that paternal job loss was one of the life events that discriminated between children who developed serious behavior problems (e.g., delinquency) and children who were free of such problems. Lempers et al. (in press) found no direct link between economic hardship and delinquency-drug use. Rather, economic hardship led to more delinquency-drug use by increasing inconsistent and punitive discipline by parents. Research also indicates that problem behavior in children experiencing economic loss is greater if economic strain as perceived by parents is high (Perrucci & Targ, in press), if parental acceptance of the child is low (Galambos & Silbereisen, 1987b), if the family lacks cohesion (Flanagan, 1988b; Walper & Silbereisen, 1987), and if the marriage is weak (Rockwell & Elder, 1982).

Though the paucity of longitudinal data precludes firm conclusions, economic loss during childhood appears to have few long-term psychological effects. Buss and Redburn (1983), who interviewed college-age children of laid-off and employed steelworkers during the four years following the closing of the steel mills, reported no effects. Elder (1979) found few enduring effects of economic hardship on psychological health, though men who were economically deprived as very young children, compared with their nondeprived counterparts, were more worried, emotionally distant, and lethargic at midlife. They also had higher levels of alcohol consumption and were more likely to use professional therapy.

Aspirations and Expectations

Parents experiencing economic hardship are more pessimistic about their lives and the future of their children (Galambos & Silbereisen, 1987a; Ginsburg, 1942), feel less confident about helping their children prepare for future work roles, and are less likely to encourage college matriculation (Flanagan, 1988a). They also report more negative changes in educational plans for their children (Larson, 1984). These parental dispositions and behaviors appear to dampen children's aspirations and expectations. Adolescents in families experiencing economic loss express more financial worries, are less likely to expect to go to a four-year college, and are more likely to expect to go into vocational training after high school (Flanagan, 1988a), though their work values (i.e., ratings of the importance of job prestige and security, monetary rewards, etc.) appear unaffected (Isralowitz & Singer, 1986).

Girls are especially prone to reduce their aspirations and expectations of job success, and this seems to be in response to the father's pessimism and rejection (Elder et al., 1985; Galambos & Silbereisen, 1987a). Furthermore, economic adversity is more likely to lead to a downward shift in parents' educational plans for daughters than for sons (Mott & Haurin, 1982). These factors, combined with parental expectations of lower achievement in daughters than sons even in a favorable economic climate (Parsons, Adler, & Kaczala, 1982) and increased pressure during early adolescence to conform to feminine sex-role stereotypes (Galambos & Silbereisen, 1987a), constrict girls' aspirations and discourage feelings of self-adequacy.

If children's work aspirations diminish, education may come to be seen as irrelevant to the future and the child's academic performance may suffer. As one Detroit student put it after both her mother and father lost jobs:

The future stinks. You're supposed to spend your childhood preparing for the real life of being an adult. But what if that real life is no good? What's the sense? Look at my parents. They always did everything the way you're supposed to. Now look at them—nobody will give them a job. . . . What's the sense of trying in school. There's no jobs for my dad or my mom. Why should I believe there will be jobs for me when I get out [of school]? ("Children of the Unemployed," 1983, p. 3)

Research from the 1930s and the 1980s reports declines in the academic performance of children in families experiencing economic hardship. This may be the result of reduced educational and occupational expectations, emotional problems that reduce attention span, poor physical health, lack of parental assistance with homework, or a combination of these factors (Eisenberg & Lazarsfeld, 1938; Elder, 1979). Teachers perceive children from families experiencing economic loss to be less well adjusted to school than children from economically stable families (Flanagan, 1988a).

However, economic hardship may not be a strong predictor of occupational success. Elder (1979) found that though men from economically deprived families were less likely to complete college, they were more likely than nondeprived men to match or exceed career expectations based on level of education. Factors that appear to have fostered resilience in the deprived men who suffered psychological impairment during adolescence include entry into college, late marriage and child bearing, military service, a rewarding work life, and the emotional support of marriage and family life.

Physical Health

Children of job losers are at increased risk of illness including respiratory infections, gastrointestinal infections, immunological diseases such as asthma and eczema, and trauma (Margolis & Farran, 1981). This may be attributable to a decline in the quality of food, the disruption of social support, and a decrease in the use of medical care because many displaced workers lose employer-financed health insurance along with their jobs (Podgursky & Swaim, 1987). The impact of economic decline on children's physical health also may be mediated through the father's behavior. Children often learn how to behave in different situations and become aware of the consequences of events and behavior by observing the behavior of others (Bandura, 1977). Deterioration in the father's health following job and income loss may become a communicable social phenomenon to the extent that the child models the symptomatic behavior of the father (Kelly et al., 1985). Kelly et al. (1985) found no direct link between parental job loss and the child's physical health status. Rather, job loss adversely affected the child's physical health through its elevation of the parent's health problems. In Buss and Redburn's (1983) study, the somatic complaints of the children of unemployed steelworkers and managers paralleled those of the fathers.

Summary

Studies of contemporary families and families of the 1930s Depression are consistent in demonstrating that paternal job and income loss affect children's development primarily through the changes they produce in the father's behavior and disposition. The amount of psychological distress experienced by unemployed fathers and the extent to which this distress adversely affects the father's treatment of the child depend on several cognitive, personality, and environmental factors. Negative fathering behavior increases the child's risk of socioemotional problems, deviant behavior, and reduced aspirations and expectations.

A great deal more study is needed of those factors that account for variation in the child's response to economic hardship in the contemporary context. Degree of material deprivation, social support, family decision-making style, adolescent employment, developmental status, and the child's causal attributions about the parent's loss of employment or income are obvious factors that need to be considered. The contemporary mother, more so than mothers of the Depression, shares her role as socializer and caregiver with others (e.g., father or day care worker), often because she is employed. Whether she is as potent as mothers of the Depression in insulating the child against the negative impact of economic hardship is not known. Studies are needed to determine long-term effects and how these are related to the child's work values and causal attributions about economic decline. Our knowledge base should be expanded to include Afro-American and Hispanic families because their risk of economic decline is high.

Maternal Job and Income Loss

Research on the impact of economic decline focuses almost exclusively on displaced men and their children, despite significant numbers of married and single mothers who are unemployed and seeking work. Women were less affected than men by the two recent recessions because their employment is concentrated in the steadily growing service-producing sector, but they were not immune. Of those workers displaced between 1981 and 1986 from jobs they had held at least three years, about a third were women (Horvath, 1987). Compared with married men, married women appear to be spared at least some of the psychological costs of unemployment, apparently because the alternative roles of wife and mother provide self-gratification and self-definition that men do not derive from their roles as husbands and fathers (Warr & Parry, 1982). On the assumption that children's responses to job loss are conditioned by parents' responses, one would expect children to be less affected by maternal job loss than paternal job loss if it occurs in the context of marriage. However, more substantial effects may result if work is a major source of a mother's identity, self-esteem, and psychological fulfillment or if her wages are a significant determinant of the family's income and standard of living.

Two factors make it difficult to be sanguine about children living in households headed by single women who have suffered economic losses. First, they have fewer financial resources and face a high risk of falling into poverty (Rosen, 1983). Because there are fewer persons of working age, on average, in female-headed families, these families are less likely to have a second wage earner whose income can cushion the impact of job and income loss. Since 1976, the proportion of unemployed women who head families that include an employed person has never exceeded 22% (Klein, 1983). Second, irrespective of employment status, single mothers generally are at greater risk of anxiety, depression, and health problems than other marital status groups (Guttentag, Salasin, & Belle, 1980; Kelly et al., 1985). Thus, they probably have fewer psychological resources to cope with economic setbacks, and this is likely to increase the risk of punitive and harsh treatment of the child. These considerations justify special concern about the children of single women who experience job and income loss.

REFERENCES

Bakke, E. (1940). *Citizens without work.* New Haven, CT: Yale University.

Bandura, W. (1977). *Social learning theory.* Englewood Cliffs, NJ: Prentice-Hall.

Bishop, J. (1977). *Jobs, cash transfers, and marital instability: A review of the evidence.* Madison: University of Wisconsin Institute for Research on Poverty.

Blechman, E. (1982). Are children with one parent at psychological risk? A methodological review. *Journal of Marriage and the Family, 44,* 179–196.

Bowman, P. (in press). Post-industrial displacement and family role strains: Challenges to the black family. In P. Voydanoff & L. Majka (Eds.), *Families and economic distress.* Beverly Hills, CA: Sage.

Buss, T., & Redburn, F. S. (1983). *Mass unemployment: Plant closings and community mental health.* Beverly Hills, CA: Sage.

Caplovitz, D. (1979). *Making ends meet: How families cope with inflation and recession.* Beverly Hills, CA: Sage.

Cavan, R. S. (1959). Unemployment—crisis of the common man. *Marriage and Family Living, 21,* 139–146.

Cohn, R. (1978). The effect of employment status change on self-attitudes. *Social Psychology, 41,* 81–93.

Coopersmith, S. (1967). *The antecedents of self-esteem.* San Francisco: Freeman.

Cunningham, S. (1983, January). Shock of layoff felt deep inside family circle. *APA Monitor,* p. 14.

Children of the unemployed. (1983, March 8). *Detroit Free Press,* p. 3.

Dew, M., Bromet, E., & Schulberg, H. (1987). A comparative analysis of two community stressors' long-term mental health effects. *American Journal of Community Psychology, 15,* 167–184.

Dooley, D., & Catalano, R. (1980). Economic change as a cause of behavioral disorder. *Psychological Bulletin, 87,* 358–390.

Duncan, G. (1984). *Years of poverty, years of plenty.* Ann Arbor, MI: Institute for Social Research.

Eisenberg, P., & Lazarsfeld, P. E. (1938). The psychological effects of unemployment. *Psychological Bulletin, 35,* 358–390.

Elder, G. (1974). *Children of the Great Depression.* Chicago: University of Chicago Press.

Elder, G. (1979). Historical change in life patterns and personality. In P. Baltes & O. Brim (Eds.), *Life span development and behavior* (Vol. 2, pp. 117–159). New York: Academic Press.

Elder, G., Caspi, A., & Nguyen, T. (1986). Resourceful and vulnerable children: Family influence in hard times. In R. K. Silbereisen, K. Eyferth, & G. Rudinger (Eds.), *Development as action in context* (pp. 167–186). New York: Springer-Verlag.

Elder, G., Liker, J., & Cross, C. (1984). Parent–child behavior in the Great Depression: Life course and intergenerational influences. In P. Baltes & O. Brim (Eds.), *Life span development and behavior* (Vol. 6, pp. 109–158). Orlando, FL: Academic Press.

Elder, G., Nguyen, T., & Caspi, A. (1985). Linking family hardship to children's lives. *Child Development, 56,* 361–375.

Flaim, P., & Sehgal, E. (1985). Displaced workers of 1979–83: How well have they fared? *Monthly Labor Review, 108,* 3–16.

Flanagan, C. (1988a, April). *The effects of a changing economy on the socialization of children's academic and vocational aspirations.* Paper presented at the American Educational Research Association, New Orleans.

Flanagan, C. (1988b). *Parents' work security and the young adolescent's development.* Unpublished manuscript, University of Michigan, Dearborn.

Furstenberg, F. (1981). The social consequences of teenage parenthood. In F. Furstenberg, R. Lincoln, & J. Menken (Eds.), *Teenage sexuality, pregnancy, and childbearing* (pp. 184–210). Philadelphia: University of Pennsylvania Press.

Fusfeld, D., & Bates, T. (1984). *The political economy of the urban ghetto.* Carbondale, IL: Southern Illinois University Press.

Galambos, N., & Silbereisen, R. (1987a). Income change, parental life outlook, and adolescent expectations for job success. *Journal of Marriage and the Family, 49,* 141–149.

Galambos, N., & Silbereisen, R. (1987b). Influences of income change and parental acceptance on adolescent transgression proneness and peer relations. *European Journal of Psychology of Education, 1,* 17–28.

Gary, L. (1985). Correlates of depressive symptoms among a select population of black men. *American Journal of Public Health, 75,* 1220–1222.

Ginsburg, S. W. (1942). What unemployment does to people. *American Journal of Psychiatry, 99,* 439–446.

Goldsmith, R., & Radin, N. (1987, April). *Objective versus subjective reality: The effects of job loss and financial stress on fathering behaviors.* Paper presented at the biennial meeting of the Society for Research in Child Development, Baltimore, MD.

Gore, S. (1978). The effect of social support in moderating the health consequences of unemployment. *Journal of Health and Social Behavior, 19,* 157–165.

Greenberger, E. (1987). Children's employment and families. In N. Gerstel & H. Gross (Eds.), *Families and work* (pp. 396–406). Philadelphia: Temple University Press.

Guttentag, M., Salasin, S., & Belle, D. (1980). *The mental health of women.* New York: Academic Press.

Herrenkohl, R., Herrenkohl, E., & Egolf, B. (1983). Circumstances surrounding the occurrence of child maltreatment. *Journal of Consulting and Clinical Psychology, 51,* 424–431.

Hetherington, M. (1979). Divorce: A child's perspective. *American Psychologist, 34,* 859–865.

Hill, R. (1958). Generic features of families under stress. *Social Casework, 39,* 139–150.

Horvath, F. (1987). The pulse of economic change: Displaced workers of 1981–85. *Monthly Labor Review, 110,* 3–12.

Horwitz, A. (1984). The economy and social pathology. *Annual Review of Sociology, 10,* 95–119.

Isralowitz, R., & Singer, M. (1986). Unemployment and its impact on adolescent work values. *Adolescence, 21,* 145–158.

Jahoda, M. (1979). The impact of unemployment in the 1930s and the 1970s. *Bulletin of the British Psychological Society, 32,* 309–314.

Jahoda, M. (1982). *Employment and unemployment: A social-psychological analysis.* Cambridge: Cambridge University Press.

Johnson, L., & Abramovitch, R. (1985). *Unemployed fathers: Parenting in a changing labour market* (ISBN 0-919456-30-8). Toronto, Canada: Social Planning Council of Metropolitan Toronto.

Johnson, L., & Abramovitch, R. (1986). *Between jobs: Paternal unemployment and family life* (ISBN 0-919456-29-4). Toronto, Canada: Social Planning Council of Metropolitan Toronto.

Kanter, R. (1977). *Work and family in the United States: A critical review and agenda for research and policy.* New York: Russell Sage.

Kasl, S. V., & Cobb, S. (1979). Some mental health consequences of plant closings and job loss. In L. Ferman & J. Gordus (Eds.), *Mental health and the economy* (pp. 255–300). Kalamazoo, MI: Upjohn Institute for Employment Research.

Kelly, R., Sheldon, A., & Fox, G. (1985). The impact of economic dislocation on the health of children. In J. Boulet, A. M. DeBritto, & S. A. Ray (Eds.), *The impact of poverty and unemployment on children* (pp. 94–108). Ann Arbor: University of Michigan Bush Program in Child Development and Social Policy.

Kessler, R., House, J., & Turner, J. (1987). Unemployment and health in a community sample. *Journal of Health and Social Behavior, 28,* 51–59.

Kessler, R., Turner, J., & House, J. (in press-a). Intervening processes in the relationship between unemployment and health. *Psychological Medicine.*

Kessler, R., Turner, J., & House, J. (in press-b). The effects of unemployment on health in a community sample: Main, modifying, and mediating effects. *Journal of Social Issues.*

Klein, D. (1983). Trends in employment and unemployment in families. *Monthly Labor Review, 106,* 21–25.

Komarovsky, M. (1940). *The unemployed man and his family.* New York: Dryden Press.

Kutscher, R. (1987). Overview and implications of the projections to 2000. *Monthly Labor Review, 110,* 3–9.

Larson, J. (1984). The effect of husband's unemployment on marital and family relations in blue-collar families. *Family Relations, 33,* 503–511.

LeGrande, L. (1983). *Unemployment during the Great Depression and the current recession* (Report #83-15-E). Washington, DC: Library of Congress Congressional Research Service.

Lempers, J., Clark-Lempers, D., & Simons, R. (in press). Economic hardship, parenting, and distress in adolescence. *Child Development.*

Liem, R. (1981). Unemployment and mental health implications for human service policy. *Policy Study Journal, 10,* 354–364.

Liem, R. (1983). *Unemployment: Personal and family effects.* Unpublished manuscript, Boston College.

Little, C. B. (1976). Technical–professional unemployment: Middle-class adaptability to personal crisis. *Sociological Quarterly, 17,* 262–274.

Margolis, L., & Farran, D. (1981). Unemployment: The health consequences for children. *North Carolina Medical Journal, 42,* 849–850.

Moen, P. (1983). Unemployment, public policy, and families: Forecasts for the 1980s. *Journal of Marriage and the Family, 45,* 751–760.

Moen, P., Kain, E., & Elder, G. (1983). Economic conditions and family life: Contemporary and historical perspectives. In R. R. Nelson & F. Skidmore (Eds.), *American families and the economy: The high costs of living* (pp. 213–259). Washington, DC: National Academy Press.

Mott, F., & Haurin, R. (1982). Variations in the educational progress and career orientations of brothers and sisters. In F. Mott (Ed.), *The employment revolution: Young American women in the 1970's* (pp. 19–44). Cambridge, MA: MIT Press.

Parke, R., & Collmer, C. (1975). Child abuse: An interdisciplinary review. In E. M. Hetherington (Ed.), *Review of child development research* (Vol. 5, pp. 509–590). Chicago: University of Chicago Press.

Parsons, J., Adler, T., & Kaczala, C. (1982). Socialization of achievement attitudes and beliefs: Parental influences. *Child Development, 53,* 310–321.

Perrucci, C., & Targ, D. (in press). Effects of a plant closing on marriage and family life. In P. Voydanoff & L. Majka (Eds.), *Families and economic distress.* Beverly Hills: Sage.

Perrucci, C., Targ, D., Perrucci, R., & Targ, H. (1987). Plant closing: A comparison of effects on women and men workers. In R. Lee (Ed.), *Redundancy, layoffs, and plant closures* (pp. 181–207). Wolfeboro, NH: Croom Helm.

Podgursky, M., & Swaim, P. (1987). Health insurance loss: The case of the displaced worker. *Monthly Labor Review, 110,* 30–33.

Powell, D. H., & Driscoll, P. F. (1973). Middle-class professionals face unemployment. *Society, 10,* 18–26.

Radin, N., & Goldsmith, R. (in press). The involvement of selected unemployed and employed men with their children. *Child Development.*

Ray, S. A., & McLoyd, V. C. (1986). Fathers in hard times: The impact of unemployment and poverty on paternal and marital relations. In M. Lamb (Ed.), *The father's role* (pp. 339–383). New York: Wiley.

Rockwell, R., & Elder, G. (1982). Economic deprivation and problem behavior: Childhood and adolescence in the Great Depression. *Human Development, 25,* 57–64.

Rosen, E. (1983, September). *Laid off: Displaced blue collar women in*

New England. Paper presented at annual meeting of the Society for the Study of Social Problems, Detroit, MI.

Rutter, M. (1979). Protective factors in children's responses to stress and disadvantage. In M. Kent & J. Rolf (Ed.), *Primary prevention of psychopathology* (Vol. 3, pp. 49–74). Hanover, NH: University Press of New England.

Schlozman, K. L., & Verba, S. (1978). The new employment: Does it hurt? *Public Policy, 26,* 333–358.

Shamir, B. (1986). Unemployment and household division of labor. *Journal of Marriage and the Family, 48,* 195–206.

Sheldon, A., & Fox, G. (1983, September). *The impact of economic uncertainty on children's roles within the family.* Paper presented at meeting of the Society for the Study of Social Problems, Detroit, MI.

Siegal, M. (1984). Economic deprivation and the quality of parent-child relations: A trickle-down framework. *Journal of Applied Developmental Psychology, 5,* 127–144.

Simms, M. (1987). How loss of manufacturing jobs is affecting blacks. *Focus: The Monthly Newsletter of the Joint Center for Political Studies, 15,* 6–7.

Tauss, V. (1976). Working wife-house husband: Implications for counseling. *Journal of Family Counseling, 4,* 52–55.

Theorell, T., Lind, E., & Floderus, B. (1975). The relationships of disturbing life changes and emotions to the early development of myocardial infarction and other serious illness. *International Journal of Epidemiology, 4,* 281–293.

Thomas, L. E., McCabe, E., & Berry, J. (1980). Unemployment and family stress: A reassessment. *Family Relations, 29,* 517–524.

Voydanoff, P. (1983). Unemployment and family stress. In H. Lopata (Ed.), *Research in the interweave of social roles: Jobs and families* (Vol. 3, pp. 239–250). Greenwich, CT: JAI Press.

Walper, S., & Silbereisen, R. (1987, April). *Economic loss, strained family relationships, and adolescents' contranormative attitudes.* Paper presented at the biennial meeting of the Society for Research in Child Development, Baltimore, MD.

Warr, P., & Parry, G. (1982). Paid employment and women's psychological well-being. *Psychological Bulletin, 91,* 498–516.

Warr, P., & Payne, R. (1983). Social class and reported changes in behavior after job loss. *Journal of Applied Social Psychology, 13,* 206–222.

Weiss, R. (1979). Growing up a little faster: The experience of growing up in a single-parent household. *Journal of Social Issues, 35,* 97–111.

Werner, E., & Smith, R. (1982). *Vulnerable but invincible: A study of resilient children.* New York: McGraw-Hill.

Multiple Choice:

1. Which of the following has been shown to increase after paternal job loss?

    A. the value children place on education
    B. children's physical health
    C. child abuse
    D. marital support

2. Both McLoyd and Elder (who studied Depression families) place particular stress on the importance of which factor in mediating the effects of economic loss on children?

    A. father's behavior
    B. mother's behavior
    C. marital status of the parents
    D. child's temperament

Essay:

1. Did your father ever lose his job? If so, how were you affected? If not, what impact can you imagine it might have had? In both cases, use the model in Figure 1 to organize your response.

2. Relate the concepts of resilience and vulnerability described in Article 1 by Werner and the effects of paternal unemployment discussed by McLoyd in this article. What factors protect children, and which make them more vulnerable in this situation?

ARTICLE 22

Facts, Fantasies and the Future of Child Care in the United States

Sandra Scarr, Deborah Phillips, and Kathleen McCartney

Reprinted from: *Psychological Science*, 1990, *1*, 26-35.
Copyright © 1990 by the American Psychological Society.
Reprinted with the permission of Cambridge University Press.

It would be impossible to be unaware of the fact that child care has become a social policy issue of great concern in the United States today. The problem is often described as a "crisis." For some, the crisis refers to the fact that so many children are being cared for outside their homes and especially that they are not receiving full-time care from their mothers. For others, the crisis concerns the fact that there is not enough good quality, affordable child care available for families in need of it.

The origin of our child care problem is in one sense simple--many more mothers of young children are in the work force today than was true in previous decades. Why are so many mothers now working? There are many reasons. In part due to the feminist movement, more women are pursuing careers than in the past. Because of the economics of family life, maternal employment outside the home is a necessity for an increasing number of families. Because of our increased divorce rate, more women head up households, and they must work to support their children (especially since the record of child support by divorced fathers is dismal). There are a host of other reasons as well.

Why is finding child care such a problem? One obvious reason is that there is greater demand than ever before as more women are working outside the home. In addition, the ever-increasing mobility of our society leaves families without relatives nearby to provide child care. Also, there are not enough providers of child care services, in large part because caretakers' salaries are extremely low. As a consequence, some percentage of the available child care situations are less than optimal.

As Sandra Scarr and her co-authors note in this article, maternal employment is a fact of life in the US today, and it is not likely to change any time soon. Thus, the real issue is how we can ensure that children in child care do not suffer from that circumstance--and might even profit from it.

Given the intensity of the debate, there has been much confusion and distortion of the facts, and the authors of this article have attempted to dispel some of the fantasies that exist about children, mothers, and child care. They review the conclusions from the multitude of studies on the effects of child care, and they also discuss the social policy implications of this very important issue.

FACTS, FANTASIES AND THE FUTURE OF CHILD CARE IN THE UNITED STATES

by Sandra Scarr, Deborah Phillips, and Kathleen McCartney

Psychologists in both family practice and developmental research may be puzzled about the scientific status of research on child care as it affects children, parents, and caregivers. What conclusions can be reached about mothers in the labor force, about the advisability of various child care arrangements, about their short and long-term consequences, and what advice do we as psychologists have to offer in the public interest to parents of infants and young children? In this article, we review research on child care, and discuss its implications for the nation and for psychology as a research enterprise and a helping profession.

Child care is now as essential to family life as the automobile and the refrigerator. As of 1986, the majority of families, including those with infants, require child care to support parental employment. Yet most families find it far easier to purchase quality cars and refrigerators than to buy good care for their children.

Contemporary realities about the need for child care, captured in statistics about family income, mens' wages, maternal employment, and labor force needs, have not produced a coherent national policy on parental leaves or on child care services for working parents (Kahn & Kamerman, 1987; Scarr, Phillips, & McCartney, 1989a). Instead, our society remains ambivalent about mothers who work and about children whose care is shared, part-time, with others (McCartney & Phillips, 1988). The cost of our reluctance to shed fantasies about children's needs and parents' obligations, particularly mothers' obligations, is the failure to develop constructive social policies.

Facts and fantasies about child care arrangements influence the thinking of psychologists, other experts, parents, and those who make child care policy. It is thus imperative to reassess our ideas about children's needs and maternal roles, based especially on research. The social and demographic facts that are affecting the growing reliance on child care are now well known. They encompass documentation of declines in family income (Greenstein, 1987), dramatic changes in family structure (Cherlin, 1988), rapid increases in maternal employment and projected continuations of this trend (Hofferth & Phillips, 1987), and converging patterns of employment among mothers of all races and marital statuses (Kahn & Kamerman, 1987; Phillips, 1989). In this article we aim to dispel some of the fantasies that have prevented our nation from making appropriate provisions for the care of infants and young children, and to present research facts about child care. In conclusion, we take a brief look at current policy debates and at the future of child care that could emerge if we proceeded from facts about infants, mothers, and child care.

FANTASIES ABOUT MOTHERS

Science is, in part, a social construction (Scarr, 1985). As such, we sometimes construct fantasies about child development, the uses and implications of which can endure long beyond the time when conflicting evidence becomes available. This is most likely to occur when prior scientific results support strongly-held social values. We argue here that the field of psychology has constructed fantasies about the role of mothers in infant development that have impact on our views of child care. We label these beliefs *fantasies* because they are not supported by contemporary scientific evidence. Such fantasies can be found in thinking about mother-infant attachment, maternal deprivation, and the role of early experience for later development. The end result is that some of our fantasies about the mothers and infant development have contributed to our national ambivalence about child care as an acceptable childrearing environment.

Fantasies about Mother-Infant Attachment

Prevailing views about mother-infant attachment have their roots in psychoanalytic theory, Bowlby's theory (1951), and ethology. In some way, all these theories es-

Requests for reprints should be sent to Sandra Scarr, Department of Psychology, University of Virginia, Charlottesville, VA 22903.

pouse "monotropism" (Smith, 1980), the idea that a single relationship with a special caregiver, typically the mother, is critical for physical and social nourishment. Psychiatrists and others from a psychoanalytic tradition have most often objected to the use of child care, especially in infancy, for this reason (Fraiberg, 1977; Goldstein, Freud, & Solnit, 1973). Yet, research reveals that infants can and do develop multiple attachment relationships: with fathers (Lamb, 1980), with other family members and close friends of the family (Schaffer, 1977), and with caregivers (Ainslie & Anderson, 1984; Farran & Ramey, 1977; Howes, Rodning, Galluzzo, & Myers, 1988). Moreover, we know that most infants become securely attached to their parents, even when they live with a full-time caregiver in a kibbutz (Fox, 1977). Some research has shown that a secure attachment with a caregiver can buttress a child who otherwise might be at risk (Howes, Rodning, Galluzo & Myers, 1988). Nevertheless, little is known about children's relationships with their caregivers, whose roles in children's lives must differ from those of parents, especially because of the high turnover rates of caregivers in the United States. An enduring child-adult relationship requires at least moderate stability in caregiving.

A number of studies have compared attachment relationships between infants and their mothers as a function of maternal employment or use of child care. Currently, there is a controversy concerning whether extensive child care during infancy is a risk to infants' attachments to their mothers (Belsky, 1988). But most infants require care while their mothers work. Should we view as a "risk factor" a small mean difference in attachment security (8%; Clarke-Stewart, 1989) between children as a function of maternal employment status or child care use? When children in child care seem to fare less well, child care is said to be a risk. When children in child care fare better on assessments of social competence, independence, or school readiness (e.g., Clarke-Stewart, 1984; Gunnarsson, 1978; Howes & Olenick, 1986; Howes & Stewart, 1987), no one is prepared to call care by mothers a risk factor. All forms of care have their strengths and weaknesses, although the effect sizes are likely to be small (for a thorough review of infant care, see Clarke-Stewart, 1989).

Few would disagree that maternal employment and child are contextual issues (Bronfenbrenner, 1979, 1986), with many "ifs, ands, and buts" that depend upon the family and the child care situation. Unfortunately, expert advice to parents often fails to mention the size of effects, fails to acknowledge known moderators of effects, and fails to speculate on the possibility, indeed probability, of unknown moderators (Gerson, Alpert, & Richarson, 1984). A notable exception comes from Maurer & Maurer (1989):

Developmental psychology knows much more about babies now than it knew even ten years ago. . . . Consider, for instance, the effect upon the baby of the mother's going back to work. . . . Studies on the topic abound, and every new one yields a flurry of pronouncements, either dire or reassuring depending on the results. But look at some of the factors involved here. A baby may be cared for in his own home, or in somebody else's home, or in a day care center, by either a relative or a stranger. The caretaker may be trained or untrained, and may be looking after one baby or several babies. The mother may be an overbearing woman and the caretaker easy-going, or vice versa. The mother may be happy about going to work and relaxed about giving over her baby in the morning, or she may be distressed at having to leave him with someone else: either way she may communicate her emotions to the child. At home in the evening, the mother may not have time to play with the baby because she is swamped with housework, or the babysitter or her husband may do the housework, leaving her evenings free. Her husband may be unhappy about her returning to work, so their evenings with the child become tense, or her husband may support her. And, of course, babies differ in temperament from one to another, so they react differently to all these factors. Clearly, no one study can take all of this into account. (pp. 207-208).

No study to date has taken into account this full complement of possible influences on children's development and family functioning.

Fantasies about Early Experience

The "romance of early experience" (Scarr & Arnett, 1987) has given us the assumption that infancy provides more potent and pervasive influences than does later human experience. Although evidence for modest relations between early experience and later development exists (Caspi, Elder, & Bem, 1987; Erickson, Sroufe, & Egeland, 1985; Fagan, 1984; Funder, Block, & Block, 1983; Sigman, Cohen, Beckwith, & Parmelee, 1986), we agree with Kagan's (1979) interpretation of the data, namely that continuity does not imply inevitability. The human organism is surprisingly resilient in the face of deleterious experiences and sufficiently malleable to "bounce back" given constructive inputs. Only the most pervasive and continuous detrimental experiences have lasting, negative effects on development (Clarke & Clarke, 1976; Ernst, 1988; Lerner, 1984). Although this fact is encouraging for developmentalists, it is discouraging for interventionists, because even the most intensive early interventions appear to require some follow-up services or lasting environmental changes to assure long-term gains (Rutter, 1979; Scarr & McCartney, 1988; Valentine & Stark, 1979).

As a consequence of growing evidence for malleability, the search for critical periods has shifted toward efforts to examine relations between early and later experience, and to elucidate the mechanisms by which individuals and their environments interact to promote continuities and discontinuities in development (Brim & Kagan, 1980; Lerner, 1984; Scarr & Weinberg, 1983; Wachs & Gruen, 1982). Research on the developmental implications of child care would benefit greatly from adopting this perspective.

Fantasies about Maternal Deprivation

Images about child care include for some the notion of deprivation of maternal care. Research on "maternal deprivation" reached an emotional climax in the 1950s, when Spitz (1945), Bowlby (1951), and others claimed that institutionalized infants were retarded intellectually and socially for lack of mothering. Reanalyses and reinterpretation of the evidence (Yarrow, 1961) found that it was, in fact, lack of sensory and affective stimulation in typical institutions that led to detrimental outcomes for the orphans. Infants need someone consistently there with whom to interact and to develop a trusting relationship, but that person does not have to be the child's biological mother.

Critics of child care sometimes write as though working parents abandon their infants as orphans. For example, the term, "maternal absence," was used to describe employed mothers in the title of a recent article in the prestigious journal, *Child Development* (Barglow, Vaughn & Molitor, 1987). The terms "maternal absence" and "maternal deprivation" seem uncomfortably close and both conjure up negative images. Some seem to forget that employed mothers are typically with their babies in the mornings, evenings, weekends, and holidays, which for most fully-employed workers constitutes about half of the child's waking time.[1] And, when the child is ill, mothers are more likely than other family members to stay at home with the child (Hughes & Galinsky, 1986).

There are moderators of effects in the maternal deprivation literature as well. In his comprehensive review, Rutter (1979) concluded that it is not separation alone but separation in conjunction with other risk factors, for example, family stress, that leads to later antisocial behavior in children. A recent study by Ernst (1988) in Switzerland demonstrates Rutter's point nicely. Ernst's longitudinal study of 137 children who spent their first years in residential nurseries showed no differences between these children and the general population in IQ and in popularity. These children were two to three times more likely to develop behavior and social disorders, however. Ernst's careful analyses revealed that it was not nursery status alone that accounted for the difference. Rather, risk was associated with psychosocial factors in the environment such as parental discord, psychosocial disorder in parents, and abuse.

Early deprivation often indicates that an unfavorable situation will continue. For example, one research team has conducted a retrospective study and found that care during infancy is associated with negative outcomes at age 8 (Vandell & Corasaniti, in press). Infant care was atypical 8 years ago from a demographic perspective (Hofferth & Phillips, 1987). Thus, we must ask the follow-up questions Ernst thought to ask about psychosocial factors in the environment that might be continuous. Was the use of infant child care 8 years ago an indicator of unfavorable circumstances that continue in childhood? A search for these moderators is most likely to advance our knowledge of any identified child care effects. The quality of maternal care, just like other child care arrangements, depends on many aspects of the home situation and mothers' mental health. The fantasy that mothers at home with young children provide the best possible care neglects the observation that some women at home full-time are lonely, depressed, and not functioning well (see Crosby, 1987; Scarr, Phillips & McCartney, 1989b). Although, surely, most mothers at home are well motivated to provide good and stimulating care, they have many responsibilities other than direct child care. Time-use studies show that mothers at home full-time with preschool children spend very little time in direct interaction with them. They spend less time playing educational games and talking with the children than in many other household activities (Hill & Stafford, 1978; Hoffman, 1984; Nock & Kingston, in press; Ziegler, 1983). Child caregivers, on the other hand, usually have a majority of their time to give to their charges, although they usually have more children to care for than a mother at home. There are trade-offs: Neither home care nor out-of-home care promises quality child care. In fact, employed mothers of infants and young children spend less time in total home activities than non-employed mothers (715 versus 930 minutes, summed across one workday and a Sunday), but their actual time with their *children* is much closer to that of non-employed mothers. The largest difference in time with young children is the distribution of time between weekdays and weekends, with em-

---

1. Consider 5 working days/weeks for 49 weeks of the year: 1.5 hours in the morning, 3 hours of the child's waking time in the late afternoon and evening, for a sum of 4.5 of the approximately 14 hours of the child's daily waking time. The caregiver accounts for approximately 9 hours of which 2 hours are typically spent in a nap. (A half hour is allocated for transportation.) The sum of the work-week hours for parents employed full-time is 1102; for caregivers, 1715.

To the parental sum, add week-ends (2 days/work week) for 49 weeks, a sum of 1274. To that add 3 weeks of vacation time, and 10 days of personal and sick leave (for self and child) during the work week, a sum of 455.

By these calculations, typical, fully-employed parents spend 2831 hours with the child; caregivers spent approximately 1715.

ployed mothers concentrating their child-time on the weekends. Employed mothers scrimp on housework and on their own leisure time, rather than on time with their children (Nock & Kingston, in press). Fathers with employed wives spend more time with their infants and pre-school children than fathers with non-employed wives (580 versus 521 minutes; Nock & Kingston, in press). Thus, working parents do spend considerable time in both direct and indirect activities with their children. In addition, children of working parents have the attention of caregivers while their parents work.

RESEARCH FACTS ABOUT CHILD CARE AND CHILD DEVELOPMENT

Child care arrangements, like families, vary enormously in their abilities to promote children's development, to provide support for working families, and to give caregivers rewarding adult roles. In the research literature, however, child care is still cast as nonmaternal care by investigators who, in fact, rarely study variation in child care settings. Similarly, home care is treated uniformly as though all families were alike, and is assumed to be preferred to other child care arrangements. Thus studies often ignore the facts that families vary from abusive and neglectful of children's needs to supportive and loving systems that promote optimal development, and so do other child care arrangements. Actual child care arrangements vary from hiring a trained nanny or untrained babysitter in one's own home, to family day care in another person's home, to centers that care for more than 100 infants and children. Diversity in the quality of child care, at home and in other settings, is what matters for children. High-quality day care settings have in fact been shown to compensate for poor family environments (McCartney, Scarr, Phillips, & Grajek, 1985; Ramey, Bryant & Suarez, 1985) and, for low-income children, to promote better intellectual and social development than they would have experienced in their own homes.

Developmental Effects of Child Care

Fears about the effects of child care have centered on possible interference with infants' attachment to their mothers, on their later social development, and on their intellectual development.

Attachment Research
The earliest research on child care asked whether or not caregivers replaced mothers as children's primary attachment figures. Concerns that daily prolonged separations from mother might weaken the mother-child bond

were a direct heritage of the work on children in orphanages. But child care was not found to be a milder form of full-time institutionalization. Attachment was not adversely affected by enrollment in the university-based child care centers that provided the early child care samples. Bonds formed between children and their caregivers did not replace the mother-child attachment relationship (Belsky & Steinberg, 1978; Etaugh, 1980).

Now, almost twenty years later, the emergence of infant day care as a middle-class phenomenon among parents who themselves were reared at home by their mothers, has spawned an active debate about infant day care. The central issue here is whether full-time child care in the first year of life increases the probability of insecure attachments between mothers and infants. Some researchers have presented evidence that supports this claim (Belsky, 1986; Belsky, 1988; Belsky & Rovine, in press).

Other researchers have highlighted the many limitations of this new literature on infant day care (Clarke-Stewart, in press; Clarke-Stewart & Fein 1983; McCartney & Galanopoulos, 1988; Phillips, McCartney, Scarr, & Howes, 1987). The main limitation concerns the exclusive use of the Strange Situation (Ainsworth & Wittig, 1969) to assess attachment. Critics question whether this experimental laboratory procedure of separation from and reunion with mother is equally stressful for children with and without child care experience, because children with child care experience have daily experience with the supposed stressful procedure. Furthermore, studies with an attachment Q-sort measure (Waters & Deane, 1985) have failed to show differences between children in child care and children at home with mother (Belsky, personal communication, to K. McCartney, November 6, 1987; Weinraub, Jaeger, & Hoffman, in press). Finally, the practical significance of differences reported in the Strange Situation between child care and non-child care samples is minimal, despite press reports to the contrary (Clarke-Stewart, 1989).

Social Development
Although some studies have reported no differences in social behavior (Golden, Rosenbluth, Grossi, Policare, Freeman, & Brownlees, 1978; Kagan, Kearsley & Zelazo, 1978), others find that children who have attended child care are more socially competent (Clarke-Stewart, 1984; Gunnarsson, 1978; Howes & Olenick, 1986; Howes & Stewart, 1987; Ruopp, et al., 1979), and still others suggest lower levels of social competence (Haskins, 1985; Rubenstein, Howes, & Boyle, 1983). Positive outcomes include teacher and parent ratings of considerateness and sociability (Phillips, McCartney, &

> Senate approval in June [1989] of the Act for Better Child Care (ABC) represents the first major effort by the federal government to address the nation's child care crisis since 1971 when President Nixon vetoed the Child Development Act. It is the first of several bills in progress that deal with the long-neglected issue.
>
> —from *Child Behavior and Development Letter* (Brown University), 1989, *5*, 1.

Scarr, 1987), observations of compliance and self regulation (Howes & Olenick, 1986), and observations of involvement and positive interactions with teachers (McCartney, 1984; Ruopp, Travers, Glantz, & Coelen, 1979; Vandell & Powers, 1983).

Negative outcomes of day care experience have emphasized aggression. For example, Haskins' (1985) study of graduates from the Abecedarian project, a high-quality intervention day care program, showed that teachers in the early elementary grades rated these children higher on scales of aggression than a control group that was not enrolled in the program. However, a subgroup of the control children who were enrolled in an equivalent amount of community-based child care were found to be among the least aggressive children in the study, thereby demonstrating that the effect was not due to child care per se. A change in the curriculum of the Abecedarian project decreased aggression by 80% (Finkelstein, 1982), and by third grade, all early effects had dissipated for the initial group (Bryant, personal communication, February 1988). Here again, the story of day care effects will eventually be told through an examination of moderators, such as quality, and of trends in behavior over time.

Intellectual and Cognitive Development

Differences in intelligence between children in varying forms of day care and children cared for by their mothers have not been reported in most studies (Carew, 1980; Doyle & Somers, 1978; Kagan, Kearsley, & Zelaso, 1978; Robertson, 1982; Stith & Davis, 1984). Two studies, however, have reported that children in center care score higher on tests of cognitive competence (Clarke-Stewart, 1984; Rubenstein, Howes, & Boyle, 1981) than children in other types of child care settings. Similar evidence is provided by evaluations of early intervention programs (Lee, Brooks-Gunn, & Schnur, 1988; McCartney, Scarr, Phillips & Grajek, 1985; McKey, Condelli, Ganson, Barrett, McConkey & Plantz, 1985; Ramey & Haskins, 1981; Schweinhart & Weikart, 1980; Seitz, Apel, Rosenbaum, & Zigler, 1983), which indicate that carefully designed group programs can have substantial,

and, in some cases lasting, positive effects on children's patterns of achievement.

In sum, there is near consensus among developmental psychologists and early childhood experts that child care per se does not constitute a risk factor in children's lives; rather, poor quality care and poor family environments can conspire to produce poor developmental outcomes (National Center for Clinical Infant Programs, 1988).

Child Care as a Heterogeneous Environment

Contemporary developmental research has recognized the vast heterogeneity of child care and turned to the question of "what is *quality?*" in child care. Reliable indices of child care quality include caregiver-child ratio, group size, and caregiver training and experience. These variables, in turn, facilitate constructive and sensitive interactions among caregivers and children, which promote positive social and cognitive development (Phillips, 1987; Ruopp et al., 1979).

The caregiver-child ratio is related to decreased exposure to danger (Ruopp et al., 1979) and to increased language interactions in the child care setting. Both Bruner (1980) and Howes and Rubenstein (1985) report that children in centers with more adults per child engage in more talking and more playing. Another study (McCartney, 1984) has documented a link between verbal interaction with caregivers and children's language competence. Results of the National Day Care Study suggest that adequate ratios are particularly important for infants, with experts citing 1:4 as the threshold for good quality care.

Research on group size has revealed that the larger the group, the more management is necessary; the smaller the group, the more education and social interaction is possible. As first demonstrated in the National Day Care Study (Ruopp et al., 1979), caregivers in larger groups provide less social interaction and cognitive stimulation. Children in larger groups were found to be more apathetic and more distressed. These findings have since been replicated in other studies (Bruner, 1980; Howes, 1983; Howes & Rubenstein, 1985).

The reserach on caregiver training and education is particularly consistent. Not surprisingly, years of child-related education are associated with increased caregiver responsivity, positive affect, and ability to provide socially- and intellectually-stimulating experiences (Clarke-Stewart & Gruber, 1984; Howes, 1983; Ruopp et al., 1979; Stallings & Porter, 1980). These findings do not simply represent the effects of self-selection. Two intervention studies show that training leads to caregiver improvement (Arnett, 1989; Kaplan & Conn, 1984). Experience working with children cannot replace child-related training. Although Howes (1983) found an association between years of experience and responsiveness to children, the National Day Care Study (Ruopp et al., 1979) found that day care experience was associated with less social interaction and more apathy. Other studies have not found any important effects of experience per se (Phillips, McCartney, Scarr, & Howes, 1987; Stallings & Porter, 1980).

Research has also shown that many aspects of quality are correlated and that a good center is essentially one with good caregivers. Good caregivers are caring, able to read a baby's signals, and responsive to babies signals (McCartney, 1987). In fact, preschoolers perceive caregivers to provide the same caregiving functions as their mothers (Tephly & Elardo, 1984). The vast literature on mother-child interaction can also inform us of caregiving behaviors that are important. Although these behaviors are not legislatable, they are trainable.

Among the most recent indicators of quality to emerge from research is the stability of children's child care arrangements (Cummings, 1980; Howes & Olenick, 1986; Howes & Stewart, 1987). Children who experience multiple changes in caregivers and settings develop less optimally in social and language areas than children with stable child care, with effects lasting into the early school years (Howes, 1988). The importance of stable care stands in stark contrast with the alarmingly high turnover rates among child care workers. Between 1980 and 1990, 42% of all non-household child care workers will need to be replaced each year, just to maintain the current supply of child care providers ("New Occupational," 1984). Low pay, lack of benefits, and stressful working conditions are the major reasons cited by child care workers who leave their jobs (Jorde-Bloom, 1987; Kontos & Stremmel, 1988; Whitebook, Howes, Darrah, & Friedman, 1982). Infants and young children cannot develop stable relationships with caregivers if they are faced with new caregivers every few weeks.

Relations Between Home and Child Care

In studies of typical child care, researchers can neither assign children randomly to child care nor assign parents to varying employment patterns. As a consequence, efforts to decipher the "effects" of child care are a methodological conundrum. Pre-existing family differences—in background, traits, and beliefs—are confounded with child care arrangements.

Recent research suggests that there may be interaction effects between family characteristics and child care arrangements in maternal anxiety (Hock, DeMeis & Mc-

Bride, 1987), marital status and living arrangements (Scarr, Lande, & McCartney, 1989), such that good child care can compensate for poor home environments. There is also increasing evidence that the lowest income and most disorganized families (among the middle class) end up in the lowest quality child care programs (Howes & Olenick, 1986; Howes & Stewart, 1987; Lamb, Huang, Brookstein, Broberg, Hult, & Frodi, 1988). A number of other family variables might reasonably moderate effects, especially those related to family stress (Kontos & Wells, 1986).

A number of relationships may affect children's sense of security and thereby their adjustment. Belsky found that daughters with unemployed mothers were more likely to be insecurely attached to their fathers than daughters of employed mothers (Belsky & Rovine, in press). Using the attachment Q-sort (Waters & Deane, 1985), Howes and her colleagues (Howes, et al., 1988) have shown recently that both attachment security at home with mother and attachment security with the caregiver at day care are predictors of the child's positive interaction with caregivers and peers in day care. Interactions between family characteristics and child care have been found to affect development in the first 2 years of life. For example, Scarr, Lande, and McCartney (1989) reported negative main effects for typical center care (but not family day care) in the first 2 years of life on both intellectual and social/emotional ratings. The same children were also disadvantaged by being reared in single mother-headed households (but not in extended families with single mothers). Further, they found important interactions between households and center care, such that infants from single mother-headed households benefited from group care more than similar children in other kinds of care, including maternal care. By the age of 4 years, there were no effects of child care in the first 2 years or in the second 2 years on any child development outcome. Other research (McBride & Belsky, 1988; Weinraub, Jaeger & Hoffman, in press) has found that relations between maternal employment and attachment vary according to maternal satisfaction with child care arrangements, role satisfaction, and coping skills. Studies such as these suggest that child care must be seen in the context of the child's family life before one can interpret any effects of child care per se.

FACTS ABOUT CHILD CARE POLICY

For the first time in a decade, child care is on the national agenda. In 1988, more than 40 bills containing provisions for child care were introduced in the U.S. Congress (Robins, 1988). Driven largely by escalating rates of employment among non-poor, married mothers (Kahn & Kamerman, 1987), federal child care policies have come under intense scrutiny and numerous proposals for restructing the federal role have surfaced. These range from "supply side" proposals that emphasize improvements in the current system of child care to "demand side" proposals that offer families additional tax subsidies for purchasing child care. Parental leave policies are also being debated. In addition, the majority of states are now moving towards limited funding for school-based child care programs that typically are targeted at poor and/or disadvantaged families (Marx & Seligson, 1988).

The same demographic trends that are influencing child care policy are also creating new goals for welfare reform effects. For low-income mothers, prevailing beliefs about maternal care have traditionally led us to favor policies that enable them to stay home with their babies, through child support and public assistance (e.g., Aid to Families with Dependent Children). But the new welfare reform bill (Family Support Act of 1988: P.L. 100-483), emphasizes training, employment and women's attainment of economic independence rather than support for full-time mothering (Phillips, in press). This shift in purpose is due largely to policymakers' recognition that the majority of mothers with preschool-age children are now in the labor force. Under these circumstances, it is difficult to justify the prior exemption from training and employment programs for AFDC-eligible mothers with children under age 6. Unfortunately, even in the best of circumstances, the child care subsidies included in the Family Support Act are continued for only one year after mothers achieve the minimum wage jobs for which they are being trained.

The policy debate about child care is no longer about whether there will be support for child care or whether families will continue to rely on child care (Martinez, 1989). Instead, it has focused on relatively pragmatic questions about delivery systems, target populations, and financing. These questions, however, are not uncontroversial. For example, the high cost of market forms of child care and fears about nationalizing our child care system have generated strong resistance to legislation that ties government subsidies to use of licensed programs (i.e., centers and regulated family day care homes) or that mandates federal day care standards. For these reasons, we are unlikely ever to see child care and leave policies in the United States that resemble European or Canadian policies (see Scarr, Phillips, & McCartney, 1989a). Considerations of "who should provide child care?" are now mired in an acrimonious debate involving the schools, community-based child care programs, and

church-housed programs. And, on-going debates about whether government child care benefits should be reserved for the poor or also assist the non-poor, and about whether these benefits should purchase good quality child care (as in the Head Start program) or disregard consideration of quality are far from resolved.

The child care policies that result from today's debate will constitute some adaptation to the realities of working parents. However, the effects of our national ambivalence about working mothers will undoubtedly be felt, as well. Prevailing beliefs that mothers of very young children belong at home and that child care problems are best solved privately will assure that any new child care policy is likely to remain fragmented, marginal, and modestly funded. At a minimum, any generous policy that might actually create an incentive for those mothers who have a choice about working to use child care, will be avoided.

This is the political and social context on which research on child care has a bearing. The ways in which research questions are framed and the values that underlie our questions can challenge the assumptions that guide policy and promote policies that are based more on facts and less on fantasies.

THE FUTURE

Research on Child Care

Future research on child care influences will need to place more emphasis on the contexts in which families use child care services (Bronfenbrenner, 1986; McCartney & Galanopoulis, 1988). The ecology of child care includes the family, its choice of child care arrangements, its ability to pay for quality care, and its independent effects on child development. Contemporary researchers recognize the necessity of taking into account not only the quality of child care, but also the quality of the home environment, individual differences in children, and the history of children's experience with child care. Life is complicated, and thus requires complex models.

As part of the ecology of child care, research needs to examine the effects of the *un*availability of child care, particularly of the unavailability of good quality, consistent care. Similarly, we have no understanding of the effects of the virtual absence of parental leave policies in the United States (Scarr, Phillips, & McCartney, 1989b). What are the effects on children and families when parents do not have choices about when they return to work, and about the type and quality of the child care they offer their children?

Research on child care has also sampled a relatively narrow range of care types, with licensed centers and regulated family day care homes dominating the empirical literature. Even among center-based arrangements, we have neglected for-profit chains and centers that are exempted from state regulation (e.g., church-run centers in several states). Unregulated family day care homes and other types of care that are not covered by state licensing (e.g., nannies) are virtually unstudied. As a consequence, it is entirely possible that we have not sampled programs that represent the poorest quality care offered in this country.

Longitudinal research is necessary to determine which effects of child care are transitory and which represent enduring influences on development. So far, there are conflicting findings on the long term correlates of early child care arrangements (Scarr, Lande & McCartney, 1989; Scarr & McCartney, in preparation; Vandell & Corasaniti, in press; Vandell, Henderson & Wilson, in press).

At the very least, research is needed on: (1) the family and other mediators of development that correlate, augment, and interact with child care arrangements; (2) range of types and qualities of child care; and (3) longitudinal research on short and long term effects of child care on development, on families, and on caregivers. For these reasons, we can make few definitive statements at this time about the direct effects of child care on children. Rather, we have documented effects that appear to be caused by child care, but may be attributable to children's case histories, temperaments, families, or to complex interactions among these and other circumstances.

Conclusions

The discussion of fantasies about the nature of child care suggests that we need a closer look at the facts about children's, parents', and care providers' experiences in our current child care system—their discomforts and their satisfactions—to orient our research to the most pressing issues. As one of the reviewers of the article said,

> . . . in the circumstances prevailing in contemporary society, day care—far more often than not—plays an essential and crucial role as a support system that enables families to function and can provide important supplementary developmental experiences for children. To be sure, there are probably some circumstances, not yet fully understood, that involve some measure of risk, especially for very young children, and these risks need to be weighed, but they are hardly comparable in their probability and magnitude to those to which many children are exposed, through the unavailability of quality child care for thousands of families that desperately want and need it. (Bronfenbrenner, personal communication, December 1988)

For children, the most pressing issue is quality of care—care that will encourage and support all aspects of child development.

For parents, the most pressing issues are affordability and availability of consistent and dependable child care, and employment options that make the task of combining worker and parent roles less stressful.

For child care providers, the most pressing issues are staff wages and working conditions and public support for a system of high quality care that will meet the diverse needs of the working poor, minority families, middle income families, and even yuppie parents who want "the best."

For policy makers, at federal and state levels, the most pressing issues are how to fund a system of quality child care, regulate those aspects of quality that can be legislated and enforced, and coordinate efforts with the private sector and at all levels of government.

REFERENCES

Ainslie, R.C., & Anderson, C.W. (1984). Day care children's relationships to their mothers and caregivers: An inquiry into the conditions for the development of attachment. In R.C. Ainslie (Ed.), *The child and the day care setting*. New York: Praeger.

Ainsworth, M., & Wittig, B.A. (1969). Attachment and exploratory behavior of one-year olds in a strange situation. In B.M. Foss (Ed.), *Determinants of infant behavior*, Vol. 4. London: Methuen.

Arnett, J. (1989). Issues and obstacles in the training of caregivers. In J. Lande, S. Scarr, & N. Gunzenhauser (Eds.), *Caring for children: Challenge to . America* (pp. 241-256). Hillsdale, NJ: Erlbaum.

Barglow, P., Vaughn, B.E., & Molitor, N. (1987). Effects of maternal absence due to employment on the quality of infant-mother attachment in a low-risk sample. *Child Development, 58*, 945-954.

Belsky, J. (1986). Infant day care: A cause for concern? *Zero to Three, 6*(5), 1-9.

Belsky, J. (1988). The "effects" of infant day care reconsidered. *Early Childhood Research Quarterly, 3*, 235-272.

Belsky, J., & Rovine, M.J. (in press). Nonmaternal care in the first year of life and the security of infant-parent attachment. *Child Development*.

Belsky, J., & Steinberg, L.D. (1978). The effects of daycare: A critical review. *Child Development, 49*, 929-949.

Bowlby, J. (1951). *Maternal care and mental health*. Geneva: World Health Organization.

Bronfenbrenner, U. (1979). *The ecology of human development: Experiments by nature and design*. Cambridge, MA: Harvard University Press.

Bronfenbrenner, U. (1986). Ecology of the family as a context for human development: Research perspectives. *Developmental Psychology, 22*, 723-742.

Brim, O.G., & Kagan, J. (1980). *Constancy and change in human development*. Cambridge, MA: Harvard University Press.

Bruner, J. (1980). *Under five in Britain*. London: Methune.

Carew, J. (1980). Experience and the development of intelligence in young children. *Monographs of the Society for Research in Child Development, 45*, 6-7 (Serial No. 187).

Caspi, A., Elder, G.H., Jr., & Bem, D.J. (1987). Moving against the world: Life course patterns of explosive children. *Developmental Psychology, 23*, 308-313.

Cherlin, A.J. (Ed.). (1988). *The changing American family and public policy*. Washington, DC: The Urban Institute Press.

Clarke, A.M., & Clarke, A.D.B. (1976). *Early experience: Myth and evidence*. London: Open Books.

Clarke-Stewart, A. (1984). Day care: A new context for research and development. In M. Perlmutter (Ed.), *The Minnesota Symposia on Child Psychology: Vol. 27. Parent-child interaction and parent-child relations in child development* (pp. 61-100). Hillsdale, NJ: Erlbaum.

Clarke-Stewart, A. (1989). Infant day care: Malignant or maligned? *American Psychologist*.

Clarke-Stewart, A., & Fein, G. (1983). Early childhood programs. In P.H. Mussen (Series Ed.) & M. Haith and J. Campos (Vol. Eds.), *Handbook of child psychology: Vol. II. Infancy and developmental psychobiology* (pp. 917-1000). New York: Wiley.

Clarke-Stewart, A., & Gruber, C. (1984). Day care forms and features. In R.C. Ainslie (Ed.), *The child and the day care setting* (pp. 35-62). New York: Praeger.

Crosby, F.J. (Ed.). (1987). *Spouse, parent, worker: On gender and multiple roles.* New Haven: Yale University Press.

Cummings, E.H. (1980). Caregiver stability and day care. *Developmental Psychology, 16,* 31-37.

Doyle, A., & Somers, K. (1978). The effects of group and family day care on infant attachment behaviors. *Canadian Journal of Behavioral Science, 10,* 38-45.

Erickson, M.F., Sroufe, L.A., & Egeland, B. (1985). The relationship between quality of attachment and behavior problems in preschool in a high-risk sample. In I. Bertherton & E. Waters (Eds.), Growing points in attachment theory and research. *Monographs of the Society for Research in Child Development, 50,* 147-166.

Ernst, D. (1988). Are early childhood experiences overrated? A reassessment of maternal deprivation. *European Archives of Psychiatry and Neurological Sciences, 237,* 80-90.

Etaugh, C. (1980). Effects of nonmaternal care on children: Research evidence and popular views. *American Psychologist, 35,* 309-319.

Fagan, J.F. (1984). The intellectual infant: Theoretical implications. *Intelligence, 8,* 1-9.

Farran, D., & Ramsey, C. (1977). Infant day care and attachment behaviors toward mothers and teachers. *Child Development, 48,* 1112-1116.

Finkelstein, N. (1982). Aggression: Is it stimulated by day care? *Young Children, 37,* 3-9.

Fox, N. (1977). Attachment of kibbutz infants to mothers and metapelet. *Child Development, 48,* 1228-1239.

Fraiberg, S. (1977). *Every child's birthright: In defense of mothering.* New York: Basic Books.

Funder, D., Block, J.H., & Block, J. (1983). Delay of gratification: Some longitudinal personality correlates. *Journal of Personality and Social Psychology, 44,* 1198-1213.

Gerson, J., Alpert, J.L., & Richardson, M. (1984). Mothering: The view from psychological research. *Signs, 9,* 434-453.

Golden, M., Rosenbluth, L., Grossi, M.T., Policare, H.J., Freeman, H., Jr., & Brownlee, E.M. (1978). *The New York City infant day care study.* New York: Medical and Health Research Association of New York City.

Goldstein, J., Freud, A., & Solnit, A.J. (1973). *Beyond the best interests of the child.* New York: Free Press.

Greenstein, R. (1987). Testimony presented before the Income Security Task Force Committee on the Budget, U.S. House of Representatives, Washington, D.C., November 9, 1987.

Gunnarsson, L. (1978). *Children in day care and family care in Sweden* (Research Bulletin, No. 21). Gothenburg, Sweden: University of Gothenburg.

Haskins, R. (1985). Public school aggression among children with varying day care experience. *Child Development, 56,* 689-703.

Hill, C.R., & Stafford, F.P. (1978). Parental care of children: Time diary estimates of quantity, predictability, and variety. *Institute for Social Research Working Paper Series.* Ann Arbor: University of Michigan.

Hock, E., DeMeis, D., & McBride, S. (1987). Maternal separation anxiety: Its role in the balance of employment and motherhood in mothers of infants. In A. Gottfried, & A. Gottfried (Eds.), *Maternal employment and children's development: Longitudinal research* (pp. 191-229). New York: Plenum.

Hofferth, S.L., & Phillips, D.A. (1987). Child care in the United States, 1970 to 1995. *Journal of Marriage and the Family, 49,* 559-571.

Hoffman, L.W. (1984). Maternal employment and the child. In M. Perlmutter (Ed.), *The Minnesota Symposia on Child Psychology: Vol. 17. Parent child interaction and parent-child relations in development* (pp. 101-127). Hillsdale, NJ: Erlbaum.

Howes, C. (1983). Caregiver behavior in center and family day care. *Journal of Applied Developmental Psychology, 4,* 99-107.

Howes, C. (1988). Relations between early child care and schooling. *Developmental Psychology, 24,* 53-57.

Howes, C., and Olenick, M. (1986). Child care and family influences on compliance. *Child Development, 57,* 202-216.

Howes, C., Rodning, C., Galluzzo, D., & Myers, L. (1988). Attachment and child care: Relationships with mother and caregiver. *Early Childhood Research Quarterly, 3,* 403-416.

Howes, C., & Rubenstein, J. (1985). Determinants of toddlers' experience in daycare: Age of entry and quality of setting. *Child Care Quarterly, 14,* 140-151.

Howes, C., & Stewart, P. (1987). Child's play with adults, toys, and peers: An examination of family and child-care influences. *Developmental Psychology, 23,* 423-430.

Hughes, D., & Galinsky, E. (1986). Maternity, paternity, and parenting policies: How does the United States compare. In S.A. Hewlett, A.S. Ilchman, & J.J. Sweeney (Eds.), *Family and work: Bridging the gap* (pp. 53-66). Cambridge, MA: Ballinger.

Jorde-Bloom, P. (1987, April). *Factors influencing overall job commitment and facet satisfaction in early childhood work environments.* Paper presented at the meeting of the American Education Research Association, Washington, D.C.

Kagan, J. (1979). Family experience and the child's development. *American Psychologist, 34,* 886-891.

Kagan, J., Kearsley, R.B., & Zelaso, P.R. (1978). *Infancy: Its place in human development.* Cambridge, MA: Harvard University Press.

Kahn, A.J., & Kamerman, S.B. (1987). *Child care: Facing the hard choices.* Dover, MA; Auburn House.

Kaplan, M., & Conn, J. (1984). The effects of caregiver training on classroom setting and caregiver performance in eight community day care centers. *Child Study Journal, 14,* 79-93.

Kontos, S., & Stremmel, A.J. (1988). Caregivers' perceptions of working conditions in a child care environment. *Early Childhood Research Quarterly, 3,* 77-90.

Kontos, S., & Wells, W. (1986). Attitudes of caregivers and the day care experiences of families. *Early Childhood Research Quarterly, 1,* 47-67.

Lamb, M. (1980). The development of parent-infant attachments in the first two years of life. In F. Pederson (Ed.), *The father-infant relationship: Observational studies in the family setting.* New York: Praeger.

Lamb, M., Hwang, C., Bookstein, F.L., Broberg, A., Hult, G., & Frodi, M. (1988). Determinants of social competence in Swedish preschoolers. *Developmental Psychology, 24,* 58-70.

Lee, V.E., Brooks-Gunn, J., & Schnur, E. (1988). Does Head Start work? A 1-year follow-up comparison of disadvantaged children attending Head Start, no preschool, and other preschool programs. *Developmental Psychology, 24,* 210-222.

Lerner, R.M. (1984). *On the nature of human plasticity.* New York: Cambridge University Press.

Martinez, S. (1989). Child care and federal policy. In J. Lande, S. Scarr, & N. Gunzenhauser (Eds.), *Caring for children: Challenge to America* (pp. 111-124). Hillsdale, NJ: Erlbaum.

Marx, F., & Seligson, M. (1988). *The public school early childhood study. The state survey.* New York: Bank Street College of Education.

Maurer, C., & Maurer, D. (1988). *World of the newborn.* New York: Basic.

McBride, S., & Belsky, J. (1988). Characteristics, determinants, and consequences of maternal separation anxiety. *Developmental Psychology, 24,* 407-414.

McCartney, K. (1984). The effect of quality of day care environment upon children's language development. *Developmental Psychology, 20,* 244-260.

McCartney, K. (1987, July/August). Quality: A child's point of view. *Child Care Action News,* Newsletter of the Child Care Action Campaign, 4(4).

McCartney, K., & Galanopoulis, A. (1988). Child care and attachment: A new frontier the second time around. *American Journal of Orthopsychiatry, 58,* 16-24.

McCartney, K., & Phillips, D. (1988). Motherhood and child care. In B. Birns & D. Hay (Eds.), *Different faces of motherhood* (pp. 157-183). New York: Plenum Press.

McCartney, K., Scarr, S., Phillips, D., & Grajek, S. (1985). Day care as intervention: Comparisons of varying quality programs. *Journal of Applied Development Psychology, 6,* 247-260.

McKey, R.H., Condelli, L., Ganson, H., Barrett, B.J., McConkey, C., & Plantz, M.C. (1985). *The impact of Head Start on children, families, and communities: Final report of the Head Start evaluation, synthesis, and utilization project.* Washington, D.C.: CSR Inc.

National Center for Clinical Infant Programs. (1988). *Infants, Families and Child Care.* Washington, D.C.: Author. Brochure.

New occupational separation data improve estimates of job replacement needs. (1984, March). *Monthly Labor Review, 107*(3), 3-10.

Nock, S.L., & Kingston, P.W. (in press). Time with children: The impact of couples' work-time commitments. *Social Forces.*

Phillips, D. (Ed.). (1987). *Quality in child care: What does research tell us?* Washington, D.C.: National Association for the Education of Young Children.

Phillips, D. (1989). Future directions and need for child care in the United States. In J.S. Lande, S. Scarr, & N. Gunzenhauser (Eds.), *Caring for children: Challenge to America* (pp. 257-275). Hillsdale, NJ: Erlbaum.

Phillips, D. (in press). With a little help: Children in poverty and child care. In A. Huston (Ed.), *Children and Poverty.* New York: Cambridge University Press.

Phillips, D., McCartney, K., & Scarr, S. (1987). Child-care quality and children's social development. *Developmental Psychology, 23,* 537-543.

Phillips, D., McCartney, K., Scarr, S., & Howes, C. (1987, February). Selective view of infant day care research: A cause for concern! *Zero to Three, 7,* 18-21.

Ramey, C.T., Bryant, D.M., & Suarez, T.M. (1985). Preschool compensatory education and the modifiability of intelligence: A critical review. In D. Detterman (Ed.), *Current topics in human intelligence* (pp. 247-296). Norwood, NJ: Ablex.

Ramey, C.T., & Haskins, R. (1981). The causes and treatment of school failure: Insights from the Carolina Abecedarian Project. In M.J. Begab, H.C. Haywood, & H.L. Garber (Eds.), *Psychosocial influences in retarded performance: Strategies for improving competence.* Baltimore: University Park Press.

Robertson, A. (1982). Day care and children's response to adults. In E. Zigler & E.W. Gordon (Eds.), *Day care: Scientific and social policy issues* (pp. 152-173). Boston: Auburn House.

Robins, P. (1988). Child care and convenience: The effects of labor market entry cost on economic self-sufficiency among public housing residents. *Social Science Quarterly, 69,* 122-136.

Rubenstein, J., Howes, C., & Boyle, P. (1981). A two year follow-up of infants in community based day care. *Journal of Child Psychology and Psychiatry, 22,* 209-218.

Ruopp, R., Travers, J., Glantz, F., & Coelen, C. (1979). *Children at the center: Final results of the National Day Care Study.* Boston: Abt. Associates.

Rutter, M. (1979). Maternal deprivation, 1972-1978: New findings, new concepts, new approaches. *Child Development, 50,* 283-291.

Scarr, S. (1985). Constructing psychology: Making facts and fables for our times. *American Psychologist, 40,* 499-512.

Scarr, S., & Arnett, J. (1987). Malleability: Lessons from intervention and family studies. In J.J. Gallagher (Ed.), *The malleability of children* (pp. 71-84). New York: Brooke.

Scarr, S., Lande, J., & McCartney, K. (1989). Child care and the family: Cooperation and interaction. In J. Lande, S. Scarr, & N. Gunzenhauser (Eds.), *Caring for children: The future of child care in the United States* (pp. 1-21). Hillsdale, NJ: Erlbaum.

Scarr, S., & McCartney, K. (in preparation). Follow-up studies of early child care experiences at school age.

Scarr, S., & McCartney, K. (1988). Far from home: An experimental evaluation of the mother-child home program in Bermuda. *Child Development, 59,* 531-543.

Scarr, S., Phillips, D., & McCartney, K. (1989a). Dilemmas of child care in the United States: Employed mothers and children at risk. *Canadian Psychology, 30*(2), 126-139.

Scarr, S., Phillips, D., & McCartney, K. (1989b). Working mothers and their families. *American Psychologist,* June.

Scarr, S., & Weinberg, R.A. (1983). The Minnesota adoption studies: Genetic differences and malleability. *Child Development, 54,* 260-267.

Schaffer, H.R. (1977). *Attachments.* Cambridge, MA: Harvard University Press.

Schweinhart, L., & Weikart, D. (1980). The effects of the Perry Preschool Program on youths through age 15. *Monographs of the High/Scope Educational Research Foundation No. 7.*

Seitz, V., Apfel, N., Rosenbaum, L., & Zigler, E. (1983). Long term effects of Projects Head Start and Follow Through: The New Haven Project. In Consortium for Longitudinal Studies, *As the twig is bent. Lasting effects of preschool programs* (pp. 299-332). Hillsdale, NJ: Erlbaum.

Sigman, M., Cohen, S.E., Beckwith, L., & Parmelee, A.H. (1986). Infant attention in relation to intellectual abilities in childhood. *Developmental Psychology, 22,* 788-792

Smith, P.K. (1980). Shared care of young children: Alternative models to monotropism. *Merrill-Palmer Quarterly, 26,* 371-389.

Spitz, R. (1945). Hospitalism: An inquiry into the genesis of psychiatric conditions in early childhood. *Psychoanalytic Study of the Child, 1,* 53-74.

Stallings, J., & Porter, A. (1980, June). *National Day Care Home Study: Observation component* (Final Report of the National Day Care Home Study, Vol. III). Washington, DC: Dept of Health, Education and Welfare.

Stith, S., & Davis, A. (1984). Employed mothers and family day care substitute caregivers. *Child Development, 55,* 1340-1348.

Tephly, J., & Elardo, R. (1984). Mothers and day care teachers: Young children's perceptions. *British Journal of Developmental Psychology, 2,* 251-256.

Valentine, J., & Stark, E. (1979). The social context of parent involvement in Head Start. In E. Zigler, & J. Valentine (Eds.), *Project Head Start: A legacy of the War on Poverty.* (pp. 291-314). New York: Free Press.

Vandell, D.L., & Corsaniti, M.A. (in press). Child care in the family: Complex contributions to child development. In K. McCartney (Ed.), *New directions in child development research, Vol. 20: The social ecology of child care.* New York: Jossey-Bass.

Vandell, D.L., Henderson, V.K., & Wilson, K.S. (in press). A longitudinal study of children with varying quality day care experiences. *Child Development.*

Vandell, D.L., & Powers, C.P. (1983). Day care quality and children's free play activities. *American Journal of Orthopsychiatry, 53,* 493-500.

Wachs, T.D., & Gruen, G.E. (1982). *Early experience and human development.* New York: Plenum Press.

Waters, E., & Deane, K.E. (1985). Defining and assessing individual differences in attachment relationships: Q-methodology and the organization of behaviors in infancy and childhood. In I. Bertherton & E. Waters (Eds.), Growing points in attachment theory and research. *Monographs of the Society for Research in Child Development, 50,* 41-65.

Weinraub, M., Jaeger, E., & Hoffman, L. (in press). Predicting infant outcome in families of employed and non-employed mothers. *Early Childhood Research Quarterly.*

Whitebook, M., Howes, C., Darrah, R., & Friedman, J. (1982). Caring for the caregivers: Staff burnout in child care. In L. Katz (Ed.), *Current topics in early childhood education* (Vol. 4, pp. 211-235). Norwood, NJ: Ablex.

Yarrow, L. (1961). Maternal deprivation: Toward an empirical and conceptual evaluation. *Psychological Bulletin, 58,* 459-490.

Ziegler, M.E. (1983). *Assessing parents' and children's time together.* Paper presented at the annual meeting of the Society for Research in Child Development, Detroit, Michigan.

Multiple Choice:

1. Which of the following is characterized as a child care "fantasy" in this article?

    A. the idea that maternal employment threatens infants' attachments to their mothers
    B. the assumption that the effects of experience in infancy are especially potent and persistent
    C. the belief that maternal employment constitutes maternal deprivation
    D. all of the above

2   Which of the following is true about how parents spend time with their children?

    A. Mothers who are at home full-time spend several hours a day in direct interaction with their preschool children.
    B. Employed mothers decrease time with their children in order to get their housework done.
    C. Fathers with employed wives spend more time with their young children than do fathers whose wives do not work outside the home.

3. Studies comparing the social development of children who have and have not attended child care have reported:

    A. no difference between the two groups.
    B. children who have attended child care are more socially competent.
    C. children who have not attended child care are more socially competent.
    D. all of the above.

Essay:

1. When (and if) you are looking for child care arrangements for your own child, what kinds of information would you want to know about the prospective child care situation?

2. Imagine you are on the staff of a Senator on a Congressional committee conducting hearings on the need for increased federal support for child care. Based on this article, what would you tell your Senator about research on child care and development? How would you try to influence him or her to vote on the issue? Why?

ARTICLE 23

A Developmental Perspective on Antisocial Behavior

G. R. Patterson, Barbara D. DeBaryshe, and Elizabeth Ramsey

Reprinted from: *American Psychologist*, 1989, *44*, 329-335.

Why do boys go bad? In other words, what are the antecedents of antisocial behavior and delinquency? As has been true in several other articles in this book, the answer is that many different variables interact to produce this developmental outcome. This article focuses on the contribution of a youngster's family to the development of antisocial behavior.

Patterson and his colleagues see delinquency as the sad result of a series of steps involving the child's behavior, his family's reaction to his behavior, his reaction to their reaction, their consequent reaction, and so on. These authors believe that children are trained in antisocial behavior by other members of their family. As you will see, this training takes several forms, the most important of which is the child's learning to avoid unpleasant interactions with other family members by using coercive behaviors--behaviors whose goal is to force another person to do something.

In families of delinquent boys, coercion attempts often escalate into the use of physical force. Having learned to use coercion to deal with the folks at home, many boys try the same approach outside the family. Because of their antisocial behaviors and their lack of prosocial skills, these children are often rejected by peers and experience failure in school. They may, in turn, become members of a deviant peer group that further reinforces their antisocial and delinquent behavior. The first figure in the article clearly depicts the sequence through which a boy can be socialized into an antisocial person.

The authors broaden their frame to consider contextual variables that can influence general family functioning, and thereby influence the child's antisocial tendencies. They are nicely summarized in the second figure. The effect of stressors depends on the prior state of the individual and his family. Families that are already weak and individuals with few personal resources are more likely to suffer adverse effects from added stress.

As several of the articles in this reader have also shown, the family within which an individual develops plays a crucial role in his or her development. Families can provide powerful protective buffers against external stresses, or they can themselves be a source of stress and further undermine the individual's development.

A Developmental Perspective on Antisocial Behavior

G. R. Patterson, Barbara D. DeBaryshe, and Elizabeth Ramsey
Oregon Social Learning Center

ABSTRACT: A developmental model of antisocial behavior is outlined. Recent findings are reviewed that concern the etiology and course of antisocial behavior from early childhood through adolescence. Evidence is presented in support of the hypothesis that the route to chronic delinquency is marked by a reliable developmental sequence of experiences. As a first step, ineffective parenting practices are viewed as determinants for childhood conduct disorders. The general model also takes into account the contextual variables that influence the family interaction process. As a second step, the conduct-disordered behaviors lead to academic failure and peer rejection. These dual failures lead, in turn, to increased risk for depressed mood and involvement in a deviant peer group. This third step usually occurs during later childhood and early adolescence. It is assumed that children following this developmental sequence are at high risk for engaging in chronic delinquent behavior. Finally, implications for prevention and intervention are discussed.

In 1986, more than 1.4 million juveniles were arrested for nonindex crimes (e.g., vandalism, drug abuse, or running away) and almost 900,000 for index crimes (e.g., larceny–theft, robbery, or forcible rape; Federal Bureau of Investigation, 1987). The United States spends more than $1 billion per year to maintain our juvenile justice system. The yearly cost of school vandalism alone is estimated to be one-half billion dollars (Feldman, Caplinger, & Wodarski, 1981). These statistics are based on official records and may represent only a fraction of the true offense rate. Data on self-reported delinquent acts indicate that police records account for as little as 2% of the actual juvenile law violations (Dunford & Elliott, 1982).

Of course, not all costs can be counted in dollars and cents. Antisocial children are likely to experience major adjustment problems in the areas of academic achievement and peer social relations (Kazdin, 1987; Walker, Shinn, O'Neill, & Ramsey, 1987; Wilson & Herrnstein, 1985). Follow-up studies of antisocial children show that as adults they ultimately contribute disproportionately to the incidence of alcoholism, accidents, chronic unemployment, divorce, physical and psychiatric illness, and the demand on welfare services (Caspi, Elder, & Bem, 1987; Farrington, 1983; Robins, 1966; Robins & Ratcliff, 1979).

Antisocial behavior appears to be a developmental trait that begins early in life and often continues into adolescence and adulthood. For many children, stable manifestations of antisocial behavior begin as early as the elementary school grades (see Farrington, Ohlin, & Wilson, 1986; Loeber, 1982; and Olweus, 1979, for reviews). As Olweus noted, stability coefficients for childhood aggression rival the figures derived for the stability of IQ. Findings that early behaviors such as temper tantrums and grade school troublesomeness significantly predict adolescent and adult offenses suggest the existence of a single underlying continuum. If early forms of antisocial behavior are indeed the forerunners of later antisocial acts, then the task for developmental psychologists is to determine which mechanisms explain the stability of antisocial behavior and which control changes over time.

From a policy standpoint, a serious social problem that is predictable and understandable is a viable target for prevention. The purpose of this article is to present an ontogenic perspective on the etiology and developmental course of antisocial behavior from early childhood through adolescence. Evidence is presented in support of the notion that the path to chronic delinquency unfolds in a series of predictable steps. This model is presented in detail by Patterson, Reid, and Dishion (in press). In this model, child behaviors at one stage lead to predictable reactions from the child's social environment in the following step. This leads to yet further reactions from the child and further changes in the reactions from the social environment. Each step in this action–reaction sequence puts the antisocial child more at risk for long-term social maladjustment and criminal behavior.

A Developmental Progression for Antisocial Behavior

Basic Training in the Home

There is a long history of empirical studies that have identified family variables as consistent covariates for early forms of antisocial behavior and for later delinquency. Families of antisocial children are characterized by harsh and inconsistent discipline, little positive parental involvement with the child, and poor monitoring and supervision of the child's activities (Loeber & Dishion, 1983; McCord, McCord, & Howard, 1963).

Two general interpretations have been imposed on these findings. Control theory, widely accepted in sociology (Hirschi, 1969), views harsh discipline and lack of supervision as evidence for disrupted parent–child bonding. Poor bonding implies a failure to identify with parental and societal values regarding conformity and work. These omissions leave the child lacking in internal control. Several large-scale surveys provide correlational data consistent with this hypothesis. The correlations show

Copyright 1989 by the American Psychological Association, Inc. 0003-066X/89/$00.75
Vol. 44, No. 2, 329–335

253

that youths who have negative attitudes toward school, work, and authority tend to be more antisocial (Elliott, Huizinga, & Ageton, 1985; Hirschi, 1969). The magnitude of these correlations tends to be very small. Because the dependent and independent variables are often provided by the same agent, it is difficult to untangle the contribution of method variance to these relations.

In contrast, the social–interactional perspective takes the view that family members directly train the child to perform antisocial behaviors (Forehand, King, Peed, & Yoder, 1975; Patterson, 1982; Snyder, 1977; Wahler & Dumas, 1984). The parents tend to be noncontingent in their use of both positive reinforcers for prosocial and effective punishment for deviant behaviors. The effect of the inept parenting practices is to permit dozens of daily interactions with family members in which coercive child behaviors are reinforced. The coercive behaviors are directly reinforced by family members (Patterson, 1982; Snyder, 1977; Snyder & Patterson, 1986). While some of the reinforcement is positive (attend, laugh, or approve), the most important set of contingencies for coercive behavior consists of escape-conditioning contingencies. In the latter, the child uses aversive behaviors to terminate aversive intrusions by other family members. In these families, coercive behaviors are functional. They make it possible to survive in a highly aversive social system.

As the training continues, the child and other family members gradually escalate the intensity of their coercive behaviors, often leading to high-amplitude behaviors such as hitting and physical attacks. In this training, the child eventually learns to control other family members through coercive means. The training for deviant behaviors is paralleled by a lack of training for many prosocial skills. Observations in the homes of distressed families suggest that children's prosocial acts are often ignored or responded to inappropriately (Patterson, 1982; Patterson, Reid, & Dishion, in press; Snyder, 1977). It seems that some families produce children characterized by not one, but two problems. They have antisocial symptoms and they are socially unskilled.

A series of structural equation modeling studies by Patterson and his colleagues support the theory that disrupted parent practices are causally related to child antisocial behavior. They used multiple indicators to define parental discipline and monitoring practices, child coercive behavior in the home, and a cross-situational measure of the child antisocial trait. In four different samples, involving several hundred grade school boys, the parenting practices and family interaction constructs accounted for 30–40% of the variance in general antisocial behavior (Baldwin & Skinner, 1988; Patterson, 1986; Patterson, Dishion, & Bank, 1984; Patterson et al., in press). For-

gatch (1988) used a quasi-experimental design based on data from families referred for treatment of antisocial boys. She showed that changes in parental discipline and monitoring were accompanied by significant reductions in child antisocial behavior. There were no changes in antisocial child behavior for those families who showed no changes in these parenting skills.

Social Rejection and School Failure

It is hypothesized that coercive child behaviors are likely to produce two sets of reactions from the social environment. One outcome is rejection by members of the normal peer group, and the other is academic failure.

It is consistently found that antisocial children show poor academic achievement (Hawkins & Lishner, 1987; Wilson & Herrnstein, 1985). One explanation for this is that the child's noncompliant and undercontrolled behavior directly impedes learning. Classroom observations of antisocial children show they spend less time on task than their nondeviant peers (Shinn, Ramsey, Walker, O'Neill, & Steiber, 1987; Walker et al., 1987). Earlier classroom observation studies showed that they were also deficient in academic survival skills (e.g., attending, remaining in seat, answering questions) necessary for effective learning (Cobb, 1972; Cobb & Hops, 1973; Hops & Cobb, 1974). Two studies showed a significant covariation between antisocial behavior and failure to complete homework assignments (Dishion, Loeber, Stouthamer-Loeber, & Patterson, 1983; Fehrmann, Keith, & Reimers, 1987).

The association between antisocial behavior and rejection by the normal peer group is well documented (Cantrell & Prinz, 1985; Dodge, Coie, & Brakke, 1982; Roff & Wirt, 1984). Experimental studies of group formation show that aggressive behavior leads to rejection, not the reverse (Coie & Kupersmidt, 1983; Dodge, 1983). Rejected children are also deficient in a number of social–cognitive skills, including peer group entry, perception of peer group norms, response to provocation, and interpretation of prosocial interactions (Asarnow & Calan, 1985; Dodge, 1986; Putallaz, 1983).

It is often suggested that academic failure and peer rejection are causes rather than consequences of antisocial behavior. However, a stronger case may be made that antisocial behavior contributes to these negative outcomes. For example, some investigators have predicted that successful academic remediation will lead to a reduction in antisocial behavior (e.g., Cohen & Filipczak, 1971). However, it has been repeatedly demonstrated that programs improving the academic skills of antisocial youths have not achieved reductions in other antisocial symptoms (Wilson & Herrnstein, 1985); similar findings have been obtained for social skills training (Kazdin, 1987).

Deviant Peer Group Membership

Antisocial behavior and peer group rejection are important preludes to deviant peer group membership (Dishion, Patterson, & Skinner, 1988; Snyder, Dishion, & Patterson, 1986). These analyses also suggest that lax parental su-

We gratefully acknowledge the support of National Institute of Mental Health Grants 2 R01 MH 37940 and 5 T32 MH 17126 in the preparation of this article.

Correspondence concerning this article should be addressed to G. R. Patterson, Oregon Social Learning Center, 207 East 5th Ave., Suite 202, Eugene, OR 97401.

pervision also accounts for unique variance to the prediction of deviant peer affiliation.

A large number of studies point to the peer group as the major training ground for delinquent acts and substance use (Elliott et al., 1985; Hirschi, 1969; Huba & Bentler, 1983; Kandel, 1973). Peers are thought to supply the adolescent with the attitudes, motivations, and rationalizations to support antisocial behavior as well as providing opportunities to engage in specific delinquent acts. There are, however, only a small number of studies designed to investigate the hypothesized training process. One study in an institutional setting showed that delinquent peers provided considerable positive reinforcement for deviant behavior and punishment for socially conforming acts (Buehler, Patterson, & Furniss, 1966).

It seems, then, that the disrupted family processes producing antisocial behavior may indirectly contribute to later involvement with a deviant peer group. This particular product may function as an additional determinant for future antisocial behavior. In effect, the deviant peer group variable may be thought of as a positive feedback variable that contributes significantly to maintenance in the process. Common adult outcomes for highly antisocial youths include school dropout, uneven employment histories, substance abuse, marital difficulties, multiple offenses, incarceration, and institutionalization (Caspi et al., 1987; Huesmann, Eron, Lefkowitz, & Walder, 1984; Robins & Ratcliff, 1979).

Figure 1 depicts the relation among the concepts discussed up to this point.

Some Implications of the Development Perspective

Early Versus Late Starters

Boys starting their criminal career in late childhood or early adolescence are at the greatest risk of becoming chronic offenders (Farrington, 1983; Loeber, 1982). Studies of prison populations have shown that recidivists are generally first arrested by age 14 or 15, whereas one-time offenders are first arrested at a later age (Gendreau, Madden, & Leipciger, 1979). Farrington found that boys first arrested between 10 and 12 years of age average twice as many convictions as later starters (Farrington, Gallagher, Morley, St. Ledger, & West, 1986); this comparison holds into early adulthood.

One implication of the aforementioned developmental perspective is that early forms of age-prototypic antisocial behavior may be linked to the early onset of official juvenile offenses. Following this logic, the child who receives antisocial training from the family during the preschool and elementary school years is likely to be denied access to positive socialization forces in the peer group and school.

On the other hand, the late starter would be someone committing his or her first offense in middle to late adolescence. This individual lacks the early training for antisocial behaviors. This implies that he or she has not experienced the dual failure of rejection by normal peers and academic failure.

Only about half the antisocial children become adolescent delinquents, and roughly half to three quarters of the adolescent delinquents become adult offenders (Blumstein, Cohen, & Farrington, 1988; Farrington, 1987; Robins & Ratcliff, 1979). At some point in late adolescence, the incidence of delinquent acts as a function of age group begins to drop; the drop continues into the late 20s. One interpretation of these data is that many of the delinquent offenders drop out of the process. We assume that many of these dropouts are late starters, but more research is clearly needed to specify what factors determine the probability of an individual's dropping out of the antisocial training process. A proper developmental theory of antisocial behavior must delineate not only the variables that lead a child into the process but those that cause some of them to drop out of it.

Contextual Variables for Family Disruption

Because parent–child interaction is a central variable in the etiology of antisocial behavior, it is important to de-

Figure 1
A Developmental Progression for Antisocial Behavior

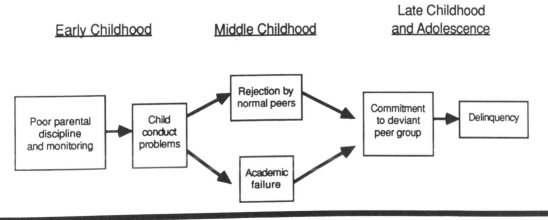

termine why a minority of parents engage in highly maladaptive family management practices. A number of variables, which shall be referred to as disruptors, have negative effects on parenting skill. These variables also correlate with the probability of children's antisocial behavior. Thus, the effect of disruptors on children's adjustment is indirect, being mediated through perturbations in parenting. Potential disruptors include a history of antisocial behavior in other family members, demographic variables representing disadvantaged socioeconomic status, and stressors—such as marital conflict and divorce—that hamper family functioning.

Antisocial Parents and Grandparents

There is a high degree of intergenerational similarity for antisocial behavior (Farrington, 1987; Robins & Ratcliff, 1979). As a predictor of adult antisocial personality, having an antisocial parent places the child at significant risk for antisocial behavior; having two antisocial parents puts the child at even higher risk (Robins & Earls, 1985). Concordance across three generations has also been documented (Elder, Caspi, & Downy, 1983; Huesmann et al., 1984; Robins, West, & Herjanic, 1975).

There is considerable evidence that parental discipline practices may be an important mediating mechanism in this transmission. Our set of findings shows that antisocial parents are at significant risk for ineffective discipline practices. Ineffective discipline is significantly related to risk of having an antisocial child. For example, Elder et al. (1983) found a significant relation between retrospective accounts of grandparental explosive discipline and paternal irritability. Irritable fathers tended to use explosive discipline practices with their own children who tended to exhibit antisocial behavior. Patterson and Dishion (1988) also found a significant correlation between retrospective reports of grandparental explosive reactions in the home and parental antisocial traits. Furthermore, the effect of the parents' antisocial trait on the grandchildren's antisocial behavior was mediated by parental discipline practices.

Family Demographics

Demographic variables such as race, neighborhood, parental education, income, and occupation are related to the incidence of antisocial behavior, particularly in its more severe forms (Elliott et al., 1985; Rutter & Giller, 1983; Wilson & Herrnstein, 1985). We presume that the effect of social class on child adjustment is mediated by family management practices.

The empirical findings linking social class to parenting practices are not consistent. But, in general, middle-class parents seem more likely to use reasoning and psychological methods of discipline, allow their children more freedom of choice and self-direction, show egalitarian parenting styles, express positive affect toward their children, verbalize, and support cognitive and academic growth (Gecas, 1979; Hess, 1970). Lower class parents are more likely to use physical discipline, be controlling of their child's behavior, exhibit authoritarian parenting styles, and engage in less frequent verbal and cognitive stimulation.

The findings from the at-risk sample at the Oregon Social Learning Center are in keeping with the trends in the literature (Patterson et al., in press). Uneducated parents working in unskilled occupations were found to be significantly less effective in discipline, monitoring, problem solving, positive reinforcement, and involvement.

Family Stressors

Stressors impinging on the family such as unemployment, family violence, marital discord, and divorce are associated with both delinquency (Farrington, 1987) and child adjustment problems in general (Garmezy & Rutter, 1983; Hetherington, Cox, & Cox, 1982; Rutter, 1979). Although stressors may well have direct and independent effects on child behavior, we assume that the major impact of stress on child adjustment is mediated by family management practices. If the stressors disrupt parenting practices, then the child is placed at risk for adjustment problems. For example, in the case of divorce, postseparation behavior problems occur with diminished parental responsiveness, affection, and involvement, and increased parental punitiveness and irritability (Hetherington et al., 1982; Wallerstein & Kelley, 1981). Structural equation modeling using data from a large sample of recently separated families provided strong support for the relation among stress, disrupted discipline, and antisocial behavior for boys (Forgatch, Patterson, & Skinner, in press).

We assume that antisocial parents and parents with marginal child-rearing skills are perhaps most susceptible to the disrupting effects of stressors and socioeconomic disadvantage. Elder, Caspi, and Nguyen (in press) described this interaction as an *amplifying effect.* External events are most disabling to those individuals who already exhibit negative personality traits or weak personal resources because stressors amplify such problems in adjustment. The interaction between the aforementioned disruptors and parental susceptibility is presented in Figure 2.

When antisocial parents or parents with minimal family management skills are faced with acute or prolonged stress, nontrivial disruptions in family management practices are likely to occur. It is these disruptions that are thought to place the child at risk for adjustment problems. A recent study by Snyder (1988) provided strong support for the mediational hypothesis. Roughly 20 hours of observation collected in the homes of three mother–child dyads showed significant covariation across days between stress and both disrupted maternal discipline and maternal irritability. Days characterized by high stress prior to the observation showed higher rates of disrupted behavior for the mother and increased child problem behaviors. A similar covariation was shown in the study by Wahler and Dumas (1984).

Is Prevention a Possibility?

Reviews of the literature summarizing efforts to intervene with antisocial adolescents invariably lead to negative

Figure 2
Disruptors of Effective Parenting

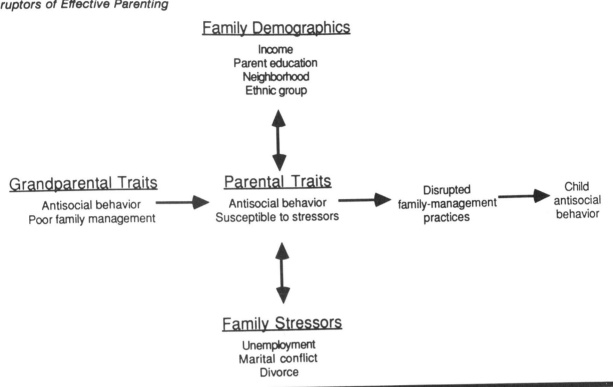

Family Demographics
Income
Parent education
Neighborhood
Ethnic group

Grandparental Traits
Antisocial behavior
Poor family management

Parental Traits
Antisocial behavior
Susceptible to stressors

Disrupted
family-management
practices

Child
antisocial
behavior

Family Stressors
Unemployment
Marital conflict
Divorce

conclusions (Kazdin, 1987; Wilson & Herrnstein, 1985). At best, such interventions produce short-term effects that are lost within a year or two of treatment termination. For example, efforts to apply behavior modification procedures in a halfway house setting (Achievement Place) showed no treatment effects after youths returned to their homes and communities (Jones, Weinrott, & Howard, 1981). Similarly, systematic parent training for families of delinquent adolescents produced reductions in offenses, but this effect did not persist over time (Marlowe, Reid, Patterson, Weinrott, & Bank, 1988).

Successful intervention appears to be possible for preadolescents, with parent-training interventions showing the most favorable outcomes (Kazdin, 1987). Parent training refers to procedures in which parents are given specific instructions in ways to improve family management practices (e.g., Forehand, Wells, & Griest, 1980; Patterson, Reid, Jones, & Conger, 1975). As shown in the review by Kazdin (1987), the parent-training programs have been evaluated in a number of random assignment evaluation studies including follow-up designs (six-month to four-year intervals). In general, the findings support the hypothesis that parent training is effective when applied to younger antisocial children. That several major studies failed to show a treatment effect led most investigators to conclude that parent training techniques *and* soft clinical skills are necessary for effective treatment. Current intervention studies have expanded their scope to include teaching academic and social–relational skills

in addition to parent training. In order to alter both the problem child's lack of social skills and his or her antisocial symptoms, it seems necessary to design these more complex interventions.

We believe that prevention studies are now feasible. It seems reasonable to identify children in the elementary grades who are both antisocial and unskilled. Successful programs would probably include three components: parent training, child social-skills training, and academic remediation.

REFERENCES

Asarnow, J. R., & Calan, J. R. (1985). Boys with peer adjustment problems: Social cognitive processes. *Journal of Consulting and Clinical Psychology, 53,* 80–87.
Baldwin, D. V., & Skinner, M. L. (1988). *A structural model for antisocial behavior: Generalization to single-mother families.* Manuscript submitted for publication.
Blumstein, A., Cohen, J., & Farrington, D. P. (1988). Criminal career research: Its value for criminology. *Criminology, 26,* 1–35.
Buehler, R. E., Patterson, G. R., & Furniss, J. M. (1966). The reinforcement of behavior in institutional settings. *Behavior Research and Therapy, 4,* 157–167.
Cantrell, V. L., & Prinz, R. J. (1985). Multiple predictors of rejected, neglected, and accepted children: Relation between sociometric status and behavioral characteristics. *Journal of Consulting and Clinical Psychology, 53,* 884–889.
Caspi, A., Elder, G. H., & Bem, D. J. (1987). Moving against the world: Life course patterns of explosive children. *Developmental Psychology, 23,* 308–313.
Cobb, J. A. (1972). The relationship of discrete classroom behavior to fourth grade academic achievement. *Journal of Educational Psychology, 63,* 74–80.

Cobb, J. A., & Hops, H. (1973). Effects of academic skill training on low achieving first graders. *Journal of Educational Research, 63,* 74–80.

Cohen, H. L., & Filipczak, J. (1971). *A new learning environment.* San Francisco: Jossey Bass.

Coie, J. D., & Kupersmidt, J. B. (1983). A behavioral analysis of emerging social status in boys' groups. *Child Development, 54,* 1400–1416.

Dishion, T. J., Loeber, R., Stouthamer-Loeber, M., & Patterson, G. R. (1983). Social skills deficits and male adolescent delinquency. *Journal of Abnormal Child Psychology, 12,* 37–54.

Dishion, T. J., Patterson, G. R., & Skinner, M. L. (1988). *Peer group selection processes from middle childhood to early adolescence.* Manuscript in preparation.

Dodge, K. A. (1983). Behavioral antecedents of peer social status. *Child Development, 54,* 1386–1399.

Dodge, K. A. (1986). A social information processing model of social competence in children. In M. Perlmutter (Ed.), *Minnesota symposium on child psychology* (Vol. 18, pp. 77–125). Hillsdale, NJ: Erlbaum.

Dodge, K. A., Coie, J. D., & Brakke, N. P. (1982). Behavior patterns of socially rejected and neglected preadolescents: The roles of social approach and aggression. *Journal of Abnormal Child Psychology, 10,* 389–410.

Dunford, F. W., & Elliott, D. S. (1982). *Identifying career offenders with self-reported data* (Grant No. MH27552). Washington, DC: National Institute of Mental Health.

Elder, G. H., Jr., Caspi, A., & Downey, G. (1983). Problem behavior in family relationships: A multigenerational analysis. In A. Sorensen, F. Weinert, & L. Sherrod (Eds.), *Human development: Interdisciplinary perspective* (pp. 93–118). Hillsdale, NJ: Erlbaum.

Elder, G. H., Jr., Caspi, A., & Nguyen, T. V. (in press). Resourceful and vulnerable children: Family influences in stressful times. In R. K. Silbereisen & K. Eyferth (Eds.), *Development in context: Integrative perspectives on youth development.* New York: Springer.

Elliott, D. S., Huizinga, D., & Ageton, S. S. (1985). *Explaining delinquency and drug use.* Beverly Hills, CA: Sage.

Farrington, D. P. (1983). Offending from 10 to 25 years of age. In K. T. Van Dusen & S. A. Mednick (Eds.), *Prospective studies of crime and delinquency* (pp. 17–37). Boston: Kluwer-Nijhoff.

Farrington, D. P. (1987). Early precursors of frequent offending. In J. Q. Wilson & G. C. Loury (Eds.), *From children to citizens: Vol. III. Families, schools, and delinquency prevention* (pp. 27–51). New York: Springer-Verlag.

Farrington, D. P., Gallagher, B., Morley, L., St. Ledger, R. J., & West, D. J. (1986). *Cambridge study in delinquent development: Long term follow-up.* Unpublished annual report, Cambridge University Institute of Criminology, Cambridge, England.

Farrington, D. P., Ohlin, L. E., & Wilson, J. Q. (1986). *Understanding and controlling crime: Toward a new research strategy.* New York: Springer-Verlag.

Federal Bureau of Investigation. (1987). *Crime in the United States: Uniform crime reports, 1986.* Washington, DC: Government Printing Office.

Fehrmann, P. G., Keith, T. Z., & Reimers, T. M. (1987). Home influences on school learning: Direct and indirect effects of parental involvement in high school grades. *Journal of Educational Research, 80,* 330–337.

Feldman, R. A., Caplinger, T. E., & Wodarski, S. S. (1981). *The St. Louis conundrum: Prosocial and antisocial boys together.* Unpublished manuscript.

Forehand, R., King, H. E., Peed, S., & Yoder, P. (1975). Mother–child interactions: Comparison of a non-compliant clinic group and a non-clinic group. *Behaviour Research and Therapy, 13,* 79–85.

Forehand, R., Wells, K., & Griest, D. (1980). An examination of the social validity of a parent training program. *Behavior Therapy, 11,* 488–502.

Forgatch, M. S. (1988, June). *The relation between child behaviors, client resistance, and parenting practices.* Paper presented at the Earlscourt Symposium on Childhood Aggression, Toronto.

Forgatch, M. S., Patterson, G. R., & Skinner, M. (in press). A mediational model for the effect of divorce on antisocial behavior in boys. In E. M. Hetherington (Ed.), *The impact of divorce and step-parenting on children.* Hillsdale, NJ: Lawrence Erlbaum Assoc.

Garmezy, N., & Rutter, M. (Eds.). (1983). *Stress, coping, and development in children.* New York: McGraw Hill.

Gecas, V. (1979). The influence of social class on socialization. In W. R. Burr, R. Hill, F. I. Nye, & I. L. Reiss (Eds.), *Contemporary theories about the family* (Vol. 1, pp. 365–404). New York: Free Press.

Gendreau, P., Madden, P., & Leipciger, M. (1979). Norms and recidivism rates for social history and institutional experience for first incarcerates: Implications for programming. *Canadian Journal of Criminology, 21,* 1–26.

Hawkins, J. D., & Lishner, D. M. (1987). Schooling and delinquency. In E. H. Johnson (Ed.), *Handbook on crime and delinquency prevention* (pp. 179–221). New York: Greenwood Press.

Hetherington, E. M., Cox, M., & Cox, R. (1982). Effects of divorce on parents and children. In M. Lamb (Ed.), *Nontraditional families* (pp. 233–288). Hillsdale, NJ: Erlbaum.

Hess, R. D. (1970). Social class and ethnic influences on socialization. In P. H. Mussen (Ed.), *Charmichael's manual of child psychology* (Vol. 2, pp. 457–558). New York: Wiley.

Hirschi, T. (1969). *Causes of delinquency.* Berkley, CA: University of California Press.

Hops, H., & Cobb, J. A. (1974). Initial investigations into academic survival-skill training, direct instruction, and first-grade achievement. *Journal of Educational Psychology, 66,* 548–553.

Huba, G. J., & Bentler, P. M. (1983). Causal models of the development of law abidance and its relationship to psychosocial factors and drug use. In W. S. Laufer & J. M. Day (Eds.), *Personality theory, moral development and criminal behavior* (pp. 165–215). Lexington, MA: Lexington Books.

Huesmann, L. R., Eron, L. D., Lefkowitz, M. M., & Walder, L. O. (1984). Stability of aggression over time and generations. *Developmental Psychology, 20,* 1120–1134.

Jones, R. R., Weinrott, M. R., & Howard, J. R. (1981). *The national evaluation of the Teaching Family Model.* Unpublished manuscript, Evaluation Research Group, Eugene, OR.

Kandel, D. B. (1973). Adolescent marijuana use: Role of parents and peers. *Science, 181,* 1067–1081.

Kazdin, A. E. (1987). Treatment of antisocial behavior in children: Current status and future directions. *Psychological Bulletin, 102,* 187–203.

Loeber, R. (1982). The stability of antisocial and delinquent child behavior: A review. *Child Development, 53,* 1431–1446.

Loeber, R., & Dishion, T. J. (1983). Early predictors of male delinquency: A review. *Psychological Bulletin, 94,* 68–99.

Marlowe, H. J., Reid, J. B., Patterson, G. R., Weinrott, M. R., & Bank, L. (1988). *Treating adolescent multiple offenders: A comparison and follow up of parent training for families of chronic delinquents.* Manuscript submitted for publication.

McCord, W., McCord, J., & Howard, A. (1963). Familial correlates of aggression in nondelinquent male children. *Journal of Abnormal and Social Psychology, 62,* 79–93.

Olweus, D. (1979). Stability of aggressive reaction patterns in males: A review. *Psychological Bulletin, 86,* 852–875.

Patterson, G. R. (1982). *A social learning approach: 3. Coercive family process.* Eugene, OR: Castalia.

Patterson, G. R. (1986). Performance models for antisocial boys. *American Psychologist, 41,* 432–444.

Patterson, G. R., & Dishion, T. J. (1988). Multilevel family process models: Traits, interactions, and relationships. In R. Hinde & J. Stevenson-Hinde (Eds.), *Relationships within families: Mutual influences* (pp. 283–310). Oxford: Clarendon Press.

Patterson, G. R., Dishion, T. J., & Bank, L. (1984). Family interaction: A process model of deviancy training. *Aggressive Behavior, 10,* 253–267.

Patterson, G. R., Reid, J. B., & Dishion, T. J. (in press). *Antisocial boys.* Eugene, OR: Castalia.

Patterson, G. R., Reid, J. B., Jones, R. R., & Conger, R. E. (1975). *A social learning approach to family intervention: Vol 1. Families with aggressive children.* Eugene, OR: Castalia.

Putallaz, M. (1983). Predicting children's sociometric status from their behavior. *Child Development, 54,* 1417–1426.

Robins, L. N. (1966). *Deviant children grown up: A sociological and psychiatric study of sociopathic personality.* Baltimore: Williams & Wilkins.

Robins, L. N., & Earls, F. (1985). A program for preventing antisocial behavior for high-risk infants and preschoolers: A research prospectus. In R. L. Hough, P. A. Gongla, V. B. Brown, & S. E. Goldston (Eds.), *Psychiatric epidemiology and prevention: The possibilities* (pp. 73–84). Los Angeles: Neuropsychiatric Institute.

Robins, L. N., & Ratcliff, K. S. (1979). Risk factors in the continuation of childhood antisocial behavior into adulthood. *International Journal of Mental Health, 7*(3–4), 96–116.

Robins, L. N., West, P. A., & Herjanic, B. L. (1975). Arrests and delinquency in two generations: A study of black urban families and their children. *Journal of Child Psychology and Psychiatry, 16,* 125–140.

Roff, J. D., & Wirt, R. D. (1984). Childhood aggression and social adjustment as antecedents of delinquency. *Journal of Abnormal Child Psychology, 12,* 111–116.

Rutter, M. (1979). Protective factors in children's responses to stress and disadvantage. In M. W. Kent & J. E. Rolfe (Eds.), *Primary prevention of psychopathology: 3. Social competence in children.* Hanover, NH: University Press of New England.

Rutter, M., & Giller, H. (1983). *Juvenile delinquency: Trends and perspectives.* New York: Penguin Books.

Shinn, M. R., Ramsey, E., Walker, H. M., O'Neill, R. E., & Steiber, S. (1987). Antisocial behavior in school settings: Initial differences in an at-risk and normal population. *Journal of Special Education, 21,* 69–84.

Snyder, J. J. (1977). Reinforcement analysis of interaction in problem and nonproblem families. *Journal of Abnormal Psychology, 86,* 528–535.

Snyder, J. J. (1988). *An intradyad analysis of the effects of daily variations in maternal stress on maternal discipline and irritability: Its effects on child deviant behaviors.* Manuscript in preparation.

Snyder, J. J., Dishion, T. J., & Patterson, G. R. (1986). Determinants and consequences of associating with deviant peers during preadolescence and adolescence. *Journal of Early Adolescence, 6*(1), 20–43.

Snyder, J. J., & Patterson, G. R. (1986). The effects of consequences on patterns of social interaction: A quasi-experimental approach to reinforcement in natural interaction. *Child Development, 57,* 1257–1268.

Wahler, R. G., & Dumas, J. E. (1984). Family factors in childhood psychopathology: Toward a coercion neglect model. In T. Jacob (Ed.), *Family interaction and psychopathology.* New York: Plenum Press.

Walker, H. M., Shinn, M. R., O'Neill, R. E., & Ramsey, E. (1987). Longitudinal assessment and long-term follow-up of antisocial behavior in fourth-grade boys: Rationale, methodology, measures, and results. *Remedial and Special Education, 8,* 7–16.

Wallerstein, J. S., & Kelley, J. B. (1981). *Surviving the breakup: How children and parents cope with divorce.* New York: Basic Books.

Wilson, J. Q., & Herrnstein, R. J. (1985). *Crime and human nature.* New York: Simon & Schuster.

Multiple Choice:

1.   Which of the following statements is correct?

    A.   Most antisocial children become teen delinquents.
    B.   Boys who engage in criminal activity at an early age tend to get it "out of their system" and are less likely to become adult criminals than are boys whose first criminal activity occurs later.
    C.   The incidence of delinquent acts begins to drop in late adolescence.
    D.   All of the above.

2.   Which of the following is *not* identified as a factor contributing to the development of antisocial behavior?

    A.   academic failure
    B.   membership in a deviant peer group
    C.   ineffective parental discipline
    D.   parental reinforcement of prosocial behavior

3.   According to Patterson et al., families train children in antisocial behavior. A particularly important role is played by:

    A.   coercive behaviors.
    B.   ridicule.
    C.   lack of attention.
    D.   overly contingent reinforcement.

Essay:

1.   Make up a family history that illustrates the developmental paths shown in Figures 1 and 2. Start with a mythical set of grandparents, a family with particular characteristics undergoing certain stressors, etc. Tell how a variety of factors might interact to result in a delinquent teen. Explicitly consider the concept of an *amplifying effect*.

2.   Think about your own developmental history. How many factors can you identify that protected you from an antisocial outcome? Could things easily have been different, or do you think that many aspects of your family life would have to have been different for you to have become a delinquent?

ARTICLE 24

Peer Rejection: Origins and Effects on Children's Development

John D. Coie and Antonius H. N. Cillessen

Reprinted from *Current Directions*, 1993, *2*, 89-92
Copyright © 1993 by the American Psychological Society.
Reprinted with the permission of Cambridge University Press.

Have you ever wondered why some children are more popular than others? When you were young, were there some children in your class who no one wanted to play with? In this article, John Coie and Antonius Cillessen tell us how psychologists study popularity by using a method called *sociometrics*. The authors also review the research in this area and discuss what psychologists have found out about both the origins, or causes, of being rejected by peers and the consequences, or effects, of peer rejection on children's later development.

With respect to the causes of peer rejection, it appears that aggressive behavior, particularly when coupled with poor social skills, is especially likely to lead to rejection by peers. Early parenting also influences peer relations: Children of warm, positive parents develop better peer relations than do children whose parents are cold. Further, parents influence their children's abilities to both interpret and express emotions. These abilities are related to how well children get along with peers, that is, kids who are better at expressing their emotions and understanding the emotions of others are more popular with other children.

Coie and Cillessen's exploration of the short and long-term consequences of peer rejection reveals that peer rejection in early childhood is related to not wanting to go to school and poor school performance in the short-term. In the long term, it is related to delinquency, school drop-out and possibly psychopathology (such as depression). These consequences are most pronounced for children who are both rejected and aggressive.

The authors suggest that because of the serious consequences of peer rejection, we should develop interventions to help rejected children, particularly those who are aggressive.

Peer Rejection: Origins and Effects on Children's Development

John D. Coie and Antonius H.N. Cillessen

Research over the past 20 years has brought a growing consensus among developmentalists that peer relations are a very influential factor in child development. Entry into school marks the beginning of a sig-

John D. Coie is Professor of Psychology at Duke University and a member of the faculty of the Carolina Consortium on Human Development. **Antonius H.N. Cillessen** is a postdoctoral fellow at Duke University. Address correspondence to John D. Coie, Department of Psychology: Social & Health Sciences, Duke University, P.O. Box 90085, Durham, NC 27708-0085; e-mail: djcoie@dukemvs or dtoon@dukemvs.

nificant increase in the amount of time children spend with peers. As important as the time a child spends with peers is the way these peers feel about that child. It is now widely accepted that adequate relations with peers form an important social context in which children acquire many of their social skills.

A significant number of children, however, lack access to a peer context that serves this developmental function. Consider Michael, for instance, an 8-year-old boy whose parents and school teacher have become very concerned about his frequent anger and aggression in interactions with other children. Michael tends to be bossy, dominating, and disruptive. He also frequently starts fights with other children. Often, he gets angry and upset with other children without adequate reason. As a result of this behavior, Michael's classmates have started to dislike him, and as the school year progresses they consistently try to avoid him.

A second example is Sean, another 8-year-old boy in Michael's class. When other children come to school in an irritable mood, Sean is an easy victim for them to pick on. Other children do not seem to be very concerned when this happens. In fact, the other children often tease Sean and exclude him from their play. When Sean is around other children, he appears anxious and often says embarrassing things that make them uncomfortable being with him. For the most part, however, peers ignore Sean, and he is usually by himself on the playground.

Although their ways of interacting with peers are notably different,

Michael and Sean have something important in common: Neither is well liked by peers. In fact, both are actively disliked by other children. Children who are rejected by their peers often lack the opportunity to acquire socially competent skills in their interactions with other children. Although we do not yet know all of the causal mechanisms involved, longitudinal data indicate that rejected children are at serious risk for various forms of social maladjustment in later life,[1] even when some antisocial characteristics of the children, such as aggression, are taken into account. Because of these findings, peer rejection in childhood has been given increasing research attention over the last two decades.

Peer social rejection typically is measured by sociometric methods, that is, by asking children to name three peers that they like the most, as well as three that they like the least.[2] These votes are summed across peers for each child. Those children who receive a high number of liked-least votes and a low number of liked-most votes are classified as rejected. Conversely, those children receiving many liked-most and few liked-least votes are considered popular. Although this is the essence of a sociometric method, several variations of this methodology have been introduced and investigated. One alternative to peer nominations is the use of Likert-type ratings children make of each other. Another important methodological development is the use of an unlimited number, instead of a fixed number, of peer nominations. Following these methodological changes, refinements have also taken place in the complex statistical procedures used to derive sociometric group classifications from the continuous liked-most and liked-least scores.[2]

The way peer rejection is assessed points to an important aspect of this concept: Social rejection is a statement of a relationship between an individual child and his or her school peers. While characteristics of the individual child, such as frequent aggressive behavior, may form a partial basis of that child's rejection by the group, being disliked is not simply a property of the individual. It is a response of the group to that individual and describes an aspect of the relationship between the individual and the group. There also is evidence that once an individual is rejected by a group, the group tends to maintain that perception. Two levels of analysis are thus involved in understanding social rejection. Individual characteristics usually are one essential factor in a child's being rejected by peers, but group dynamics play an important role in the maintenance of that rejected status. There is also some evidence that matches or mismatches between the characteristics of individuals and groups can be important determinants of rejection or acceptance by the group.

ORIGINS OF PEER REJECTION

Methods for resolving questions about the determinants of rejection have evolved dramatically over the past 20 years, from simple field studies in which observed behavior was correlated with peer status, to more complex experimental paradigms involving children being brought together for the first time so that video sequences of the acquaintance process can be analyzed. A common early method for studying the factors that are related to childhood peer rejection was to identify rejected children by means of classroom sociometric measures and then to observe these children in various school contexts in order to compare their behavior to that of children who were not rejected. Using this method, researchers related social rejection to aggression, disruptiveness, hyperactivity, social intrusiveness, bossi-

ness, and anxious-withdrawn behavior. But behavioral differences discovered in this way do not necessarily mean that these differences cause peer rejection. The problem with this method is that it does not permit investigators to determine which behaviors contribute to rejection and which are the result of being rejected.

More recently, a number of investigators have studied peer rejection as it emerges in experimentally created peer groups of children who were previously unacquainted. Observations of these small groups have documented the negative peer consequences of aggressiveness, social intrusiveness, disruption, and, to some extent, social fearfulness. There is, in fact, some evidence for two general subcategories of rejected children; one of these subtypes is illustrated by the description of Michael, and the other is illustrated by Sean.

Several studies indicate that around 40% to 50% of rejected children are highly aggressive. Aggression seems to be more of a contributing factor to rejection among boys than girls, and as children move into later childhood and adolescence, other factors besides aggression begin to take prominence. Aggression has been studied as a basis for rejection more intensely than social withdrawal or other factors. Dodge and his colleagues have found several ways that aggressive-rejected children process social information differently than other rejected children or nonrejected children.[3] Aggressive-rejected children are more likely to impute hostile intentions to peers when having difficult social interactions with them than are non-aggressive-rejected or nonrejected children. They also are more inclined to overemphasize the functional value of aggressive solutions to social problems. More detailed observations of aggression episodes involving aggressive-rejected boys suggest that they are more punitive

Published by Cambridge University Press

and less forgiving in such situations than aggressive boys who are not rejected by peers.[4]

Asher and his colleagues have argued that there is more to becoming rejected than is accounted for simply by categories of behavior such as aggression; they contend that it is the continuation of these behaviors along with deficits in important prosocial capacities that is critical.[5] Another way to think of this point is that some children who are highly aggressive may not be rejected by peers because their aggressiveness is balanced by socially redeeming characteristics. They can be fun to play with, be athletically gifted, or have important leadership skills, for example.

The search for an understanding of the origins of peer rejection has moved from an investigation of the behavior patterns leading to rejection to the study of early parenting influences.[6] Putallaz concluded that children of warm, positive parents develop a social orientation toward peers that is also warm and positive. Conversely, mothers who are disagreeable and controlling have children of lower social status. Parental influence on emotional development also has been related to early social status. Parents influence their children's ability to read and express emotion effectively, and this ability is related to peer status. In research on children's peer relations, the role of family variables is a relatively new area of investigation that is expected to expand in the future. Parallel to this trend, there also will be increased attention to the role of the family context in intervention programs for children who are rejected by their peers.

MAINTENANCE OF REJECTION

Although rejection by peers is not stable for some children, other children remain rejected over time, even when they move to a new peer group. In one study,[7] almost half the children rejected in fifth grade continued to be rejected when they were followed from year to year over a 5-year period. Some of this stability may be attributed to the stability of those personal behaviors and characteristics that lead a child to be rejected. However, there also is evidence that peer group dynamics contribute to the stability of peer rejection and that group processes play a role in maintaining existing social status distinctions.[8] In a study of the way children explain the behavior of other children, Hymel found that children made notably different causal attributions for rejected peers than for nonrejected peers. Children explained the negative behavior of a rejected child in terms of stable characteristics of that child. However, the same behaviors in a nonrejected child were said to be caused by more temporary characteristics. Children also held nonrejected peers less responsible than rejected children for negative outcomes. Thus, biased perceptions of a rejected peer lead children to interpretations of that peer's behavior that serve to maintain the negative feelings they have about him or her.

These biases are not limited to the level of children's social cognitions. They also operate on the level of actual social interactions. When children have negative expectations of another child, they act more negatively toward that child. This negative behavior then seems to trigger a reciprocally negative reaction from the target child that, in turn, fulfills the negative bias of the perceiving child. In this way, a self-fulfilling prophecy is created by some of the interactions between rejected children and their peers. By tracing children's expectations, behavioral exchanges, and interpretations over time, researchers have been able to document the existence of such self-perpetuating cycles of cognitions

and behavior. It is now clear that children who are rejected repeatedly by peers over time are confronted with consistently negative expectations, behavioral initiatives, and interpretations of their behavior by their peers. This group process contributes to the stability of the rejected child's poor social reputation.

An important implication of these studies is that even if rejected children change their behavior, they still face a difficult time recovering accepted positions in the peer group. If their behavior is subject to negative interpretations by other children, they will be treated by these peers in ways that may challenge their motivation to try to behave positively with peers. Peer ridicule can also undermine the confidence necessary for them to try out newly acquired skills. There also is some very interesting research evidence suggesting that when rejected children think other children are going to like them, they behave more appropriately in subsequent interactions with new acquaintances and actually are more well liked by these new acquaintances. Consequently, it seems that in addition to changing the behavior of the rejected target child, intervention efforts may need to attack the biased perceptions of the child's peers.

CONSEQUENCES OF REJECTION

One major reason for the study of the origins and maintenance of peer rejection is that children who are rejected by their peers are at risk for a series of negative consequences, both immediately and over the course of a longer time period. For aggressive-rejected children like Michael, the immediate social consequences of their behavior may not be so obvious to them. Because their aggressiveness makes them a threat to peers, these peers may not give them direct feedback about their negative regard. Thus, they may not be rejected overtly. There is some evidence that they are not noticeably isolated from peers,[4] and they do not report being as lonely or as aware of peer dislike as are more submissive-rejected children.[5] The social consequences of rejection appear to be more immediate for the withdrawn or submissive children like Sean. These children recognize that other children do not like them, and they describe themselves as lonely and wanting help with friendships. Perry and his colleagues have found that a significant percentage of rejected children, like Sean, are the targets of peer bullying and abuse.[9]

In addition to these immediate social consequences, peer rejection has further negative effects emerging as early as the first year in school. Ladd found that children who are rejected by their peers after 2 months in kindergarten are at risk for adjustment problems by the end of that first school year.[10] Early rejection in this study predicted less favorable attitudes toward school, increased avoidance of school, and lower levels of performance over the course of kindergarten. Ladd argued that peer rejection interferes with children's early adjustment in school because it is a serious stressor in the early school environment.

The immediate negative consequences of rejection are related to research questions about the continuing negative consequences of peer rejection over the course of a child's school career and beyond. In fact, there is important evidence for long-term consequences of peer rejection, in line with its immediate consequences. These long-term negative consequences fall into three main categories: delinquency, school dropout, and psychopathology. Aggressive-rejected children are the ones who are most at risk for delinquency problems and school dropout, although nonaggressive-rejected children also have more of

these problems than nonrejected children. Less is known about psychopathology, but aggressive-rejected children show a similarly high prevalence of internalizing disorders as well as externalizing disorders.[1] Internalizing disorders are also an important category of long-term outcomes of peer rejection, and Rubin has evidence that some nonaggressive-rejected children are at high risk for depression.[11]

CONCLUSION

The long-term correlates of peer rejection suggest that it is an important factor to be considered in designing prevention programs for a variety of serious problems in adolescence. This is particularly true for aggressive-rejected children, although there is also evidence that nonaggressive-rejected children are at greater long-term risk than children who are neither rejected nor aggressive.[1] The immediate consequences of rejection, however, are obvious in nonaggressive-rejected children and call for some form of help for them, too. Their experience is painful. Perhaps because of this pain, many nonaggressive-rejected children may get help. Their pain may motivate them to change their behavior if help is offered, unlike their aggressive counterparts who create more pain for others. If, in fact, many of these nonaggressive children are successful in getting help in changing their peer relations, this may be one reason there is less strong evidence for serious adjustment problems in later life for this group of rejected children than for children who are both aggressive and rejected.

Acknowledgments—Some of the research reported here was supported by Grants R01MH39140 and K05MH00797 from the Prevention Branch and Grant R01MH38765 from the Violence and Antisocial Behavior Branch of the National Institute of Mental Health.

Notes

1. J.G. Parker and S.R. Asher, Peer relations and later personal adjustment: Are low-accepted children at risk? *Psychological Bulletin, 102,* 357–389 (1987); J.D. Coie, J.E. Lochman, R. Terry, and C. Hyman, Predicting early adolescent disorder from childhood aggression and peer rejection, *Journal of Consulting and Clinical Psychology, 60,* 783–792 (1992).

2. J.D. Coie, K.A. Dodge, and H. Coppotelli, Dimensions and types of social status: A cross-age perspective, *Developmental Psychology, 18,* 557–571 (1982); J.D. Coie and K.A. Dodge, Continuities and changes in children's social status: A five-year longitudinal study, *Merrill-Palmer Quarterly, 29,* 261–282 (1983); R. Terry and J.D. Coie, A comparison of methods for defining sociometric status among children, *Developmental Psychology, 27,* 867–880 (1991).

3. See K.A. Dodge and E. Feldman, Issues in social cognition and sociometric status, in *Peer Rejection in Childhood,* S.R. Asher and J.D. Coie, Eds. (Cambridge University Press, New York, 1990).

4. J.D. Coie, K.A. Dodge, R. Terry, and V. Wright, The role of aggression in peer relations: An analysis of aggression episodes in boys' play groups, *Child Development, 62,* 812–826 (1991).

5. S.R. Asher and G.A. Williams, Helping children without friends in home and school, in *Children's Social Development: Information for Teachers and Parents* (ERIC Clearing House on Elementary and Early Childhood Education, Urbana, IL, 1987); J.T. Parkhurst and S.R. Asher, Peer rejection in middle school: Subgroup differences in behavior, loneliness, and interpersonal concerns, *Developmental Psychology, 28,* 231–241 (1992).

6. M. Putallaz and A.H. Heflin, Parent-child interaction, in *Peer Rejection in Childhood,* S.R. Asher and J.D. Coie, Eds. (Cambridge University Press, New York, 1990); J. Cassidy, R.D. Parke, L. Butkovsky, and J.M. Braungart, Family-peer connections: The roles of emotional expressiveness within the family and children's understanding of emotions, *Child Development, 63,* 603–618 (1992).

7. Coie and Dodge, note 2.

8. S. Hymel, Interpretations of peer behavior: Affective bias in childhood and adolescence, *Child Development, 57,* 431–445 (1986); A.H.N. Cillessen and T.J. Ferguson, *Self-perpetuation processes in children's peer relations,* manuscript submitted for publication (1993); D.L. Rabiner and J.D. Coie, Effect of expectancy inductions on rejected children's acceptance by unfamiliar peers, *Developmental Psychology, 25,* 450–457 (1989).

9. D.G. Perry, S.J. Kusel, and L.C. Perry, Victims of peer aggression, *Developmental Psychology, 24,* 807–814 (1988).

10. G.W. Ladd, Having friends, keeping friends, making friends, and being liked by peers in the classroom: Predictors of children's early school adjustment? *Child Development, 61,* 1081–1100 (1990).

11. K.H. Rubin, L.J. LeMare, and S. Lollis, Social withdrawal in childhood: Developmental pathways to peer rejection, in *Peer Rejection in Childhood,* S.R. Asher and J.D. Coie, Eds. (Cambridge University Press, New York, 1990).

Recommended Reading

Asher, S.R., and Coie, J.D. (Eds.). (1990). *Peer Rejection in Childhood* (Cambridge University Press, New York).

Multiple Choice:

1. The most common way of identifying popular or rejected children is to:

    A. ask children's teachers to rate children on dimensions relevant to popularity.
    B. directly observe children in interaction with their peers, recording the frequency with which each child serves as a leader or is rebuffed by other children.
    C. ask each member of the peer group to nominate two or three children they especially like and others they especially dislike.
    D. ask children to respond to a standardized paper-and-pencil test that taps ability to generate solutions to interpersonal problems.

2. According to the article by Coie and Cillessen, children who fall into the _____ category of peer acceptance are the ones who are most likely to suffer serious adjustment problems later in life such as school drop-out and delinquency.

    A. aggressive rejected
    B. isolated or neglected
    C. nonaggressive rejected
    D. "controversial"

Essay:

1. What role do parents play in their children's popularity and the development of social skills? What can parents do to facilitate the development of their children's social skills?

2. What are some of the ways that the peer group contributes to the stability of peer rejection over time?

ARTICLE 25

Changes in Adolescents' Daily Interactions With Their Families From Ages 10 to 18: Disengagement and Transformation

Reed W. Larson, Maryse H. Richards, Giovanni Moneta, Grayson Holmbeck, and Elena Duckett

Reprinted from *Developmental Psychology*, 1996, *32*, 744-754.
Copyright © 1996 by the American Psychological Association. Reprinted with permission.

Does family become less important to children as they enter adolescence and become more concerned with their peers? Are adolescents' relationships with their parents fraught with conflict and bickering? The stereotypical view of adolescence is indeed one in which children reject the ways of their parents for those of their peers. But how accurate is this view?

In this article, Reed Larson and his colleagues are concerned with how the time children spend with their parents changes as they enter adolescence. To examine this issue, these investigators had children ranging from 10 to 14 years report on what they were doing every two hours while they were awake for an entire week. Four years later when these children were 14 to 18 years old, they did the same thing again.

Consistent with the view that family becomes less important during adolescence, the children in the study spent less time with their families as they got older. However, this was not due to increased conflict with their parents, but to the fact that they had more opportunities to do things on their own. Opportunities like being able to drive and having a job took them away from their families. Although the overall time children spent with their family decreased, they continued to spend time talking with their parents one on one; and these conversations were not colored by conflict and bickering. In fact, adolescent girls were more likely to talk to their mothers about their relationships than when they were younger, suggesting that girls may actually have gotten closer to their mothers.

The results of this study are important for several reasons. For one thing, they tell us about how adolescents spend their time on a daily basis. The methods used by the researchers were quite in-depth in that adolescents were contacted with a beeper up to eight times a day and asked to report on what they were doing at the moment, and this went on for an entire week. Second, because the investigators followed these children over four years, the results tell us about *changes* children experienced over a fairly long time period. Third, the findings help to dispel the myth that adolescence is a time fraught with conflict between children and their parents.

Developmental Psychology
1996, Vol. 32, No. 4, 744–754

Changes in Adolescents' Daily Interactions With Their Families From Ages 10 to 18: Disengagement and Transformation

Reed W. Larson
University of Illinois at Urbana–Champaign

Maryse H. Richards
Loyola University of Chicago

Giovanni Moneta
Institute of Occupational Health

Grayson Holmbeck and Elena Duckett
Loyola University of Chicago

In a cross-sequential study spanning 5th–12th grade, 220 White working- and middle-class youth provided reports on their experience at 16,477 random moments in their lives. Amount of time spent with family was found to decrease from 35% to 14% of waking hours across this age period, indicating disengagement. However, transformation and continued connection were evident in stability across age in time talking and alone with parents; an age increase in family conversation about interpersonal issues, particularly for girls; and with age, adolescents' more frequent perception of themselves as leading interactions. After a decrease in early adolescence, older teens reported more favorable affect in themselves and others during family interactions. Last, the age decline in family time was found to be mediated not by internal family conflict but by opportunities and pulls an adolescent experiences from outside the family.

Two prominent theses have been advanced about developmental changes in adolescents' family relationships. The traditional view was that adolescence is a time of growing disengagement from family, associated with the process of becoming an independent adult. Havighurst (1953) identified emotional autonomy from parents as a developmental task of Western adolescence, and psychoanalytic writers portray adolescents as driven to individuate from their parents (Blos, 1967; Freud, 1946; Lidz, 1969). Steinberg and Silverberg (1986) obtained evidence that, with age, a sample of U.S. adolescents perceived themselves to be more emotionally and behaviorally independent of their parents.

A more recent thesis asserts that even as disengagement occurs, there is a transformation in adolescents' relationships with their parents that maintains continued closeness and warmth. Offer and Offer (1975) found continuity in most adolescent–parent relationships through the teenage years. Youniss (1980) found evidence that adolescent–parent relationships improve in later adolescence and hypothesized that a process of renegotiation takes place, leading to a more symmetric and mutual rela-

tionship, at least with mothers (Youniss & Smollar, 1985). Numerous authors have contended that the developmental task of adolescents is achievement of psychological independence from parents but with continued connectedness (Grotevant & Cooper, 1986; Hauser, 1991; Hill & Holmbeck, 1987; Youniss & Smollar, 1985).

An important yet neglected level at which these two developmental theses must be evaluated is that of daily interactions. Interactions are the forum in which relationships are enacted: It is through interactions that relationships are maintained, improve, or go sour (Kelley et al., 1983). Although it is useful to know that older adolescents continue to feel warm toward their families, it may be more valuable to know how often they actually see or talk with them. Whereas it is helpful to know that adolescents come to view their relationship with their parents as more mutual, it may be more important to know whether they experience themselves to be on an equal footing during actual interactions. To evaluate disengagement and transformation, we need information on how often and in what circumstances teenagers engage with their families: Is there disengagement and transformation within their daily interactions?

This article examines how basic parameters of adolescents' daily family interactions change across the 5th to 12th grade period. We used time-sampling data, obtained from a longitudinal sample of European American middle and working class youth, first, to examine developmental changes in the quantity of time and contexts of adolescents' family interactions, and second, to examine age changes in adolescents' subjective experience of these interactions: what they feel and how they perceive family members. Third, we evaluate the role of variables such as puberty, family conflict, and adolescents' opportunities outside the family in driving these changes.

This article is a follow-up to a prior article that examined age changes in social interactions across early adolescence (Larson

Reed W. Larson, Department of Human and Community Development, University of Illinois at Urbana–Champaign; Maryse H. Richards, Department of Psychology, Loyola University of Chicago; Giovanni Moneta, Institute of Occupational Health, Helsinki, Finland; Grayson Holmbeck and Elena Duckett, Department of Psychology, Loyola University of Chicago.

This research was partially supported by National Institute of Mental Health Grant 1 R01 MH38324. We are grateful to Marcelo Diversi for assistance on the manuscript.

Correspondence concerning this article should be addressed to Reed W. Larson, Department of Human and Community Development, University of Illinois, 1105 West Nevada Street, Urbana, Illinois 61801. Electronic mail may be sent via Internet to larsonr@uiuc.edu.

& Richards, 1991). The earlier article used Time 1 data from the current study to map age differences in the full range of social (and asocial) experience—including time with friends, with family, and alone—across the span from the fall of 5th grade to the winter of 9th grade. Several findings from that article are pertinent to the issues of this article: (a) Across this age span, amount of time spent with family declined by 40%; (b) this decline was largely due to less time in group interactions with family and was attributable to more time spent alone rather than more time away from home; and (c) the emotional states adolescents reported during family interactions became less positive across this age period, although for boys these states were more positive again in the ninth grade. The large decline in time and the less favorable affect suggest disengagement; however, continued engagement was suggested by the findings that amount of one-on-one time with parents did not decrease with age and that boys' emotional states with their families appeared to improve in middle adolescence.

The current article covers the 8-year period from 5th through 12th grade and focuses solely on family interactions, going into more depth. By extending the analysis to comprise the high school years, we include an important period when access to cars and the granting of new freedoms by parents (Feldman & Quatman, 1988) may further diminish family interaction; yet it is also a period when, according to prior research, renegotiation of family relationships is likely to occur. To detect changes in adolescents' level of engagement in family interactions, we evaluate age differences in the activities teens share with their families. In particular, we are interested in whether the amount of time spent communicating with family members decreases along with time in less interactive activities. To examine renegotiation, we examine age differences in how friendly adolescents perceive other family members to be and whom they perceive to be the leader during family interactions.

In addition to describing processes of disengagement and renegotiation within daily interactions, we evaluate variables that might drive these changes. The process of disengagement is often attributed to factors that are internal to adolescents' family relationships, factors that repel teens out of the family sphere. Psychoanalysts have sometimes put this in extreme terms, arguing that a felt need to individuate drives adolescents to partly or wholly repudiate their families (Freud, 1946; Lidz, 1969). Steinberg (1989, 1990) took a more moderate view, arguing that bickering and conflict increase at the age of puberty and lead to somewhat greater psychological distance between parents and adolescents. In one article, he suggested that there may be a built-in biological mechanism, across primate species, that stimulates distancing between offspring and parents at puberty in order to discourage endogenous mating (Steinberg, 1989). To evaluate this line of reasoning, we test whether puberty, family conflict, and other qualities of family relationships might be mediators of age differences in adolescents' family interactions.

Factors external to the family, however, may also play a role in changing adolescents' family interactions: Disengagement might result from as much pull as push. Older adolescents may spend less time with their families simply because they have more competing opportunities apart from the family sphere, either at home or away from home. If this is the case, diminished family time might be linked to life-situational factors that make it more attractive or easier for older adolescents to spend time apart from the family, such as having a private bedroom and a phone or TV in one's room, a later curfew, a job, or a driver's license and a car. In this study, therefore, we evaluate whether these kinds of life-situational factors are mediators of age differences in family interactions. Given the limits of our data set, these analyses of mediators should not be seen as conclusively testing a causal model but only as providing preliminary evidence.

In sum, the objective of this article is to examine processes of disengagement and transformation at the level of adolescents' everyday family interactions. We look at three sets of questions: (a) Does the amount of time and context of family interactions change across this age period? (b) Does adolescents' subjective experience of these interactions change? (c) Are these age changes related to factors internal to the adolescent and family relationships, or are they related to external factors that may pull the adolescent away from the family? Past research leads us to expect that boys' and girls' interactions with their families may differ (Collins & Russell, 1991; Youniss & Smollar, 1985), hence we consider gender as a moderating variable throughout the analyses.

Method

Sample

Participants were 220 middle- and working-class youth from a cross-sequential longitudinal study of adolescent development. At Time 1 of the study, these youth were in the 5th to 8th grades (ages 10–14). At Time 2, 4 years later, they were in the 9th to 12th grades (ages 13–18).

The initial sample was randomly selected from four elementary or junior high schools in the Chicago suburbs. Two schools were in a working class, blue-collar community on the edge of the city, and two were in an outlying, middle-class bedroom community. The population of both communities was European American. A stratification procedure was used to obtain equal numbers of students by grade, gender, and community. The students in the longitudinal sample, analyzed here, were a subset from those in a larger cross-sectional Time 1 sample (see Larson, 1989a; Larson & Richards, 1989). Students from this larger sample who were ninth graders at Time 1 or who participated during the summer at Time 1 were not studied at Time 2.

Attrition reduced the number of students in the final longitudinal sample. From an initial pool of 438 randomly drawn students, 328 (75%) participated at Time 1, and 220 (67%) of these participated at Time 2. Reasons for nonparticipation included refusal or failure to obtain parental permission ($n = 110$), family moved and was unreachable at Time 2 ($n = 67$), death between Time 1 and 2 ($n = 3$), and providing data at Time 1 or Time 2 that was judged to be of poor quality ($n = 38$). Population data at Time 1 indicated that attrition was not related to community, parents' socioeconomic status (SES), or sociometric ratings of the youth made by other students; however, attrition was somewhat higher among youth with lower self-esteem and those in remarried families (Larson, 1989a). Nonparticipation at Time 2 was somewhat higher among boys (the final sample consists of 97 boys and 123 girls) and among youth with scores at 13 or above on Kovacs's (1985) Children's Depression Inventory (attrition between Time 1 and 2 was 39% for these depressed youth, as compared with 33% for nondepressed).

Census data showed the divorce rates in these two communities to be considerably below the national average. At Time 1, 179 of the youth lived with both of their original parents, 15 lived in remarried families, and 26 lived in one-parent families. At Time 2, 173 lived with both parents, 13 lived in remarried families, and 34 lived in one-parent families.

Procedure

At both Times 1 and 2, participants carried pagers for 1 week and provided reports on their situation and experience at random times when signaled, following the procedures of the experience sampling method (ESM; Csikszentmihalyi & Larson, 1987). One signal was sent at a random time within each 2-hr block of time, with 7 to 8 signals per day. At Time 1, signals were sent between 7:30 a.m. and 9:30 p.m. for all days of the week. This closely approximated their waking hours (Larson, 1989a). At Time 2, signals were sent between 7:30 a.m. and 10:30 p.m. on weekdays and between 8:00 a.m. and 12:00 a.m. on weekends. Although this approximated their waking hours, small amounts of waking time before and after these hours were missed by this schedule for some youth.[1]

Reports were provided for the great majority of the ESM time samples. Participants responded to an average of 85% of the signals at Time 1 and 76% of the signals at Time 2 by completing a report. About 6% of these missed signals were attributable to mechanical failure of the pager, with the remaining attributable to a wide range of reasons from forgetting the pager at home or in one's room to the signal occurring during an activity that could not be interrupted, such as a test or participation in a sporting event (Larson, 1989a). In total, the students provided an average of 40.2 reports per person at Time 1 and 34.7 reports per person at Time 2, resulting in a total of 16,477 reports across the two data collections.

After completing the ESM procedure at each time, participants filled out a packet of questionnaires. Data were also obtained from one parent, typically the mother, and from the schools. To randomize time-of-year effects, some students participated in the fall, some in the winter, and some in the spring.

ESM Measures

Being with family. At the time of each ESM signal, participants checked off whom they were with from a list of possible companions. For the purposes of these analyses, we divided their reports into times they indicated being with and not with family members. In addition, we divided occasions with family into seven mutually exclusive categories: (a) being with a parent group (this includes any combination of family members that includes both mother and father); (b) being alone with mother only; (c) being alone with father only; (d) being with one or more siblings only; (e) being with mother and one or more siblings; (f) being with father and one or more siblings; and (g) being with extended family (includes any extended family member, and nuclear family members may or may not be present).

Activity, topic of conversation, location. On the ESM questionnaire, participants also responded to open-ended questions asking their activity, topic of conversation, and location each time they were signaled. Their activities were coded into 127 categories (interrater agreement was maintained at 94%). We have collapsed these into nine categories representing major groupings of family activities: homework, chores, eating, transportation, personal maintenance, watching TV, active leisure, talking, and idling. On occasions when students were talking, they were asked to report their topic of conversation. Responses to this item have been divided into two categories: times they were and times they were not talking about an interpersonal topic. Interrater agreement for this coding was 97%. Locations were initially coded into 68 categories (interrater agreement = 99%). For this variable, we were solely concerned about whether they were at home or away from home.

Subjective experience. Students rated their emotional state at each ESM signal on a scale of Affect, computed from three 7-point semantic differential items (happy–unhappy, cheerful–irritable, friendly–angry). This scale has strong internal reliability (α = .75 at the level of the self-report) and construct validity (Larson, 1989b). Values for this scale were z scored within person separately for Time 1 and Time 2 such that a value of 0.0 corresponds to each person's mean for that time and an increment of 1.0 corresponds to that person's standard deviation. With this transformation, values for affect represent a person's feeling relative to his or her overall distribution of affect scores.

Students also rated their perception of the people they were with at the time of each signal. They were given a 7-point semantic differential scale to rate people from *very unfriendly* (1) to *very friendly* (7). These values were also converted to z scores. In addition, participants were asked on the ESM form who was "the leader" at the moment of the signal. The fixed response choices were "nobody," "yourself," and "someone else."

Questionnaire Measures

Pubertal status. Data on each participant's pubertal status were collected at Time 1 only. Students rated their level of physical development by comparing themselves with drawings created by Morris and Udry (1980) that represent five stages of development articulated by Tanner (1975). Boys rated themselves on two sequences of drawings depicting stages of pubic hair and genitalia development. We created a single puberty scale for boys by summing these two highly correlated (.85) ratings. Girls rated themselves on two sequences of drawings depicting pubic hair and breast development. We summed these two highly correlated (.71) ratings to create a single puberty scale for girls. Boys' and girls' ratings on these drawings have shown correlations with physicians' ratings ranging from .57 to .81 (Morris & Udry, 1980).

Family relationships. Information on family conflict and family relationships was obtained from the adolescent and parent questionnaires. Both adolescents and parents responded to the Conflict and Cohesion scales of the Family Environment Scale (Moos & Moos, 1986). In addition, adolescents responded to a scale assessing how close they felt to their mother (α = .89) and father (α = .91; Blyth, 1982).

Life-situation variables. At Time 2 students completed a questionnaire asking about situational factors in their lives that might be related to the amount of time they spent with their families. We have grouped these to create two scales. The first includes factors related to being apart from the family at home. It includes items asking whether they had their own bedroom and whether they had their own TV, VCR, CD player or stereo, phone, and phone number. The scale assessing factors related to being away from home includes whether they had a driver's license, whether they owned or had access to a motorcycle or car, whether they had a job and how many hours they worked per week, and the hour at which their parents expected them to be home on weekdays and weekends. Responses were adjusted according to the standard deviations for each item and summed to create the two scales.

School grade (versus chronological age). Because grade in school was part of the sampling design, we used it as our index of age. Our prior analyses suggested that this measure of social age is often a better index of developmental status than is chronological age.

Analyses

Analytic techniques were chosen to accommodate the nested or multilevel structure of the ESM data. Our data set included reports on

---

[1] On a questionnaire administered at Time 2, students were asked when they usually got up and went to bed. For weekdays, the average wake-up time was 6:26 a.m. and bedtime was 10:45 p.m. For weekends, the average wake-up time was 9:31 a.m. and bedtime was 12:46 p.m. There were significant grade trends, with 12th graders reporting bedtimes of 38 min later than 9th graders on weekdays and 80 min later on weekends.

16,477 moments in time, but these reports were not statistically independent; they were provided by 220 adolescents, each of whom may have shown distinct patterns. Thus the structure of the data involves two levels: Level 1, constituted by the 16,477 ESM reports, and Level 2, constituted by the 220 adolescents.

When possible we have used multilevel modeling, a regression procedure for modeling data with this hierarchical structure (Goldstein, 1987; Prosser, Rabash, & Goldstein, 1991; see also hierarchical linear modeling, developed by Bryk & Raudenbush, 1992). Through an iterative process, multilevel modeling fits separate regressions for each higher level grouping (in our case, each person) as a step toward arriving at a regression solution for the entire sample. The advantage of this procedure is that it makes full use of the degrees of freedom provided by the 16,477 time samples while taking into account the variation in patterns among the 220 persons. More extensive discussion of the use of multilevel modeling with ESM data is provided by Moneta and Csikszentmihalyi (in press).

Our hypotheses concern the relationship between day-to-day experience and developmental level as indexed by school grade. We were also interested in how these relationships might vary by gender. Thus for our central analyses, we tested multilevel models with the following form:

$$Y = \beta 1 + \beta 2 * \text{Grade} + \beta 3 * \text{Sex} + \beta 4 * (\text{Grade} * \text{Sex}),$$

in which Y was some aspect of family experience. The dependent variable, Y, was based on ESM reports, thus it was a Level 1 variable; sex was a Level 2 variable; and because participants took part in the study at two periods, 4 years apart, their grade in school varied both within a participant's reports and across participants, making it both a Level 1 and a Level 2 variable. Grade and the intercept were defined as random effects for Level 2.

Our strategy with each dependent variable was to first test this fundamental model, then to evaluate whether addition of other independent variables contributed significantly. In addition to this basic set of predictor variables, we evaluated a quadratic variable for school grade and the interaction of this quadratic variable with sex. Before computing these quadratic terms, we subtracted the mean for grade (8.5), so that these variables were less correlated with the linear variable for grade (Draper & Smith, 1981). In preliminary analyses, we also evaluated a variable, time, that indicated whether a data point came from Time 1 or Time 2. This variable was not significant when grade was also included, thus we concluded that there was at most a minimal test–retest effect from participating in the ESM twice.

To make our findings most useful, we report the raw values for betas (except where otherwise indicated), and we report them using the same units we use to discuss Y. Thus in the example in which Y is the likelihood of being with one's family at each ESM signal—a variable we report as a percentage—values for beta are reported as the percentage change in the likelihood of being with one's family for each grade increment. In other words, a raw beta value of -2.00 indicates that time with family drops by two percentage points per year. To obtain beta values comparable to percentages, we used dichotomous dependent variables that were coded 0 and 100 rather than the typical 0 and 1.

In several instances multilevel modeling could not be used, so we used more conventional analyses, following guidelines described by Larson and Delespaul (1992) for analyzing ESM data. In some analyses that used only a subset of the ESM data points, the multilevel program, ML3 (Prosser et al., 1991), could not converge on a solution because there were insufficient data points per person. In these instances we used standard regression, disregarding the hierarchical structure of the data but using a more stringent alpha of $p < .01$ to compensate for the inflated N. In other instances in which our questions dealt primarily with the person as the unit of analysis, we created person-level variables from the ESM data (e.g., amount of time spent with family) and performed analyses at that level.

Results

Age Changes in the Amount of Time, Context, and Content of Family Interactions

Total time. Our first question was whether the amount of time adolescents spent with their families decreased across the adolescent years. To evaluate this prediction, we performed a multilevel regression equation in which being with family was the dependent variable, and grade, sex, and the interaction of grade and sex were the independent variables.

This analysis showed a large linear decline in time spent with family that continued from early through late adolescence. In the regression, grade was found to be a significant predictor of spending time with family. The value of beta for grade was -2.74 ($SE = .40$, $p < .001$), indicating that the amount of time spent with family decreased by an estimate of 2.74% per year across the 5th to 12th grade period. Twelfth graders spent approximately two fifths as much of their waking hours with their families as did 5th graders. The addition of a quadratic term for grade did not add significantly to the equation, and the interaction between grade and sex was not significant.

This large drop in family time was evident across all times of the week. The largest decline in family time was on Friday and Saturday nights, with large declines also evident for weekday afternoons and evenings and declines during daytime hours on weekends. The most frequent time for family interaction for both age groups was Sunday evening after 6:00 p.m.

Time in family subsystems. The next question was whether this decline in family time occurred across all groupings of family members. To test this, a dichotomous dependent variable was created for each of the seven categories of family members, and separate multilevel regressions were run for each.

We found that time spent alone with mother and alone with father did not decline significantly across this 8-year age period. Time spent with mother only remained stable across grade at approximately 3.0% of waking time; time spent with father only remained stable at approximately 1.6% of waking time. Time spent in all other family groupings showed linear declines with age. Grade was a significant predictor for time with parent group ($\beta = -.79$, $SE = .14$, $p < .001$); mother and one or more siblings ($\beta = -.44$ $SE = .10$, $p < .001$); father and one or more siblings ($\beta = -.08$, $SE = .03$, $p < .05$); one or more siblings only ($\beta = -.60$, $SE = .15$, $p < .01$); and extended family ($\beta = -.41$, $SE = .16$, $p < .01$). For the regression predicting time with father and one or more siblings, there was also a significant sex effect ($\beta = -.58$, $SE = .23$, $p < .05$) attributable to boys spending more time in this family subsystem. For all of these equations, the addition of a quadratic term for grade was not significant.

The full set of age changes in adolescents' time with each family subsystem is summarized in Figure 1. The graph as a whole shows the substantial cumulative decrease in the total volume of time spent with family.

Activities and topic of conversation with family. Our next question was whether the decline in family time would be uniform across all activities or whether there might be less decline in activities that involve communication. To evaluate this we created dichotomous dependent variables to represent each of the nine categories of activities and included these as dependent

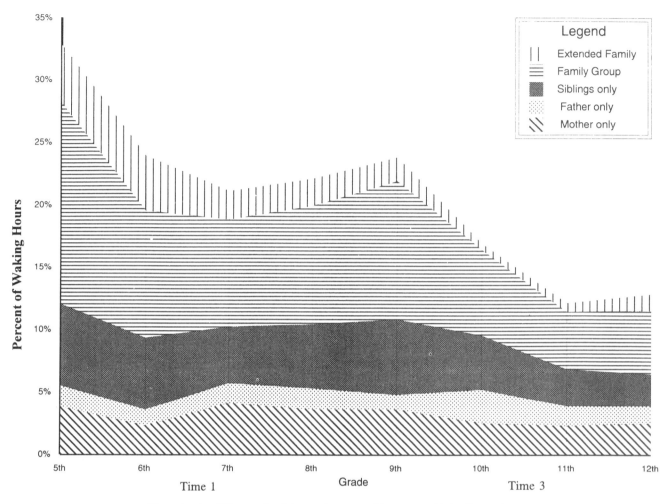

Figure 1. Age differences in adolescents' amount of time spent with family members.

variables in separate multilevel regression analyses in which grade, sex, and their interaction were predictors.

These analyses revealed significant linear declines with grade for all activities with family, except talking and transportation (Table 1). The most substantial decline appeared in leisure activities with family, including TV viewing and active leisure. These analyses also revealed a significant sex effect for frequency of talking ($\beta = 1.35$, $SE = .36$, $p < .001$), with girls reporting more frequent talking. None of the sex by grade interactions and none of the quadratic trends for grade were significant.

We next evaluated whether the rate of talking was stable across all family subsystems. For this analysis, only ESM self-reports when the students were in each subsystem were included, thus the findings address the rate of talking within that subsystem (not as a proportion of all time). Talking versus not talking was the dichotomous dependent variable; because of the reduced sample sizes for these analyses, multilevel regressions did not converge, so we used standard regressions, with an alpha level of .01.

These analyses suggested that talking increased within family subsystems that included mother (Table 2). Rate of talking rose

at a significant rate when the adolescent was with mother and one or more siblings. It increased at a close-to-significant rate when the adolescent was with a parent group or with mother only. These analyses also suggested that girls reported talking more frequently than did boys when with mother only and when with one or more siblings only. A close-to-significant interaction between grade and sex for parent groups was attributable to an increased rate of talking for girls (from 10% in the 5th–6th grades to 21% in the 11th–12th grades) with little change for boys (8% and 11%, respectively).

Further analysis showed that the topics of this talk became more interpersonal with age, particularly for girls. The pool of self-reports for this analysis included all occasions with family in which a topic of conversation was reported. The dichotomous dependent variable represented whether the topic was interpersonal or not. Again, the limited number of cases prevented us from testing this trend with multilevel regressions, so we used standard regression with the more stringent alpha of .01. This analysis found that grade was a significant predictor of interpersonal conversation, $\beta = 1.04$, $SE = .25$, $p < .001$. This regression also yielded a significant main effect for sex, $\beta = 7.05$, $SE = 1.20$, $p < .001$, attributable to girls talking more about inter-

Table 1
Percentage of ESM Reports in Different Activities With Family, by Grade

| | % of ESM reports by grade level | | | | | | | | |
Activity	5	6	7	8	9	10	11	12	β for grade trend
Homework	3.1	1.4	1.5	2.2	1.7	0.9	0.3	0.4	$-.31***$
Chores	1.5	1.8	1.7	1.4	2.0	1.2	0.9	1.1	$-.11*$
Eating	3.9	2.6	1.8	2.6	2.2	1.6	1.4	1.8	$-.22***$
Transportation	1.5	1.5	0.9	1.1	1.6	1.4	0.9	0.8	$-.06$
Personal maintenance	3.5	2.1	1.7	2.0	2.1	1.6	1.1	1.7	$-.18**$
Watching TV	9.9	7.6	6.0	6.7	6.9	4.5	2.9	3.4	$-.87***$
Active leisure	5.4	3.4	3.5	2.0	2.4	1.2	0.5	1.2	$-.56***$
Talking	2.3	3.1	2.8	2.7	3.0	2.2	2.1	2.3	$-.11$
Idling	2.1	1.3	1.3	0.8	1.6	1.1	0.5	0.4	$-.18***$

Note. ESM = experience sampling method.
$* p < .05.$ $** p < .01.$ $*** p < .001.$

personal topics. It also yielded a significant grade by sex interaction, $\beta = 1.86$, $SE = .95$, $p < .05$; separate regressions for girls and boys found that the grade increase was significant for girls, $\beta = 2.90$, $SE = .75$, $p < .001$, but not for boys, $\beta = -.23$, $SE = 1.04$, *ns*.

In sum, although total time with family declined substantially across adolescence, the amount of time spent in communication with family, especially with mothers, did not drop, and for girls, the proportion of this communication addressed to interpersonal issues increased.

Age Changes in Adolescents' Experience of Family Interactions

Our next question was whether adolescents' subjective experience of their interactions with family changed with age. Did their emotional state become less positive, did they perceive family members to be more friendly, and did they experience greater equality in who was leading the interactions? It should be noted that individuals' aggregated scores for these experience variables were found to be unrelated to the amount of time each spent with his or her family, thus age changes in the quality of family experience appear to be independent of age changes in quantity of time.

Affect. To evaluate whether adolescents' emotional states with family changed as a function of age, we tested a series of multilevel regressions in which ESM reports of affect constituted the dependent variable. Age changes in adolescents' overall emotional states were controlled by using z scored values for affect, as described in the *Analyses* section earlier. Only self-reports during family interactions were included.

These analyses indicated that adolescents' affect with family decreased in early adolescence and then increased in late adolescence. We first tested a simple model with linear terms for grade, sex, and their interaction as the independent variables. This multilevel regression yielded no significant findings. We then added a quadratic term for grade, which was strongly significant ($\beta = 1.24$, $SE = .37$, $p < .01$). Affect with family decreased in the early adolescent years. When we added a cubic term to the equation, we found a significant interaction between this cubic term and gender ($\beta = .89$, $SE = .41$, $p < .05$). A graph of the age by sex interaction indicates that boys and girls both showed a drop in affect with their families between the 5th–6th and 7th–8th grades; however, in the 9th–10th grade period girls' affect remained low, whereas boys' affect improved (Figure 2). The decrease in affect appeared to last longer for girls.

Further analyses suggested that this early adolescent decrease in affect was more evident in some family activities than others.

Table 2
Grade and Sex Differences in Rates of Talk Within Family Subsystems

| | | | Regression predicting rate of talk (unstandardized β) | | |
Family subsystem	Number of reports	Rate of talk (%)	Grade	Sex of child	Sex by grade
Parent groups	877	10.9	.96*	5.61*	1.86*
Mother only	502	16.3	1.49*	9.88**	-.07
Mother and sibling(s)	538	11.2	2.45***	.13	1.37
Father only	257	12.5	-.33	9.13*	1.57
Father and sibling(s)	123	8.9	.74	6.27	1.37
Sibling(s) only	783	9.8	.47	8.76***	1.86
Extended family	375	15.2	1.45	8.01	1.27

$* p < .05.$ $** p < .01.$ $*** p < .001.$

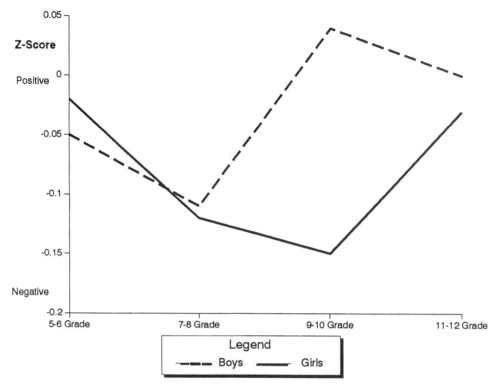

Figure 2. Grade trends in affect reported with family members.

We examined the relationship of grade and sex to affect within each of the nine categories of family activities. In a standard regression, we found that affect during family talk was significantly related to a quadratic term for grade ($\beta = 3.16$, $SE = 1.17$, $p < .01$). This quadratic effect did not approach significance for any of the other activities, including activities with *n*s that were similar to or larger than for talking (i.e., eating, personal maintenance, media, active leisure). Thus this early-adolescent decrease in affect appeared to be most apparent during talk, an activity in which interaction with family is probably most direct. Similar analyses failed to differentiate trends by family subsystem.

Friendliness of others. Age change in the perceived friendliness of family members was evaluated in multilevel regressions identical to those used to evaluate affect and showed a similar decrease in early adolescence. The regression yielded a significant quadratic effect for grade ($\beta = 1.28$, $SE = .43$, $p < .01$) that was due to a drop in the perceived friendliness of family members in early adolescence. It also yielded a significant main effect for sex ($\beta = -.117$, $SE = .048$, $p < .01$) attributable to girls' perceiving family members to be less friendly than boys. Other terms, including the cubic term for grade and interactions between sex and grade, were not significant.

Perceived leader. Consistent with the hypothesis of renegotiation, we found an age trend, with older adolescents perceiving themselves to be the leader more often during family interactions. We first tested whether there were age changes in adolescents' reporting that there was a leader. The grade term for this multilevel regression was not significant: No leader was reported for approximately 66% of reports across all grades. We

then evaluated a similar multilevel regression with a dependent variable of self versus other as leader. In this analysis there was a significant linear effect for grade ($\beta = 1.50$, $SE = .72$, $p < .05$), with all other effects nonsignificant. In 5th–6th grade, the students reported themselves to be leader in 6.1% of their family reports; in 11th–12th grade this number was 12.8%.

This age trend in adolescents' perception of themselves as the leader was most evident in interactions with siblings. Standard regressions, conducted for the reports within each subsystem, revealed significant trends for time with mother and one or more siblings ($\beta = 2.20$, $SE = .46$, $p < .001$) and time with one or more siblings only ($\beta = 2.50$, $SE = .73$, $p < .001$). The regressions for other family subsystems yielded betas for grade that were smaller and did not approach significance.

Factors Mediating Grade Changes in Family Interaction

The most prominent grade changes we found earlier are a dramatic decline in the amount of time adolescents spent with their families and a curvilinear pattern in the affect they reported during this time. Grade per se, however, is probably not the cause of these changes, but rather variables that are related to grade. Our final question is whether these grade trends are attributable to variables that are internal or external to adolescents' family relationships; that is, are they related to factors that affect family relationships from within, such as puberty and family conflict, or are they related to factors that pull adolescents out of the family, such as opportunities in one's bedroom or away from home?

In essence we wanted to know whether these internal and ex-

Table 3

Regressions Evaluating Possible Mediators of the Relationship Between Grade and Family Time

Mediator	Regression prediction (standardized β)				
		Family time from mediator	Family time from grade	Family time from	
	Mediator from grade			Grade	Mediator
Pubertal status[a]					
Boys	.63***	−.41***	−.39***	−.18	−.32**
Girls	.62***	−.23*	−.22*	−.12	−.16
Family conflict					
Reported by adolescent	.19***	−.06	−.45***	−.45***	.03
Reported by parent	−.05	−.03	−.45***	−.45***	−.06
Life-situation factors[b]					
For separation at home	.12	−.16*	−.29***	−.28***	−.14*
To be away from home	.56***	−.32***	−.26***	−.12	−.26**

[a] 5th–8th grade only.   [b] 9th–12th grade only.
* $p < .05$.   ** $p < .01$.   *** $p < .001$.

ternal variables mediated the relationship we have found between grade and family experience. Baron and Kenny (1986) defined a mediator as "a third variable, which represents the generative mechanism through which the focal independent variable [grade, in this case] is able to influence the dependent variable of interest [family experience]" (p. 1173). We used Baron and Kenny's criteria to evaluate mediation (Table 3). For each possible mediating variable we asked the following questions: Is it associated with the independent variable, grade (Column 1)? Is it related to the dependent variable, amount of family time or average experience with family (Column 2)? Is the beta for the independent variable, grade, reduced or eliminated in a regression that includes the mediator (is the beta in Column 4 smaller than the beta in Column 3)? And does the mediator significantly predict family time or experience in a regression that controls for grade (Column 5)? Given the limits of our data, these tests cannot prove that a mediator is the "generative mechanism," but failure to meet all four tests is evidence that it is not the mechanism, or that it is, at best, a weak contributor.

Mediators of changes in family time. We first evaluated whether the internal factors met criteria as mediators of the grade changes in family time. These analyses suggested that in early adolescence pubertal status was a mediator of the decline in family time for boys but not girls. For boys, pubertal status met all four criteria (Table 3): It was strongly related to grade; negatively related to amount of time spent with family; and in a regression including grade as a predictor, the contribution of grade became nonsignificant and pubertal status was a strong independent predictor of family time. These findings are consistent with the hypothesis that puberty rather than grade drives boys' decline in family time during early adolescence. For girls, the fourth criteria was not met: With grade included in the equation, pubertal status was not an independent predictor of family time. However, grade was also not a significant predictor in this equation, leaving it ambiguous whether grade or pubertal status might drive the age decline in family time for girls. Separate analyses with our larger sample of fifth to ninth graders

indicated that grade but not pubertal status was an independent predictor of family time for girls during this age period.[2] Thus puberty may make little contribution to girls' diminished time with family.

Next we found that family conflict was not related to the age changes in family time, nor did any of the other family relationship variables meet criteria as mediators of this change. Our analyses of these relationship variables included the entire 5th to 12th grade period and used data for each person at each time period as the unit of analysis (n = 440). Surprisingly, family conflict (as reported by the adolescent and by the parent) was not related to amount of family time—youth with more conflict did not spend less time with their families (Table 3)—thus, it could not be a mediator. Similar analyses with the other relationship variables also failed to meet the criteria as mediators (not shown). Tests of quadratic trends for grade also failed to show mediation. Because the literature has sometimes found different patterns for girls and boys, we also tested these relationships separately for each gender and found that the patterns differed little for boys and girls.

Factors that are "external" to family relationships fared better as mediators of the age changes in adolescents' family time. For the 9th to 12th grade period, the score representing life situation opportunities for separation at home did not meet all the criteria. However, the score representing opportunities to be away from home did (Table 3). This later score included whether the student had a driver's license, a job, and other factors that might make him or her more likely to be away from home. Consistent with mediation, this score was related positively to grade and negatively to family time. In a regression

[2] We repeated the final step of these pubertal analyses with the larger Time 1 sample of 483 young adolescents that we have used in other publications (cf. Larson & Richards, 1989). For girls, grade was found to be a significant independent predictor of family time, with a standardized $\beta = -.38$, $p < .001$, but not pubertal status, $\beta = -.03$, *n s*. For boys, pubertal status was found to be a significant predictor of family time, $\beta = -.31$, $p < .001$, but not grade, $\beta = -.14$, $p < .10$.

including both this score and grade as independent variables, only this score was a significant predictor of family time. Thus, for the senior high school period, this score—which represents opportunities and pulls to be away from home—meets criteria as a mediator of the decline in family time.

An additional set of analyses helped illuminate this last finding. We found that amount of time spent away from home did not change during the 5th to 9th grade period, remaining stable at about 55% of waking hours. During this early adolescent period, declining family time was replaced primarily by time spent alone at home. It was only in the high school years that time apart from home showed an increase, rising to 63% in the 10th grade and to 66% in the 11th and 12th grades. This suggests that pulls away from home mediate the age decline in family time only for the older age period; during early adolescence, factors that draw an adolescent to be alone may be more important.

Mediators of changes in family experience. None of the internal and external factors met the criteria as mediators of the early adolescent decrease in affect and perceived friendliness with family nor the age changes in perceived leader.

Discussion

The focus of this research was on age changes in the mundane, daily interactions between adolescents and their families for this sample of European American youth. We were interested in the quality and quantity of contact that take place after school, at the supper table, or when family members do chores on the weekend. The findings showed that, with age, there is both disengagement and transformation in these kinds of daily interactions.

Disengagement

Disengagement was evident in the total quantity of time teens spent with their families. These working- and middle-class youth exhibited a steady and dramatic drop in their family time: from 35% of waking hours in 5th grade to 14% in 12th grade. By the end of senior high school, these teenagers were spending much less time in leisure and daily maintenance activities with their families. The decline was greatest for time with groups of family members and time with siblings. Evidence from other studies cautions that we should not generalize this pattern to adolescents from non-European backgrounds, for whom centripetal forces to the family may be stronger (Cooper & Baker, 1991; Feldman & Quatman, 1988). Nonetheless, for these European American adolescents, the progressive withdrawal from daily family life is striking.

Contrary to some theories, this disengagement did not appear to be driven by factors internal to family relationships that repel adolescents outward. We failed to find that measures of family relationships met criteria as mediators of this age decline in family time. Our questionnaire measures of family conflict were unrelated to the age differences in amount of family time (see also Montemayor, 1982), as were our measures of family cohesion and adolescents' closeness to mother and father. The immediate affect that adolescents reported with their families was also not correlated with their amount of family time. Such findings suggest that negative experience with family is as likely to be a stimulus for continued interaction—like one might see in an embattled, enmeshed family—as it is to be a stimulus for physical withdrawal.

The findings did indicate that in early adolescence this disengagement was related to puberty for boys. This relationship resembles, in less extreme form, the pattern for many other primates, among whom there is a dramatic drop for male individuals in time spent with family members at puberty (Caine, 1986; Pusey, 1983). In other primates, however, this disengagement is related to bickering and conflict, which appear to drive pubertal males from the natal group (Caine, 1986; Steinberg, 1989). But for the male human adolescents in this study, family conflict appeared not to be related to the reduction in family time.

Instead, the decline in adolescents' family time was related to pulls from outside the family. In early adolescence, diminishing family time was replaced by time spent alone at home. At this age, teens begin spending more time alone in their bedrooms, and although this time typically brings less favorable affective states, they appear to be drawn to it (Larson, 1990; Larson & Richards, 1991). During the high school years, the continuing decline in family time within our sample was related to increasing pulls from outside the home. After the ninth grade, these adolescents begin spending more time away from home: They stay late at school or go out with friends and thus are with their families less often. Our findings showed that life-situation factors that required or made it easier to be away from home were related to the decline in family time for this older age period. A composite of variables, including having a car, having a job, and having permission from parents to stay out later, met the criteria to be considered a mediator of the age reduction in family time, indeed it eliminated the contribution of grade to predicting family time.

We are thus led to the conclusion that most adolescents do not feel driven out of their families, rather their increasing involvement in outside activities may crowd out or displace family time. In short, the decline with age in family interactions appears to have little to do with the family. In fact, our findings suggest various ways in which teens and their families may try to compensate for loss of shared time.

Continuity and Transformation

Concurrent with this disengagement from daily interactions, we see elements of continued engagement and transformation in the time these adolescents did spend with their families. Although overall family time declined, certain categories of family time did not, suggesting that withdrawal from family was discriminate. The quantity of time these adolescents spent alone with their mothers and the smaller quantity of time they spent alone with their fathers both remained stable across this age period. The stability of this one-on-one time with parents suggests that adolescents, or their parents, may be deliberately selecting their shared time in order to maintain more intimate interaction.

This priority of maintaining direct interaction was further suggested by shifts in the activities that older adolescents reported with their families. With age, adolescents showed the largest declines in family activities involving less communication, such as TV watching, whereas time spent talking did not decline. In fact, for girls, amount of time spent in conversations about interpersonal issues increased significantly. This shift for girls is parallel to shifts in their interactions with peers (Raffaelli & Duckett, 1989), suggesting that it reflects a general growth in girls' capacity for and interest in interactions around interpersonal issues.

Transformation was also indicated by age shifts in adolescents' perceptions of who was leading family interactions. Across ages, these youth reported that no one was leading for about two thirds of the time. However, at older ages they saw themselves as the leader more often during the remaining one third of the time, and by age 18 they saw themselves as the leader nearly as often as they saw other family members to be the leader, especially when they were with siblings or with mother and siblings. This finding provides support, at the level of daily interactions, for Youniss's (1980) thesis that adolescents' relationships with their parents, at least with their mothers, change in the direction of becoming less unilateral and more symmetric in late adolescence.

Finally, we saw signs of transformation in these adolescents' changing emotional experience with their families. The emotional states they reported became less positive in early adolescence, especially during talk, and they experienced family members as less friendly. But these states and perceptions of others became more favorable in the early high school years for boys and in the late high school years for girls. These curved trends—based on adolescents' in vivo experiences—reinforce findings from interview, questionnaire, and observational studies suggesting that early adolescence is often the most strained period in adolescent–parent relationships (Holmbeck & Hill, 1991; Offer & Offer, 1975; Steinberg, 1981). The more positive affect we found in late adolescence is a sign that the renegotiation described by other scholars has led to improved relationships at this age period. Older adolescents report becoming better able to tolerate or even enjoy their parents' company as a result of better communication and greater mutual understanding and respect (Freeman, Csikszentmihalyi, & Larson, 1986).

Therefore, even as these adolescents' family time is diminishing, it is being transformed. The shrinking portion of time that adolescents spend with their families involves more dyadic and direct interaction with parents; it is perceived as less unilateral; and after an early adolescent period of less favorable affect, it is experienced more favorably in late adolescence. Of course, these findings reflect only group trends: Some individuals did not demonstrate transformation; for some, irritability and conflict continues into late adolescence and beyond (cf. Hauser, 1991). We also cannot be certain whether these trends would have been evident for the substantial group of students from the original random sample who declined to take part or for adolescents other than the working- and middle-class European Americans whom we studied. Nonetheless, within the confines of our sample, the findings clearly support the thesis that adolescents are not just disengaging from daily family interaction, but rather these interactions are being altered to maintain family connectedness.

References

Baron, R. M., & Kenny, D. A. (1986). The moderator–mediator variable distinction in social psychological research: Conceptual, strate-

gic, and statistical considerations. *Journal of Personality and Social Psychology, 51,* 1173–1182.

Blos, P. (1967). The second individuation process of adolescence. *The Psychoanalytic Study of the Child, 22,* 162–186.

Blyth, D. A. (1982). Mapping the social world of adolescents: Issues, techniques, and problems. In F. Serafica (Ed.), *Social cognition, context, and social behavior: A developmental perspective* (pp. 240–272). New York: Guilford Press.

Bryk, A., & Raudenbush, S. W. (1992). *Hierarchical linear models: Applications and data analysis methods.* Newbury Park, CA: Sage.

Caine, N. G. (1986). Behavior during puberty and adolescence. In J. Erwin (Series & Vol. Ed.) & G. Mitchel (Vol. Ed.), *Comparative primate biology: Vol. 2, Part A. Behavior, conservation, and ecology* (pp. 327–361). New York: Liss.

Collins, W. A., & Russell, G. (1991). Mother–child and father–child relationships in middle childhood and adolescence: A developmental analysis. *Developmental Psychology, 25,* 550–559.

Cooper, C. R., & Baker, H. (1991, July). *Ethnic perspectives on individuality and connectedness in adolescents' relationships with family and peers.* Paper presented at the meetings of the International Society for the Study of Behavioral Development, Minneapolis.

Csikszentmihalyi, M., & Larson, R. (1987). The experience sampling method. *Journal of Nervous and Mental Disease, 175,* 526–536.

Draper, N. R., & Smith, H. (1981). *Applied regression analyses.* (2nd ed.). New York: Wiley.

Feldman, S. S., & Quatman, T. (1988). Factors influencing age expectations for adolescent autonomy: A study of early adolescents and parents. *Journal of Early Adolescence, 8,* 325–343.

Freeman, M., Czikszentmihalyi, M., & Larson, R. (1986). Adolescence and its recollection: Toward an interpretive model of development. *Merrill-Palmer Quarterly, 32,* 167–185.

Freud, A. (1946). *The ego and the mechanisms of defence.* New York: International Universities Press.

Goldstein, H. (1987). *Multilevel models in educational and social research.* New York: Oxford University Press.

Grotevant, H. D., & Cooper, C. R. (1986). Individuation in family relationships: A perspective on individual differences in the development of identity and role-taking skill in adolescence. *Human Development, 29,* 82–100.

Hauser, S. T. (with Powers, S. I., & Noam, G. G.). (1991). *Adolescents and their families: Paths of ego development* (pp. 231–243). New York: Free Press.

Havighurst, R. J. (1953). *Human development and education.* New York: McKay.

Hill, J. P., & Holmbeck, G. N. (1987). Familial adaptation to biological change during adolescence. In R. M. Lerner & T. T. Foch (Eds.), *Biological-psychosocial interactions in early adolescence* (pp. 207–223). Hillsdale, NJ: Erlbaum.

Holmbeck, G. N., & Hill, J. P. (1991). Conflictive engagement, positive affect, and menarche in families with seventh-grade girls. *Child Development, 62,* 1030–1048.

Kelley, H. H., Berscheid, E., Christensen, A., Harvey, J. H., Huston, T. L., Levinger, G., McClintock, E., Peplau, L. A., & Peterson, D. R. (Eds.). (1983). *Close relationships.* New York: Freeman.

Kovacs, M. (1985). The Children's Depression Inventory. *Psychopharmacology Bulletin, 21,* 995–998.

Larson, R. W. (1989a). Beeping children and adolescents: A method for studying time use and daily experience. *Journal of Youth and Adolescence, 18,* 511–530.

Larson, R. W. (1989b). *The factor structure of moods and emotions in a sample of young adolescents.* Unpublished manuscript, University of Illinois, Urbana–Champaign.

Larson, R. W. (1990). The solitary side of life: An examination of the time people spend alone from childhood to old age. *Developmental Review, 10,* 155–183.

Larson, R. W., & Delespaul, P. (1992). Analyzing experience sampling data: A guidebook for the perplexed. In M. deVries (Ed.), *The experience of psychopathology: Investigating mental disorders in their natural setting* (pp. 58–78). Cambridge, England: Cambridge University Press.

Larson, R. W., & Richards, M. H. (Eds.). (1989). The changing life space of early adolescence (Special issue). *Journal of Youth and Adolescence, 18,* 501–626.

Larson, R. W., & Richards, M. H. (1991). Daily companionship in late childhood and early adolescence: Changing developmental contexts. *Child Development, 62,* 284–300.

Lidz, T. (1969). The adolescent and his family. In G. Caplan & S. Lebovici (Eds.), *Adolescence: Psychosocial perspectives* (pp. 105–112). New York: Basic Books.

Moneta, G. B., & Csikszentmihalyi, M. (in press). The effect of perceived challenges and skills on the quality of subjective experience. *Journal of Personality, 64.*

Montemayor, R. (1982). The relationship between parent–adolescent conflict and the amount of time adolescents spend alone and with parents and peers. *Child Development, 53,* 1512–1519.

Moos, R. H., & Moos, B. S. (1986). *Family environment scales manual* (2nd ed.). Palo Alto, CA: Consulting Psychologists Press.

Morris, N. M., & Udry, J. R. (1980). Validation of a self-administered instrument to assess stage of adolescent development. *Journal of Youth and Adolescence, 9,* 271–280.

Offer, D., & Offer, J. B. (1975). *Teenage to young manhood: A psychological study.* New York: Basic Books.

Prosser, R., Rasbash, J., & Goldstein, H. (1991). *Software for three-level analysis* London: University of London, Institute of Education.

Pusey, A. E. (1983). Mother–offspring relationships in chimpanzees after weaning. *Animal Behavior, 31,* 363–377.

Raffaelli, M., & Duckett, E. (1989). "We were just talking . . .": Conversations in early adolescence. *Journal of Youth and Adolescence, 18,* 567–582.

Steinberg, L. (1981). Transformations in family relations at puberty. *Developmental Psychology, 17,* 833–840.

Steinberg, L. (1989). Pubertal maturation and parent–adolescent distance: An evolutionary perspective. In G. R. Adams, R. Montemayor, & T. P. Gullotta (Eds.), *Biology of adolescent behavior and development* (pp. 71–97). Newbury Park, CA: Sage.

Steinberg, L. (1990). Autonomy, conflict, and harmony in the family relationship. In S. S. Feldman & G. R. Elliot (Eds.), *At the threshold: The developing adolescent* (pp. 255–276). Cambridge, MA: Harvard University Press.

Steinberg, L., & Silverberg, S. B. (1986). The vicissitudes of autonomy in early adolescence. *Child Development, 57,* 841–851.

Tanner, J. M. (1975). Growth and endocrinology of the adolescent. In L. J. Gardner (Ed.), *Endocrine and diseases of childhood* (2nd ed., pp. 14–64). Philadelphia: Saunders.

Youniss, J. (1980). *Parents and peers in social development.* Chicago: University of Chicago Press.

Youniss, J., & Smollar, J. (1985). *Adolescent relations with mothers, fathers, and friends.* Chicago: University of Chicago Press.

Received March 3, 1995
Revision received July 24, 1995
Accepted November 3, 1995 ∎

Multiple Choice:

1. An *innovative* feature of this research was:

    A. pubertal status was assessed.
    B. children were paged every day for one week.
    C. children were asked about family conflict.
    D. children's grade in school was used instead of their chronological age.

2. This study found that:

    A. as children entered adolescence, they were more likely to be the leader in family interactions.
    B. as children entered adolescence, the time they spent with their mothers alone and their fathers alone did not change.
    C. once children entered adolescence, there were greater opportunities for them to take part in activities outside of the home.
    D. all of the above.

Essay:

1. What might the consequences be for adolescents of spending less time with their families in the way depicted by this article? Do you think that the consequences might differ for children of different socio-economic status, gender, and ethnicity?

2. What effects might the decrease in time adolescents spend with their family have on parents? Do you think it would influence how parents treat their children?

Answers to Multiple Choice Questions

Article 1
1. B
2. B
3. C

Article 2
1. C
2. B

Article 3
1. B
2. A

Article 4
1. D
2. A

Article 5
1. D
2. C
3. A

Article 6
1. B
2. B

Article 7
1. B
2. C
3. A

Article 8
1. B
2. A

Article 9
1. A
2. D

Article 10
1. D
2. E

Article 11
1. D
2. C
3. D

Article 12
1. E
2. C

Article 13
1. D
2. A
3. A

Article 14
1. A
2. C

Article 15
1. B
2. B

Article 16
1. C
2. C

Article 17
1. B
2. A

Article 18
1. A
2. D

Article 19
1. A
2. A

Article 20
1. B
2. C

Article 21
1. C
2. C

Article 22
1. C
2. A

Article 23
1. D
2. C
3. D

Article 24
1. C
2. D
3. A

Article 25
1. C
2. A

Article 26
1. B
2. D